VOLUME ONE

THE TRADITIONAL WORLD

# THE SHAPING OF WESTERN CIVILIZATION

VOLUME ONE

THE TRADITIONAL WORLD

# THE SHAPING OF WESTERN CIVILIZATION

Edited by


LUDWIG F. SCHAEFER
Carnegie-Mellon University

DANIEL P. RESNICK
Carnegie-Mellon University

GEORGE L. NETTERVILLE, III
Southern University



HOLT, RINEHART AND WINSTON, INC.
New York • Chicago • San Francisco • Atlanta • Dallas • Montreal • Toronto

# Copyright Acknowledgments


Library of Congress Catalog Card Number:
70-93266
**SBN: 03-074135-1**
Printed in the United States of America
0 1 2 3 31 9 8 7 6 5 4 3 2 1

**Text Design and Maps
by Plasencia Design
Associates, Inc.,
New York**

Cover: Photographie Giraudon; p. xxii: Dominique Lajoux from Rapho-Guillumette Photos, Inc.; p. 4: Musée Calvet, Avignon; p. 5: Violette Cornelius, ABC Press-Amsterdam, from Black Star Publishing Co., Inc.; p. 8: from *Prehistoric Societies,* by Grahame Clark and Stuart Piggott. Copyright 1965 by Alfred A. Knopf, Inc. Reprinted by permission of Alfred A. Knopf, Inc.; p. 13: from *Prehistoric Societies,* by Grahame Clark and Stuart Piggott. Copyright 1965 by Alfred A. Knopf, Inc. Reprinted by permission of Alfred A. Knopf, Inc.; p. 23: Dr. Georg Gerster, Zurich, from Black Star; p. 31: Ernst Haas from Magnum Photos, Inc.; p. 28: From p. 239 *Prehistory and the Beginnings of Civilization,* by J. Hawkes and Sir Leonard Woolley. Copyright 1963 by Harper & Row. By permission of Harper & Row; p. 39: Dominique Lajoux from Rapho-Guillumette Pictures; p. 43: Courtesy of the American Museum of Natural History; p. 44: Dr. Georg Gerster, Zurich, from Rapho-Guillumette; p. 46: Courtesy of the Oriental Institute, University of Chicago; p. 53: Editorial Photocolor Archives, Inc.; p. 57: Kunsthistorisches Museum, Vienna; p. 58: Elliott Erwitt from Magnum; p. 60: Louvre, Paris (Service de Documentation Photographique de la Réunion des Musées Nationaux, Versailles); p. 65: The Shrine of the Book, The Israel Museum, Jerusalem: D. Samuel and Jeane H. Gottesman Center for Biblical Manuscripts; p. 70: Alinari; p. 71: Jean Roubier from Rapho-Guillumette; p. 76: Acropolis Museum, Athens (Hirmer Fotoarchiv München); p. 80: Joan Menschenfreund; p. 83: The Metropolitan Museum of Art, New York: Rogers Fund, 1907; p. 104: Bruce Davidson from Magnum; p. 122: Antikenabtellungen, Staatliche Museen, Berlin; p. 123: Acropolis Museum, Athens (Hirmer Fotoarchiv München); p. 130: Palazzo dei Conservatori: Museo Nuovo, Rome (Alinari); p. 135: Vatican Museum, Rome; pp. 142–143: Rev. Raymond V. Schoder, S. J.; p. 151: *Thesaurus of Judaean Coins,* Bialik Institute, Jerusalem; p. 163: Museum, Trier (Alinari); p. 184: Bibliothèque Nationale, Paris: Ms. Grec 510 (Roger-Jean Ségalat); p. 187: Colonna Antonina, Rome (Alinari); p. 206: Colonna Antonina, Rome (Alinari); p. 212: The Bettmann Archive; p. 219: Bibliothèque Nationale, Paris: Ms. Nouv. Acq. Fr. 1098 (Roger-Jean Ségalat); p. 224: Michal Heron; p. 225; Biblioteca del Monasterio, El Escorial, Madrid (MAS); p. 230; top left: Uffizi, Florence (Alinari); p. 230, top right: Louvre, Paris (Service de Documentation); p. 230, bottom: Bibliothèque Nationale, Paris: Ms. Nouv. Acq. Lat. 1539 (Roger-Jean Ségalat); p. 232: Musée Condé, Chantilly: Jean Foucquet, *Heures d'Etienne Chevalier* (Giraudon); p. 233, top: Bibliothèque Publique de Dijon: Ms. 170; p. 233, bottom left: Courtesy of the Trustees of the British Museum, London: Ms. Cotton Claud. E. IV, Part I (R. B. Fleming & Co., Ltd.); p. 233, bottom right: Courtesy of the Trustees of the British Museum, London: Ms. Sloane; p. 236: Kunsthistorisches Museum, Vienna; p. 246: Louvre, Paris (Service de Documentation); p. 243: Charles S. Anderson, *Augsburg Atlas of Christianity In The Middle Ages and Reformation;* Augsburg, 1967; p. 252, left: Bibliothèque Nationale, Paris: Coislin 79 (Hirmer Fotoarchiv München); p. 252, right: Bibliothèque Nationale, Paris: Ms. Lat. 1141 (Roger-Jean Ségalat), p. 257: Pierpont Morgan Library, New York: Ms. 736, fol. 9v.; p. 259: J. Allan Cash from Rapho-Guillumette; p. 263: Bibliothèque Nationale, Paris; Ms. Lat. 4772 (Roger-Jean Ségalat); p. 266: Bibliothèque Nationale, Paris: Ms. Nouv. Acq. Lat. 1390 (Roger-Jean Ségalat); p. 268: Courtesy of the Trustees of the British Museum, London: Ms. Roy. 15 E. II (R. B. Fleming); p. 272, left: Courtesy of the Trustees of the British Museum, London: Ms. Roy. 15 E. II (R. B. Fleming); p. 272, right: Pierpont Morgan Library, New York: Ms. 399, November; p. 274: Giraudon; p. 282, top: The Bettmann Archive; p. 282, bottom:

Giraudon; p. 286: Bibliothèque Nationale, Paris: Ms. Lat. 1 (Roger-Jean Ségalat); p. 294: Pierpont Morgan Library, New York: Ms. 638, fol. 23v.; pp. 299–300: Bildarchiv Foto Marburg (Art Reference Bureau); p. 301: Apostolic Library, Vatican, Rome: Vat. Lat. 4922; p. 306: Bibliothèque Nationale, Paris: Ms. Lat. 17716 (Roger-Jean Ségalat); p. 308: Courtesy of the Trustees of the British Museum: Ms. Add. 23923 (R. B. Fleming); p. 313: Staatliche Museen, Berlin; p. 314: Picture Collection, New York Public Library; p. 326: Biblioteca del Monasterio, El Escorial, Madrid (MAS); p. 330: Bibliothèque Nationale, Paris: Ms. Fr. 22495 (Roger-Jean Ségalat); p. 331: Bibliothèque Nationale, Paris: Ms. Fr. 352 (Roger-Jean Ségalat); p. 331, right: Joan Menschenfreund; p. 333: Bildarchiv Foto Marburg (Art Reference Bureau); p. 334: Courtesy of the Trustees of the British Museum, London: Ms. Sloane 1977 (R. B. Fleming); pp. 342–343: Giraudon; p. 344: Photographie Bulloz; p. 345: Bibliothèque Nationale, Paris: Ms. Fr. 25425 (Roger-Jean Ségalat); p. 346: Prado, Madrid (MAS); p. 347: Alinari; p. 350: University Library, Heidelberg: Codex Manesse Liederhandschrift; p. 352: Bibliothèque de l'Arsenal: Ms. 3516 (Giraudon); p. 358: Bibliothèque Royale de Belgique, Brussels: Ms. 13076–7; p. 359: Château de Versailles (Service de Documentation); p. 360: Archives Photographiques, Paris; p. 362: Picture Collection, New York Public Library; p. 363: The Metropolitan Museum of Art, New York: Rogers Fund, 1921; p. 364: Alinari; p. 366: Courtesy of the Trustees of the British Museum, London: Ms. Harley 1319 (R. B. Fleming); p. 369: Prado, Madrid (MAS); p. 371, top and bottom left: Pierpont Morgan Library, New York: PML 20684; p. 371, bottom right: The Metropolitan Museum of Art, New York: Rogers Fund, 1913; p. 374: The Metropolitan Museum of Art, New York: Harris Brisbane Dick Fund, 1934; p. 479: de Vries, Lugkx, and Henderson, *An Atlas of World History,* Nelson, 1965; p. 381, left: Editorial Photocolor Archives, Inc.; p. 381, right: Emmett Bright, Time, Inc.; p. 383: Photographie Bulloz; p. 384: Courtesy of the Trustees of the British Museum, London: Ms. Roy. 15 E. II (R. B. Fleming); p. 388, top: The Metropolitan Museum of Art, New York: Fletcher Fund, 1947 (The A. W. Bahr Collection); p. 388, bottom: The Metropolitan Museum of Art, New York: Rogers Fund, 1918; p. 394: Louvre, Paris (Alinari); p. 395: Courtesy of the Trustees of the British Museum: Ms. Add. 27695; p. 397: Herzog Anton Ulrich Museum, Braunschweig; p. 398: The Bettmann Archive; p. 412: Alinari; p. 416: H.M. the Queen; p. 418: Libreria Piccolomini, Duomo, Siena (Alinari); p. 419: Vatican Museum (Alinari-Anderson); p. 420: Alinari-Anderson; p. 423: Alinari; p. 427, left: Staatsbibliothek, Berlin; p. 427, right: The Metropolitan Museum of Art, New York: Harris Brisbane Dick Fund, 1934; p. 428: Rare Book Division, New York Public Library (Astor, Lenox and Tilden Foundations); p. 434, top left: National Gallery of Art: Kress Collection; pp. 434, 435, 437: Alinari; p. 453: Roland Bainton (Courtesy American Heritage); p. 459, left: Alte Pinakothek, Munich (Bruckmann-Giraudon); p. 459, right: The Metropolitan Museum of Art, New York: Rogers Fund, 1919; p. 460: Culver Pictures, Inc.; p. 467: Bibliothèque Publique et Universitaire, Geneva; p. 470: Picture Collection, New York Public Library; p. 484: Bibliothèque Nationale, Paris (Giraudon); p. 493: R. R. Palmer, *Atlas of World History,* Rand McNally & Company, Chicago, 1957; p. 494: Rare Book Division, New York Public Library (Astor, Lenox and Tilden Foundations); p. 495: Picture Collection, New York Public Library; p. 498: Bibliothèque Nationale, Paris: Ms. Port. 1 (Roger-Jean Ségalat); p. 499: Victoria & Albert Museum, London; p. 500: Editorial Photocolor Archives, Inc.; p. 502: Lauros-Giraudon; p. 504, top: Ohio State University; p. 504, bottom: Picture Collection, New York Public Library.

Portfolios: following p. 58: Rev. Raymond V. Schoder, S. J.; 3 through 13, Harry Burton, The Metropolitan Museum of Art, New York; André Held; following page 90: Alinari; 2 through 8, Hirmer Fotoarchiv München; Martin von Wagner-Museum der Universität Würzburg; Bibliothèque Nationale, Paris (Giraudon); Royal Ontario Museum, Toronto; Royal Ontario Museum, Toronto; Museum of Fine Arts, Boston: Gift of Mrs. George M. Bett; Courtesy of the Oriental Institute, University of Chicago; following page 186: Alinari; Museo Capitolino, Rome, Alinari; Museo Vaticano, Rome, Alinari; Museo Profano, Laterano, Rome, Alinari; Museo, Plazzo Vaticano, Rome, Alinari; Inge Morath from Magnum; Vatican Museum; Hirmer Fotoarchiv München; Pan American; Hirmer Fotoarchiv München; Hirmer Fotoarchiv München; Edizione Enrico Verdesi, Rome; Alinari; following page 474: Rare Book Division, New York Public Library (Astor, Lenox and Tilden Foundation); National Gallery, London; The Metropolitan Museum of Art, New York: Gift of R. Thornton Wilson, 1954, Florence Ellsworth Wilson; Rijksmuseum, Amsterdam; Rare Books Division, New York Public Library (Astor, Lenox and Tilden Foundations); Rare Books Division, New York Public Library (Astor, Lenox and Tilden Foundations); Picture Collection, New York Public Library; Schoenfeld Collection, Three Lions Inc.; Picture Collection, New York Public Library; Courtesy of the Trustees of the British Museum, London; Picture Collection, New York Public Library; Musée Guimet, Paris (Service de Documentation Photographique de la Réunion des Musées Nationaux, Versailles); Victoria and Albert Museum, London. Crown Copyright.

# Preface

The editors of this book have attempted to examine the varieties and tensions of the Western experience through the eyes and minds of laymen and scholars, contemporary participants and historians whose task is to demonstrate the relevance of the past. The result is a set of considered arguments about our myths, traditions, ideals, and achievements. It is our hope that we have brought some critical perspective to these developments and will have helped Westerners to understand the continuing process of modernization throughout the world, for which the West has served as an experimental laboratory and in which she has been both victor and victim. The encounter with lively and sometimes angry minds has been stimulating for us, and we hope that it will be fresh and instructive for those who open these pages now.

The text is divided into chapters and topics. Each topic generally includes an introductory narrative, primary sources, and interpretive selections. Each topic has been designed as a single assignment—its unifying theme briefly stated in an introduction. For these assignments, the editors have prepared a Guide to Study that can be of special value. Assignment sheets in the guide provide three reading options of increasing length and sophistication, with appropriate study questions and exercises. Although designed as an integral text, it may also serve as a book of readings or provide topics for class discussions.

The readings are the product of an experimental course in Western Civilization designed, under a grant from the Carnegie Corporation of New York, to develop more effective approaches to the teaching of history. Without this assistance the project would scarcely have been possible, and we wish to thank the many individuals associated with the Carnegie Corporation who have encouraged and supported our efforts.

Those who have collaborated with us in a Cooperative Program in History include representatives from Catholic colleges, community colleges, predominantly Negro colleges of the South, and other private and state-related institutions. Versions of the course have been taught at Coker College (S.C.), the Community College of Allegheny County (Pa.), Fontbonne College (Mo.), Grambling College (La.), Houston-Tillotson College (Tex.), Johnson State College (Vt.), Norfolk State College (Va.), Southern University (La.), Texas Southern University (Tex.), Virginia Union University (Va.), and Xavier University (La.), as well as at Carnegie-Mellon. Numerous suggestions from faculty and students of these institutions have enriched this work, in particular those of Hunter Brooks, William Doyle, Charles Grose, Muriel Holmes, Roscoe Leonard, Colin Loader, Earl Mills, and Nancy Ropp.

To our colleagues Pearle Mankins, Benjamin Moskowitz, and James and Virginia Welch must go an expression of special appreciation for their contributions. Mary Zarroli typed much of the manuscript; Helen Prine smilingly performed the innumerable duties connected with providing material for a thousand students scattered from Vermont to Texas; Judith Sichel is responsible for many research details and for the review section of the Guide to Study.

A pioneering work of this sort requires creative backing from its publishers. To Susan Vannucci and Enid Klass we are indebted for imaginative photo research; to Raymond Gill for conscientious and concerned editing; and to Clifford Snyder for his vision and support. To them and others we are properly grateful.

Ludwig F. Schaefer
Daniel P. Resnick
George L. Netterville, III

Carnegie-Mellon University
Southern University
January 1970

# Contents Volume One

VOLUME ONE

THE TRADITIONAL WORLD

# THE SHAPING OF WESTERN CIVILIZATION

# Chapter 1

## The Ancient World: Roots of Western Civilization

The story of man begins fourteen to fifteen million years ago with our earliest ancestors, whose existence is recorded in the earth that provided their home. Only in the past five or six thousand years has the story of man appeared in written records; the vast eons of time before constitute prehistory. Prehistoric man was faced with basic demands that still concern human beings today and he undoubtedly also asked the great questions of life, the answers to which form the core of history. The answers that prehistoric men found, however, remain locked as secrets in the unwritten past, and can be deduced only from anthropological and archeological finds, inference drawn from later history, and study of the culture of such primitive peoples as still exist today.

The readings in Chapter 1 distinguish between primitive culture and the ancient civilization in which the roots of Western civilization can be found. No attempt is made to cover all or even a large segment of the distant past. Instead the readings focus on the Sumerians, Babylonians, Egyptians, and Hebrews. A few large questions are asked. What is civilization? How did it originate? What was the relationship between man and the unknown? How was society organized? What were the dominant notions of law, justice, morality, and power?

A handful of readings are obviously insufficient to present a picture of the history of these thousands of years. Here the reader will not find pages on the rise and fall of ancient empires, involved narrative of dynasties, or detailed enumeration of place names, gods and legends. Instead it is hoped that he may find a comprehensible statement of the beginnings of the ideas and practices that have influenced the shaping of the modern world.

TOPIC 1

# PREHISTORY: THE ORIGINS OF MAN

The origins of man are today an exciting study in the social as well as the natural sciences. In history, archaeology, and anthropology, as in geology and biology, a rewarding search is in progress. That search has taken scholars to distant continents and led them to the most challenging kinds of discovery and speculation. In these readings we examine how students of prehistory gather their evidence and where their speculation leads. From their work we may gain a better understanding of the evolution of man and his culture.



## John Pfeiffer: Man Through Time's Mists

From John Pfeiffer, "Man Through Time's Mists," *Saturday Evening Post* (December 3, 1966), pp. 41–44, 48–52, 65. Reprinted by special permission of *The Saturday Evening Post.*


### I

Man has been around a long time, much longer than was suspected as recently as three or four years ago, and he has spent more than 99 per cent of his time on earth roaming the wilderness and competing with other meat-eaters for available supplies of game. . . .

Human evolution turns out to be a long and exceedingly subtle process. As far as we know there was no "magic moment" when our ancestors crossed the line from pre-man to man. It was a gradual change resembling the transition from twilight to evening or from childhood to adolescence. We are the latest members of a family that arose more than 15 million years ago in the forests of the Old World, descendants of primates that were neither monkeys nor apes nor men but something quite different and outside our experience—men in the making. They were primarily vegetarians, but for reasons we can only guess at, they gave way to creatures that consumed greater and greater quantities of raw meat, and, as they learned to kill bigger animals, evolved into human beings.

Among those leading the current research boom are adventurers, men with strong personalities and a willingness to spend their lives following up leads and hunches. . . .

Not surprisingly, the number of investigators who can meet these qualifications is small; perhaps 50 specialists throughout the world devote a major part of their time to work on human origins. They spend about $500,000 a year, a modest figure in these days of billion-dollar science budgets. Most of the money for American studies comes from grant-giving agencies such as the National Science Foundation and New York's Wenner-Gren Foundation for Anthropological Research—and goes for a wide variety of activities from excavating with dental picks and paintbrushes and fitting pieces of bone together to making stone tools (often at the price of a bashed finger) or studying monkeys so long and so closely that the observer almost becomes a member of the troop.

The accent at present is on techniques, on the art of getting the evidence and making the most of it. First, of course, you have to find your site, which generally involves hunting in Africa, where our closest living relatives, the chimpanzee and gorilla, survive and where the earliest human remains have been discovered. Every lead must be followed up. There are local rumors about bones in haunted caves,

"The Creation of the World," by Joseph Belline, a sixteenth-century view.

the diaries of explorers and travelers, and fossils uncovered during the building of roads and railways. Geological maps indicate ancient lake shores and river beds and exposed deposits; aerial photographs, examined through stereo viewers, provide miniature three-dimensional pictures of the territory to be searched.

Luck also plays a major role. A chunk of fossil-bearing rock blasted loose by a quarryman's dynamite charge, light falling at just the right angle on a bit of dusty bone, likely-looking cliff formations seen through a spyglass from the deck of a lake steamer running off course—these are some of the coincidences that have led to significant finds, clues to the story of man. The Olduvai Gorge itself was discovered in 1911 by a German entomologist named Kattwinkel, who nearly fell over one of its cliffs while chasing a butterfly.

But in the long run luck generally comes to the most patient searchers, and I learned firsthand what patience means when I visited an expedition in the wilds of Malawi not long ago. Desmond Clark of the University of California at Berkeley, head of the expedition and an authority on African prehistory, has been exploring the southern end of the Great Rift Valley, a series of deep gashes in the earth which run north more than 4,000 miles to the Sea of Galilee in Israel. In one day we tramped eight dry and dusty hours through brush and brambles and down steep gullies under a blazing sun. (The only other kind of weather in Africa, the rainy season, is too much even for paleontologists.) We had only one small canvas bag of water between us because our African water carriers, with some logic, considered us crazy and managed to "lose" us early in the morning. Furthermore, we had had a total of little more than half an hour of rest, taken in all-too-brief snatches, and I protested weakly toward the end of the hike. "You can't be tired, really," Clark replied in the surprised tone of someone who has just started a stroll along a comfortable English lane. "There's a lot more to look at. The army, you know, allows only five minutes of rest for every hour of marching."

Clark explained that he and his colleagues are looking for something special: "We need more sealed-in living sites which have been preserved in about their original condition ever since prehistoric times. The excavation of such sites is extending our knowledge in a way that would hardly have been believed possible twenty years ago. The next step is to be able to select meaningful patterns and interpret them. That's the real problem."

Anthropologists examine finds in a cave near Pegue in West Africa. The cave contained a number of conical towers built of finger-imprinted clay rolls. A great number of human bones and skulls were excavated from these towers along with fragments of finely woven cloth and basketwork.

The marks of man are surprisingly persistent. Objects covered by the gentle action of falling volcanic ash or lake sediments may remain in position, in context, for hundreds of thousands of years—like the pieces of an intricate mosaic. The trick is to excavate sites so that you do not miss the messages, the so-called "living-floor" patterns. So, once you find an undisturbed site in mint condition, you approach it with almost surgical care and precision. Removing the top cover of rock and soil exposes underlying layers, and from there on things may proceed very slowly. Indeed, you can spend entire days on your knees digging two to four inches deep in an area not much bigger than the page of a newspaper. Furthermore, the position of every object, every bit of bone and stone, must be measured and noted and eventually plotted on living-floor diagrams.

The most impressive sites excavated to date lie near the bottom of the Olduvai Gorge, some 300 feet below the surrounding East African plains. Mary Leakey, who learned precise digging techniques during her student days at a hill-fort site in England, spent months exposing material in an area about the size of a tennis court. Her final diagram reveals a feature of unusual interest. Extending most of the way around a saucer-shaped area are piles of rock arranged in a semicircle, perhaps a crude wall or windbreak. This hardly rates as an architectural milestone, but it happens to be about two million years old, which makes it the oldest artificial structure known.

The earth yields further clues to skilled investigators. An eye for jigsaw-puzzle pieces of bone and the details of tooth structure is required to reconstruct our extinct predecessors as well as the animals they hunted and avoided. I remember the exclamation of a South African anatomist as he inspected a fossil tooth through a jeweler's magnifying lens: "My poor child—you're so sickly!" He was reading a medical record that has endured more than 1,000 millennia, enamel defects which showed that the child had three separate attacks of a long-lasting illness (possibly gastroenteritis) at the approximate ages of two, four, and four and a half.

The color and consistency of soils indicate weathering, erosion and climatic changes. Certain types of black soil are signs of wet periods with thick forests; angular, split particles show the effects of frost. Ancient pollen is preserved in such fine detail that an expert with a microscope can identify oak, birch, spruce, holly, date palms, juniper and dozens of other plants—and reconstruct past landscapes with great accuracy. In one pollen study the sudden decline of an oak forest, coinciding with the appearance of grasses and early man, suggests the accidental spread of fires started by hunters to stampede game.

There are even invisible timekeepers in the earth, natural clocks whose "ticking" is the explosion of radioactive atoms. Bits of volcanic glass are scattered over many sites and may contain traces of U-238, the radioactive form of uranium involved in the production of early atomic weapons. U-238 atoms split at a regular rate, leaving "fission tracks" in the glass, which resemble tiny grooves under the microscope and can be counted to provide a measure of the time elapsed since the glass cooled. General Electric researchers used this recently developed method to calculate the figure of 2,000,000 for the age of lava at the bottom of Olduvai Gorge, where the semicircle of piled stones was found (more precisely, they estimated 2,030,000 give or take 280,000). Another valuable clock, found in certain types of lava, depends on the steady accumulation of the inert gas argon as a product of the breakdown of radioactive potassium atoms. Still another involves the decay of C-14, a radioactive variety of carbon.

Living prehistory is another increasingly important source of information, involving a whole complex of new techniques. For some time investigators have realized that fossils and other dug-up materials alone are not enough, that an intimate feeling for the ways of our extinct predecessors can come only from firsthand studies of existing species.

According to one recent estimate, more than 100 scientists in a dozen countries are engaged in such long-term studies in the wilderness, and they have already made some striking discoveries. For one thing, they expected to see considerable violence among wild monkeys and apes, because animals observed in laboratories and zoos often fight viciously and to the death. But violence turns out to be an effect of life in cages rather than an innate primate characteristic. Although wild primates frequently threaten and chase one another, pitched battles are extremely rare and killing is even rarer, a finding which tends to deflate the theory that human violence is a built-in trait inherited from subhuman ancestors.

Studies of past human behavior are also based on a sort of Stanislavsky approach to prehistory, on the theory that doing what our ancestors did is one way of identifying with them and understanding them better. A number of prehistorians have become experts at making and using stone and bone tools, traps, snares and other devices. . . .

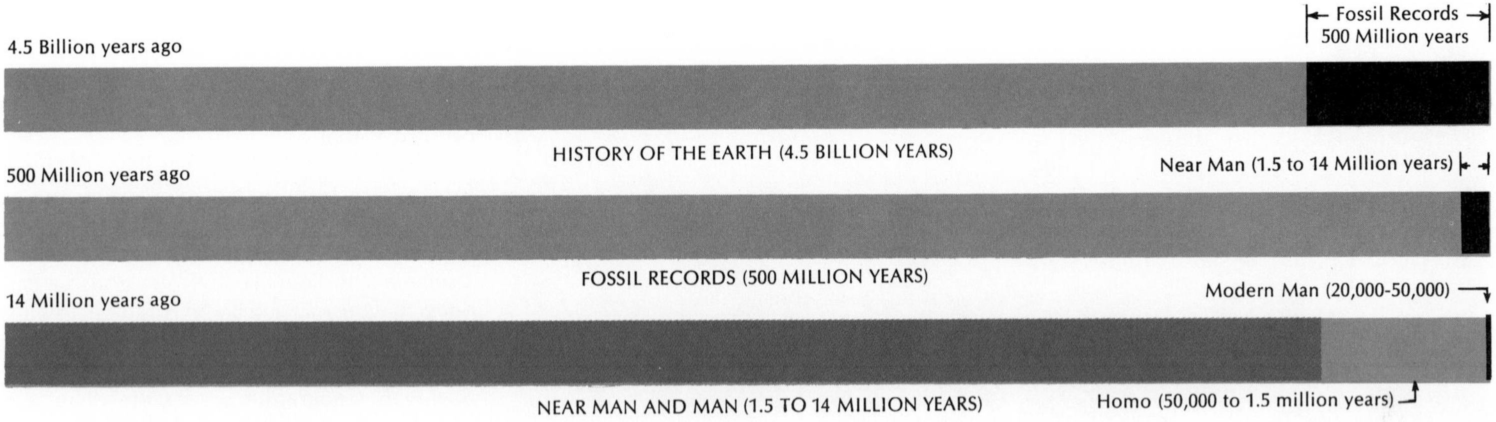


## II

Our story starts about 14 million years ago . . . in the abundant subtropics of Asia and Africa. The savannas, yellow-brown grasslands, were wide as oceans then—rolling in all directions to the horizon and beyond, penetrated here and there by dark peninsular stretches of forest. It might have been an Eden of a sort except for, or perhaps because of, the fact that man had not yet appeared.

His coming was imminent, however. According to one theory, the line that would lead to us had already begun in a marginal zone along the irregular border between forest and savanna. Most forest animals lived enclosed lives snug inside "green caves" of leaves and branches, tunneling along time-worn trails through the underbrush, moving high in the canopies of tall trees, and generally avoiding the bright uneasy places where savanna grasses rustled at the very edges of the woods. But one type of animal had begun exploring the open spaces, seeking food in the traditional hunting territories of stronger and swifter predators. It probably looked something like a small chimpanzee, and had the nimble hands and general agility of a monkey.

RAMAPITHECUS

This species has been studied by a young Kansas-born, Texas-raised scientist specializing in primate evolution. Elwyn Simons started collecting bones when he was 10, and is now curator of vertebrate paleontology at Yale University's Peabody Museum, which houses a collection of more than 100,000 fossil specimens. His examinations of teeth and jaw fragments gathered during the past half century in India, East Africa, China, Germany and Spain suggest the existence of a widespread species distinguished by, among other things, a short face and small canine teeth. It is known officially as Ramapithecus, because the first specimens to be recognized came from the Siwalik Hills of northwest India ("Rama" is the name of a hero in Hindu mythology, the incarnation of the diety Vishnu; *pithekos* is Greek for "ape").

The size of the teeth is especially significant. Apes, like such carnivores as lions and

**MANKIND DURING THE ICE AGE**

The shaded area marks the territory to which mankind was confined by the movement of the tremendous glaciers during the Pleistocene era, more than 130,000 years ago. Triangles indicate some of the important sites at which remains of near men belonging to an early stone age culture have been found.

tigers, have long and large canines—formidable ripping and tearing implements for shredding food, or for fighting. But at least one prehuman primate apparently did not require such weapons. "Ramapithecus wasn't feeding the way apes feed," Simons points out, "and that indicates it prepared its food and defended itself in some other way, presumably by using its hands. Furthermore, the implication is that it walked upright and fashioned tools of a simple type, although we need a great deal more evidence before we can prove that."

Some indirect evidence has been obtained from observations of the chimpanzee. Among the leading investigators of primate behavior is an attractive blond, Jane Goodall. Formerly a secretary to Louis Leakey, she is also a baroness, having married Baron Hugo van Lawick, a Dutch photographer who met her among the chimpanzees during an assignment for the *National Geographic* magazine. She has visited and revisited the forests of northwest Tanzania many times, watching and living among wild chimpanzees, and her observations do much to weaken the old notion that man is the only maker of tools. At the beginning of the rainy season in late October, when worker termites burrow passages from the depths to the surface of their hills, a chimpanzee will take a straw or bit of vine, trim it neatly by pulling off leaves and side shoots, break it off to a length of about a foot—and approach the termite hill with a glint of anticipation in his eyes. After licking the stick he pokes it into one of the burrowed holes, and waits a moment or two. When he draws the stick out, it is covered with a glob of clinging termites which he licks off as gleefully as a child licking a lollipop. The presumption is strong that Ramapithecus, the earliest known (but not the earliest) member of the family of man, was at least as ingenious as contemporary chimpanzees.

We have only a fleeting glimpse of Ramapithecus, the equivalent of a few frames clipped from a feature-length motion picture. The next view comes some 12 million years later and it is more than a glimpse, bringing us to sites in the Olduvai Gorge, where some big changes have occurred. Ever since the discovery of the skull in 1959, work has been active at Olduvai, where the Leakeys maintain an unusual establishment. Last time I visited the gorge I arrived in the evening after a magnificent 10-hour Land Rover drive from Nairobi, past Mount Kilimanjaro and up three steep palisades . . . and then down from Ngorongoro Crater into the Serengeti Plain.

Louis Leakey greeted me and led the way to an open thatched-roof structure, a dining room and laboratory and the work center of the camp. A big weather-beaten man of 63, with a shock of white hair and the drive of a high-pressure executive, Leakey was reared in Kenya by English-missionary parents as the only white child among the Kikuyu, who initiated him into their tribe. Thirteen years ago, during the Mau Mau uprisings, he ran a special police unit and risked his life helping to bring about a settlement.

Our company now included, besides the Leakeys and myself, two students and a small zooful of lesser species—crickets, flies, praying mantises and other insects attracted by our lamps, four Dalmatians, one terrier, one dormouse, a young wildebeest that had lost its mother and was being fed from a nippled brandy bottle, a tame but rambunctious monkey named Simon, and a large poisonous snake kept in a cotton bag hanging near the table. The work area and surrounding tents were protected by a ring of branches and brambles to discourage rhinoceroses and other animals from wandering into the camp. (That night a leopard came too near the barrier, and was chased off by two of the Dalmatians.)

Next morning it was up at six and down a steep trail into the gorge with Leakey: "Sometimes we come across rhinos down here, but they won't bother you." We stopped at an area on the bottom carefully covered by tarpaulin, the place where the semicircle of piled stones had recently been found. Some distance away, about 15 feet above the lava floor and near the branching part of the Y-shaped gorge, was the site of the 1959 find, marked by a concrete memorial slab. "We did a lot of work here, mostly on our hands and knees," Leakey recollected. "In one thirteen-month period, with the support of the National Geographic Society, we moved more than twice as much dirt and rock, about seven thousand tons, as we had in all our previous seasons of digging.

During the past five years or so the Leakeys have found the skull of a female referred to as "Cinderella," "Poor George" (a skull trampled to bits by Masai cattle), and remains of more than a dozen other individuals, ranging in age from about a million to a million and a half years. I later saw Poor George, also known as "Olduvai George," at the Leakey's home outside Nairobi. Mary opened a safe in her study, removed the domeshaped top of a skull, and set it down gingerly. "We spent a couple of months recovering hundreds of bone fragments after the cattle came through, and I've put about two hundred of them together in this specimen. I worked over a period of eight and a half months, on odd Sun-

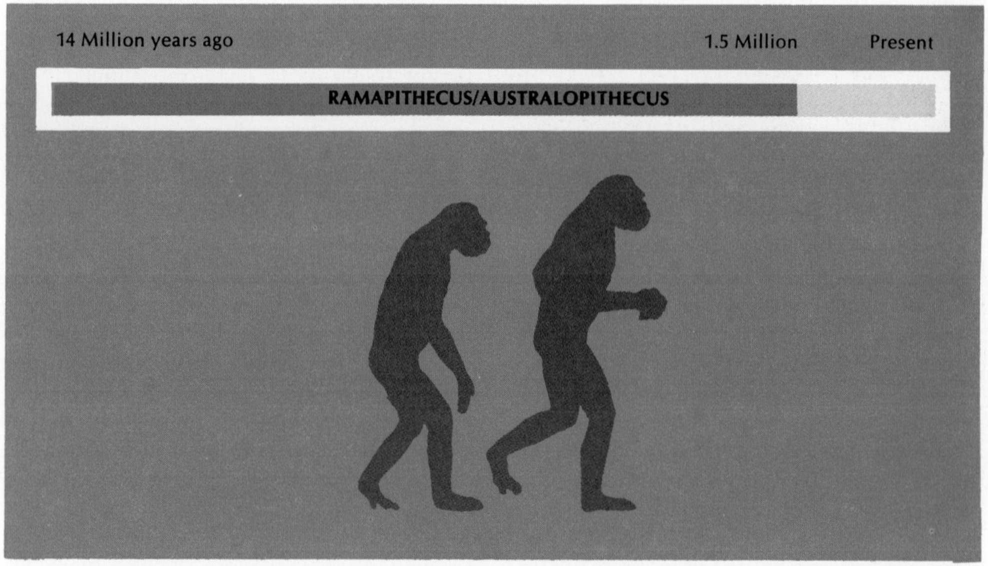


Ramapithecus, a manlike primate, is thought by many experts to be the oldest in the direct line of man's ancestors. Remains of Australopithecus, who walked upright and was capable of using stones for defense, have been found at Olduvai gorge.

days and times like that. It would drive you crazy doing that all the time!"

A highly technical debate is currently under way over which of the Olduvai individuals deserve the coveted title of *Homo*. In general, Leakey and his supporters tend to bestow the honor more readily than their opponents. But there is no argument on one point—several species of higher primates roamed the region at various times, including creatures well on the way to becoming full-fledged human beings.

These primates, call them near-men for convenience, combined archaic and advanced features, something like a high-fendered Model-T chassis fitted with bucket seats and automatic transmission. They stood about four feet high, smaller than today's pygmies, and probably had hands resembling those of a young gorilla. But their feet were basically like ours, and the odds are that they walked and ran about as efficiently. Their brain was on the small side, weighing perhaps a pound or so compared with some three pounds for modern man, although size measurements do not take into account the quality or organization of cerebral tissue.

Such creatures get credit for almost all the really clever work uncovered at Olduvai. They probably built the semi-circular structure, and new studies indicate that they used more kinds of tools than previously suspected. They stored large quantities of rubble or unworked rocks, perhaps to hurl at marauding animals at night, and the most common item in their tool kit was a stone with flakes knocked off on one or both sides to form a rough cutting edge. But as far back as two million B.C. they were also making scrapers, gougers, borers and other implements that were not supposed to have been invented for another million years or so. "At first it was rather a shock to us," Mary Leakey says. "We had a hard time believing that such tools could have been made so early. Now it should be easy to believe practically anything!"

No one knows what the near-men were doing with all those tools, but there are clues to one especially significant use. An Olduvai living-floor provides a vivid picture of the carnage left behind when they got up from dinner. It includes an area about two or three feet in diameter that is packed with the remnants of hearty meals, bones broken to bits for the marrow inside, and chips and flakes from the tools used to smash the bones. Around this area the debris thins out, except for one place nearby which contains bigger bones such as skull and jaws. You can almost see the diner, squatting on the ground where the shattered material is concentrated, tossing the unbroken bones over his shoulder. He was an enthusiastic meat-eater. Most of the bones found . . . are those of rodents, hares, birds, lizards and the young of antelopes and other large animals—in other words, small game.

One key question at this stage of human evolution is why our ancestors took up meat-eating in the first place. Apes are more or less vegetarians, living predominantly on fruits and grass shoots and other plant foods, and it is a safe bet that at one time our ancestors did the same. But somewhere along the line they began acquiring a taste for red meat. Work in the field of living prehistory offers a basis for further shrewd guesses. Experience in African game parks suggests that scavenging may have been the rule at first. Jackals can be scattered easily; vultures are more of a problem, but they will retreat before a vigorous man wielding a stick. Even driving away the killers themselves is not out of the question. Tribesmen in northern India still scan the skies for vultures, rush to the spot, and almost always manage to drive tigers away by shouting and generally making nuisances of themselves. So prehuman primates could have used similar tactics to compete successfully with other species for the leavings of more formidable predators.

Recent findings indicate that, whether or not they scavenged, they did some killing on their own. Several years ago Sherwood Washburn, of the University of California at Berkeley, descendant of a long line of Puritan theologians and one of the most imaginative of current anthropologists, started studying wild baboons in Kenya. He selected the place and the species for special reasons. Kenya contains wide, grassy savannas, dry, open country with trees concentrated near occasional streams and waterholes, the sort of environment where early man lived—and where baboons thrive. Washburn's co-worker was Irven DeVore, one of his graduate students who is now a professor at Harvard.

They eventually noted meat-eating among baboons. In a typical case an individual baboon would be walking along through the grass, come across a nest of fledgling birds, and scoop up the contents without breaking stride. In other words, it was usually an act performed in passing. But not always. Something less casual took place in 1964 when I spent several weeks with DeVore in Kenya. One July afternoon we were driving through the Nairobi National Park, looking for baboons as usual, and heading for a shallow stream. All of a sudden we saw a large male baboon with a freshly killed hare in its mouth, a noteworthy event in itself since meat-eating is rarely observed. But there was more to come. A whole troop was crossing the stream, and a few seconds later another large male passed with another hare, and not long after that a third male carrying the remains of a small antelope.

"I've never seen anything like this," DeVore remarked as he left the truck to look at the passing troop. "It certainly indicates some sort of group activity, although not necessarily hunting. The troop members all seemed aroused, jittery. Since baboons eat such small animals in a matter of minutes, these animals must all have been killed recently and almost simultaneously, suggesting that the sight of one individual catching an animal aroused fellow troop members to go after other animals in the vicinity. The result could have been the triggering of a kind of brief, spontaneous bloodlust episode."

These studies permit further deductions about behavior in the past. For example, given a stretch of open territory with clumps of bushes and tall grasses where lions may be lurking, what is the best way of organizing a group of individuals for effective defense? A baboon troop represents a living solution to this problem. As it moves through dangerous areas, large males are spread out in front and in rear, while the center is occupied by females and infants and the biggest and most dominant adult males. Covered-wagon trains employed such strategies in crossing hostile Indian territory, and so did destroyer-escorted convoys during World War II. We have every reason to believe that man's forerunners moved in the same sort of protective patterns as they roamed in search of food. Also, like baboons, they may have slept chiefly in trees or perhaps on cliff ledges. Large-scale cave-dwelling probably came later, after they had learned to use fire to drive out predators and keep them out.

Of course it is one thing to show that near-men hunted, and something else again to figure out how they did it. One way of exploring the possibilities is to try doing it yourself. Leakey, the world's leading expert in this field, described some of his tactics to me: "You try to think, observe, move and outguess your prey the way hunters might have done it two million years ago. You try to understand their feelings and the way their minds worked."

Once, near a lake outside Nairobi, he prepared to stalk a small gazelle. First he camouflaged himself with leafy branches around his head and waist, "mainly to break up the shape of my body"; then he started to advance, "never moving my arms or legs sideways, since that changes your shape and frightens animals, but always straight ahead." He moved very, very slowly, changing direction as the gazelle wandered from place to place, coming forward a few steps at a time when its head was lowered for grazing, stopping when it raised its head to look around. "You can tell just beforehand when the head is coming up; the animal makes a subtle movement, raising one shoulder a bit higher than the other."

Leakey played a double role as he advanced. Part of the time he tried to put himself in the gazelle's mind and anticipate its actions; part of the time he was a hungry hunter whose life depended on what he could catch. He stopped several times waiting for birds, which might have given alarm calls, to fly away. It took at least two hours to reduce the original distance from 250 yards to about six feet—at which point the prehistorian brought down the gazelle with a perfectly timed flying tackle.

He has also gone after hares with his bare hands. "When you see a hare, it runs straight away, and you run straight after it. It has its ears back, but not all the way back. The ears go all the way back when it's about to dodge, a sharp right or a sharp left. If you're right-handed, you always dash to the right anticipating a dodge to the right. That means the odds are fifty-fifty, and you should catch half the hares you chase. If you've guessed correctly, the hare runs by instinct directly at you and you can scoop it up fielding a fast grounder. If it happens to get past you, stop and watch. It will probably dart under a bush and freeze there, assuming it has gotten rid of you. Then you can go over and simply pick it up."

Once you have your animal, you need more than teeth to dismember it, as Leakey knows from experience. So he has learned to make tools like the ones unearthed at the oldest Olduvai site and he has also learned to use them. In fact, one Christmas Eve at his camp, before an audience of entranced Masai herdsmen, he spent half a minute making a chopper out of a pebble and another 20 minutes skinning and cutting up the carcass of a freshly-killed antelope.

The do-it-yourself approach to prehistory can never provide final answers. Early men may not have been so clever as Leakey, and if they had been, we would undoubtedly be considerably more civilized today. On the other hand, they had good brains for the times and lived as animals among animals, and knowing the ways of animals was a matter of life or death. Furthermore, this approach emphasizes the value and power of the close, intensive observation which must have distinguished all prehistoric hunters and prepared the way for the next great step in human evolution—the shift from small-game to big-game hunting.

A hunter operating strictly on his own could catch a small animal, kill it, and devour it on the spot. But sooner or later he began to realize that it makes more sense to go after meat in large packages, and that taking on bigger and stronger animals with stone weapons is no job for a lone man. Ten hunters working together can get appreciably more than ten times as much meat as a loner, and sheer evolutionary efficiency dictated a change. The change came slowly, taking more than a thousand millennia, but it created a new way of life.

Big-game hunting demanded cooperation, the devising of traps and pitfalls and ambushes, sharing the kill, and other activities that put a premium on increased intelligence. It demanded a new species with larger brains, *Homo erectus,* the first human being. The change came about so gradually that there are many in-between forms, and it is not easy to tell the differences between an advanced ape-man or near-man and a primitive man. But anthropologists are generally convinced that going after big animals played a major role in the process.

This phase of prehistory is currently of special interest to 41-year-old Clark Howell of the University of Chicago. His youthful appearance and a certain innocence of expression are misleading, for his knowledge is formidable. Trained in anthropology and biology, he can more than hold his own in geology, prehistoric archaeology and paleontology, a distinct advantage when it comes to modern interdisciplinary studies of early man. He has dug in Africa and plans to dig there again. But right now he is focusing on material obtained from two sites occupied by big-game hunters who swept out of Africa and roamed over most of the Old World.

The sites are located in a valley cut into a 3,000-foot plateau in north-central Spain, near the village of Torralba. Discovered in 1888 by railroad workers linking the region to the main Madrid-to-Barcelona line, it was partly excavated by a Spanish nobleman and amateur archaeologist. Howell decided to extend the excavations about five years ago. "We started more with hope than anything else, and sometimes hope doesn't pan out. We were lucky."

Evidence from pollen, fossils and other sources permits an unusually complete reconstruction of a camping and butchering site 400,000 to 500,000 years old, a site in a broad valley near a sluggish, meandering stream and sedge-covered swamplands. In one area most of the bones of a big bull elephant lie close together with a few isolated bones of two other elephants, an infant and a young female. Bones of other elephants, as well as horses and red deer and wild ox, lie scattered over the area. Among the bones is an abundant supply of stone tools. The animals had been bogged down in thick mud either by accident or, more likely, driven there by hunters. Whatever happened, the hunters came in to kill and dismember the trapped animals. Other patterns, Howell points out, are more "enigmatic." For example, why would prehistoric man whittle a pencil-sharp point on the tip of an elephant tusk over four feet long? This

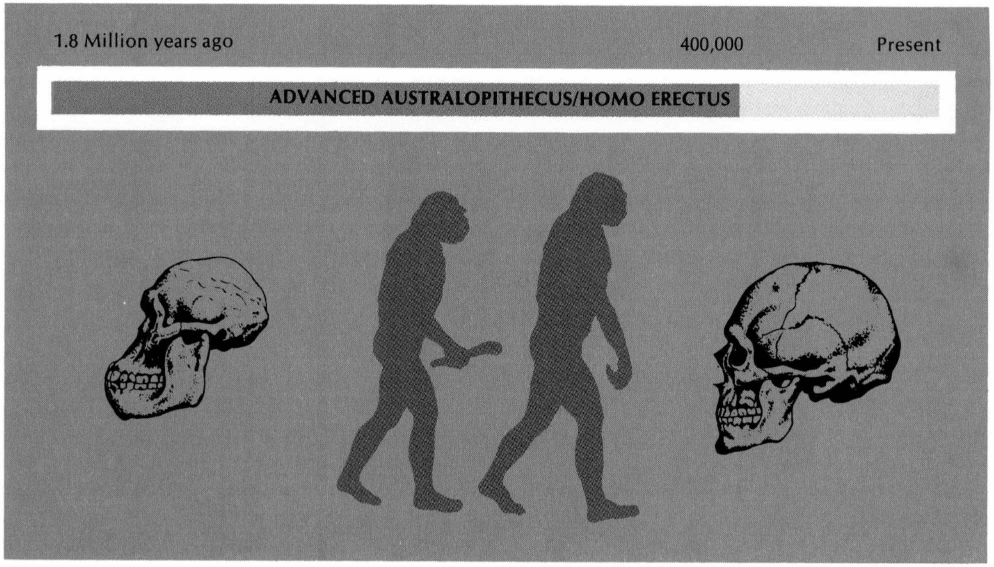


Brain capacity became larger as these types succeeded one another over more than a million years. While primitive tools have been found at sites used by the former, indications are that only Homo Erectus went on to use fire and share in a group life.

puzzling object was found not far from a row of large elephant bones and a tusk, next to a smashed elephant skull. Could some of the remains be a support for a shelter of hides held down at one edge by the aligned bones and held up at the other edge by sharpened tusks driven into the ground to serve as posts?

*Homo erectus* had a brain nearly double the size of the brain of Dart's Taung child [Australopithecus, skull section discovered by Raymond Dart in South Africa, 1924], which puts it within the range of modern brain sizes, and a new way of life. Apes and other primates that live mainly on plants confine themselves to relatively restricted areas. 15 to 20 square miles at the most. But the world widens for primates who go out into the savanna to find and follow herds, and the new men may have had hunting territories of 500 to 1,000 square miles.

Hunting heightened the division of labor, the differences between the sexes. Men went away in groups and stayed away longer, perhaps all night. Women became the "other sex" in a sense that is true for no other primate, the first females to be left behind. Physical changes included a widening of the pelvis to permit the delivery of bigger-brained infants, who remained helpless longer and required longer periods of maternal care. (Infant dependency probably lasted about five years for *Homo erectus* as compared with three or four years for chimpanzees and six to eight years for modern man.) A wider pelvis also meant that women became somewhat more dependent themselves, since it decreased their running ability.

## GROWTH OF BRAIN SIZE IN THE EVOLUTION OF PRIMATES

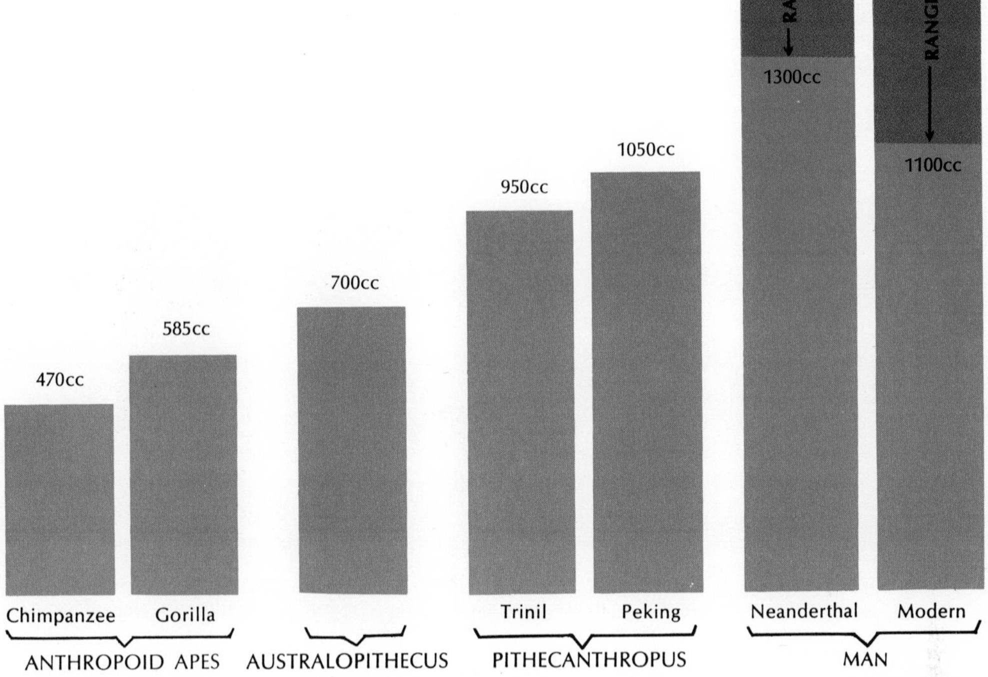


There was also the fire to take care of. . . . [Early] evidence for the use of fire, at least fire hearths and fire-cracked stones, comes from recent excavations at a site in southern France which is probably about a million years old. We can imagine men fleeing before great natural fires set by volcanic embers or lightning, and noticing even in their panic the panic of other fleeing animals, especially the big cats and other predators. A plausible next step would have been to bring fire into camp for protection, to keep carnivores and scavengers away at night. More aggressive uses, such as driving animals out of caves and stampeding herds during the hunt, probably came later.

Fire brought important advantages—warmth, for one thing, cooking and above all, light. For the first time men had the power to change the ancient and powerful rhythm of sleeping and waking. They no longer had to end their days with the setting sun, but could gather inside the bright circles of hearth and make tools and perhaps tell tall hunting tales. Certainly fire provided some leisure and an opportunity for the growth of language, a trend already fostered by the need to devise new plans and strategies for the hunt.

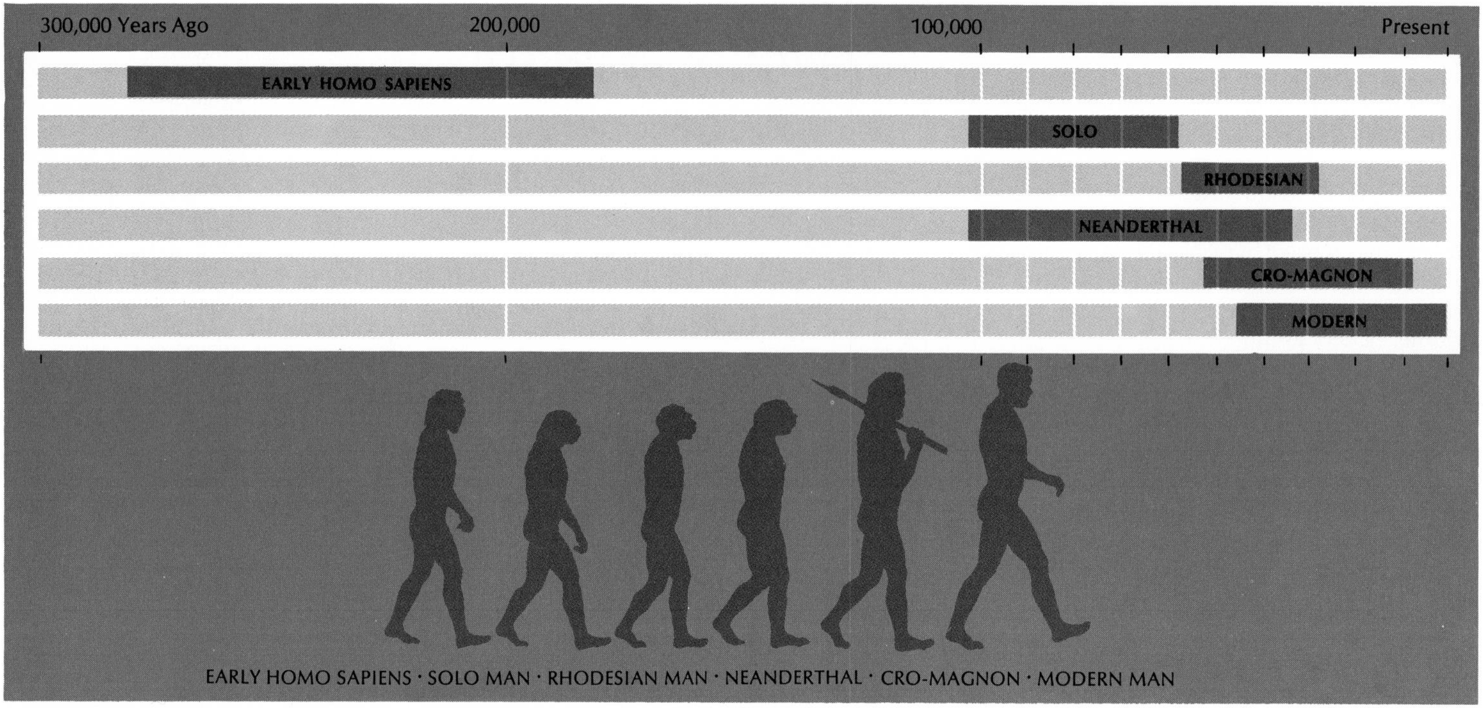


Early Homo Sapiens came within range of modern man's brain capacity but no continuous record allows us to trace a direct line. Solo, Rhodesian, and Neanderthal Man are long extinct. Cro-Magnon Man, culturally closest to our own genus, has left us cave paintings, carved figures, and engravings in stone. Modern man is only 20,000 to 50,000 years old.

At this point we have covered some 90 per cent of man's past, the all-important formative period during which human beings emerged gradually from prehuman primates that have been extinct for millions of years. It is also the period about which we know least. The rest of the story, only yesterday on the time scale of human development, occupies the last few hundred thousand years, years which have seen the appearance of *Homo sapiens.* It is more solidly documented.

### III

Neanderthal man [the first discovered skeleton of *Homo sapiens,* found in the Neander Valley of Germany in 1856] appears to have invented religion, a finding which hardly jibes with the lingering notion that he was an apelike savage. One of his most spectacular sites lies at the foot of a mountain south of Rome, close by the Mediterranean surf. Here, deep inside a cave, a Neanderthal skull was found surrounded by a ceremonial ring of stones. Other burial sites in Europe and the Middle East contain whole skeletons and include rings of goat and cave-bear skulls, as well as meat and tools left at the graveside for the use of the deceased in an afterlife.

Among prehistory's greatest mysteries is the vanishing of Neanderthal man. He seems to have been wiped out or absorbed by Cro-Magnon and other later peoples, and after that the pace of things quickened even more. By 10,000 or 15,000 years ago man had developed tool kits including a wide variety of blades and harpoons and arrows—and prehistoric art had reached its high point in the cave paintings and carvings found mainly in France and Spain. The invention of agriculture, the resulting population explosion, the first towns and temples and cities—these are some of the major advances of the last few millennia. Prehistory ends officially with the invention of writing some five thousand years ago.

Where do we stand today in the perspective of prehistory? Although we have developed cooperation and social organization to an unprecedented degree, we still harbor opposing tendencies which could become our undoing. We are hunters who have created a world which no longer has any place for hunters. After more than two million years of killing and avoiding killers, we have been struggling to civilize ourselves for perhaps five millennia (a very generous estimate)—which is about the same thing as a man trying to reform in a few weeks after a lifetime of crime.

It is no wonder that in moments of stress our responses may be those of people still on the prowl in prehistoric times, of wanderers in a wide and alien wilderness where death comes suddenly and often without apparent cause. A hatred for strangers and people who look different, a limited capacity for caring really deeply about anyone outside our immediate circle, an easily aroused aggressiveness, an almost pathological fear of uncertainty and the unknown and being wrong—such reactions make a great deal of sense in a small and tightly organized little band fighting for survival in hostile surroundings. But they are dangerously inappropriate for the 20th century. . . .

The scope of research in prehistory is becoming broader and broader. It is part of man's increasing effort to see himself and his problems more objectively, as he prepares to invade and inhabit space. He arose in times of grave physical danger and hardly any social change, living pretty much as his ancestors had lived for hundreds of thousands of years. His problem today is that of a species still trying to adjust to a world where predators are few, but where social changes are taking place at an accelerating rate. How you figure his chances of making the adjustment or failing depends on whether you are an optimist or a pessimist. But so far at least he has consistently shown a genius for getting out of, as well as into, trouble—and the possibility exists that we may be the representatives of the first species to avoid extinction, and to evolve indefinitely.

# Paul Bohannon: Africa, the "Home" of Mankind

Paul Bohannon, an American social anthropologist, spent several years in field work in Nigeria and Kenya. The book from which this reading was taken tried to place African culture in modern perspective for a Western audience. From *Africa and Africans,* by Paul Bohannon. 

## I

### Early Man

Africa, for all that it was the last continent to be "explored"—which means that it remained longest unknown to modern Western civilization—has nevertheless yielded the oldest "human" remains and artifacts yet discovered. According to our present information, the earliest anthropoid forms that could have begun the systematic invention of culture are indisputably associated with Africa.

To say that Africa is the "home" of mankind does not mean, however, that Africans as we know them today were the first human beings—indeed, it seems likely that except for a handful of "Boskopoids" or "Bushmanoids," the peopling of Africa has all been recent.

In any discussion of early man, the knotty question always emerges early: When is a man a man? In the apt phrase of Professor Raymond Dart, the earliest culture-creating anthropoid forms were "trembling on the verge of humanity." The question becomes: When did they topple over?

The usual answer to this question is made on the basis of an extension of activities rather than of the animal body. It is not the shape or the physique of the creature that defines man, but rather it is what he does. For decades, anthropologists have defined man as a tool-making animal, and said that every ape that makes a tool is human. If such a definition is maintained, both chimpanzees and gorillas are today "trembling on the verge of humanity," for both of them make tools of a crude sort. A tool is any creation, external to the physical body, that is made in order to accomplish something else. Elephants break off branches of trees in order to swish flies, but the branch is usually not considered to be a tool, for it is not worked specifically (although it is obvious that such a position can rapidly deteriorate into a quibble). Chimpanzees do alter the shape of the proto-tools that they create. They do not, however, shape them to a pattern and such students of early man as L. S. B. Leakey have preserved toolmaking as the criterion of the human—the point at which pithecus (ape) becomes anthropos (man)—by adding the criterion of tool pattern. A man is a hominid who shapes tools to a pattern.

Mankind, if such be the definition of him, shares a great many physical characteristics with the great apes, as well as the more general ones with all of the mammals of all of the animal world, and ultimately all the world of the living. The major blood types found among human beings are also found in the

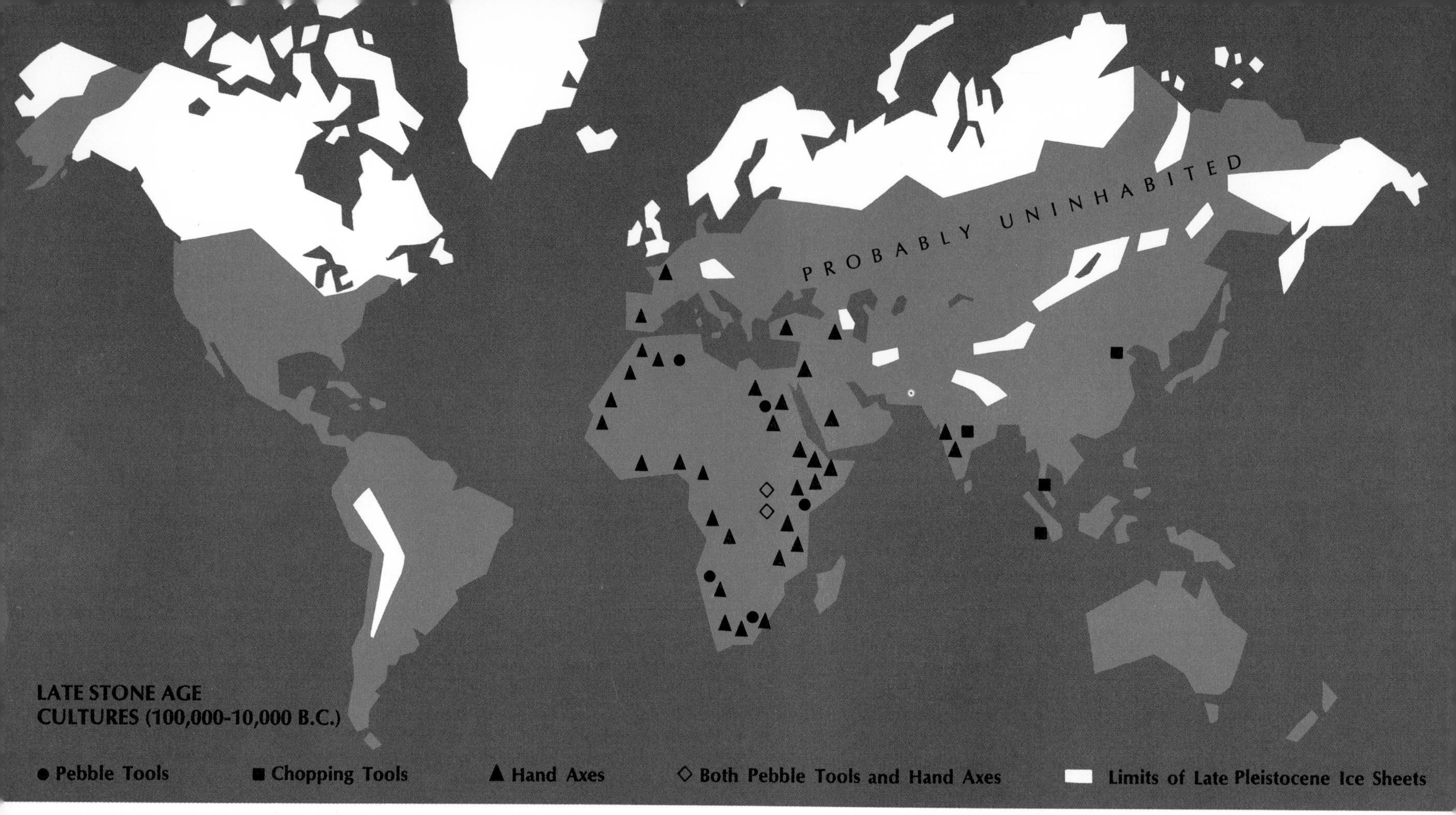


four great apes—gorilla, chimpanzee, orangutan, and gibbon. The body musculature is largely the same—the differences arise from such distinctive human features as the head being balanced more comfortably on the spine and so needing fewer heavy muscles to hold it up, and the fact that the bipedal locomotion has led to musculature development in the lower back, the legs, and the knot of muscle in the buttocks which none of the great apes shares with man. The great apes, some monkeys, and human beings are the only menstruating animals, showing again the closeness of their relationship. Other factors, such as the rhesus factor and the M-N factor in the blood, the shape of the skull, and the shape of the feet, are very different. The question emerges: What physical factor or combination of factors is correlated with the tool-making proclivities that define a beast as a man?

The argument rages, and it is this argument that lies behind the difficulty in understanding the problems of early man. When we ask "Was he a man?" we usually mean "Was he like me?" And to answer that question demands extensive examination of the degree of self-knowledge and even of narcissism in the human outlook. It also brings up another problem: the only remains of early man that have ever been found are bone. When, in the course of reconstruction, the flesh and the external appearance is guessed at (and it is never anything but a more or less educated guess), the early man must be given features that resemble in one way or another at least some aspects of the presently existing races. What was the color of Java man? What was the hair texture? We do not know.

The only answer to these riddles is that we must begin to think of ourselves as part of a continuum of the living; we must also realize that the races we know are ephemeral and (a small minority of scholars to the contrary) that races change more rapidly than do species. We must also recognize the narcissism inherent in whatever reconstructions we make. Early man may be cast in the image of the man we most admire; he may, just as readily, be cast in the image of the man we least admire, in order that we can dissociate ourselves from the disadmired type.

What is true, however, is that man and the culture by which he lives evolved together. The development of one cannot be considered in the absence of the other. Man did not evolve a large brain and then discover culture. . . . Neither did pre-man first discover culture and then evolve because of the benefits it conferred. Rather, the development of culture and the evolutionary changes in the beast counteraffected one another. Man and culture are indistinguishable historically—the distinction is valid only as a simplifying device for purposes of scientific study. . . .

## II

## Stone Age Man in Africa

The Old Stone Age, or Paleolithic, cultures of Africa began with the well-known pebble tools that the Leakeys finally pinned down when they discovered them in association with the skeletal remains of Zinjanthropus, the prime Australopithecine. These rough stone tools were, in the course of aeons, supplanted by the so-called "hand-ax" type of cultures which developed as the human animal himself developed. Man and the cultures of the Stone Age developed one another just as, today, man and culture are still developing one another.

A hand-ax is now known not to have been an ax, but the name has been current for so long that changing it becomes as difficult as changing an image like "blood relative," simply because we now know it is genes rather than blood that carry biological relationship. It seems likely that the hand-ax was used for skinning and cutting up game, and perhaps for rough working of wooden implements: a general-purpose tool that was so easy to make that it was in all likelihood seldom carried from one place to another, but simply made anew on the spot where one was needed.

The hand-axes are of many styles and types, and they spread over most of the African continent, Europe, and Asia Minor, and into India, and over hundreds of thousands of years of time. While the type-sites, that is, the excavations which give the "culture" names to the types of implements, are those of Chelles and Acheul in France, hand-axes would seem (at least insofar as our knowledge at present allows us to generalize) to have come earliest into use in the highland area of present-day Kenya. These tools come to be mixed with, and finally superseded by, a whole series of more specialized and locally limited additions of scrapers, awls, points, barbs, and other stone tools in the very late Old Stone Age and the Middle Stone Age periods. . . .

TOPIC 2

# THE POLAR ESKIMOS: A PRIMITIVE CULTURE

Our knowledge of prehistoric peoples is not limited to what can be gathered from fossils and artifacts, to the larger-scale reconstructions which this evidence makes possible, or even to the recognition of the continuities in our human development. We can also gain insight into prehistoric life by examining the islands of primitive culture that cluster on the peripheries of the contemporary world. The Polar Eskimos provide an example of one such culture. Gene Lisitzky, the author of the reading, gives a good explanation in his introduction of why we have chosen his selection.

"These primitive cultures seem insignificant today only because we see them as tiny remnants struggling hopelessly to survive in the nooks and crannies of a world rapidly being taken over by our own more powerful civilization. But against the background of the history of mankind, they are vastly more representative of human culture than are we. What we call "civilization"—the culture of cities, of writing and metals, of advanced agriculture—is only a few thousand years old. For many hundreds of thousands of years before that, for practically its whole lifetime, mankind lived only in small wandering groups by gathering wild plants and hunting animals. . . . It is we who are the exceptions in the ways of mankind. . . . The tribes who still live as they did are our last, fast disappearing chance to find out how they lived and felt."

Reading 3

## Gene Lisitzky: The Polar Eskimos

Gene Lisitzky is an American anthropologist whose book, *Four Ways of Being Human*, compares the cultures of four primitive peoples, the rain forest Semang of Malaya, the Maori islanders of New Zealand, the Hopi Indians in the deserts of southwestern United States, and the Eskimos. From *Four Ways of Being Human* by Gene Lisitzky. 

### I

The Eskimo people are not numerous, as nations go. There are less than forty thousand of them altogether—the population of a small city—but they inhabit a truly vast domain. Scattered a third of the way round the top of the globe, they can claim as their home the millions of square miles from Alaska to Greenland, the whole upper edge of North America that lies within the Arctic zone. Until the coming of the white man in modern times, there was for perhaps two thousand years no one to dispute with them their sole possession of this inhospitable empire of extreme cold and barren, treeless ice. There was nothing to tempt any invader, not even the warlike Indians to the south. Nor was there anything to tempt the Eskimos from their own wintry world, to which they were so well adapted that in softer climes they would have felt lost, they would have had to stop being Eskimos. . . .

In this vast, drafty corner of the world the average temperature for the whole year is well below the freezing point. In winter it often falls in many places to seventy degrees below zero. There are other parts of the world where the winter cold is as intense, or even more so, but here what we call winter lasts nine months of the year. For three months of that winter, the sun never rises at all. Even during the three months of summer, when the sun, by shining twenty-four hours a day, finally brings the temperature above the freezing point, the melting snow and ice keep the air fairly cool. Winter is the time of constant howling winds and violent blizzards, with never a tree to break their force. If weather means everything to the civilized hunter or camper, it can be imagined what it must mean to a people whose whole life is one long hunting trip.

This climate has remorselessly driven out every animal not especially equipped by nature to cope with the cruel, enduring cold and the sparseness of food. It was only some thousands of years ago that the mighty mastodon was wiped out. There remain only the heavily furred polar bears, wolves, foxes, hares. Even the domesticated dogs wear thick pelts. The seals, walruses, and whales carry a thick layer of fat or blubber under their skins to keep their blood warm and muscles active in the icy waters, which are anyhow warmer than the air over the land. The birds are only summer visitors.

Yet the Eskimo has hung on. With skin and flesh no different from any European's or African's, his fingers and toes are as easily frozen off. He cannot by nature run any faster, swim any longer, or do with less food or sleep than they. The natural equipment issued to him is the same, and yet it has sufficed, for it has included the same priceless fingers and, to guide them, the same resourceful brain. With these as his guarantees of survival he has devised his own special arctic equipment. Long ago he invented out of the most unpromising of materials some of the most elaborate and ingenious habitations, tools, and weapons known among primitive people anywhere in the world. . . .

## The Igloo

How [a man might wonder] is it possible to carry on a human existence so deep in the Arctic? He did not, of course, mean merely staying alive . . . on a hunting trip. He meant family living, with women and children and old people, in sickness as well as in health, in winter as in summer, in the performance of other work besides hunting, the kind of work that must be done in warmth and in leisure time. In short, he meant home life.

(1) The Polar Eskimos could have answered that. For this climate and for their needs they had ideal homes. Their little villages were usually to be found on gently sloping beaches, close to stretches of protected water that would freeze into smooth ice in winter, instead of into storm-tossed hummocks and ridges. Thus the dog sledges would have no difficulty in hauling heavy seal and walrus carcasses across the sea ice up to the very huts.

There was no wood, and even in summer the earth, a few inches below the surface, was frozen too solid for easy digging. Nevertheless, there were building materials, for permanent houses. On the beaches could be found slabs of sandstone or other rock. These, the best of insulating materials, were laid out in a rough oval to make the walls; the chinks between them were stuffed with turf. The ceiling consisted of two layers of skin with moss stuffed between, resting on rafters of long whalebone; it was topped with a roof of turf. Usually the back of the house was dug into a hillside. The front, with its single entrance and lone window, faced the sea.

The low arched doorway in front of the single room had no door in it and did not lead directly outside. Instead, one stepped down into a covered passageway or tunnel and crawled on all fours down a gradual incline ten to thirty feet long. This made the simplest, yet most efficient, of heat locks. Since the entrance to the house was below its floor level, the warm air inside, always rising, was trapped among the well-insulated walls. It could not escape with a rush into the frigid night outside, as it certainly would if entry were made by swinging doors or tent flaps. . . .

And of course all Eskimos knew how to use the most abundant housing material of all—snow and ice. When we think of igloos, it is usually these snow huts that come to mind, because our imaginations are captured by the sheer cleverness of fighting cold and snow with snow and ice. The Polar Eskimos could build these snow huts, which they called *iglooiaks,* but they did so only in an emergency, for temporary use on the trail for a few weeks at most. For their more permanent homes they had plenty of stone houses, built long ago by their more numerous ancestors on all the better wintering sites. . . .

No hunter or family ever went on the trail in winter without snow knives. When time came to make camp, a site was selected where

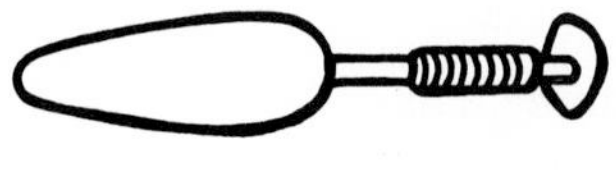

the snow was of just the right kind for building. It must not be too grainy lest it crumble in handling, or too newly fallen lest it be too soft to hold its carved shape in carrying. With the bone or ivory snow knives, foot-thick blocks were cut out of the drifts and set up on edge around the builder in a circle from six to twelve feet in diameter, depending on the size of the party. The builder stayed inside the circle as he laid the blocks round and round himself in a continuous spiral that gradually sloped inward. It took a good eye to cut each succeeding block to just the right-fitting shape, for no two could be alike.

When the builder had completely walled himself in, and had built a dome overhead that might be nine feet high, and before the final block had been put in place, he could cut himself a low arch out of which to crawl. Meanwhile, others outside had been packing soft snow into all cracks and crevices, as a mortar to cement the blocks together. They had also been digging a tunnel through the drift up to this entrance, below the level of the igloo floor, so that one would have to step up into the room. A house for a family to live in for weeks could be built by experienced Eskimos in a few hours.

A hunter or wayfarer caught in a blizzard, even if he knew that his destination was somewhere only a short distance away, would not ordinarily risk exhausting himself in aimless wandering through the blinding storm. Quickly he would build himself a one-man shelter of this kind, maybe six feet in diameter, and wait out the storm, for days if need be, till the stars or prevailing winds or known landmarks could show him his way. . . .

## The Eskimo's Lamp

Of all his simple yet efficient devices for keeping warm, the Eskimo's lamp perhaps looked the most primitive. Yet it too was quite a remarkable invention. It was nothing but a big shallow bowl or dish carved out of soft soapstone in the shape of a half-moon and standing on three or four small stones for legs. Its length could vary from one to over three feet. For fuel it burned the oil crushed from the blubber of sea animals. This was stored and carried in a waterproof bag made from a whole sealskin that had been stripped off the seal with a minimum of cuts and slits. The lamp wick was dried moss which had been reduced to a powder by being rolled in the palm of the hands, then carefully laid, like a narrow trail of gunpowder, along the straight edge of the half-moon, in a ridge about a quarter of an inch high. As the wick sucked up the oil from the very shallow bowl, it burned in a long straight line of steady little flames, bright enough to give a soft yellow light to the room and warm enough to let the family take off their clothes in any weather. . . .

Besides being the source of all the light and warmth of the house, the lamps were its only cookstove and its only water tap. Practically the only method of cooking was by boiling in stone pots that were suspended over the lamp flames by thongs tied to a square framework of wood or bone. Fresh water was made by placing clumps of ice or blocks of packed snow on an inclined stone over the blubber lamp and letting the melting water drip into a sealskin cup. People on an exclusive meat diet need lots of drinking water, and this was a tedious process for getting it. Fortunately for the housewife, bathing was all but unknown among the Eskimos. (Indeed, some people might have regarded the Eskimos as a rather dirty, verminous folk, but it could not be said that they did not have a good excuse. Among the more dangerous things that could happen in this climate was getting wet, and the avoidance of unnecessary wetting could easily become as much second nature to a fur-clad man as it is first nature to a cat.)

## Hunters of the North

Normally when we ask how some creature manages to live in a certain environment, we are thinking of its food—what it is and how it is gotten. It is only because of the extraordinary conditions of the Arctic that here our first thoughts were of dwellings and clothing, the problem of protection from the climate. We have seen how successfully the Polar Eskimo solved that problem, indoors and out. His family warmly sheltered behind stone and ice, himself warmly clad from head to toe in arctic furs, he was now ready to pursue his main business in life—the hunt.

(2) It bears repeating that any people who chose to live on the resources of this land would have to hunt and fish, not only for its food but also for almost everything else that makes human life possible. There is no possibility of living by gathering plants, let alone by cultivating them. For all practical purposes, the only natural resource is the animal life. Hunting must supply not only the total diet, indoor fuel, and outdoor clothes, but also the means of hunting—the materials for the hunter's weapons.

Chief among the Eskimo's weapons was his harpoon, considered to be among the most remarkable of primitive inventions. . . . When you consider how this complex big-game weapon had to be assembled with almost machine-like precision—so that it would fly through the air as a single piece, true as a lance, and yet so that each part would do its separate job on contact—don't forget that it was invented by men of the Stone Age. The straightness and balance of the shaft had to be achieved by scraping with a sharp stone. The work of nails, screws, and hinges was done with lashings of skin string. . . .

[The] Eskimos' principal quarry was the seal. Its flesh was their staple diet, its blubber at once their bread and their lamp fuel, its skin their most important material for clothing, bedding, lines, and almost everything else for which other people use textiles and fibers.

And yet, in the long winter, no early white explorer would ever have guessed that this was seal country. For then the seals stayed hidden away in the warmer water under the thick ice. The Eskimos knew, however, that a seal must feed fairly close to shore and that, at least every quarter-hour, it has to come up for air. That does not make the seals any more visible, for they have their own inconspicuous way of doing this. In the short autumn, when the ice is still thin, each seal makes itself a series of breathing holes, which it keeps open all through the winter by returning to them very regularly for a draft of air. At each round of visits, it scratches and gnaws away the new ice that has meanwhile formed over its blow-holes. Then it pushes only its nostrils up through the blanket of drifting snow that helps keep the ice from forming too thickly.

In doing this, however, as the Eskimos knew, the seal also leaves a scent for the hunter's dog. When a dog flushed such a blow-hole, the hunter carefully scraped away the covering snow, and could tell at once from the thinness of the ice whether the hole was in regular use. If it seemed promising, he would gently push the snow back over the hole and stick a bone pointer into it. The seal would have to move this when it thrust its muzzle through for air. Then the hunter might have to wait patiently for several hours for the seal's return visit to that hole. That is why this form of hunting was called *maupok,* meaning "he waits."

It was in fact rather more like fishing than hunting. The hunter brought a little stool with him to sit on, or he might sit it out on a cake of ice, after building a snow wall as a windbreak for his back. He kept his harpoon ready to hand; he must be ready at the first tremor of the pointer to thrust the weapon through the snow and the small hole in the ice, directly into the muzzle of the invisible seal. As the seal plunged wildly into the sea, carrying the detachable harpoon head with it, the Eskimo paid out his line and drew it in, exactly as one plays big fish, until he could pull the exhausted, air-starved animal back up to the breathing hole. Then he must chop in the ice—which was sometimes several feet thick—a hole big enough to bring in his catch. Obviously, under such conditions, the most high-powered rifle in the world would not have been a satisfactory substitute for the Eskimo's harpoon.

With the break-up of the ice in spring, the seals came out into the open, basking in the sun at the edge of the ice. Then the Eskimos could engage in a type of hunting that seems more familiar to us—*utok,* or "he stalks." The hunter crawled slowly and noiselessly forward, belly flat on the wet ice, hiding behind rocks and hummocks where he could, pretending to be a seal in all his gestures and movements when he could not hide, until he was close enough to launch his harpoon. Here too the harpoon was necessary not only to kill the seal but to hold it lest its body topple off the ice edge and be lost in the sea.

Since *utok* also took hours of patience and alertness, there was a special hazard from the glare on the ice reflecting the low rays of the spring sun. This could in a short time blind a man for days. Hence the hunter came equipped with still another special Eskimo invention—snow goggles. These were simply spectacles, with "lenses" made of thin strips

of bone, ivory, or wood, in which were cut slits just barely wide enough to see through yet narrow enough to shut out the glare. One naturally squints one's eyelids into narrow slits to cut down too dazzling a light and to protect the more sensitive parts of the retina of the eye, but this action also makes for fuzzy vision and eyestrain. The Eskimo snow goggles were simply a device for permitting the hunter to keep his eyes wide open, without strain and without loss of clarity, while protecting his retinas. . . .

In winter the women made and tended the snares for arctic hares and foxes and such small game. The hares were caught in slip nooses hanging from lines stretched across their most frequented runways. The foxes were killed in stone deadfalls or captured in stone box traps.

In summer the women, as well as the children, the infirm, and the aged, spent most of their time catching birds with hand nets on long poles or with small spears. The whole village would pitch their skin tents near the cliffs where the northern birds congregated and nested in vast numbers—the dovekies, which were the most numerous; the flightless auks, which needed only to be knocked on the head to be taken; the black eider duck, from whose down the women made undershirts. All this small game, besides being valuable for furs and feathers, provided a welcome change from the monotonous winter diet of seal and walrus.

(3) The surplus, even the eggs, could be cached away for some special feast, or for needier days, when the hunters would be stormbound in the igloos. In winter, too, if the lucky hunter brought down more than the day's needs, or if it was more than he could carry and store at home, he would find some pit or build a stone cairn, safe from marauding foxes or bears, and stow the surplus in it. In this climate, these caches could well serve as a deep-freeze, and meat might often be preserved in them for a year or more. Even if a sudden thaw should unfreeze the meat for a while, the Eskimo would not consider that great harm had been done. He was not finicking about overripeness in meat. Often the hunter would set up a whole string of caches on the trails he most regularly followed. In case of real need it was perfectly proper for any other hunter to help himself from any cache he might find.

Except when the game sought was too big for the resources and equipment of one man, the Eskimo was ordinarily a lone hunter. If you asked him about such things, he would tell you that he was alone responsible for the feeding of his family, and that what he caught was his own. Yet he did not mean by such ideas and words what they might mean to us. There is an old children's custom among us that is closer to the Eskimo way of thinking than our grown-up point of view is to either of them. If one of our boys finds a coin or other valuable treasure, he may say, "Finders keepers!" But if another boy happens to be along, he has the right to cry, "Halvies!" and to share in the finder's luck as a partner.

So, on a group hunting expedition there were strict rules and fixed customs for the division of all spoils. After an animal was killed, it was cut up into as many portions as there were heads of families in the party. The man who had actually made the kill or who had first harpooned it was entitled to choose his portion first. Second choice went to the man who first placed his hand on the game after the kill, the next choice to the second man who did so, and so on. But, in fact, almost anyone standing around when an animal was caught or brought home could expect a piece of it, especially if he helped to tow it onto the beach. Thus, calling the hunter's game "his" did not give him an absolute property right in it, to do with as he pleased, but seemed more a way of showing who were the good hunters, deserving the respect of the village. The honor was "his," not necessarily the meat.

(4) Even after the hunter had brought his meat home, his lucky household was expected to share generously with the families of those that were not so lucky. It is undoubtedly this custom of sharing food that has kept the small race of Eskimos surviving for these thousands of years. If every hunter had to depend entirely on his own skill and luck, instead of sharing in and contributing to the luck and skill of the whole village, a hostile nature would very shortly have picked them off one by one, for in the Arctic no hunter's fortune can be consistently good for several years running. The Eskimo took the greatest pride in being a good hunter because his village gave its best hunters the greatest respect, and the village did this because the life and well-being of everyone depended on his efforts. To refuse to share with those in need would have undermined the hunter's very pride in his skill. He would at the very least have lost an appreciative audience for his favorite stories—his accounts of his own breathtaking exploits.

## II

### The Dog Sledge

In this land where man's "bread" was scattered thinly over so wide an expanse and moved so swiftly on legs and flippers, his survival would have been unthinkable without the Eskimo dog team and sledge. Only because of these could he range as far and as fast as the game he chased. Because he had this means of transporting heavy loads, he could maintain a permanent base of operations for his family while he went great distances in pursuit of big animals. In winter he could hunt far out on the sea ice that bridged the many offshore islands and his narrow coastal homeland.

The sledge was a typically Eskimo piece of ingenuity in the way it turned difficulties into advantages. No wheeled vehicle could possibly have stood up to the terrain. Built low to the ground, the sledge was easy to keep from overturning even when it careened over the roughest ice. Light in weight, it could be carried over chasms that it could not jump. Intricately fitted together from many pieces of driftwood, bone, and ivory lashed together by thongs, it was as flexible as a snake, taking the contours of the land under it like the caterpillar treads of a tractor.

At the rear end were two upright guiding handles, often of caribou antlers, by which the driver steered the sledge and held it down to the ground right side up. Otherwise it was a

Still the main means of transportation for the Eskimo, the dog sledge is well adapted to Arctic conditions.

simple narrow affair of two runners, five to fifteen feet long, held together by many crossbars lashed between them. The runners could be made of odds and ends of wood pieced out with bone, or even of frozen hide shod with ivory.

When the sledging was over soft or powdery snow, the runners would stick as if in sand or pick up uneven lumps of snow unless they were "iced" to make them glide more lightly. Since ice breaks off too easily from polished bone or wood, the driver would first cover his runners with a more cushiony layer of frozen mud, moss, or even seal's blood. Onto this, just before setting out on his journey, he would squirt mouthfuls of melted snow. Then, immediately, before this could turn back into ice, he must quickly smooth the already freezing water over the runners with mittens or bare hands. In a temperature of thirty to fifty degrees below zero, his hands had to move fast if they were not to freeze to the runners. Where the snow was level and soft, this layer of ice let the sledge skim over the ground like skates on a pond. But when the going was over sharp ridges of hard ice, the shoeing would of course break off and the whole process might have to be done all over again.

On a long trip the Eskimo would lay over the crossbars of the sledge big slabs of frozen blubber and meat a half-inch thick to serve as a kind of flooring. Over this he could, with pliant cords of walrus hide, strap a bearskin rug. Thus stowed away, the cargo of food would not spill if the sledge rolled over, and was safe from the voracious dogs. When he stopped for a meal, all the traveler had to do was turn the light sledge upside down and cut himself a slice of blubber from between the crossbars. Often, too, he would use a slab of meat, frozen as hard as a plank, for his seat.

In the sledge the Eskimo again tackled and solved his problem in the typical Eskimo way. Just as with the snow house, difficulty was turned into opportunity, the enemy made into a useful ally. The very qualities that made snow and ice so very difficult for foot travel were what made them ideal for sledges. The efficiency of this invention *depended* on the extreme cold. Indeed, if there was one thing an Eskimo driver on the trail dreaded as much as an orchard grower dreads an unseasonable frost, it was an unseasonable thaw. Then, not only could he lose the icing off his runners, but also the skin lashings holding his sledge together would grow damp and begin to stretch, and his runners might flatten out altogether, leaving him with an unwieldy raft in place of a trim, efficient, speedy craft.

The sledge could of course be dragged by men at their own plodding pace, but what made it the fast, wide-ranging vehicle of the hunter was the team of dogs. The dog is man's earliest domesticated animal, and has gone with man into every part of the world. But no primitive people has ever made better use of its companionship than the Eskimos. Frobisher's chronicler did not list the dog among the "riches" of the Eskimo, probably because Frobisher came in the summertime and could not see the huskies at work. Yet they were undoubtedly the Eskimo's most valuable possession, though the only one he did not acquire by trapping and killing. On the contrary, he had often to spend as much time hunting food for his dogs as for his family. Whenever possible, he fed the dogs as well as he fed himself, for on his dog sledge depended his having any food at all. . . .

### III

## Fear

There was no Eskimo family that had not suffered some tragedy—a father lost at sea, a mother frozen to death, a child starved, stricken by a mysterious disease, buried under an avalanche, engulfed by a glacier. Undeniably it was a life haunted by the twin fears of ever-threatening hunger and cold.

January and February were nearly always months of more or less severe privation. When the last morsel of food was gone from the igloos and caches, and the village hunters had again and again returned without meat from their perilous forays into the storm and dark—then the battle to stay alive until spring would become desperately grim. Little by little, the family's possessions and necessities would go into the cooking pot. Now it was indeed fortunate that nearly all its belongings were taken from the animals, for in need these could all be eaten. First to be boiled and eaten would be any spare sealskins the housewife had been saving for new clothes or much-needed mending, then trimmings from clothes already made, the sleeping rugs, the lashings of skin and sinew from tools. The man might have to give up the long whiplash of which he was so proud, and perhaps even the skin from his kayak.

Now when the hunter returned from fruitless sitting on the ice, waiting for the seal that had so strangely disappeared, there would be no welcoming gleam from the window of his igloo to guide him home, and no warmth when he got there. The lamp blubber would long ago have been eaten. Feeling the strength leaving his own body, looking at the pale thin woman who had been his round-cheeked wife, at his once plump greasy children now listless and without strength to play, the man would finally be faced by a truly desperate decision. Without his dogs, he would not be able to hunt, but the dogs were also starving and would soon be eating one another. So they would be killed and eaten, one by one, in the hope that some of them might be permitted to survive. Finally, as we have seen, even more terrible things might happen.

Though such terrors were by no means the usual experience, they were always possible. It is no great wonder, therefore, that, when one Eskimo was asked what their religion was, what they believed in, he should answer, "We do not believe. We only fear. . . . We fear those things that are about us and about which we have no sure knowledge, as the dead, and the malevolent ghosts, and the secret misdoings of the heedless ones among ourselves."

Hunting is an activity full of unpredictable accidents, of pure luck, good and ill. Even the most reasonable of men, when he is hunting becomes a little superstitious. Secretly he begins to believe that his success may depend on something he is wearing or on some words spoken by someone else or on the attitude toward him of the game—in short, something altogether irrelevant or impossible. Now consider a primitive hunter, whose very life depends on his success, and who has moreover been taught to believe that the animals he hunts are animated by wise spirits who know all there is to be known about him. Is it so strange that he should go about in deadly fear of saying or doing the wrong thing, even unknowingly? "Bad luck" is after all not an ex-

*planation* of disaster. It *is* the disaster. And since a man, or a community, should rightly get what he or it deserves, it follows that for every piece of bad luck or hardship someone must be at fault. Someone, knowingly or unwittingly, must have offended the powers in charge of such things.

(5) The Polar Eskimos had no form of what we would recognize as government, no chiefs or headmen whose commands must be obeyed, no council to lay down laws either for the tribe as a whole or for any village. For a people who were so clever at meeting the challenges of nature, they had done remarkably little to develop the machinery of living together in groups. Every family was free to come and go as it pleased, and the only restraints on a man seemed to be the good opinion of his neighbors and relatives. But if there were no outward forms of government, no judges or police, each man had implanted in him from early childhood an ever-watchful internal governor to tell him right from wrong and to make it extremely uncomfortable for him when he did wrong.

(6) This was, of course, his belief in the world of spirits. True, these spirit powers, not being human, might have their own strange ideas of right and wrong. Being nevertheless Eskimo, their ideas usually revolved around food. A man might murder another and expect no worse punishment than being murdered in turn by his victim's relatives. But the sins that roused the spirits' wrath had mostly to do with food taboos. Every Eskimo tribe was forbidden to eat some particular animal or part of animal. In addition, there might be special taboos for women, unmarried women, married women, mothers, children, boys, girls, young men, old men, and even individuals. Food taboos, and harsh punishments for violating them, are as a matter of fact common among primitive peoples throughout the world.

The great female spirit Sedna lives at the bottom of the sea, and all the sea animals are her children, for the seals and walruses were created from her chopped-off fingers. Out of her kindness, she sends her children to be caught and killed by the Eskimos, so that human beings may have food. But let them beware of angering her by some thoughtless act she happens not to like. Let some wife in the village secretly commit the sin of working with caribou skin after her husband has brought home seal meat, and Sedna will wreak a terrible vengeance on all the village. She may withhold all her seals and walruses; she may whip up such a storm that there can be no hunting until the village has starved to death; she may smite the husband of the evildoer with a strange spirit-sickness.

(7) Then the village would have to turn to the angakok, to find out what was wrong and who had sinned. The angakok, man or woman, was the one person with authority among these people without a government. This sorcerer was respected and feared because of his magic powers, which he had earned with great suffering and cruel privation. He had been initiated into his dread profession by another angakok, who had made him fast for weeks, alone, in a freezing little igloo until he had seen visions. Then the spirits had appeared and given him the power to travel to their country and to speak to them in their own language. They had taught him magic tricks to astound the other Eskimos.

Now all the village is gathered around the angakok in the yellow lamplight of the igloo. He begins by saying how poor are his powers, how foolish his tricks, all lies and humbug. Then he sings strange songs, accompanying himself on his little drum. He performs little tricks of magic. He jumps around and speaks in "spirit language." He grows more and more excited, his movements become more and more uncontrollable, until he falls down into a hysterical trance.

His soul leaves his body and journeys far into the spirit world. There powerful spirits, perhaps including Sedna herself, tell him who has committed a secret crime and what should be done about it. His soul comes back. He awakes, shaken and exhausted. He calls upon the wrongdoer to confess.

A woman whose husband has lain mysteriously ill for a long time steps forth and confesses what she knows can no longer be concealed. She has eaten liver, knowing it was forbidden her until she should have borne five children. She has already been punished, but this is as nothing to what she will suffer from the horror of her neighbors.

Eventually the wind shifts, the storm blows over, and the men go out and find seal again. The sick man recovers. All credit and honor to the angakok. . . .

TOPIC 3

# THE ORIGINS OF CIVILIZATION

The origins of civilization stretch back into the prehistoric past. Primitive man at first lived at the margin of survival, but with the gradual development of weapons, tools, and techniques he was able to achieve a degree of personal security. Later, an adaptation to agriculture made possible the growth of a surplus of food and, in favored valleys, the emergence of urban settlement. It was then possible for civilization, which required a relatively high level of cultural and technological attainment, to bud and unfold. The readings introduce the environmental setting of two early civilizations and follow their first flowering in the Tigris-Euphrates and Nile river valleys.

**Reading 4**

## Shepard Clough: The Earliest Cultures

Seeking to explain what civilization is, Professor Shepard Clough (1901-    ) of Columbia University found it necessary to examine the factors that shaped its first appearance. From Shepard B. Clough, *The Rise and Fall of Civilization: An Inquiry into the Relationship between Economic Development and Civilization* (New York: Columbia University Press, 1961), pp. 21-30, 32, 35-37.

### THE NEOLITHIC AGRICULTURAL REVOLUTION

When the earliest form of man appeared on this planet, he probably lived much like a wild animal. Although we lack information concerning his earliest economy, archaeological evidence seems to indicate that 140,000 years ago, as the last glacial period was approaching, man was a food gatherer rather than a food producer. He hunted game, sought fruit and nuts, and collected the seeds of plants for grain. He relied similarly on such products of nature as caves for shelter and on animal skins for clothing.

In the course of time man added to the technology by which he sustained life. He commenced to make use of fire and probably developed ways of producing it. He chipped pieces of stone from rocks in order to get weapons and tools with which to perform his elementary tasks more effectively and more expeditiously. Stone implements, which gave this earliest form of civilization its name of Paleolithic or Old Stone Age, were gradually improved in quality and beauty and became differentiated in design (ax, spear, and knife) for the performance of special jobs. Subsequently Paleolithic man added bones, horns, and ivory to the list of raw materials for tools and weapons. He caught fish with hook and line, used the dog in the chase, employed rotary motion for drilling holes even in stone, utilized the principle of the lever and fulcrum for moving heavy objects, and invented the bow and arrow, the first composite mechanism made by human kind.

Yet the development of these tools and weapons made possible the accumulation of but a very small surplus, probably just enough to provide minimum human needs during the unproductive months of the year. They did not lead to any extensive division of labor, to any important trade, or to any residual body of aesthetic works. When men moved, as they frequently did, they could carry their belongings on their backs or draw them on sledges. Yet, in spite of the low level of accomplishment, one very important ideology became established in many societies—man wanted to increase his control over his physical environment so that he would not suffer from want. This desire is clear from improvements in techniques and from the character of supplications to supernatural powers. In nearly all primitive religions, there are prayers, rites, spells, and incantations to the totem to make the hunting good or to assist the supplicant one way or another in overcoming some material difficulty.

About 10,000 years ago important changes took place which were to lead to the creation of economic surplus and to the achievement of higher levels of civilization. With the melting of the northern ice sheets at the end of the last glacial period, the steppes and tundras of Europe were transformed into temperate forests and the prairies south of the Mediterranean and in Hither Asia were converted into deserts with oases. Consequently hunting in these areas became poorer, and man sought a new way to provide himself with sustenance. In the solution of his problem he effected one of the major technological revolutions in history—the domestication of grains and animals. This agricultural revolution came with the beginning of a new age in history—the New Stone or Neolithic Age.

Probably the first grains to be sowed and harvested for human food were related to wheat and barley; and they were selected from a number of wild seed plants and tubers which had been gathered by Paleolithic man in his quest for food. To wheat and barley were added in various places rice, millet, Indian corn or maize, yams, manioc, and squash. The first animals to be brought under control, cared for, and used to aid in the chase or to supplement its rewards were dogs, sheep, goats, cattle, and pigs. They were chosen either because they had not fled to the north like the reindeer, because they were relatively docile, or because they were particularly productive of the things men wanted.

The domestication of plants and animals had far-reaching effects. Tools were improved and further differentiated. Polishing of stone was more generally resorted to in order to get a finer edge for harvesting grain, cutting wood, and slaughtering animals. The hoe and sickle, the polished stone ax, and better knives bear testimony of the trend. The cultivation of plant crops involved new problems of food storage and led to the creation of the earthen pot which was far superior for this purpose to bags of skins, horns, or woven baskets. Fermentation was discovered, which allowed Neolithic man to make beverages with which to enliven festive occasions or to relieve the boredom of rainy days. Spinning and weaving were developed, which made possible a substitute for animal skins as clothing. And bodily decoration with shells and beads, which indicated the existence of aesthetic considerations, became more common.

As can readily be imagined, the new agricultural technology placed a premium upon readily arable and fertile land. Oases and naturally drained marsh areas along rivers or around lakes were probably the most desirable, for there, few if any trees had to be cleared away. In such areas caves did not exist, so man began to turn to other types of housing—to tents made from hides, to shelters from branches or grass, and to wooden or sod houses. Such structures made possible the establishment of villages of the fixed settlement type, which had the advantages of being convenient to the place of work, of facilitating social intercourse, of accumulating human aesthetic achievements and knowledge, and of providing protection. On the last score, the need was apparently very great, for in times of poor crops and threatened famine people migrated in search of greener pastures which, if need be, they would take by force. Then, too, people who lived on the periphery of settled communities preyed upon their neighbors. These nomadic and seminomadic people were for long a serious problem, for inasmuch as they lived as food gatherers and later as shepherds they had to contend with wild beasts and keep their fighting ability at a high level. They were the "barbarians" who invaded settled areas.

## THE TECHNOLOGICAL REVOLUTION IN THE AGE OF COPPER

Important as was settled agriculture as a foundation for the production of a surplus which would provide that leisure which man needs for intellectual and artistic pursuits, the Neolithic Age failed to meet some of the basic conditions of economic progress. It did not have sufficiently effective or specialized tools to permit much of a division of labor. It did not employ animal or mechanical power on a large enough scale to supplement human effort to a meaningful degree. It had only the beginnings of a social or political system which could organize the collective efforts of a group for effecting major capital improvements. And it did not have means of transportation adequate for the development of extensive commerce.

The Age of Copper, or, as it is more elaborately called, the Chalcolithic Age, marked an advance in most of these respects. It inaugurated a "technological revolution" during the 1,000 years prior to 3000 B.C., which was, in the opinion of many, more far-reaching in its consequences than any other prior to 1600 A.D. Improvements in techniques made possible important gains in production per capita and laid the foundation for an urban development that was essential to forward strides in intellectual and cultural endeavour.

The geographical area within which the technological revolution of the Copper Age took place is bounded on the west by the Sahara and the Mediterranean Sea, on the east by the Thar Desert and the Himalayas, on the north by the Balkan, Caucasus, Elburz, and Hindu Kush Mountains, and on the south by

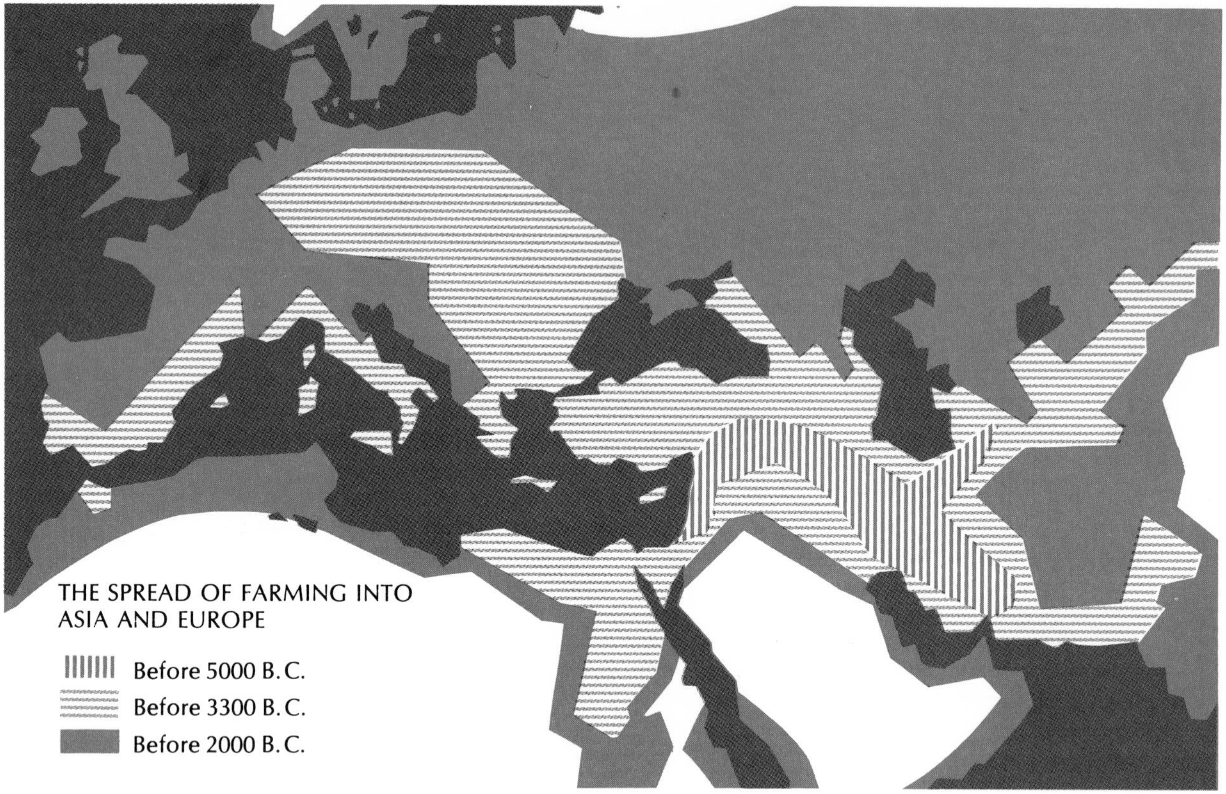


the Tropic of Cancer. It is a region in which a surplus had to be provided for nonproductive seasons. It had fertile land around oases, along river valleys, and in mountain passes. It had the wild grapevine, dependable crops of dates, figs, and olives with which man could supplement his cultivated crops. It had easily navigable waterways for commerce. It was comparatively well protected from mass migrations from outside. And it had relatively cloudless skies, which facilitated observation of the heavens—observation which led to the acquisition of knowledge useful in guiding the traveler on his way and in keeping track of the seasons.

Settled agriculture within this area was carried on most successfully near oases and along the Nile, at the mouth of the Tigris and Euphrates Rivers, and along the Indus River. Agricultural surpluses were exchanged along the rivers and with the wilder food gatherers on the fringes of settlement. Commerce of this kind made men familiar with new products turned out by their neighbors and whetted a demand for new utilitarian and luxury goods. Furthermore problems of drainage and irrigation in river agriculture contributed to cooperative effort on a relatively large scale. Out of this experience came organization for the pooling of human resources, leadership in productive enterprise, some division of labor, and a recognition of the necessity of "investment" of present energies for the purpose of future gain. Gradually the desire for more products, the possibility of obtaining them in exchange for surplus agricultural goods, and the need for control over the use of water created a situation conducive to technological change.

As the reader has already assumed from the name of the age which we are examining, one of the major technological developments in this period consisted in the discovery and use of copper. This metal had obvious advantages over stone. It was less fragile, could be more easily repaired, took a better edge, made lighter and stronger tools, and could be more readily shaped by hammering or casting into a greater variety of products. Although it was not so universally distributed over the earth's surface as stone, its lightness and consequent ease of transport gave it a preferred position in areas, like the delta of the Tigris and Euphrates, which had no stone. Its cost was high, however, which restricted its use, especially in districts like Egypt where flint was readily available. Nevertheless, we find it being used among the Sumerians in the delta of the Tigris and Euphrates for tools, weapons, vessels, and seals with which to indicate the ownership of goods.

Probably the first copper was found in a relatively pure state in nature, but by 3000 B.C. the metal was being reduced from ore in furnaces fired with charcoal. It was placed in crucibles which would withstand high temperatures; it was handled with tongs; and it was cast in molds. The production of copper provided techniques essential to the manufacture of a large number of metals, and therefore it is not strange that we find silver, lead, and tin being produced by similar methods almost at once. And before long tin began to be added to copper to make bronze.

Important as were these technological advances in metallurgy, they were rivaled in significance by changes in ceramics. Pottery made from clay and fired to obtain greater durability was inherited from earlier times. Within the time span under discussion Egyptians developed ways of glazing and decorating pottery to make the more durable and beautiful faience. The inhabitants of Hither Asia invented the potter's wheel which made possible extremely rapid manufacture of fine products of perfectly symmetrical design. The invention appears to have reached Egypt by 2700 B.C. and the Indus by 2500 B.C. The principle of the wheel was in itself of greatest moment, for it is essential in the transmission of power and in the reduction of friction. Wheeled vehicles were in use in Mesopotamia, for example, by 3000 B.C., in India before 2500 B.C., in Crete by 2000 B.C., in Egypt by 1600 B.C., and in China and Sweden by 1000 B.C. Curiously enough, they were never developed in the Maya, Inca, or Aztec civilizations, nor was the principle of the wheel used in them for anything except toys!

Among other technological developments mention should be made of the manufacture of brick, at first sun-dried but in India by 2500 B.C. fired in kilns. Wooden plows appeared in Egypt and Mesopotamia about 3000 B.C. and soon afterward in India, although not in China until about 1400 B.C. Plows required animal power for efficient traction, and oxen were equipped with yokes that fitted on the broad shoulders or horns of the beast to pull them.

This union of livestock with the cultivation of crops meant not only the addition of animal energy to human energy in agriculture, but it also meant the production of more humus for the soil and the beginning of a new form of transportation. By 3000 B.C. camels and asses, or horses, were known to the people of Hither Asia and were gradually put to use by others, the horse having been introduced into Egypt between 1800 and 1600 B.C. Unfortunately, the collar for the horse, probably adopted from the ox yoke, was so constructed that it choked the animal when he pulled a heavy load. For this reason and because the ass and horse were much smaller than now, they were not used as draft animals in ancient times except for light vehicles like chariots but were employed as pack and riding animals. It was not until the ninth or tenth century A.D. that the breastplate and later the collar were adjusted to fit on the shoulders of the horse rather than on his throat. For his part, the ox was not very efficient for transport, because he was slow; his load was limited by friction of the wheels on dirt roads; and his hoofs, like the horse's, wore out on hard surfaces. Not until the tenth century A.D. were iron shoes with nails used to overcome this last difficulty.

Finally, the period of which we are speaking witnessed a considerable improvement in water transport. Although Neolithic men had at least rafts and canoes with which they made hazardous journeys, it was probably not until a little before 3000 B.C. that craft capable of carrying substantial cargoes were constructed and that the sail was used to propel them; and it was not until about 2200 B.C. that the rudder came to supplement the steering oar. The sail was a major invention, because it increased the productive efficiency of man by adding to his technology one of the earliest methods of harnessing inorganic energy—a source of power which was in modern times to revolutionize man's economic life.

Technological advances of the Age of Copper had two major economic consequences—they helped bring about a greater amount of trade and a greater division of labor. The latter development is particularly clear in the case of coppersmiths, pottery makers, and to a degree carpenters. The metallurgical process of refining and working copper required specialized knowledge, equipment, and concentration of activity, which took it out of the hands of farmers working at home. Coppersmiths devoted their labors almost exclusively to their craft. By restricting information about their skill to a limited number of apprentices, they retained for themselves enough of the market to keep themselves steadily employed. There is evidence that at least in the making of finished products many of the smiths were itinerants or were employed in noble or priestly households.

Similarly, the potter possessed a skill that was learned only with patience and practice, and he too was frequently an itinerant worker. He carried his wheel to suitable clay near a market, for that was easier than trying to transport finished and fragile products over long distances. Carpentry, masonry, and brickmaking were somewhat less specialized, for farmers could perform in a rough way at least the major tasks of these crafts. As more elaborate tools came into use, as more refined products were demanded, and as the effective demand of the market became larger, a division of labor and a great increase in productivity per worker took place. . . .

## THE URBAN REVOLUTION OF THE EARLY BRONZE AGE

The first cities of which we have record were established prior to 2500 B.C. in the three river valleys that have been mentioned as the earliest centers of advanced civilization. Somewhat later, cities appeared in other river valleys, like that of the Yellow River in China at places producing such goods as copper and at commercial centers around the fringes or along trade routes between the earlier cultures. . . .

That the establishment of cities should be glorified by the term "urban revolution" requires a word by way of explanation. . . . Cities have been the loci for the creation of the great intellectual and cultural works of man, and hence the establishment of urban centers is a significant part of our story. Second, these early cities witnessed an intensification of economic activity on a large scale, a greater concentration of capital than had ever before been known, the growth of new techniques of production and distribution, a division of labor, and the beginnings of such important economic institutions as money, banking, and a law of contracts. Third, these early cities developed writing and systems of numerical notation which made possible the ready communication of ideas and the accumulation of man's experience for the benefit of posterity. . . .

What impresses us most in these early cities is, however, the concentration of capital, in the broadest sense of the word. In Sumer this concentration was effected primarily by the temples, in Egypt by the pharaohs, and in India probably by a bourgeois class. In Sumer, for which more complete information is available than for the other areas, the temples owned land which they leased to tenants; they granted advances (loans) of seed and implements to tillers of the soil in return for a charge which in essence was interest; they built and maintained drainage and irrigation ditches; they planned production; they employed craftsmen in their own shops and sold the goods thus produced; and they catered to those engaged in trade. From this activity they were able to amass a surplus which could be and was used for expanding production. They were not, however, responsible for the defense of the city, this task being left to the city governor or king.

In Egypt the situation seems to have been somewhat different. Here a political leader was the chief agent in the concentration of wealth, although he assumed god-like prerogatives which fortified his claim to ultimate ownership of land and to goods and services from the people. From payments made him and from profits in the crafts in his extensive household economy, he accumulated great amounts of capital. A relatively large part of it seems to have been employed in nonproductive activity, like the construction of elaborate tombs and the burial of wealth with the dead. The Great Pyramid, for example, constructed between 2420 and 2270 B.C., contains 2,300,000 stone blocks weighing an average of $2\frac{1}{2}$ tons apiece and required, according to Herodotus, the labor of 100,000 men working over a twenty-year period. But some of the wealth of the pharaohs was used to build canals and cities, to exploit the copper deposits at Sinai, to outfit trading expeditions, or to expand production in the royal workshops.

With the appearance of cities, the concentration of capital, a greater division of labor, and increased trade, money came into being. Money, which may be defined as a medium of exchange, a store of wealth, and a measure of value, albeit a fluctuating one, was in the form of metals (gold, silver, or copper) which were weighed out at each transaction. Subsequently bars of metal had the amount of their contents stamped on them. Only much later (*circa* 700 B.C.) were pieces of metal (coins) of fixed weight and fineness issued and guaranteed by political states. Money, although used in a limited degree in this period, was

This scene from the movie, "The Egyptian," while contemporary, conveys some sense of the human labor expended in constructing the pyramids. Each labor gang pulls a single block.

a tremendous convenience, for goods could readily be exchanged for it. Under a system of barter a person with goods to exchange must find someone who has goods which he wants and who wants what he has—an operation which is at best cumbersome. Because money was a boon to trade, it deepened and widened the division of labor. It also facilitated the amassing of surplus, or capital formation, for it could be stored more easily and with less deterioration than, let us say, wheat. Finally it could be brought together from many more sources than could real products, because it was easier to transport, and hence aided in tapping the savings of more people. . . .

The question now remains, did the more adequate combining of many of what we have called factors of economic progress actually result in a larger production of goods and services per capita? Of course we have no direct statistical data as a basis for a firm reply, but all the circumstantial evidence indicates that the answer should be in the affirmative. The cities seem to have brought with them a higher standard of living. People were better housed in the brick and stone buildings than they had been previously in mud and reed huts. In some places there are indications of organized sewage disposal and water supply. City granaries held stores of food which could be, and were, used to alleviate local famines, and the upper classes enjoyed luxuries in greater abundance than ever before. Finally, there was an increase in population which, so long as there is no diminution of goods per capita, is an indication of economic progress. . . .

# Sir Leonard Woolley: The Urbanization of Society

Sir Leonard Woolley (1880–1960), noted British archeologist, was famed for his excavation of the city of Ur in the Tigris-Euphrates delta and his findings of the Minoan culture in the Mediterranean. In this reading he explains why civilization began in the two great river valleys of Mesopotamia and Egypt. From "The Urbanization of Society," *The Beginnings of Civilization,* Part II by Sir Leonard Woolley, in *The History of Mankind* by Jacquetta Hawkes and Sir Leonard Woolley. Copyright © 1963 by UNESCO. By permission of Harper & Row, Publishers and George Allen & Unwin Ltd., pp. 414–420.

It is an axiom of economic history that real civilization can begin only in regions where the character of soil and climate makes surplus production possible and easy; only so is man relieved from the necessity of devoting all his energies and all his thought to the problem of mere survival, and only so is he enabled to procure from others by means of barter those things which minister to well-being and promote advance but are not naturally available in his own land; moreover, such conditions must prevail over an area large enough to maintain not merely a small group of individuals but a population sufficiently numerous to encourage occupational specialization and social development. So does civilization begin. Most of the community continue to devote their energies to actual food-production, but men whose gifts or tastes are of another sort become artisans, specialists in production of a different but scarcely less necessary kind, making those things without which the agricultural worker cannot get on. Increasing wealth and the uneven growth of private property lead to the development of technical knowledge, of art and of government, evolve an apparatus of law which is calculated to maintain order within the community and to defend it from outside aggression. The higher progress is the direct outcome of acquired skills and techniques, but those skills and techniques can be developed only where natural conditions make possible the surplus production of foodstuffs.

In two countries of the Middle East, in Mesopotamia and Egypt, these conditions were amply fulfilled and in those two countries Middle Eastern civilization accordingly began. Great emphasis has been laid by many writers on the fact that in them, as in none of the neighbouring lands, nature supplied precisely what was requisite for progress; in both there is a long valley of vast extent filled with water-borne silt which as agricultural soil is of amazing richness; in both a great river running through the centre of the flat plain brings the water that is essential in a sun-scorched land, floods it and leaves behind a silt that further enriches the soil, and can be tapped by canals to secure fertility throughout the year. So described, Mesopotamia and Egypt would appear to be exactly parallel in the opportunities that they afforded to early man, and therefore one might have expected early man in the two countries to develop along parallel lines, especially when, as we have seen, the two were in contact and Mesopotamia exercised a considerable influence upon the beginnings of Egyptian civilization. But in point of fact the two people progressed along lines wholly divergent. Nothing could be more unlike the mosaic of city states that divided between them the valley of the Euphrates and the Tigris than the unified kingdom of Egypt in which the city was really non-existent. The whole basis of society is radically different in the two countries, and the historian cannot ascribe this to 'the different mentality' of the two peoples because we know nothing of their respective mentalities so far as they had been formed at the outset of our period; and when later on they had been formed and we can fairly contrast them, they must be considered as the results just as much as, if not more than, the possible cause of the opposing conditions of life. The course of history can only be properly understood when it is realized that the similarity in the physical conditions of Egypt and Mesopotamia is only partial; actually the two valleys differ fundamentally, and in such a way as to impose upon their inhabitants quite different modes of life, and widely divergent religious views.

## EGYPT

The valley of the Nile, lying between hills of sandstone and limestone, is in profile slightly concave and slopes towards the sea with an average fall of 1 : 13,000. The annual flood, depositing the heavier silt close to the stream's course, raises the banks a little above the level of the bottom of the hollow through which the river runs, and at normal times the surface of the water is well below that of the ground on either side, the channel being deeply cut and the amount of sediment deposited on the river bed being negligible. At flood time the river rises slowly, spreading over the valley, or at least over the lower part of it, and falls slowly, draining away, thanks to the ground contours, and leaving behind it no stagnant water but a fairly uniform deposit of silt (clay with up to 20 per cent of sand) which is free of salt and an excellent fertilizer; and again, because of the gentle rise and fall and because of the ground's slope, which ensures the draining-away of the flood water, the sediment does very little in the way of silting up canals. But the most important feature of the Nile is that its flood in the first place is remarkably regular, so that its coming is predictable and—since it is gradual—can be observed in the river's upper courses in good time to give exact warning to the inhabitants of the valley downstream; and in the second place it occurs in the autumn, lasting from about August 15th into early October. This means that the flood comes long after the harvest has been gathered and, when the ground is parched and hard, irrigates it, covers it with fresh sediment and withdraws as winter sets in and gives the signal for sowing; the soil holds enough moisture for the winter-sown crops to come to maturity, and for later sowings a very simple system of short canals tapping the stream higher up will assure a summer harvest.

All that the earliest settlers had to do was to sow their seed along the riverside as soon as the flood waters receded and wait for the crop to grow and ripen; by such a simple means a single isolated homestead would obtain more than enough foodstuff to support itself. As the population increased, the relatively small area of naturally irrigated soil would no longer suffice and had to be expanded artificially; but to do so was an easy task. The primitive farmer had made the obvious discovery that the effects of the flood could be supplemented if necessary by cutting through the natural dyke of the river's bank a channel that would lead fresh water on to the growing crop, and when the ground had been thoroughly saturated the gap could be closed and the surplus water drained off by cutting the bank lower downstream. On this simple process was based the whole economy of after times, i.e. the basin irrigation of the Nile valley. The principle is that the land along the river is divided into compartments—basins—by embankments thrown up at right-angles to the river's course; a canal started from upstream conducts water from the river to the basin, where smaller canals and ditches spread it evenly over the compartment; another canal drains the excess water off to a second basin or to the river downstream. Basin irrigation can produce only one crop in the year because when the river sinks below a certain level the lead-off canals dry up; but with the rich soil of Egypt one crop is sufficient, and the system has the advantages of short canals, simple upkeep and very low silt-

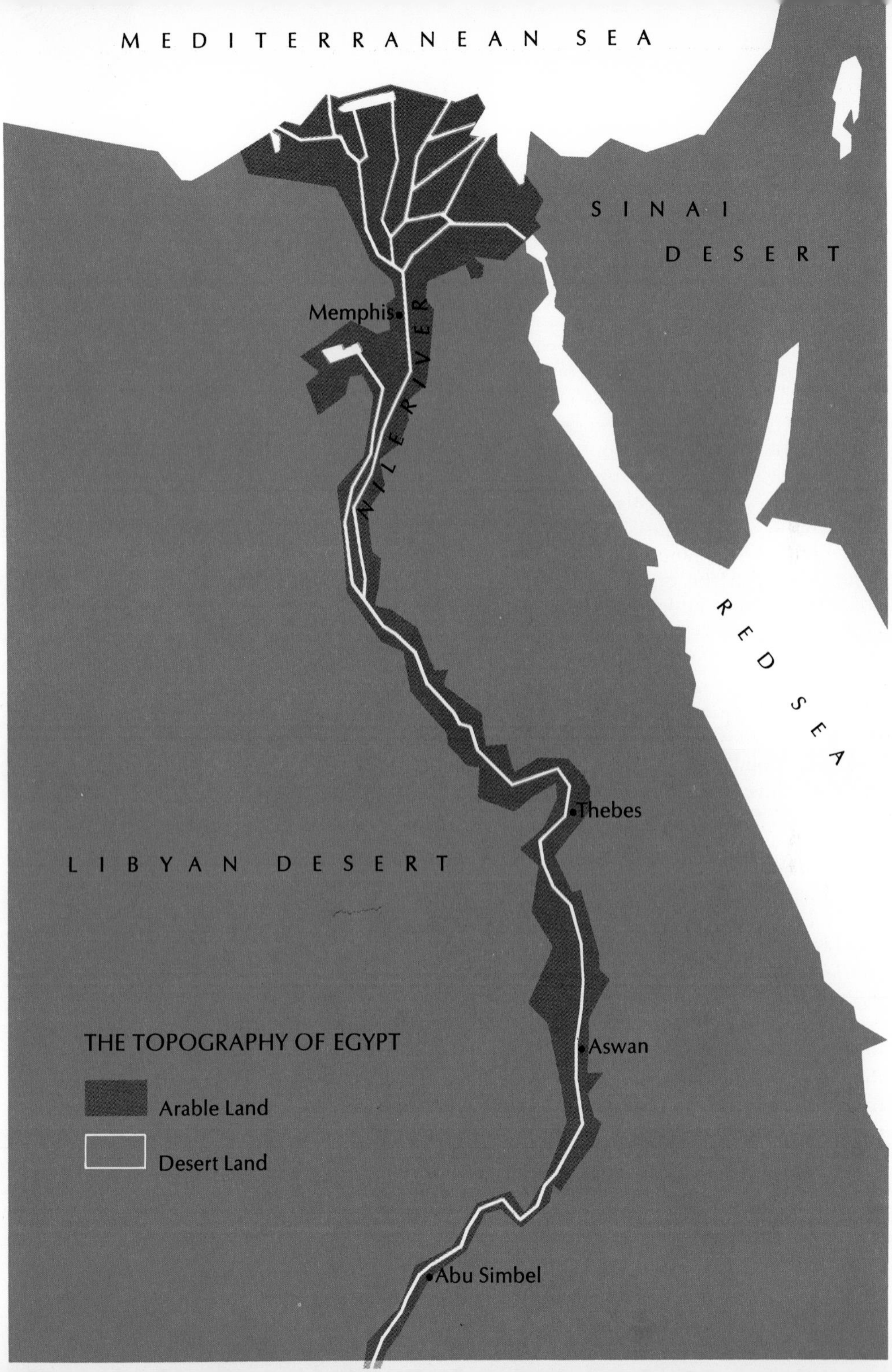

ing-up of the channels. This means that every village was economically independent in that the labour necessary for the surplus production of food was well within the scope of a small social unit, left indeed a fair amount of leisure and allowed for the specialization of handicrafts. Obviously there was an interest in having some kind of market where the produce of different villages could be exchanged, and this would lead to the growth of market towns, the existence of which would imply a certain amount of local administration; but with that the requirements of the village would be satisfied. Egypt in the pre-Dynastic period must be envisaged as a land of village communities each primarily concerned with the cultivation of its own fields by its own efforts; it is possible and indeed likely that the existence of particularly holy centres of worship acted to some extent as a centralizing influence and served to divide the country into major groupings, but these 'nomes', though they might supply a rallying point and leadership in times of crisis, had not, so far as we know, developed into administrative capitals. It is safe to say that there were no pre-Dynastic cities. With the unification of Egypt the king was at pains to regularize the happy-go-lucky irrigation system of the old days; Nilometers were built and observers attached to them to give due warning of the coming of the annual flood; the king himself performed the ceremony of cutting the dykes, as is shown on the macehead of Khasekhamui; a land-registry office in the interests of government taxation measured and counted the fields whose boundaries might have been obliterated by the mud of the inundation; forced labour was imposed on the peasants to dig canals on a more ambitious scale so as to bring into bearing the higher land beyond the reach of the flood waters. But though the once free farmer was now the drilled and regimented serf of the divine Pharaoh, his basic manner of life was but little changed and for him at least social conditions remained the same; Egypt was still an agricultural country of villages and market towns wherein, apart from the temporary capital arbitrarily set up by the dynasty of the time, there were no cities overshadowing the countryside.

## MESOPOTAMIA

To Egypt Mesopotamia affords a striking contrast. Between hills of marl containing salt and gypsum lies a wide plain which in cross-section is absolutely flat and has a seaward slope (1 : 26,000) only half that of the Nile valley. Of the two rivers which run through the length of the plain the Tigris, on its eastern marge, is of relatively little use for irrigation because it has a deeply-cut bed and the normal level of its waters lies too low beneath that of the surrounding country for the stream to be tapped by any simple system of canalization. The Euphrates it is that makes agriculture possible in a land where the rainfall is as scanty as in Egypt and the climate even less equable, with greater extremes both of heat and of cold.

From its source in the Anatolian mountains down to the rocky barrier below Hit the Euphrates has a violent current (at Carchemish, for instance, it flows at a rate of five miles an hour), and in consequence its turbid waters carry about five times as great a content of sediment—loam mixed with a large proportion of lime—as does the Nile. When it enters the flat alluvium of the delta the current is naturally slowed up and much of the sediment is dropped on to the bed of the river and especially along its edges where the main force of current is less; the bed is raised thereby and high banks are formed on either side, and in time the whole river runs above the level of the plain. Clearly this high-running water can be tapped for the benefit of the fields alongside, and clearly also the natural banks of the river must be maintained and strengthened if those fields are not to be submerged at the wrong time. To cut the bank is only too easy, and the Euphrates' water, like that of the Nile, will not only irrigate but with its silt will enrich the soil; the difficulty in this flat plain is rather to get rid of the superfluous water, which is prone to lie in pools and stagnant swamps and, if it be merely dried out by the sun, impregnate the earth with salts and alkaline compounds which in time will make it barren. Drainage in Mesopotamia is as essential as irrigation.

But the chief difference between the Euphrates and the Nile is in the date of the annual floods. No one can foretell precisely when the Euphrates flood is to be expected, because that depends upon weather conditions in the far-distant mountainous regions of Anatolia, the flood being caused by the melting of the winter snows there. It comes in the late spring, at some time between the beginning of April and early June, and the rise of the waters is sudden. Now from the farmers' point of view no time could be worse than this. Crops must be sown according to the climate, and by April the wintersown crops are well advanced and the summer crops are in; if at this state the fields were to be drowned beneath two or three feet of water all hope of a harvest would vanish, and after the flood waters had dried it would be too late for a fresh sowing. In Egypt, Hapi, the god of the inundation, was a beneficent deity by whose help man was able to eat bread; in Mesopotamia the flood was the enemy of man and Nin-Girsu and Tiamat who ruled over the chaos of the waters were to that extent malevolent powers. The flood had to be fought, to be kept in check at all costs; some of its waters might indeed be led off to fill the reservoirs or natural depressions on the edge of the higher desert, but the fertility of the country—and it was wonderfully fertile—depended on the river's normal flow when it could be profitably tapped by irrigation canals, and was only endangered by its rise.

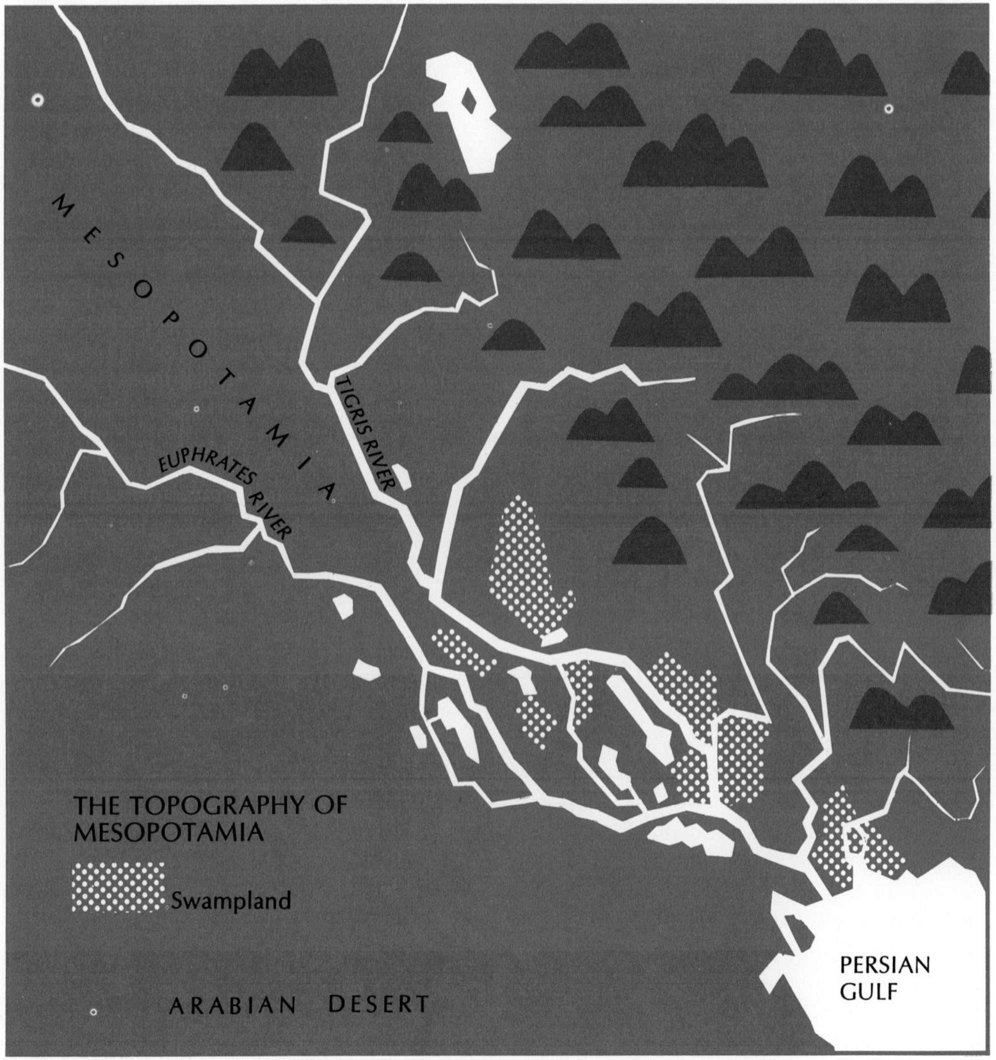

THE TOPOGRAPHY OF MESOPOTAMIA

The Mesopotamian agriculturalist was compelled by nature to adopt the system of perennial irrigation. Because the river bed was high above the cultivated plain, water could be brought to the latter all through the dry season and he could therefore count on having two harvests in the year ripened by the torrid sun. But against this tremendous advantage was set the colossal amount of labour involved. Because the river ran at a high level, the canals leading from it had also to be high, so as to obviate a too-sudden rush of water, seeing that such would tend to destroy the canals, built as they were of fine light silt (sometimes it was thought worth while to strengthen the canal banks with layers of reed matting, as was more often done in the case of the river banks); and since distances had to be great and the wastage of water was considerable, size was an important consideration, and the main canals therefore might be as much as 25 yards in width, navigable channels making inland voyages possible and so facilitating transport as well as irrigating the soil. From the main channels smaller canals and ditches distributed the water; but again there had to be drainage canals which served the further purpose of cleaning the soil by washing out the superfluity of salt deposited with the silt.

All this meant not only a vast amount of manual labour but also an elaborate organization. It was not a case of a peasant watering his own small holding; individual work of that sort was possible only in the immediate vicinity of the river and would have limited agriculture to a narrow strip of soil doomed to be destroyed by the flood. If any reasonable area was to be cultivated, water had to be carried far inland, and only communal labour could achieve the task. A network of subsidiary canals had to be planned which would ensure an equal distribution of water over the largest possible extent of arable land. Constant supervision was necessary to prevent one landowner exploiting the canal-borne water to the detriment of his neighbours. There had to be due authority for enforcing and directing labour to build the canals in the first place, to clean them when, as happened very quickly, they were choked with silt, and, above all, to prevent the breaching of the Euphrates' banks in floodtime. The Mesopotamian delta held out to early man the promise of a better and a richer life than could be found in any neighbouring land, but it was a conditional promise; its fulfilment required a cooperative effort and a centralization of control quite beyond the scope of a village community. The very nature of the country and of the river forced the inhabitants to make common cause throughout a territory whose size was decided by the limits of an interdependent canalization system, and the planning and upkeep of the canals required the direction of a regional authority enjoying absolute powers. By the mere logic of circumstances the Euphrates delta was from the outset parcelled out into a number of agricultural-irrigational units each having its own centre of administration, and the development of the city state was due not to the peculiar mentality of the Sumerian people but to the physical character of Sumer.

The surplus production of foodstuffs leads almost inevitably to occupational distinctions, the non-agriculturalist following his natural bent in manufacturing something that is in general demand and exchanging his handiwork for the food produced by others, and this specialization leads to distinctions of class. In the most primitive communities we are likely to find an 'intellectual' minority enjoying a more or less privileged ascendancy over the 'labouring' classes, and as the 'professions' become more sharply differentiated from each other and from the workers on the soil there must result a social organism in which functions are regularized and there is an admitted system of government. But while such development is essential to the urbanization of a society, it is not the sole condition; by itself it does not necessarily lead to the growth of cities or the birth of the civic spirit. In Egypt class distinctions were at least as sharply defined as they were in Mesopotamia, but in the manner and degree of urbanization the contrast between the two countries is profound. . . .

# Lewis Mumford: Development of the City

Lewis Mumford (1895–      ), a native of New York City, has written on many subjects. Often taken for an architect because of his books and articles on architecture and city planning, he calls himself a social philosopher who early recognized the function of the city in civilization as "storehouse and powerhouse." Excerpted from *The City in History*, © 1961, by Lewis Mumford, pp. 17, 18, 25, 27–32. Reprinted by permission of Harcourt, Brace & World, Inc.

## THE CONTRIBUTION OF THE VILLAGE

Let us look more closely at the early village, as one must picture it in Mesopotamia and the Valley of the Nile between, say, 9000 and 4000 B.C. A heap of mud huts, baked, or of mud-and-reed construction, cramped in size, at first little better than a beaver's lodge. Around these villages lie garden plots and patches, all the dimensions modest; not yet the broad but bounded fields, rectangular in shape, that come in with the plow. Nearby, in swamp and river, are birds to snare, fish to net, extra food to tide over a bad crop or enrich the daily diet. But even in the most primitive hamlet, such as the delta village of Merimdeh Beni-Salameh, there was a "jar sunk into the flooring to drain off the rainwater coming through the roof," as John A. Wilson observed. In addition "the village had a communal granary, consisting of woven baskets sunk into the ground." . . .

Everywhere, the village is a small cluster of families, from half a dozen to threescore perhaps, each with its own hearth, its own household god, its own shrine, its own burial plot, within the house or in some common burial ground. Speaking the same tongue, meeting together under the same tree or in the shadow of the same upstanding stone, walking along the same footway trodden by their cattle, each family follows the same way of life and participates in the same labors. If there is any division of labor, it is of the most rudimentary kind, determined more by age and strength than vocational aptitude: whoever looks into his neighbor's face sees his own image. For the most part, time has dissolved the material structure of the village into the landscape; only its shards and shells claim permanence;

but the social structure has remained tough and durable, for it is based on precepts, laws, family histories, heroic examples, moral injunctions, treasured and passed on without deviation from the old to the young.

As the routine of neolithic agriculture became more successful, it probably tended to become more fixed and conservative. By the end of this period, all the adventurous experiments that distinguished food plants from indigestible or poisonous ones, that had discovered the secrets of rooting and seeding and cross-fertilization and selection, that had picked out the docile and tractable animals which became man's helpers, had tapered off, if not come to an end. Conformity, repetition, patience, were the keys to this culture, once it had solidified. Doubtless it took thousands of years for the neolithic economy to establish its limits: but once it reached them, it had little impulse to further development. "Hold fast to what is good and seek no further" was the formula for its contentment. . . .

What actually happened before the city came into existence can only be conjectured. Perhaps residual paleolithic hunting groups and the new neolithic settlers, each still too sparse to have the upper hand, began to occupy the same territory and stayed together long enough to absorb some of each other's ways and interchange some of their kit of tools. If one dare to call this a marriage of the two cultures, they were probably at first equal partners, but the relationship became increasingly onesided, as the weapons and coercive habits of the aggressive minority were re-enforced by the patient capacity for work that the stone-grinding neolithic peoples showed. As often happens, the rejected component of the earlier culture (hunting) became the new dominant in the agricultural community, but it was now made to do duty for the governance of a superior kind of settlement. Weapons served now not just to kill animals but to threaten and command men. . . .

The city, then, if I interpret its origins correctly, was the chief fruit of the union between neolithic and a more archaic paleolithic culture. In the new proto-urban milieu, the male became the leading figure; woman took second place. Her digging stick and hoe were replaced by the more efficient plow, capable, with ox-drawn power, of cleaving the heavier soils of the bottom lands. Even the female goddesses yielded in some degree to Osiris and Bacchus, precisely in the realms of agriculture and invention where woman had been most active. Woman's strength had lain in her special wiles and spells, in the mysteries of menstruation and copulation and childbirth, the arts of life. Man's strength now lay in feats of aggression and force, in showing his ability to kill and his own contempt for death: in conquering obstacles and forcing his will on other men, destroying them if they resisted.

As a result of this union of the two cultures, the widest sort of crossbreeding and intermixture probably took place all along the line. This gave the city potentialities and capabilities that neither the hunter, the miner, the stockbreeder, nor the peasant would ever, if left to themselves in their regional habitat, have been able to exploit. Where hoe culture supported hamlets, plow culture could support whole cities and regions. Where local effort could build only minor embankments and ditches, the large scale co-operations of the city could turn a whole river valley into a unified organization of canals and irrigation works for food production and transport—shifting men, supplies, and raw material about, as need dictated. . . .

In the city, new ways, rigorous, efficient, often harsh, even sadistic, took the place of ancient customs and comfortable easy-paced routine. Work itself was detached from other activities and canalized into the 'working day' of unceasing toil under a taskmaster: the first step in that 'managerial revolution' which has reached its climax in our day. Struggle, domination, mastery, conquest were the new themes: not the protectiveness and prudence, the holding fast or the passive endurance of the village. With this all-too-plenteous enlargement of power, the isolated village—even a thousand isolated villages—could not cope: it existed as a container for more limited functions and more strictly maternal and organic concerns. But that part of village culture which was capable of having a share in this development was drawn into the city and systematically harnessed to its new mode of life. . . .

## THE FIRST URBAN TRANSFORMATION

The city came as a definite emergent in the paleo-neolithic community: . . . On the new plane, the old components of the village were carried along and incorporated in the new urban unit; but through the action of new factors, they were recomposed in a more complex and unstable pattern than that of the village—yet in a fashion that promoted further transformations and developments. The human composition of the new unit likewise became more complex: in addition to the hunter, the peasant, and the shepherd, other primitive types entered the city and made their contribution to its existence: the miner, the woodman, the fisherman, each bringing with him the tools and skills and habits of life formed under other pressures. The engineer, the boatman, the sailor arise from this more generalized primitive background, at one point or another in the valley section: from all these original types still other occupation groups develop, the soldier, the banker, the merchant, the priest. Out of this complexity the city created a higher unity.

This new urban mixture resulted in an enormous expansion of human capabilities in every direction. The city effected a mobilization of manpower, a command over long distance transportation, an intensification of communication over long distances in space and time, an outburst of invention along with a large-scale development of civil engineering, and, not least, it promoted a tremendous further rise in agricultural productivity.

That urban transformation was accompanied, perhaps preceded, by similar outpourings from the collective unconscious. At some moment, it would seem, the local familiar gods, close to the hearth fire, were overpowered and partly replaced, certainly outranked, by the distant sky gods or earth gods, identified with the sun, the moon, the waters of life, the thunderstorm, the desert. The local chieftain turned into the towering king, and became likewise the chief priestly guardian of the shrine, now endowed with divine or almost divine attributes. The village neighbors would now be kept at a distance: no longer familiars and equals, they were reduced to subjects, whose lives were supervised and directed by military and civil officers, governors, viziers, tax-gatherers, soldiers, directly accountable to the king.

Even the ancient village habits and customs might be altered in obedience to divine command. No longer was it sufficient for the village farmer to produce enough to feed his family or his village: he must now work harder and practice self-denial to support a royal and priestly officialdom with a large surplus. For the new rulers were greedy feeders, and openly measured their power not only in arms, but in loaves of bread and jugs of beer. In the new urban society, the wisdom of the aged no longer carried authority. . . . Though family connections still counted in urban society, vocational ability and youthful audacity counted even more, if it gained the support of the king.

When all this happened, the archaic village culture yielded to urban 'civilization,' that peculiar combination of creativity and control, of expression and repression, of tension and release, whose outward manifestation has been the historic city. From its origins onward, indeed, the city may be described as a structure specially equipped to store and transmit the goods of civilization, sufficiently condensed to afford the maximum amount of facilities in a minimum space, but also capable of structural enlargement to enable it to find a place for the changing needs and the more complex forms of a growing society and its cumulative social heritage. The invention of such forms as the written record, the library, the archive, the school, and the university is one of the earliest and most characteristic achievements of the city. . . .

In this emergence of the city, the dynamic element came, as we have seen, from outside the village. Here one must give the new rulers their due, for their hunting practices had accustomed them to a wider horizon than village culture habitually viewed. Archaeologists have pointed out that there is even the possibility that the earliest grain-gatherers, in the uplands of the Near East, may have been hunters who gathered the seeds in their pouch, for current rations, long before they knew how to plant them. The hunter's exploratory mobility, his willingness to gamble and take risks, his need to make prompt decisions, his readiness to undergo bitter deprivation and intense fatigue in pursuit of his game, his willingness to face death in coming to grips with fierce animals—either to kill or be killed—all gave him special qualifications for confident leadership. These traits were the foundations of aristocratic dominance. Faced with the complexities of large-scale community life, individualistic audacity was more viable than the slow communal responses that the agricultural village fostered.

In a society confronting numerous social changes brought on by its own mechanical and agricultural improvements, which provoked serious crises that called for prompt action, under unified command, the hoarded folk wisdom born solely of past experience in long-familiar situations was impotent. Only the self-confident and adventurous could in some degree control these new forces and have sufficient imagination to use them for hitherto unimaginable purposes. Neolithic 'togetherness' was not enough. Many a village, baffled and beset by flooded fields or ruined crops, must have turned away from its slow-moving, overcautious council of elders to a single figure who spoke with authority and promptly gave commands as if he expected instantly to be obeyed.

Doubtless the hunter's imagination, no less than his prowess, was there from the beginning, long before either flowed into political channels: for surely there is a more commanding esthetic sense in the paleolithic hunter's cave than there is in any early neolithic pottery or sculpture. Nothing like the same superb esthetic flair as we find in the Aurigna-

The "superb aesthetic flair" of late paleolithic man, noted by Mumford, can be seen in these hunting scenes from the cave of Jarbaren at Tassili n'Ajjer in Algeria (3000–2500 B.C.).

cian caves came back till the stone-and-copper age. But now heroic exertions, once confined mainly to the hunt, were applied to the entire physical environment. Nothing the mind projected seemed impossible. What one singularly self-assured man dared to dream of, under favor of the gods, a whole city obedient to his will might do. No longer would wild animals alone be subdued: rivers, mountains, swamps, masses of men, would be attacked collectively at the King's command and reduced to order. Backbreaking exertions that no little community would impose on itself, so long as nature met its customary needs, were not undertaken: the hunter-hero, from Gilgamesh to Herakles, set the example in his superhuman acts of strength. In conquering hard physical tasks every man became a bit of a hero, surpassing his own natural limits—if only to escape the overseer's lash.

The expansion of human energies, the enlargements of the human ego, perhaps for the first time detached from its immediate communal envelope the differentiation of common human activities into specialized vocations, and the expression of this expansion and differentiation at many points in the structure of the city, were all aspects of a single transformation: the rise of civilization. . . .

TOPIC 4

# AN ANCIENT CIVILIZATION: SUMER

Civilization is older than history which first begins when man developed writing, or more accurately when he left written records that described his society. The first people to have left such records of their activities were the Sumerians who inhabited the southern part of the Tigris-Euphrates river valley some six thousand years ago. The readings describe the civilization of the Sumerians, an astounding people the record of whose accomplishments has been established by scholars only in the past century.

Reading 7

## Samuel Kramer: The Sumerians

Samuel Kramer is a respected member of the small body of Sumerologists, that is, those scholars who have devoted their professional lives to the study of the ancient Sumerians. Such study can depend only in part on conventional scholarly research. Professor Kramer's sources are in the excavations of Iraq (as the area is now called where once Sumeria was) and the museums of Europe, especially in Turkey (which controlled the Tigris-Euphrates plain in the nineteenth century when interest in the Sumerians first awakened). His knowledge was largely gathered by piecing together and translating random fragments of cuneiform tablets. The material, he admits, is "seasoned with my blood, toil, tears and sweat." But the drudgery of a Sumerologist's work is rewarded by the fact that he "more than most other scholars, is in a position to satisfy man's universal quest for origins—for firsts in the history of civilization." From "The Sumerians" by Samuel Noah Kramer. Reprinted with permission. 

### I

The Tigris-Euphrates plain is a hot, arid land. Six thousand years ago it was a wind-swept barren. It had no minerals, almost no stone, no trees, practically no building material of any kind. It has been described as a land with "the hand of God against it." Yet it was in this desolate region that man built what was probably the first high civilization. Here were born the inventions of writing, farming technology, architecture, the first codes of law, the first cities. Perhaps the very poverty of the land provided the stimulus that mothered these inventions. But the main credit must go to the people who created them—a most remarkable people called the Sumerians.

These Sumerians, as now revealed by long archaeological research, were a surprisingly modern folk. In many ways they were like the pioneers who built the U.S.—practical, ambitious, enterprising, jealous of their personal rights, technologically inventive. Having no stone or timber, they built with marsh reeds and river mud, invented the brick mold and erected cities of baked clay. They canalled the waters of the Tigris and Euphrates rivers into the arid fields and turned Sumer into a veritable Garden of Eden. To manage their irrigation systems they originated regional government, thus emerging from the petty social order of the family and village to the city-state. They created a written language and committed it to permanent clay tablets. They traded their grain surpluses to distant peoples for metals and other materials they lacked. By the third millenium B.C. the culture and civilization of Sumer, a country about the size of the state of Massachusetts, had spread its influence over the whole Middle East, from India to the Mediterranean. And there is hardly an area of our culture today—in mathematics or philosophy, literature or architecture, finance or education, law or politics, religion or folklore—that does not owe some of its origins to the Sumerians.

One might suppose that the story of the Sumerians and their accomplishments would be one of the most celebrated in history. But the astonishing fact is that until about a century ago the modern world had no idea that Sumer or its people had ever existed. For more than 2,000 years they had simply vanished from the human record. Babylonia and ancient Egypt were known to every history student, but the earlier Sumerians were buried and forgotten. Now, thanks to a century of archaeological labor and to the Sumerians' own cuneiform tablets, we have come to know them intimately—as well as or better than any other people of the early history of mankind. The story of how the lost Sumerian civilization was discovered is itself a remarkable chapter. This article will review briefly how the history of the Sumerians was resurrected and what we have learned about them.

II

### The Cuneiform Tablets

Modern archaeologists began to dig in Mesopotamia for its ancient civilizations about a century ago. They were looking for the cities of the Assyrians and Babylonians, who of course were well known from Biblical and Greek literature. As the world knows, the diggers soon came upon incredibly rich finds. At the sites of Nineveh and other ancient Assyrian cities they unearthed many clay tablets inscribed with the wedge-shaped writing called cuneiform. This script was taken to be the invention of the Assyrians. Since the Assyrians were apparently a Semitic people, the language was assumed to be Semitic. But few clues were available for decipherment of the strange cuneiform script.

Then came a development which was to be as important a key to discovery in Mesopotamia as the famous Rosetta Stone in Egypt. In western Persia, notably on the Rock of Behistun, European scholars found some cuneiform inscriptions in three languages. They identified one of the languages as Old Persian, another as Elamite, and the third as the language of the Assyrian tablets. The way was now open to decipher the cuneiform writing—first the Old Persian, then the Assyrian, of which it was apparently a translation.

When scholars finally deciphered the "Assyrian" script, they discovered that the cuneiform writing could not have been originated by the Assyrian Semites. Its symbols, which were not alphabetic but syllabic and ideographic, apparently were derived from non-Semitic rather than Semitic words. And many of the cuneiform tablets turned out to be written in a language without any Semitic characteristics whatever. The archaeologists had to conclude, therefore, that the Assyrians had taken over the cuneiform script from a people who had lived in the region before them.

Who were these people? Jules Oppert, a leading 19th-century investigator of ancient Mesopotamia, found a clue to their name in certain inscriptions which referred to the "King of Sumer and Akkad." He concluded that Akkad was the northern part of the country (indeed, the Assyrians and Babylonians are now called Akkadians), and that Sumer was the southern part, inhabited by the people who spoke the non-Semitic language and had invented cuneiform writing.

So it was that the Sumerians were rediscovered after 2,000 years of oblivion. Oppert resurrected their name in 1869. In the following decades French, American, Anglo-American and German expeditions uncovered the buried Sumerian cities—Lagash, Nippur, Shuruppak, Kish, Ur (Ur of the Chaldees in the Bible), Erech, Asmar and so on. The excavation of ancient Sumer has proceeded almost continuously for three quarters of a century; even during World War II the Iraqi went on digging at a few sites. These historic explorations have recovered hundreds of thousands of Sumerian tablets, great temples, monuments, tombs, sculptures, paintings, tools, irrigation systems and remnants of almost every aspect of the Sumerian culture. As a result we have a fairly complete picture of what life in Sumer was like 5,000 years ago. We know something about how the Sumerians looked (from their statues); we know a good deal about their houses and palaces, their tools and weapons, their art and musical instruments, their jewels and ornaments, their skills and crafts, their industry and commerce, their *belles lettres* and government, their schools and temples, their loves and hates, their kings and history.

Let us run quickly over the history. The area where the Sumerians lived is lower Mesopotamia, from Baghdad down to the Persian Gulf. . . . It is reasonably certain that the Sumerians themselves were not the first settlers in this region. Just as the Indian names Mississippi, Massachusetts, etc., show that North America was inhabited before the English-speaking settlers came, so we know that the Sumerians were preceded in Mesopotamia by another people because the ancient names of the Tigris and Euphrates rivers (*Idigna* and *Buranum*), and even the names of the Sumerian cities (Nippur, Ur, Kish, etc.), are not Sumerian words. The city names must be derived from villages inhabited by the earlier people.

The same kind of clue—words that turn up in the Sumerian writing but are plainly not

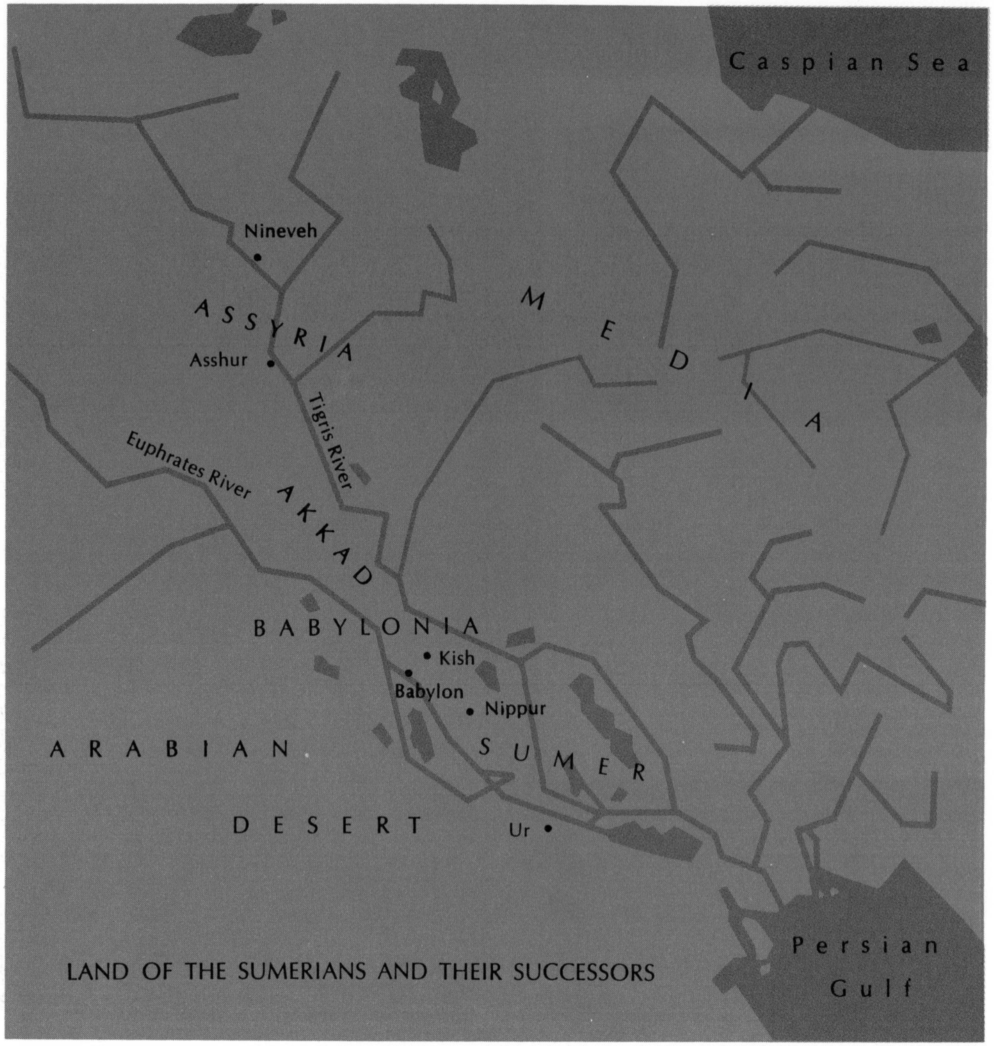

LAND OF THE SUMERIANS AND THEIR SUCCESSORS

Sumerian in origin—tells us something about those first settlers in Sumer. As Benno Landsberger of the University of Chicago, one of the keenest minds in cuneiform research, has shown, among these pre-Sumerian words are those for farmer, herdsman, fisherman, plow, metal smith, carpenter, weaver, potter, mason and perhaps even merchant. It follows that the predecessors of the Sumerians must already have developed a fairly advanced civilization. This is confirmed by excavations of their stone implements and pottery.

The dates of Sumer's early history have always been surrounded with uncertainty, and they have not been satisfactorily settled by tests with the new method of radiocarbon dating. According to the best present estimates, the first settlers occupied the area sometime before 4000 B.C.; new geological evidence indicates that the lower Tigris-Euphrates Valley, once covered by the Persian Gulf, became an inhabitable land well before that date. Be that as it may, it seems that the people called Sumerians did not arrive in the region until nearly 3000 B.C. Just where they came from is in doubt, but there is some reason to believe that their original home had been in the neighborhood of a city called Aratta, which may have been near the Caspian Sea: Sumerian epic poets sang glowingly of Aratta, and its people were said to speak the Sumerian language.

Wherever the Sumerians came from, they brought a creative spirit and an extraordinary surge of progress to the land of Sumer. Uniting with the people who already inhabited it, they developed a rich and powerful civilization. Not long after they arrived, a king called Etana became the ruler of all Sumer: he is described in Sumerian literature as "the man who stabilized all the lands," and he may therefore be the first empire builder in human history. Sumer reached its fullest flowering around 2500 B.C., when its people had developed the cuneiform symbols and thereby originated their finest gift to civilization—the gift of written communication and history. Their own history came to an end some 800 years later: about 1720 B.C. In that year Hammurabi of Babylon won control of the country, and Sumer disappeared in a Babylonian kingdom.

III

## Life in Sumer

The Sumarians' writings and disinterred cities . . . make it possible to reconstruct their life in great detail. Their civilization rested on agriculture and fishing. Among their inventions were the wagon wheel, the plow and the sailboat, but their science and engineering went far beyond these elementary tools. For irrigation the Sumerians built intricate systems of canals, dikes, weirs and reservoirs. They developed measuring and surveying instruments, and a sexagesimal number system (*i.e.*, based on the number 60) with a place notation device not unlike our decimal system. Their farming was highly sophisticated: among their tablets is a veritable farmer's almanac of instructions in agriculture.

In the crafts, the Sumerians' inventions included the potter's wheel, metal casting (of copper and bronze), riveting, soldering, engraving, cloth fulling, bleaching and dyeing. They manufactured paints, leather, cosmetics, perfumes and drugs. Prescriptions recorded on some of the tablets show that the Sumerian physician had command of a large assortment of *materia medica,* prepared from plants, animals and inorganic sources.

Although the Sumerians' economy was primarily agricultural, their life was centered mainly in the cities. Here lived many of the farmers, herdsmen and fishermen, as well as merchants, craftsmen, architects, doctors, scribes, soldiers and priests. Artisans and traveling merchants sold their products in the central town market, and were paid in kind or in money—usually silver coin in the form of a disk or ring. The dozen or so cities in Sumer probably ranged from 10,000 to 50,000 in population. Each was enclosed by a wall and surrounded with suburban villages and hamlets.

The dominant feature of every Sumerian city was a massive temple mounted on a high terrace. It usually had the form of a ziggurat, Sumer's most distinctive contribution to religious architecture. This is a pyramidal tower with a series of ascending terraces winding around the outside. To break the unattractive blankness of the temple's mudbrick walls, the Sumerian architects introduced buttresses and recesses, and they also beautified the building with columns decorated in colored mosaics. Inside the temple were rooms for the priests and a central shrine with a niche for the statue of the god. Each city in Sumer had a different tutelary god, and the Sumerians considered the city the god's property. Thus the city of Nippur, for example, belonged to Enlil, the god of the air. Nippur became Sumer's chief religious and cultural center, and Enlil was elevated to the highest rank as father of all the gods.

A street in a Sumerian city. This modern reconstruction of Ur about 2000 B.C. (in the American Museum of Natural History) shows a ziggurat in the background.

Originally the cities were governed by the citizens themselves, presided over by a governor of their selection. On all important decisions the citizens met in an assembly divided into two chambers—the "elders" and the "men." But for military reasons they gradually relinquished this democratic system. Each city acquired a ruler—at first elected, later hereditary—who organized its defense against the other cities and against foreign invaders. In the course of time the king rivaled the city's religious leaders in wealth and influence. The rulers of Sumer's dozen or so city-states also contended with one another for control of the whole country, and the history of Sumer is largely a record of bitter conflicts among its cities, which eventually led to its downfall.

The life of the individual citizen in a Sumerian city was remarkably free and prosperous. The poorest citizen managed to own a farm and cattle or a house and garden. To be sure, slavery was permitted, and a man could sell his children or his entire family to pay off his debts. But even slaves had certain legal rights: they could engage in business, borrow money and buy their freedom. (The average price for an adult slave was 10 shekels—less than the price of an ass.) The great majority of Sumerians were free citizens, going about their business and the pursuit of happiness with a minimum of restrictions. This did not, however, apply to children, who were under the absolute authority of their parents, could be disinherited or sold into slavery, and had to marry mates chosen by the parents. But in the normal course of events Sumerian families cherished their children and were knit closely together by love and mutual obligations. Women had many legal rights, including the right to hold property and engage in business. A man could divorce his wife on comparatively slender grounds, or, if they had no children, he was allowed to take a second wife.

A Sumerian couple of the first half of the third millenium B.C. strike modern viewers by their grace, proportion and surreal eyes. Statues from the Abu Temple, Tell Asmar, now in the Baghdad Museum.

Most Sumerian families lived in a one-story, mud-brick house consisting of several rooms grouped around an open court. The well-to-do had two-story houses of about a dozen rooms, plastered and whitewashed inside and out; these houses boasted servants' rooms and sometimes even a private chapel. Often the house had a mausoleum in the basement where the family buried its dead. The Sumerians believed that the souls of the dead traveled to a nether world where existence continued more or less as on earth. They therefore buried pots, tools, weapons and jewels with the dead. When a king died, the palace sometimes buried with him some of his courtiers and servants and even his chariot and animals.

Sumerian men were often clean-shaven, but many of them wore a long beard and had long hair parted in the middle. In early times their usual dress was a flounced skirt and felt cloak; later these were replaced by a long shirt and a big fringed shawl draped over the left shoulder, leaving the right arm bare. The common dress for women was a long shawl covering the body from head to foot, except for the right shoulder. Women usually braided their hair into a heavy pigtail and wound it around the head, but on important occasions they wore elaborate headdresses consisting of ribbons, beads and pendants.

Music apparently occupied a large place in the life of the Sumerians—at home, in school and in the temple. Beautifully constructed harps and lyres were found in the royal tombs at Ur. Research has turned up references to drums, tambourines, reed and metal pipes, and hymns written on tablets. Some of the important personages in the palaces and temples of Sumerian cities were musicians. . . .

## Religion

The Sumerians lived by a simple, fatalistic theology. They believed that the universe and their personal lives were ruled by living gods, invisible to mortal eyes. The chief gods were those of water, earth, air and heaven, named respectively Enki, Ki, Enlil and An. From a primeval sea were created the earth, the atmosphere, the gods and sky, the sun, moon, planets and stars, and finally life. There were gods in charge of the sun, moon and planets, of winds and storms, of rivers and mountains, of cities and states, of farms and irrigation ditches, or the pickax, brick mold and plow. The major gods established a set of unchangeable laws which must be obeyed willy-nilly by everything and everybody. Thus the Sumerians were untroubled by any question of free will. Man existed to please and serve the gods, and his life followed their divine orders. Because the great gods were far away in the distant sky and had more important matters to attend to, each person appealed to a particular personal god, a "good angel," through whom he sought salvation. Not that the people neglected regular public devotions to the gods. In the Sumerian temples a court of professionals, including priests, priestesses, musicians and eunuchs, offered daily libations and sacrifices of animal and vegetable fats. There were also periodic feasts and celebrations, of which the most important was a royal ceremony ushering in each new year.

This ceremony is traceable to the cycle of nature in Mesopotamia. Every summer, in the hot, parched months, all vegetation died and animal life languished. In the autumn the land began to revive and bloom again. The Sumerian theology explained these events by supposing that the god of vegetation retired to the nether world in the summer and returned to the earth around the time of the new year; his sexual reunion with his wife Inanna, the goddess of love and procreation, then restored fertility to the land. To celebrate this revival and ensure fecundity, the Sumerians each year staged a marriage ceremony between their king, as the risen god, and a priestess representing the goddess Inanna. The marriage was made an occasion of prolonged festival, ritual, music and rejoicing.

The Sumerians considered themselves to be a chosen people, in more intimate contact with the gods than was the rest of mankind. Nevertheless they had a moving vision of all mankind living in peace and security, united by a universal faith and perhaps even by a universal language. Curiously, they projected this vision into the past, into a long-gone golden age, rather than into the future. As a Sumerian poet put it:

Once upon a time there was no snake,
  there was no scorpion,
There was no hyena, there was no lion,
There was no wild dog, no wolf
There was no fear, no terror,
Man had no rival.

Once upon a time . . .
The whole universe, the people in unison,
To Enlil in one tongue gave praise. . . .

## Cuneiform

But the Sumerians' chief contribution to civilization was their invention of writing. Their cuneiform script is the earliest known system of writing in man's history. The cuneiform system served as the main tool of written communication throughout western Asia for some 2,000 years—long after the Sumerians themselves had disappeared. Without it, mankind's cultural progress would certainly have been much delayed.

The Sumerian script began as a set of pictographic signs devised by temple administrators and priests to keep track of the temple's resources and activities. They inscribed the signs in clay with a reed stylus, and this accounts for the curious wedge-shaped characters. In the course of the centuries Sumerian scholars developed the signs into purely phonetic symbols representing words or syllables.

More than 90 per cent of the tablets that have been excavated in Sumer are economic, legal and administrative documents, not un-

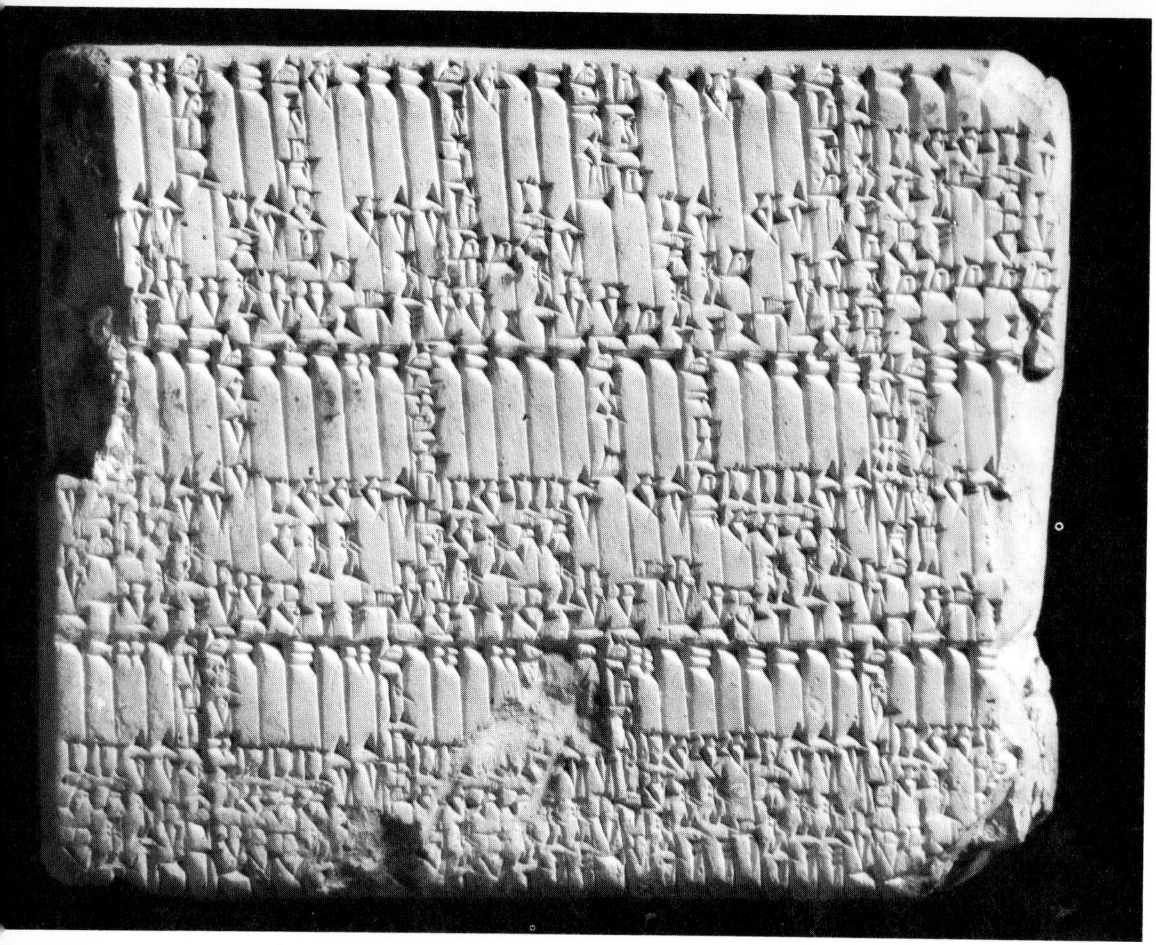

The cuneiform inscription on this Sumerian tablet of about 2000 B.C. offers an official account of the disposal of dead cattle at the court of Ur.

like the commercial and governmental records of our own day. But some 5,000 of the finds are literary works: myths and epic tales, hymns and lamentations, proverbs, fables, essays. They qualify as man's oldest known literature—nearly 1,000 years older than the *Iliad* and the Hebrew Bible. In addition the tablets include a number of Sumerian "textbooks," listing the names of trees, birds, insects, minerals, cities, countries and so forth. There are even commemorative narratives which constitute mankind's first writing of history.

From the Sumerians' invention of writing grew the first formal system of education—another milestone in human intellectual progress. They set up "professional" schools to train scribes, secretaries and administrators; in time these vocational schools became also centers of culture where scholars, scientists and poets devoted their lives to learning and teaching.

The head of the school was called "the school father"; the pupils, "school sons." Among the faculty members were "the man in charge of drawing," "the man in charge of Sumerian," "the man in charge of the whip." There was no sparing of the rod. The curriculum consisted in copying and memorizing the lists of words and names on the textbook tablets, in studying and composing poetic narratives, hymns and essays and in mastering mathematical tables and problems, including tables of square and cube roots.

Teachers in ancient Sumer seem to have been treated not unlike their counterparts in the U.S. today: their salaries were low and they were looked upon with a mixture of respect and contempt. The Sumerians were an aggressive people, prizing wealth, renown and social prestige. As their tablets suggest, they were far more concerned with accounts than with academic learning. . . .

The Sumerians firmly believed that when man died, his emasculated spirit descended to a dark, dreary nether world. The spirit and fame of this proud vigorous people certainly suffered a remarkable eclipse after their empire fell. But what their minds created survives throughout the living corpus of present day civilization: it appears in the form of a Biblical proverb, a statutory law, a heroic folktale, an Aesopic fable, a zodiacal sign, a Euclidean theorem, the weight of a coin, the degree of an angle. And in the cuneiform tablets which were the Sumerians' pre-eminent gift we have found the earliest intellectual record of man's strivings toward civilization.

# Their Tablets Tell of Sumerian Life

The four documents in this reading are samples of the findings from Sumerian clay tablets. In the first the gods, overburdened with labor, decide to create mortal beings to serve them. In the second the gods, dissatisfied with these mortals, determine to destroy all of them except Ziusudra, a pious god-fearing king. The third is a legal document concerning inheritance; the fourth, excerpts from detailed instructions on how to farm. The first two documents are from Samuel Noah Kramer, *History Begins at Sumer* (New York: Doubleday & Co., 1959), pp. 108–109, 152–154. The last two documents are from Samuel Noah Kramer, *The Sumerians* (Chicago: University of Chicago Press, 1964). Copyright © 1964 by the University of Chicago.

## I. CREATION OF MAN

[An exchange between Nammu, the goddess of the ocean, and Enki, her son, the water god and god of wisdom.]

"Oh my son, rise from your bed, from your wise work,
Fashion servants of the gods, may they produce their doubles."

"O my mother, the creature whose name you uttered, it exists,
Bind upon it the image of the gods;
Mix the heart of the clay that is over the abyss,
The good and princely fashioners will thicken the clay,
You, do you bring the limbs into existence;
Ninmah (the earth-mother goddess) will work above you,
The goddesses (of birth) . . . will stand by you at your fashioning;
O my mother, decree its (the newborn's) fate,
Ninmah will bind upon it the image of the gods,
It is Man. . . ."

## II. THE FLOOD

Ziusudra, standing at [the holy wall's] side, listened.
"Stand by the wall at my left side . . .,
By the wall I will say a word to you, take my word,
Give ear to my instructions:
By our [word missing on tablet] . . . a flood will sweep over the cult centers;
To destroy the seed of mankind [words missing]
Is the decision, the word of the assembly of the gods.
By the word commanded by An and Enlil,
Its kingship, its rule (will be put to an end)."

All the windstorms, exceedingly powerful, attacked as one,
At the same time, the flood sweeps over the cult centers.

After, for seven days and seven nights,
The flood had swept over the land,
And the huge boat had been tossed about by the windstorms on the great waters,
Utu came forth, who sheds light on heaven and earth,
Ziusudra opened a window on the huge boat,
The hero Utu brought his rays into the giant boat.

Ziusudra, the king,
Prostrated himself before Utu,
The king kills an ox, slaughters a sheep.

An and Enlil uttered "breath of heaven," "breath of earth," by their [word missing] . . . it stretched itself,
Vegetation, coming up out of the earth, rises up.

Ziusudra, the king,
Prostrated himself before An and Enlil.
An and Enlil cherished Ziusudra,
Life like a god they give him:
Breath eternal like a god they bring down for him.
Then, Ziusudra the king,
The preserver of the name of vegetation and of the seed of mankind,
In the land of crossing, the land of Dilmun, the place where the sun rises, they caused to dwell."

## III. A COURT DECISION

Innashagga, the wife of Dudu, the son of Titi, bought a house . . . with her own money. As long as Dudu lived, Ur-Eninnu, the son of Dudu, had possession of his house. Since Innashagga had bought the house, he (Ur-Eninnu) had the tablet (recording) the purchase of the house made over to him by Innashagga. Innashagga took the oath that she bought the house with her own money (and) not with the property of Dudu.

Dudu had given Ninana, the son of Niza, the goldsmith, (as a slave) to Innashagga, his wife. After the death of Dudu, the heirs of Dudu, . . . claimed title (to the slave) from her.

[Witnesses] testified that Dudu had given the slave to Innashagga; (and) the heirs of Dudu confirmed this testimony. Since (their statements) were confirmed by the statements of the heirs, the witnesses were not compelled to take the oath.

(Therefore) Ninana, the son of Niza, (and) the house were then confirmed (as belonging to) Innashagga, the wife of Dudu.

Geme-Tirash, Magina, (and) Sag-Bautuku, the daughters of Ninana, the son of Niza, were given their freedom by Innashagga, the wife of Dudu, before the judges. The heirs of Dudu swore by the name of the king that they would not change their mother's word.

Urbagara, the son of Ur—. . .—the *mashkim.*

Lu-Shara, Ludingirra, (and) Ur-Sataran—their judges (that is, of the lawsuits here recorded).

(Date-formula follows.)

### IV. FARMERS' ALMANAC

In days of yore a farmer instructed his son (as follows):

When you are about to take hold of your field (for cultivation), keep a sharp eye on the opening of the dikes, ditches, and mounds (so that) when you flood the field the water will not rise too high in it. When you have emptied it of water, watch the field's water-soaked ground that it stay virile ground for you. Let shod oxen (that is, oxen whose hooves are protected one way or another) trample it for you; (and) after having its weeds ripped out (by them) (and) the field made level ground, dress it evenly with narrow axes weighing (no more than) two-thirds of a pound each. (Following which) let the pickax wielder eradicate the ox hooves for you (and) smooth them out; have all crevices worked over with a drag, and have him go with the pickax all around the four edges of the field.

While the field is drying, let your obedient (household) prepare your tools for you, make fast the yoke bar, hang up your new whips on nails, and let the hanging handles of your old whips be mended by the artisans. Let the bronze . . . your tools "heed your arm"; let the leather "headbinder," goad, "mouth-opener," (and) whip uphold you (in matters requiring discipline and control); let your *bandu*-basket crackle; (all this) will make a mighty income for you.

When your field has been supplied with what is needed, keep a sharp eye on your work. After adding an extra ox to the plow-ox—when one is harnessed to another ox, their plow is larger than (an ordinary) plow—make them . . . one *bur;* they will make for you a . . . like a storm, so that three *gur* barley will be planted in that one *bur*. Sustenance is in a plow! (Thus) having had the field worked with the *bardil*-plow—(yes) the *bardil*-plow—(and then) having had it worked over with the *shukin*-plow, repeat (the process). (After) having had it (the field) harrowed (and) raked three times and pulverized fine with a hammer, let the handle of your whip uphold you; brook no idleness. Stand over them (the field laborers) during their work, (and) brook no interruptions. Do not [distract] your field workers. Since they must carry on by day (and by) heaven's stars for ten (days), their strength should be spent on the field, (and) they are not to dance attendance on you. . . .

After the sprout has broken through (the surface of) the ground, say a prayer to the goddess Ninkilim, (and) shoo away the flying birds. When the barley has filled the narrow bottom of the furrow, water the top seed. When the barley stands up high as (the straw of) a mat in the middle of a boat, water it (a second time). Water (a third time) its royal barley. If the watered barley has turned red, what you say is: "It is sick with the *samana*-disease." But if it has succeeded in producing kernel-rich barley, water it (a fourth time), (and) it will yield you an extra measure of barley in every ten. . . .

When you have heaped up the barley, say the "prayer of the (still) uncleaned barley." When you winnow the barley, pay attention to the men who lift the barley from the ground—two "barley-lifters" should lift it for you. On the day the barley is to be cleaned, have it laid on sticks, (and) say a prayer evening and night. (Then) have the barley "unloosed" (from the chaff) like (with) an overpowering wind, (and) the "unloosed" barley will be stored for you.

(These are) the instructions of Ninurta, the son of Enlil. O Ninurta, trustworthy farmer of Enlil, your praise is good!

# Henri Frankfort: The Role of Myth in the Ancient World

Dutch-born orientalist Henri Frankfort (1897–1954) is the author and editor of books on the culture of ancient Egypt and Babylonia. Frankfort was interested in all aspects of life in the ancient Near East, in its philosophy as well as its visual arts. He believed visual arts should be appreciated for their own sake and not only as "antiquarian evidence." In this reading he examines the role myth played in the ancient world. From H. and H. A. Frankfort, John A. Wilson, Thorkild Jacobsen, William A. Irwin, *The Intellectual Adventure of Ancient Man* (Chicago: University of Chicago Press, 1946). Copyright © 1946 by the University of Chicago.

### I

The world appears to primitive man neither inanimate nor empty but redundant with life;

and life has individuality, in man and beast and plant, and in every phenomenon which confronts man—the thunderclap, the sudden shadow, the eerie and unknown clearing in the wood, the stone which suddenly hurts him when he stumbles while on a hunting trip. Any phenomenon may at any time face him, not as "It," but as "Thou." In this confrontation, "Thou" reveals its individuality, its qualities, its will. "Thou" is not contemplated with intellectual detachment; it is experienced as life confronting life, involving every faculty of man in a reciprocal relationship. Thoughts, no less than acts and feelings, are subordinated to this experience. . . .

. . . In other words, the ancients told myths instead of presenting an analysis or conclusions. We would explain, for instance, that certain atmospheric changes broke a drought and brought about rain. The Babylonians observed the same facts but experienced them as the intervention of the gigantic bird Imdugud which came to their rescue. It covered the sky with the black storm clouds of its wings and devoured the Bull of Heaven, whose hot breath had scorched the crops.

In telling such a myth, the ancients did not intend to provide entertainment. Neither did they seek, in a detached way and without ulterior motives, for intelligible explanations of the natural phenomena. They were recounting events in which they were involved to the extent of their very existence. They experienced, directly, a conflict of powers, one hostile to the harvest upon which they depended, the other frightening but beneficial: the thunderstorm reprieved them in the nick of time by defeating and utterly destroying the drought. The images had already become traditional at the time when we meet them in art and literature, but originally they must have been seen in the revelation which the experience entailed. They are products of imagination, but they are not mere fantasy. . . .

The irrational aspect of myth becomes especially clear when we remember that the ancients were not content merely to recount their myths as stories conveying information. They dramatized them, acknowledging in them a special virtue which could be activated by recital.

Of the dramatization of myth, Holy Communion is a well-known example. Another example is found in Babylonia. During each New Year's festival the Babylonians re-enacted the victory which Marduk had won over the powers of chaos on the first New Year's Day, when the world was created. At the annual festival the Epic of Creation was recited. It is clear that the Babylonians did not regard their story of creation . . . as an intellectually satisfying account of how the world came to be as it is. Ancient man had not thought out an answer; an answer had been revealed to him in a reciprocal relationship with nature. If a question had been answered, man shared that answer with the "Thou" which had revealed itself. Hence, it seemed wise that man, each year, at the critical turn of the seasons, should proclaim the knowledge which he shared with the powers, in order to involve them once more in its potent truth. . . .

II

## The Nature of Reality in the Ancient and Modern Worlds

We shall find that if we attempt to define the structure of mythopoeic [myth-making] thought and compare it with that of modern (that is, scientific) thought, the differences will prove to be due rather to emotional attitude and intention than to a so-called prelogical mentality. The basic distinction of modern thought is that between *subjective* and *objective*. On this distinction scientific thought has based a critical and analytical procedure by which it progressively reduces the individual phenomena to typical events subject to universal laws. Thus it creates an increasingly wide gulf between our perception of the phenomena and the conceptions by which we make them comprehensible. We see the sun rise and set, but we think of the earth as moving round the sun. We see colors, but we describe them as wave-lengths. We dream of a dead relative, but we think of that distinct vision as a product of our own subconscious minds. Even if we individually are unable to prove these almost unbelievable scientific views to be true, we accept them, because we know that they can be proved to possess a greater degree of objectivity than our sense-impressions. In the immediacy of primitive experience, however, there is no room for such a critical resolution of perceptions. Primitive man cannot withdraw from the presence of the phenomena because they reveal themselves to him in the manner we have described. Hence the distinction between subjective and objective knowledge is meaningless to him.

Meaningless, also, is our contrast between reality and appearance. Whatever is capable of affecting mind, feeling, or will has thereby established its undoubted reality. There is, for instance, no reason why dreams should be considered less real than impressions received while one is awake. On the contrary, dreams often affect one so much more than the humdrum events of daily life that they appear to be more, and not less, significant than the usual perceptions. The Babylonians, like the Greeks, sought divine guidance by passing the night in a sacred place hoping for a revelation in dreams. And pharaohs, too, have recorded that dreams induced them to undertake certain works. Hallucinations, too, are real. We find in the official annals of Assarhaddon of Assyria a record of fabulous monsters—two-headed serpents and green, winged creatures—which the exhausted troops had seen in the most trying section of their march, the arid Sinai Desert. We may recall that the Greeks saw the Spirit of the Plain of Marathon arisen in the fateful battle against the Persians. As to monsters, the Egyptians of the Middle Kingdom, as much horrified by the desert as are their modern descendants, depicted dragons, griffins, and chimeras among gazelles, foxes, and other desert game, on a footing of perfect equality.

Just as there was no sharp distinction among dreams, hallucinations, and ordinary vision, there was no sharp separation between the living and the dead. The survival of the dead and their continued relationship with man were assumed as a matter of course, for the dead were involved in the indubitable reality of man's own anguish, expectation, or resentment. . . .

Symbols are treated in the same way. The primitive uses symbols as much as we do; but he can no more conceive them as signifying, yet separate from, the gods of powers than he can consider a relationship established in his mind—such as resemblance—as connecting, and yet separate from, the objects compared. Hence there is coalescence of the symbol and what it signifies, as there is coalescence of two objects compared so that one may stand for the other.

In a similar manner we can explain the curious figure of thought *pars pro toto,* "a part can stand for the whole"; a name, a lock of hair, or a shadow can stand for the man because at any moment the lock of hair or shadow may be felt by the primitive to be pregnant with the full significance of the man. It may confront him with a "Thou" which bears the physiognomy of its owner.

An example of the coalescence of a symbol and the thing it stands for is the treating of a person's name as an essential part of him—as if it were, in a way, identical with him. We have a number of pottery bowls which Egyptian kings of the Middle Kingdom had inscribed with the names of hostile tribes in Palestine, Libya, and Nubia; the names of their rulers; and the names of certain rebellious Egyptians. These bowls were solemnly smashed at a ritual, possibly at the funeral of the king's predecessor; and the object of this ritual was explicitly stated. It was that all these enemies, obviously out of the pharaoh's reach, should die. But if we call the ritual act of the breaking of the bowls symbolical, we miss the point. The Egyptians felt that *real* harm was done to the enemies by the destruction of their names. The occasion was even used to cast a propitious spell of wider scope. After the names of the hostile men, who were enumerated "that they should die," were added such phrases as: "all detrimental thought, all detrimental talk, all detrimental dreams, all detrimental plans, all detrimental strife," etc. Mentioning these things on the bowls to be smashed diminished their actual power to hurt the king or lessen his authority.

For us there is an essential difference between an act and a ritual or symbolical performance. But this distinction was meaningless to the ancients. Gudea, a Mesopotamian ruler, describing the founding of a temple, mentions in one breath that he molded a brick in clay, purified the site with fire, and consecrated the platform with oil. When the Egyptians claim that Osiris, and the Babylonians that Oannes, gave them the elements of their culture, they include among those elements the crafts and agriculture as well as ritual usages. These two groups of activities possess the same degree of reality. It would be meaningless to ask a Babylonian whether the success of the harvest depended on the skill of the farmers or on the correct performance of the New Year's festival. Both were essential to success. . . .

TOPIC 5

# THE STRUCTURE OF NEAR EASTERN SOCIETY

Religion and the king's power were the two central elements that held together ancient society. Kingship itself was sacred and the state long was able to enjoy the benefits of this connection. But even beyond such bonds, the divine left its mark on human affairs in law, administration, and conquest. The readings examine the association of political leadership with the gods in the ancient Near East, especially Egypt and Babylonia, and the kind of law and government that followed from this relationship.

**Reading 10**

## The Transmission of Civilization

This selection was contributed by the editors.

We are all familiar with the ways in which ideas, techniques, beliefs and institutions spread from one people to another. These distinguishing features of a civilization may be sought after and borrowed by interested peoples, or imposed against their will. In the ancient world, more than today, transmission required personal contact. The principal means of contact in the ancient world were provided by migration, conquest, and trade. These permitted the circulation of the specific gifts and ideas of the ancient peoples—writing, religion, art, architecture, and science.

The Egyptians of the Old Kingdom (3000–2200 B.C.) enjoyed eight hundred years in relative isolation from the rest of the world. Although the Nile River which fed their valley civilization emptied into the Mediterranean, there was no push toward expansion or discovery. Free from invasions during these centuries, the Pharaohs were able to govern with little challenge along the entire length of the river. This was the period during which their civilization took form—in public architecture, writing, art, administration, and agriculture. The basic conceptions of divine kingship and an afterlife were elaborated during those years.

The first external challenge to the stability of Egypt came at the end of the Middle Kingdom (2000–1792 B.C.). During the Middle Kingdom there had again been no foreign invasion, but in contrast to the Old Kingdom, an increase in foreign trade. The new trade lines had run to Nubia in Africa to the south, and into the Mediterranean to peoples along its northern and eastern shores. Perhaps most importantly, tin had been brought in and had been added to the copper production of the mines at Sinai to allow the production of bronze. About 1670 B.C., invaders of unknown origin—the Hyksos— moved in from the north through Palestine and conquered Egypt with superior arms. In shaking off the Hyksos one hundred years later, Egypt under the New Kingdom (1570–525 B.C.) entered a period of expansion. Her armies left the Nile Valley and extended Egyptian authority to Palestine, Syria and even to the edge of the Euphrates Valley. Thus under the New Kingdom for the first time, Egyptians mingled with the peoples of the Fertile Crescent. Some were brought back to Egypt as slaves, among them the Hebrews, whose captivity is described in *Exodus,* the second book of the Bible. Although there were periods of strong rule during the thousand years of the New Kingdom, the later Pharaohs could not defend these broad frontiers against successive invasion from the North. The Hittites of Asia Minor were followed as invaders by the Assyrians, the Persians, the Greeks, and finally the Romans. Through the violence of conquest, the civilization of Egypt became the common property of many peoples.

The other great river valley civilization, that of the Tigris and Euphrates, does not offer the same example of more than a thousand years of calm, continuity, and isolation. There—through settlement and conquest in the land of Mesopotamia—other peoples came to share in the heritage of Sumerian civilization. The separate cities of Sumer were first brought together by Sargon (about 2400 B.C.), but at his death the city-states with their separate gods and bitter rivalries emerged once more. Four hundred years passed before this land was again the territory of an empire. The Babylonian Empire (c.2000–c.1600 B.C.) was created by Amorites, a Semitic tribe that pushed eastward to capture the Sumerian city of Babylon and make this small city their capital. Their great royal law-giver was Hammurabi, and his influence, like that of the Sumerian law-makers before him, outlasted his period of rule. The Babylonians held the land for four hundred years. After 1600 B.C., they were increasingly less able to defend their territory against raids from the north and west.

Thirteen centuries before the birth of Christ a fierce people called the Assyrians, who lived on the mountain borders of Mesopotamia in the north, were drawn to the rich cities in the valley. By the year 1000 B.C. through a combination of superior armed force and ruthless military practices, and capitalizing on the weaknesses of Mesopotamia and Egypt, they had gained control of a vast territory that extended from the Persian Gulf along the Fertile Crescent southward to the Upper Nile, bringing the two river valley civilizations together for the first time under one imperial rule. As a Mesopotamian people, their law codes and religion had much in common with those of Sumer and Babylonia. . . . Today no trace of a separate Assyrian people or civilization remains, though many cuneiform tablets filled with information about these early centuries have been found in the ruins of Nineveh, their capital on the Euphrates. The Assyrians seem to have been completely wiped out by an alliance of neighboring peoples that captured Nineveh in 612 B.C.

In less than a century, however, the territory of the great Assyrian Empire was reconstituted and greatly extended by Cyrus, a Persian prince, who became King of the Medes (549 B.C.), a people living in the mountains east of the Fertile Crescent. Cyrus conquered Babylonia and then pushed the boundary of his Empire in successive campaigns to the Mediterranean and up into Asia Minor (present-day Turkey). Under his successor, Egypt was added to the Persian Empire, which by 500 B.C. stretched from the Caspian Sea to the Greek city-states on the Aegean. By conquest and commerce, the two ancient river valley civilizations were thus brought into closer contact with one another, and to the edge of the infant West.

# Three Rulers in the Ancient Near East

The political thought of the ancient Near East is sampled in these selections from temple, tomb, and commemorative inscriptions. In all of the ancient cultures, kingship had its origin in some relationship with the gods. An understanding of the origins and nature of the power of the state in ancient society can be reached by examining primary sources.

Pharaoh Rameses II has best been commemorated in the temple of Abu Simbel, recently saved by international action from the waters of the Nile flooding behind the Aswan High Dam. It is one of the "Wonders of the World," the entrance guarded by four mighty (67 foot high) statues of Rameses.

Hammurabi was a famous king of Babylonia, the state that succeeded Sumer as the great Mesopotamian power.

Darius of Persia reigned over most of the Near East twelve centuries after Hammurabi and seven centuries after Rameses. Darius ordered his account of how he restored the rule of his family over Persia carved on a great mountain cliff for all passers-by to see. From George Willis Botsford, *A Source-Book of Ancient History* (New York, 1912), pp. 10–12, 28–29, 57–59.

## I. RAMESES II, PHARAOH OF EGYPT (13th CENTURY B.C.)

Thus speaks Ptah-Totunen with the high plumes, armed with horns, the father of the gods, to his son who loves him. . . .

Num and Ptah have nourished thy childhood, they leap with joy when they see thee made after my likeness, noble, great, exalted. The great princesses of the house of Ptah and the Hathors of the temple of Tem are in festival, their hearts are full of gladness, their hands take the drum with joy, when they see thy person beautiful and lovely like my Majesty. . . . King Rameses, I grant thee to cut the mountains into the statues immense, gigantic, everlasting; I grant that foeign lands find for thee precious stone to inscribe the monuments with thy name.

The Temple of Rameses II at Abu Simbel on the Nile River. It was built by the Pharaoh during his lifetime. How does such a structure reflect the position of the king in ancient Egypt?

I give thee to succeed in all the works which thou hast done. I give thee all kinds of workmen, all that goes on two or four feet, all that flies and all that has wings. I have put in the heart of all nations to offer thee what they have done; themselves, princes great and small, with one heart seek to please thee, King Rameses. Thou has built a great residence to fortify the boundary of the land, the city of Rameses; it is established on the earth like the four pillars of the sky; hast constructed within a royal palace, where festivals are celebrated to thee as is done for me within. I have set the crown on thy head with my own hands, when thou appearest in the great hall of the double throne; and men and gods have praised thy name like mine when my festival is celebrated.

Thou hast carved my statues and built my shrines as I have done in times of old. I have given thee years by periods of thirty; thou reignest in my place on my throne; I fill thy limbs with life and happiness, I am behind thee to protect thee; I give thee health and strength; I cause Egypt to be submitted to thee, and I supply the two countries with pure life. King Rameses, I grant that the strength, the vigor, and the might of thy sword be felt among all countries; thou castest down the hearts of all nations; I have put them under thy feet; thou comest forth every day in order that be brought to thee the foreign prisoners; the chiefs and the great of all nations offer thee their children. I give them to thy gallant sword that thou mayest do with them what thou likest. King Rameses, I grant that the fear of thee be in the minds of all and thy command in their hearts. I grant that thy valor reach all countries, and that the dread of thee be spread over all lands; the princes tremble at thy remembrance, and thy majesty is fixed on their heads; they come to thee as supplicants to implore thy mercy. Thou givest life to whom thou wishest, and thou puttest to death whom thou pleasest; the throne of all nations is in thy possession. . . .

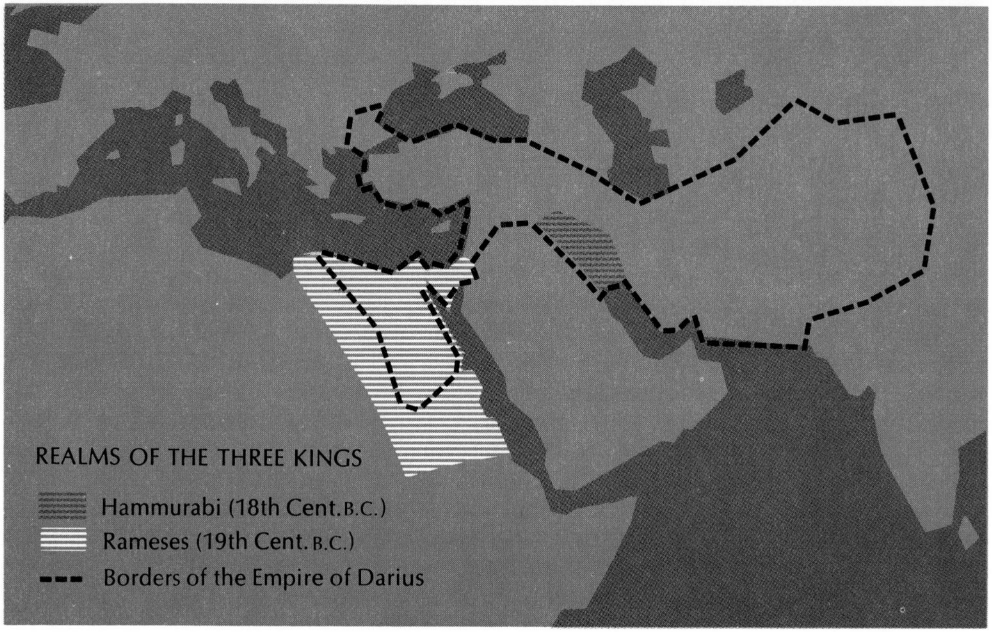


The empire of Darius, stretching from India to the Aegean Sea, covered most of the territory ruled in earlier centuries by Rameses and Hammurabi.

King Rameses, I have exalted thee through such marvelous endowments that heaven and earth leap for joy and those who are within praise thy existence; the mountains, the water, and the stone walls which are on the earth are shaken when they hear thy excellent name, since they have seen what I have accomplished for thee. . . .

## II. HAMMURABI, KING OF BABYLON (18TH CENTURY B.C.)

Hammurabi, the exalted King, the King of Babylon, the King renowned throughout the world, conqueror of the enemies of Marduk [chief god of Babylon], the King beloved by his heart am I.

The favor of god and Bel gave the people of Sumer and Accad unto my government. Their celestial weapons unto my hand they gave. The canal Hammurabi, the joy of men, a stream of abundant waters, for the people of Sumer and Accad excavated. Its banks, all of them, I restored to newness; new supporting walls I heaped up; perennial waters for the people of Sumer and Accad I provided.

The people of Sumer and Accad, all of them, in general assemblies I summoned. A review and inspection of them I ordained every year. In joy and abundance I watched over them, and in peaceful habitations I caused them to dwell.

By the divine favor I am Hammurabi, the exalted King, the worshipper of the supreme deity.

With the prosperous power which Marduk gave me, I built a lofty citadel on a high mound of earth, whose summits rose up like mountains, on the bank of Hammurabi river, and the joy of men.

### III. DARIUS, KING OF PERSIA (6TH CENTURY B.C.)

Says Darius the king: Afterward there was one man, a Magian, Gaumata by name: . . . he thus deceived the people [saying]; I am Bardiya the son of Cyrus, brother of Cambyses; afterward all the people became estranged from Cambyses and went over to him, both Persia and Media and the other provinces; he seized the kingdom; 9 days in the month Garmapada were in course—he thus seized the kingdom; afterwards Cambyses died by a self-imposed death.

Says Darius the king: This kingdom which Gaumata the Magian took from Cambyses, this kingdom from long ago was the possession of our family; afterwards Gaumata the Magian took from Cambyses both Persia and Media and the other provinces; he seized the power and made it his own possession; he became king.

Says Darius the king: There was not a man neither a Persian nor a Median nor any one of our family who could make Gaumata the Magian deprived of the kingdom; the people feared his tyranny; they feared he would slay the many who knew Bardiya formerly; for this reason he would slay the people, "that they might not know me that I am not Bardiya the son of Cyrus"; anyone did not dare to say anything against Gaumata the Magian until I came; afterwards I asked Auramazda for help; Auramazda bore me aid; 10 days in the month Bagayadish were in course—I thus with few men slew that Gaumata the Magian and what men were his foremost allies; . . . I took the kingdom from him; by the grace of Auramazda I became king; Auramazda gave me the kingdom.

Says Darius the king: The kingdom which was taken away from our family, this I put in its place; I establish it on its foundations; as it was formerly so I made it; the sanctuaries which Gaumata the Magian destroyed I restored; for the people, the revenue and the personal property and the estates and the royal residences which Gaumata the Magian took from them I restored; I established the state on its foundation, both Persia and Media and the other provinces; as it was formerly, so I made it; I labored by the grace of Auramazda that Gaumata the Magian might not take away our royal house. . . .

Says Darius the king: For this reason Auramazda bore me aid and the other gods which are, because I was not an enemy, I was not a deceiver, I was not a wrong-doer, neither I nor my family; according to rectitude I ruled; I [did not make] my power an oppression to those who praise me; the man who helped my house, him who should be well esteemed I esteemed; the man who would destroy it, him who should deserve punishment, I punished.

# The Mesopotamian City-States

From H. and H. A. Frankfort, John A. Wilson, Thorkild Jacobsen, and William A. Irwin, *The Intellectual Adventure of Ancient Man* (Chicago: University of Chicago Press, 1946). 

### GODS AND GOVERNMENT IN THE MESOPOTAMIAN CITY-STATE

The subject with which we are to deal is "the function of the state," that is, the particular function which the human state in Mesopotamia was thought to fulfil in the functioning of the universe as a whole. Before we go any further, however, it will be well to consider our modern term "state", lest it trip us up when we apply it to ancient Mesopotamian concepts. When we speak of a state, we usually imply inner sovereignty and independence of all external control. Moreover, we think of a state as dominating a specific territory, and we see as its chief aim the protection of its members and the furthering of their well-being.

Now in the Mesopotamian view of the world, these attributes do not—indeed, cannot—belong to any human organization. The only truly sovereign state, independent of all external control, is the state which the universe itself constitutes, the state governed by the assembly of the gods. This state, moreover, is the state which dominates the territory of Mesopotamia; the gods own the land, the big estates, in the country. Lastly, since man was created especially for the benefit of the gods, his purpose is to serve the gods. Therefore no human institution can have its primary aim in the welfare of its own human members; it must seek primarily the welfare of the gods. . . .

Throughout the third millennium B.C. Mesopotamia was made up of small political units, the so-called "city-states." Each such state consisted of a city with its surrounding territory, cultivated by the people of the city. Sometimes a city-state included more than one city. There might be two or three towns and a number of villages which were dependent on and administered by the chief city. From time to time conquerors arose who succeeded in uniting most of the city-states into a single large national state under their rule; but these national states usually lasted for a relatively short time, after which the country would divide into city-states again.

Central in the city-state was the city, and central in the city was the temple of the city god. The temple of the city god was usually the greatest landowner in the state, and it cultivated its extensive holdings by means of serfs and sharecroppers. Other temples belonging to the city god's spouse, to their divine children, and to deities associated with the chief god similarly had large land holdings, so that it has been estimated that around the middle of the third millennium B.C. most of the lands of a Mesopotamian city-state were temple lands. The larger part of the inhabitants were accordingly earning their livelihood as sharecroppers, serfs, or servants of the gods.

In this situation lie the economic and political realities expressed in the Mesopotamian myths which state that man was created to relieve the gods of toil, to work on the gods' estates. . . .

To carry out [his] orders the city god had at his disposal a large staff of divine and human servants. The human servants worked in the house and in the fields and were organized accordingly. The divine servants, minor gods, served as overseers of the work. Each such minor god had his own special province in the running of the estate; and here he infused his divine powers into the labor of his human underlings, so that it prospered and bore fruit. . . .

The fact that the Mesopotamian universe was conceived of as a state—that the gods who owned and ruled the various city-states were bound together in a higher unity, the assembly of the gods, which possessed executive organs for exerting outward pressure as well as for enforcing law and order internally—had far-reaching consequences for Mesopotamian history and for the ways in which historical events were viewed and interpreted. It vastly strengthened tendencies toward political unification of the country by sanctioning even the most violent of means used toward that end. For any conqueror, if he was successful, was recognized as the agent of Enlil. It also provided—even at times when national unity was at a low ebb and the many city-states were, for all practical purposes, independent units—a background on which international law could work. We see, already at the dawn of history, that a boundary dispute between the neighboring city-states Lagash and Umma was viewed as a dispute between two divine landowners, Ningirsu, the god of Lagash, and Shara, the god of Umma. As such it could be taken to court and adjudicated by Enlil in Nippur. Enlil implemented his decision through the ruler who was then his human representative, Mesilim, king of Kish. Mesilim measured the disputed territory and marked the boundary line which Enlil had designated.

In a similar manner other "kings" throughout Mesopotamian history acted as mediators and judges in disputes between city-states, fulfilling their tasks as Enlil's representatives. Thus Utuhegal of Uruk, after he had freed and united Shumer, settled boundary disputes between Lagash and Ur. Again, Urnammu, the first king of the Third Dynasty of Ur, brought a similar dispute before the judge of the gods, the sun-god Utu, and "in accordance with the righteous verdict of Utu he had the facts cleared up and confirmed (by witnesses)."

This tendency to view what was, in purely human terms, a naked conflict of force as a legal procedure in the state of the gods, as an execution of a devine verdict, appears in full light in an inscription in which Utuhegal tells how he liberated Shumer from its Gutian oppressors. After an introduction stating the misrule which the Gutians had instituted, Utuhegal tells how Enlil gave a verdict deposing them. Then follows Enlil's commission to Utuhegal, a divine deputy is assigned to him to accompany him and authorize his action as that of a legally empowered agent. And, finally, we hear about his campaign and victory. . . .

# The Vizier of Egypt Is the Eyes and Ears of Pharaoh

The vizier was the chief official of Egypt under the pharaoh. Rekh-mi-Re, the subject of the following article, lived in the fifteenth century B.C. This information about him was carved into the walls of his impressive tomb. From *The Tomb of Rekh-Mi-Re at Thebes* (New York: The Metropolitan Museum of Art, 1943). 

## I

I was summoned again into the presence of the good god, King Men-kheper-Re [Thutmose III]—may he live forever. . . .

"So then His Majesty opened his mouth and spake his words before me: 'Behold, my eyes send me to my heart, forasmuch as My Majesty knows that decisions are many and there is no end to them, and the Judgment of cases never flags. Mayest thou act according as I say; then will Maet [truth] rest in her place.' He admonished me very greatly: 'Armor thyself; be strong in action; weary not; accuse evil.'

". . . I acted according as he had ordained. He gave me a court of justice under my authority, and none of them could overrule me. Then I strode forth, acting with stick on back; the dogs were not let loose; my voice went up to heaven. . . .

"I was the heart of the Lord, the ears and eyes of the Sovereign. Yea, I was his own skipper, and knew not slumber night or day. Whether I stood or sat, my heart was set upon prow rope and stern rope, and the sounding-pole never was idle in my hands. I was watchful for any chance of stranding. Every king of Upper and Lower Egypt is a god by whose guidance men live. He is the father and mother of all men, alone by himself, without an equal. I did not suffer evil to overtake me. No neglect of mine led to misfortune.

". . . I judged poor and rich alike. I rescued the weak from the strong. I opposed the rage of the ill-disposed and quelled the covetous in his hour. I checked the passionate moment of the infuriated. I restrained weeping by replacing it with an avenger. I defended the husbandless widow, I established the son and heir on the seat of his father. I gave bread to the hungry, water to the thirsty, meat and ointment and clothes to him who had nothing. I relieved the old man, giving him my staff, and causing the old women to say, 'What a good action!' I hated iniquity, and wrought it not, causing false men to be fastened head downwards. I was innocent before God. No one who knew said concerning me, 'What has he done?' I judged great matters. . . . I caused both parties to go forth at peace. I did not pervert justice for reward. I was not deaf to the empty-handed, nay more, I never accepted anyone's bribe. . . .

Sebekemsaf, an Egyptian official whose high devotion to his duties is recounted by the inscription on this black granite figurine, served the Thirteenth Dynasty about 1700 B.C.

". . . I was clever in all undertakings, deliberate in counsel, ready to listen. I was skilled in past matters, and the condition of yesterday caused me to know tomorrow.

"I judged the suppliant. I did not incline to one side. I paid no attention to rewards. I was not angry with him who came as a suppliant. I did not rebuff him. I tolerated him in his moment of passion. I rescued the timid man from the violent." . . .

II

## The Duties of the Vizier

Regarding the exact procedure of His Excellency the Vizier when he gives a hearing in the hall of the vizier—he is to sit on a backed chair, a reed mat being on the ground, the chain of office on him, a skin under his back, another under his feet, and a matwork cape on him, a baton near him, forty leathern rods laid out before him, the Chiefs of Ten of Upper Egypt before him on either hand, the chamberlain on his right hand, the Controller of Ingress on his left, and the scribes of the vizier near him. . . .

Report is to be made to him [the vizier] of the closing of repositories at the proper time and of their opening at the proper time. Report is to be made to him of the condition of the strongholds of the South and the North and of the outgoing of all that goes out from the Royal Demesne. Report is to be made to him of the incoming of all that comes into the Royal Demesne. Report is to be made to him too of all incomings and outgoings to and from the grounds of the Residence, they that enter and they that leave. . . . Superintendents of bailiffs, and superintendents of landholdings are to report their affairs to him. . . .

It is he who dispatches any courier and all commissions of the Royal Demesne. It is he who appoints anyone from the bureaucracy as superintendent of Upper or Lower Egypt, the Front of the South, or the Great Territory (the province of Abydos). They are to report to him all that has happened in their zones at the beginning of each four-monthly season, and they are to bring to him the official scribes attached to them and their council.

It is he who sees that soldiers mobilize and move as an escort of the monarch when he sails north or south. It is he who appoints to vacancies whether in the Southern City or in the Residence, following a decision of the Royal Demesne. There shall be brought before

Egyptian workers harvesting and thrashing grain under supervision. This detailed fourteenth-century wall painting was found in the tomb of Menna, scribe of the fields, an official of the Eighteenth Dynasty. Note that the illustration of a worker being whipped (in the first panel) has been placed in front of the figure of the supervisor.

1 General approach to the desolate and forbidding area in the Valley of the Kings where Tutankhamen's tomb is located.

## An Ancient Tomb Reveals the Splendors of Egypt

A city of the dead has lain for thousands of years exposed to searing heat and human greed near ancient Thebes. Here, in the Valley of the Kings on the west bank of the Nile River, an English archaeologist made the most important tomb discovery in the history of Egyptology. Howard Carter, in 1922, after six years of preliminary exploration with Lord Carnarvon, scraped away the dirt and debris that lay before the sealed burial vault of King Tutankhamen. The tomb of this youthful monarch, a lesser figure among the royalty of the Eighteenth Dynasty, overflowed with riches of great historic and aesthetic value, and the mummy itself was found as the royal embalmers prepared it thirty-three hundred years ago. An American photographer, Harry Burton, followed in the footsteps of the archaeologist to record the stages of discovery. Some of his photographs of the interior of the tomb are among those that follow.

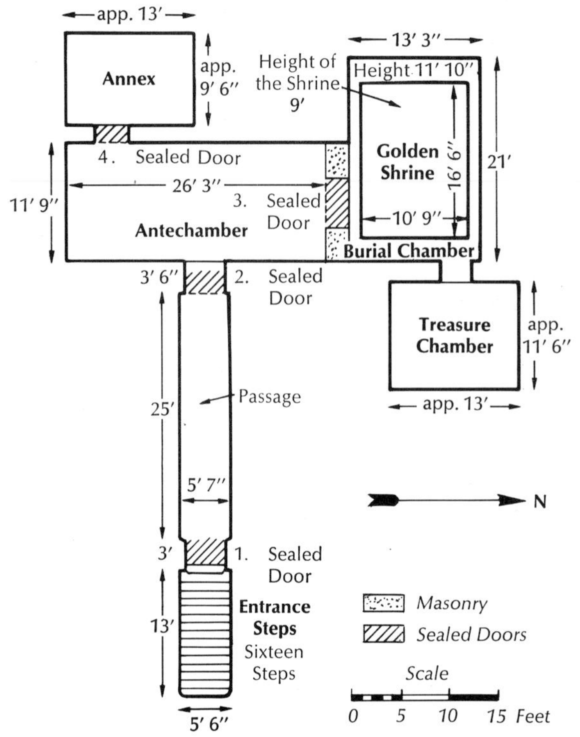


2 Diagram of Tutankhamen's tomb. The antechamber and annex were penetrated by grave robbers on at least two occasions before the end of the second millennium B.C. Unlike most of the tombs of the pharaohs, however, no further pilfering seems to have occurred. The burial chamber itself, sealed about 1350 B.C., remained untouched for 3300 years.

3 A part of the tomb showing the disorder the thieves left. Jackal-headed figure with a shawl is Anubis, god of the dead.

4 Gilded figures of goddesses found surrounding the large coffer in the Treasury.

5 One of the three golden couches with animal-shaped supports found in the antechamber.

6 Alabaster jar lids fashioned as busts of Tutankhamen.

7 Scene from the rear panel of the throne showing the pharaoh, who died at the age of eighteen, with his young wife. A small bouquet of flowers, believed to be her gift, was found next to the mummy.

8 Detail of chariot body, showing African and Near Eastern prisoners. Four enormous chariots covered with gold had been brought into the tomb. Every bit of the gold covering was either embossed, hammered, or inlaid—some with abstract designs and others with scenes of the hunt or war.

9 Offering cakes, found among the gifts for the dead in the inner chambers.

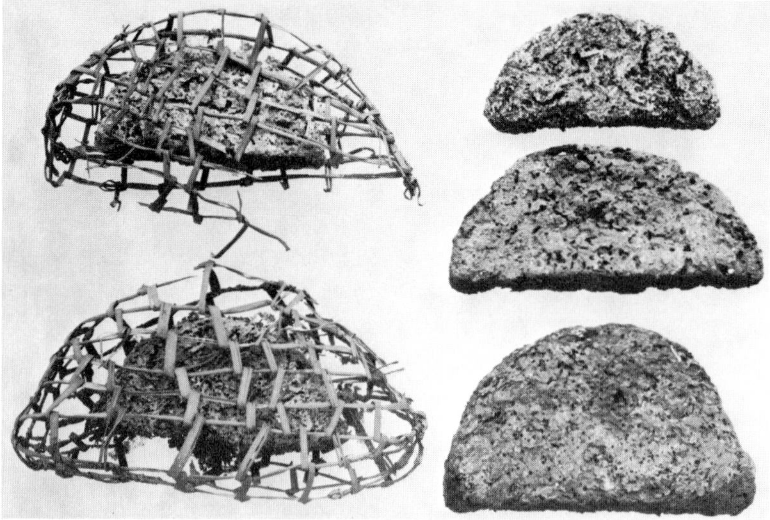

10 Tutankhamen's yellow quartzite sarcophagus with the outermost of three man-shaped coffins visible within. This sarcophagus was itself discovered inside the smallest of four enclosing and protective shrines.

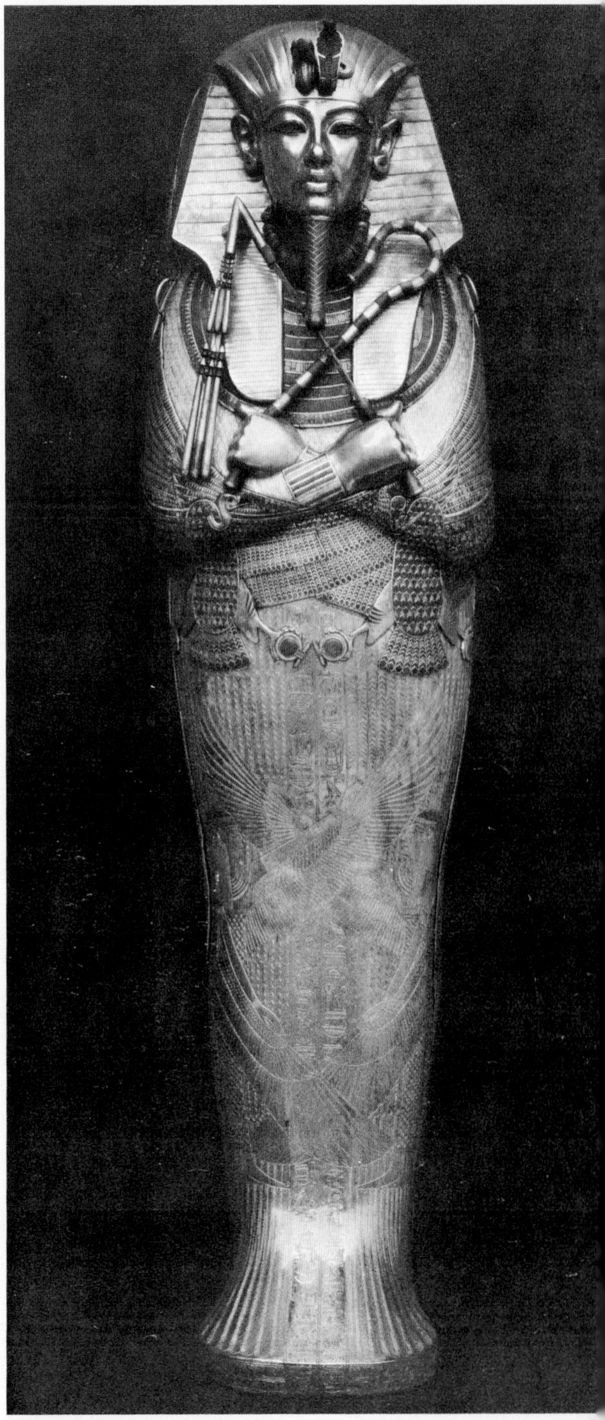

12 Lid of the third of the three nested coffins, after cleaning. The king is represented with the crook and flail, symbols of his authority.

11 Howard Carter and an Egyptian assistant remove the sticky unguent material which covered the space between the second and third coffins. The third coffin, made entirely of gold, contained the mummy.

13 The mummified head of Tutankhamen.

14 Golden mask which lay over the head and shoulders of the mummy. It is made of polished gold and inlaid with pieces of many-colored glass, lapis lazuli, alabaster, and obsidian.

him the guild of victualers to the Ruler, that his hall and the military council may be supplied and that the army regulation may be issued to them. . . .

It is he who sends out men to cut down sycamores, following a decision of the Royal Demesne. It is he who sends out the councillors of the nome [provinces into which Egypt was divided] to make irrigation canals throughout the entire land. It is he who dispatches mayors and heads of divisions for summer tillage. It is he who appoints superintendents of bailiffs in the hall of the Royal Demesne. It is he who appoints one who shall hear the case of mayors and heads of divisions and who shall go on circuit in his [the vizier's] name to Upper or Lower Egypt. Report is to be made to him of all legal cases.

. . . It is he who is to fix the boundaries of any nome, any additional marshland, any temple fief, and any entry on possession. . . .

. . . It is he who makes inventories of all oxen of which inventories have to be made. It is he who inspects the water supply on the first of every ten-day period. . . . Report is to be made to him on the ascent of Sirius [bright star which annually became visible at about the time the Nile began to flood] and the slackening of the Nile. Report shall be made to him of rains. . . .

# Pharaoh and the Officials of the Empire

When rulers of Egypt and the other great empires of the Near East conquered foreign territories, they frequently left these areas under the local control of their native princes. These princes recognized their land as belonging to the king, paid taxes, and supported the imperial armies. Within their district the princes performed services similar to that of the vizier in Egypt and, like him, shared in both the advantages and problems of power. From George Steindorff and Keith C. Steele, *When Egypt Ruled the East* (Chicago: University of Chicago Press, 1957), pp. 105–106. Copyright © 1957 by the University of Chicago.

Intercourse between Egypt and the Syrian vassal princes was maintained through the medium of royal couriers who traveled from city to city, collected the tribute, delivered written orders from the pharaoh, and carried letters from the princes to the Egyptian court. We are quite well informed about this correspondence, which was carried on in the cuneiform writing of the Akkadian language, for in the year 1887 a portion of it, together with numerous letters of Babylonian and other western Asiatic kings, was discovered in the ruins of Amarna in Upper Egypt. . . . Their content is of the most varying character. A prince assures the pharaoh in the humblest possible terms of his abiding loyalty, requests aid against his enemies, complains when after numerous pressing demands it does not arrive, or announces to the king the peace and safety of the region intrusted to his care. Above all, eloquent expression is found in these letters of the quarrels and intrigues among the various princes, each of whom is, of course, more faithful than any of his fellows. Thus Prince Abdihepa of Jerusalem defends himself against charges of treason which have been reported at court in the following communication:

> To the king, my lord, speaks Abdihepa, your servant: Seven and seven times do I fall at the feet of the king, my lord. What have I done to the king, my lord? They are calumniating me before the king, saying, "Abdihepa has fallen away from the king, his lord." But see, neither my father nor my mother has set me in this place, but the mighty hand of the king has invested me with the house of my father. Why then should I commit a crime against the king, my lord? As long as the king, my lord, lives I shall say to the commissar of the king, my lord, "Why do you love the Habiru and hate the resident vassal prince?" And that is why they are slandering me before the king, my lord.

Full of obsequiousness is, likewise, the following epistle which Prince Ammunira of Beirut addressed

> to the king, my lord, my sun, my gods, and the breath of my life. . . . I have heard the words of the tablets of the king, my lord, my sun, my gods, the breath of my life, and the heart of your servant, the dust under the feet of the king, my lord, my sun, my gods, and the breath of my life, rejoices very, very much because the breath of the king, my lord, my sun, my gods, has gone forth to his servant and the dust under his feet. When, furthermore, the king, my lord, my sun, wrote to his servant and the dust under his feet, "Make everything ready for the troops of the king, your lord," I have understood it completely. And behold, I have prepared everything, my horses, my chariots, everything of mine which the ser-

vant of the king, my lord, possesses, for the troops of the king, my lord. May the troops of the king, my lord, my sun, my gods, crush the head of his enemies. And may the two eyes of your servant look upon the life of the king, my lord.

# Hammurabi Issues a Law Code

The collection of laws ordered by the great Babylonian law-giver, Hammurabi, survives today on stone tablets and has been dated to the eighteenth century B.C. The code is remarkable for the variety of relationships it seeks to regulate and for its strictness. By no means the first body of laws in the history of the countries existing in the Fertile Crescent, it is nonetheless the one that has been preserved in greatest detail. Like all law codes, it provides insight into the values of the society in which it was conceived. From Louis Cohn-Haft, *Source Readings in Ancient History, Vol. I: The Ancient Near East and Greece* (Chicago: The University of Chicago Press, 1965), pp. 81–84, 86, 89, 91, 93, 96–98, 102. Copyright © 1965 by the University of Chicago.

I

## Prologue

When the lofty Anu, king of the Anunnaki, and Enlil, lord of heaven and earth, who determines the destinies of the land, committed the rule of all mankind to Marduk, the first-born son of Ea, and made him great among the Igigi; when they pronounced the lofty name of Babylon, made it great among the quarters of the world and in its midst established for him an everlasting kingdom whose foundations were firm as heaven and earth—at that time Anu and Enlil named me, Hammurabi, the exalted prince, the worshipper of the gods, to cause righteousness to prevail in the land, to destroy the wicked and the evil, to prevent the strong from plundering the weak, to go forth like the sun over the black-headed race, to enlighten the land and to further the welfare of the people. . . . The ancient seed of royalty, the powerful king, the sun of Babylon, who caused light to go forth over the lands of Sumer and Akkad; the king who caused the four quarters of the world to render obedience; the favorite of Innanna am I. When Marduk sent me to rule the people and to bring help to the land, I established law and justice in the language of the land and promoted the welfare of the people.

Hammurabi, his right hand raised in respect, stands before Shamash, god of justice. Shoulders aflame, the god holds in his right hand a rod and large ring, attributes of power. Shamash is seated high on a mountain, indicated by the ridged mound under his feet, and is dictating the Law to the Babylonian ruler. This eighteenth-century B.C. black basalt stele (stone pillar) has engraved upon it 282 clauses of Hammurabi's Code.

II

## The Laws

15. If a man aid a male or a female slave of the palace, or a male or a female slave of a common man, to escape from the city, he shall be put to death.

25. If a fire break out in a man's house and a man who goes to extinguish it cast his eye on the household property of the owner of the house, and take the household property

of the owner of the house, that man shall be thrown into the fire.

26. If either an officer or a constable who is ordered to go on an errand of the king do not go . . . that officer or constable shall be put to death. . . .

42. If a man rent a field for cultivation and do not produce any grain in the field, because he has not performed the necessary work on the field they shall convict him, and he shall give to the owner of the field grain on the basis of the adjacent fields.

45. If a man rent his field to a tenant for rent and receive the rent of his field and later Adad [the storm god] inundate the field, or carry away the produce, the loss is the tenant's.

48. If a man owe a debt and Adad inundate the field or the flood carry the produce away, or, through lack of water, grain have not grown in the field, in that year he shall not make any return of grain to the creditor, he shall alter his contract-tablet and he need not pay the interest for that year.

53. If a man neglect to strengthen his dike, and do not strengthen his dike, and a break be made in his dike and he let the water carry away the farmland, the man in whose dike the break has been made shall restore the grain which he has damaged.

54. If he be not able to restore the grain, they shall sell him and his goods, and the farmers whose grain the water has carried away shall divide the results of the sale.

87. If he put out money at interest, for one shekel of silver he shall receive one-fifth of a shekel as interest.

128. If a man take a wife and do not draw up a contract with her, that woman is not a wife.

150. If a man make his wife a present of field, garden, house, and goods and deliver to her a sealed deed, after the death of her husband her children may not make any claim against her. The mother after her death may give them to her child whom she loves, but to a brother she may not give them.

168. If a man set his face to disinherit his son and say to the judges, "I will disinherit my son," the judges shall inquire into his past, and if the son have not committed a crime sufficiently grave to cut him off from sonship, the father may not cut off his son from sonship.

195. If a man strike his father, they shall cut off his hand.

196. If a man destroy the eye of another man, they shall destroy his eye.

197. If he break a man's bone, they shall break his bone.

198. If he destroy the eye of a common man or break a bone of a common man, he shall pay one mina of silver.

199. If he destroy the eye of a man's slave or break a bone of a man's slave, he shall pay one-half his price.

200. If a man knock out a tooth of a man of his own rank, they shall knock out his tooth.

201. If he knock out a tooth of a common man, he shall pay one-third mina of silver.

202. If a man smite on the cheek a man who is his superior, he shall receive sixty strokes with an oxtail whip in public.

203. If the son of a gentleman smite the son of a gentleman of his own rank, he shall pay one mina of silver.

205. If a man's slave smite the son of a gentleman on the cheek, they shall cut off his ear.

215. If a physician make a deep incision upon a man with his bronze lancet and save the man's life; or if he operate on the eye socket of a man with his bronze lancet and save that man's eye, he shall receive ten shekels of silver.

216. If it were a common man, he shall receive five shekels.

217. If it were a man's slave, the owner of the slave shall give two shekels of silver to the physician.

218. If a physician make a deep incision upon a man with his bronze lancet and cause the man's death, or operate on the eye socket of a man with his bronze lancet and destroy the man's eye, they shall cut off his hand.

219. If a physician make a deep incision upon a slave of a common man with his bronze lancet and cause his death, he shall substitute a slave of equal value.

224. If a veterinary surgeon make a deep incision upon an ox or an ass and save its life, the owner of the ox or ass shall give to the surgeon as his fee one-sixth of a shekel of silver.

225. If he make a deep incision upon an ox or an ass and cause its death, he shall give to the owner of the ox or ass one-fourth of its value.

229. If a builder erect a house for a man and do not make its construction firm, and the house which he built collapse and cause the death of the owner of the house, that builder shall be put to death.

230. If it cause the death of a son of the owner of the house, they shall put to death a son of that builder.

232. If it destroy property, he shall restore whatever he destroyed, and because he did not make the house which he built firm and it collapsed, he shall rebuild the house which collapsed from his own property.

282. If a male slave say to his master, "Thou art not my master," his master shall prove him to be his slave and shall cut off his ear.

# M. Rostovtzeff: Political, Social, and Economic Organization of the Eastern Empires

Michael Rostovtzeff (1870–1952) climaxed his career as a noted historian, first in Russia and then in the United States, with his election as the president of the American Historical Association. Rostovtzeff believed in change by evolution and presented a strong case for change in antiquity through psychological phenomena, erosion of the vital energy of a group, and class conflict. In this reading, however, he deals with the power of the king over ancient society. From M. Rostovtzeff: *A History of the Ancient World,* I, pp. 144–145, 147–149. Reprinted by permission of the Clarendon Press, Oxford.

The ties which bind a kingdom and community into one whole are, first, religion and, secondly, the king's power, which is closely connected with religion. The king's power from the first takes an absolute form: it is unlimited, divine, and responsible to heaven alone; it demands blind obedience from the subjects and relies upon the army, the officials, and the priesthood. The first of these is the most obedient instrument in the king's hands. Originally, the army consists of a militia which includes the whole population. In cases where a kingdom was formed by conquest, the adult men of the predominant people form the nucleus of the army. In Egypt . . . and in Assyria, liability to military service was universal. . . . Further, a special standing force is created for the personal protection of the king—his bodyguard, which generally consists of the strongest and most active members of the ruling nation. . . .

The officials and the priesthood were less trustworthy as supporters of the king's power. . . . Whenever the centralized kingdom prospers, the officials and the priests are obedient instruments in the king's hands; they are his personal agents and entirely dependent upon him. But when the central power is weak, the officials and priests, who act for the king in civil and religious business, try to secure greater independence of action, relying on their wealth and personal influence with the population, and finally succeed in forcing the central authority to concede rights and privileges, which break down the unity of the kingdom, by making certain officials and priests independent rulers in the districts committed to their charge. But . . . even in feudal Eastern kingdoms the government of parts of the realm is founded on the principle of absolute obedience to their superior on the part of officials; so that each feudal ruler, within his own domains, is just as absolute a monarch as the king of a united kingdom, and requires complete subservience from his own officials and priests and from his subjects in general.

The general population played no political part at all. We hear nothing of popular risings or revolutions with the aim of securing a right to share in the government. The people did not even conceive the possibility of any political and social system, except that which had been formed by the passage of centuries. To them the power of the god and the king was not a subject for discussion but an article of belief. To the government, that is to the god and the king, belonged full and unlimited right to dispose of the person, labour, and property of the subject. It might require of him military service, just as it thought good. For tilling the land of the king and the god, for making canals and dikes, for constructing roads, for transporting men and goods required by the government, the subject was bound to give his time and labour without a murmur, and also the labour of the animals belonging to him. Finally, the subject was also bound to surrender to the government part of the produce of his labour: the court must be maintained, the worship of the gods must be performed, new temples or palaces or royal tombs must be built, military expenses must be defrayed. If the work was too heavy or food not forthcoming for the men summoned to forced labour, the only means of protest was a strike. But there was no germ whatever of political protest in these strikes.

Within the limits of this relation between government and people we observe certain differences, mainly formal and theoretical, in the different countries. In Egypt, but for some temporary and exceptional arrangements, the king considered himself the sole owner of the soil, recognizing in the subject no right except that of using it for a time; but in Babylonia the government recognized and upheld the right of private property in land. In spite, however, of this theoretical difference, the practice, as regards the possession of land, became identical in all the Eastern monarchies. . . . The king, the temples, and the higher classes were lords of the soil. It was tilled by serfs bound to the soil which they tilled and the place where they lived, and forced, not only to surrender part of the produce to the government and landowner, but also to labour at such public works as irrigation, roads, bridges, temples, and palaces; they had also to provide for transport. In industry we observe the same conditions. The workshops were owned by the king, the temples, and a group of wealthy merchants; the artisans were either serfs or slaves. Industry was closely connected with the large estates and came under the same management. Trade, large and small, was more independent of the king, the temples, and the large landowners; but the trader, unless he was agent of one of these powers, had to pay various taxes.

Agriculture was the basis of economic life. Industry and trade were concentrated round the temples and the palace. The ruling aristocracy, the royal bodyguard, the merchants and craftsmen lived in close proximity to the king and the god, and converted the settlement round the temple and palace into a city defended by walls. These city-states, ruled by the god and the king, were the earliest germs of political life over all the East. . . . Within the city, indeed, a certain unity grew up between men of the same profession and social standing, such as the royal bodyguard, the officials, the priests, the artisans, the merchants. These might form a sort of corporation, chiefly on a religious basis.

As separate cities developed into kingdoms, certain traditions and forms of self-government grew up simultaneously in the cities. The kings, representatives of the central principle, observed a cautious attitude toward such traditions. Even in great centralized empires like Egypt, and still more in Assyria and Persia, the kings were forced to reckon with these traditions and the set form which time had given to the life of these cities. The result is that in the great monarchies the cities are granted a certain measure of self-government, sometimes, as in Assyria, assured by charters, and referring especially to taxes and imports levied on the population. But this self-government does not go beyond certain definite limits. The mastery of the city remains with the king; as he chooses, he can extend or maintain existing rights; he can grant self-government to new cities or take it away from those which have enjoyed it. In the eye of the government, a city is the centre of a given territory and the residence of the ruling power; any rights that have grown up in the course of history are not binding on the king. And this is the fundamental difference which divides the Eastern empires from the Hellenistic monarchies and the Roman Empire. Within the East there was no tradition of self-government upheld by the city population. The king of Assyria or Persia was the heir, not of the sovereign power of the people inhabiting a certain city, but of his predecessors, who were god-kings like himself.

In the East government was identified with the king. He was the fountain and centre of power. The legislative, judicial, and executive powers were concentrated in his hands. He might bind himself by the laws he had himself made by the inspiration of the god; but he was free to change these laws and to interpret them as he liked. Part of his power he might transfer to others; but their power owned the king as its source, and his officials acted exclusively in his name. . . .

TOPIC 6

# THE HEBREWS

In the writings commonly known to the Christian world as the Old Testament, an invaluable record has been preserved of the history, leadership, and struggle for survival of the ancient Hebrews. Although they were only one of the many peoples caught between the pincers of the great powers in the river valleys, they managed to preserve their identity and make a significant contribution to the religious and moral foundations of Western civilization. The readings trace the Hebrew image of God, their confrontations with His presence, and their effort to lead a life shaped by His law.

Reading 17

## History of the Jews

From Crane Brinton, John B. Christopher, and Robert Lee Wolff, *A History of Civilization, Volume One: Prehistory to 1715,* 2nd ed., © 1960. Reprinted by permission of Prentice-Hall, Inc. Englewood Cliffs, New Jersey.

### I

The Jews have left us a remarkable account of their part in the ancient history of the Near East. This account is known to Christians as the Old Testament. For fundamentalists of both Christian and Jewish faiths today it is the word of God, an exact account of the creation of the earth and of the subsequent history of God's chosen people, the sons of Abraham. For the ancient Jews, of course, these writings were revelations of God's will; for those scholars today who take the naturalistic-historical approach the Old Testament is simply the Jewish national record, more complete and consecutive in a single work than any other record we possess from that region, but nevertheless a historical document and one to be criticized by the canons of historical science. . . . The latest such scholarship, greatly helped by modern archaeological research, has tended to . . . regard the Jewish holy writings as on the whole much more historically accurate than they appeared to be to scholars only a generation ago. . . . Thus it seems to scholars now that Abraham did live, that Terah his father did migrate from Ur of the Chaldees to northwestern Mesopotamia, that Abraham did migrate southward, that the Jews did live long in the hill country now Transjordan, and that they were also long established in the Delta region of Egypt, that they there sank into a state of servitude, that there was a historical Moses (the name is Egyptian), and that he did lead the Israelites out of bondage at least to the edge of Canaan, the Promised Land.

Nevertheless, what Christians call the Old Testament remains, from the point of view of the naturalistic historian, a great but varied body of writings. The account of the patriarchs, and of the age of Moses, remains an epic. To this epic material have been added some actual historical chronicles, a great deal of material on ritual and other priestly concerns, and material more purely literary—lyrical poems like the Song of Solomon, tales like that of Ruth, philosophical poems like the Book of Job, aphorisms and reflections on man's fate like the "wisdom" books. Finally, to all these was added the work of the prophets. These spiritual leaders sought to understand why the Jews were being overcome by the great powers round about them, and sought to spur their people to resistance, or to spiritual conquests. The Old Testament as we know it was thus put together—*edited,* in fact—by Jewish scholars who had known the dark days of the exile in Babylon, who had seen the beginnings of the uprooting of the Jews from their homeland, or, as it is tamely called, the Diaspora or "scattering abroad."

Seen in the light of history, the Jews were a Semitic tribe that may have originated in the Arabian desert, and that was closely related to such nomads as the Arabs of later history.

The oldest surviving fragments of the Old Testament were discovered in 1947 in caves near the Dead Sea. These date as far back as 200 B.C. Fragment from the Qumran manuscripts.

About the third quarter of the twentieth century B.C. they left the region of Ur for the western hill country and the Negeb. Some of them later settled in Egypt. Under Moses the Israelites emerged from Egypt some time shortly after 1300 B.C. They were still simple folk, semi-nomads, herdsmen, without the skills of townsmen, with no clear and important noble class, and already with a monotheistic god, Yahweh, our Jehovah. In the next few centuries they invaded the more urban and more sophisticated land of Canaan; were tempted by the Canaanite wealth and Canaanite polytheistic religion; in short, were ready to assume the full burden of their history as religious pioneers. An established Jewish kingdom reached its height of prestige in the tenth century under David and Solomon. Even at its height, however, this ancient kingdom was no more than a relatively minor state, which, under Solomon, enjoyed particularly good commercial and diplomatic relations with neighboring Egypt and Phoenicia.

This prosperity and unity did not last. In the tenth century the northern tribes seceded and formed the Kingdom of Israel (933–722 B.C.). The southern tribes, retaining the sacred city of Jerusalem, formed the Kingdom of Judah (933–586 B.C.). The two rival kingdoms struggled together and took part in the balance-of-power politics in the Near East, which as we have seen was dominated by the rivalry of great powers in Mesopotamia and in Egypt. Had the power-centers in these two great valleys remained substantially equal, the Jews, like the modern Swiss, might have continued

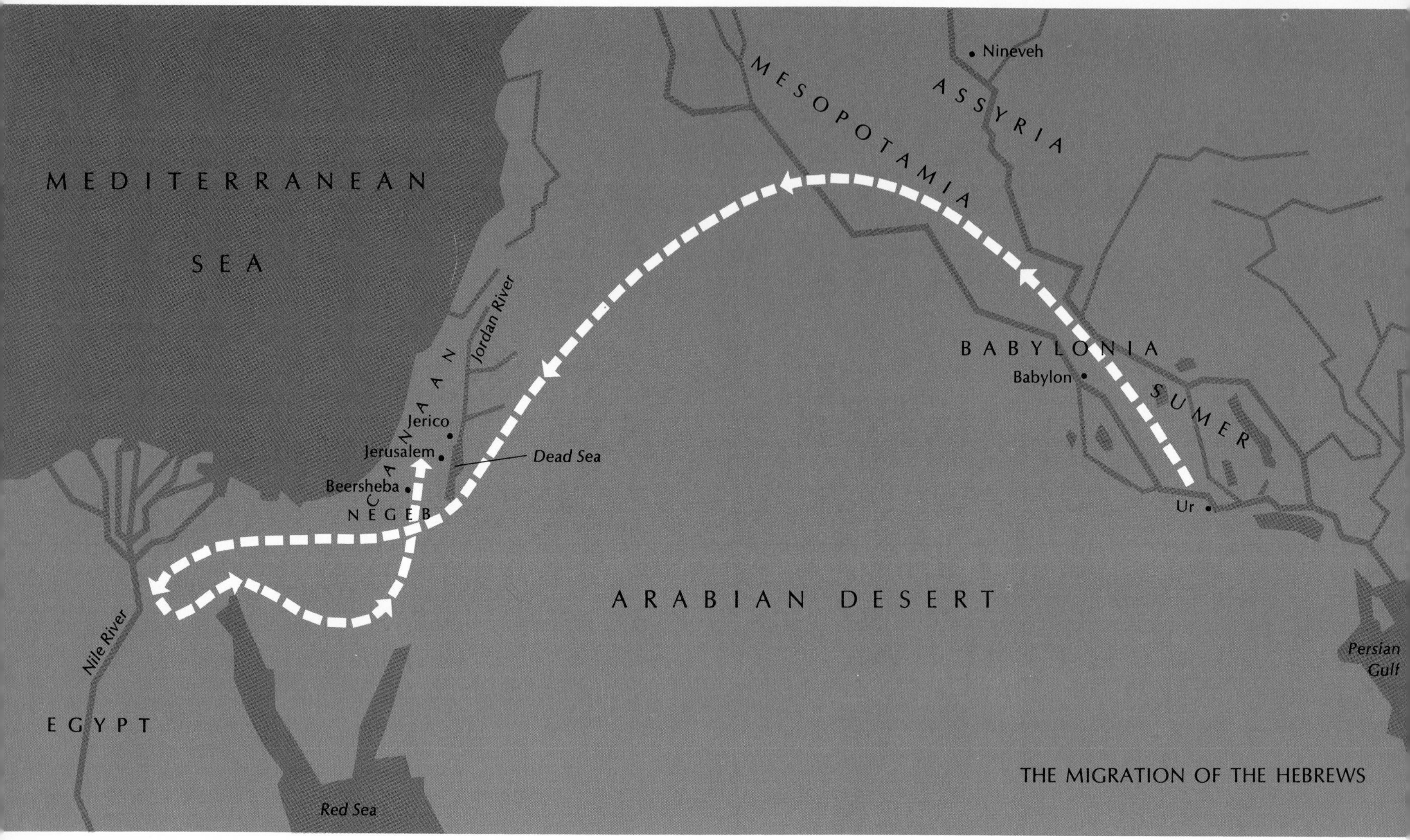


independent. As it was, Assyria, Babylonia, and Persia all rose to international supremacy, and as we should say, "annexed" Palestine, the land of the Jews. Israel fell in 722 to Assyria, and Judah fell to Nebuchadnezzar II of Babylonia in 586. Because the Jews had been particularly stiff-necked in their resistance in Jerusalem, Nebuchadnezzar determined to stamp out the Jewish nuisance once and for all. He destroyed city and temple, and deported ten thousand or more Jews—the intellectuals, the elite—to Babylon.

Under Persian rule, the Jews sifted back and restored Jerusalem after a fashion. Under Nehemiah in the fifth century the walls were rebuilt, and Jerusalem was started on a new period of material prosperity as part of the increasingly mature world of trade, war, and advanced culture that culminated in the One World of the Roman Empire. But the restored Jewish kingdom, though politically independent from 142 to 63 B.C., was for most of this period no more than a client or satellite state, a subordinate part of some great imperial system, Persian, Hellenistic, or Roman. The political greatness of Solomon was never restored.

### The Uniqueness of the Jews

Yet the Jews, unlike the hundreds of tribes of the Near East, persisted. Their survival is hardly to be explained in terms of any single factor. Certainly no simple geographical or other environmental factor will do at all, for these they shared with the forgotten tribes. Modern biological and historical knowledge makes it unlikely that the sons of Abraham enjoyed a hereditary racial toughness, or that they kept their race pure. The fact is that the Jews have been held together by their *beliefs,* by a faith, by a hard core within the individual Jew that has been toughened, not worn away, by persecution.

The Jews were the first people of our western civilization to attain a belief in one God: this belief was brought home to every Jew, and lodged firmly in his whole personality, by the full ritual and legal force of community education. The Jewish tribal God, Yahweh, the Jehovah of our biblical transliteration, was at first no more than another tribal god, the protector of his own, but still no more than one god in a Near East full of roving peoples, settled peoples, and gods of all sorts. Very early, however, the worship of Jehovah became an exclusive worship enjoined on the Jews. No Jew could even hedge a bit by an occasional sacrifice to some other god. The first commandment reads: Thou shalt have no other gods before me.

The second commandment forbids the children of Israel to make graven images or idols, "for I the Lord thy God am a jealous God." That is, not only was the developed Jewish faith monotheistic, it was also resolutely turned against naturalistic or anthropomorphic (manlike) notions of divinity. Jehovah was not only the sole God of the Jews; he was a being so awful, so majestic, so unlike us humans that he must not be conceived in any earthly form or symbol, let alone portrayed. This was a greater emancipation from things of this earth than Ikhnaton had attained; for his one god, Aton, though a pure and powerful being, was nonetheless a sungod who was plainly symbolized by a sun and rays, and was therefore nearer the material universe than the developed Jewish concept of Jehovah.

The Old Testament records at length the Law of the Jews, the religious practices that made and kept the Jew aware of his membership in the faith, of the burden and discipline put upon him by the choice of Jehovah. We know that the Jew may not eat pork, that the Jewish boy must be circumcised, and that the Jew must fast on certain holy days. How far this religious organization, as contrasted with religious ideas, or theology, is responsible for the way the Jews have held together is a question of the kind that human beings love to ask. But there is no effective religion without *both* theology and church organization, *both* spirit and letter, faith and works. The Jewish faith was built over the centuries into a kind of prescribed but freely accepted behavior that most Jews would rather die than abandon. This faith survived, and the Jews survived.

It was a faith that foreshadows much of the later religions of the West. Its God, though infinitely above men, was also close to them, bound to them by a covenant (agreement) which men could rely on; if men lived up to the covenant—that is, if they lived up to moral standards and to ideas of justice recognizably like our own—they would be justified, they would be good men; later, perhaps under some eastern influences, that justification came to be seen as a personal immortality in another and happier world; finally, some generations before the birth of Christ, this concept of the future state (an "eschatology") came to include a Messiah, a divinely appointed leader who should bring the Jewish people, as leaders of humanity, into the New Jerusalem, the perfect state on earth.

## II

### The Beginnings of a Universal Faith

One more element was added to Jewish faith at the very end of the period with which this chapter is concerned. The earlier books of the Old Testament, even after their editing by later Jewish scholars, do not make Jehovah a universal God, nor even a God who was clearly more powerful *throughout the universe* than the pagan gods were. Jehovah is the sole God for a Jew, but not by any means for an Egyptian; the Egyptian had better stick to Isis and Osiris and their family. It was hardly a nice family and the Jews, who had always some touch of what we call "puritanism," could not approve of its ways; but in these early days the Jews would not think of Isis and the rest as frauds. Yet by the time of the prophets, roughly in the years just before and after the fall of Jerusalem in 586, writers like the author of the second part of the Book of Isaiah saw Jehovah as the sole God, the beginning and the end of the universe, a God for the whole human race.

> Ye are my witnesses, saith the Lord, and my servant whom I have chosen: that yet may know and believe me, and understand that I am he; before me there was no God formed, neither shall there be after me. I, even I, am the Lord; and beside me there is no saviour. I have declared, and I have saved, and I have shewed, and there was no strange God

among you: therefore ye are my witnesses, . . . and I am God. . . .*

The life of the good religious Jew was not just a series of adjustments to the desires and habits of gods who were no more than irresponsible men with unlimited powers, like the gods of neighboring peoples. Especially for the sensitive and intelligent, life became a series of adjustments to the will of a being so much above mere men that he could not be known at all in human terms, in terms of buying and selling, persuading other people to do what we want, contriving better ways of spinning or cooking or raising food. God's plan was not the plan of common sense, nor even of what under the Greeks became the plan of natural science. No man could really *know* God's plan.

This indeed is the conclusion of the philosophic poem we call the Book of Job. In this poem, Job is a rich and happy man whom God afflicts with disasters of all sorts. Job does not really rebel or lose faith, but he does begin to wonder why God has thus afflicted him, an innocent man, a righteous man. But he learns to regret the pride that made him question, and the book closes (save for a prose epilogue in which Job recovers wealth and happiness) with the words:

Therefore have I uttered that which I understood not,
Things too wonderful for me, which I knew not.
Hear, I beseech thee, and I will speak.
I will demand of thee, and declare thou unto me.
I had heard of thee by the hearing of the ear;
But now mine eye seeth thee;
Wherefore I abhor myself, and repent
In dust and ashes. . . .**

*Isaiah 43:11.

**Job 42:3-6

# H. Frankfort: The Hebrew Concept of Yahweh

From H. and H. A. Frankfort, John A. Wilson, Thorkild Jacobsen, William A. Irwin, *The Intellectual Adventure of Ancient Man* (Chicago: University of Chicago Press, 1946). 

The differences between the Egyptian and Mesopotamian manners of viewing the world are very far-reaching. Yet the two peoples agreed in the fundamental assumptions that the individual is part of society, that society is embedded in nature, and that nature is but the manifestation of the divine. This doctrine was, in fact, universally accepted by the peoples of the ancient world with the single exception of the Hebrews.

The Hebrews arrived late upon the scene and settled in a country pervaded by influences from the two superior adjacent cultures. One would expect the newcomers to have assimilated alien modes of thought, since these were supported by such vast prestige. Untold immigrants from deserts and mountains had done so in the past; and many individual Hebrews did, in fact, conform to the ways of the Gentiles. But assimilation was not characteristic for Hebrew thought. On the contrary, it held out with a peculiar stubbornness and insolence against the wisdom of Israel's neighbours. It is possible to detect the reflection of Egyptian and Mesopotamian beliefs in many episodes of the Old Testament; but the overwhelming impression left by that document is one, not of derivation, but of originality.

The dominant tenet of Hebrew thought is the absolute transcendence of God. Yahweh is not in nature. Neither earth nor sun nor heaven is divine; even the most potent natural phenomena are but reflections of God's greatness. It is not even possible properly to name God:

> And Moses said unto God, Behold, when I come unto the children of Israel and shall say unto them, The God of your fathers hath sent me unto you; and they shall say to me: What is his name? what shall I say unto them?
>
> And God said unto Moses: I AM WHAT I AM [Hebrew: Yhwh]: and he said, Thus shalt thou say unto the children of Israel, I AM hath sent me unto you (Exod. iii, 13-14).

This God of the Hebrews is pure being, unqualified, ineffable. He is *holy*. That means that he is *sui generis*. It does not mean that he is taboo or that he is power. It means that all values are ultimately attributes of God alone. . . .

This conception of God represents so high a degree of abstraction that, in reaching it, the Hebrews seem to have left the realm of mythopoeic thought. The impression that they did so is strengthened when we observe that the Old Testament is remarkably poor in mythology of the type we have encountered in Egypt and Mesopotamia. But this impression requires correction. The processes of mythopoeic thought are decisive for many sections of the Old Testament. . . . Even the great conception of an only and transcendent God was not entirely free from myth, for it was not the fruit of detached speculation but of a passionate and dynamic experience. Hebrew thought did not entirely overcome mythopoeic thought. It created, in fact, a new myth—the myth of the Will of God.

Although the great 'Thou' which confronted the Hebrews transcended nature, it stood in a specific relationship to the people. For when they were freed from bondage and roamed in 'a desert land . . . the waste howling wilderness . . . the Lord alone did lead (them) and there was no strange God with (them)' (Deut. xxxii, 10-12). And God had said:

> But thou, Israel, art my servant, Jacob whom I have chosen, the seed of Abraham my friend. Thou whom I have taken from the ends of the earth, and called thee from the chief men thereof, and said unto Thee, Thou art my servant; I have chosen thee, and not cast thee away (Isa. xli, 8–9).

Thus God's will was felt to be focused on one particular and concrete group of human beings; it was asserted to have manifested itself at one decisive moment in their history and ceaselessly and relentlessly to have urged, rewarded, or chastised the people of its choice. For in Sinai, God had said, 'Ye shall be unto me a kingdom of priests and an holy nation' (Exod. xix, 6).

It is a poignant myth, this Hebrew myth of a chosen people, of a divine promise made, of a terrifying moral burden imposed—a prelude to the later myth of the Kingdom of God, that more remote and more spiritual 'promised land'. For in the myth of the chosen people the ineffable majesty of God and the worthlessness of man are correlated in a dramatic situation that is to unfold in time and is moving toward a future where the distant yet related parallels of human and divine existence are to meet in infinity.

Not cosmic phenomena, but history itself, had here become pregnant with meaning; history had become a revelation of the dynamic will of God. The human being was not merely the servant of the god as he was in Mesopotamia; nor was he placed, as in Egypt, at a pre-ordained station in a static universe which did not need to be—and, in fact, could not be—questioned. Man, according to Hebrew thought, was the interpreter and the servant of God; he was even honoured with the task of bringing about the realization of God's will. Thus man was condemned to unending efforts which were doomed to fail because of his inadequacy. In the Old Testament we find man possessed of a new freedom and of a new burden of responsibility.

# God Creates Earth and Heaven

The five readings that follow are drawn from the Bible. Like the clay tablets of the Sumerians or the inscriptions of the Persians, a collection of religious precepts provides invaluable information for the historian. This is particularly true of the rich documentation of Hebrew history found in the Old Testament. From *The Jerusalem Bible*. Copyright © 1966 by Darton, Longman and Todd, Ltd. and Doubleday & Company, Inc. Reprinted by permission of the publishers.

### GENESIS 1:1-1:27

In the beginning God created the heavens and the earth. Now the earth was a formless void, there was darkness over the deep, and God's spirit hovered over the water.

God said, 'Let there be light', and there was light. God saw that light was good, and God divided light from darkness. God called light 'day', and darkness he called 'night'. Evening came and morning came: the first day.

God said, 'Let there be a vault in the waters to divide the waters in two. And so it was. God made the vault, and it divided the waters above the vault from the waters under the vault. God called the vault 'heaven'. Evening came and morning came: the second day.

God said, 'Let the waters under heaven come together into a single mass, and let dry land appear.' And so it was. God called the dry land 'earth' and the mass of waters 'seas', and God saw that it was good.

God said, 'Let the earth produce vegetation: seed-bearing plants, and fruit trees bearing fruit with their seed inside, on the earth'. And so it was. The earth produced vegetation: plants bearing seed in their several kinds, and trees bearing fruit with their seed inside . . . God saw that it was good. Evening came and morning came: the third day.

God said, 'Let there be lights in the vault of heaven to divide day from night, and let them indicate festivals, days and years. Let them be lights in the vault of heaven to shine on the earth'. And so it was. God made the two great lights: the greater light to govern the day, the smaller light to govern the night, and the stars. God set them in the vault of heaven to shine on the earth, to govern the day and the night and to divide light from darkness. God saw that it was good. Evening came and morning came: the fourth day.

God said, 'Let the waters teem with living creatures, and let birds fly above the earth within the vault of heaven'. And so it was.

In a famed Renaissance painting by Michelangelo Buonarroti (1475–1564), God gives life to man, fashioned in God's own image. Detail of the Sistine Chapel ceiling.

God created great sea-serpents and every kind of living creature with which the waters teem, and every kind of winged creature. God saw that it was good. God blessed them, saying, 'Be fruitful, multiply, and fill the waters of the seas; and let the birds multiply upon the earth'. Evening came and morning came: the fifth day.

God said, 'Let the earth produce every kind of living creature: cattle, reptiles, and every kind of wild beast'. And so it was. God made every kind of wild beast, every kind of cattle, and every kind of land reptile. God saw that it was good.

God said, 'Let us make man in our own image, in the likeness of ourselves, and let them be masters of the fish of the sea, the birds of heaven, the cattle, all the wild beasts and all the reptiles that crawl upon the earth!'

God created man in the image of himself,
in the image of God he created him,
male and female he created them.

# Yahweh Sends a Flood To Rid the Earth of Wickedness

From Genesis 6:5–8, 12–14; 7:1–5, 17–24. Excerpts from *The Jerusalem Bible*. Copyright © 1966 by Darton, Longman and Todd, Ltd. and Doubleday & Company, Inc. Reprinted by permission of the publishers.

Yahweh saw that the wickedness of man was great on the earth, and that the thoughts in his heart fashioned nothing but wickedness all day long. Yahweh regretted having made man on the earth, and his heart grieved. 'I will rid the earth's face of man, my own creation,' Yahweh said 'and of animals also, reptiles too, and the birds of heaven; for I regret having made them.' But Noah had found favour with Yahweh. . . .

God said to Noah, 'The end has come for all things of flesh; I have decided this, because the earth is full of violence of man's making, and I will efface them from the earth. Make yourself an ark out of resinous wood. Make it with reeds and line it with pitch inside and out.' . . .

Yahweh said to Noah, 'Go aboard the ark, you and all your household, for you alone among this generation do I see as good man in my judgement. Of all the clean animals you must take seven of each kind, both male and female; of the unclean animals you must take two, a male and its female (and of the birds of heaven also, seven of each kind, both male and female), to propagate their kind over the whole earth. For in seven days' time I mean to make it rain on the earth for forty days and nights, and I will rid the earth of every living thing that I made.' Noah did all that Yahweh ordered. . . .

The flood lasted forty days on the earth. The waters swelled, lifting the ark until it was raised above the earth. The waters rose and swelled greatly on the earth, and the ark sailed on the waters. The waters rose more and more on the earth so that all the highest mountains under the whole of heaven were submerged. The waters rose fifteen cubits higher, submerging the mountains. And so all things of flesh perished that moved on the earth, birds, cattle, wild beasts, everything that swarms on the earth, and every man. Everything with the breath of life in its nostrils died, everything on dry land. Yahweh destroyed every living thing on the face of the earth, man and animals, reptiles, and the birds of heaven. He rid the earth of them, so that only Noah was left, and those with him in the ark. The waters rose on the earth for a hundred and fifty days.

Noah's Ark. Stone carving from the Cathedral of Autun, early twelfth century.

# Obligations of a Chosen People

From Genesis 12:1-8; 17:1-11; Exodus 19:1-25; 20:1-24. Excerpts from *The Jerusalem Bible.* 

## I. GOD GIVES A LAND TO ABRAHAM

Yahweh said to Abram, 'Leave your country, your family and your father's house, for the land I will show you. I will make you a great nation; I will bless you and make your name so famous that it will be used as a blessing.

I will bless those who bless you:
I will curse those who slight you.
All the tribes of the earth
shall bless themselves by you.

So Abram went as Yahweh told him, and Lot went with him. Abram was seventy-five years old when he left Haran. Abram took his wife Sarai, his nephew Lot, all the possessions they had amassed and the people they had acquired in Haran. They set off for the land of Canaan, and arrived there.

Abram passed through the land as far as Shechem's holy place, the Oak of Moreh. At that time the Canaanites were in the land. Yahweh appeared to Abram and said, 'It is to your descendants that I will give this land.' So Abram built there an altar for Yahweh who had appeared to him. From there he moved on to the mountainous district east of Bethel, where he pitched his tent, with Bethel to the west and Ai to the east. There he built an altar to Yahweh and invoked the name of Yahweh.

## II. GOD MAKES A COVENANT WITH ABRAHAM

When Abram was ninety-nine years old Yahweh appeared to him and said, 'I am El Shaddai. Bear yourself blameless in my presence, and I will make a Covenant between myself and you, and increase your numbers greatly.'

Abram bowed to the ground and God said this to him, 'Here now is my Covenant with you: you shall become the father of a multitude of nations. You shall no longer be called Abram; your name shall be Abraham, for I make you father of a multitude of nations, and your issue shall be kings. I will establish my Covenant between myself and you, and your descendants after you, generation after generation, a Covenant in perpetuity, to be your God and the God of your descendants after you. I will give to you and to your descendants after you the land you are living in, the whole land of Canaan, to own in perpetuity, and I will be your God.'

God said to Abraham, 'You on your part shall maintain my Covenant, yourself and your descendants after you, generation after generation.' . . .

## III. THE TEN COMMANDMENTS

Three months after they came out of the land of Egypt . . . on that day the sons of Israel came to the wilderness of Sinai. From Rephidim they set out again; and when they reached the wilderness of Sinai, there in the wilderness they pitched their camp; there facing the mountain Israel pitched camp.

Moses then went up to God, and Yahweh called to him from the mountain, saying, 'Say this to the House of Jacob, declare this to the sons of Israel, "You yourselves have seen what I did with the Egyptians, how I carried you on eagle's wings and brought you to myself. From this you know that now, if you obey my voice and hold fast to my covenant, you of all the nations shall be my very own for all the earth is mine. I will count you a kingdom of priests, a consecrated nation." Those are the words you are to speak to the sons of Israel.' So Moses went and summoned the elders of the people, putting before them all that Yahweh had bidden him. Then all the people answered as one, 'All that Yahweh has said, we will do.' And Moses took the people's reply back to Yahweh.

Yahweh said to Moses, 'I am coming to you in a dense cloud so that the people may hear when I speak to you and may trust you always'. And Moses took the people's reply back to Yahweh.

Yahweh said to Moses, 'Go to the people and tell them to prepare themselves today and tomorrow. Let them wash their clothing and hold themselves in readiness for the third day, because on the third day Yahweh will descend on the mountain of Sinai in the sight of all the people. You will mark out the limits of the mountain and say, "Take care not to go up the mountain or to touch the foot of it. Whoever touches the mountain will be put to death. No one must lay a hand on him: he must be stoned or shot down by arrow, whether man or beast; he must not remain alive." When the ram's horn sounds a long blast, they are to go up the mountain.'

So Moses came down from the mountain to the people and bade them prepare themselves; and they washed their clothing. Then he said to the people, 'Be ready for the third day; do not go near any woman.'

Now at daybreak on the third day there were peals of thunder on the mountain and lightning flashes, a dense cloud, and a loud trumpet blast, and inside the camp all the people trembled. Then Moses led the people out of the camp to meet God; and they stood at the bottom of the mountain. The mountain of Sinai was entirely wrapped in smoke, because Yahweh had descended on it in the form of fire. Like smoke from a furnace the smoke went up, and the whole mountain shook violently. Louder and louder grew the sound of the trumpet. Moses spoke, and God answered him with peals of thunder. Yahweh came down on the mountain of Sinai, on the mountain top, and Yahweh called Moses to the top of the mountain; and Moses went up. Yahweh said to Moses, 'Go down and warn the people not to pass beyond their bounds to come and look on Yahweh, or many of them will lose their lives. The priests, the men who do approach Yahweh, even these must purify themselves, or Yahweh will break out against them.' Moses answered Yahweh, 'The people cannot come up the mountain of Sinai because you warned us yourself when you said, "Mark out the limits of the mountain and declare it sacred." ' 'Go down,' said Yahweh to him 'and come up again bringing Aaron with you. But do not allow the priests or the people to pass beyond their bounds to come up to Yahweh, or he will break out against them.' So Moses went down to the people and spoke to them. . . .

Then God spoke all these words. He said, 'I am Yahweh your God who brought you out of the land of Egypt, out of the house of slavery.

'You shall have no gods except me.

'You shall not make yourself a carved image or any likeness of anything in heaven or on earth beneath or in the waters under the earth; you shall not bow down to them or serve them. For I, Yahweh your God, am a jealous God and I punish the father's fault in the sons, the grandsons, and the great-grandsons of those who hate me; but I show kindness to thousands of those who love me and keep my commandments.

'You shall not utter the name of Yahweh your God to misuse it, for Yahweh will not leave unpunished the man who utters his name to misuse it.

'Remember the sabbath day and keep it holy. For six days you shall labour and do all your work, but the seventh day is a sabbath for Yahweh your God. You shall do no work that day, neither you nor your son nor your daughter nor your servants, men or women, nor your animals nor the stranger who lives with you. For in six days Yahweh made the heavens and the earth and the sea and all that these hold, but on the seventh day he rested; that is why Yahweh has blessed the sabbath day and made it sacred.

'Honour your father and your mother so that you may have a long life in the land that Yahweh your God has given to you.

'You shall not kill.

'You shall not commit adultery.

'You shall not steal.

'You shall not bear false witness against your neighbour.

'You shall not covet your neighbour's house. You shall not covet your neighbour's wife, or his servant, man or woman, or his ox, or his donkey, or anything that is his.'

All the people shook with fear at the peals of thunder and the lightning flashes, the sound of the trumpet, and the smoking mountain; and they kept their distance. 'Speak to us yourself' they said to Moses 'and we will listen; but do not let God speak to us, or we shall die.' Moses answered the people, 'Do not be afraid; God has come to test you, so that your fear of him, being always in your mind, may keep you from sinning.' So the people kept their distance while Moses approached the dark cloud where God was.

Yahweh said to Moses, 'Tell the sons of Israel this, "You have seen for yourselves that I have spoken to you from heaven. You shall not make gods of silver or gods of gold to stand beside me; you shall not make things like this for yourselves.

"You are to make me an altar of earth, and sacrifice on this . . . from your flocks or herds. In every place in which I have my name remembered I shall come to you and bless you." . . .

# A King Replaces the Judge of Israel

From I Samuel 8:1–22; 9:1–2; 14–17; 10:1; 11:1–15. Excerpts from *The Jerusalem Bible*. 

When Samuel grew old, he appointed his two sons as judges over Israel. . . . But his sons did not follow his ways; they wanted money, taking bribes and perverting justice. Then all the elders of Israel gathered together and came to Samuel at Ramah. 'Look,' they said to him 'you are old, and your sons do not follow your ways. So give us a king to rule over us, like the other nations.' It displeased Samuel that they should say, 'Let us have a king to rule us,' so he prayed to Yahweh. But Yahweh said to Samuel, 'Obey the voice of the people in all that they say to you, for it is not you they have rejected; they have rejected me from ruling over them. All they have done to me from the day I brought them out of Egypt until now—they deserted me and served other gods—they are doing now to you. Well then, obey their voice; only, you must warn them solemnly and instruct them in the rights of the king who is to reign over them.'

All that Yahweh had said Samuel repeated to the people who were asking him for a king. He said, 'These will be the rights of the king who is to reign over you. He will take your sons and assign them to his chariotry and cavalry, and they will run in front of his chariot. He will use them as leaders of a thousand and leaders of fifty; he will make them plough his ploughland and harvest his harvest and make his weapons of war and the gear for his chariots. He will also take your daughters as perfumers, cooks and bakers. He will take the best of your fields, of your vineyards and olive groves and give them to his officials. He will take the best of your manservants and maidservants, of your cattle and your donkeys, and make them work for him. He will tithe your flocks, and you yourselves will become his slaves. When that day comes, you will cry out on account of the king you have chosen for yourselves, but on that day God will not answer you.'

The people refused to listen to the words of Samuel. They said, 'No! We want a king, so that we in our turn can be like the other nations; our king shall rule us and be our leader and fight our battles.' Samuel listened to all that the people had to say and repeated it in the ears of Yahweh. Yahweh then said to Samuel, 'Obey their voice and give them a king.' Samuel then said to the men of Israel, 'Go back, each to your own town.'

Among the men of Benjamin there was a man named Kish son of Abiel, son of Zeror, son of Becorath, son of Aphiah; a Benjaminite and a man of rank. He had a son named Saul, a handsome man in the prime of life. Of all the Israelites there was no one more handsome than he; he stood head and shoulders taller than the rest of the people. . . .

So they [Saul and a servant] went up to the town, and as they were going through the gate Samuel came out in their direction on his way to the high place. Now Yahweh had given Samuel a revelation the day before Saul came, saying, 'About this time tomorrow I will send to you a man from the land of Benjamin; you are to anoint him as prince over my people Israel, and he will save my people from the power of the Philistines; for I have seen the distress of my people and their crying has come to me.' When Samuel saw Saul, Yahweh told him, 'That is the man of whom I told you; he shall rule my people'. . . .

Samuel took a phial of oil and poured it on Saul's head; then he kissed him, saying, 'Has not Yahweh anointed you prince over his people Israel? You are the man who must rule Yahweh's people, and who must save them from the power of the enemies surrounding them.' . . .

About a month later, Nahash of the Ammonite marched up and laid siege to Jabesh-gilead. All the men of Jabesh said to Nahash, 'Make a treaty with us and we will be your subjects.' But Nahash the Ammonite said to them, 'I will make a treaty with you on this condition, that I put out all your right eyes; I shall inflict this disgrace on the whole of Israel.' The elders of Jabesh said to him, 'Give us seven days' grace while we send messengers throughout the territory of Israel, and if no one comes to our help, we will go over to you.' The messengers came to Gibeah of Saul, and reported this to the people, and all the people began to lament and weep.

Now Saul was just then coming in from the fields behind his oxen, and he said, 'What is wrong? Why are the people weeping?' They explained to him what the men of Jabesh had said. And the spirit of Yahweh seized on Saul when he heard these words, and his fury was stirred to fierce flame. He took a yoke of oxen and cut them in pieces which he sent by messengers throughout the territory of Israel with these words: 'If anyone will not march with Saul, this shall be done with his oxen!' At this, a dread of Yahweh fell on the people and they marched out as one man. He inspected them at Bezek; there were three hundred thousand Israelites and thirty thousand of Judah. He then said to the messengers who had come, 'This is what you must say to the men of Jabesh-gilead, "Tomorrow by the time the sun is hot help will reach you." The messengers went and reported this to the men of Jabesh who were overjoyed; they said to Nahash, 'Tomorrow we will go over to you and you can do what you like to us.'

The next day, Saul disposed the army in three companies; they burst into the middle of the camp in the last watch of the night and struck down the Ammonites until high noon. The survivors were so scattered that not two of them were left together.

The people then said to Samuel, 'Who said, "Is Saul to reign over us?" Hand the men over for us to put them to death.' 'No one is to be put to death today' Saul replied 'for today Yahweh has brought victory to Israel.' Then Samuel said to the people, 'Come, let us go to Gilgal and reaffirm the monarchy there.'

So all the people went to Gilgal and there they proclaimed Saul king before Yahweh at Gilgal. They offered . . . sacrifices there before Yahweh; and Saul and all the men of Israel rejoiced greatly.

## Psalm in Praise of the Divine Law

From Psalms 119:1–8, 129–136, 145–160. Excerpts from *The Jerusalem Bible*. Copyright © 1966, by Darton, Longman and Todd, Ltd. and Doubleday & Company, Inc. Reprinted by permission of the publishers.

Ah, how happy those of blameless life
  who walk in the Law of Yahweh!
How happy those who respect his decrees,
  and seek him with their whole heart,
and, doing no evil,
  walk in his ways!
You yourself have made your precepts known,
  to be faithfully kept.
Oh, may my behaviour be constant
  in keeping your statutes.
If I concentrate on your every commandment,
  I can never be put to shame.
I thank you from an upright heart,
  schooled in your rules of righteousness.
I mean to observe your statutes;
  never abandon me. . . .

Your decrees are so wonderful
  my soul cannot but respect them.
As your word unfolds, it gives light,
  and the simple understand.
I open my mouth, panting
  eagerly for your commandments.
Turn to me please, pity me,
  as you should those who love your name.
Direct my steps as you have promised,
  let evil win no power over me.
Rescue me from human oppression;
  I will observe your precepts.
Treat your servant kindly,
  teach me your statutes.
My eyes stream with tears,
  because others disregard your Law. . . .

Sincere, my call—Yahweh, answer me!
  I will respect your statutes.
I invoke you, save me,
  I will observe your decrees.
I am up before dawn to call for help,
  I put my hope in your word.
I lie awake throughout the night,
  to meditate on your promise.
In your love, Yahweh, listen to my voice,
  let your rulings give me life.
My cruel persecutors are closing in,
  how remote they are from your Law!
But, Yahweh, you are closer still
  and all your commandments are true.
Long have I known that your decrees
  were founded to last for ever.

Take note of my suffering and rescue me,
  for I do not forget your Law.
Take up my cause, defend me,
  give me life as you have promised.
You will never save the wicked,
  if they do not study your statutes,
but many are your mercies to me, Yahweh,
  by your rulings give me life.
Many hound me and oppress me,
  but I do not swerve from your decrees.
The sight of these renegades disgusts me,
  they do not observe your promise;
but, Yahweh, see how I love your precepts,
  and lovingly give me life.
Faithfulness is the essence of your word,
  your righteous rulings hold good for ever.

# Chapter 2

## The Greeks and Romans: Ancient Civilization Moves Westward

The movement to settled agriculture and to the birth of cities represents a great triumph for man, whose history the preceding chapter traced from early beginnings in Africa to the flourishing river valley civilizations of the Near East. Chapter Two is concerned with the transmission of this civilization westward and its fusion, in the millennium before the birth of Christ, with another strain of civilization developing in the Mediterranean.

The achievements of the Greeks and Romans, the inspiration behind their struggle to found and maintain a civilization, and the way in which they defined man, nature, and the unknown, are vital for the development of Western civilization. The Greeks were the first "Westerners" in their attempt to pierce the mystery of religion, probe the secrets of nature, and establish a political community based on participation. The decline of their city-states was balanced by the dispersion of their culture and its mergence with the older civilization of the Near East. Under Alexander the Great the Greeks conquered the mighty Persian empire and carried Greek practices into Asia and Africa.

A century later the Romans, a vigorous Western Mediterranean people, began a series of conquests that eventually made them masters of the entire Mediterranean world, and the heirs of the Western and Eastern societies that had preceded them. The Roman Empire, created by practical men, builders, planners, and soldiers, was thus a blending of Roman, Greek, and Eastern cultures and exhibited both the zeal and the tensions of a conquering system. The Roman struggle to maintain the legal and moral basis of their civilization, given the burdens and behavior required by imperial rule, the dependence upon slavery, and the unique challenge posed by Christianity, has made their history particularly instructive for the twentieth century.

TOPIC 7

# THE GREEKS EXAMINE THE GODS

Political history is but one way of understanding a culture. Instead of beginning the study of Graeco-Roman civilization by describing its geographic and political setting, the readings that follow spotlight the Greeks as a people wrestling with the problem of man's relation to the supernatural. In so doing they provide an opportunity for the reader to compare the Greek approach to that of earlier societies. Topic 11 will introduce the political history of Greece.



## Crane Brinton: The Greek Experiment in Civilization

The late Crane Brinton retired in 1968 after forty-five years of teaching history at Harvard University. Professor Brinton's interests range over the gamut of Western civilization, most particularly in intellectual history and the how and why of revolutions. In *Ideas and Men* he was concerned about the nature of the big questions that Western man has asked about the universe and his place in it. Brinton's conclusion that the Greeks played a unique role in the development of such questioning makes the following selections from the book a logical starting point for a study of their place in Western civilization. From Crane Brinton, *Ideas and Men: The Story of Western Thought,* ©1950. Reprinted by permission of Prentice-Hall, Inc., Englewood Cliffs, N.J.

There have survived writings in classic, or ancient, Greek, dating very roughly from 750 B.C. to 1000 A.D., which cover almost the whole range of thinking men have done in the fields of [non-scientific] knowledge. Greek philosophers, Greek observers of nature, Greek historians, Greek men of letters have expressed in some form or other almost all the kinds of intellectual and emotional experience Western men have recognized and named. This may seem an extreme statement, and is not of course a denial of the force, weight, beauty, wisdom, and in many senses, originality of medieval or modern achievement in these fields.

You can test this assertion in almost any field. In literature, the Greeks tried all of what we call the genres, including, toward the end, something very close to the novel. Especially in epic, lyric, and dramatic poetry and in history they set standards never yet surpassed—some would say, never yet equaled. In philosophy, their schools put all the Big Questions—being and becoming, the one and the many, mind and body, spirit and matter—and gave all the big answers. Among the Greek philosophers were idealists, materialists, rationalists, monists, pluralists, skeptics, cynics, relativists, absolutists. Their painting has not survived physically; the decline in most phases of civilization that followed the breakup of the Graeco-Roman world was so great that men could not, at any rate did not, take care of these paintings. There is some doubt whether Greek painting was as great an art as Greek sculpture and Greek architecture; there is no doubt of the greatness of these latter, which have managed to survive, though often in imperfect condition, from the very solidity of their materials. Finally, in science or cumulative knowledge the Greeks, building in part on earlier achievements in Egypt and Mesopotamia, carried to high development the theo-

Sturdy Ionic columns support the temple of Athene Nike on the Acropolis overlooking Athens.

retical side of mathematics and astronomy and did creditably in physics and in medicine; the Romans, building in part on Greek achievements, attained high standards in engineering. In political and economic life, this culture attained great complexity. These people, in short, were fully "civilized."

Indeed, so great was the prestige acquired by this classical civilization that it was not until nearly 1700 A.D., in France and in England, that writers and thinkers came to wonder whether they, the moderns, couldn't come somewhere near the old Greeks and Romans as writers, artists, scientists—in short, as civilized human beings. The prestige of the "classical" in this sense has now, however, almost disappeared in mid-twentieth-century America. In formal education, the classicists have lost even the rear-guard actions. Greek is no longer taught in secondary schools, and Latin survives as hardly more than a genteel formality.

Although many educated Americans are wholly ignorant of an achievement that once meant so much to all educated men, the Greek achievement remains an essential part of the capital stock of our culture. . . . If from Greek sources the psychologists have named their Oedipus complex, their narcissism, their phobias and their manias, it is because the so-called mythology of the Greeks is in fact an amazingly rich treasury of realistic, and in the unromantic sense of the word, imaginative, observations on human behavior, on human aspirations, on that never-to-be-exhausted commonplace, human nature. . . . We cannot know ourselves well if we know the Greeks not at all. Moreover, the Graeco-Roman experiment in civilization was in some senses completed; it exhibits, as philosophers of history all remind us, something like a full cycle, from youth to age and death, from spring to winter; it has a beginning and an ending.

Finally, in this civilization was matured the Christian religion. Christianity clearly has Jewish origins largely outside Greek influences. But in its growth and organization it was an integral part of the Graeco-Roman world in the last few centuries of that civilization's active life. We cannot understand Christianity today unless we understand Christianity then.

The origins of the Greeks are unrecorded in history, but are clearly reflected in Greek legend and mythology and in archaeological remains. It is clear that the Greek-speaking peoples were outsiders, Northerners from the Danube basin or even further north, and related by language at least to the Germans, the Celts, and the Slavs. In various waves, of which the latest, the Doric, finished its wanderings almost in historic time, at the beginning of the first millennium before Christ, these Greeks—or Hellenes, as they called themselves—came down on an earlier native culture we now call Minoan. [See map.] Almost certainly Hellenes and Minoans mixed their genes and their cultures, with the Hellenes the dominant group, and with the usual falling off of cultural standards that accompanies the conquest of more civilized by less civilized peoples. For the Minoans had a high civilization, as we can tell from their architectural and sculptural remains. From this dark age the Greeks emerged clearly by the eighth century B.C., already traders as well as fighters, already artists, perhaps even thinkers, and already organized in the most famous of Greek institutions, the *polis,* or self-governing, sovereign city-state. In the *polis* was bred the classical culture of Greece. Athens and its surrounding territory, Attica, had in the fifth century B.C., the century of its greatness, a population of at most 200,000—the size of a modest American city today.

The thousand years of the classical civilization of the Mediterranean offer something we cannot afford to turn down—a chance to see a kind of trial run of ideas that are still part of our daily living. Perhaps we behave as we do more because of what a great many generations of our ancestors did as prehistoric men than because of what the relatively few generations of our ancestors did as members of this classical Mediterranean culture; human bodies, from liver to brain, were twenty-five hundred years ago substantially what they are today. Many of our habits of mind, our sentiments, our psychological needs, were no doubt formed long before the Greeks were

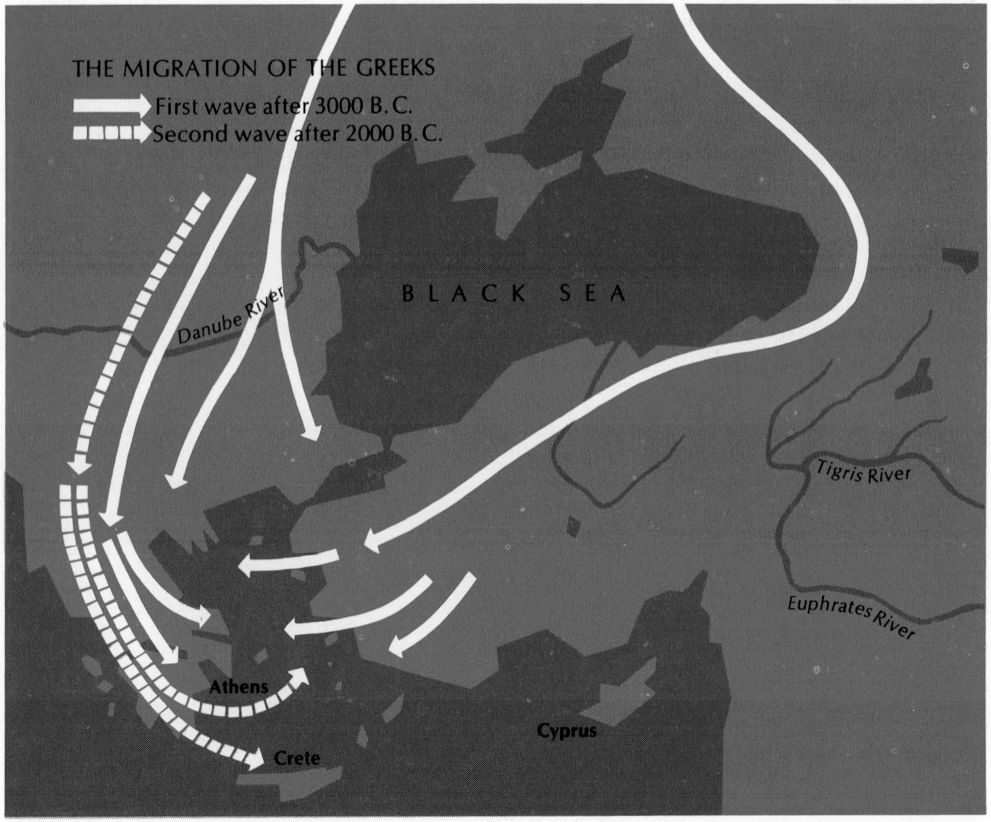

ever heard of, but history can tell us little of these, intellectual history least of all. Indeed, Western intellectual history in a great measure begins with the Greeks, for they were the first to use the mind in a striking and novel way. The Greeks have left the first permanent and extensive record in our Western society of the kind of thinking we all do a great deal of (sometimes rather against the grain) in our lives. There is no good, unambiguous word for this kind of thinking; let us simply call it *objective reasoning.*

Now the Greeks were by no means the first people to think, nor even the first to think scientifically: Egyptian surveyors and Chaldean [Mesopotamean] stargazers used mathematics, and therefore thought scientifically. But the Greeks first reasoned about the whole range of human experience. The Greeks even reasoned about how they should behave. Perhaps every human being tries to do what the Greeks did by reasoning—that is, adjust himself to the strange, bewildering, sometimes hostile universe that is clearly not himself, that seems to run on most of the time with no regard for him, that seems to have will, strength, purpose often at odds with his. Probably Australian Bushmen, Iroquois, Kalmucks, and all other peoples reason about these matters, and if we really knew how their minds worked we could understand them. But the point is, some of the Greeks, as early as the great age, did it *our way.* Their minds worked the way ours work.

Their own primitive ancestors had not done it quite our way. They had heard thunder, and seen lightning, and been frightened. The thunder and lightning were clearly not human, they realized, but they must be alive—everything, for some primitive men, is alive. So they ultimately came to believe that a powerful being, whom they called the god Zeus, was hurling his monster bolts through the sky and causing all the row. Sometimes, they thought, he was hurling them at other gods, sometimes just displaying his anger, sometimes, of course, hurling them at mortal men, whom he thus struck dead. A good Greek believed, or hoped, that if he showed proper respect for Zeus, the god would not throw thunderbolts at him. For right into the great days of Athenian culture, the man in the street believed in Zeus and his thunderbolts.

Note that the early Greek "explained" the thunderstorm. He explained almost everything by the actions of gods, or spirits, or nymphs, or giants, or the kind of supermen he called heroes. But some Greeks—we do not know just where and when—come to the conclusion that a good deal went on in the universe without any god's doing anything about it. They became convinced, for instance, that the weather made itself. They did not know much about electricity, certainly not enough to connect the simple instances of magnetism they had observed with anything as potent as thunder and lightning. But they did believe, as we might put it, that a thunderstorm was a natural phenomenon, subject to a reasonable and scientific explanation.

The conflict between the older, supernatural explanation and the newer, natural explanation is recorded in a play of Aristophanes, *The Clouds,* first performed in 423 B.C. In spite of the burlesque and deliberate nonsense in which the playwright puts the scientific case, you can gather that some Athenians held the respectable meteorological theory that winds go from high-pressure areas to low-pressure areas. Aristophanes was—or to cater to the popular audience perhaps pretended to be—shocked at these newfangled ideas, and leaves the impression that the old Zeus theory was sounder. But in spite of the absurdities he puts in the mouth of the philosopher Socrates, for him the type of the new thinker, you can see the Greek mind at work, trying to understand the weather. . . .

# The Myths of Greece

*The Myths of Greece, Life* Magazine, January, 18, 1963, © 1963 Time Inc.

The myths of Greece weave around the modern imagination like a golden garland. At one time or other everyone has dreamily surrendered to the classical world of windswept plain and wine-dark sea, where Jason's *Argo* threaded the white foam in quest of the Golden Fleece, where Hercules labored and wily Odysseus outwitted the Cyclops, where the laughter-loving gods feasted on snow-capped Olympus, and Troy at their feet glittered with the clash of shining arms and the deeds of heroes. . . .

Myths to the Greeks were the living tissue that fleshed out the bare bones of their official religion, the cult of the Olympian gods. Whole anthologies in marble encrusted their temples and adorned their homes on painted vases. Altars and statues of their heroes stood in every public place. Their sanctuaries dotted the countryside. Many a hilltop, valley, grove and spring had its resident divinity, from Delphi, where Apollo spoke through lips of his oracle, to Delos, where ancient stone lions still guard the approach to Apollo's birthplace.

Such landmarks were big tourist attractions in ancient Greece. The places where Orestes

Two fifth-century Athenian vases. The first shows Apollo, god of music and poetry, and his twin sister Artemis, goddess of hunting and of the moon, before an altar. The body of the second vase depicts a battle between Greeks and Amazons.

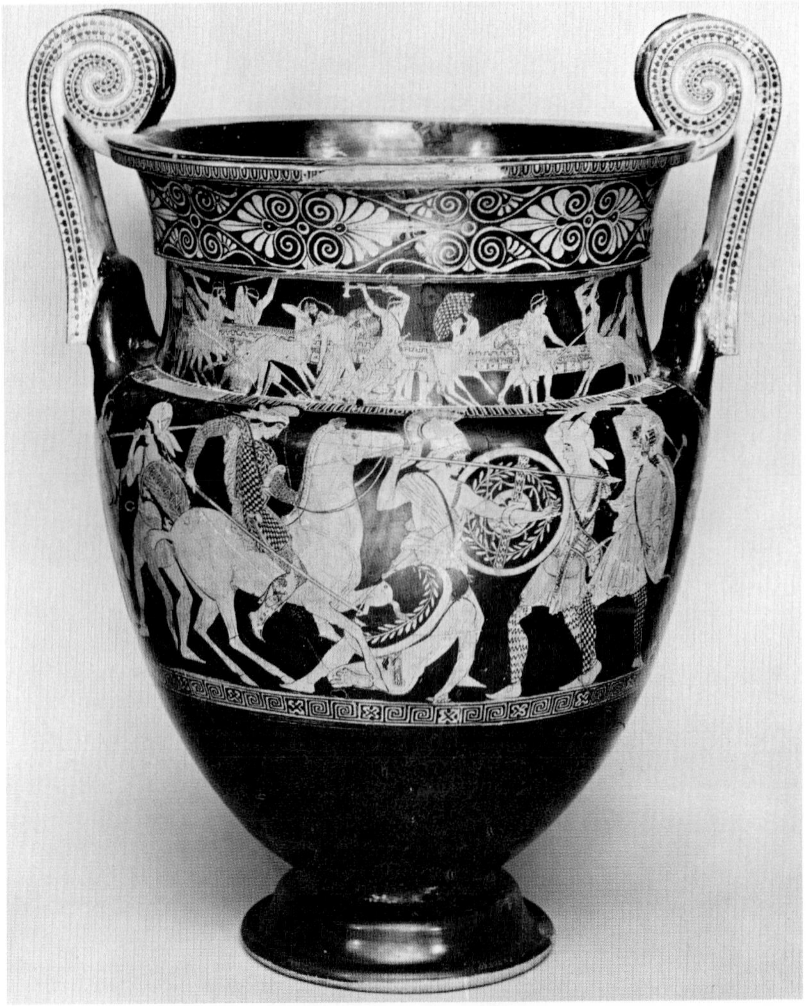

sought refuge in flight from the Furies were devoutly visited. At Troy Alexander the Great was shown the shield supposedly carried by Achilles in the Trojan War nearly a thousand years before. Alexander piously removed the relic and took it into every battle from Palestine to the Punjab.

What made the myths real to Alexander, and all Greeks, was the genius of one man: the blind poet Homer. In the dawn of Greek history, around 800 B.C. Homer hammered out images of gods and heroes that defined them forever. When they imagined ideal manhood Greeks thought of Homer's heroes. When they prayed to Zeus, they thought of Homer's words: "Zeus bowed his sable brows. The ambrosial locks rolled forward from the head of the King, and high Olympus shook."

Homer glorified gods and heroes alike, but he also made them believable; in his hands Greek myth took on a human naturalness that set it apart from every other mythology in the world. And the Greeks understood how much they owed to Homer. They venerated the *Iliad* and the *Odyssey* like a bible. Even Aeschylus is said to have described his own great tragedies as nothing more than "slices from Homer's banquet."

Homer did not invent the myths. Nor did his rustic contemporary, Hesiod, who traced the lineage of the gods back to creation. Behind both poets move older, darker forms that stretch back for unknown distances into the past.

Just what these forms are, and what the myths really mean, has been heatedly disputed for generations. The Greeks assumed that they were based on historical fact—at least the legends of the heroes. The idea has seemed less childish ever since an ardent amateur archaeologist named Heinrich Schliemann went to Asia Minor in 1871 and dug up the remains of a city that fitted Homer's description of ancient Troy.

History's trail has led to the gods as well. Even Zeus's love affairs, once dismissed as so much Hellenic dalliance, have been decoded. Zeus worship came in with the tribes who swept down into Greece during the second millennium B.C. The many nymphs that Zeus loved and left were probably local goddesses of an older race whom the invaders conquered, and whose feminine cults were taken over by Zeus.

The myths have been thought to describe the beginnings of things—like the story of Prometheus, for example, telling how civilization started. They have been interpreted as explanations of natural events like rain, thunder, earthquakes and the cycle of sun and seasons. They have even been explained as an elaborate system of astronomical data which the Greeks somehow picked up from the ancient Babylonians.

Some anthropologists have claimed that the myths are nothing but propaganda aimed at keeping members of the tribe in line by means of customs like ancestor worship. There may be some truth in this. The heroes were always held up as models of behavior. When the statesman Cleisthenes redistricted Athens in 508 B.C., each new district got a brand-new ancestral hero, whose statue was duly set up in the market place.

All Greek myths, some scholars say, evolved in one way or another from fertility rituals. Other scholars detect fetishism, the worship of inanimate objects, in the sacred character the Greeks attributed to certain rocks, plants and places. (One stone at Delphi was believed by the Greek's to be the earth's navel.) But the minor gods and nymphs, who personify rivers, groves, and springs, also smack of animism, which endows objects in nature with souls. There is even a whiff of totemism, the worship of ancestral animals, in the eagle of Zeus and the owl of Athena.

The latest to join the scholarly fray are psychologists. Noting that mythical motifs keep cropping up in people's dreams, the famous Swiss psychiatrist Carl Gustav Jung concluded that a deep layer of fantasy was shared by all mankind as part of man's biological inheritance. Myths, he insisted, are primordial images blindly cast up from the depths of the "collective unconscious."

It now appears that the myths did not have a single root but many. The wanderings of Hercules, for instance, may dramatize the migrations of the Doric Greek tribe who took Hercules as their patron hero. His self-sacrificing struggles express the Doric virtues of courage, perseverance and duty. Yet his famous Twelve Labors are also connected with the 12 divisions of the zodiac.

But Greek myths owe their beauty and vitality to a single, unquestioned source: a genius for storytelling. Taken simply as stories, they are the most imaginative ever told.

## PROMETHEUS, CHAMPION OF MAN

Prometheus is the archrebel and archmartyr of all humanity. His might was as great and his fall as terrible as Lucifer's. But his suffering was almost as sublime as the passion of Christ. Wherever the human spirit is oppressed by tyranny and injustice, men resurrect Prometheus as the symbol of their anguish.

Prometheus fell because he had dared to challenge the power of the gods. He himself was not a god but a Titan, the immortal race that had ruled supreme for aeons until the gods overwhelmed them in a horrendous battle.

Prometheus survived the cataclysm but he nursed a secret hatred for the gods and made himself the champion of man. Some say that he created man, fashioning him out of earth from a river in central Greece, where in historic times the Greeks thought that the clay still smelled like human flesh.

When men sacrificed animals to Zeus, Prometheus tricked Zeus into choosing fat and bones as his portion, so that men might keep the tastiest meat for themselves. When Zeus retaliated by withholding the civilizing gift of fire, Prometheus stole the fire when Zeus's back was turned.

Infuriated, Zeus nailed Prometheus to a lofty crag where an eagle daily tore his new-healed flesh to rags and feasted on his blackened liver, winter and summer, year after year. But the fettered Titan's defiance never weakened. Zeus might rack his body; Zeus could not break his spirit. . . .

## PANDORA'S DEADLY JAR

Man's attempts to explain the presence of evils are as old as evil itself. The seductive beauty and boundless curiosity of women have always seemed to qualify them as ideal agents for mischief. Christians and Jews blame it on Eve, the Greeks on Pandora.

As the poet Hesiod tells it, Zeus, before punishing Prometheus, first turned against man and thought of a clever plan to give the human race its comeuppance. He invented woman, a lovely tempter of innocent mankind. The craftsman-god Hephaestus fashioned her, most of the other gods and goddesses contributed some grace toward her perfection and they named her Pandora, "gift of all."

Pandora's beauty dazzled even the gods, and each desired her. But Zeus offered her to Epimetheus, slow-witted brother of Prometheus. Epimetheus happily took her, in spite of his brother's warning to beware of gifts from Zeus.

Epimetheus soon regretted it, for Pandora proved to be vain and frivolous. She was also insatiably curious, especially about the sealed jar (often misnamed a box) that the gods had given her and warned her never to open. Inevitably Pandora gave in to her curiosity and one day opened the jar. Instantly a cloud of demons billowed out and spread across the earth. The demons were Old Age, Disease, Insanity, Passion, Envy, Spite, Revenge, Cruelty, and every other plague that brings mischief and misery to man.

The last demon may have been the solitary blessing that made the others endurable, or it may have been the worst demon of all—Hope, which makes men willing to suffer all the other demons forever.

## PERSEPHONE AND THE CYCLE OF THE CROPS

Persephone was the daughter of the goddess of the crops, Demeter. One day, as she was gathering flowers . . . the earth opened at her feet and Hades, god of the Underworld, swept up in his chariot, seized the girl and plunged with her down to his realm.

When she heard what had happened, Demeter was overcome by grief. She left the company of the gods, and, shrouding herself like an old woman, wandered aimlessly over the earth. In the fields the grain ceased to sprout. The land lay blighted and barren, and men were close to perishing of hunger.

Zeus had hesitated to interfere for fear of offending his powerful brother, Hades. But he agreed at last to restore Persephone to earth—provided she had not tasted any food during her captivity. Persephone rose out of the earth to a joyful reunion with her mother. At once fields were fertile again and the famine was ended. But then Persephone confessed: during her captivity she had tasted some pomegranate seeds. Because of this, Zeus decreed, Persephone had condemned herself to leave her mother for four months every year, and preside at Hades' side over the gloomy world of the dead.

In every primitive agricultural community the sprouting of the new crop is an annual miracle, a divine act that must have a divine explanation. The Greeks explained it with the myth of Persephone, whose yearly leaving and returning represents the cycle of the crops.

Persephone personifies the grain crop itself. She descends to the Underworld in June, when the harvested seed corn was also placed underground in large buried storage jars. Persephone remains in the Underworld during the arid summer months, when the fields are scorched by the sun and not a single green shoot shows. Then, in October, when the seed grain is brought up out of storage for fall sowing, Persephone rises to rejoin her waiting mother.

The myth also suggests the idea of death and rebirth, and Persephone's reunion with Demeter became the basis of an important cult centered in Eleusis, 13 miles from Athens. It was called the Eleusinian Mysteries, because no one ever revealed what ceremonies took place. Little is known about the mysteries except that they taught a doctrine of resurrection, and offered a spiritual and emotional release that the Greeks never experienced in their official religion. Thousands pilgrimaged to Eleusis to share the mystical joy of the sacred reunion and thereby discover hope of happiness after death.

## OEDIPUS

Oedipus, King of Thebes, was only a minor figure in Greek myth until Sophocles, through his tragedy *Oedipus Rex,* made him the most famous of tragic heroes and the harrowing example for all time of man's inability to escape his fate.

Oedipus' fate was fixed before he was born. His father, Laius, had been warned by an oracle that any son born to him would murder his father and marry his mother. So when Jocasta, his queen, gave birth to a son, Laius gave the infant to a shepherd with orders to expose it on Mount Cithaeron. But the shepherd, in pity, passed the baby on, and it was brought to Corinth, whose king adopted the foundling.

Years later, Oedipus himself learned of the grim prophecy from the oracle at Delphi. Not daring to return to his supposed parents at Corinth, he struck out across the hills. The first man he met was his real father, Laius, whom he unknowingly killed in a trivial quarrel on the narrow mountain road.

Oedipus hurried on to Thebes. He found the city harassed by the Sphinx, who challenged travelers with a riddle—"What walks on four legs in the morning, on two at noon, and on three in the evening?"—and when they could not answer, the Sphinx devoured them. Confronting the Sphinx, Oedipus gave the correct answer: Man—who crawls in infancy, walks erect in adulthood, and hobbles with a stick in old age.

Defeated, the Sphinx hurled itself to death from a cliff. Oedipus was made king by the grateful citizens. He married Queen Jocasta, his own mother, and the fateful prophecy was fulfilled.

Years later Thebes was struck by a devastating plague which, the oracle warned, could not be checked until the murderer of Laius had been found. Full of civic fervor, Oedipus took charge of the search, only to find, to his horror, that all clues led directly to himself. When the old shepherd who had rescued him confessed, the truth in all its enormity broke upon the wretched king. Jocasta hanged herself. In the extremity of despair and self-abasement, Oedipus tore out his own eyes. "What shall I do with eyes," he cried, "where all is ugliness?"

His tragic destiny fulfilled, Oedipus was cast out like a vile pollution to suffer an anguished old age as a blind beggar in the wilderness.

In modern times Oedipus has become namesake of the Oedipus complex, an unconscious state of mind, described by Freud, that impels some men to desire their mother and compete jealously with their father. (Freud expressly absolved Oedipus from the complex.) But the Greeks of Sophocles' day took the hero's deeds at face value. As they saw it, they were the most frightful crimes imaginable, and called for severe atonement. To some Greeks, and to people today, Oedipus was a man rescued from a lifelong delusion who finally faced and accepted a painful truth. His fulfillment could be gained only through self-knowledge, and self-knowledge only through suffering.

# Edith Hamilton: Early Greek Views on Creation

In *Mythology* Edith Hamilton (1867–1963) retold in modern form the ancient Greek myths gathered from oral tradition by Homer and Hesiod. On her ninetieth birthday Miss Hamilton was made an honorary citizen of Athens in appreciation of her lifelong efforts to recreate the world of Greeks and Romans for contemporary Westerners. From *Mythology* by Edith Hamilton by permission of Little, Brown and Company. Copyright 1942 by Edith Hamilton.

First there was Chaos,
the vast immeasurable abyss,
Outrageous as a sea, dark,
wasteful, wild.

These words are Milton's, but they express with precision what the Greeks thought lay back of the very first beginning of things. Long before the gods appeared, in the dim past, uncounted ages ago, there was only the formless confusion of Chaos brooded over by unbroken darkness. At last, but how no one ever tried to explain, two children were born to this shapeless nothingness. Night was the child of Chaos and so was Erebus, which is the unfathomable depth where death dwells. In the whole universe there was nothing else; all was black, empty, silent, endless.

And then a marvel of marvels came to pass. In some mysterious way, from this horror of blank boundless vacancy the best of all things came into being. A great playwright, the comic poet Aristophanes, describes its coming in words often quoted:—

. . . Black-winged Night
Into the bosom of Erebus dark and deep
Laid a wind-born egg, and as the seasons rolled
Forth sprang Love, the longed-for, shining, with
wings of gold.

From darkness and from death Love was born, and with its birth, order and beauty began to banish blind confusion. Love created Light with its companion, radiant Day.

What took place next was the creation of the earth, but this, too, no one ever tried to explain. It just happened. With the coming of Love and light it seemed natural that the earth also should appear. The poet Hesiod, the first Greek who tried to explain how things began, wrote,—

Earth, the beautiful, rose up,
Broad-bosomed, she that is the steadfast base
Of all things. And fair Earth first bore
The starry Heaven, equal to herself,
To cover her on all sides and to be
A home forever for the blessed gods.

In all this thought about the past no distinction had as yet been made between places and persons. Earth was the solid ground, yet vaguely a personality, too. Heaven was the blue vault on high, but it acted in some ways as a human being would. To the people who told these stories all the universe was alive with the same kind of life they knew in themselves. They were individual persons, so they personified everything which had the obvious marks of life, everything which moved and changed: earth in winter and summer; the sky with its shifting stars; the restless sea, and so on. It was only a dim personification: something vague and immense which with its motion brought about change and therefore was alive.

But when they told of the coming of love and light the early storytellers were setting the scene for the appearance of mankind, and they began to personify more precisely. They gave natural forces distinct shapes. They thought of them as the precursors of men and they defined them far more clearly as individuals than they had earth and heaven. They showed them acting in every way as human beings did; walking, for instance, and eating, as Earth and Heaven obviously did not. These two were set apart. If they were alive, it was in a way peculiar to them alone.

The first creatures who had the appearance of life were the children of Mother Earth and Father Heaven (Gaea and Ouranos). They were monsters. Just as we believe that the earth was once inhabited by strange gigantic creatures, so did the Greeks. They did not, however, think of them as huge lizards and mammoths, but as somewhat like men and yet unhuman. They had the shattering, overwhelming strength of earthquake and hurricane and volcano. In the tales about them they do not seem really alive, but rather to belong to a world where as yet there was no life, only tremendous movements of irresistible forces lifting up the mountains and scooping out the seas. The Greeks apparently had some such feeling because in their stories, although they represent these creatures as living beings, they make them unlike any form of life known to man.

Three of them, monstrously huge and strong, had each a hundred hands and fifty heads. To three others was given the name of *Cyclops* (the Wheel-eyed), because each had only one enormous eye, as round and as big as a wheel, in the middle of the forehead. The Cyclops, too, were gigantic, towering up like mighty mountain crags and devastating in their power. Last came the Titans. There were a number of these and they were in no way inferior to the others in size and strength, but they were not purely destructive. Several of them were even beneficent. One, indeed, after men had been created, saved them from destruction.

It was natural to think of these fearful creations as the children of Mother Earth, brought forth from her dark depths when the world was young. But it is extremely odd that they were also the children of Heaven. However, that was what the Greeks said, and they made Heaven out to be a very poor father. He hated the things with a hundred hands and fifty heads, even though they were his sons, and as each was born he imprisoned it in a secret place within the earth. The Cyclops and the Titans he left at large; and Earth, enraged at the maltreatment of her other children, appealed to them to help her. Only one was bold enough, the Titan Cronus. He lay in wait for his father and wounded him terribly. The Giants, the fourth race of monsters, sprang up from his blood. From this same blood, too, the Erinyes (the Furies) were born. Their office was to pursue and punish sinners. They were called "those who walk in darkness," and they were terrible of aspect, with writhing snakes for hair and eyes that wept tears of blood. The other monsters were finally driven from the earth, but not the Erinyes. As long as there was sin in the world they could not be banished.

From that time on for untold ages, Cronus, he whom as we have seen the Romans called Saturn, was lord of the universe, with his sister-queen, Rhea (Ops in Latin). Finally one of their sons, the future ruler of heaven and earth, whose name in Greek is Zeus and in Latin Jupiter, rebelled against him. He had good cause to do so, for Cronus had learned that one of his children was destined some day to dethrone him and he thought to go against fate by swallowing them as soon as they were born. But when Rhea bore Zeus, her sixth child, she succeeded in having him secretly carried off to Crete, while she gave her husband a great stone wrapped in swaddling clothes which he supposed was the baby and swallowed down accordingly. Later, when Zeus was grown, he forced his father with the help of his grandmother, the Earth, to disgorge it along with the five earlier children, and it was set up at Delphi where eons later a great traveler, Pausanias reports that he saw it about 180 A.D.: "A stone of no great size which the priests of Delphi anoint every day with oil."

There followed a terrible war between Cronus, helped by his brother Titans, against Zeus with his five brothers and sisters—a war that almost wrecked the universe. . . .

The Titans conquered, partly because Zeus released from their prison the hundred-handed monsters who fought for him with their irresistible weapons—thunder, lightning, and earthquake—and also because one of the sons of the Titan Lapetus, whose name was Prometheus and who was very wise, took sides with Zeus. [After a few more unsuccessful attempts to revolt against them] Zeus and his brothers and sisters ruled, undisputed lords of all. . . .

# Plato Attacks Myths

**(4th Century B.C.)**

Plato (427–347) was one of the world's most famous philosophers. Like his teacher Socrates, Plato was concerned with the relation between knowledge, living "justly," and happiness. In his greatest work, *The Republic,* he tried to define such basic concepts as justice, truth, and what constitutes the good life, by setting up a model of an ideal state in which such concepts are made real. In the following excerpt from *The Republic,* the philosopher [Plato] and a companion discuss the education of the members of this ideal state. From *The Republic* in *The Dialogues of Plato,* trans. B. Jowett (New York, 1892), Vol. III, pp. 58–67.

## I

[Plato] How are [the citizens of the ideal state] to be reared and educated? Is not this an inquiry which may be expected to throw light on the greater inquiry which is our final end—How do justice and injustice grow up in States? . . .

The first thing will be to establish a censorship of the writers of fiction, and let the censors receive any tale of fiction which is good, and reject the bad; and we will desire mothers and nurses to tell their children the authorized one only. Let them fashion the mind with such tales, even more fondly than they mould the body with their hands; but most of those which are now in use must be discarded.

Of what tales are you speaking? he said. . . .

[Plato] Those, I said, which are narrated by Homer and Hesiod, and the rest of the poets, who have ever been the great story-tellers of mankind.

But which stories do you mean, he said; and what fault do you find with them?

[Plato] A fault which is most serious, I said; the fault of telling a lie, and, what is more, a bad lie.

But when is this fault committed?

[Plato] Whenever an erroneous representation is made of the nature of gods and heroes,—as when a painter paints a portrait not having the shadow of a likeness to the original. . . .

If we mean our future [citizens] to regard the habit of quarrelling among themselves as of all things the basest, should any word be said to them of the wars in heaven, and of the plots and fightings of the gods against one another, for they are not true. No, we shall never mention the battles of the giants, or let them be embroidered on garments; and we shall be silent about the innumerable other quarrels of gods and heroes with their friends and relatives. If they would only believe us we would tell them that quarrelling is unholy, and that never up to this time has there been any quarrel between citizens; this is what old men and old women should begin by telling children; and when they grow up, the poets also should be told to compose for them in a similar spirit. But the narrative of Hephaestus binding . . . his mother, or how on another occasion Zeus sent him flying for taking her part when she was being beaten, and all the battles of the gods in Homer—these tales must not be admitted into our State, whether they are supposed to have an allegorical meaning or not. For a young person cannot judge what is allegorical and what is literal; anything that he receives into his mind at that age is likely to become indelible and unalterable; and therefore it is most important that the tales which the young first hear should be models of virtuous thoughts. . . .

II

[Plato] God is always to be represented as he truly is, whatever be the sort of poetry, epic, lyric or tragic, in which the representation is given.

Right.

[Plato] And is he not truly good? and must he not be represented as such?

Certainly.

[Plato] And no good thing is hurtful?

No, indeed. . . .

[Plato] And the good is advantageous?

Yes.

[Plato] And therefore the cause of well-being?

Yes.

[Plato] It follows therefore that the good is not the cause of all things, but of the good only?

Assuredly.

[Plato] Then God, if he be good, is not the author of all things, as the many assert, but he is the cause of a few things only, and not of most things that occur to men. For few are the goods of human life, and many are the evils, and the good is to be attributed to God alone; of the evils the causes are to be sought elsewhere, and not in him.

That appears to me to be most true, he said.

[Plato] Then we must not listen to Homer or to any other poet who is guilty of the folly of saying that two casks

> Lie at the threshold of Zeus, full of lots, one of good, the other of evil lots, . . . [Iliad]

And again—

> Zeus, who is the dispenser of good and evil
> to us. . . .

Let this then be one of our rules and principles concerning the gods, to which our poets and reciters will be expected to conform,—that God is not the author of all things, but of good only.

That will do, he said.

[Plato] And what do you think of a second principle? Shall I ask you whether God is a magician, and of a nature to appear insidiously now in one shape, and now in another—sometimes himself changing and passing into many forms, sometimes deceiving us with the semblance of such transformations; or is he one and the same immutably fixed in his own proper image?

I can not answer you, he said, without more thought. . . .

[Plato] But surely God and the things of God are in every way perfect?

Of course they are.

[Plato] Then he can hardly be compelled by external influence to take many shapes?

He can not.

[Plato] But may he not change and transform himself?

Clearly, he said, that must be the case if he is changed at all.

[Plato] And will he then change himself for the better and fairer, or for the worse and more unsightly?

If he change at all he can only change for the worse, for we can not suppose him to be deficient either in virtue or beauty.

[Plato] Very true, Adeimantus; but then, would any one, whether God or man, desire to make himself worse?

Impossible.

[Plato] Then it is impossible that God should ever be willing to change; being, as is supposed, the fairest and best that is conceivable, every god remains absolutely and forever in his own form.

That necessarily follows, he said, in my judgment.

[Plato] Then, I said, my dear friend, let none of the poets tell us that—

> The gods, taking the disguise of strangers from other lands, walk up and down cities in all sorts of forms; . . .

Neither must we have mothers under the influence of the poets scaring their children with a bad version of these myths—telling how certain gods, as they say—"Go about by night in the likeness of so many strangers and in divers forms;" but let them take heed lest they make cowards of their children, and at the same time speak blasphemy against the gods.

Heaven forbid, he said.

[Plato] But although the gods are themselves unchangeable, still by witchcraft and deception they may make us think that they appear in various forms?

Perhaps, he replied.

[Plato] Well, but can you imagine that God will be willing to lie, whether in word or deed, or to put forth a phantom of himself?

I can not say, he replied. . . .

[Plato] Or perhaps he may tell a lie because he is afraid of enemies?

That is inconceivable.

[Plato] But he may have friends who are senseless or mad?

But no mad or senseless person can be a friend of God.

[Plato] Then no motive can be imagined why God should lie?

None whatever.

[Plato] Then the superhuman and divine is absolutely incapable of falsehood?

Yes.

[Plato] Then is God perfectly simple and true both in word and deed; he changes not; he deceives not, either by sign or word, by dream or waking vision.

Your thoughts, he said, are the reflections of my own.

[Plato] You agree with me then, I said, but this is the second type or form in which we should write and speak about divine things. The gods are not magicians who transform themselves, neither do they deceive mankind in any way.

I grant that.

[Plato] Then, although we are admirers of Homer, we do not admire the lying dream which Zeus sends to Agamemnon; neither will we praise the verses of Aeschylus in which Thetis says that Apollo at her nuptials—

> Was celebrating in song her fair progeny whose days were to be long, and to know no sickness. And when he had spoken of my lot as in all things blessed of heaven he raised a note of triumph and cheered my soul. And I thought that the word of Phoebus, being divine and full of prophecy, would not fail. And now he himself who uttered the strain, he who was present at the banquet, and who said this—he it is who has slain my son.

[Plato continuing] These are the kind of sentiments about the gods which will arouse our anger; and he who utters them shall be refused a chorus; neither shall we allow teachers to make use of them in the instruction of the young, meaning, as we do, that our guardians, as far as men can be, should be true worshippers of the gods and like them. . . .

## Empire and Art
## Greek Art and the Hellenistic Age

The conquests of Alexander were accompanied by the widespread diffusion of Hellenic civilization into Africa, into the Near East, and even into the borderlands of India. The Greeks and Macedonians who populated the new cities established by the conqueror and his successors brought with them the artistic standards of their homeland. Dress, architecture, literature, theater, and art all reflected the Hellenic tradition, tempered by the culture of the earlier civilizations that were being displaced. The Hellenistic Age was a wayward child of its Hellenic parent. Greek values, nurtured in the freedom of a small-scale city-state society, were adjusted to serve the needs of a vast, oriental, autocratically organized area governed by a small cosmopolitan upper class. These values in art sharply contrasted with the classic Greek search for balanced harmony and aloofness from the passions of the everyday world. Hellenistic art was absorbed in movement, sensation and a rather excessive realism—and it was fascinated by scenes of daily life and of foreign peoples.

1 Hellenistic style set the artistic tone for the Mediterranean world. As the eastern empires fell before the vigorous Roman armies in the second and first centuries B.C., the Romans themselves willingly assimilated the culture of their subjects. Educated Greek slaves served as tutors in rich Roman homes, and the walls of these homes were decorated with paintings either taken from the East or dealing in some way with Greek and oriental themes. This Roman panel, which pictures the mythical Greek figure Hercules (right) finding his lost son Telephus (being suckled by a deer), was found in Herculaneum near Naples. Herculaneum was buried in the eruption of Mt. Vesuvius (79 A.D.) that destroyed Pompeii. The lute player behind the representation of the local goddess, Arcadia, may be African.

1

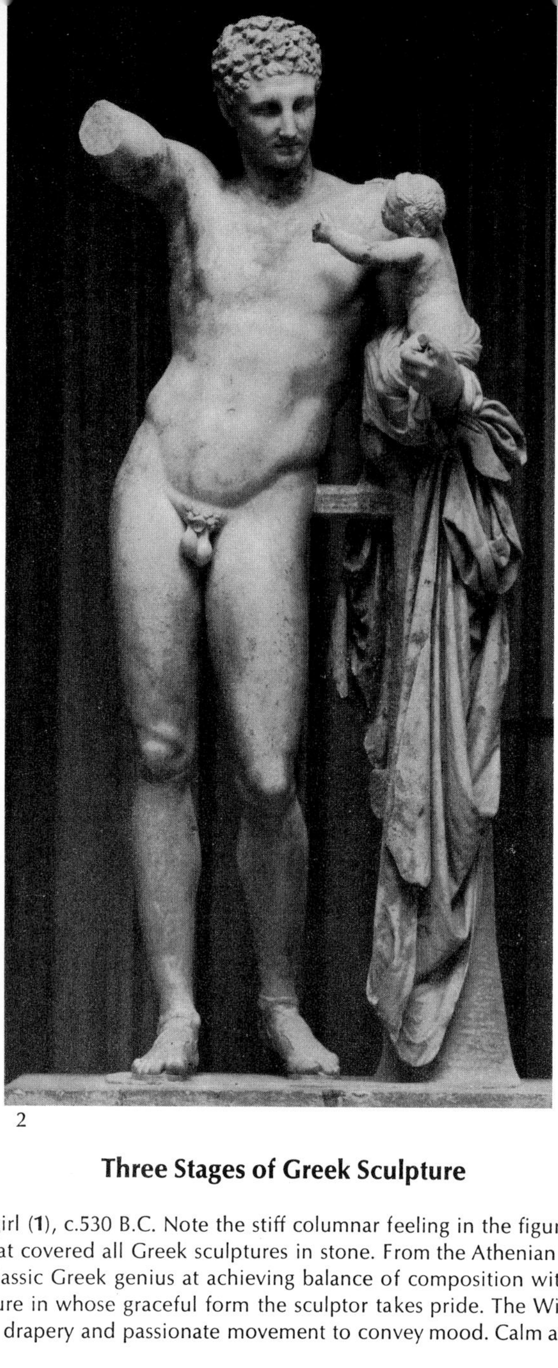
2

3

## Three Stages of Greek Sculpture

An early figure of a draped standing girl (**1**), c.530 B.C. Note the stiff columnar feeling in the figure that is essentially a monolith. This is one of the few existing statues to retain traces of the paint that covered all Greek sculptures in stone. From the Athenian Acropolis. The famous statue of the god Hermes (**2**), c.320 B.C. This statue by Praxiteles reveals the classic Greek genius at achieving balance of composition within the bounds of the sculpture. Hermes is passionless, calm, reflective, a restrained aristocratic figure in whose graceful form the sculptor takes pride. The Winged Victory or Nike from the island of Samothrace (**3**), c.190 B.C. The Hellenistic sculptor has used drapery and passionate movement to convey mood. Calm and balance are no longer the standard.

6 Bronze head of man from the island of Delos, c.100 B.C. This is a face modeled from life and not that of an inhabitant of an ideal world. The Hellenistic sculptor obviously has striven to capture the lined features and quizzical expression of his subject.

4 A closer side view of the standing girl reveals serene composure and a set smile. The face, restrained and removed from the concerns of everyday life, hints at an Eastern origin. Some historians theorize that archaic Greek art was influenced by the Egyptians (by way of Crete). 5 Hermes' face is more plastic, though equally idealized. In the manner of the art of the Golden Age, the eyes express a feeling of thoughtfulness.

1 Two third-century girls play knucklebones, the ancient counterpart of the game of jacks. These clay figurines were found in southern Italy.

## Scenes of Daily Life and Representations of Non-Greeks

2 Many works portrayed the non-Greeks who lived in the far-flung Hellenistic world. This squatting figure of an African (late third century B.C.) is actually a flask.

3 Bronze statuette of black youth singing to the music of an instrument, now missing. Second century B.C.

1

## Influence on the Depiction of Buddha

One unusual effect of Alexander's invasion of Central Asia was to provide a Greek model for later depictions of Buddha. Representation of the Buddha's physical image had been avoided in the centuries after his death (c.480 B.C.), but sculptors in the Indian frontier province of Gandhara (now in Pakistan) were evidently impressed by the statues of Apollo introduced by the Greeks. Apollo had, over time, been associated with the arts of civilization, youth, and the sun's light. Images of Buddha that are clearly inspired by this sort of statue of Apollo appear in the second century A.D. Compare the marble head of the Apollo Belvedere (**1**) (fourth century B.C.) with the Gandhara head of the Buddha in stucco (**2**) (fourth or fifth century A.D.). Hair and features are remarkably similar; chiefly, the more contemplative expression of the Buddha separates the two.

2

3

Somewhat more oriental features grace this standing Buddha of the second or third centuries A.D. (**3**), but he wears a topknot typical of Apollo and is draped in a Greek *himation,* or mantle.

1 Alexander and his successors quickly began to exploit the oriental practice of deifying rulers. This Thracian silver coin of the 280s B.C. (**1**) depicts Alexander the Great with the ram's horns that were the symbol of both the chief Greek god, Zeus, and the Egyptian god of Thebes, Amon-Ra. Since both controlled the heavens and the weather, they were easily assimilated. It was at the oracle of Amon in the Libyan desert that the priests first hailed Alexander in the winter of 332–331 as the son of the god.

## Shared Images of Authority

2 A carving in the temple of Luxor in Egypt (**2**) shows Alexander presenting an offering to Amon (right). The Macedonian king is dressed as an Egyptian.

# The Fable of the Hawk and the Nightingale

In one of the earliest works of Western literature the poet Hesiod captured the folk wisdom of a farmer's almanac, including the story of the Greek gods as it had been passed down by word of mouth over the centuries. Hesiod appears to have been cheated of some inherited property by his brother Perses, and the fable of the hawk and nightingale alludes to this loss. The tale has much more significant implications, however, for an understanding of the reasoned Greek view of the relation of the human to the divine. Hesiod's *Works and Days* was composed about 700 B.C., a century before the composition of the Hebrew *Book of Job,* which also sought to comprehend this relationship. Reprinted by permission of the publishers and the Loeb Classical Library from *Hesiod, The Homeric Hymns, and Homerica,* trans. H. G. E. White (Cambridge, Mass.: Harvard University Press).

And now I will tell a fable for princes who themselves understand. Thus said the hawk to the nightingale with speckled neck, while he carried her high up among the clouds, gripped fast in his talons, and she, pierced by his crooked talons, cried pitifully. To her he spoke disdainfully: "Miserable thing, why do you cry out? One far stronger than you now holds you fast, and you must go wherever I take you, songstress as you are. And if I please I will make my meal of you, or let you go. He is a fool who tries to withstand the stronger, for he does not get the mastery and suffers pain besides his shame." So said the swiftly flying hawk, the long-winged bird.

But you, Perses, listen to right and do not foster violence; for violence is bad for a poor man. Even the prosperous cannot easily bear its burden, but is weighed down under it when he has fallen into delusion. The better path is go by on the other side towards justice; for Justice beats Outrage when she comes at length to the end of the race. But only when he has suffered does the fool learn this. For Oath keeps pace with wrong judgements. There is a noise when Justice is being dragged in the way where those who devour bribes and give sentence with crooked judgements take her. And she, wrapped in mist, follows to the city and haunts of the people, weeping, and bringing mischief to men, even to such as have driven her forth in that they did not deal straightly with her.

But they who give straight judgements to strangers and to the men of the land, and go not aside from what is just, their city flourishes, and the people prosper in it: Peace, the nurse of children, is abroad in their land, and all-seeing Zeus never decrees cruel war against them. Neither famine nor disaster ever haunt men who do true justice; but light-heartedly they tend the fields which are all their care. The earth bears them victual in plenty, and on the mountains the oak bears acorns upon the top and bees in the midst. Their woolly sheep are laden with fleeces; their women bear children like their parents. They flourish continually with good things, and do not travel on ships, for the grain-giving earth bears them fruit.

But for those who practice violence and cruel deeds far-seeing Zeus, the son of Cronos, ordains a punishment. Often even a whole city suffers for a bad man who sins and devises presumptuous deeds, and the son of Cronos lays great trouble upon the people, famine and plague together, so that the men perish away, and their women do not bear children, and their houses become few, through the contriving of Olympian Zeus. And again, at another time, the son of Cronos either destroys their wide army, or their walls, or else makes an end of their ships on the sea.

You princes, mark well this punishment you also; for the deathless gods are near among men and mark all those who oppress their fellows with crooked judgements and reck not the anger of the gods. For upon the bounteous earth Zeus has thrice ten thousand spirits, watchers of mortal men, and these keep watch on judgements and deeds of wrong as they roam, clothed in mist, all over the earth. And there is virgin Justice, the daughter of Zeus, who is honoured and reverenced among the gods who dwell on Olympus, and whenever anyone hurts her with lying slander, she sits beside her father, Zeus the son of Cronos, and tells him of men's wicked heart, until the people pay for the mad folly of their princes who, evilly minded, pervert judgement and give sentence crookedly. Keep watch against this, you princes, and make straight your judgements, you who devour bribes; put crooked judgements altogether from your thoughts.

He does mischief to himself who does mischief to another, and evil planned harms the plotter most.

The eye of Zeus, seeing all and understanding all, beholds these things too, if so he will, and fails not to mark what sort of justice is this that the city keeps within it. . . .

But you, Perses, lay up these things within your heart and listen now to right, ceasing altogether to think of violence. For the son of Cronos has ordained this law for men, that fishes and beasts and winged fowls should devour one another, for right is not in them; but to mankind he gave right which proves far the best.

TOPIC 8

# THE REACHES AND LIMITS OF GREEK SCIENCE

The inquiring Greek mind, seeking answers to great cosmological and ethical questions, and not fully satisfied by the conventional responses of myth and tradition, turned to an exploration of the seemingly chaotic state of nature in which man lived. The accumulation of knowledge is as old, and older, than civilization itself. The Greeks, however, as the following readings demonstrate, were the first to make a science of the search for knowledge. Brilliant as Greek achievements in science were, the readings also raise the question of what prevented full exploitation of their potential.



**Reading 29**

## The Big Questions



Although the Mesopotamians and Egyptians acquired a considerable body of organized and accurate information about the nature of things, it was the Greeks who first arrived at the *idea* of a science. Until the idea was formed, the development of the sciences was impeded by the lack of any general notion of their aim. It is one thing to know, as the men of the ancient East knew, that lines in the ratio 3 : 4 : 5 will make a right triangle. It is quite another thing to say, as the Greeks said, "If the sum of the squares on two sides of a triangle equal the square on the third side, the triangle is always a right triangle." To arrive at such a generalization, they had to ask themselves a general question: "What is the relation among the sides of any right triangle?" The Greeks developed a remarkable skill in raising such general questions, and in doing so they laid the foundations of scientific thought and of philosophy.

**A Right Triangle**

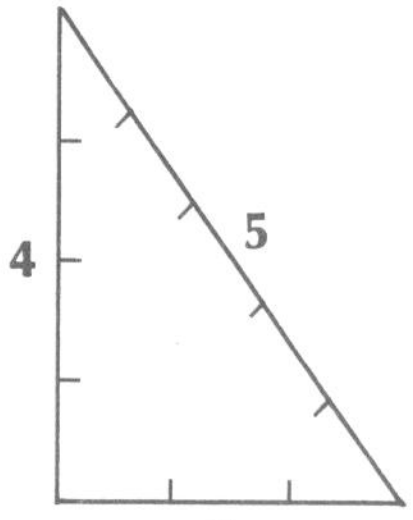


The Greeks' long career of question-asking seems to have begun in Ionia. It is possible that the Ionian Greeks picked up a good deal of scientific knowledge from the advanced civilizations of the Orient, for there was much contact between the trading towns on the coast of Ionia and the East. Since they did not share the Oriental religions, to which much of that knowledge was merely auxiliary, they could take the facts and leave the myths, and the fund of wholly non-mythical knowledge that they eventually built up may have set them off on their quest to know the nature of the world around them.

Many civilized peoples, faced with the great catastrophes and recurring cycles of nature, ask, "Who did it?" The Greeks, as we can judge from their myths, had once asked that question too, and had given the usual answer: "Such and such a god did it." But Homer had so humanized the Greek gods that it was hard for the Greeks to think of them as all-powerful beings. Every aristocratic clan claimed descent from one god or another, so the gods were right in the family—rather too much in the family, in fact, to provide a satisfactory explanation of the major mysteries of nature.

The decisive question that stood at the beginning of Greek thought about the nature of things was asked, it seems, by three men who lived in Miletus in Ionia from about the beginning through the middle of the sixth century B.C. The question was, "What sort of stuff is the world really made of?" Or, more simply, "What is real?" The three Milesians who tried to answer the question were Thales, Anaximander, and Anaximenes, and their answers, respectively, were that the world is made of water, of the unlimited, and of air. Though their answers differed, the three agreed that what underlay all things was a material stuff and that it was one, not many. But if you start with one stuff, why does this one stuff look like so many different things—trees, and sky, and tables, and hair, and so on? It is clear that each of the Milesians picked a stuff that is capable of transformation without the assistance of a god. The basic stuff water, for example, can become "air" (steam) or "earth" (ice). In avoiding mythical explanations of the world, they were establishing a fundamental rule of rational scientific explanation. Each chose his fundamental stuff with a view to explaining the observed facts, to making sense of them rather than making a myth about them.

The Ionians, then, had begun a new era in the history of the human mind by trying to fathom what stuff the world was made of and by selecting things that seemed versatile enough to become other things, apparently unlike the basic stuff. The Ionians, however, appear to have had nothing to say about a major problem. We do not experience the world as several different general and vague states of stuff (liquids, solids, gases) any more than we experience it as a single stuff. What we experience are things with definite shapes and sizes and colors. From this point of view, what really matters is not the unlimited supply of stuff of which things are made but the force or principle that transforms that dull homogeneous stuff into the kinds of things that exist. What force changes water into steam? What force changes the unlimited into a table?

A group of men called Pythagoreans made the first effort to cope with this problem. Pythagoras, their leader, lived toward the end of the sixth century. He began life in Ionia but migrated to Italy, where he became the head of a religious-philosophical cult that long survived him. Pythagoras seems to have combined mysticism with a flair for scientific and mathematical investigation. His followers were faith healers, physicians, mathematicians, and also the first students of acoustics, the science of sound. In their study of music these students discovered that, by vibrating lengths of string that were in proportions of 2:1, 3:2, and 4:3, they always got a concord, while with other proportions they got discords. They also noted other curious relationships among numbers. For example, if you increase numbers [units] successively from 1 (1 plus 2 plus 3 plus 4. . .), you get a triangle [see illustration below], and 1, 3, 6, 10 . . . become in a sense triangular numbers. If you add the successive *odd* numbers [units] to 1 (1 plus 3 plus 5 plus 7. . .), you develop a series of squares, and the sums of this progression, 1, 4, 9, 16, . . . are in this sense square numbers [see illustration].

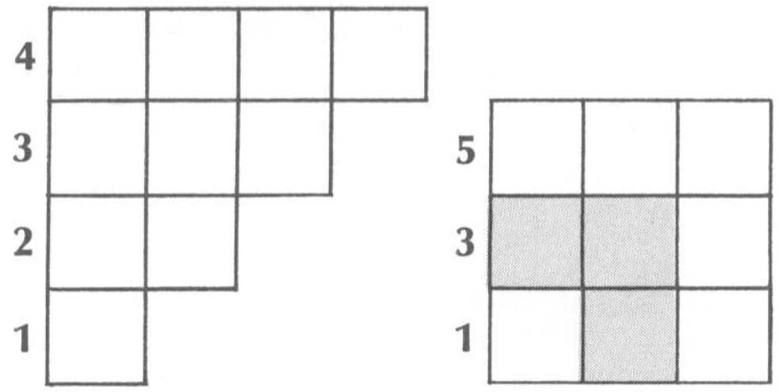


**Triangular Numbers** **Square Numbers**

On the basis of the peculiar internal harmonies that they thus discovered in the number series and from the external numerical harmonies that they discovered in music, the Pythagoreans made one of those amazing leaps to conclusions that the Greeks seem to have specialized in. They concluded that what made sense of the world—what made it regular or subject to rule—was the imposition of limit or form on the boundless stuff of the universe, and they further decided that the regularity was numerical. In other words, the forms that rule the world, that make it orderly rather than chaotic, are relationships among numbers like the harmonic ratio revealed by the study of music. The way to the highest truth, then, lies through the search for the ruling numbers that determine the world order. The search for ruling numerical relationships led some of the followers of Pythagoras through all the superstitious nonsense of magic squares, lucky and unlucky numbers—the whole folderol of number magic. But it led others to develop the magnificent generalized systems of plane and solid geometry still called, after a later Greek compiler, Euclidean. It also led to attempts to discover numerical formulas that would describe regularities in the physical world. It was along this path, first opened by the Pythagoreans, that the Western world at last found its way to one of its incomparable achievements—modern physical science.

As the speculative Greek probed into the mysteries of the world around him, he encountered an ever-increasing number of problems about the nature of things. Everything changes, but can a constantly changing thing really be said to exist? If there is only *one* real thing in the world—air, water, or whatever—can there be any change? If so, what makes it change? Is there really only one stuff in the world? May there not be several or even an infinite number? The Greeks eventually reached answers to all these questions—frequently wholly contradictory answers. *Everything* that is moves and changes constantly, said Heraclitus; nothing *real* ever moves or changes, said Parmenides; there is *one* stuff, said the Ionians; there are *four* stuffs or elements—earth, air, fire, and water—said Empedocles; there are an *infinite* number of stuffs or atoms, and all that happens is the result of their random bumpings about in the empty space through which they are falling, said Leucippus. And so it went with brilliant insight and yet with endless disagreement. It was the disagreements and the apparent lack of any means to resolve them that gave rise to two new questions: (1) How do you know that what you say about the nature of things is so? (2) In any case, of what use is such knowledge to men in conducting their lives? The Greek quest for understanding through reason raised the questions of what the world is really made of, how it changed, how men could know things, how they should behave, and, finally how any answer to any of these questions could be made to stick. In so doing the Greeks threw open to human inquiry almost every great problem of life. At the same time they rejected the answers given by men of other civilizations, most of which boiled down to: "The gods did it or commanded it, because they wanted to." Such answers simply did not satisfy the Greek thinkers, who would have demanded how one knew what the gods did or commanded, or what kind of gods there were and how one knew *that*. Thus, beginning in the sixth century B.C. with the first big question of the Ionians, "What is real?," Greek thought in about a century and a half got around to asking questions about almost everything that men have since felt important and to demanding sensible answers to all these questions. The Greeks embarked man on a great endless adventure of thought, engaging him in the attempt to make rationally intelligible the widest possible range of his own experience. . . .

# Aristotle's Contribution to Knowledge

From pp. 177–178, *Western Civilization: Paleolithic Man to the Emergence of European Powers,* edited by William Langer. Copyright © 1968 by William L. Langer, Paul MacKendrick, Deno J. Geanakoplos, J. H. Hexter, and Richard Pipes. By permission of Harper & Row, Publishers.

Plato's best student was Aristotle (384–322 B.C.), son of the Macedonian court physician and later tutor to Alexander. Aristotle agreed with Plato about the important questions for the mind to explore, and himself started from Plato's proposed answers. He was the best kind of disciple; on the basis of what he had learned in the Academy, he explored new ground and developed new solutions for perennial problems. Aristotle's solutions had an amazing history: they lie at the root of the dominant philosophy of the three great religions of the West—Islam, Judaism, and Christianity. . . .

To know the real was . . . to understand the processes of change and growth. In order to know, one did not try by a leap of thought to escape the actual world, since only in it were to be found the objects of knowledge; one must, rather, study them in an orderly organized way. For orderly study, Aristotle thought, two things are essential: order in the student's thinking (*logic*), and recognition of the order of nature (*classification*).

If we are to know anything worth knowing, Aristotle believed, we must think straight. I may know that most workingmen and most Communists share a dislike of bosses, but this knowledge will only confuse me if I conclude from this shared dislike that it follows that most workingmen are Communists. Aristotle early developed a method which, if adhered to, would prevent such confusion. He carefully explored the particular circumstances under which it would be correct to say that one assertion *followed* from another. The rules he discovered he called logic, the science of using words to make valid inferences. For 2,000 years, until the seventeenth century, Aristotelian logic formed the basis for accurate thinking.

How is one to avoid getting wholly lost amid the infinite variety of things in whose study lies the way to truth? Aristotle's way was to know something about the kinds of things there are. Each thing, of course, is different from every other, being made up of a different mess of matter. But insofar as it is different, we cannot know or say much about it; we cannot do much more than point to it. It is only the *likenesses* between things that enable us to think about them effectively. Moreover, for such thinking, some traits of things are more important than others. To recognize the brownness of a cow is not very important since nothing much follows from its being brown. To recognize its "cowness," however, *is* important, for then I know about this particular creature what I know about cows in general. But cows share traits with other cud-chewing creatures—mammals that feed their young with milk from the mother, and so on. Thus, as we classify things we add to the number of true things we can say about them, and at the same time we get farther and farther away in thought from the specific material individual and ascend a sort of staircase of forms, groupings of increasing generality. So knowledge grows by following nature's course from the specific (species) to the general (genus), by recognizing or discovering the significantly general in the particular, the form that is in or joined to the matter. Aristotle himself showed the gain in knowledge to be derived from a sound system of classification by recognizing that a whale was not a fish but a mammal, since it did not lay eggs but bore its young in its body.

With his logic and his system of classification, Aristotle had equipped himself to make all knowledge his province: physics, biology, and astronomy as well as politics, ethics, and poetry. For just as there are different kinds of motion and of living creatures, so too there are different kinds of states, and the state is one kind of association. (The best kind of state, Aristotle decided, would be of medium size, the citizens middle class and habituated to the life of reason through systematic, universal, and public education.) There are also different kinds of virtue (the best being a mean between extremes) and different kinds of poetry (the most interesting being tragedy). Orderly discourse about any of these has to classify them properly to avoid violating the rules of logic.

In his impulse toward synthesis and his concept of an educated, responsible ruling class, Aristotle represented the best minds of his age, but he towers above it as the center of the revolution from the classical to the Hellenistic world.

Given Aristotle's rather down-to-earth approach to ways of knowing, he naturally disagreed with the pattern of teaching at Plato's Academy. Encouraged by Alexander, he set up his own school in Athens, the Lyceum (335 B.C.). Given his notion of method, the Lyceum naturally resembled the present-day graduate school by developing specialists. For 2,000 years after Aristotle, no one anywhere added much to what he had known about certain sciences: embryology, for example. He first developed the experimental method, most successfully in embryology. By breaking open one egg each day in the time between laying and hatching, he was able to describe with remarkable accuracy the development of the chick. He proceeded no further in experiment, partly because he lacked rudimentary apparatus (thermometer, barometer, microscope, telescope), partly for lack of time, partly because of his own prejudices. . . .

# Aristotle Explains Why Men Desire Knowledge

Aristotle (384–322 B.C.), a pupil of Plato and, in turn, teacher of Alexander the Great, the conqueror of the great empires of the Near East, conducted a school in Athens modelled on Plato's Academy. Like Plato, Aristotle tried to understand and explain the workings of the human mind and pinpoint the nature of knowledge. He wrote a large number of books covering the gamut of human knowledge, and his impact on Western thought was immense for many centuries. In fact, concentrated attacks on the traditional authorities who dogmatically held to the letter of his conclusions (while misconstruing his methodology) were necessary before the modern world could emerge in the sixteenth and seventeenth centuries. From *The Metaphysics of Aristotle,* trans. J. F. McMahon in *Aristotle: On Man in the Universe,* pp. 5–11 (New York, Walter J. Black, 1943).

## I

All men by nature have a desire to know. A sign of this is the joy we take in our senses, for quite apart from their usefulness we love them for their own sake, and the sense of sight above all. For not only as a help in action but also when we have no intention of acting we value our sight above almost everything else. The reason for this is that of all the senses sight makes knowledge most possible for us and shows us the many differences between things. . . .

Animals [too] live by impressions and memories but have little in the way of connected experience, whereas the human race lives by art and reasoning as well. In man, experience is a result of his memory, for many memories of doing the same thing end in creating a sense of a single experience. Experience seems almost the same as science and art. But in fact science and art come to men through experience. . . .

Men of experience know that a thing is so but do not know why it is so, while the others know the why and the cause. Therefore we think that the masters in every craft deserve more honor and know more and are wiser than the handworkers, because they know the reasons for the things that are done. But the handworkers seem like certain lifeless things that act, but act without knowing what they are doing—as fire does when it burns. Lifeless things perform their functions because of some nature in them, and handworkers perform theirs through habit. But we call the masters wiser, not because they can do things but because they grasp the theory and understand the causes. . . .

## II

The theme of our present remarks is this, that all men believe that what we call wisdom has to do with first causes and principles of things. Accordingly, as we have just said, the man of experience is considered wiser than those who know only sensations of whatever kind, and the artist wiser than the man of experience, the master than the handworker and the theoretical science than the practical. Patently then wisdom is knowledge of principles and causes.

Since we are investigating this kind of knowledge, we must ask what are the causes and what are the principles the knowledge of which is wisdom. If we take our conception of a wise man, perhaps the answer to this question will seem clearer. In the first place, we expect a wise man to know all things, as far as that is possible, without, however, knowing each of them in individual detail. Secondly, we think he is one who understands difficult things, not easy for men to comprehend. . . . Furthermore, we think that in every branch of knowledge the wiser a man is, the more exact he is and the better able to teach the causes of things. Among the sciences too we call that one nearer to wisdom that is worth learning for its own sake and for the sake of knowing than the one that is desirable for the results to be got from it. A superior science also is nearer than one that is merely contributory. So too a wise man ought not to receive orders but to give them; nor should he obey another but the less wise should obey him. . . .

One who desires knowledge for its own sake will desire above all what is most genuinely knowledge and that is the knowledge of what is best to know. And the things best to know are first principles and causes. For through them and from them all other things may be known but not they through the things covered by them. Supreme then among the sciences and superior to all subordinate science is that which knows the end for which everything takes place, which is the good for each thing and, as a whole, the highest good for all nature. According then to everything we have said, the name of wisdom belongs to this same science; for it must be that which investigates first principles and causes, since the good as the end and aim of things is one of the causes.

That this is not a science for producing things is plain from the story of the earliest philosophers. For it was wonder that made men first start to philosophize and still makes them today, wondering originally about the problems close at hand and then little by little advancing to strain their minds over the great perplexities, such as the changes of the moon and sun, the stars and the origin of the universe. And a man who is puzzled and wondering sees himself as ignorant. . . . Then as men framed systems of philosophy to escape from their ignorance, it is clear they were pursuing knowledge in order to understand and not for any practical use to which they might put it. The facts themselves support our statement, for it was not until after almost everything necessary for life, comfort, and recreation had been provided that this kind of knowledge began to be sought. . . .

## III

Manifestly then we seek this knowledge for no utilitarian end but, even as we call a man free who lives for his own sake and not for another's, so we call this the only free science, for it alone exists for itself.

For this very reason mastery of this science may be justly regarded as beyond human power. . . . God only can enjoy this privilege and man ought by rights to try for just that knowledge that is suited to him. If, indeed, the poets were right and if God were by nature jealous, he would most probably be especially so on grounds of this kind and all men who excel in knowledge would be doomed to misfortune. But the Deity cannot be jealous and, as the proverb says, "The poets tell many a lie." . . .

The study of truth is partly hard and partly easy. A proof of this is the fact that no one man is able to grasp it adequately. Yet they do not all entirely fail. Each says something about the nature of the world, and, though individually he adds little or nothing to our understanding of it, still from the combination of all something considerable is accomplished. Hence, as truth seems to be like the door which, the proverb says, no one can fail to hit, in that respect our study of it is easy. But the fact that we can have some notion of it as a whole, but not of the particular part we want, shows it is difficult. Perhaps too the difficulty is of two kinds and its cause is not so much in the things themselves as in us. For as the eyes of bats are to the brightness of daylight, so is the reason in our soul to the things that by nature are the clearest of all. . . .

It is right that philosophy should be called the knowledge of truth. For the object of theoretical knowledge is truth, whereas of practical knowledge it is action. (Even if practical men do ask *how* a thing is as it is, they are not trying to understand eternal being but only something relative and immediate.) But we do not know truth without some knowledge of its causes. . . .

# Aristotle on Animals

From book IX, Chap. 1 of "History of Animals" trans. D'Arcy Wentworth Thompson from *The Oxford Translation of Aristotle,* ed. J. A. Smith and W. D. Ross, Vol. IV, 1910, by permission of the Clarendon Press, Oxford. Reprinted as pp. 637–640 in *The Basic Works of Aristotle,* ed. Richard McKeon, published by Random House, Inc.

There is enmity between such animals as dwell in the same localities or subsist on the same food. If the means of subsistence run short, creatures of like kind will fight together. Thus it is said that seals which inhabit one and the same district will fight, male with male, and female with female, until one combatant kills the other, or one is driven away by the other; and their young do even in like manner.

All creatures are at enmity with the carnivores, and the carnivores with all the rest, for they all subsist on living creatures. . . . One may go so far as to say that if there were no lack or stint of food, then those animals that are now afraid of man or are wild by nature would be tame and familiar with him, and in like manner with one another. This is shown by the way animals are treated in Egypt, for owing to the fact that food is constantly supplied to them the very fiercest creatures live peaceably together. The fact is they are tamed by kindness, and in some places crocodiles are tame to their priestly keeper from being fed by him. And elsewhere also the same phenomenon is to be observed.

The eagle and the snake are enemies, for the eagle lives on snakes; so are the ichneumon and the venom-spider, for the ichneumon prays upon the latter. In the case of birds, there is mutual enmity between the poecilis, the crested lark, the woodpecker and the chloreus, for they devour one another's eggs; so also between the crow and the owl; for, owing to the fact that the owl is dim-sighted by day, the crow at midday preys upon the owl's eggs, and the owl at night upon the crow's, each having the whip-hand of the other, turn and turn about, night and day. . . .

The snake is at war with the weasel and the pig; with the weasel when they are both at home, for they live on the same food; with the pig for preying on her kind. The merlin is at war with the fox; it strikes and claws it, and, as it has crooked talons, it kills the animal's young. The raven and the fox are good friends, for the raven is at enmity with the merlin; and so when the merlin assails the fox the raven comes and helps the animal. The vulture and the merlin are mutual enemies, as being both furnished with crooked talons. The vulture fights with the eagle, and so, by the way, does the swan; and the swan is often victorious: moreover, of all birds swans are most prone to the killing of one another. . . .

Elephants fight fiercely with one another, and stab one another with their tusks; of two combatants the beaten one gets completely cowed, and dreads the sound of his conqueror's voice. These animals differ from one another to an extraordinary extent in the way of courage. Indians employ these animals for war purposes, irrespective of sex; the females, however, are less in size and much inferior in point of spirit. An elephant by pushing with his big tusks can batter down a wall, and will butt with his forehead at a palm until he brings it down, when he stamps on it and lays it in orderly fashion on the ground. Men hunt the elephant in the following way: they mount tame elephants of approved spirit and proceed in quest of wild animals; when they come up with these they bid the tame brutes to beat the wild ones until they tire the latter completely. Hereupon the driver mounts a wild brute and guides him with the application of his metal prong; after this the creature soon becomes tame and obeys guidance. Now when the driver is on their back they are all tractable, but after he has dismounted, some are tame and others vicious; in the case of these latter, they tie their front-legs with ropes to keep them quiet. The animal is hunted whether young or full grown.

Thus we see that in the case of the creatures above mentioned their mutual friendship or enmity is due to the food they feed on and the life they lead.

# Hippocrates Investigates the Nature of Disease

Hippocrates (c. 460–c. 370 B.C.) was a Greek doctor, commonly considered the father of modern medicine. Hippocrates' great achievement lay in separating the treating of disease from superstitious practices of the past by demanding a scientific examination of the individual patient's condition. The Hippocratic Oath, still taken by doctors today, may not actually have been written by him but it certainly reflects his principles. From *The Greek Mind,* by Walter R. Agard. Copyright © 1957, by Walter R. Agard, by permission of Van Nostrand Reinhold Company.

## UNDERSTANDING DISEASE

The so-called "sacred disease" (epilepsy) has natural causes like other diseases. No disease is beyond being understood or incapable of being cured.

The material on which medicine works has always been right at hand, and methods have been worked out by which many important discoveries have been made. What is still undiscovered will be found out if those who study it are competent.

To understand disease we must study the general nature of mankind, individual differences, the disease itself, the treatments used, and the doctor who applies them. The more we know of such matters, the easier it will be to make a sound judgement. Climate and local peculiarities of weather must be considered; then the particular patient—his habits, occupation, and age; his manner of talking and keeping silent; his temperament; his sleep or inability to sleep; the time and type of his dreams; his gestures, his fears. Finally we must record during the course of the disease the movements of the bowels and the urine, the spitting and vomiting; we must follow every stage of the disease and note what occurs and the result in recovery or death. During its course we must observe carefully every detail so as to decide what direction the disease will take.

## A CASE HISTORY

Name: Philiscus. Residence: near the city wall. The first day he had an acute fever with sweating, went to bed, was distressed all night. Second day: worse, but took an enema and got some sleep. Third day: he seemed to be over his fever in the morning, but in the afternoon it came on again, higher than before; sweating, thirst, parched tongue, dark-colored urine. Had a bad night, sleepless and delirious. Fourth day: worse, urine still dark, but he felt more comfortable at night. Fifth day: slight nosebleed, granules in urine, small bowel movement after taking laxative. Bad night, delirium, extremities cold. Toward morning he got some sleep. Hereafter unable to speak. Heavy sweat, extremities turning grayish color. Sixth day: died at noon, after period of slow, painful breathing. His spleen was swollen. Disease marked by cold sweats. He felt worse every even-numbered day.

## THE HIPPOCRATIC OATH

I swear (by Apollo and the other divinities of healing) that according to my ability I will keep this oath: to regard the man who taught me the art of medicine as dear to me as my own parents; to follow that system of treatment which I believe will help my patients, and to refrain from anything that is harmful to them. I will give no deadly drug if I am asked to do so, nor will I recommend any such thing; I will not practice abortion. In purity and holiness I will practice the art of medicine. Whatever I see or hear which should not be divulged, I will keep secret. While I continue to keep this oath may I enjoy life and the practice of my profession, respected at all times by all men.



# Euclid and Archimedes Make Discoveries in Science

Euclid and Archimedes were Greeks who lived in the third century B.C. Euclid was a mathematician who incorporated the mathematical knowledge of his time into a book entitled *Elements,* which is still today used as a textbook in geometry by many people, even though some of its conclusions are no longer valid. Archimedes was an inventor, as well as a mathematician and physicist, who lived in Syracuse, a Greek city on the island of Sicily. From *The Greek Mind,* by Walter R. Agard. Copyright © 1957, by Walter R. Agard, by permission of Van Nostrand Reinhold Company. And from "The Principle of Archimedes" from Vitruvius, *On Architecture, IX,* 9–12, in Paul MacKendrick and Herbert M. Howe, editors, *Classics in Translation,* Volume I (Madison: The University of Wisconsin Press; © 1959 by the Regents of the University of Wisconsin), pp. 312–313.

## 1. EUCLID: AXIOMS

Equals of the same thing are equal to each other. If equals be added to equals, the wholes are equal. If equals be taken away from equals, the remainders are equal. If equals be added to unequals, the wholes are unequal. If equals be taken away from unequals, the remainders are unequal. Doubles of the same thing are equal to each other. Halves of the same thing are equal to each other. The whole is greater than the part. A proposition (Book I, 20)—Parallels to the same straight line are also parallel to each other. Let there be AB and CD, each parallel to EF. I say that AB is also parallel to CD. For let a straight line GHI intersect them. When GHI intersects the parallels AB and EF, the angle AGI is equal to the angle GHF. Again, when GHI intersects the parallels EF and CD, the angle GHF is equal to the angle GID. It has been shown that the angle AGI is equal to the angle GHF. Therefore the angle AGI is also equal to the angle GID, and they are interchangeable. Therefore AB is parallel to CD. (See illustration.) Therefore parallels to the same straight line are also parallel to each other. Which is precisely what had to be demonstrated.

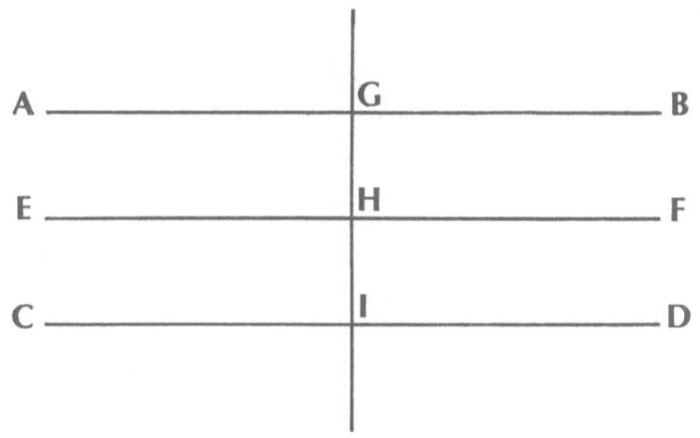


**Parallel Lines**

## 2. ARCHIMEDES TAKES A BATH

The discoveries of Archimedes were many and ingenious, in widely different fields, but of them all that which I am now going to describe seems to me best to display his unlimited cleverness.

Since the affairs of King Hiero of Syracuse had prospered and his power had been much increased, he decided to offer a golden crown in a certain temple in thanks to the immortal gods. He therefore let out a contract to a goldsmith, to whom he paid a fee for making the crown and enough beside for the exact weight of the gold that would be necessary. At the proper time the goldsmith presented a beautifully made crown to the king, having, to judge by the weight of the crown, used all the gold that had been issued to him. But a little later the king got wind of a story that the goldsmith had abstracted some of the gold and replaced it with an equal weight of silver. Hiero was furious at having been tricked, but he saw no way to prove the theft; he therefore asked Archimedes to think over his problem.

While Archimedes was considering the matter, he went one day to the city baths. There he went into a small pool (with an overflow pipe), and while in it he reflected that the submerged part of his body made its own volume of water overflow. Realization of this showed him the principle on which his whole problem hinged, and in his delight he leaped from the pool and ran home without bothering about his clothes, announcing in a loud voice that he had found what he was looking for. For as he hurried along he kept shouting in Greek, "I've got it! I've got it!" (Eureka! Eureka!)

The story goes on that after he had made this start he took a slab of silver and another of gold, each weighing the same as the crown. He then filled a large pot to the brim with water and dropped in the silver. Water equal in bulk to the silver ran over the edge of the pot; after removing the slab he measured the amount of water it took to refill the pot. Thus he found what weight of silver equaled that of a known bulk of water.

Next he dropped in his slab of gold, removed it, and measured the amount of water needed to replace the overflow; it was much less than had been the case with the silver—a difference corresponding to the smaller bulk of the gold, compared with the same weight of silver. Finally, he lowered in the crown, and found that more water ran over than had done for the pure gold, although their weights were the same. From the difference in overflows of the crown and the pure gold Archimedes calculated the amount of silver alloyed with the gold in the crown, and thus proved the guilt of the goldsmith.

Another highly scientific toy designed by Heron appears to the left. Hercules kneeling on a platform aims an arrow at a dragon coiled around a tree. When the plug is pulled up from the receptacle in the center, an attached cord and pully release the arrow which strikes the dragon that hisses as it is shot. The pipe running up into the tree below the dragon was a whistle that provided the hissing sound. The top half of the platform was filled with water and the lower half with air. When the plug was lifted it allowed the water to fill the lower section and forced the air up through the pipe which consequently whistled. Why didn't the ancients use their considerable scientific know-how in more productive ways?

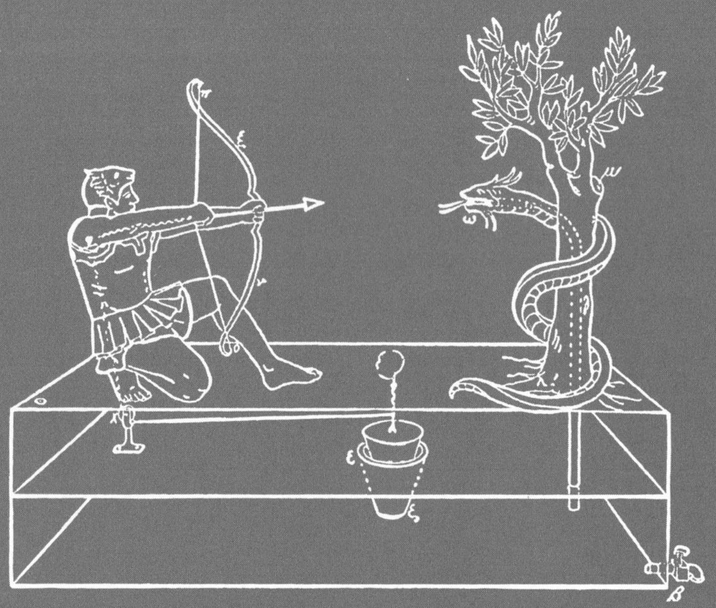

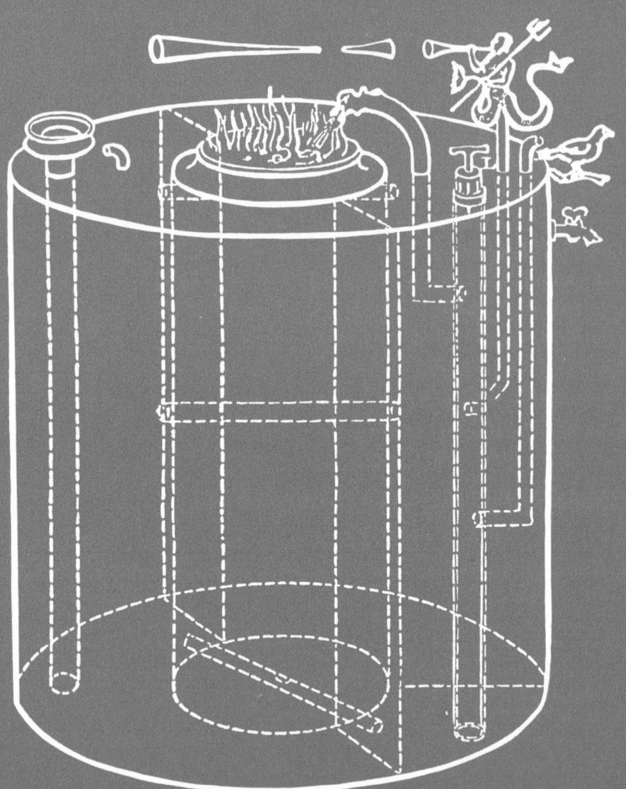

The Graeco-Roman world was not lacking in inventive individuals. Heron of Alexandria, whose life dates are uncertain but may go back as far as the second century B.C., left two works *Pneumatica* and *Automata* which provide a treasury of early inventiveness. Heron is credited with being the father of the steam engine, and his sketch for a steam boiler appears to the right. To illustrate the uses of steam power he included three figures on top of his design: a blackbird that sings, a sea god that blows a horn, and a serpent that blasts hot air into the fire. What explains the identification by the ancients of scientific apparatus with instruments of play and leisure?

# Ludwig Edelstein: Motives and Incentives for Science in Antiquity

Professor Ludwig Edelstein (1902–1965) was particularly interested in the history of medicine and in classical philosophy. In a chapter of a book concerned with scientific change he raised the question of why ancient science remained relatively impractical. Excerpts from "Motives and Incentives for Science in Antiquity" by Ludwig Edelstein, in *Scientific Change,* edited by Alistair Crombie, © Heinemann Educational Books Ltd. 1963, Basic Books, Inc., Publishers, New York.

## UNDERDEVELOPMENT OF GREEK SCIENCE

One cannot deny that applied science, as all ancient technology, did not advance as far as it could conceivably have done. During the thousand years of scientific studies in which the intellect on its "flight through the universe" revolutionized man's understanding of nature and achieved ever greater triumphs, the forms of daily existence changed relatively little, less perhaps than during the later Middle Ages, surely much less than in some of the decades since the middle of the nineteenth century. That the usefulness of science in Graeco-Roman times was comparatively unexploited, that it was, strictly speaking, no motive for developing scientific knowledge, is due I think mainly to three factors.

## LACK OF AN EXPERIMENTAL TRADITION

First, the "empirical" scientists, who considered speculation and theory of less importance, if of importance at all, and who on account of their prevalent concern with reality might have taken a special interest in applying their knowledge, were the ones to curtail research and thereby to curtail also the chances of mastering the phenomena. For in the Hellenistic theory of empiricism, the possibility of comprehending nature is severely narrowed down. Everything inaccessible to the senses is regarded as hidden from exploration and thus closed to scientific study. It was the empirical physician who denied that anatomy and physiology could become sciences and rendered useful for medical treatment. Also, reading of books—the treasured-up experience of the past—for him took precedence over making new experiments and accumulating more data. Extension of knowledge, the opening-up of new opportunities for applied science, was therefore left almost exclusively to the "theoretical" scientists—the "dogmatists" as they were derisively called by their opponents, and yet in fact the only ones to venture beyond the already known. But with them, of course, knowledge for the sake of knowledge was the prime motive and the prime concern.

## DOMINATION OF PHILOSOPHY

Second, one must not forget that ancient sciences have by their very nature so to say a slant towards the theoretical rather than the practical. Some, physics and psychology for instance, were really "philosophical" sciences. For they remained in the domain of the philosopher and were studied by him as part of his analysis of the physical world and of human nature. When the original unity of philosophy and all the sciences obtaining in the pre-Socratic period, dissolved, and independent, particular sciences were established—sciences pursued by specialists—they still kept in close touch with philosophy. Their first principles, their methodology rested on philosophical grounds. The issue between mechanism and teleology, the controversy about the respective values of empirical observation and theoretical reasoning were fought not with scientific but with philosophical arguments, and these discussions occupied a much larger part of scientific writing than they would in later science. Not that the scientist slavishly followed the dictates of a philosophic law-giver. Rather he took an active interest in philosophy, he became himself a philosopher. The title of Galen's essay "That the best physician is also a philosopher" epitomizes the prevailing attitude. On the other hand, there was a feeling that men of experience, as Aristotle says, are better in practical matters, better equipped to handle particulars, than is the scientist who knows the universals. Thus the improvement of the technical apparatus remained largely in the hands of artisans and craftsmen, who changed things slowly and cautiously in their traditional conservative manner.

## BOUNDARIES OF KNOWLEDGE

Last though not least, the relative neglect of the practical must I think be viewed against the background of the ancients' general attitude towards life, of which it seems characteristic that they acknowledged and respected boundaries set to their actions. They would, to be sure, aim at perfection in rational insight and in right conduct; they would fashion their cities or states in accordance with political ideals; they would above all civilize human existence so that it became truly human. They did not feel that it was their business to take the world over altogether. Men no more claimed than did their gods to be creators out of nothing, to act with a free will that imposes its law on things that have no nature of their own. Rather did they feel called upon to shape matter that was given and, here below at any rate, refractory to reason. The gods but mould, or to use a Platonic phrase, persuade the physical universe to accommodate itself to their wishes as far as possible. It does not stand otherwise with that universe which men build. Having accomplished what appeared possible and essential, the pagans were satisfied to use knowledge mostly for taking care of their daily wants which were modest, for defending their country when there was need, for adorning temple services . . . for increasing pleasure through play and amusement.

It is mainly for such reasons, I think, that ancient science remained relatively useless, that changes which in principle were within reach were actually not made. . . .

TOPIC 9

# THE GREEK WAY OF LIFE

The last two topics have presented a remarkable extension of the human mind. The conviction that the well-lived life should consist of a continuing search for truth required, however, a viable social organization that permitted the leisure time needed for contemplative activities. The Greeks maintained that their way of life, intellectual, esthetic, social, and political, differed from that of any of their contemporaries and from all peoples who had preceded them. The readings below examine this contention by focusing on the Greek institution of the *polis.* They consider two of the most vital city-states—Athens and Sparta—but are concerned with the weaknesses of the Greek system as well as its strengths.

**Reading 36**

## The Greek City-States

From Crane Brinton, John B. Christopher, Robert Lee Wolff, *Civilization in the West,* © 1964. Reprinted by permission of Prentice-Hall, Inc., Englewood Cliffs, New Jersey.

About four thousand years ago, the Greeks descended into the peninsula at the southeastern extremity of Europe that still bears their name, moved out into islands of the Aegean Sea, and soon across it to the western shores of Asia Minor. They later planted many colonies westward along the Mediterranean and northeastward along the Black Sea. But their homeland was the Aegean world, the natural bridge between the ancient Near Eastern civilizations, from which the Greeks would borrow, and the Western civilization still to come, which they would do so much to shape.

Blue seas, a many-harbored shore-line, mountains, and islands characterized these Aegean lands, which were, however, often too barren or too dry for farming. In the warm, generally mild climate men could live outdoors for much of the year and grow olives and grapes. Besides oil and wine their farms

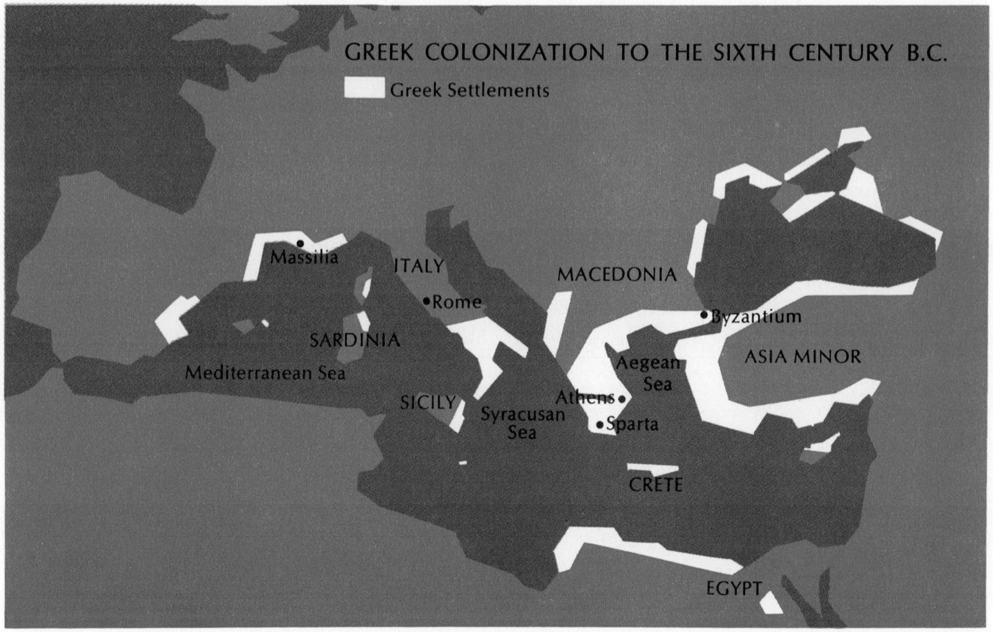

This view of the Athenian Acropolis illustrates its protective relationship to the city below.

produced some barley and other grain but relatively little else. The rugged coastline invited the Greek to sail. No part of the Aegean Sea was more than fifty miles from land, and vessels could journey hundreds of miles without losing sight of the shore. Travel by ship was swifter, cheaper and more comfortable than an up-hill and down-dale journey overland. Very soon, the Greeks began an active maritime trade, exchanging their olive oil and wine for the wheat and metal and slaves they needed. . . .

## CITY-STATES AND COLONIZATION

Partly fostered by the physical features of the land that conspired to isolate small regions from each other, the individual Greek town (*polis*) with its surrounding countryside tended to raise itself into a state of its own. Usually small in area and, by modern standards, in population, these city-states multiplied until they numbered well over a hundred. Often the town itself grew up around some natural fortress: a rock that was easy to defend, the "high city," or Acropolis, as at Athens. Between about 800 and 600 B.C., the city-states of Greece developed their own political institutions at home, and founded many colonies abroad; it was an age of colonization. From about 600 to 400 B.C., the city-state civilization as a whole reached its height. After 400 B.C. political decline set in, and in the late fourth century the rising empire of Macedonia under King Philip and his son Alexander the Great conquered and absorbed the city-states. Two hundred years after *that,* Rome took over from Macedonia.

The age of colonization saw the planting of Greek settlements northeastward from the Aegean into the straits between Europe and Asia and along the coasts of the Black Sea, and as far west in the Mediterranean as the coasts of what we now call France and Spain. Byzantium (later named Constantinople and, today, Istanbul) and Massilia (Marseilles) are two of the colonies founded in these years. So thoroughly did the Greeks colonize most of Sicily and the toe and heel of Italy that the Romans later called the area *Magna Graecia* (Great Greece).

It was not the Greek people acting as a nation that embarked on this program of colonization but the individual Greek city-states. Soon the "daughter" cities became politically independent, retaining only a sentimental tie to the original founding "mothers." No doubt Greek land-hunger, over-population, and constant internecine warfare stimulated the emigration. Even in the remotest colony, the population remembered its Greek origin and maintained its traditional feeling of superiority to those not speaking Greek, the "barbarians" who made noises like "ba-ba-ba" when they talked.

With colonization went commerce, which created its own problems. Greece proper needed grain, which was grown overseas, and so concentrated on oil and wine for export, a policy that gave large landowners a great advantage and depressed the small farmer. The shipowner and merchant, on the one hand, and the ordinary sailor and dockworker, on the other, complicated the earlier simple social structure. All sought to share in the political power that the landowner had hitherto monopolized.

The introduction of metallic coinage in the seventh century accelerated the enrichment of the few. The landowning nobility seems to have lost both its old-fashioned paternal generosity and its skill at government and war. The seventh century saw political upheaval in one *polis* after another, as individual dictators, called "tyrants," seized power by force in some of the states. A "tyrant" was not necessarily tyrannical: Often he would put through a vigorous reform program that struck at the abuses to which the discontented objected. Some city-states kept "tyranny" permanently; others turned to it temporarily as a transition to a more popular form of government; and still others never had tyrants.

## SPARTA

In Sparta, one of the most celebrated city-states, only the upper 5 to 10 per cent of the population were citizens; descendants of the Dorian conquerors, they were the rulers and soldiers. The overwhelming majority of the people belong to the *helot* class, farm laborers bound to the soil, or servants of the ruling group, descendants of the original population. In between was a free class called *perioikoi* (dwellers around), descendants of the pre-Dorian residents of neighboring areas, who lived in the villages under Spartan control, and had personal freedom but no right to participate in politics or to intermarry with the Spartans. Naturally the ruling Spartans lived in constant fear of revolution, and indeed barely managed to put down a helot uprising in the late seventh century. Spartan citizens were thus "a garrison permanently stationed among a hostile population."

The constitution, which the Spartans attributed to a divinely-inspired law-giver, Lycurgus, provided that there should be two kings, descendants of two rival Dorian families, but that real political power rested with five *ephors* (overseers) elected annually by an assembly of all Spartan citizens over 30, excluding, of course, all women, helots, and *perioikoi*. In addition, there was a kind of council representing the more powerful families.

War dominated Spartan thinking. The citizens led lives of self-denial and lived under military discipline from early childhood, when a boy was taken from his parents and taught reading and music and running and fighting. Weak-looking babies were abandoned to die. So that there might be healthy children, girls too were given strenuous training. Adult males lived in the barracks until they were 30, and dined in the mess-hall until they were 60. It was a harsh, bleak life, "Spartan" in its merits and in its defects. The army was excellent and the citizens patriotic and able to bear misfortune, but the city contributed almost nothing to the Greek economy or to Greek literature and art.

The Spartans kept their secret agents planted among the helots to report subversive talk. They discouraged visitors from outside. Yet their own limited numbers (only 4000 citizens at their height in the 5th century B.C.) prevented their expansion beyond a certain point, and their policies forbade recruitment of new citizens. A barracks-state, defensive and conservative, living in constant fear, Sparta suggests modern totalitarianism.

## ATHENS

Athens, however, the *polis* that had come to dominate most of the surrounding province of Attica, gradually developed a political system that did not depend on fear, that rested on a wide freedom, and that became, as its famous fifth-century leader Pericles once called it, the "school" for the rest of Greece. Until about 600 B.C. the ancient landed families supplied the nine *archons* who governed Athens, and dominated its chief judicial and policy-making body, the Council of the Areopagus (the hill of Ares, god of war). The dominant class twice tried in a cautious way to allay the discontent of the debt-ridden farmers. In 621 B.C. they published the first written law-code, called after its compiler, Draco, and celebrated for the harshness of its penalties; and in the 590's, the archon Solon cancelled the peasants' debts and forbade the enslavement of free debtors. Solon opened most important political offices to rich landowners not of ancient family. He may also have tried to balance the power of the Areopagus by increasing that of a more popular body, the Assembly, and by setting up popular courts of justice.

Members of his own class found Solon too radical, and the unprivileged found him too timid. Like many other Greek city-states, Athens passed into the hands of a tyrant: Peisistratus seized power about 560 B.C. He exiled the members of the aristocracy and divided their lands among the peasants. He forbade the unprofitable growing of grain, and commanded the farmers to specialize in olives and grapes, so that they might export oil and wine. He exploited the local silver mines, and first issued the famous Athenian coins stamped with an owl, the bird of the city's protectress, Athena, goddess of wisdom. He patronized the arts. Yet, though Peisistratus greatly strengthened the economy, he and his sons, who succeeded him, seem not to have reformed the antique machinery of government. It was Cleisthenes, a new tyrant, appearing in 508 after a brief interlude of renewed aristocratic rule, who was the true founder of Athenian democracy.

Cleisthenes abolished the traditional four tribes or clans, each with its firm territorial base along the coast, on the plain, or in the hills; he thereby shattered the old loyalties that had often outweighed the individual's loyalty to Athens as such. Cleisthenes' ten new tribes had no territorial base, for each was composed of numerous *demes,* or local units, scattered here and there in the territory of Athens. About 200 in all, the demes had the right of local self-government; we may think of them as wards within the city-state. Moreover, the demes chose, by lot from among their own members, the Council of 500, which carried on the government of the state, and in practice exercised the authority of the Assembly, which Cleisthenes enlarged to include all male citizens, and which was therefore too big to handle everyday affairs. He also allowed noncitizens to acquire citizenship in the new demes, and so to participate in the workings of the central government. In the decades which followed, the old aristocratic institutions, the archons and Aeropagus, became chiefly ornamental.

During the fifth century, when Athenian democracy was at its height, the Assembly met in the open air at least ten times a year. It voted all the laws, and it alone could exile a discredited leader—usually for a ten-year period—by the famous process of *ostracism,* so-called from the *ostraka* or pieces of tile used as ballots. Though open to abuse, ostracism served as a check on threats of renewed dictatorship by a tyrant. Executive power rested with the Council of 500, which was divided into ten 50-member committees, each governing for a tenth of a year, transacting routine business and referring more important questions to the full Council. Since nobody could sit on the Council of 500 for more than two years, each citizen had a good chance of serving on it once during his lifetime.

Athens, then, was governed by amateurs, not by professional bureaucrats. There was one exception: the Assembly elected every year the ten generals in command of the army and navy; since a general could run for office as often as he liked, he might serve for years and exert great influence over political as well as military affairs. The great Pericles was elected general every year for 30 years, and enjoyed an authority comparable with that of President of the United States, Secretary of State and Secretary of Defense all rolled into one. But he was no tyrant: He had to be re-elected annually.

In judicial procedure, the Athenians carried their democratic practices further than anywhere else. The demes elected 6000 men each year to act as judges (who also performed the function of jury), and those needed to hear cases were selected by lot. Athens believed there was safety in numbers: even a minor case had to be heard by 201 judges; and more important cases by 501, or even 1501, so that personal prejudice would not affect the outcome.

Athenian democracy was direct, not representative democracy. The Athenians, except in the case of the generals, did not believe that any citizen was better qualified for office than any other; and they themselves did not really like their own habit of re-electing generals, feeling it to be a necessary but unfortunate hangover from the old aristocratic period. Pericles referred to men who shirked the responsibility of citizenship as "useless." The state furnished daily allowances and free meals to those who attended the Council and the courts, but not, of course, the Assembly of all citizens.

Only a fraction of the citizenry, however, attended the Assembly, and, since farmers no doubt hesitated to sacrifice a day's work to walk to Athens, the city-dwellers tended to dominate it. By no means all the male inhabitants were citizens: there were about as many noncitizens—*metics* (resident aliens) and slaves. Metics were often business men with foreign connections; after Pericles they could no longer be naturalized or own real estate. The Athenians bought or captured their slaves. Those who labored in the silver mines worked in chains and suffered severely; but a household slave often received good treatment as a virtual member of the family, and might later become free as a metic.

# H. D. F. Kitto: The Polis

H. D. F. Kitto (1897– ), a famous English classical scholar, sought to make clear to contemporary Westerners that the ancient Greeks themselves believed that they had found the best of all possible ways to live. The social and political heart of the Greek way of life was the "polis," a broad concept difficult to relate to modern society. From H. D. F. Kitto, *The Greeks* (London: Penguin Books Ltd, 1951), pp. 64-67, 73-74, 78-79.

"Polis" is the Greek word which we translate "city-state." It is a bad translation, because the normal polis was not much like a city, and was very much more than a state. But translation, like politics, is the art of the possible; since we have not got the thing which the Greeks called "the polis," we do not possess an equivalent word. From now on, we will avoid the misleading term "city-state," and use the Greek word instead. . . . We will first enquire how this political system arose, then we will try to reconstitute the word "polis" and recover its real meaning by watching it in action. It may be a long task, but all the time we shall be improving our acquaintance with the Greeks. Without a clear conception of what the polis was, and what it meant to the Greeks, it is quite impossible to understand properly Greek history, the Greek mind, or the Greek achievement. . . .

It is important to realize their size. The modern reader picks up a translation of Plato's *Republic* or Aristotle's *Politics;* he finds Plato ordaining that his ideal city shall have 5,000 citizens, and Aristotle that each citizen should be able to know all the others by sight; and he smiles, perhaps, at such philosophic fantasies. But Plato and Aristotle are not fantasts. Plato is imagining a polis on the normal Hellenic scale; indeed he implies that many existing Greek poleis are too small—for many had less than 5,000 citizens. Aristotle says, in his amusing way—Aristotle sometimes sounds very like a don—that a polis of ten citizens would be impossible, because it could not be self-sufficient, and that a polis of a hundred thousand would be absurd, because it could not govern itself properly. And we are not to think of these "citizens" as a "master-class" owning and dominating thousands of slaves. The ordinary Greek in these early centuries was a farmer, and if he owned a slave he was doing pretty well. Aristotle speaks of a hundred thousand citizens; if we allow each to have a wife and four children, and then add a liberal number of slaves and resident aliens, we shall arrive at something like a million—the population of Birmingham; and to Aristotle an independent "state" as populous as Birmingham is a lecture-room joke. Or we may turn from the philosophers to a practical man, Hippodamas, who laid out the Piraeus in the most up-to-date American style; he said that the ideal number of citizens was ten thousand, which would imply a total population of about 100,000.

In fact, only three poleis had more than 20,000 citizens—Syracuse and Acragas (Girgenti) in Sicily, and Athens. At the outbreak of the Peloponnesian War the population of Attica was probably about 350,000, half Athenian (men, women and children), about a tenth resident aliens, and the rest slaves. Sparta, or Lacedaemon, had a much smaller citizen-body, though it was larger in area. The Spartans had conquered and annexed Messenia, and possessed 3,200 square miles of territory. By Greek standards this was an enormous area: it would take a good walker two days to cross it. The important commercial city of Corinth had a territory of 330 square miles—about the size of Huntingdonshire. The island of Ceos, which is about as big as Bute, was divided into four poleis. It had therefore four armies, four governments, possibly four different calendars, and, it may be, four different currencies and systems of measures—though this is less likely. Mycenae was in historical times a shrunken relic of Agamemnon's capital, but still independent. She sent an army to help the Greek cause against Persia at the battle of Plataea; the army consisted of eighty men. Even by Greek standards this was small, but we do not hear that any jokes were made about an army sharing a cab.

To think on this scale is difficult for us, who regard a state of ten million as small, and are accustomed to states which, like the U.S.A. and the U.S.S.R., are so big that they have to be referred to by their initials; but when the adjustable reader has become accustomed to the scale, he will not commit the vulgar error of confusing size with significance. The modern writer is sometimes heard to speak with splendid scorn of "those petty Greek states, with their interminable quarrels." Quite so; Plataea, Sicyon, Aegina and the rest are petty, compared with modern states. The Earth itself is petty, compared with Jupiter—but then, the atmosphere of Jupiter is mainly ammonia, and that makes a difference. We do not like breathing ammonia—and the Greeks would not much have liked breathing the atmosphere of the vast modern state. They knew of one such, the Persian Empire—and thought it very suitable, for barbarians. Difference of scale, when it is great enough, amounts to difference of kind. . . .

We have now learned enough about the word polis to realize that there is no possible English rendering of such a common phrase as, "It is everyone's duty to help the polis." We cannot say "help the state," for that arouses no enthusiasm; it is "the state" that takes half our incomes from us. Not "the community," for with us "the community" is too big and too various to be grasped except theoretically. One's village, one's trade union, one's class, are entities that mean something to us at once, but "work for the community," though an admirable sentiment, is to most of us vague and flabby. In the years before the war, what did most parts of Great Britain know about the depressed areas? How much do bankers, miners and farmworkers understand each other? But the "polis" every Greek knew; there it was, complete, before his eyes. He could see the fields which gave it its sustenance—or did not, if the crops failed; he could see how agriculture, trade and industry dove-tailed into one another; he knew the frontiers, where they were strong and where weak; if any malcontents were planning a *coup,* it was difficult for them to conceal the fact. The entire life of the polis, and the relation between its parts, were much easier to grasp, because of the small scale of things. Therefore to say "It is everyone's duty to help the polis" was not to express a fine sentiment but to speak the plainest and most urgent common sense. Public affairs had an immediacy and a concreteness which they cannot possibly have for us.

One specific example will help. The Athenian democracy taxed the rich with as much disinterested enthusiasm as the British, but this could be done in a much more gracious way, simply because the State was so small and intimate. Among us, the payer of super-tax (presumably) pays much as the income-tax payer does: he writes his cheque and thinks, "There! *That's* gone down the drain!" In Athens, the man whose wealth exceeded a certain sum had, in a yearly rota, to perform certain "liturgies"—literally, "folk-works." He had to keep a warship in commission for one year (with the privilege of commanding it, if he chose), or finance the production of plays at the Festival, or equip a religious procession. It was a heavy burden, and no doubt unwelcome, but at lease some fun could be got out of it and some pride taken in it. There was satisfaction and honour to be gained from producing a trilogy worthily before one's fellow citizens. So, in countless other ways, the size of the polis made vivid and immediate, things which to us are only abstractions or wearisome duties. Naturally this cut both ways. For example, an incompetent or unlucky commander was the object not of a diffused and harmless popular indignation, but of direct accusation; he might be tried for his life before an Assembly, many of whose past members he had led to death. . . .

Aristotle made a remark which we most inadequately translate "Man is a political animal." What Aristotle really said is "Man is a creature who lives in a polis"; and what he goes on to demonstrate, in his *Politics,* is that the polis is the only framework within which man can fully realize his spiritual, moral and intellectual capacities.

Such are some of the implications of this word: we shall meet more later, for I have deliberately said little about its purely "political" side—to emphasize the fact that it is so much more than a form of political organization. The polis was a living community, based on kinship, real or assumed—a kind of extended family, turning as much as possible of life into family life, and of course having its family quarrels, which were more bitter because they were family quarrels.

This it is that explains not only the polis but also much of what the Greek made and thought, that he was essentially social. In the winning of his livelihood he was essentially individualist: in the filling of his life he was essentially "communist." Religion, art, games, the discussion of things—all these were needs of life that could be fully satisfied only through the polis—not, as with us, through voluntary associations of like-minded people, or through *entrepreneurs* appealing to individuals. (This partly explains the difference between Greek drama and the modern cinema.) Moreover, he wanted to play his own part in running the affairs of the community. When we realize how many of the necessary, interesting and exciting activities of life the Greek enjoyed through the polis, all of them in the open air, within sight of the same acropolis, with the same ring of mountains or of sea visibly enclosing the life of every member of the state—then it becomes possible to understand Greek history, to understand that in spite of the promptings of common sense the Greek could not bring himself to sacrifice the polis, with its vivid and comprehensive life, to a wider but less interesting unity. . . .

# Pericles Praises Athens as a Model Community

Pericles (c. 495–429 B.C.), the dominant political figure in Athens from 461 B.C. until his death, was a great patron of the arts and presided over the Golden Age of Athens. He also followed a policy of political and economic expansion and used other Greek cities (which had been formed into a league, to oppose Persia) for Athenian benefit. Pericles' policies are largely responsible for the outbreak of the bitter Peloponnesian War in 431 B.C. The losses of the first year of that war were commemorated in a famous oration in 430, which the Athenian statesman utilized to extoll the virtues of his native city. He died in the following year, a victim of the great plague which swept Athens. From *Funeral Oration of Pericles* in George Willis Botsford, *A Source-Book of Ancient History* (New York, 1912), pp. 206–209.

Our form of government does not enter into rivalry with the institutions of others. We do not copy our neighbors, but are an example to them. It is true that we are called a democracy, for the administration is in the hands of the many and not of the few. But while the law secures equal justice to all alike in their private disputes, the claim of excellence is also recognized; and when a citizen is in any way distinguished, he is preferred for the public service, not as a matter of privilege, but as a reward of merit. Neither is poverty a bar, but a man may benefit his country whatever be the obscurity of his condition. There is no exclusiveness in our public life, and in our private intercourse we are not suspicious of one another, nor angry with our neighbor if he does what he likes; we do not put on sour looks at him which, though harmless, are not pleasant. While we are thus unconstrained in our private intercourse, a spirit of reverence pervades our public acts; we are prevented from doing wrong by respect for authority and for the laws, having a special regard to those which are ordained for the protection of the injured as well as to those unwritten laws which bring upon the transgressor of them the reprobation of the general sentiment.

And we have not forgotten to provide for our weary spirits many relaxations from toil; we have regular games and sacrifices throughout the year; at home the style of our life is refined; and the delight which we daily feel in all these things helps to banish melancholy. Because of the greatness of our city the fruits of the earth flow in upon us; so that we enjoy the goods of other countries as freely as of our own. . . .

If then we prefer to meet danger with a light heart but without laborious training, and with a courage which is gained by habit and not enforced by law, are we not greatly the gainers? Since we do not anticipate the pain, although when the hour comes, we can be as brave as those who never allow themselves to rest; and thus too our city is equally admirable in peace and in war. For we are lovers of the beautiful, yet simple in our tastes, and we cultivate the mind without loss of manliness. Wealth we employ, not for talk and ostentation, but when there is a real use for it. To avow poverty with us is no disgrace: the true disgrace is in doing nothing to avoid it. An Athenian does not neglect the state because he takes care of his own household; and even those of us who are engaged in business have a very fair idea of politics. We alone regard a man who takes no interest in public affairs, not as a harmless, but as a useless character; and if few of us are originators, we are all sound judges of a policy. The great impediment to action is, in our opinion, not discussion, but the want of that knowledge which is gained by discussion preparatory to action. For we have a peculiar power of thinking before we act and of acting too, whereas other men are courageous from ignorance but hesitate upon reflection. And they are surely to be esteemed the bravest spirits who, having the clearest sense both of the pains and pleasures of life, do not on that account shrink from danger. In doing good, again, we are unlike others; we make our friends by conferring, not by receiving favors. Now he who confers a favor is the firmer friend, because he would fain by kindness keep alive the memory of an obligation; but the recipient is colder in his feelings, because he knows that in requiting another's generosity he will not be winning gratitude, but only paying a debt. We alone do good to our neighbors not upon a calculation of interest but in the confidence of freedom and in a frank and fearless spirit.

To sum up, I say that Athens is the school of Hellas, and that the individual Athenian in his own person seems to have the power of adapting himself to the most varied forms of action with the utmost versatility and grace. This is no passing and idle word, but truth and fact; and the assertion is verified by the position to which these qualities have raised the state. For in the hour of trial Athens alone among her contemporaries is superior to the report of her. No enemy who comes against her is indignant at the reverses which he sustains at the hand of such a city; no subject complains that his masters are unworthy of him. And we shall assuredly not be without witnesses; there are mighty monuments of our power which will make us the wonder of this and of succeeding ages; we shall not need the praises of Homer or of any other panegyrist whose poetry may please for the moment, although his representation of the facts will not bear the light of day. For we have compelled every land and every sea to open a path for our valor, and have everywhere planted eternal memorials of our friendship and of our enmity.

# Greek Slavery

The fact that Greek civilization was based on the institution of human slavery has disturbed most champions of the Greek way of life. Professor T. G. Tucker in the first section of this reading examines why the freedom-loving Athenians should find nothing wrong in having slaves. Oxford University Professor Antony Andrewes in the second section looks at the place of slavery in the Greek way of life. (I) From T. G. Tucker, *Life in Ancient Athens* (London: Macmillan, 1927), pp. 72–74. (II) From *The Greeks,* by Antony Andrewes.  This is published in Canada by Hutchinson Publishing Group Ltd.

## I. T. G. TUCKER: WHY DID THE GREEKS TOLERATE SLAVERY?

It is a strange puzzle that a people so ardent for personal freedom as were the Athenians, a people who valued above all things liberty and freedom of speech, should nevertheless see nothing wrong or unreasonable in slavery. That they did not, is beyond all doubt. Never were there minds more free from cant and pretense than the minds of the Athenians, and particularly those of Socrates, Plato and Aristotle. Yet not one of these declares against the institution. If they had unequivocally thought it wrong, they would unequivocally have said so. On the contrary, they thought it part of the natural order of things. All ancient people had slaves. The Athenians had possessed them from time immemorial. This might perhaps be no logical defence. But Aristotle remarks, in his matter-of-fact way, that some men were born to be masters and others to obey, and that we should see this clearly enough, if nature had made the difference of their mental powers as visible as the difference of their bodies. And here steps in that everlasting disturber of true reason—national conceit. There is nothing more obtuse than national or racial pride. What the Gentiles were to the Jews, that the outer world was to the Greeks; its people were *barbaroi,* fit enough to have their own distinctions at home, but, as soon as they came in contact with the Greeks, only fit to be tools and instruments for the superior Greek intellect to work with. "A slave," says Aristotle, "is a live implement" of the higher intelligence. . . .

Slaves came into Greece from various sources. Some, but comparatively few, were born of the slaves already existing. In the second place they were obtained by conquest in war. Once on a time it was taken as a matter of course that the conquered people were simply the property of the conqueror. In our period this was still the theory, but in practice it did not properly apply within the charmed circle of the Greek world itself. When a Greek state conquered a Greek state, it was only in a fit of extreme exasperation that the vanquished were absolutely enslaved. It was becoming abhorrent to Greek sentiment for Greeks to enslave Greeks. Ransom was accepted instead. When no ransom was forthcoming, however, the inevitable must take place, and Aristotle's doctrine of superior and inferior intelligences must go to the wall. Many Athenian slaves were therefore Greeks. When the war was not with Greeks, but with other peoples, there were no scruples at all about enslaving. The captives were simply sold to the highest bidder. Most of the slaves, however, were bought from dealers, who picked them up or kidnapped them in Asia Minor, Syria, and the East or in the Northern Balkans and round the Black Sea. . . .

## II. ANTONY ANDREWES: HOW ESSENTIAL WAS SLAVERY TO THE GREEKS?

We must now turn to slavery, never an entirely comfortable subject for the admirer of ancient Greek civilisation. Respectable scholars have allowed themselves, a little helplessly, to feel that Greek slavery must somehow have been a more humane institution than it looks; and if that form of distortion is now less prevalent, confusion is still caused by controversy about the character of negro slavery in America, and by Marxist concentration on slavery as the basis of ancient civilisation. In the broadest terms, slavery was basic to Greek civilisation in the sense that, to abolish it and substitute free labour, if it had occurred to anyone to try this one, would have dislocated the whole society and done away with the leisure of the upper classes of Athens and Sparta. The ordinary Athenian had a very deeply ingrained feeling that it was impossible for a free man to work directly for another as his master. While it is true that free men, as well as slaves, engaged in most forms of trade and industry, the withdrawal of slaves from these tasks would have entailed a most uncomfortable reorganisation of labour and property. But the question whether it could have been otherwise must not too much preoccupy us. The first question is how the institution actually worked.

Estimates of the total slave population of Attica vary greatly, but perhaps the most probable is some 80,000—100,000 at the time of Athens' greatest prosperity and highest citizen population—an average of about one and a half slaves to every adult citizen, or about one in four of the entire population. A large part of the slave labour went in domestic service. This was not merely a matter of the gentlemen keeping a proper state: it goes down to much lower levels, as in the case of the comparatively small man who appears as hero in so many of Aristophanes' comedies and constantly calls on his slave or slaves. A single family tilling a small plot of land would normally own slaves; in this typical small unit they would turn their hands to all tasks, domestic or agricultural, working alongside their masters, and the domestic tasks would include baking and weaving. (There is a large difference here from the plantation system in the southern states of America, where most of the slaves were owned by a small minority of the white population, while the remaining whites, less comfortably, managed their own concerns.) Off the land, a free man would hope to have a slave to help him in his trade, or even to take it over. A much quoted and certainly significant instance is the cripple for whom Lysias wrote a speech, defending before the Council his right to a minute dole from the state: the cripple remarks in passing that he has difficulty in practising his trade himself, and has not yet been able to buy a slave to take it over. On public buildings, again, citizens and metics and their slaves worked side by side in small groups.

In work like this, though all were doing the same kind of job for the same wage, the slave's wage went to his master, whose profit consisted in the difference between this wage and the slave's keep. . . . Another regular way of making an income was to leave the slave to work on his own at his trade, responsible for his own keep but paying in a regular sum to his master. This was especially prevalent at Athens, where "living apart" became a technical term for slaves working on these conditions; and some of them prospered conspicuously. Another variant was the hiring out of slaves to a free employer, who again saw to the slave's keep himself and paid an agreed sum to the owner for the slave's labour. This might be done on a very small scale: indeed, we meet the case of a man setting out on a longish journey to collect the hiring-money of a single slave. But a rich man might invest heavily, as the Athenian general, Nicias, did in the late fifth century, who was said to own a thousand such slaves.

Figures like these might seem to take us back to the possibility of large contractors employing a large labour force. There is one area, the silver mines in Laurium, where slave labour was used extensively, though probably not any very large single gang in a single mine. These mines were heavily exploited from the early fifth century down to the later stages of the Peloponnesian War, and again, after a period of less activity, in the fourth century. Like other mines in the Greek world, they were somehow state property, though it is not clear whether the surface land was in private ownership or belonged to the state. The democracy . . . let them out on fairly short leases to individual operators, most of them on quite a small scale, who used their own or a neighbour's surface installations and took what profit their luck gave them, after paying their royalty to the state. . . .

The question is often raised, why the ancient world never developed a more efficient technology—why, for instance, the steam-engine devised by Hero of Alexandria never became anything more than an interesting toy—and whether slavery had anything to do with this apparent retardation. The same question can be asked in varying measure about any civilisation previous to our Industrial Revolution, and that is enough to show that slavery was not the only cause at work. Slavery was, no doubt, part of the cause, in that cheap imported slaves were the main means by which the upper classes of Athens had raised themselves above the necessity of devoting most of their time to subsistence agriculture, and so had gained the leisure whose fruits we still admire. Their mind and taste thus satisfactorily engaged, they were less tempted to look again at the foundation of this leisure and ask whether it might be improved. . . .

No easy generalisation is possible about the relations between slave and master in the

Greek world, since the slave's view, as usual, is not known. In the close quarters of Greek domestic life, no distance could be preserved like that which English middle-class families used to keep between themselves and their servants—and the Greek was unlikely to refrain from talking under any circumstances. The closer relation of nurse and child, tutor and pupil, easily ripened into affection, nor need we doubt stories of the loyal slave saving his master's life on the battlefield, and the like. But at its best the relationship was bound to have unhappy elements, as that when a slave was punished it was with physical blows of the kind that a free man had the right to resent. . . .

The domestic slave who was on good terms with his master stood some chance of liberation, and the slave "living apart" and practising his trade might hope to earn enough to buy his release. Manumission was by no means uncommon, though the practice and the formalities differed a good deal from place to place. The master often retained the right to certain services for a fixed period, or for his own lifetime. Some of those "living apart" prospered conspicuously, giving rise to disgruntled oligarchic comment that slaves in the streets of Athens might be better dressed than free men. An outstanding instance was the early fourth-century banker, Pasion, who achieved not only his freedom but Athenian citizenship. But the domestic slave with a bad master was in poor case, with little hope of redress, and the prospects were altogether bleaker for those who were hired out to the mines and other work—and we are not given even a distorted reflection of their feelings. But, after the Spartans had fortified their post outside Athens in 413, Thucydides tells us that over 20,000 slaves deserted to the enemy, the bulk of them "craftsmen" (the word would cover any sort of skilled labour and need not be confined to the miners of Laurium, though no doubt many of the deserters were from there). We do not know what promises the invaders had held out to them, still less what eventually became of them, but the suggestion is clear that the life of even a skilled slave was one which he was ready to fly from on a very uncertain prospect. . . .

In the generation of Socrates, when everything was questioned, the justice of slavery was questioned also Isolated voices were heard to say that all men were equally men, and that slavery was against nature. The defence of Aristotle, that some were naturally slaves, incapable of full human reason and needing the will of a master to complete their own, rings hollow to us, quite apart from the accident that "naturally free" Greeks might be enslaved by the chances of war. But this was a world in which slavery, in some form or other, was universal, and no nation could remember a time when it had not been so. It is not surprising that there was no clamour for emancipation. It has been convincingly argued that the margin over bare subsistence in Greece was so small that the surplus which was needed to give leisure to the minority could only be achieved with artificially cheap labour. If that is right, there was not much alternative for Greece. For Athens, it had come, by the opening of the sixth century, to a choice between reducing citizens to slavery or extensive import of chattel slaves from abroad. Only a greatly improved technology, something like an industrial revolution, could effectively have altered these conditions.

# Socrates Looks Down upon Manual Labor

Xenophon (c.430–c.355 B.C.) was an Athenian soldier and historian who had been a disciple of Socrates. In his book, the *Economist,* which is written in dialogue form, he used his master to express the views of a cultivated Greek toward manual labor. From *The Economist of Xenophon,* ed. and trans. A. D. Wedderburn and W. G. Collingwood (London, 1876), pp. 22–23.

But why need you show me them all, Socrates? said Critobulus: for neither do we want to get men who are fair hands at all the arts alike, nor can one man become an adept in all. No; those arts which are thought the noblest, and which would be most suitable for me to engage in, are what I would have you show me, together with those who practise them; and in this, as far as you can, let me have the advantage of your teaching.

Well said, Critobulus! exclaimed Socrates; for not only are the arts which we call mechanical generally held in bad repute, but States also have a very low opinion of them, —and with justice. For they are injurious to the bodily health of workmen and overseers, in that they compel them to be seated and indoors, and in some cases also all the day before a fire. And when the body grows effeminate, the mind also becomes weaker and weaker. And the mechanical arts, as they are called, will not let men unite with them care for friends and State, so that men engaged in them must ever appear to be both bad friends and poor defenders of their country. And there are States, but more particularly such as are most famous in war, in which not a single citizen is allowed to engage in mechanical arts. . . .

# Sebastian de Grazia: The Greek Idea of Leisure

This commentary on the part played by leisure in Greek life is taken from the introductory chapter of a general study on the nature of leisure in modern industrial society. From Sebastian de Grazia, *Of Time, Work and Leisure,* Twentieth Century Fund, New York, 1962.

Aristotle in the *Politics* says a curious thing. The Spartans remained secure as long as they were at war; they collapsed as soon as they acquired an empire. They did not know how to use the leisure that peace brought.

In Aristotle the words "peace" and "leisure" come together often. They repeat his thesis that wars are fought to have peace, and peace is needed for leisure. Sparta trained its citizens for war. It designed its laws principally with war in mind. Leisure and peace were used to prepare for war. The Spartans made another mistake. A well-ordered state manages to secure leisure or freedom from the necessity of labor. Now the Spartans did obtain leisure, but in a wrong way. They wrung it from a system of serfdom. What leisure could there be when Helots lay in ambush waiting for a chance at their masters? The moral is plain. Sparta had not discovered the best mode of governing for a life of leisure.

One more charge against Sparta: the men by their military life were educated to discipline, which at least tided them along in times of peace and leisure, but the women were given absolutely no education in self-control. With the men absent for long periods, the women abandoned themselves to license and luxury. Legislators like Lycurgus tried to bring them, as well as the men, within range of the law, but they opposed him and he had to abandon the attempt. The results brought misfortune to Sparta—the growth of luxuriousness, avarice, maldistribution of property, shortage of warriors, and a female population that in war caused more confusion than the enemy.

These then are the charges. A citizenry unprepared for leisure will degenerate in prosperous times. Women, too, are liable to fall on evil ways. Furthermore, leisure based on serfdom is so insecure as to be no leisure at all.

The Greeks took the question of leisure seriously. Their ideas are worth attention for they not only examined many of the problems confronting us today but asked questions we have not dared to ask ourselves. Who today would say that a nation could collapse because it didn't know how to use its leisure? Who today so predicts the downfall of the United States or of China? But Aristotle not only lived in but was preceded by a century interested in leisure. His Greece, his Athens, pulled back the curtains to offer the West an ideal. . . .

Contemplation in the Greek sense is so close to leisure that in describing one and the other repetition is inevitable. Plato first developed the idea in the *Republic.* His models were the Ionian philosophers, whose absorption in knowledge for its own sake inspired Plato's academy and Aristotle's Peripatetic school. Thales of Miletus was one of these philosophers. Plato has told us his story, of how gazing at the stars he fell into a well, and of the little maid who, standing by, laughed at the sport. The idea of contemplation itself in those days seemed to be groping for its true meaning. Our word comes from the Latin but the Latin is a translation from the Greek *theorein,* to behold, to look upon. *Theōria* was also the word for theory, and was used in the phrase "the theoretical life," which in Latin became "the contemplative life," both of which have a fast friendship with the life of leisure.

Contemplation for Plato and Aristotle was the best way of truth-finding. They prized it above all other activities. It was the only activity in which they could picture the gods. The contemplator looks upon the world and man with the calm eye of one who has no design on them. In one sense he feels himself to be close to all nature. He has not the aggressive detachment or unfeeling isolation that comes from scrutinizing men and objects with a will to exploiting them. In another sense he is truly detached because he looks on none of them with intent to manipulate or control or change, on neither man nor beast nor nature. Whoever does look on the world with design, who wishes to subdue or seduce others, to gain money, to win fame, cannot see much beyond the slice he is cutting. His aim on the world puts lenses before his eyes. He doesn't even know his sight is distorted.

When Plato describes the ideal education of those who should be the rulers of the country, he has them passing every test and trial with honors, so that finally they can "lift up the eye of the soul and fix it upon that which gives light to all things." In contemplation they can see the essence of the good and take it for their pattern. They can see things and how they fit together so well because, as rulers, they are free of all necessity to take an oblique view. They do not have the compulsion of those who must make money or win honors. Take the mechanic or anyone who has to work for his living. He is the one who must watch his job and tools and his boss, who must have relief from toil and calculate how best to sell his wares or his services, and who gets caught up in a futile flurry of activities that lead nowhere. How can he see true and carry truth forward to the outer reaches of the cosmos circled by man's eye?

Contemplation, like leisure, or being itself leisure, brings felicity. Aristotle in the *Ethics* contends that happiness extends only so far as contemplation does. Those who can contemplate are the most truly happy. Indeed, happiness must be some form of contemplation. The activity of God, surpassing all others in blessedness, must be contemplative. Those men who most cultivate the mind are most akin to the gods and therefore dearest to them. The man in contemplation is a free man. He needs nothing. Therefore nothing determines or distorts his thought. He does whatever he loves to do, and what he does is done for its own sake. . . .

We begin to grasp how leisure is related to politics. If a man is at leisure only when he is free, the good state must exist to give him leisure. What he does in this leisure can be equated with what we today call the good life. Surprisingly few political philosophers have seen the connection between freedom and leisure as ends of the state. The prevalence of work in modern times, as we shall see, partly explains the oversight. Aristotle took it for granted: the life of leisure was the only life fit for a Greek.

TOPIC 10

# FROM HELLENIC TO HELLENISTIC AGE

The Golden Age of Greece covered only a few generations. The exhausting Peloponnesian War hastened the end of the fragile political balance among the Greek city-states, and they eventually fell subject to the semi-Greek forces of Macedon to the north. It would be excessive, however, to speak of an overall decline in the Greek way of life. The fourth century was after all that of Plato and Aristotle and many gifted artists and playwrights. Alexander the Great spread Greek ideas and institutions throughout the Eastern empires that he conquered. Yet the theories of Plato and Aristotle were sharply critical of the actual conditions of their time. And Alexander's conquests infused the Greek world with massive doses of oriental culture. This, then, was a period of readjustment to changing conditions. The readings pursue the reasons for such readjustment, the direction change took and its implications for the further shaping of Western civilization.

**Reading 42**

## Greek History from Persian Invasions to Macedonian Conquests

This selection was contributed by the editors.

In the fifth century B.C., the very loose organization of Greek city-states was put to a test by the sprawling Persian Empire, which had gradually extended its control over those Greek cities along the coast of Asia Minor. Amazed by the encouragement to revolt incited by the Greek cities in Europe, the Persians determined to subjugate them as well. Three major invasions were attempted. Athenians defeated the more numerous Persians at Marathon (490 B.C.), just 20 miles from home, in the first round of an eleven year struggle. In the second round, Persians routed Greeks under Spartan leadership at Thermopylae (480 B.C.). Athens was sacked and the Persians prepared to invade the Peloponnesus. But the naval forces of Athens won a victory over the Persian armada in the Bay of Salamis. The third round was also marked by battles fought on both land and sea. Persian land forces were defeated at Platea (479 B.C.), and the Persian navy was decisively defeated off Cape Mycale by the fleets of Athens and the Ionian city-states that had risen in rebellion against a shaken Persia.

The War against the Persians had demonstrated the need for the city-states to coordinate their policies and strategy in order to overcome the threat of invasion. It had also demonstrated the rivalry between city-states, and the ability of an outside power to play off states and factions against one another.

Athens tried at the end of the Persian Wars to establish a league for the defense of the Aegean islands, an effort that would require construction of a fleet for their common protection. Sparta and some of her neighbors refused to join the league, and Athens, under the leadership of Pericles, actually used the Delian League which it dominated to create an Athenian Empire. Tribute money was exacted from the members, whose governments became the pawns of Athens. Their continued membership in the League was compelled ultimately by Athens' superior force. Sparta and Corinth, threatened by Athens, launched an attack; the war of the Athenian Empire against Sparta and her allies, known as the Peloponnesian War, lasted twenty-six years (431–405 B.C.). Sparta was able to capitalize on the resentment against Athens' economic domination, her errors in strategy, and her increasingly cruel tactics as the war proceeded. Of considerable help, too, was the interest of Persia in weakening Athens by helping Sparta. The result was a vanquished Athens and the end of the Golden Age of Greece.

The Greek city-state system lasted for less than a century after the end of the Peloponnesian War. The Persians were content to see the Greek cities remain weak and divided, but by the middle of the fourth century a new power—the border Greek kingdom of Macedonia—arose in the north and by 338 B.C. had conquered the whole of Greece. For Philip of Macedon, however, the final goal was not

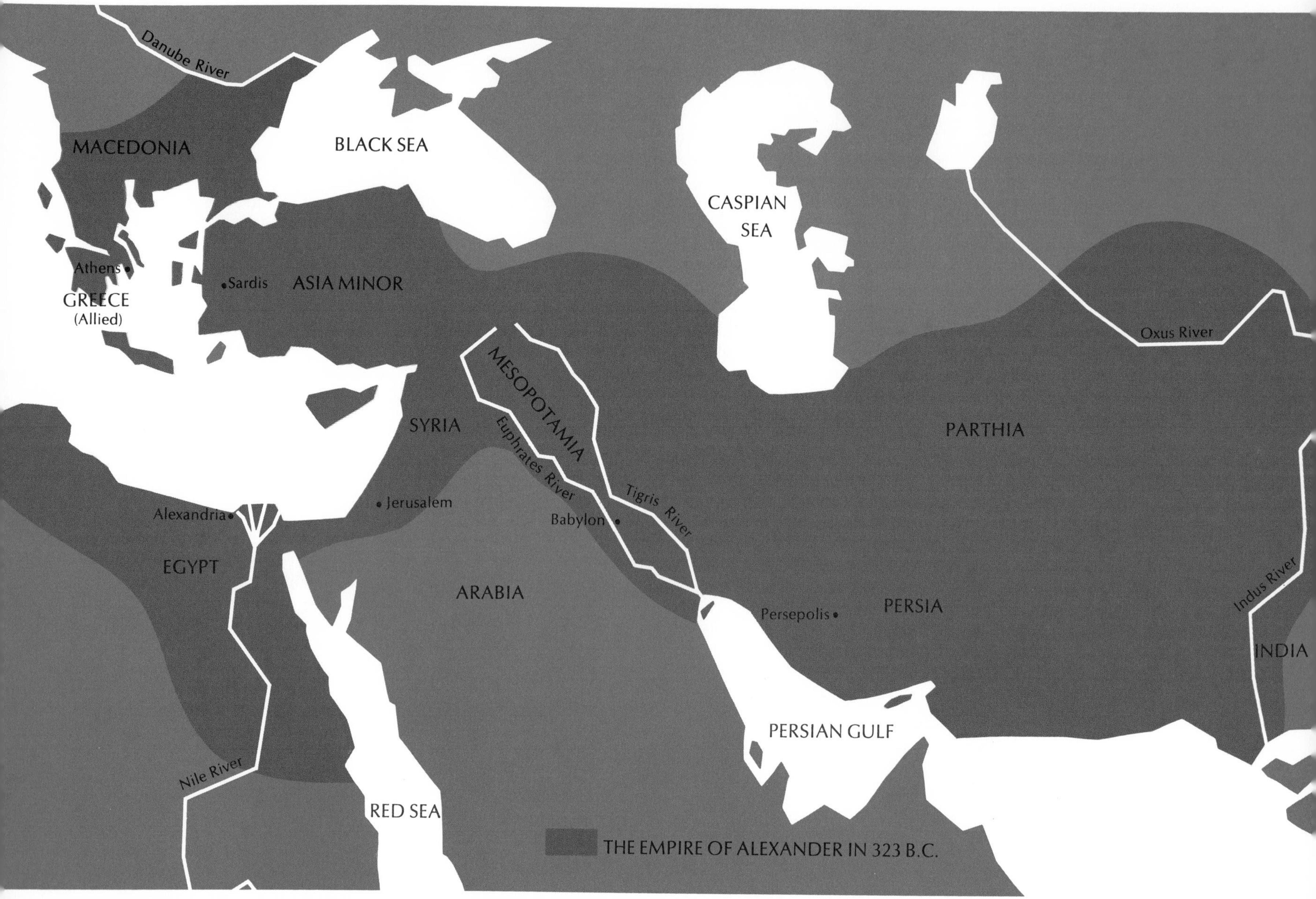
Danube River
MACEDONIA
BLACK SEA
CASPIAN SEA
Athens
GREECE
(Allied)
Sardis
ASIA MINOR
Oxus River
MESOPOTAMIA
SYRIA
Euphrates River
PARTHIA
Tigris River
Jerusalem
Alexandria
Babylon
EGYPT
ARABIA
Persepolis
PERSIA
Indus River
INDIA
PERSIAN GULF
Nile River
RED SEA
THE EMPIRE OF ALEXANDER IN 323 B.C.

a united Greece but the conquest of Asia. His son Alexander, known in history as "the Great" (336–323 B.C.), made the vision of an empire straddling Europe and Asia a reality. Alexander is an intriguing figure. Only twenty years old when he became king, he spent the twelve years of his reign (he died at thirty-two of a sudden fever in Babylon) in a vast and improbable military campaign during which the Greeks penetrated deeply into Africa and Asia (reaching the western and northern bounds of India) and destroyed the mighty Persian Empire.

The conquests of Alexander carried Greek institutions and colonists into the heartland of the old civilization of the Near East. Alexander had wanted to merge Greeks and Persians into one world community. Thus he encouraged intermarriage between Greeks and Asiatics, himself wedding a Persian princess. He founded a score of new Greek cities on the Nile and in the Fertile Crescent, settled by colonists from Greece and Macedonia, and, where he could, introduced Greek ideas to his new Oriental subjects. After Alexander's death the grand empire was divided among his generals, but the intermixing of East and West continued. The Greek language (in somewhat altered form) became the common tongue of the upper classes; Greek law and concepts of philosophy were accepted in the East. Similarly Asian and Egyptian ideas and institutions spread westward. The eastern Mediterranean became the center of flourishing commercial life. The centuries of fusion after Alexander's conquests when Greek and Eastern civilizations worked on one another are known collectively as the Hellenistic Age.

# M. I. Finley: The Decline of Sparta and Athens

English historian M. I. Finley suggests that the economic and political problems of Greece were too critical to permit more than a brief flourishing of the Greek way of life. From *The Ancient Greeks* by M. I. Finley. 

Spartan discipline and Spartan military prowess—the Spartans were a professional army in a world of citizen militias and mercenary bands—elevated Sparta into a major power, far beyond what her size would otherwise have warranted. Her first and only unwavering concern was peace at home in the Peloponnese. This she never fully achieved, but she came near enough through the instrumentality of the Peloponnesian League. The League gave Sparta military assistance, and it was this help, together with armies from among the *perioikoi* [secondary citizens], which built her strength, in numerical terms, to major proportions. In the sixth century Sparta became beyond question the greatest Greek military force on land, and her allies provided adequate naval support too, until that arm was surpassed by the creation of the all-powerful Athenian fleet.

Yet the fact remains that, from the Persian Wars on, Spartan history is one of decline, despite her coalition victory (aided by Persian gold) over Athens in 404. Her xenophobic society was marked by a steadily decreasing population, for she stubbornly refused to recruit new citizens even when the need for manpower became desperate, preferring to arm freed helots, all sorts of social outcasts and even mercenaries. The Peloponnesian War put unbearable pressure not only on manpower but also on leadership: continuous campaigning by numbers of armies had not been provided for in the system, and some of the new commanders, most notably Lysander, who achieved the final victory, revealed no virtues other than ruthless military competence tied to ugly personal ambition. Lack of vision and mental inflexibility, whether in politics or social matters, proved most ruinous in times of success. Even Sparta's famed egalitarianism turned out to be incomplete and finally unworkable. Kings and commanders quarrelled frequently, among themselves or with the ephors, and the suspicion seems justified that the disagreements were not merely over tactics or policy. Abroad Spartans were quickly corrupted and unmanageable. The property system broke down, though we do not quite know how: an increasing number of Spartans lost their land allotments, held by them from the state and worked for them by helots, and with their land they automatically lost their status as full Spartiates. Others accumulated wealth, though that could be done only illegally. Herodotus suggests the widespread accessibility of Spartans to bribery as early as the beginning of the fifth century, with their kings commanding the highest price.

The Sparta which won the Peloponnesian War proved to be far more hollow than any contemporary could reasonably have guessed. . . . In 371 came the defeat by Thebes. . . . Thereafter, though Sparta still played a role in Greek politics, it was as a ghost of past glory. In a real crisis—as Philip of Macedon saw—she was only a minor state, like hundreds of others, no longer a serious force in the real world. And in the third century, finally and ironically, she virtually blew up in one of the most virulent civil wars in all Greek history. But the myth of Sparta was nevertheless strong and tenacious. The brilliance of Athens must not blot out the fact that there were Greeks (and men in all later ages too) for whom Sparta was the ideal. She was the model of the closed society, admired by those who rejected an open society with its factional politics, its acceptance of the *demos* [people] as a political force, its frequent "lack of discipline," its recognition of the dignity and claims of the individual.

After the battle of Chaeronea in 338, Philip II of Macedon was effectively the master of Greece (excluding the Sicilian and other western Greeks). He then summoned all the states to a congress in Corinth, where a League of the Hellenes was founded, with the king as head and commander-in-chief. . . . The success of Philip, repeated by his son Alexander, illustrated once again, and for the last time, the rule that the political difficulties which were rooted in the fragmentation of Hellas were susceptible only to an imposed solution, whether by a more powerful Greek state or by a powerful outsider. No one, not even the proponents of pan-Hellenic peace and coalition, suggested political integration of the city-states into larger units, for example. And no one was able to suggest, even hypothetically, how to overcome the poverty of natural resources and the low level of technology, except by moving out against Persia. Whenever in Greek history economic difficulties became critical, and that meant agrarian crisis, they were solved either by revolutionary means or by looking abroad, whether by emigration to new lands, as in the long colonization period, or by one or another form of pressure on other Greeks. Now, in the fourth century, the areas open to expansion abroad were severely restricted, and the relative weakness of the once great states gave much scope for intra-Hellenic warfare almost without end. Not even the sanctuaries were immune: in 356 the Phocians seized Delphi and used its treasure to hire a mercenary force of 10,000 and become for a fleeeting moment the greatest military power in all Greece.

The available evidence suggests that in the period 399-375 there were never less than 25,000 Greek mercenaries in active service somewhere, and that later the figure rose to 50,000. The significance of these numbers is underscored by matching them against the low population figures as a whole, and by noticing how widely the mercenaries ranged, how indifferent they were to "national" considerations in their search for employment. The century opened with the most famous of all Greek mercenary armies, the "Ten Thousand" of Xenophon's *Anabasis* who marched east on behalf of the younger brother of the Persian king in his unsuccessful attempt to seize the throne. In 343 we find another 10,000 Greeks—1000 from Thebes, 3000 from Argos, and 6000 from Asia Minor—in the army with which the Persians recaptured Egypt for their empire. . . .

All this movement, . . . marked a failing of the community, and therefore of the *polis*. The more the *polis* had to hire its armed forces; the more citizens it could no longer satisfy economically, and that meant above all with land, so that they went elsewhere in order to live; the more it failed to maintain some sort of equilibrium between the few and the many; the more the cities were populated by outsiders, whether free migrants from abroad or emancipated slaves (who can be called metaphorically free migrants from within)—the less meaningful, the less real was the community. "Decline" is a tricky and dangerous word to use in this context: it has biological overtones which are inappropriate, and it evokes a continuous downhill movement in all aspects of civilization which is demonstrably false. Yet there is no escaping the evidence: the fourth century was the time when the Greek *polis* declined, unevenly, with bursts of recovery and heroic moments of struggle to save itself, to become, after Alexander, a sham *polis* in which the preservation of many external forms of *polis* life could not conceal that henceforth the Greeks lived, in Clemenceau's words, "in the sweet peace of decadence, accepting all sorts of servitude as they came.". . .

Even fourth-century Athens was not free from signs of the general decline. Contemporary political commentators themselves made much of the fact that whereas right through the fifth century political leaders were, and were expected to be, military leaders at the same time, so that among the ten generals were regularly found the outstanding political figures (elected to the office because of their political importance, not the other way round), in the fourth century the two sides of public activity, the civil and the military, were separated. The generals were now professional soldiers, most of them quite outside politics or political influence, who often served foreign powers as mercenary commanders as well as serving their own *polis*. There are a number of reasons for the shift, among which the inadequate finances of the state rank high, but, whatever the explanation, the break was a bad thing for the *polis,* a cleavage in the responsibility of the members to their community which weakened the sense of community without producing visibly better generalship. In the navy the signs took a different form. A heavy share of the costs still fell on the richest 1200 men and the navy continued to perform well, but there was more evasion of responsibility, more need than before to compel the contributions and to pursue the defaulters at law. The crews themselves were often conscripted; voluntary enlistment could no longer provide the necessary complements. No doubt that was primarily because the treasury was too depleted to provide regular pay for long periods, just as the unwillingness of some to contribute their allotted share of the expenses resulted from an unsatisfactory system of distributing the burden, rather than from lack of patriotism. Wherever the responsibility lay, however, the result was again a partial breakdown in the *polis.*

There is no need to exaggerate: Athens nearly carried it off, and the end came because Macedon, or at least Alexander, was simply too powerful. But Macedon did exist, and so did Persia and Carthage, and later Rome. The *polis* was developed in such a world, not in a vacuum or in Cloud-Cuckoo-Land, and it grew on poor Greek soil. Was it really a viable form of political organization? Were its decline and disappearance the result of factors which could have been remedied, or of an accident—the power of Macedon—or of inherent structural weaknesses? These questions have exercised philosophers and historians ever since the late fifth century (and it is noteworthy how the problem was being posed long before the *polis* could be thought of as on its way out in any literal sense). Plato wished to rescue it by placing all authority in the hands of morally perfect philosophers. Others blame the *demos* and their misleaders, the demagogues, for every ill. Still others, especially in the past century or so, insist on the stupid failure to unite in a national state. For all their disparity, these solutions all have one thing in common: they all propose to rescue the *polis* by destroying it, by replacing it, in its root sense of a community which is at the same time a self-governing state, by something else. The *polis,* one concludes, was a brilliant conception, but one which required so rare a combination of material and institutional circumstances that it could never be realized; that it could be approximated only for a very brief period of time; that it had a past, a fleeting present, and no future. In that fleeting moment its members succeeded in capturing and recording, as man has not often done in his history, the greatness of which the human mind and spirit are capable.

# Aristotle Considers the Forms of Government

From Aristotle, *Politics* in G. W. Botsford, *A Source Book of Ancient History* (New York, 1912) pp. 100–101.

We have next to consider how many forms of government there are, and what they are; and in the first place what are the true forms; for what they are determines the perversions of them, as will at once be apparent. . . . The government which is the supreme authority in states must be in the hands of one or of a few or of many. The true forms of government therefore are those in which the one, or the few, or the many govern with a view to the common interest; but governments which rule with a view to the private interest, whether of the one, or of the few, or of the many, are perversions. For citizens, if they are truly citizens, ought to participate in the advantages of a state. We call that [form of government in which one rules] kingship or royalty; that in which more than one but not many rule, aristocracy ("the rule of the best"); and it is so called either because the rulers are the best men or because they have at heart the best interests of the state and of the citizens. But when the citizens at large administer the state for the common interest, the government is called by the generic name—[a constitutional government]. And there is a reason for this use of language. One man or a few may excel in virtue, but . . . there are many kinds [of virtue] and as the number increases it becomes more difficult for them to attain perfection in every kind, though they may in military virtue, for this is found in the masses. Hence, in a constitutional government the fighting men have the supreme power, and those who possess arms are the citizens.

Of the above-mentioned forms, the perversions are as follows:—of royalty, tyranny; of aristocracy, oligarchy; of constitutional government, democracy. For tyranny is a kind of monarchy which has in view the interest of the monarch only; oligarchy has in view the interest of the wealthy; democracy [the interest] of the needy; none of them the common good of all.

The first governments were kingships; probably for this reason, because of old, when cities were small, men of eminent virtue were few. They were made kings because they were benefactors, and benefits can only be bestowed by good men. But when many persons equal in merit arose, no longer enduring the pre-eminence of one, they desired to have a commonwealth, and set up a constitution. The ruling class soon deteriorated and enriched themselves out of the public treasury; riches became the path to honor, and so oligarchies naturally grew up. These passed into tyrannies and tyrannies into democracies; for love of gain in the ruling classes was always tending to diminish their number, and so to strengthen the masses, who in the end set upon their masters and established democracries. Since cities have increased in size, no other form of government appears to be any longer possible.

# Plutarch Marvels at the Achievements of Alexander

Plutarch (c. 46–120 A.D.) was a Greek essayist and biographer in the days of the Roman Empire. His biographies of famous Greeks and Romans provide one of the best existing records of the lives and characters of ancient leaders. His birthplace, Chaeronea, was the site of Philip of Macedon's decisive battle in 338 B.C. over the Greek city-states, a battle as Plutarch wrote, "fatal to Greek liberty." Do not let the many foreign names in this selection detract from what Plutarch is saying. The Hyrcanians, Arachosians, and so forth, are non-Greeks conquered and Hellenized (influenced by Greek culture) under Alexander. Reprinted by permission of the publishers and the Loeb Classical Library, from Plutarch, *Moralia,* trans. F. C. Babbitt (Cambridge, Mass: Harvard University Press, 1936), IV, pp. 393–405. Somewhat simplified by the editors.

If you examine the results of Alexander's instruction, you will see that he educated the Hyrcanians to respect the marriage bond, and taught the Arachosians to till the soil, and persuaded the Sogdians to support their parents, not to kill them, and the Persians to revere their mothers and not to take them in wedlock. O wondrous power of Philosophic Instruction, that brought the Indians to worship Greek gods, and the Scythians to bury their dead, not to devour them! . . . When Alexander was civilizing Asia, Homer was commonly read, and the children of the Persians, of the Susianians, and of the Gedrosians learned to chant the tragedies of Sophocles and Euripides. . . . Through Alexander, Bactria and the Caucasus learned to revere the gods of the Greeks. Plato wrote a book on the One Ideal Constitution, but because of its forbidding character he could not persuade anyone to adopt it; Alexander established more than seventy cities among savage tribes, and sowed all Asia with Grecian [judges], and thus overcame its uncivilized and brutish manner of living. Although few of us read Plato's *Laws,* yet hundreds of thousands have made use of Alexander's laws, and continue to use them. Those who were vanquished by Alexander are happier than those who escaped his hand; for these had no one to put an end to the wretchedness of their existence, while the victor compelled those others to lead a happy life. . . .

For Alexander did not follow Aristotle's advice to treat the Greeks as if he were their leader, and other peoples as if he were their master; to have regard for the Greeks as for friends and kindred, but to conduct himself toward other peoples as though they were plants or animals; for to do so would have been to encumber his leadership with numerous battles and banishments and festering seditions. [Since] he believed that he came as a heaven-sent governor to all, and as a mediator for the whole world, those whom he could not persuade to unite with him, he conquered by force of arms, and he brought together into one body all men everywhere, uniting and mixing in one great loving-cup, as it were, men's lives, their characters, their marriages, their very habits of life. He bade them all consider [the whole inhabited earth] as their fatherland, [his camp] as their stronghold and protection, [all good men] as [related] to them, and [only the wicked] as foreigners. . . . They should not distinguish between Greek and foreigner by Grecian cloak . . . or [Persian] jacket, but the distinguishing mark of the Greek should be seen in virtue, and that of the foreigner in iniquity; clothing and food, marriage and manner of life they should regard as common to all, being blended into one by ties of blood and children. . . .

I would gladly have been a witness of that fair and holy marriage-rite, when he brought together in one golden-canopied tent an hundred Persian brides and an hundred Macedonian and Greek bridegrooms, united at a common hearth and board. He himself, crowned with garlands, was the first to raise the marriage hymn as though he were singing a song of truest friendship over the union of the two greatest and most mighty peoples; for he, [bridegroom] of one maid, . . . and at the same time [escort] of all the brides, . . . united them in the bonds of wedlock as a father and sponsor. Indeed at this sight I should have cried out for joy, "O dullard Xerxes, stupid fool that spent so much fruitless toil to bridge the Hellespont! [King Xerxes directed the Persian invasion of Greece in 480 B.C.] This is the way that wise kings join Asia with Europe; it is not by beams nor rafts, nor by lifeless and unfeeling bonds, but by the ties of lawful love and chaste nuptials and mutual joy in children that they join the nations together."

Considering carefully this order of affairs, Alexander did not favour the Median raiment, but preferred the Persian, for it was much more simple than the Median. Since he deprecated the unusual and theatrical varieties of foreign adornment, such as the tiara and full-sleeved jacket and trousers, he wore a composite dress adapted from both Persian and Macedonian fashion, as Eratosthenes has recorded. As a philospher what he wore was a matter of indifference, but as sovereign of both nations and benevolent king he strove to acquire the goodwill of the conquered by showing respect for their apparel, so that they might continue constant in loving the Macedonians as rulers, and might not feel hate toward them as enemies. . . . Alexander desired to render all upon earth subject to one law of reason and one form of government and to reveal all men as one people, and to this purpose he made himself conform. If the deity that sent down Alexander's soul into this world of ours had not recalled his quickly [Alexander was 32 at the time of his sudden death], one law would govern all mankind, and they all would look toward one rule of justice as though toward a common source of light. . . .

# Hellenistic Civilization

Reprinted *From Western Civilizations, Their History and Their Cultures,* Seventh Edition by Edward McNall Burns. By permission of W. W. Norton & Company, Inc.  pp. 187–190, 192–197, 202–203.

## I

### A New Stage in World History

The death of Alexander the Great in 323 B.C. constituted a watershed in the development of world history. Hellenic civilization as it had existed in its prime now came to an end. Of course, the old institutions and ways of life did not suddenly disappear, but Alexander's career had cut so deeply into the old order that it was inconceivable that it could be restored intact. The fusion of cultures and intermingling of peoples resulting from Alexander's conquests accomplished the overthrow of many of the ideals of the Greeks in their Golden Age of the fifth and fourth centuries. Gradually a new pattern of civilization emerged, based upon a mixture of Greek and Oriental elements. To this new civilization, which lasted until about the beginning of the Christian era, the name Hellenistic is the one most commonly applied.

Though the break between the Hellenic and Hellenistic eras was as sharp as that between any two other civilizations, it would be a mistake to deny all continuity. The language of the new cultured classes was predominantly Greek, and even the hordes of people whose heritage was non-Greek considered it desirable to have some Hellenic culture. Hellenic achievements in science provided a foundation for the great scientific revolution of the Hellenistic Age. Greek emphasis upon logic was likewise carried over into Hellenistic philosophy, though the objectives of the latter were in many cases quite different. In the spheres of the political, social, and economic the resemblances were few indeed. The classical ideal of democracy was now superseded by despotism perhaps as rigorous as any that Egypt or Persia had ever produced. The Greek city-state survived in some parts of Greece itself, but elsewhere it was replaced by the big monarchy, and in the minds of some leaders by notions of a world state. The Hellenic devotion to simplicity and the golden mean gave way to extravagance in the arts and to a love of luxury and riotous excess. Golden Age intensity of living was superseded by a craving for novelty and breadth of experience. In the economic realm the Athenian system of small-scale production was supplanted largely by the growth of big business and vigorous competition for profits. In view of these changes it seems valid to conclude that the Hellenistic Age was sufficiently distinct from the Golden Age of Greece to justify its being considered the era of a new civilization.

### Political and Social History

When Alexander died in 323 B.C, he left no legitimate heir to succeed him. His nearest male relative was a feeble-minded half brother. Tradition relates that when his

friends requested him on his deathbed to designate a successor, he replied vaguely, "To the best man." After his death his highest-ranking generals proceeded to divide the empire among them. Some of the younger commanders contested this arrangement, and a series of wars followed which culminated in the decisive battle of Ipsus in 301 B.C. The result of this battle was a new division among the victors. . . . Finally, between 146 and 30 B.C. nearly all of the Hellenistic territory passed under Roman rule.

The dominant form of government in the Hellenistic Age was the despotism of kings who represented themselves as at least semi-divine. Alexander himself was recognized as a son of God in Egypt and was worshipped as a god in Greece. His most powerful successors, the Seleucid kings in western Asia and the Ptolemies in Egypt, made systematic attempts to deify themselves. A Seleucid monarch, Antiochus IV, adopted the title "Epiphanes" or "God Manifest." The later members of the dynasty of the Ptolemies signed their decrees "Theos" (God) and revived the practice of sister marriage which had been followed by the Pharaohs as a means of preserving the divine blood of the royal family from contamination. Only in the kingdom of Macedonia was despotism tem-

Hellenistic artistic extravagance becomes obvious when this bas-relief on the second-century B.C. Pergamon altar is compared with a frieze from the classic fifth-century B.C. Parthenon.

pered by a modicum of respect for the liberties of the citizens. . . .

According to the available evidence, the Hellenistic Age, during the first two centuries at least, was a period of prosperity. Although serious crises frequently followed the collapse of speculative booms, they appear to have been of short duration. But the prosperity that existed seems to have been limited chiefly to the rulers, the upper classes, and the merchants. It certainly did not extend to the peasants or even to the workers in the towns. The daily wages of both skilled and unskilled workers in Athens in the third century had dropped to less than half of what they had been in the Age of Pericles. The cost of living, on the other hand, had risen considerably. To make matters worse, unemployment in the large cities was so serious a problem that the government had to provide free grain for many of the inhabitants. Slavery declined in the Hellenistic world, partly because of the influence of the Stoic philosophy, but mainly for the reason that wages were now so low that it was cheaper to hire a free laborer than to purchase and maintain a slave.

An interesting result of social and economic conditions in the Hellenistic Age was the growth of metropolitan cities. Despite the fact that a majority of the people still lived in the country, there was an increasing tendency for men to become dissatisfied with the dullness of rural living and to flock into the cities, where life, if not easier, was at least more exciting. But the chief reasons are to be found in the expansion of industry and commerce, in the enlargement of governmental functions, and in the desire of former independent farmers to escape the hardships of serfdom. Cities multiplied and grew in the Hellenistic empires almost as rapidly as in ninteenth- and twentieth-century America. Antioch in Syria quadrupled its population during a single century. Seleucia on the Tigris grew from nothing to a metropolis of several hundred thousand in less than two centuries. The largest and most famous of all the Hellenistic cities was Alexandria in Egypt, with over 500,000 inhabitants and possibly as many as 1,000,000. No other city in ancient times, not even Rome, surpassed it in size or in magnificence. Its streets were well paved and laid out in regular order. It had splendid public buildings and parks, a museum, and a library of 750,000 volumes. It was the most brilliant center of Hellenistic cultural achievement, especially in the field of scientific research. The masses of its people, however, were a disorganized mob without any share in the brilliant and luxurious life around them, although it was paid for in part out of the fruits of their labor.

II

## Hellenistic Philosophy

Hellenistic philosophy exhibited two trends that ran almost parallel throughout the civilization. The major trend, exemplified by Stoicism and Epicureanism, showed a fundamental regard for reason as the key to the solution of man's problems. This trend was a manifestation of Greek influence, though philosophy and science, as combined in Aristotle, had now come to a parting of the ways. The minor trend, exemplified by the Skeptics, Cynics, and various Oriental cults, tended to reject reason, to deny the possibility of attaining truth, and in some cases to turn toward mysticism and a reliance upon faith. Despite the differences in their teachings, the philosophers of the Hellenistic Age were generally agreed upon one thing: the necessity of finding some way of salvation for man from the hardships and evils of his existence.

Epicureanism and Stoicism both originated about 300 B.C. The founders were, respectively, Epicurus (342–270) and Zeno (fl. after 300), who were residents of Athens; the former was born on the island of Samos, and the latter was a native of Cyprus, probably of Phoenician descent. Epicureanism and Stoicism had several features in common. Both were individualistic, concerned not with the welfare of society primarily, but with the good of the individual. Both were materialistic, denying categorically the existence of any spiritual substances; even divine beings and the soul were declared to be formed of matter. In Stoicism and Epicureanism alike there were definite elements of universalism, since both implied that men are the same the world over and recognized no distinctions between Greeks and "barbarians." . . .

But in many ways the two systems were quite different. Zeno and his principal disciples taught that the cosmos is an ordered whole in which all contradictions are resolved for ultimate good. Evil is, therefore, relative; the particular misfortunes which befall human beings are but necessary incidents to the final perfection of the universe. Everything that happens is rigidly determined in accordance with rational purpose. Man is not master of his fate; his destiny is a link in an unbroken chain. He is free only in the sense that he can accept his fate or rebel against it. But whether he accepts or rebels, he cannot overcome it. The supreme duty of man is to submit to the order of the universe in the knowledge that that order is good; in other words, to resign himself as graciously as possible to his fate. Through such an act of resignation he will attain to the highest happiness, which consists in tranquillity of mind. The individual who is most truly happy is therefore the man who by the assertion of his rational nature has accomplished a perfect adjustment of his life to the cosmic purpose and has purged his soul of all bitterness and whining protest against evil turns of fortune. . . .

The ethical philosophy of the Epicureans was based upon the doctrine that the highest good for man is pleasure. But they did not include all forms of indulgence in the category of genuine pleasure. The so-called pleasures of the debauched man should be avoided, since every excess of carnality must be balanced by its portion of pain. On the other hand, a moderate satisfaction of bodily appetites is permissible and may be regarded as a good in itself. Better than this is mental pleasure, sober contemplation of the reasons for the choice of some things and the avoidance of others, and mature reflection upon satisfactions previously enjoyed. The highest of all pleasures, however, consists in serenity of soul, in the complete absence of both mental and physical pain. This end can be best achieved through the elimination of fear, especially fear of the supernatural, since that is the sovereign source of mental pain. Man must recognize from the study of philosophy that the soul is material and therefore cannot survive the body, that the universe operates of itself, and that the gods do not intervene in human affairs. The gods live remote from the world and are too intent upon their own happiness to bother about what takes place on earth. Since they do not reward or punish men either in this life or in a life to come, there is no reason why they should be feared. The Epicureans thus came by a different route to the same general conclusion as the Stoics—the supreme good is tranquillity of mind.

The ethics of the Epicureans as well as their political theory rested squarely upon a utilitarian basis. In contrast with the Stoics, they did not insist upon virtue as an end in itself but taught that the only reason why man should be good is to increase his own happiness. In like manner, they denied that there is any such thing as absolute justice; laws and institutions are just only in so far as they contribute to the welfare of the individual. Certain rules have been found necessary in every complex society for the maintenance of security and order. Men obey these rules solely because it is to their advantage to do so. . . . The wise man will recognize that he cannot eradicate the evils in the world no matter how strenuous and intelligent his efforts; he will therefore withdraw to "cultivate his garden," study philosophy, and enjoy the fellowship of a few congenial friends.

A more radically defeatist philosophy was that propounded by the Skeptics. . . . The chief source of inspiration of the Skeptics was the Sophist teaching that all knowledge is derived from sense perception and therefore must be limited and relative. From this they deduced the conclusion that we cannot prove anything. Since the impressions of our senses deceive us, no truth can be certain. All we can say is that things *appear* to be such and such; we do not know what they really *are*. We have no definite knowledge of the supernatural, of the meaning of life, or even of right and wrong. It follows that the sensible course to pursue is suspension of judgment; this alone can lead to happiness. If man will abandon the fruitless quest for absolute truth and cease worrying about good and evil, he will attain that equanimity of mind which is the highest satisfaction that life affords. . . . The Skeptics were even less concerned than the Epicureans with political and social problems. Their ideal was the typically Hellenistic one of escape for the individual from a world he could neither understand nor reform.

The nonrational trend in Hellenistic thought reached its farthest extreme in the philosophies of Philo Judaeus and the Neo-Pythagoreans in the last century B.C. and the first century A.D. The proponents of the two systems were in general agreement as to their basic teachings, especially in their predominantly religious viewpoint. They believed in a transcendent God so far removed from the world as to be utterly unknowable to mortal minds. They conceived the universe as being sharply divided between spirit and matter. They considered everything physical and material as evil; man's soul is imprisoned in his body, from which an escape can be effected only through rigorous denial and mortification of the flesh. Their attitude was mystical and nonintellectual; truth comes neither from science nor from reason but from revelation. Philo maintained that the books of the Old Testament were of absolute divine authority and contained all truth; the ultimate aim in life is to accomplish a mystic union with God, to lose one's self in the divine. . . .

## III

## Religion in the Hellenistic Age

If there was one aspect of the Hellenistic civilization which served more than others to accent the contrast with Hellenic culture, it was the new trend in religion. The civic religion of the Greeks as it was in the age of the city-states had now almost entirely disappeared. For the majority of the intellectuals its place was taken by the philosophies of Stoicism, Epicureanism, and Skepticism. . . . Among the masses a tendency to embrace emotional religions was even more clearly manifest. . . .

The worship of the Egyptian mother-goddess Isis threatened for a time to become dominant throughout the Near Orient. The astral religion of the Chaldeans likewise spread rapidly, with the result that its chief product, astrology, was received with fanatical enthusiasm throughout the Hellenistic world. But the most powerful influence of all came from the offshoots of Zoroastrianism. [The followers of the Persian prophet, Zoroaster, held that life consisted of a constant struggle between the gods of good and evil.] While all of the cults of Oriental origin resembled each other in their promises of salvation in a life to come, [these] had a more ethically significant mythology, a deeper contempt for this world, and a more clearly defined doctrine of redemption through a personal savior. These were the ideas which satisfied the emotional cravings of the common people, convinced as they were of the worthlessness of this life and ready to be lured by extravagant promises of better things in a world to come. If we can judge by conditions in our own time, some of the doctrines of these cults must have exerted their influence upon members of the upper classes also. Even the most casual observer of modern society knows that pessimism, mysticism, and otherworldliness are not confined to the downtrodden. In some cases the keenest disgust with this life and the deepest mystical yearnings are to be found among those whose pockets bulge with plenty.

A factor by no means unimportant in the religious developments of the Hellenistic Age was the dispersion of the Jews. As a result of Alexander's conquest of Palestine in 332 B.C. and the Roman conquest about three centuries later, thousands of Jews migrated to various sections of the Mediterranean world. It has been estimated that 1,000,000 of them lived in Egypt in the first century A.D. and 200,000 in Asia Minor. They mingled freely with other peoples, adopting the Greek language and no small amount of the Hellenic culture which still survived from earlier days. At the same time they played a major part in the diffusion of Oriental beliefs. . . .

# W. W. Tarn: Alexander and the Brotherhood of Man

Sir William Tarn (1869–1957), a noted Hellenistic specialist, saw Alexander's greatness in his dreams even more than in his deeds. Special attention is given to his vision of a larger world to which man might belong. From Sir William Tarn, *Alexander the Great* (New York: Cambridge University Press, 1948), pp. 145–147.

Whatever else [Alexander] was, he was one of the supreme fertilising forces of history. He lifted the civilised world out of one groove and set it in another; he started a new epoch; nothing could again be as it had been. He greatly enlarged the bounds of knowledge[1] and of human endeavour, and gave to Greek science and Greek civilisation a scope and an opportunity such as they had never yet possessed. Particularism was replaced by the idea of the "inhabited world," the common possession of civilised men; trade and commerce were internationalised and the "inhabited world" bound together by a network both of new routes and cities, and of common interests. Greek culture, heretofore practically confined to Greeks, spread throughout that world; and for the use of its inhabitants, in place of the many dialects of Greece, there grew up the form of Greek known as the *koine*, the "common speech." The Greece that taught Rome was the Hellenistic world which Alexander made; the old Greece counted for little till modern scholars re-created Periclean Athens. So far as the modern world derives its civilisation from Greece, it largely owes it to Alexander that it had the opportunity. If he could not fuse races, he transcended the national State; and to transcend national States meant to transcend national cults; men came to feel after the unity which must lie beneath the various religions. Outwardly, this unity was ultimately satisfied in the official worship of the Roman Emperor, which derived from the worship of Alexander after his death; but beside this external form there grew up in men's hearts the longing for a true spiritual unity. And it was Alexander who created the medium in which the idea, when it came, was to spread. For it was due to him that Greek civilisation penetrated western Asia; and even if much of the actual work was done by his successors, he broke the path; without him they would not have been. Consequently, when at last Christianity showed the way to that spiritual unity after which men were feeling, there was ready at hand a medium for the new religion to spread in, the common Hellenistic civilisation of the "inhabited world"; without that, the conquests made by Christianity might have been as slow and difficult as they became when the bounds of that common civilisation were overpassed.

But if the things he did were great, one thing he dreamt was greater. We may put it that he found the Ideal State of Aristotle, and substituted the Ideal State of Zeno. It was not merely that he overthrew the narrow restraints of the former, and in place of limiting men by their opportunity, created opportunities adequate for men in a world where none need be a pauper and restrictions on population were meaningless. Aristotle's State had still cared nothing for humanity outside its own borders; the stranger must still be a serf or an enemy. Alexander changed all that. When he declared that all men were alike sons of one Father, when he prayed at Opis that Macedonians and Persians might be partners in the commonwealth and that the peoples of his world might live in harmony and in unity of heart and mind, he proclaimed for the first time the unity and brotherhood of mankind. Perhaps he gave no thought to the slave world—we do not know; but he, first of all men, was ready to transcend national differences, and to declare, as St. Paul was to declare, that there was neither Greek nor barbarian. . . .

# Donald Kagan: The Idea of Kingship in the Hellenistic Age

In the course of a study of the interrelatedness of Greek political thought, Professor Donald Kagan of Cornell University reveals the close connection between political events and political theory. In this selection he discusses the Hellenistic theory of kingship that succeeded and replaced that of the *polis*. Reprinted with permission of The Macmillan Company from *The Great Dialogue: History of Greek Thought* by Donald Kagan. 

At Alexander's death his great empire, devoid of any competent legitimate ruler, became a battleground on which his ambitious generals fought for supremacy. After two decades of continued warfare the empire was permanently divided into three great kingdoms—Egypt under the Ptolemies, Syria under the Seleucids, and Macedonia under the Antigonids. In Egypt and Syria a small number of Macedonians and Greeks ruled over a vast and mixed native population; even in Europe the Greeks did not accept Macedonian rule gladly. The fact is that each kingdom had little meaning apart from the power and personal qualities of its king. Boundaries between them were not clear and were constantly the subject of dispute and warfare. The Seleucid empire, in particular, had no consitution, no natural center of focus apart from the king himself, but the other kingdoms also placed central emphasis on the importance of the king. . . .

The rationale for Hellenistic monarchy which was likely, "the official political philosophy of the Hellenistic age," comes to us in the form of a few fragments . . . [one of which] is attributed to Archytas of Tarentum. We find the familiar insistence that the king must be "understanding and powerful in ruling well," a lover of men, who is lawful. His knowledge will permit him to judge correctly, his power to correct and punish wrongdoing. He must rule according to law and reason. His rule must be unselfish and he must rule only for the sake of his subjects. All this, of course, is completely in accord with views expressed by Xenophon, Isocrates, Plato, and Aristotle. . . .

The monarchial theorists of the fourth century had found the king's relationship to law a stumbling block. In general they would subordinate him to the law, but this was not fully satisfactory. So Isocrates says, "Obey the laws which kings lay down, but bear in mind that the mightiest law is the king's disposition" (*To Demonicus*). Plato in the *Politicus* puts the statesman-king above the law, and Aristotle recognizes that a naturally superior man must be permitted to rule free of law. All, however, are troubled by the conflict, which none resolves adequately. There was, in addition, the old problem of the written law versus the unwritten, statutory versus customary law, the law of nature versus the law of man. All these problems were solved by Archytas' device of making the king and the law identical. The ruler is Animate Law; as such he is justice itself, using or amending customary law by virtue of his knowledge of the unwritten law, which he embodies. He is more even than the "Seeing Law" of Xenophon.

But how may we know whether an actual king in fact meets the qualification of justice, knowledge, and lawfulness? Diotogenes, another Pythagorean, provides an answer based on the Hellenistic assumption that the king is animate law. . . .

> For the best must be honored by the best man, and the Governing principle by one who is a governor. So just as God is the Best of those things which are most honorable by nature, likewise the king is best in the earthly and human realm. Now the king bears the same relation to the state as God to the world; and the state is in the same ratio to the world as the king is to God. For the state, made as it is by a harmonizing together of many different elements, is an imitation of the order and harmony of the world, while the king who has an absolute rulership, and is himself Animate Law, has been metamorphosed into a deity among men.

As a god among men the king must have godlike qualities and carry out almost divine functions. Like a pilot whose job is to save the ship, like a charioteer who saves the chariot, like the physician who saves his patient, so the King "is to save those who are in danger in war." In his role as judge, "it is right for the king to act as does God in his leadership and command of the universe." He must be a harmonizer and benefactor of his subjects. Even his avarice is justified, for he needs wealth to benefit his subjects. He must be preeminent not only in virtue, benefaction, and grace, but also in majesty, which inspires fear in his subjects. "For majesty, a godlike thing, can make him admired and honored by the multitude; graciousness will make him popular and beloved; while the ability to inspire fear will make him terrible and unconquerable in his dealings with enemies, but magnanimous and trustworthy toward his friends." He must reserve himself from human passions, "and draw himself up closer to the gods." The very sight of him clothed in majesty, self-control, and preeminence should have an effect on the souls of his viewers, "no less than a flute or harmony." In short, he must have the attributes of Zeus. . . .

The legitimacy, transcendental power, and infallibility of the king have been established. It remains to describe the positive role he plays in the lives of his subjects. We must remember that the view that government is a negative force instituted only to prevent wrongdoing was never more than a minority opinion among the Greeks. Most men looked to the state for positive aid in making men better morally. We have seen that the *polis,* through its laws and style of life, had always claimed this function. The Hellenistic monarch, as Animate Law, had in fact become the state, and he now assumed the duty formerly performed by the *polis.* . . .

Thus, to amend Aristotle in accordance with Hellenistic theory, the king (not the *polis*) is necessary for life. What is more, the king is the source of the good life. He distributes justice according to his intelligence and virtue. . . .

Hellenistic monarchs often took symbolic names to indicate the positive role they played in the lives of their subjects; *Euergetês* (Benefactor), *Soter* (Savior), *Epiphanes* (The God Manifest) were among those frequently used. The fragments in Stobaeus make clear the deeper meaning of these names. The monarchs were benefactors not only in a worldly sense but in a spiritual one as well. They were saviors not only from worldly dangers but from sin; they were God and the logos made manifest. As Goodenough puts it:

> So we have, perhaps, at last grasped the meaning which lies behind the conception of the Animate Law; it means that the king is personally the constitution of the realm, that all the laws of localities under him must be ultimately moulded by and express his will. But more, he is a saviour of his subjects from their sins, by giving them what the Hellenistic world increasingly wanted more than anything else, a dynamic and personal revelation of deity.

And so the history of Greek political thought has come fully around to the oriental view from which it revolted after the fall of the Mycenaean monarchies. Law is no longer embodied in custom or dependent on the conscious consent of a free citizenry, but descends from God and is embodied in a being closer to God than any man, the king. He is the source of all safety, benefaction, spiritual salvation. The *polis* is dead not only in fact but in theory. . . .

TOPIC 11

# THE VALUES OF THE ROMAN REPUBLIC

Centuries before the conquests of Alexander the Great and the establishment of the Graeco-Oriental successor states whose history composed the Hellenistic Age, an obscure Western Mediterranean people, the Latins, began the process of expansion that culminated in the absorption of the greater part of the ancient world. For hundreds of years until 27 B.C. these Latins with their capital of Rome lived under a republican form of government. Possessed of a practical nature and an extraordinary personal discipline, they gradually conquered an empire that stretched from Britain to Mesopotamia. The readings inquire into the values of the early Romans that contributed to their success and note the effect that expansion had upon these values.

**Reading 49**

## Saga of the Roman Republic

From "The Stormy Road to Grandeur," by Edward Kern, *Life* Magazine, March 11, 1966, © 1966 Time Inc.

In the Sixth Century before Christ, something shook the human race out of its timeless slumber, as if, like Michelangelo's Adam, it had been touched by a mysterious hand. Everywhere the fixed, familiar surface of things cracked apart as new ideas and forces flooded up to quicken the world. Buddha and Confucius were awakening the Orient, and Zoroaster the Persian heartland. The Jews, in Babylonian captivity, were in the throes of spiritual rebirth. Outsiders broke into the locked world of the Pharaohs. Greece was ready to explode into the golden age of Pericles. The Mediterranean was being gathered for the first time into the arms of a single power, Carthage. And in Italy, in 509 B.C., a small country town on the banks of the Tiber threw out its foreign Etruscan king and declared itself a republic. Rome set out on a long stormy road to power and grandeur—as a republic until 27 B.C., then as an empire.

The republican revolution in Rome went unnoticed by the outside world which, indeed, hardly knew the place existed. Italy was on the fringe of the civilized world. Its only claim to attention was its foreigners: Etruscans —probably immigrants from Asia Minor— who had carved out a domain in the north; and Greeks whose cities laced the southern seaboard. The Romans were locals, peasants of Italic stock living in the plain of Latium.

When, centuries later, Rome had become great, the Romans felt that the gods must have had a hand in their success and they invented those legends about Rome's supernatural birth that have become some of the best-known stories in the world; how Romulus and Remus, twin sons of Mars, were suckled by a fierce she-wolf; how Romulus, following divine command, founded Rome by marking out the city limits with a furrow and killed Remus for jumping over it; how Romulus engineered the Rape of the Sabine women to procure wives for his young settlers.

Not a glimmer of divine grace brightens the bleak record of the Romans' early days—unless it was their luck in holding on to the little they had. For over two centuries, under their half-legendary Seven Kings, and for a century more after the Republic was born, the Romans were embroiled with their neighbors. Every summer, with tiresome regularity, Etruscans or rough tribesmen came sweeping down from the hills, and Roman farmers had to drop their plows, snatch up their swords and oxhide shields, and drive them off. It was not always easy and Rome existed on the margin of survival: Horatius' one-man stand against the Etruscans may be just another legend, but it shows how close Rome sometimes came to destruction.

To add to its troubles, the Republic was distracted by the interminable struggle of the people—the plebs—to win civil rights. Though Rome was a republic, political rights were determined by how much property a citizen owned and the real power lay with

Left to die in the Tiber River, the infants Romulus and Remus were said to have been rescued and reared by a she-wolf. This ancient Etruscan sculpture commemorates the legend.

the haughty, domineering patricians who filled the Senate, monopolized public offices, including the two annual consulships, and ran the state. Republican government was not only inequitable but also inefficient. In serious emergencies the whole machinery had to be shelved and dictators appointed.

The most famous dictator was the staunch old patriot, Lucius Cincinnatus, who was summoned in an hour of peril when the armies of the Republic were surrounded. He was toiling on his three-acre farm when the officers of the Senate found him. Cincinnatus wiped the honest sweat from his brow and sent his wife to fetch his toga. Fifteen days later, after crushing the foe in a decisive battle, Cincinnatus dutifully laid down his powers and went back to his fields.

The Republic was just getting its feet on the ground—its nearest enemies had been subdued, the plebs had succeeded through campaigns of massive civil disobedience in getting laws published and tribunes elected to protect their rights—when a disaster overwhelmed Rome and changed the course of its history. In 390 B.C. marauding Gauls from the north surprised and sacked the city. Only the Capitoline Hill was saved, so the story goes, by the honking of a flock of sacred geese which alerted the garrison. Even at that, the Romans had to buy all the barbarians with a hefty ransom.

The shock, the humiliation, the thought of the hard work of centuries undone in a single blow, seared the Roman mind with an indelible purpose: to make Rome so strong and its territories so wide that no enemy could ever reach it again. The Romans marshaled their citizen legions and marched forth to conquer.

Their first step was to master Italy, and it took them more than a hundred years of stubborn fighting to do it. Once a whole Roman army was trapped in a canyon by Samnite mountaineers and driven captive under the yoke. But no setback could stop the Romans now. One by one the people of Italy submitted and were either induced or forced to enlist as allies and fellow soldiers. The Greek cities to the south, watching the Roman steamroller coming, hired a Greek general, Pyrrhus, to help them stop the Romans.

To the Greeks, the Romans were barbarians, and Pyrrhus expected to scatter them like chaff. He was a fine soldier and the first professional the Romans had come up against. But despite his superior tactics and his terrifying war elephants, the unshakable legions made his triumphs so costly that even Pyrrhus had to confess, after one bloody clash, that another victory like that would undo him. Three years and several Pyrrhic victories later, Pyrrhus in 275 B.C. sailed home discouraged and the Romans mopped up the rest of Italy south of the River Rubicon.

Boss of a tight federation of Italian tribes and cities, Rome was now the strongest and most compact state in the West. The only power great enough to match it was the maritime empire of Carthage. Carthage itself was at a distance, on the North African shore. But Sicily, a Carthaginian stronghold, was less than two miles from Italy. The Romans saw Sicily as a dagger, poised and near. The Carthaginians saw the Romans as a threat to their mercantile dominion. And in their mutual rivalry, the two titans collided in a 63-year struggle that shook the ancient world, drove the contestants beyond all limits of sacrifice and exhaustion, and came close to wrecking both of them.

The first Punic War with Carthage—so-called because the Carthaginian spoke Punic—was won in 241 B.C. by the Romans, who turned themselves into salt water sailors to beat the Carthaginians in their own element. But it was only a curtain-raiser. Next time the Carthaginians had as commander a great military genius—Hannibal.

As a boy, Hannibal had sworn before the altar of his gods to punish Rome. Now, in 218 B.C., he led his mercenary host up out of Carthage-held Spain, forced his way across the snowbound Alps—an astounding feat—and plunged into the heart of Italy.

He had lost half his troops and all but one of his war elephants crossing the mountains. He was desperately sick and had lost an eye. Yet the news of his approach threw Rome into a panic. Wailing women swept the temple floors with their hair. Statues, they said, sweated blood. Consuls and armies marched off to face the invader, only to be overwhelmed by Hannibal's amazing tactics and finally annihilated, at Cannae.

Hannibal's army was too small to storm Rome itself, so he tried to get Rome's Italian allies to desert. A few did, but most of them stuck loyally to Rome. Repeatedly Hannibal tried to lure the Romans into battle. But the legions, under the wary consul Fabius Cunc-

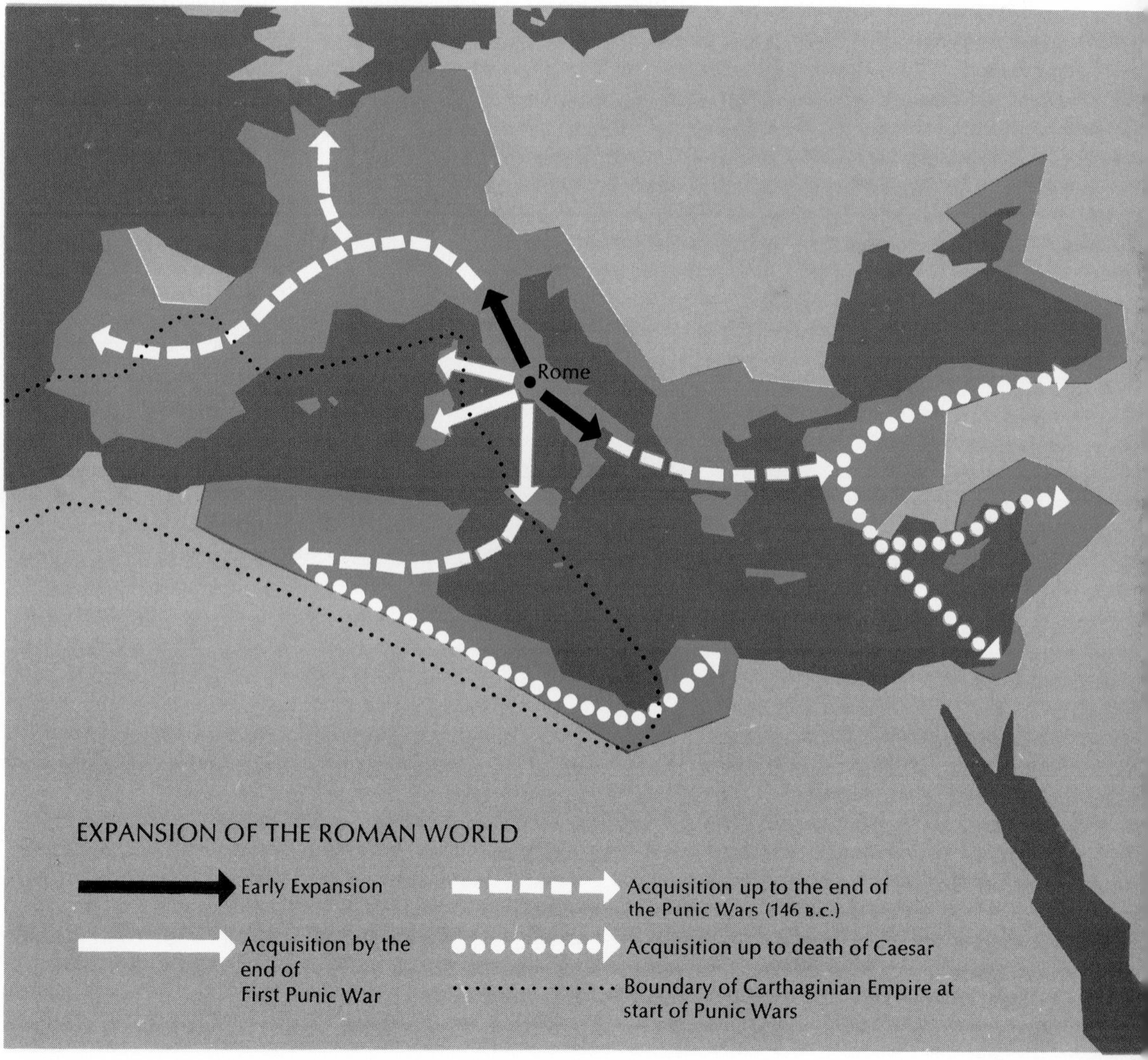

tator—"the Delayer"—learned never to risk one.

For 15 years Hannibal prowled up and down Italy as if he owned it, unable to force a decision. A whole generation of Romans grew up in the shadow of his presence. But the Romans' Fabian tactics gradually paid off. Unable to get help from home, watching his ragged army dwindle from disease and desertion, Hannibal slowly lost the war.

By 202 B.C. the Romans felt ready to challenge Carthage on home ground and shipped an army to Africa under Scipio Africanus. Hannibal was forced to sail home. On the plain of Zama south of Carthage he at last met his match. Defeated by Scipio, Hannibal fled to the East where he eventually took poison rather than fall into the hands of the Romans.

Carthage lost its empire—the Romans gained their first provinces and unchallenged mastery of the western Mediterranean. Never again until the distant day of the Fall, would Rome have to fight literally for its life. To the Romans, the struggle with Carthage was their great national experience. It marked Rome's fateful passage from nationhood to empire.

At the eastern end of the Mediterranean a jumble of densely populated, rich Greek kingdoms and cities—all of them fragments of Alexander's empire—had been fighting among themselves ever since their great founder had died. Rome became overnight the bright star in the West. Every interest wanted the invincible Romans on their side, and Hannibal had hardly been beaten before Rome was besieged by smooth-tongued Easterners loaded with flattery and bribes.

The Romans at first were reluctant to extend their empire. They were exhausted and needed time to consolidate their gains. They also feared that their simple Roman ways might get contaminated. In the Senate, Cato constantly gibed at slippery "Greeklings." Still, the Romans felt a countryman's awe for the urbane glories of Greece, if not for its decadent heirs. The political mess appalled their tidy minds. Most of all, they saw in the East a chance to satisfy a newly awakened appetite for money. Half against their better judgment, the Romans let themselves be dragged into eastern quarrels.

Time and again the Roman legions clanked eastward to discipline this or that misbehaving monarch. After a while, a warning was usually enough. When Syria's King Antiochus in 168 B.C. was on his way to invade Egypt, he was met by a Roman emissary who told him to turn back or risk war with Rome. Drawing a circle around the startled king, the Roman curtly ordered him to make up his mind before he stepped out of it. Antiochus meekly marched back to Syria.

But eastern machinations eventually wore out Roman patience. Roman arrogance enraged the Easterners. There were more wars, and little by little the rich lands that had been Rome's allies and protégés became Rome's provinces. Resistance was useless. Bowing to the inevitable, one king in Asia Minor simply left his whole kingdom to Rome in his will.

Rome brought order to the East; but the East literally revolutionized Roman life. As the sluice gates opened, the Romans were nearly buried under an avalanche of gold and luxuries, intellectuals and artists, priests, knaves and slaves. The Senate tried to stem the torrent. It suppressed the imported orgies of eastern Bacchus and expelled every Greek philosopher from the city. But they all came back, to make Greek a second language for every educated Roman, and to undermine the simple Roman mind with worldly skepticism. Cato's worst fears had come true; in little more than a generation Rome changed from a decent country town to a metropolis as corrupt and luxurious as any eastern capital.

The change was not all bad. There was a new refinement. Greek literature inspired the Romans to develop their own. But sudden wealth and power was more than the Romans could cope with. Freed from prudent restraints, they showed a new cruelty in dealing with others. In 146 B.C., Cato, who had been thundering for years that Carthage must be finally destroyed, got his way: the unoffending city was beseiged and razed to the ground. The same year, the Greek city of Corinth was wantonly sacked, plundered and burned, and its citizens sold into slavery. The eastern provinces were picked clean by swarms of Roman carpetbaggers.

At home the specter of civil strife raised its head again. On one side were senators and generals, gorged with eastern booty, with extravagant villas, huge plantations, hordes of political retainers and armies of slaves. On the other were the peasant soldiers of Italy, who came home after long campaigns to their neglected farms, only to be forced off the land by wealthy land-grabbers and wind up in Rome as an idle, destitute and irresponsible proletariat.

When Tiberius Gracchus (in 133 B.C.) tried to promote land reforms and appealed to the masses, the Senate in blind rage butchered him and 300 of his followers in the streets and flung their corpses into the Tiber. It was the first blood that Rome had shed in civil strife in 400 years. The rootless mobs of Rome discovered their strength, and from now on the deepening tragedy of the Roman Republic was played out against the backdrop of spreading class warfare—the rich "optimates" versus the underprivileged "populares."

The main source of Rome's troubles was political. As a government the Republic might be fit to run a small federation of rustic tribes; it was hopelessly unfit to run a rich world empire. There was no professional government, no civil service. The governors sent out to the provinces got their plush jobs through influence and connections. They were supposedly responsible to the Senate and the people. But the people were a fickle mob and the once-solid Senate had become a disorderly battlefield of rival family cliques who stopped at nothing—deceit, bribery, extortion, the courting of the city masses—to win money and power. Governorships and military commands, instead of serving the provinces and the Republic, became the tools of personal ambitions, a chance to accumulate fortunes and trained armies that could be thrown into political warfare at home. It was a cynical saying that a governor could extort enough from his province in his first year to pay off his political debts; enough in his second to bribe a future jury into acquitting him of extortion; and enough in his third to allow him to live like a king for the rest of his life. All through the last century B.C. the Republic was overshadowed by strongmen whose rivalries plunged Rome and Italy into bloody civil wars. . . .

[Typical of the] contenders were Pompey and Julius Caesar. Pompey came on first. His success against the pirates infesting the Mediterranean made Pompey a popular hero. His spectacular successes as supreme commander in the restive eastern theater of the empire gave him more power and prestige than any Roman had ever enjoyed before him. Caesar came up from behind. He used Pompey to get himself started. Then he conquered Gaul to get the money and the seasoned army he needed to challenge him. . . . After Caesar had suppressed the Gauls, crossed the Rubicon into Italy and routed Pompey, Caesar contemptuously dismissed the tattered Republic as null and void, and had himself made dictator for life.

Everything indicated that Rome was headed for one-man rule. But Caesar was a little premature. So long as it could still field a speaker like Cicero to articulate its ideals and men of action like Brutus and Cassius to strike a blow for them, the Republic was not ready to die; and Caesar paid the price of misjudgment with his life.

It was the last pair of contenders who finally dispatched the Republic: Octavian, Caesar's sickly, scheming, cold-blooded great-nephew and heir, and Antony, Caesar's bluff, simple-minded general. Cooperating at first, they crushed Caesar's assassins and purged the last of the great Republican families. But once they had divided the empire between them, their partnership dissolved.

In the East, Antony married Cleopatra, Caesar's erstwhile mistress, adopted the grand style of an Oriental monarch and dreamed of an eastern empire. In the West, Octavian smoothly settled disorders, nailed down his inheritance and methodically prepared for the inevitable showdown with Antony. It came, in 31 B.C., at the sea battle of Actium off the western coast of Greece. Antony and Cleopatra fled back to Egypt where their soldiers deserted them and they both committed suicide; Octavian was left, alone amid the ashes, to face the enormous task of constructing a new order and infusing a new and higher purpose into the weary world of Rome. . . .

It was as if the longings of millions, accumulated over decades of chaos and bloodshed, had suddenly found a voice and a focus, in the person of one frail young man. Octavian did not fail them. On Jan. 16, 27 B.C. he was given the title of Augustus and began his lifelong task of reshaping the Roman world.

# W. W. Fowler: The Roman Character

William Warde Fowler (1847–1921), Oxford classicist, characterized the Romans as the world's most practical people and thus a necessary complement to the civilizing work of the Greeks. In this reading he comments on the factors influencing their "hard and practical turn of mind." From W. W. Fowler, *Rome* (New York, 1912), pp. 12, 55–59, 63.

There must have been a quality in this people, individually and as a whole, fitting them to withstand so much storm and stress, and to emerge from disaster with renewed strength to take in hand the work of conquest and government. . . .

We have to do . . . with a people not of imagination, but of action: a people intensely alive to the necessities and difficulties of human life. The Romans were, in fact, the most practical people in history; and this enabled them to supply what was wanting to the civilisation of the Mediterranean basin in the work of the Greeks. They themselves were well aware of this quality, and proud of it. We find it expressed by the elder Cato quite at the beginning of the best age of Roman literature; his ideal Roman is *vir fortis et strenuus*—a man of strong courage and active energy. Tacitus, in the later days of that literature, says that all designs and deeds should be directed to the practical ends of life. . . .

Discipline and duty are the two words which best explain [the Romans]; the habit of obedience to authority, which is the necessary condition of the power of governing, and that sense of duty which lies at the root of the habit and the power. This aptitude for discipline and this sense of duty can be traced both in the private and the public life of early Rome, in the life of the family and in the life of the State. Let us be clear at once that the individual as such was not as yet an important item of society; society was a system of groups, and the individual played no part in it in these early times except as the member of a group. . . . But the only group with which we are concered . . . was the *familia,* another of those immortal words which we have inherited from the Latin language. . . .

This word *familia* did not mean exactly what we mean by family; household would perhaps come nearer to it, if we understand by household a group of individuals supporting itself on the land. It meant not only father, mother, and children, but also their dependents, whether bond or free. These, if bond, were slaves (*servi*), prisoners of war and the children of such prisoners, or persons who had forfeited their liberty by debt: if free, they were clients, who for some reason had become attached to the *familia* in an inferior position, and looked to it for subsistence and protection. And our picture is not complete unless we take into account also the divine members of the group, dwelling in the house or on the land, to whom the human members looked for protection and prosperity in all the walks of life. Chief among these were the spirit of the hearth-fire, Vesta; Penates, the spirits of the store-closet and its contents; the Lar, the guardian spirit of the cultivated land, or, as some think, of a departed ancestor; and the Genius of the head of the family, which enabled him to beget children and so continue the collective life of the group. Though these spirits—they are hardly yet deities—naturally seem to us mere fancies of the primitive Roman mind, they were to that mind itself as real and active as any human member of the group, and we must try to think of them as such, for they played a very important part in the development of the quality we wish to realise.

Now this group, or rather the human part of it, lived under a very simple and effective form of government. It was under absolute control of a head, the father and husband; or, if more than one family lived together, the oldest living father and husband. Over wife and children he had a father's power (*patria potestas*), and they were said to be in his *hand;* over the slaves he has a master's power (*dominium*); to his clients he was *patronus,* or quasi-father. His power over wife and children was absolute, but it was kept from being arbitrary by a wholesome custom, of immense importance in all its results throughout Roman history, of seeking the advice of a council of relations before taking any extreme step in the way of punishment for serious offences. This was an obligation, a duty, on his part, enforced by no law, but by what may be well called an even more powerful sovereign than law—the custom of the ancestors. . . .

What of the education which should perpetuate these habits? Unluckily we have no contemporary record of it for these early times, and must guess at it chiefly from what we know of the bringing up of his son by the elder Cato, a strenuous believer in the old methods, in the second century B.C. As we might expect, it seems to have been an education in the active practical life of the farm, and in reverence, obedience, and modesty of demeanour. Cato taught his boy not only to work, to ride, to box, and to swim, but to shun all indecency; and was himself "as careful not to utter an indecent word before his son, as he would have been in the presence of the Vestal virgins." He wrote histories for his son in large letters, so that he might learn something of the illustrious deeds of the ancient Romans, and of their customs. In his time an education of the mind was beginning to come into vogue, as well as one of the will; but in the period we have been surveying this must have been of the most meagre kind. Yet it is possible that the idea of active duty to the State and its deities, as well as to the family and its presiding spirits, was all the more vividly kept up in the absence of intellectual interests. As life in the city became more usual, the boys of good families had more opportunity of learning what was meant by duty to the State; they accompanied their fathers to hear funeral orations on eminent citizens, and were even admitted to meetings of the Senate. In this way they must have developed a shrewdness and practical sagacity invaluable to them in after life. . . .

# Plutarch Praises The Life of Cato

Plutarch (c. 46–120 A.D.) wrote forty-six *Parallel Lives* contrasting Greek and Roman soldiers, statesmen, and heroes. Cato the Elder (234–149 B.C.), whose life Plutarch describes in this reading, held most of the important offices of the Republic, although he was a "new man" and not a member of the Roman aristocracy. Patronized by the head of one of Rome's leading families, the Valerii, he tried to reform and rebuild Roman life. His own fourfold career as landowner, soldier, lawyer, and officeholder typified the traditional Roman virtues. His hatred for foreign ways was strong, as witnessed by his successful efforts to annihilate Carthage even after it had lost its power to threaten Rome. For years he ended every speech in the Senate with the words, "And Carthage must be destroyed," finally inciting the Third Punic War (149–146 B.C.), that removed every trace of the city from the earth. From Plutarch, *Lives of Illustrious Men,* trans. John Dryden (New York, n.d.) I, pp. 526–530, 540–546. Simplified by the editors.

## I

Marcus Cato's . . . ancestors seem to be almost entirely unknown. He himself praises his father Marcus, as a worthy man and a brave soldier, and Cato, his great-grandfather, as a man who had often obtained military awards and once, having lost five horses under him in battle, received their value from the public treasury, on account of his bravery. Now it being the custom among the Romans to call those who, not being members of the upperclass families, raised themselves by their own efforts, new men or upstarts; this is what they called Cato, which he admitted himself to be as fair as any public distinction was concerned, but yet asserted that in the exploits and virtues of his ancestors he was very ancient. . . .

He built up his body in early life by working with his own hands and living temperately and serving in war; and seemed to have an equal proportion both of health and strength. And he exerted and practised his ability to speak well through all the neighborhood and little villages; thinking this as necessary for him as a second body, and an all but necessary organ to one who looks forward to something above a mere humble and inactive life. He would never refuse to be counsel for those who needed him, and was, indeed, early reckoned a good lawyer, and soon as a capable orator.

Thus his solidity and depth of character showed itself gradually, more and more to those with whom he had something to do, and justified, as it were, his employment in great affairs and places of public command. He neither took fees for his counsel and legal work nor seemed to put any high price on the honor which proceeded from such kind of civilian combats, for he seemed much more desirous to make a name for himself in military camp and in real fights. While yet a youth, his breast was already covered with scars he had received from the enemy, being (as he himself says) but seventeen years old when he made his first campaign, in the time when Hannibal in the height of his success was burning and pillaging all Italy. In engagements he would strike boldly, without flinching, stand firm to his ground, fix a bold countenance upon his enemies, and with a harsh threatening voice attack them; rightly thinking that such a rugged kind of behavior sometimes terrified the enemy more than the sword itself. In his marches, he carried his own weapons on foot, while only one servant followed him to carry the provision for his table. He is said never to have been angry

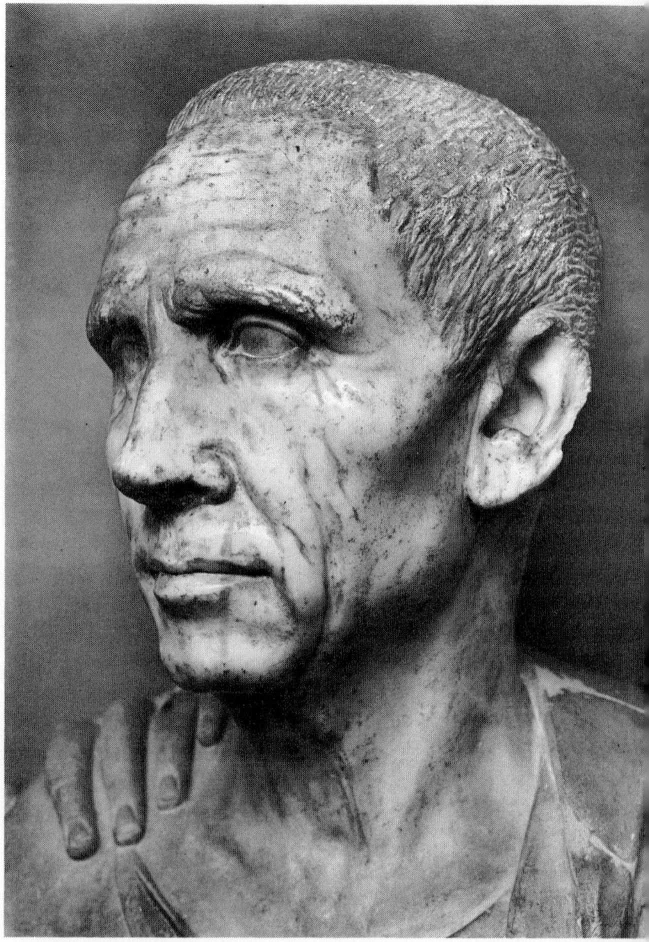

The character and personality of Romans such as Cato emerge in this work by a contemporary sculptor, now in the Vatican Museum.

or hasty with this servant while the latter made ready his dinner or supper, but would for the most part when he was free from military duty, assist and help him himself to prepare it.

There was a man of the highest rank, and very influential among the Romans, called Valerius Flaccus, who was extremely skillful in recognizing future potential in young people, and much disposed to help such men rise in the world. He, it seems, had lands bordering upon Cato's and he could not help but admire him when he understood from Cato's servants the manner of his living, how he labored with his own hands, went on foot sometimes in the morning to the courts to assist those who wanted his counsel, how, returning home again, when it was winter, he would throw a loose cloak over his shoulders, and in the summer time would labor in working clothes among his servants, sit down with them, eat of the same bread, and drink of the same wine. When these servants spoke of other good qualities, his fair dealing and moderation, mentioning also some of his wise sayings, Valerius ordered that Cato should be invited to supper. Becoming personally convinced of his fine temper and his superior character which, like a plant, seemed only to require care and better situation, he urged him to apply himself to state affairs at Rome. There, henceforth, he went, and by his work as a lawyer soon gained many friends and admirers. With Valerius as the chief force behind his advancement, he first got appointed tribune in the army and afterwards was made quaestor, or treasurer. And now becoming eminent and noted, he passed, with Valerius himself, through the greatest commands, being first his colleague as consul, and then censor. . . .

Cato grew more and more powerful by his eloquence, so that he was commonly called the Roman Demosthenes; but his manner of life was even more famous and talked about. For all young men studied and sought oratorical skill, but the person was very rare who would cultivate the old habits of bodily labor, or prefer a light supper and a breakfast which never saw the fire, or be in love with poor clothes and a simple lodging, or could set his ambition rather on doing without luxuries than on possessing them. For now the state, unable to keep its purity by reason of its greatness, and having so many affairs, and people from all sections under its government, tended to admit many mixed customs and new examples of living rather than sticking with Roman habits. With reason, therefore, everybody admired Cato, when they saw others fail under the load of their work and grow effeminate by too many luxuries and yet saw him unconquered by either, and that not only when he was young and ambitious but also when old and grey-headed, after a consulship and triumph. Like some famous victor in the athletic games, he persevered in his exercise and maintained his character to the very last. . . . He did all this for the sake of his country so that his body might be the hardier for war. . . .

## II

Ten years after his consulship, Cato stood for the office of censor, which was indeed the summit of all honor, and in a way the highest step in civil affairs; for besides all other power, it had also that of an inquisition into every one's life and manners. For the Romans thought that no marriage or rearing of children, nay, no feast or drinking-bout ought to be permitted according to just anybody's appetite or fancy, but should first be examined and inquired into. They were of the opinion that a man's character was much sooner perceived in things of this sort than in what is done publicly and in open day. They chose, therefore, two persons, one out of the patricians, the other out of the commons, who were to watch, correct, and punish, if anyone ran too much into sensualness, or transgressed the usual manner of life of his country; these they called Censors. They had power to take away a horse, or expel out of the senate any one who lived intemperately and out of order. It was their own business to make an estimate of what everyone was worth, and to write down for the records everybody's birth and quality; besides many other prerogatives. And therefore the chief opposed Cato's desire for this office. Jealousy prompted the patricians, who thought that it would be a stain to everybody's nobility if men of no original birthright should rise to the highest dignity and power; while others conscious of their own evil practices, and of the violation of the laws and customs of their country, were afraid of the austerity of the man; which, in an office of such great power, was likely to prove most uncompromising and severe. And so, consulting among themselves, they brought forward seven candidates in opposition to him, who sedulously set themselves to court the people's favor by fair promises, as though what they wished for was indulgent and easy-going government. Cato, on the contrary, promising no such mildness but plainly threatening evil livers, openly declared his position and, exclaiming that the city needed a great and thorough cleansing, called upon the people if they were wise not to choose the gentlest but the roughest of physicians. Such a one, he said, he was. . . .

He added that he saw all the rest trying to win the office with ill intent, because they were afraid of those who would exercise it justly as they ought. And it would seem that the Roman people were so truly great and so worthy of great men to be its leaders that they did not fear the severity and grim countenance of Cato. Rejecting those smooth promisers who were ready to do all things to ingratiate themselves, they elected him and Flaccus. . . .

He gave most general annoyance, by cutting down people's luxury; for though (most of the youth being thereby already corrupted) it seemed almost impossible to take it away with an open hand and directly, yet, going as it were obliquely around, he caused all dress carriages, women's ornaments, household furniture, whose price exceeded one thousand five hundred drachmas, to be rated at ten times as much as they were worth; intending by making the assessments greater to increase the taxes paid upon them. . . .

And thus, on the one side, not only those were disgusted at Cato, who paid the taxes in order to retain their luxuries but those too who, on the other side, gave up their luxuries to avoid the taxes. . . . Cato, notwithstanding, being little solicitous of those who exclaimed against him, increased his austerity. He caused the pipes through which some persons brought the public water into their houses and gardens to be cut, and demolished all buildings which jutted out into the public streets. He beat down also the price in contracts for public works to the lowest, and raised it in contracts for collecting the taxes to the highest sum; by which proceedings he drew a great deal of hatred upon himself. . . .

He was also a good father, an excellent husband to his wife, and an extraordinary economist. As he did not manage his affairs of this kind carelessly, because he considered them things of little moment, I think I ought to record a little further whatever was commendable in him in these points.

Whenever a son was born to him, no matter how urgently he had other things to do, unless it were some public matter, he would be present when his wife washed it and dressed it in its swaddling clothes. For she herself suckled it, nay, she often gave her breast to her servants' children, because she felt she could produce, by sucking the same milk, a kind of natural love in them to her son. As he grew up Cato himself taught him to read, although he had a servant, a very good grammarian called Chilo, who taught many others. He thought it not fitting, as he himself said, to have his son reprimanded by a slave, or perhaps pulled by the ears when found tardy in his lesson. Nor would he have his son be obligated to a servant for so great a thing as his learning. He himself, therefore (as we were saying), taught him his grammar, law, and his gymnastic exercises. Nor did he only show him how to throw a dart, to fight in armor, and to ride, but to box also and to endure both heat and cold and to swim over the most rapid and rough rivers. He says, likewise, that he wrote histories in large letters with his own hand in order that his son, without stirring out of the house, might learn to know about his countrymen and forefathers.

He purchased a great many slaves out of the captives taken in war but chiefly bought up the young ones, who were capable to be, as it were, broken and taught like puppies and colts. . . .

When a servant was at home, he was obliged either to do some work or to sleep, for Cato loved those most who used to lie down often to sleep, accounting them more easily manageable than those who were wakeful, and more fit for any thing when they were refreshed with a little slumber. Since he was also of the opinion that the great cause of the laziness and misbehavior of slaves was their running after their pleasures, he fixed a certain price for them to pay for permission to marry amongst themselves, but would suffer no relationships outside of his household. At first, when he was only a poor soldier, he would not be difficult in anything which related to his eating but looked upon it as a pitiful thing to quarrel with a servant for the belly's sake. Afterwards, when he grew richer, and held many feasts for his friends and colleagues in office, as soon as supper was over he used to go with a leathern thong and scourge those who had waited or prepared the meat carelessly. He always contrived, too, that his servants should have some difference among one another, always suspecting and fearing the consequences of good understanding among them.

# Plutarch Relates The Fate of Caesar

From Plutarch, *Lives of Illustrious Men,* trans. John Dryden (New York, n.d.) II, pp. 541-552.

Caesar was born to do great things, and had a passion after honour, and the many noble exploits he had done did not now serve as an inducement to him to sit still and reap the fruit of his past labours, but were incentives and encouragements to go on, and raised in him ideas of still greater actions, and a desire of new glory, as if the present were all spent. . . .

But that which brought upon him the most apparent and mortal hatred was his desire of being king; which gave the common people the first occasion to quarrel with him, and proved the most specious pretence to those who had been his secret enemies all along. Those who would have procured him that title gave it out that it was foretold in the Sibyls' book that the Romans should conquer the Parthians when they fought against them under the conduct of a king, but not before. And one day, as Caesar was coming down from Alba to Rome, some were so bold as to salute him by the name of king; but he, finding the people disrelished it, seemed to resent it himself, and said his name was Caesar, not King. Upon this there was a general silence, and he passed on looking not very well pleased or contented. . . .

He gave a fresh occasion of resentment by his affront to the tribunes. The [feast of] Lupercalia [was being] celebrated [in which] . . . many young noblemen. . . run up and down the city with their upper garments off, striking all they meet with thongs of hide, by way of sport; and many women, even of the highest rank, place themselves in the way, and hold out their hands to the lash, as boys in a school do to the master, out of a belief that it procures easy labour to those who are with child, and makes those conceive who are barren. Caesar, dressed in a triumphal robe, seated himself in a golden chair at the rostra to view this ceremony.

Antony, as consul, was one of those who ran this course, and when he came into the Forum, and the people made way for him, he went up and reached to Caesar a diadem wreathed with laurel. Upon this there was a shout, but only a slight one, made by the few who were planted there for that purpose; but when Caesar refused it, there was universal applause. Upon the second offer, very few, and upon the second refusal, all again applauded. Caesar, [finding that the experiment had failed] rose up and ordered the crown to be carried into the Capitol.

Caesar's statues were afterwards found with royal diadems on their heads. Flavius and Marullus, two tribunes of the people, went presently and pulled them off, and having apprehended those who first saluted Caesar as king committed them to prison. The people followed them with acclamations, and called them by the name of Brutus, because Brutus was the first who ended the succession of kings, and transferred the power which before was lodged in one man into the hands of the senate and people. Caesar so far resented this, that he displaced Marullus and Flavius; and in urging his charges against them, at the same time ridiculed the people, by himself giving the men more than once the names of Brutes. . . .

Fate, however, is to all appearance more unavoidable than unexpected. For many strange prodigies and apparitions are said to have been observed shortly before [Caesar's assassination]. As to the lights in the heavens, the noises heard in the night, and the wild birds which perched in the Forum, these are not perhaps worth taking notice of in so great a case as this. Strabo, the philosopher, tells us that a number of men were seen, looking as if they were [on fire] contending with each other; that a quantity of flame issued from the hand of a soldier's servant, so that they who saw it thought he must be burnt, but that after all he had no hurt. [When] Caesar was sacrificing [an animal], the victim's heart was missing, a very bad omen, because no living creature can subsist without a heart. One finds it also related by many that a soothsayer bade him prepare for some great danger on the Ides of March. When this day was come, Caesar, as he went to the senate, met this soothsayer, and said to him [jokingly] "The Ides of March are come," [to which the soothsayer answered softly], "Yes, they are come, but they are not past." . . .

After this, when he was sleeping with his wife, all the doors and windows of the house flew open together, he was startled at the noise and the light which broke into the room, and sat up in his bed, where by the moonshine he perceived Calpurnia fast asleep, and heard her utter in her dream some indistinct words and inarticulate groans. She [was dreaming] that she was weeping over Caesar, and holding him butchered in her arms. . . . When it was day, she begged of Caesar, if it were possible, not to stir out [of the house] but to adjourn the senate to another time; and if he [was not impressed by] her dreams, that she would be pleased to consult his fate by sacrifices and other kinds of divination. Nor was he himself without some suspicion and fears; for he never before discovered any womanish superstition in Calpurnia, whom he now saw in such great alarm. Upon the report which the priests made to him, that they had killed several sacrifices, and still found them [unfavorable] he resolved to send Antony to dismiss the senate.

In this junture, Decimus Brutus, surnamed Albinus, one whom Caesar had such confidence in that he made him his second heir, who nevertheless was engaged in the conspiracy with the other Brutus and Cassius, fearing lest if Caesar should put off the senate to another day the [plot] might [be disclosed], spoke scoffingly and in mockery of the diviners, and blamed Caesar for giving the senate [such a good] occasion of saying he had slighted them . . . . They were ready to vote unanimously that he should be declared king of all the provinces out of Italy, and might wear a diadem in any other place but Italy, by sea or land. If any one should be sent to tell them they [should] break up for the present, and meet again when Calpurnia should chance to have better dreams, what would his enemies say? Or who would with any patience hear his friends, if they should presume to defend his government as not arbitrary and tyrannical? But if he was possessed so far as to think this day unfortunate, yet it were more decent to go himself to the senate, and to adjourn it in his own person. . . .

When Caesar entered, the senate stood up to show their respect to him, and [some] of Brutus' confederates, came about his chair and stood behind it, [while] others met him, pretending to add their petitions to those of Tillius Cimber, in behalf of his brother who was in exile; and they followed him with their joint applications till he came to his seat. When he was sat down, he refused to comply with their requests, and upon their urging him further began to reproach them severely, . . . when Tillius, laying hold of his [toga] with both hands, pulled it down from his neck, which was the signal for the assault.

Casca gave him the first cut in the neck, which was not mortal nor dangerous, coming from one who at the beginning of such a bold action was probably very much disturbed. Caesar immediately turned about, and laid his hand upon the dagger and kept hold of it. And both of them at the same time cried out, he that received the blow, in Latin, "Vile Casca, what does this mean?" and he that gave it, in Greek, to his brother, "Brother, help!"

Upon this first onset, those who were not [in on the plan] were astonished, and their horror and amazement at what they saw were so great that they did not dare flee, nor assist Caesar, nor so much as speak a word. But those who came prepared for the business enclosed him on every side, with their naked daggers in their hands. Whichever way he turned he met with blows, and saw their swords levelled at his face and eyes, and was encompassed, like a wild beast in the toils, on every side.

For it had been agreed they should each make a thrust at him, and flesh themselves with his blood; for which reason Brutus also gave him one stab in the groin. Some say that he fought and resisted all the rest, shifting his body to avoid the blows, and calling out for help, but that when he saw Brutus's sword drawn, he covered his face with his [toga] and [fell to the ground]. . . .

When Caesar was [killed], Brutus [stepped] forth to [explain] what they had done. The senate would not hear him but flew out of doors in haste, and filled the [populace] with so much alarm and distraction, that some shut up their houses, others left their counters and shops. All ran one way or the other, some to the place to see the sad spectacle, others back again after they had seen it. Antony and Lepidus, Caesar's most faithful friends, [stole off] and hid themselves in some friends' houses.

Brutus and his followers, being yet hot from the deed, marched in a body from the senate house to the Capitol with their drawn swords, not like persons who thought of escaping, but with an air of confidence and assurance, and as they went along, called to the people that liberty [had been restored]. . . .

# Ronald Syme: The Roman Oligarchy

In *The Roman Revolution,* Oxford Professor Ronald Syme (1903-     ) deals with the transformation of state and society in the last years of the Republic. His attention is directed to the transfer of power and property among the Roman noble families, rather than to the deeds of the strongmen, Pompey, Caesar, and Augustus. From Ronald Syme, *The Roman Revolution,* by permission of the Clarendon Press, Oxford.

When the patricians expelled the [Etruscan] kings from Rome [509 B.C.], they were careful to retain the kingly power, vested in a pair of annual magistrates [consuls]; and though impelled in time to admit the plebians to political equality, certain of the great patrician houses, Valerii, Fabii and Cornelii, nonetheless held in turn a dynastic and almost regal position. The Senate again, being a permanent body, arrogated to itself power, and after conceding sovereignty to the assembly of the People was able to frustrate its exercise. The two consuls remained at the head of the government, but policy was largely directed by ex-consuls. These men ruled, as did the Senate, not in virtue of written law, but through *auctoritas;* and the name of *principes civitatis* came suitably to be applied to the more prominent of the consulars.

The consulate did not merely confer power upon its holder and dignity for life; it ennobled a family for ever. Within the Senate, itself an oligarchy, a narrow ring, namely the *nobiles,* or descendants of consular houses, whether patrician or plebian in origin, regarded the supreme magistracy as the prerogative of birth and the prize of ambition. . . .

Not mere admission to the Senate but access to the consulate was jealously guarded by the *nobiles*. It was a scandal and a pollution if a man without ancestors aspired to the highest magistracy of the Roman Republic—he might rise to the praetorship but no higher, save by a rare combination of merit, industry and protection. The *nobilitas* did not, it is true, stand like a solid rampart to bar all intruders. No need for that—the conservative Roman voter could seldom be induced to elect a man whose name had not been known for centuries as a part of the history of the Republic. Hence the *novus homo* (in the strict sense of the term the first member of a family to secure the consulate and consequent ennoblement) was a rare phenomenon. . . .

The political life of the Roman Republic was stamped and swayed . . . by the strife for power, wealth and glory. The contestants were the *nobiles* among themselves, as individuals or in groups, open in the elections and in the courts of law, or masked by secret intrigue. As in its beginning, so in its last generation, the Roman Commonwealth, "res publica populi Romani," was a name; a feudal order of society still survived in a city-state and governed an empire. Noble families determined the history of the Republic, giving their names to its epochs. . . .

In any age of the history of Republican Rome about twenty or thirty men, drawn from a dozen dominant families, hold a monopoly of office and power. From time to time, families rise and fall: as Rome's rule extends in Italy, the circle widens from which the nobility is recruited and renewed. None the less, though the composition of the oligarchy is slowly transformed with the transformation of the Roman State, the manner and fashion of dynastic politics changes but little; and though noble houses suffered defeat in the struggle for power, and long eclipse, they were saved from extinction by the primitive tenacity of the Roman family and the pride of their own traditions. . . .

TOPIC 12

# THE ROMAN APPROACH TO EMPIRE

The term *pax romana,* the Roman peace, has come to symbolize the virtues of a world at peace under a single political authority. It refers historically to the two centuries (27 B.C.–180 A.D.) of Roman rule over the Mediterranean world. The term brings to mind a stretch of years, longest in the memory of man, in which diverse peoples, Italians, Britons, Greeks, Jews, Africans, and many others, lived together freely, securely, and harmoniously. The readings examine the basis for this image and the relationship between peace and conquest. They are concerned with how the Romans ruled and the reaction to that rule. The first readings concentrate on the example of the late Republic and use the noted Roman writer and politician Cicero to interpret the interplay between the theory and practice of imperial rule. The later readings illuminate aspects of the problem in the post-Augustan era.

**Reading 54**

# How the Romans Ruled

From "The Stormy Road to Grandeur," by Edward Kern, *Life* Magazine, March 11, 1966, 

The Roman Empire was one of the great collective achievements of the human race. As Gibbon says, it "comprehended the fairest part of the earth, and the most civilized portion of mankind." It covered an area almost exactly the size of the U.S. and supported a population of at least 70 to 90 million souls —citizens, provincials, slaves, men, women and children. At one extreme were suave Syrians and Greeks who looked down their noses at the obtuse Romans from their vantage point of a longer history, richer culture and, perhaps, quicker intelligence. At the other extreme were half-savage Britons who had only recently given up wearing animal skins and dyeing their own skins blue. And there was every shade of culture and experience in between.

The Romans, of course, felt superior to them all. They smiled at the crudities of their more barbarous subjects, sneered at servile Orientals ("A Phrygian is usually improved by whipping," runs a Roman saying), and had a curious love-hate relationship with the Greeks. For Roman ways never replaced Greek ways in the East. There Greek language and culture were so widespread as to represent a cultural division of the empire into the Greek East and the Latin West—a division which eventually became political.

But the Romans refrained from forcing conformity on their eastern constituents. So long as they paid their taxes, observed Roman laws, paid obeisance to local statues of the emperor, accepted Roman rule and Latin as the official language, they could do pretty much as they pleased.

In the more barbarous provinces of the West—Spain, Gaul, Britain—the Romans had the far greater task of lifting primitive populations to an urban level. This, too, they accomplished with surprising speed and, to their credit more by persuasion than by force.

The historian Tacitus, describing in 98 A.D. the activities of his father-in-law, the Roman general Agricola, in Britain, gives a graphic picture of Roman techniques. "To accustom a scattered, barbarous and warlike people," he wrote, "to rest and repose through the charms of luxury, Agricola gave private encouragement and public aid to the building of temples, law courts, and private houses, praising the energetic and reproving the indolent. Thus an honorable rivalry took the place of compulsion. He likewise provided a liberal education for the sons of the chiefs, and showed such a preference for the natural powers of the Britons . . . that they, who lately disdained the language of Rome, now coveted its eloquence. Hence, too, a liking sprang up for our style of dress, and the toga became fashionable." And Tacitus, a stern moralist, added: "Step by step they were led to things which dispose to vice, the lounge, the bath, the elegant banquet."

What persuaded the provincials more than anything else to adopt Roman ways was their hope for Roman citizenship, which Rome

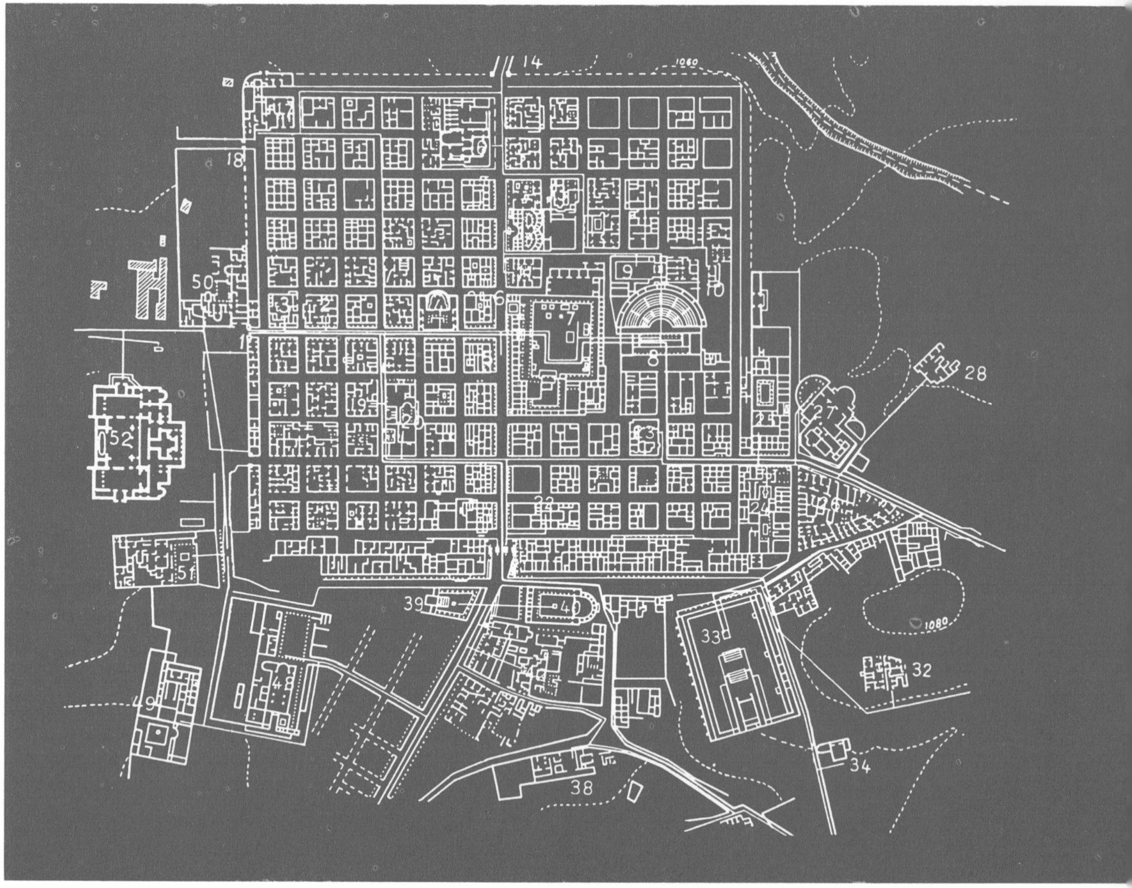


**a)** Plan of Timgad, a city located south of Constantine in modern-day Algeria. Construction of this city was begun in 100 A.D. by Trajan. It was destroyed in the seventh century and brought to light again by excavations in the 1880s.

dangled in front of them. Citizenship gave its possessor the full protection of Roman law from any arbitrary official action against his person or property, along with many other rights and privileges. Only a minority in the empire had it; all the rest competed for it—not only for its tangible benefits, but also as a kind of diploma of social acceptability. It is one of the most striking proofs of the greatness of Rome that the grandsons of the very Gauls who had fought Caesar so savagely should have come clamoring for citizenship. . . .

## THE PROVINCES

Unlike the last days of the Republic, there were no political points to be gained by plundering the provinces. Governors were directly responsible to the emperor and acted on the whole with honesty and competence. Provinces could appeal to Rome, and any offending governor was likely to find himself arraigned in Rome. There were still instances of malfeasance and occasionally of criminal outrage, and emperors were chary of exposing senators to too much temptation. One province, Egypt, on which Rome depended for much of its wheat supply, was governed by a civil servant of lower rank: senators had to have a special visa even to set foot in it.

The provinces were not organic entities like the states of the U.S. They could be expanded, contracted, divided up and reshuffled as bureaucratic convenience dictated. The real basic unit of the empire, the cells that made up its living tissue, were the cities. There may have been as many as 10,000 of them, with temples and forums, markets, public baths, libraries, theaters, amphitheaters and aqueducts—the amenities which made life worth living. Some towns, especially in the East, antedated Rome. In Africa there were old Punic towns that had been Romanized—especially rebuilt Carthage itself. Other towns were founded by Roman colonizers or grew out of old army camps where veterans stayed to marry and settle down. These considered themselves Romes in miniature and looked it, with compact thickets of colonnades, arches, niches, fountains, and neatly paved streets and squares all laid out in the standard classical style that hardly varied throughout the empire.

**b)** View along the main artery of Timgad looking toward the triumphal arch.

In each city a circle of best families dominated the little municipal senate (known as the curia) and owned most of the surrounding land—except for the vast estates of rich absentee landlords in Rome. They pursued local rivalries with neighboring towns in prestige and in the splendor of public buildings and entertainments. Sometimes zeal and civic spirt overleapt itself and got a city so heavily in debt that it could not pay its taxes. The federal government then had to step in, forgive unpaid taxes and appoint a federal official to keep an eye on municipal expenditures. But except for such emergencies, the cities were to such an extent free from federal interference in managing their own affairs that the whole Roman Empire could almost be regarded as a federation of independent cities. The cities helped out the government in Rome by maintaining order, assessing taxes, and keeping up the aqueducts, bridges, highways and the expensive post-horse system in their districts. Because so much of the work of keeping the Empire rolling along was left to them, the imperial civil service comprised a surprisingly small body of men.

At the center of the far-flung web of power sat the emperor himself, deciding every step of policy, sifting reports, making appointments and keeping in close touch with his vast dominions by couriers who carried the imperial dispatches with astonishing speed over the Roman highway system.

# Cicero Is Concerned with the Relationship between Rome and the Provinces (70 B.C.)

Marcus Tullius Cicero (106–43 B.C.) was one of the most illustrious Romans in the last years of the Republic. A gifted speaker and brilliant lawyer, he rose rapidly through the ranks of government, although like Cato he was a "new man" and not a patrician. The Orations against Verres from which this reading is taken formed the foundation stone of his reputation. Of all the Roman provinces in Cicero's day, Sicily, at the toe of Italy, conquered from the Carthaginians in the third century, was the most important. Its thriving agricultural economy made it into the breadbasket of Rome and an inviting goal for greedy officials, of whom Gaius Verres (120–43 B.C.) was the most notorious. Verres as governor of Sicily between 73 and 71 B.C. gained a reputation for corruption notable even at a time when use of public office for private gain was taken for granted. In 70, representatives of the long-suffering Sicilian cities accused him before the Senate of having extorted a fortune in taxes from them during his term of office. Cicero utilized the case to emphasize the necessity of just treatment for the provinces that contributed so significantly to Rome's power and prosperity. Verres himself fled during the trial to southern Gaul (France), where he lived in exile until his death. Both excerpts from the Verrine Orations of Cicero. I. is taken from *Second Speech Against Verres,* II, i.2–111.8, xiii. 32 in *Roman Civilization,* ed. N. Lewis and M. Reinhold (New York: Columbia University Press, 1951), I, pp. 346–348. II is reprinted by permission of the publishers and the Loeb Classical Library, from Cicero: *The Verrine Orations,* trans: L. H. Greenwood, Cambridge, Mass.: Harvard University Press, 1900.

## I. CICERO ASSERTS THE IMPORTANCE OF SICILY TO ROME

Before I speak of Sicily's distresses, I feel that I should say a little of the high position of that province, of its antiquity, and of its practical importance. Your attentive consideration, due to the interests of all our allies and all our provinces, is especially due, gentlemen, to those of Sicily for many strong reasons, the first of which is this, that Sicily was the first of all foreign nations to turn to the friendship and protection of the Roman people. She was the first of all to receive the title of province, the first such jewel in our imperial crown. She was the first who made our forefathers perceive how splendid a thing a foreign empire is. No other people has equaled her in loyal good will toward us: once the various states in the island had embraced our friendship, they never thereafter seceded from it, and most of them—and those the most notable—remained without a break our firm friends. From this province therefore it was that our forefathers took that great step in their imperial career, the invasion of Africa; for the great power of Carthage would never have been crushed so readily had not Sicily been at our disposal, supplying us with grain and affording safe harborage to our fleets. . . .

Accordingly, our relations with this province for all purposes were always such that we looked upon her various products not as growing on her soil, but as already added to our stores at home. When has she failed to pay us punctually her tribute of grain? When has she not spontaneously offered us what she believed we needed? When has she refused to supply what was ordered of her? Cato the Wise called her in consequence "the nation's storehouse, the nurse at whose breast the Roman people is fed." Nay, we in our time have found, in the critical days of the great Italic War, how Sicily has been to us no mere storehouse, but like the ancient and well-filled state treasury of our fathers' days, supplying us with hides and shirts and grain, free of cost to ourselves, to clothe, feed, and equip our great armies. Yes, and she does us services, great services, of which we, gentlemen, are I daresay not even aware. Many of our citizens are the richer for having a profitable field of enterprise in this loyal province close at hand, which they can visit so easily, and where they can carry on their business so freely. To some of these Sicily supplies merchandise, and sends them away enriched with profits; others she keeps with her, to become, according to their preference, farmers or cattlemen or businessmen, and in short to settle and make their homes there. It is a national advantage of no trifling kind that so large a number of Roman citizens should be kept so near their own country, engaged in occupations so honest and profitable. Our tributes and our provinces constitute, in a sense, our nation's landed estates; and thus, just as you, gentlemen, gain most pleasure from such of your estates as are close to Rome, so to the nation there is something pleasant in the nearness of this province to the capital.

And then again, the character of the inhabitants is such, so hardy and upright and honest, that it really reminds us of the stern old Roman manners rather than of those which have come to prevail among us today. They have none of the failings found elsewhere among Greeks; they are neither slothful nor self-indulgent; on the contrary, they are highly industrious, for their own and for the public good; plain-living and conscientious folk. Such, moreover, is their attachment to our own people that only among them is neither tax collector nor moneylender an object of hatred. Acts of oppression, again, on the part of Roman officials, they have borne so patiently time after time that never before this day have they, as a community, sought refuge in the sanctuary of the law and the stronghold of your protection. . . . It was an inherited tradition of theirs to regard Rome as so great a benefactor of the Sicilians that they must even endure oppression, if the oppressors were Romans. . . .

## II. CICERO ATTACKS MISGOVERNMENT OF THE SICILIANS

When Verres was governor of Sicily, the position of the farmers was such that they thought themselves well treated if they were allowed to vacate their farms and hand them over to Apronius [tax-collector]; they were only too eager to escape the numerous sufferings they saw in front of them. The edict required them to hand over as much corn as Apronius might declare due from them. Even if he declared more due than the whole of their crop? Yes: by Verres' edict that was what the magistrates had to extract from them. Well, the farmer had power to claim back from the collector. He had; and his claim was heard by—Artemidorus [judge appointed by Verres]. What if the farmer paid over less than Apronius demanded? He was prosecuted before a court, with a fourfold penalty if convicted. From whom was this court selected? From the high respectable members of the governor's admirable staff. Is that all? No; I next charge you with making an under-statement of your acreage; stand your trial for breaking the regulations. Trial before what court? Before a court taken from the staff aforesaid. And finally: if you are found guilty, or rather, *when* you are found guilty—for before such a court what doubt could there be of it?—you must be flogged to death. Under such terms and such conditions, will anyone be so simple as to think that those sales were sales of tithes? as to suppose that the farmer was allowed to keep nine-tenths of his corn? as not to see that the farmers' goods and property and fortunes simply went to enrich that pirate of a governor?

And now hear what Verres did order them to do, and then conceal if you can your certainty of what all Sicily saw clearly, that it was the governor himself who was the purchaser of those tithe-rights, or rather, who was the farmers' master and tyrant. He ordered the people of Agyrium to take over, as a community, the collection of the tithe, paying Apronius a bonus as well.—If Apronius bought those tithe-rights dear, may I ask you, Verres—since you are the man who looked into the value of these things so carefully, and tell us you sold those rights so dear—why should you think the purchaser ought to be paid a bonus? Oh well, you did think so: but why did you *order* that payment? What can "extortion of money" be—that clearly criminal act—if this violent abuse of your authority to force unwilling persons to pay another person a bonus—in other words, to pay him money—if this is *not* extortion?—Very well. They were ordered to pay a small trifle of bonus to the governor's particular friend Apronius. You shall believe, gentlemen, that it was Apronius to whom this was paid, if you make up your mind that it *was* a bonus for Apronius and not plunder for the governor. —You order them to take over the tithe-collection, and to pay Apronius a bonus of *thirty-three thousand* bushels of wheat. What? From the land of one town, this one town is forced, by the governor's orders, to make Apronius a present of enough corn to supply the populace of Rome for nearly a month! What, you sold the tithes at a high price—when such a profit as that was made over to the man who bought them? If you had made careful inquiry into the value of those tithes when you were selling them, I am very sure the town would have added another ten thousand bushels then, rather than 600,000 sesterces [$30,000] afterwards. . . .

Because of Roman greed and Roman injustice, all our provinces are mourning, all our free communities are complaining, and even foreign kingdoms are protesting. As far as the bounds of Ocean there is no spot now so distant or so obscure that the wanton and oppressive deeds of Romans have not penetrated thither. Not against the onset of the armies of the world in war, but against its groans and tears and lamentation, can Rome hold out no longer. When such are the facts, and such the prevailing moral standards, if any prosecuted person, upon his crimes being clearly demonstrated, shall plead that others have done the like, he will not find himself without precedents: but Rome will find herself without hope of escaping doom, if the precedents set by one scoundrel are to secure the acquittal and impunity of another. Are you satisfied that our governors shall govern as they do? satisfied that our allies should for the future be treated as you see that in recent years they have been treated? Then why am I wasting my labour here, why do you still sit on, why do you not rise and go while I am still addressing you? Would you, on the other hand, do something to reduce the unscrupulous and unprincipled villany of such men as that? Then waver no longer between the advantage of sparing one rascal for the sake of a number of rascals, and that of punishing one rascal and thereby checking the rascality of many others. . . .

# Cicero Advises His Brother How To Govern

**(60 B.C.)**

Cicero's brother Quintus was governor of the province of Asia (in western Turkey) 60–59 B.C. From Cicero, *Letters to His Brother Quintus*, Book I, No. 1, pp. 8–35 in *Roman Civilization*, ed. N. Lewis and M. Reinhold (New York: Columbia University Press, 1951).

It is a glorious thought that you should have been three years in Asia in supreme command and not been tempted by the offer of any statue, picture, plate, garment, or slave, by any fascination of human beauty, or by any pecuniary proposals—temptations with which that province of yours abounds—to deviate from the path of strict integrity and sobriety of conduct. . . .

In these matters, however, experience itself has by this time taught you that it is by no means sufficient to possess these virtues yourself, but that you must keep diligent watch around you so that in this guardianship of your province it may appear that you are responsible to the allies, the citizens, and the state not for yourself alone, but for all the officials of your government. You have as legates men who are likely to consider their own reputation [as well as yours]. . . . Your quaestor is not a man of your own deliberate selection, but one assigned you by lot; he ought to be a man of instinctive self-control, and should also comply with your policy and instructions. Among these men, should it happen that anyone could not show a clean record of conduct, you would put up with him so long as he disregarded only the regulations by which he was bound in his capacity as a private individual, but not if he abused for purposes of private lucre the powers you had vouchsafed him for the maintenance of his public position. . . .

As for those, however, whom you have chosen to be about you either in your domestic entourage or on your train of personal attendants—generally spoken of as a sort of "praetor's retinue"—in *their* case we have to be responsible not only for their every act, but for their every word. . . . Let this third year show the same standard of integrity as the preceding two, but even an increase in caution and in diligence. Let your ears be such as are reputed to hear only what they do hear, and not such as are open to false and interested whispers prompted by the hope of profit. . . . In a word, let it be recognized by the whole province that the welfare, children, reputation, and fortunes of all whom you govern are most precious to you. Finally, let it be the general impression that you will regard with disfavor not only those who have taken a bribe, but also those who have given one, if ever you get to know of it. And, as a matter of fact, there will be no giving of bribes when it is made perfectly clear that, in general, nothing is got out of you through the machinations of persons pretending to have great influence with you. . . .

These and all the other precedents of notable severity you have established in your province we should not easily justify except by the most perfect probity. For that reason be as severe as you please in administering justice, provided that your severity is not varied by partiality but kept on the same level of consistency. However, it is of little importance that your own administration of justice is consistent and careful, unless it is so administered also by those to whom you have yielded any portion of that duty. And indeed it seems to me that there is no great variety of transactions in the government of Asia, but that the entire government mainly depends upon the administration of justice; and, being thus limited, the theory of government itself, especially in the provinces, presents no difficulty; you only need to show such consistency and firmness as to withstand not only favoritism, but the very suspicion of it. In addition to this there must be civility in hearing, clemency in deciding, and careful discrimination in the satisfactory settlement of disputes. . . .

And my personal opinion is that those who govern others must guage their every act by this one test—the greatest possible happiness of the governed; and that this principle is and has been from the beginning, from the moment you set foot in Asia, of primary importance in your eyes, is a fact bruited abroad by unvarying report and in the conversation of all. And indeed it is the duty not only of one who governs allies and citizens, but also one who governs slaves and dumb animals, to be himself a slave to the interest and well-being of those he governs. And in this respect I see that there is universal agreement as to the extraordinary pains you are taking; I see that no new debt is being contracted to burden the states, whereas many of them have been relieved by you of a big and heavy debt of long standing; that several cities, demolished and almost deserted (among them Samos and Halicarnassus, the most famous cities of Ionia and Caria, respectively), have been rebuilt through your instrumentality; that there are no insurrections, no civil discords in the towns; that you are providing for the government of the states by councils of their aristocracies; that brigandage has been exterminated in Mysia, murder suppressed in various places, and peace established throughout the province; that thefts and robberies, not only those on the highways and in the country, but also (and these are far more frequent and serious) in towns and temples, have been effectually checked; that the good name, the possessions, and the peace of mind of the wealthy have been delivered from that pernicious instrument of praetorian greed—prosecution on a false charge; that the incidence of expenditure and taxation in the states bears in equal proportion upon all those who dwell within the boundaries of those states; that it is the easiest thing in the world to gain access to you; that your ears are open to the complaints of all; that no man's lack of means or of friends has ever shut him out from approaching you, not only in public and on the tribunal, but even in your very house and bedchamber; in short, that in the whole sphere of your command there is nothing harsh, nothing brutal, nothing but clemency, gentleness, and kindness of heart. . . .

And yet to all your good will and devotion to duty there is a serious obstacle in the publicans [tax collectors]; if we oppose them, we shall alienate from ourselves and from the common wealth a class that has deserved extremely well of us and been brought through our instrumentality into close association with the commonwealth; and yet, if we yield to them in everything, we shall be acquiescing in the utter ruin of those whose security, and indeed whose interests, we are bound to protect. This is the one outstanding difficulty (if we would face the question honestly) in the whole sphere of your command. For as to one's being unselfish, curbing one's passions, keeping one's staff in check, maintaining a consistently uniform policy in the administration of justice, conducting one's self with kindly courtesy in investigating cases and in giving audience to suitors and not shutting one's door to them—all that is magnificent rather than difficult to do, for it depends not upon any strenuous exertion, but upon making up one's mind and setting one's will in a certain direction.

What bitterness of feeling this question of the publicans causes the allies we have gathered from our own citizens, who recently, on the abolition of port dues in Italy, complained not so much of that impose itself as of certain malpractices on the part of the customs officers, [employees of the publicans]. I therefore know pretty well what happens to allies in distant lands from the complaints I have heard from citizens in Italy. So to conduct yourself in this connection as to satisfy the publicans, especially when they have taken over the collection of taxes at a loss, [the publicans were trying to recoup losses on a contract for which they had bid too high] and at the same time not to allow the allies to be ruined, seems to demand a sort of divine excellence—in other words, an excellence such as yours. Let us take the Greeks first; their greatest grievance is that they are subject to taxation; but they should not regard that as so very much of a grievance, for the simple reason that they put themselves in that position of their own free will by their own enactment, without any command from the Roman people. . . . And that the Greek collectors are no more gentle in enforcing the payment of taxes than our own publicans may be inferred from the fact that quite recently the Aunians and all the islands that had been made tributary by Sulla to the Rhodians fled for protection to our senate, begging that they might pay their taxes to us rather than to the Rhodians. . . . Let Asia at the same time bear this in mind, that were she not under our government, there is no disaster in the way of either foreign war or intestine discords that she would have been likely to escape. Seeing, however, that such government cannot possibly be maintained without taxes, she should not resent having to pay for perpetual peace and tranquility with some portion of what her soil produces. . . .

# Cicero as a Roman Governor: Theory versus Practice (51 B.C.)

Cicero was governor of the province of Cilicia (southern Turkey and the island of Cyprus) in the year 51–50 B.C. Here he intended to carry out the principles of government he championed. The clash between theory and practice is shown in his three letters below. The publicans of whom he speaks in the second letter were private citizens (often organized into companies) who purchased the job of collecting the taxes for the government. The publicans earned their profit by collecting more money than the sum set by the government. The desirability of such an arrangement for the men involved and the opportunities for corruption are obvious. Another source of easy income was money lending at excessive interest rates. Brutus, mentioned in the third letter, was an influential Roman Senator who had loaned money to the city of Salamis on Cyprus at 48 percent interest in the expectation of making a financial killing. From Cicero, *Letters to Atticus,* Book V, No. 16 and No. 21, and *Letters to Friends,* Book XIII, No. 9, in *Roman Civilization,* ed. N. Lewis and M. Reinhold (New York: Columbia University Press, 1951), I, pp. 366–369.

Cilicia, c. August 10, 51 B.C.

Cicero to Atticus, greeting.

My arrival in this province, which is in a state of lasting ruin and desolation, was expected eagerly. I stayed three days at Laodicea, three at Apamea, and as many at Synnas, and got here on July 31. Everywhere I heard the same story: people could not pay the poll tax; they were forced to sell out; the townspeople groaned and lamented—and all the result of the outrages of one who is no man, but rather some kind of savage beast [Cicero's predecessor as governor]. All the people are, as you may suppose, tired of life. However, the unhappy towns are relieved that they have had to spend nothing on me, my legates, a quaestor, or anyone. For I want you to know that I not only refused to accept money . . . but none of us will take firewood or anything beyond four beds and a roof; and in many places we do not accept even a roof, but remain mostly under canvas. So, extraordinary throngs of people have come to meet me from farms and villages and every homestead. Upon my word, my very coming seems to revive them. Your friend Cicero has won all hearts by his justice, self-restraint and kind bearing. . . .

Cilicia, toward the end of 51 B.C.

Cicero to Crassipes, greeting.

Although I recommended the Bithynian [tax-collecting] company to you in person as particularly as I could and understood that not only because of my recommendation, but also because that was your own inclination, you were anxious to accommodate that company in any way you could, still, since those whose interests are in question thought it of paramount importance to them that I should make it plain to you by letter also how I felt towards them, I have not hesitated to write you this note.

I would have you believe that while it has always been the greatest pleasure to me to make much of the class of publicans [tax collectors] as a whole—and considering the great services that class has rendered me, I am under obligation to do so—I am in a special sense a friend of this Bithynian company. This company, made up of members from all the other companies, constitutes a most important factor in the state by virtue of the kind of men who compose it and the class to which they belong; and, as it happens, a large proportion of its partners are on very intimate terms with myself, especially the man who is at this moment the executive head, namely Publius Rutilius, son of Publius, of the Menenian tribe, who is the manager of that company.

Such being the case, I entreat you with more than usual urgency to support with every kindness and all your generosity Gnaeus Pupius, who is in the company's employ; to see to it that his services (you will find it easy to do so) are as acceptable as possible to the partners; and to exert yourself (how much power a quaestor [official in charge of financial affairs] has in such matters I am well aware) to protect and augment the property and interests of those partners as much as possible. Not only will you greatly oblige me by so doing, but I can promise and pledge you from my own experience that, if you oblige them, you will find the Bithynian partners neither forgetful nor ungrateful.

Laodicea, February 13, 50 B.C.

Cicero to Atticus, greeting.

. . . During the six months of my administration there have been no requisitions and not a single case of billeting. Before my time this season had been devoted each year to the pursuit of gain. The richer towns used to pay large sums to escape from having soldiers billeted on them for the winter. The people of Cyprus, for example, used to pay 200 Attic talents, but under my administration they will appropriate, in literal truth, not a penny. I will accept no honors except speechifying in return for these kindnesses which have so amazed people. I permit no statues, shrines, or sculptured chariots; and I don't annoy the communities in any other respect—but perhaps I annoy you by my egotism. Bear with it out of your regard for me: it was you who wished me to act as I have. My tour through Asia was such that even the crowning misery of famine, which existed in my province owing to crop failure, gave me a welcome opportunity: wherever I went, without force, without resort to legal process, without harsh words, by my personal influence and exhortations, I induced the Greeks and the Roman citizens who had stored grain to promise a large quantity to the communities. . . .

Now let me tell you about Brutus. Some creditors of the city of Salamis in Cyprus, namely Marcus Scaptius and Publius Martinius, were warmly recommended to me by my friend Brutus as being associates of his. Martinius I have not met; Scaptius came to see me in camp. I promised that I would see to it, for Brutus' sake, that the people of Salamis paid him his money. The fellow thanked me and asked for the post of prefect. I informed him that I always refused to appoint businessmen to my staff, as I have told you. This rule Gnaeus Pompey accepted when he made a similar request. So did Torquatus, Marcus Laenius, and many others. However, I told Scaptius that if he wanted the post on account of his loan, I would see that he got paid. He thanked me and took his leave. Our "friend" Appius [the previous governor] had given him some squadrons to put pressure on Salamis, and had also given him the office of prefect. He was causing trouble to the people of Salamis. I gave orders that his cavalry should leave the island. That annoyed him.

In short, to keep faith with him I ordered the people, when they came along with Scaptius to see me at Tarsus, to pay the money. They had a good deal to say about the loan, and about the harm that Scaptius had done them. I refused to listen. I prayed and besought them to settle the business in consideration of the good I had done their city. Finally, I threatened to compel them. So far from refusing to settle, the people said that really they would be paying out of my pocket, in the sense that I had refused to take the honorarium usually given to the governor, which they admitted was more than the amount they owed Scaptius. I praised their attitude. "Very well," said Scaptius, "let us reckon up the total." Now . . . I had fixed the rate of interest at 12 per cent compounded annually. But Scaptius demanded 48 per cent in accordance with the terms of the loan. I declared that I could not break the rule laid down in my edict. But he produced a decree of the senate, passed in the consulship of Lentulus and Philippus [56 B.C.], ordering the governor of Cilicia to give judgment according to the terms of this contract! . . .

# Josephus Condemns the Judaean Revolt

**(66–73 A.D.)**

The Judaean Revolt was a striking example of the failure of Roman provincial administration and of the conflict between the *pax romana* and the ideal of freedom. Judaea, homeland of the Hebrews, had enjoyed a century of independence after the Maccabean revolt against the Hellenistic Seleucid monarchy of Persia in the second century B.C. It was conquered by the Roman general Pompey in 64 B.C. and turned into a province under Augustus. The Jews openly revolted against Roman government in 66 A.D., and many hoped to restore full independence to Judaea. The depth of the clash of Roman rule with Jewish aspirations was played down by the historian Josephus, who collaborated with the Romans in the siege of Jerusalem (in 70 A.D.), led by Titus, son of Emperor Vespasian. Josephus belonged to the group of Hellenized and assimilated Jews who distrusted and feared the elements of nationalism, religious orthodoxy, and economic discontent in the rebellion. The fall of Jerusalem did not end the struggle, for last-ditch resistance continued at the isolated fortress of Masada near the Dead Sea, and Judaea rose against the Roman occupation again in the following century. But Jewish national independence was not to be rewon until the twentieth century. Reprinted by permission of the publishers and The Loeb Classical Library from Josephus, *The Jewish War,* trans. H. Thackery and R. Marcus, Cambridge, Mass.: Harvard University Press, 1928.

### TITUS LAYS SIEGE TO JERUSALEM

The earthworks of Titus were progressing, notwithstanding the galling fire from the ramparts to which his men were exposed. The general, moreover, sent a detachment of horses with orders to lie in wait for any who issued from the town into the ravines in quest of food. . . . When caught, they were driven to resist, and after a conflict it seemed too late to sue for mercy. They were accordingly scourged and subjected to torture of every description, before being killed, and then crucified opposite the walls.

Titus indeed commiserated their fate, five hundred or sometimes more being captured daily; on the other hand, he recognized the risk of dismissing prisoners of war, and that the custody of such numbers would amount to the imprisonment of their custodians; but his main reason for not stopping the crucifixions was the hope that the spectacle might perhaps induce the Jews to surrender, for fear that continued resistance would involve them in a similar fate. The soldiers out of rage and hatred amused themselves by nailing their prisoners in different postures; and so great was their number, that space could not be found for the crosses nor crosses for the bodies.

The insurgents, however, far from relenting at these sufferings, deluded the remainder by inventing a contrary motive for them. Dragging the relatives of the deserters to the wall, together with any citizens who were anxious to accept the offer of terms, they showed them what was the fate of those who sought refuge with the Romans, asserting that the arrested victims were not captives, but suppliants. This, until the truth became known, kept back many who were eager to desert; some, however, instantly fled, as to certain punishment, regarding death at the enemy's hands as rest in comparison with starvation. But Titus now gave orders to cut off the hands of several of the prisoners, that they might not be mistaken for deserters and that their calamity might add credit to their statements, and then sent them in to Simon and John, exhorting them now at least to pause, and not compel him to destroy the city, but by repentance at the eleventh hour to gain their own lives, their magnificent city, and a temple unshared by others. At the same time he went round the embankments, urging on the workmen, as if intending shortly to follow up his threats by action.

To this message the Jews retorted by heaping abuse from the ramparts upon Caesar himself, and his father, crying out that they scorned death, which they honorably preferred to slavery; that they would do Romans every injury in their power while they had breath in their bodies; that men so soon, as he himself said, to perish, were unconcerned for their native place, and that the world was a better temple for God than this one. But, they added, it would yet be saved by Him who dwelt therein, and while they had Him for their ally they would deride all menaces unsupported by action; for the issue rested with God. . . .

## THE ROMANS DEMAND UNCONDITIONAL SURRENDER

[The defenders of Jerusalem] beaten on all sides in the war and surrounded by a wall preventing any possibility of escape, now invited Titus to a parley. Anxious with his innate humanity, at all events to save the town, and instigated by his friends, who supposed that the brigands had at length been brought to reason, Titus took up a position on the west of the outer court of the Temple; . . . The multitude stood in crowds on either side: the Jews around Simon and John, excited by hopes of pardon, the Romans beside Caesar eagerly waiting to hear their claim. Titus, after charging his troops to keep a check on their rage and their missiles, and stationing an interpreter beside him, proceeded, in token of his conquest, to address them first.

"Well, sirs, are you at length sated with your country's woes—you who, without bestowing a thought on our strength or your own weakness, have through inconsiderate fury and madness lost your people, your city, and your Temple, and are yourselves justly doomed to perish—you who from the first, ever since Pompey reduced you by force, never ceased from revolution and have now ended by declaring open war upon the Romans? Did you rely on numbers? Nay, a mere fraction of the Roman soldiery has proved your match. On the fidelity of allies? Pray, what nation beyond the limits of our empire would prefer Jews to Romans? On physical strength, perhaps? Yet you are aware that the Germans are our slaves. On the solidity of your walls? But what wall could be a greater obstacle than the ocean, encompassed by which the Britons yet do homage to the Roman arms? On the determination of spirit and the astuteness of your generals? Yet you knew that even Carthaginians were defeated.

"No, assuredly you were incited against the Romans by Roman humanity. To begin with, we allowed you to occupy this land and set over you kings of your own blood; then we maintained the laws of your forefathers and permitted you, not only among yourselves but also in your dealings with others, to live as you willed. . . .

"And after all this, most abominable wretches, do you now invite me to a parley? What have you to save comparable to what is lost? What protection do you think you deserve after losing your temple? Nay, even now you stand in arms, and at the last extremity, do not so much as pretend to be suppliants. Miserable men, on what do you rely? Is not your folk dead, your temple gone, your city at my mercy, are not your very lives in my hands? And do you yet deem it glorious bravery to die in the last ditch? I, however, will not emulate your frenzy. Throw down

A coin issued during the reign of Emperor Vespasian. On one side is a profile of the emperor; on the other a Roman officer, with a commander's baton and his foot on a helmet, stands guard over the weeping daughter of Zion. The inscription reads "Judaea captured," with "S(enatus) C(onsulto)" below. The palm-tree was the symbol of Judaea.

your arms, surrender your persons, and I grant you your lives, like a lenient master of a household punishing the incorrigible and preserving the rest for myself."

To this they replied that they could not accept a pledge from him, having sworn never to do so; but they asked permission to pass through his line of circumvallation with their wives and children, undertaking to retire to the desert and to leave the city to him. Thereupon Titus, indignant that men in the position of captives should proffer proposals to him as victors, ordered proclamation to be made to them neither to desert nor to hope for terms any longer, for he would spare none; but to fight with all their might and save themselves as best they could, because all his actions henceforth would be governed by the laws of war. He then gave his troops permission to burn and sack the city. . . .

## THE TREATMENT OF REBELS

Titus, on entering the town . . . issued orders to kill only those who were found in arms and offered resistance and to make prisoners of the rest. The troops, in addition to those specified in their instructions, slew the old and feeble, while those in the prime of life and serviceable they drove together into the Temple and shut them up in the court of the women. Caesar appointed one of his freedmen as their guard, and his friend Fronto to adjudicate upon the lot appropriate to each. Fronto put to death all the seditious and brigands, information being given by them against each other; he selected the tallest and the most handsome of the youth and reserved them for the triumph [Roman custom of ceremonial entry of the victorious general into Rome preceded by representatives of the conquered in chains]; of the rest, those over seventeen years of age he sent in chains to the mines in Egypt, while multitudes were presented by Titus to the various provinces, to be destroyed in the theaters by the sword or by wild beasts; those under seventeen were sold.

# Tacitus Views the Romanization of Britain

The conquest of Britain, begun by the Romans in 43 A.D., continued intermittently for forty years. By the 80s they had pushed to central Scotland, leaving only the arid, sea-enclosed Highlands in the hands of the Britons. Tacitus, a Roman historian writing on the campaign, described the methods adopted by the Romans to pacify the conquered population and followed this with a statement of the British position which he put in the mouth of Calgacus, a chieftain who was trying to rally a defense of the Highland area. As it happened, the need for troops elsewhere caused the recall of the bulk of the Roman armies in 84, and the Highlands were never conquered, but the Romans continued to hold most of the island. From *The Works of Tacitus,* the Oxford Translation, Revised (London, 1887), I, pp. 366, 372–373. (Somewhat simplified by the editors.)

## I. THE ROMANIZATION OF A CONQUERED LAND (83 A.D.)

The succeeding winter was employed in remedial measures. In order, by a taste of pleasures, to reclaim the natives from that rude and unsettled state which prompted them to war and reconcile them to quiet and tranquillity, [Agricola, the Roman commander,] incited them by private instigations and public encouragements to erect temples, courts of justice, and dwelling-houses. He rewarded those who were prompt in complying with his intentions and reprimanded such as were dilatory; thus promoting a spirit of imitating the Romans which had all the force of necessity. He was also attentive to provide a liberal education for the sons of their chieftains, . . . and his attempts were attended with such success that they who lately disdained to make use of the Roman language were now ambitious to speak it well. Hence Roman clothing began to be held in honour, and the toga was frequently worn. At length the [Britons] gradually deviated into a taste for those luxuries which stimulate to vice: porticos and baths and the elegance of the table; and this from their experience, they termed politeness, whilst in reality it constituted a part of their slavery.

## II. A BRITISH CHIEFTAIN EVALUATES ROMAN RULE (84 A.D.)

"When I reflect on the causes of the war and the circumstances of our situation, I am strongly persuaded that our united efforts on the present day will prove the beginning of universal liberty to Britain. For we are not yet debased by slavery; and there is no land behind us, nor does even the sea afford a refuge, whilst the Roman fleet hovers around. Thus the use of arms, at all times honourable to the brave, now even to cowards offers the only safety. Our countrymen may be deemed to have reposed their final hopes and resources in us in the battles that have been fought with various success against the Romans, for we, the noblest sons of Britain, and therefore still lighting in its most northern regions, have not even seen our fellow countrymen under subjection and hence are not polluted by the concept of slavery. We, at the furthest limits both of land and liberty, have been defended to this day by the remoteness of our situation and of our fame. The geographical extremity of Britain is now before us; and whatever is unknown becomes an object of magnitude. But there is no nation beyond us; nothing but waves and rocks and still more hostile Romans, whose arrogance we cannot escape by servility and submission. These plunderers of the world, after exhausting the land by their devastations, are rifling the ocean: stimulated by greed if their enemy be rich; by ambition if poor: unsatiated by the East and by the West: the only people who are moved to grab wealth and poverty with equal desire. To ravage, to slaughter, to usurp under false titles they call empire; and where they make a desert, they call it peace."

"Our children and relations are naturally the dearest of all things to us. These are torn away to serve in foreign lands. Our wives and sisters, even if they escape being raped, are polluted under names of friendship and hospitality. Our estates and possessions are consumed in tributes; our grain in contributions. Even our bodies are worn down amidst whippings and insults in clearing woods and draining marshes. Wretches born to slavery are once bought and afterwards maintained by their masters: Britain every day buys, every day feeds, her own servitude. And as among domestic slaves every newcomer serves for the scorn and derision of his fellows; so, in this ancient household of the world, we, as the newest and vilest, are sought out to destruction. For we have neither cultivated lands nor mines nor harbors which can induce them to preserve us for our labors. . . . Since then all hopes of mercy are vain, at length assume courage, both you to whom safety and you to whom glory is dear. . . . Shall not we, untouched, unsubdued, and struggling not for the acquisition but the security of liberty, show what men [Britain] has reserved for her defense? . . . "

# The Problems of Governing an Empire: Correspondence of Pliny and the Emperor Trajan (c. 105 A.D.)

Pliny (62– c. 113 A.D.) was governor of Bithynia in what is today northwestern Turkey. Trajan (ruler 98–117 A.D.) was one of the so-called "Five Good Emperors" who governed the empire from 98 to 180 A.D. The Pliny-Trajan correspondence provides an excellent view of the attention to detail paid by the heads of the Roman state. From Pliny, *Letters,* X. 42 in G. W. Botsford, *A Source-Book of Ancient History* (New York, 1912), pp. 503–504.

### TO THE EMPEROR TRAJAN

While I was making a journey in a different part of the province, a most destructive fire broke out at Nicomedia, which consumed not only several private houses, but also two public buildings,—the town house and the temple of Isis, though they stood on opposite sides of the street. The cause of its spreading thus wide was partly the violence of the wind, and partly the indolence of the people, who, it appears, stood fixed and idle spectators of this terrible calamity. The truth is that the city was not furnished with engines, buckets, or any single instrument for extinguishing fires. I have now, however, given directions to provide this apparatus.

You will consider, Sir, whether it may not be advisable to form a company of firemen, consisting of only a hundred and fifty members. I will take care that none but those of that occupation shall be admitted into it; and that the privileges granted them shall not be extended to any other purpose. As this corporate body will be restricted to so small a number of members, it will be easy to keep them under proper regulations.

### TRAJAN TO PLINY

You are of the opinion that it would be proper to establish a company of firemen in Nicomedia, agreeably to what has been practised in other cities. But remember that societies of this sort have greatly disturbed the peace of the provinces in general, and particularly of those cities in which they exist. Whatever name we give them, and for whatever purpose they may be instituted, they will not fail to form themselves into factious assemblies, however short their meetings may be. It will therefore be safer to provide such machines as are of service in extinguishing fires, to enjoin the owners of houses to assist in preventing the mischief from spreading, and if it should be necessary, to call in the aid of the populace.



# Appian Admires the Greatness of the Roman Empire

Appian of Alexandria (second century A.D.) was a native of the great Hellenistic city founded by Alexander. A Greek, Appian typified the cosmopolitan culture of the Empire in his strong bias for Roman ways. His history of Rome, written about the time of Trajan, has preserved many contemporary documents for later generations. From *The Roman History of Appian of Alexandria,* trans. Horace White (London, 1899), I, pp. 3–6.

From the advent of the emperors to the present time is nearly two hundred years more, in the course of which the city has been greatly embellished, its revenue much increased, and in the long reign of peace and security everything has moved toward a lasting prosperity. Some nations have been added to the empire by these emperors, and the revolts of others have been suppressed. Possessing the best part of the earth and sea they have, on the whole, aimed to preserve their empire by the exercise of prudence, rather than to extend their sway indefinitely over poverty-stricken and profitless tribes of barbarians, some of whom I have seen at Rome offering themselves, by their ambassadors, as its subjects, but the chief of the state would not accept them because they would be of no use to it. They give kings to a great many other nations whom they do not wish to have under their own government. On some of these subject nations they spend more than they receive from them, deeming it dishonorable to give them up even though they are costly. They surround the empire with great armies and they garrison the whole stretch of land and sea like a single stronghold.

No government down to the present time ever attained such size and duration. That of the Greeks . . . lasted comparatively but few years. . . . Greek power, although ardent in fighting for the Grecian hegemony, never advanced steadfastly beyond the boundaries of Greece, but took pride in holding itself unenslaved and seldom conquered. From the time of Philip and Alexander, they seem to me to have done very badly and to have been unworthy of themselves.

The mastery of Asia is not to be compared, as to labor and bravery, with that of the smallest of the countries of Europe, on account of the effeminacy and cowardice of the Asiatic peoples, as will be shown in the progress of this history. Such of the Asiatic nations as the Romans hold, they subdued in a few battles, though even the Macedonians

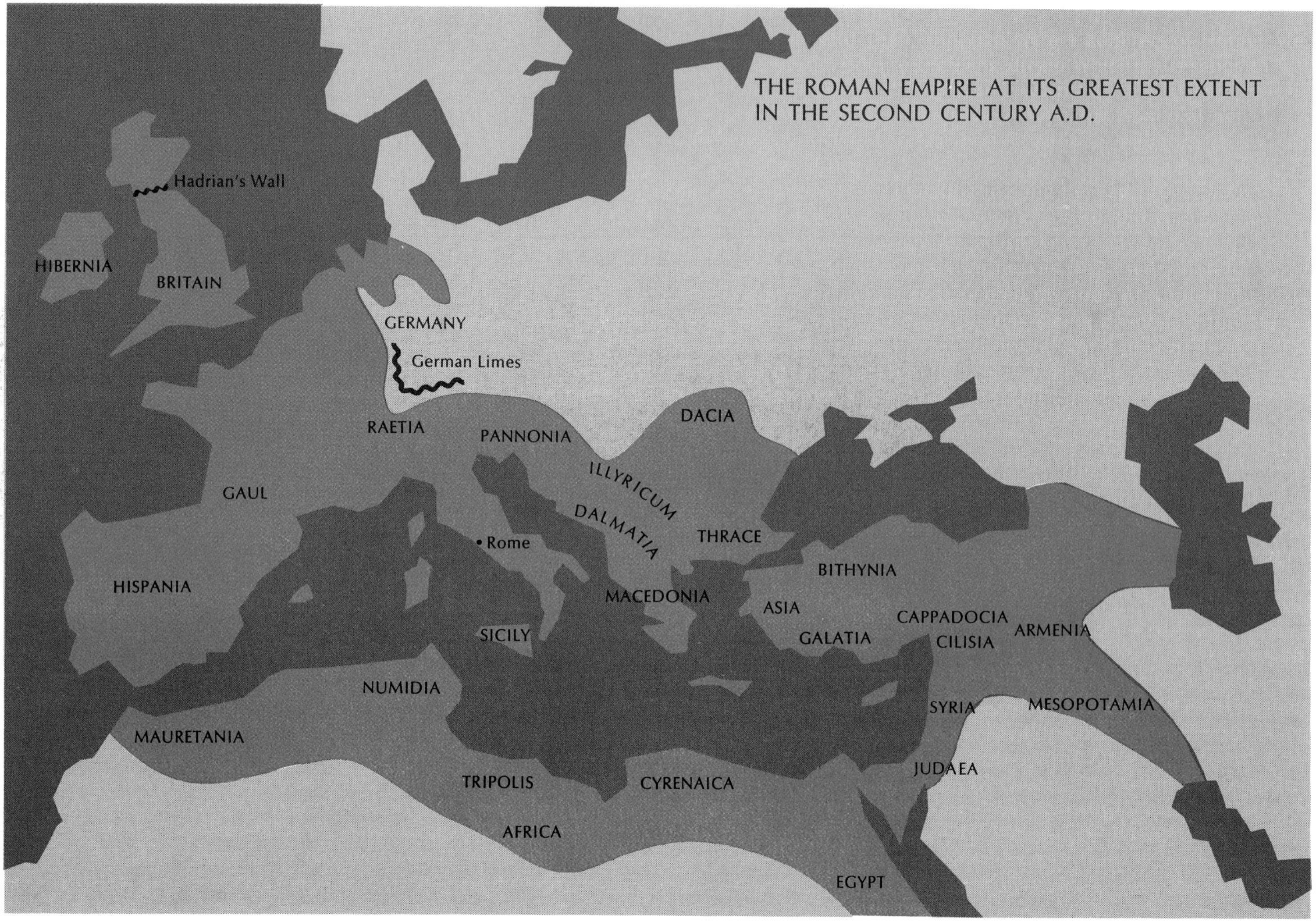

joined in the defence, while the conquest of Africa and of Europe was in many ways very exhausting. Again, the duration of the Assyrians, Medes, and Persians taken together (the three greatest empires before Alexander), does not amount to nine hundred years, which that of Rome has already reached, and the size of their empire I think was not half that of the Romans, whose boundaries extend from the setting of the sun and the Western ocean to Mount Caucasus and the river Euphrates, and through Egypt to Ethiopia and through Arabia as far as the Eastern ocean, so that their boundary is the ocean both where the sun-god rises and where he sinks, while they control the entire Mediterranean, and all its islands as well as Britain in the ocean. . . .

Through prudence and good fortune has the empire of the Romans attained to greatness and duration; in gaining which they have excelled all others in bravery, patience, and hard labor. They were never elated by success until they had firmly secured their power, nor were they ever cast down by misfortune, although . . . the city itself was often in danger. Neither famine, nor frequently recurring plague, nor sedition, nor all these falling upon them at once could abate their ardor; until, through the doubtful struggles and dangers of seven hundred years, they achieved their present greatness, having enjoyed the favors of fortune through wisdom. . . .

TOPIC 13

# ROMAN LAW AND HUMAN RIGHTS

History accords the Romans the reputation of great soldiers, knowledgeable administrators, and superb engineers, town planners, and builders. Posterity, however, is most indebted to them for their development of a legal system based on a broad science of law. Roman concepts of law underlay the functioning of the Empire; they persisted throughout the vast changes that followed the barbarian invasions that began in the third century A.D. Medieval and Renaissance interest in classics led to the revival of Roman law as the major component of contemporary civil and commercial law. Indeed the belief in natural law underlies much of the revolution of the twentieth century. The readings seek to establish the origins and nature of this Roman contribution to civilization but also examine the limits within the ancient world to a full expression of human rights.



**Reading 62**

## The Romans Develop the Foundations of Modern Law

From Crane Brinton, *Ideas and Men: The Story of Western Thought,* © 1950. Reprinted by permission of Prentice-Hall, Inc., Englewood Cliffs, New Jersey.

We moderns are well used to the notion that laws are arrangements for getting things done in human relations, and if we want to do something new, we are quite used to repealing an old law and making a new one. The eighteenth and twenty-first amendments to the American Constitution afford a neat example. The Jews, the Greeks, the Romans, all seem to have started with the notion of a revealed and unchanging Law, and they all did in practice change this Law. . . .

The Romans more definitely than any other ancient people got beyond the stage of changing their laws while pretending they were not changing them. By imperial times, indeed, the Roman Law was a complex body of doctrine that the jurists themselves acknowledged to have many sources, basically the laws of the Republic modified by statutes, by decisions of judges, by interpretations of scholarly experts, and, since Augustus, by decrees of the emperor. . . .

The Romans first clearly made law a living, growing thing consciously adapted by lawmakers to changing human demands. They have another related achievement to their credit. Law to earlier peoples, to the Jews for example, was not merely a set of divine rules, perfect and unchanging; it was a set of such rules designed *exclusively for them.* Only a Jew could obey the Mosaic Law. Only an Athenian could be tried under the Law of Athens. We have seen that the Jewish prophets rose to the conception of a Jehovah, and a divine law, shared by all mankind; and philosophically the Greeks even at the height of the independent *polis* could conceive a humanity transcending the distinction between Greeks and barbarians. The Romans, characteristically, did something of the sort not in a philosophical or theological, but in a practical way. *They extended their laws to other peoples.*

As the little *polis* on the seven hills by the Tiber, Rome seems to have had originally divine and exclusive laws, the privilege and the possession of born Roman citizens. Only gradually did the Romans come to extend the basis of Roman citizenship. Their rulers, working cautiously through the Senate, would confer Roman citizenship on individual foreigners they wished to win over, on communities, later on bigger areas. In an earlier period, they invented a sort of halfway citizenship, the Latin, in which the useful commercial and suchlike privileges were shared, but the personal, political, quasi-religious privileges of full Roman citizenship were not. And, certainly in these formative days of 500 B.C. to 100 B.C., all this was done neither in accordance with a conscious theory of widening political sovereignty nor, like the American process of citizenship by naturalization, as a kind of deliberate Romanization.

Roman citizenship, and Roman political rule generally, were widened by men of affairs trying to get things done, to lessen the tensions, the pulling and hauling, among many peoples. By the time Rome faced the international struggles of the last few centuries B.C., she had what no Greek *polis* could count on, an extended territorial area in which her rule was accepted—and in which her laws prevailed. Yet it is characteristic of the slowness of this process of political unification that as late as 90 B.C. Rome's Italian allies revolted against her, and for motives not worlds apart from those that made the allies of Athens revolt in the fifth century. Rome beat the rebels in the field—and then gave them what they wanted, full Roman citizenship. Ultimately, under the emperor Caracalla, all freeborn persons, all the mixed peoples from Britain to Syria, were made Roman citizens. . . .

Roman Law is obviously the product of generations of hard, logical thinking; and what is more, the lawyers never wholly kept from their sight the notion of an ideal, of something the law *ought to be*—of justice, in short, which is a Latin word. But they could not in the sophisticated world of later Rome retain the old simple belief that the gods had directly revealed a code of justice. Being practical and sensible men, used to responsibility, they had to believe in justice. They could not take the position that justice is a noble but unreal abstraction, or that justice is what you can get away with, or that might makes right. What they did was to put nature in place of the gods. They produced the concept of *natural law* that was to play so important a part in all subsequent political thinking.

Natural law in this sense is not a generalized description of what actually goes on in this natural world of our sense experience. It is not a law of nature in the sense that the law of gravity is a law of nature. It is, in fact, a prescription for, and a description of, a world that *ought to be*. Yet the Latin *natura,* and its Greek equivalent *physis,* certainly carry connotations of the existing, of the here-and-now, of *this* world. Perhaps one of the great reasons for the success of the concept of natural law is that though in fact it is an otherworldly concept, an ideal, it manages to suggest this world so firmly that it seems practical, not at all visionary. The natural is not only good; it seems quite possible.

Into the specific content of natural law as it was developed in the Graeco-Roman world there went several different trains of thought and experience. In a way, the ripened classical concept of natural law is one of the most successful fusions of Greek and Roman thought.

The simplest of these trains of thought is that of the practicing lawyers in Rome. We have seen that the Roman state early extended its citizenship, or part citizenship, to various individuals and groups. Some remained, however, though allies, actually foreigners. Business dealings among these individuals of varying status soon produced problems that came up for judgment in the Roman courts. The lawyers could not apply full Roman Law, which was still the property, the quasi-religious monopoly, of true Roman citizens. Yet the two litigants—a Neapolitan and a Latin, for example—themselves had grown up under different laws. What the Roman . . . judge handling such cases, did was to try to find a common rule, a sort of least common denominator in all these varying local laws, customs, usages. A business contract in one place meant one set of forms to be complied with; a business contract in another place meant quite a different set of forms. But what was common to both, what underlay both, what was a valid contract for both places? These were the questions the Roman lawyers asked themselves, and in answering them they worked out what they called the *jus gentium,* or law of peoples, as distinguished from the *jus civile,* [local law]. They arrived at this working international law, these rules for [settling] cases among men of different citizenship, or among different political units, by comparing existing national, city, or tribal laws, and trying to find what was common to them. . . .

So far, the Roman lawyers had done no more than produce a working instrument for adjusting law cases involving different legal systems. They had done no more, really, than extend to differing systems what they had done with conflicting separate rules of law within their own system. But they could hardly help feeling that their new *jus gentium* was somehow more "universal," somehow more perfect, more valid for all men, than the separate local systems they started with. And here the Greek philosophers, and especially the Stoics, came in to help them, and transform *jus gentium* into *jus naturale.*

For the Stoics had arrived at a kind of aristocratic cosmopolitanism that emphasized what men have in common as opposed to their apparent differences. That the unwise, ordinary man notices, so the Stoics reasoned, is the variegated appearance of this world and its human inhabitants. What the wise Stoic notices is the underlying unity of all God's work. He sees the permanent, not the temporary, the accidental. Nature fools the unwise into thinking she is fickle, many-sided, changing. Actually nature is, to him who can penetrate her secrets, regular, orderly, consistent, uniform. For the Stoic philosopher, the *jus gentium,* this international law common to many peoples, seemed more natural than did the various separate codes and systems of the cities, tribes, and nations. To the ruling classes of the Roman world, trained both in law and in Stoic ideas, the *jus gentium* became a kind of pattern, never wholly realized, for the *jus naturale.*

The natural is an "ought to be" which, we know from history, appealed at least to educated citizens of the most various racial origins—Britons, Gauls, Spaniards, Greeks, Romans, Egyptians, Syrians. Natural law, or what seemed its nearest early embodiment, the great system of developed Roman Law, unlike the Jewish or Athenian Law, was designed for all men; it was not an exclusive tribal possession. On the other hand, this natural law was not a mere collection of practical rules for keeping things as they are. It too was a set of ideals, a higher law, an attempt to bring justice down to earth. Natural law, the offspring of Roman Law and Greek philosophy, has been one of the most important abstract ideas in Western society. . . .

# Cicero Applies Stoic Principles to Law

Cicero (106–43 B.C.) was a complex figure, a sharp lawyer and aspiring politician who utilized his talents to promote his position, but also a scholarly idealist captivated by Hellenistic philosophy, especially Stoicism, the principles of which he tried to apply to Roman conditions. In the first reading Cicero describes his early education in Rome and Athens. The second reading contains excerpts from his great treatise on the nature of law, *De Legibus.* I. From Cicero, *Brutus,* LXXXIX-XCI in *Roman Civilization,* ed. N. Lewis and M. Reinhold (New York: Columbia University Press, 1951). II. Reprinted by permission of the publishers and The Loeb Classical Library from Cicero, *De Legibus,* trans. C. W. Keyes, Cambridge, Mass.: Harvard University Press, 1900.

## I. CICERO DESCRIBES HIS EDUCATION (91–84 B.C.)

Though I wrote and read and declaimed daily with unflagging interest, yet I was not satisfied to confine myself only to rhetorical exercises. . . . For the study of civil law I attached myself to Quintus Scaevola, the son of Quintus; he took no pupils, but the legal opinions given to his clients taught those who wished to hear him. The year following this was the consulship of Sulla and Pompey. Publius Sulpicius was tribune at that time and addressed the people daily, so that I came to know his style thoroughly. At this time Philo, then head of the Academy, along with a group of loyal Athenians, had fled from Athens because of the Mithridatic War and had come to Rome. Filled with great enthusiasm for the study of philosophy, I gave myself up wholly to his instruction. In so doing I tarried with him the more faithfully, for . . . the variety and sublimity of his subject delighted and held me. . . .

For a space of about three years the city was free from the threat of arms. . . . During all this time I spent my days and nights in study of every kind. I worked with Diodotus the Stoic, who made his residence in my house, and after a life of long intimacy died there only a short time ago. From him, apart from other subjects, I received thorough training in dialectic, which may be looked upon as a contracted or compressed eloquence. . . . But though I devoted myself to his teaching and to the wide range of subjects at his command, yet I allowed no day to pass without some rhetorical exercises. . . . This exercise I practiced much in Latin, but more often in Greek, partly because Greek, offering more opportunity for stylistic embellishment, accustomed me to a similar habit in using Latin, but partly too because the foremost teachers, knowing only Greek, could not, unless I used Greek, correct my faults nor convey their instructions. . . .

[Later] arriving at Athens I spent six months with Antiochus, the wise and famous philosopher of the Old Academy, and with him as my guide and teacher I took up again the study of philosophy, which from my early youth I had pursued, and had made some progress in, and had never wholly let drop. . . .

## II. CICERO WRITES ABOUT THE NATURE OF LAW (52 B.C.)

Out of all the material of the philosophers' discussions, surely there comes nothing more valuable than the full realization that we are born for Justice, and that right is based, not upon men's opinions, but upon Nature. This fact will immediately be plain if you once get a clear conception of man's fellowship and union with his fellow-men. For no single thing is so like another, so exactly its counterpart, as all of us are to one another. . . . However we may define man, a single definition will apply to all. This is a sufficient proof that there is no difference in kind between man and man; for if there were, one definition could not be applicable to all men; and indeed reason, which alone raises us above the level of the beasts and enables us to draw inferences, to prove and disprove, to discuss and solve problems, and to come to conclusions, is certainly common to us all, and, though varying in what it learns, at least in the capacity to learn it is invariable. For the same things are invariably perceived by the senses, and those things which stimulate the senses, stimulate them in the same way in all men; and those rudimentary beginnings of intelligence to which I have referred, which are imprinted on our minds, are imprinted on all minds alike. . . .

The next point, then, is that we are so constituted by Nature as to share the sense of Justice with one another and to pass it on to all men. . . . For those creatures who have received the gift of reason from Nature have also received the gift of Law, which is right reason applied to command and prohibition. And if they have received Law, they have received Justice also. Now all men have received reason; therefore all men have received Justice. Consequently Socrates was right when he cursed, as he often did, the man who first separated utility from Justice; for this separation, he complained, is the source of all mischief. . . .

If it were a penalty and not Nature that ought to keep men from injustice, what anxiety would there be to trouble the wicked when the danger of punishment was removed? . . . For to what lengths will that man go in the dark who fears nothing but a witness and a judge? What will he do if, in some desolate spot, he meets a helpless man, unattended, whom he can rob of a fortune? Our virtuous man, who is just and good by nature, will talk with such a person, help him, and guide him on his way; but the other, who does nothing for another's sake, and measures every act by the standard of his own advantage—it is clear enough, I think, what he will do! . . .

But the most foolish notion of all is the belief that everything is just which is found in the customs or laws of nations. Would that be true, even if these laws had been enacted by tyrants? . . . For justice is one; it binds all human society, and is based on one Law, which is right reason applied to command and prohibition. Whoever knows not this Law, whether it has been recorded in writing anywhere or not, is without Justice.

But if Justice is conformity to written laws and national customs, and if, as the same persons claim, everything is to be tested by the standard of utility, then anyone who thinks it will be profitable to him will, if he is able, disregard and violate the laws. . . . that will mean the destruction [of the virtues on which human society depends]. For where then will there be a place for generosity, or love of country, or loyalty, or the inclination to be of service to others or to show gratitude for favours received? For these virtues originate in our natural inclinations to love our fellow-men, and this is the foundation of Justice. . . . If the principles of Justice were founded on the decrees of peoples, the edicts of princes, or the decisions of judges, then Justice would sanction robbery and adultery and forgery of wills, in case these acts were approved by the votes or decrees of the populace. But if so great a power belongs to the decisions and decrees of fools that the laws of Nature can be changed by their votes, then why do they not ordain that what is bad and baneful shall be considered good and salutary? Or, if a law can make Justice out of Injustice, can it not also make good out of bad? But in fact we can perceive the difference between good laws and bad by referring them to no other standard than Nature; indeed, it is not merely Justice and Injustice which are distinguished by Nature, but also and without exception things which are honourable and dishonourable. . . .

# The Institutes of Justinian (6th Century A.D.)

Five centuries after the death of Cicero, an energetic emperor, Justinian (ruled 527–565 A.D.), ordered his officials to collect previous Roman law, judicial opinions, and imperial edicts. In this systematic statement of civil law, the Greek and Roman legal contribution—with its concern for justice—was kept alive for later Western civilization. Excerpts explaining the basis for the Code appear below. From J. B. Moyle, *The Institutes of Justinian,* by permission of the Clarendon Press, Oxford.

The imperial majesty should be armed with laws as well as glorified with arms, that there may be good government in times both of war and of peace, and the ruler of Rome may not only be victorious over his enemies, but may show himself as scrupulously regardful of justice as triumphant over his conquered foes.

With deepest application and forethought, and by the blessing of God, we have attained both of these objects. The barbarian nations which we have subjugated know our valour, Africa and other provinces without number being once more, after so long an interval, reduced beneath the sway of Rome by victories granted by Heaven, and themselves bearing witness to our dominion. All peoples too are ruled by laws which we have either enacted or arranged. . . .

The precepts of the law are these: to live honestly, to injure no one, and to give every man his due. The study of law consists of two branches, law public, and law private. The former relates to the welfare of the Roman State; the latter to the advantage of the individual citizen. Of private law then we may say that it is of threefold origin, being collected from the precepts of nature, from those of the law of nations, or from those of the civil law of Rome.

The law of nature is that which she has taught all animals; a law not peculiar to the human race, but shared by all living creatures, whether denizens of the air, the dry land, or the sea. Hence comes the union of male and female, which we call marriage; hence the procreation and rearing of children, for this is a law by the knowledge of which we see even the lower animals are distinguished. The civil law of Rome and the law of all nations, differ from each other thus. The laws of every people governed by statutes and customs are partly peculiar to itself, partly common to all mankind. Those rules which a state enacts for its own members are peculiar to itself, and are called civil law: those rules prescribed by natural reason for all men are observed by all peoples alike, and are called the law of nations. Thus the laws of the Roman people are partly peculiar to itself, partly common to all nations. . . . Whenever we speak, however, of civil law, without any qualification, we mean our own; exactly as, when "the poet" is spoken of, without addition or qualification, the Greeks understand the great Homer, and we understand Virgil. But the law of nations is common to the whole human race; for nations have settled certain things for themselves as occasion and the necessities of human life required. For instance, wars arose, and then followed captivity and slavery, which are contrary to the law of nature; for by the law of nature all men from the beginning were born free. The law of nations again is the source of almost all contracts; for instance, sale, hire, partnership, deposit, loan for consumption, and very many others.

Our law is partly written, partly unwritten, as among the Greeks. The written law consists of statutes, plebiscites, senatusconsults, enactments of the Emperors, edicts of the magistrates, and answers of those learned in the law. . . . The unwritten law is that which usage has approved: for ancient customs, when approved by consent of those who follow them, are like statute. . . . But the laws of nature, which are observed by all nations alike, are established, as it were, by divine providence, and remain ever fixed and immutable: [while] the municipal laws of each individual state are subject to frequent change, either by the tacit consent of the people, or by the subsequent enactment of another statute.

# Pliny Describes Three Roman Lawsuits

Pliny (62–c.113 A.D.) was a leading Roman lawyer who held various government positions, including that of governor of Bithynia (Reading 60). His letters, published sometime before 109 A.D., reflect Roman life and letters in his day. Many of the letters contain description of cases he argued in his legal career. The letter to Cornelianus in this reading deals with three cases held before the advisory council of Emperor Trajan. Reprinted by permission of the publishers and The Loeb Classical Library from Pliny, *Letters Vol. I*, trans. W. Hutchinson (Cambridge, Mass.: Harvard University Press, 1915).

## LETTER TO CORNELIANUS

I received lately the most exquisite entertainment imaginable at Centumcellae (as it is called), whither our Emperor had summoned me to his Privy Council. Could anything indeed afford a higher pleasure than to see the Sovereign exercising his justice, his wisdom, and his affability, and that in retirement, where they are laid most open to view? Various were the cases brought before him, which showed under several aspects the virtues of the judge.

That of Claudius Ariston came on first. He is an Ephesian nobleman, of great munificence and unambitious popularity; having thus aroused the envy of persons his opposites in character, they had spirited up an informer against him; such being the facts, he was honourably acquitted.

The next day, Galitta was tried on the charge of adultery. Her husband, a military tribune, was upon the point of standing for office, when she disgraced both him and herself by an intrigue with a centurion [junior officer]. The husband had written of this to the consul's legate, and he to the Emperor. Caesar, having well sifted the evidence, not only broke but banished the centurion. Still, justice was but half satisfied, for the crime is one in which two parties must necessarily be involved. But the husband drew back, out of fondness for his wife, and was a good deal censured for complaisance; for even after her crime was detected he had kept her under his roof, content, it should seem, with having removed his rival. He was admonished to proceed in the suit, which he did with great reluctance: it was necessary, however, that she should be condemned, even against the prosecutor's will. Condemned she was, and given up to the punishment directed by the Julian law [banishment for life]. The Emperor thought proper to specify in his judgment the name of the centurion, and to dwell upon the claims of military discipline; lest it should be supposed that he intended to try all similar causes himself.

The third day an inquiry was begun concerning the much-discussed will of Julius Tiro, part of which was plainly genuine, the other part, it was said, was forged. The persons brought under the charge were Sempronius Senecio, a Roman knight, and Eurythmus, Caesar's freedman and procurator [financial agent]. The heirs had written a joint letter to the Emperor when he was in Dacia, petitioning him to reserve the case for his own hearing. He did so, and upon his return appointed a day for the hearing; and when some of the heirs, as if from respect to Eurythmus, would have withdrawn the suit, he nobly said, "He is not Polyclitus, nor am I Nero" [a reference to the suspicious wheeling-dealing of a favorite freedman agent of the notorious Emperor Nero]. However, he complied with their request for an adjournment, and the time being expired, he now sat to hear the cause. Two only of the heirs appeared; they requested that either all the heirs might be compelled to prosecute, as all had joined in the information, or they also might have leave to desist.

Caesar spoke with great dignity and moderation; and when the counsel for Senecio and Eurythmus said that, unless the defendants were heard, they would remain under suspicion, "I do not care," said the Emperor, "whether suspicion rests upon your clients; it rests upon myself." Then, turning to us, "Advise me," said he, "what is my proper course, for you see they want to complain that they have not been allowed to prosecute." Then, by advice of the Council, he ordered notice to be given to the heirs collectively, that they should either go on with the suit, or severally show cause for not doing so; otherwise that he would at least pronounce them guilty of calumny [false charges].

Thus you see how honourably and seriously we spent our days.

# Slavery in the Roman World

From Paul Louis, *Ancient Rome at Work,* trans. E. Wareing (New York: Barnes & Noble, Inc., 1927). This is published in Canada by Routledge & Kegan Paul Ltd.

In early Rome, slaves were, in principle, chattels, but the word must not be taken in its narrowest acceptation. Law was soon to attenuate its rigours for them and . . . they were allowed to take part in the practice of religion and received decent burial—two points to which, as everyone knows, the ancient Romans attached especial importance.

Nor is that all. Although throughout several hundreds of years the servile worker was denied legal rights and remained in this respect excluded from human society, his master—from interest, no doubt, rather than from generosity—was obliged to care for his existence and provide for his elementary needs. By acting otherwise the small proprietor, whose resources were slender, who cultivated a small strip of land, but who nevertheless required the help of other hands, would have injured his own sources of income by destroying a portion of his capital. . . .

Moreover the law intervened to discourage the use of violence liable to damage the [property] of the people. Ancient enactments forbade even the killing of an ox without cause: the Twelve Tables sentenced to a heavy fine any person who struck his slave and not long afterwards the censors adopted the practice of reprimanding citizens who abused the whip. In all these measures for mitigating oppression everything was relative, but the case of slavery was the same as that of the wage-earners at a later time. Just as in the nineteenth century the lot of wage-earners became most burdensome and crushing when the large factory took the place of the small workshop, so also the slaves, confined . . . upon the huge estates and not knowing their masters, suffered a more cruel fate and were subject to more rigorous discipline. . . .

## THE GROWTH OF THE SLAVE SYSTEM

The economic revolution, which took place between 202 and 30 B.C. corresponded to a continual increase in the servile population. . . . As in the preceding centuries, the great source from which servile labour was recruited continued to be the waging of war which led to the capture of tribes and of whole nations and threw thousands and tens of thousands of human beings into the markets where they were sold by auction. The generals boasted just as loudly of their captures of slaves as of the treasures which they had pillaged from the vanquished kings or the contributions which they had levied. The yoke was imposed successively upon the Carthaginians, the Sardinians, the Cisalpine Gauls, the Syrians, the Macedonians, the Epirotes, the Achaeans, the Sicilians, the Paphlagonians, the inhabitants of Pontus and others, the rough adversaries whom Marius defeated on the Lower Rhone and those whom Caesar thrust back in Belgica. All races, Hellenic and Germanic, Phoenician and Iberian, were thrown together pell-mell in this terrible subjection of the conquered.

A few figures may be quoted to show the extent of depopulation suffered by the countries which were conquered or reconquered. Ten thousand allies of Hannibal were captured in 210, 30,000 others in 209, 4,000 in 208, 54,000 in 207 after the battle of Metaurus, 1,200 in 202, whilst 35,000 Carthaginians were enslaved after the treaty of 201. Flamininus sent back 5,000 captured Macedonians in 197 after Cynoscephalae, 80,000 Sardinians were deprived of their liberty in 177 and 150,000 Macedonians and Epirotes in 167. Scipio Aemilianus carried off 55,000 men and women after the great assault of Carthage in 147. It is no exaggeration to say that Aemilius Paulus sold Epirus by auction and Nicodemus of Bithynia spoke the truth when he replied to a request made by Marius for auxiliaries that all the Bithynians were in irons. No country, however, suffered such a fate as Caesar reserved for Gaul: 40,000 warriors were enslaved at Alesia, 55,000 at Namur, whole cargoes of Veneti were consigned to Narbonensis and to Rome and in all a million Gauls were handed over to the traders who followed in the wake of the victors and undertook to sell the captives at a large profit. For the slave traffic, provided with its raw material by war and also by piracy, or more simply by the caprice of owners, was one of the most lucrative trades.

It was above all in the Eastern markets that this human flesh was concentrated and exhibited. The traders who recruited for the *latifundia* of Sicily, Africa or Northern Italy were always certain to find there the low-caste and vigorous slaves whom the great agriculturists desired. They found there too the captives with brilliant intellectual qualities and those of comely form and elegant bearing much sought after in the fastidious circles of the capital. . . .

The *servus* (slave) was brought, his feet whitened with chalk, to the public square: above his head was hung a placard giving particulars of his origin, qualifications and any special talents which he might possess. From time to time a herald declaimed in a strident voice the merits of the wares thus exhibited to the public for hours at a time. The prospective purchaser was allowed to handle the unfortunate beings whom he was recommended to buy and he examined them as to-day an ox or a cow is examined—without any respect for human dignity, which indeed, according to the conceptions of the time, could only attach to free citizens. The contract was then concluded and the purchaser could carry off his new acquisition just as he would an animal or plant. Fathers were separated brutally from daughters and wives, if—as often happened at the end of a war—whole families were offered for sale. And in order to allow for all eventualities—for the Romans were an essentially practical race—the law permitted purchasers who felt that they had been unfairly treated to take action against the dealers for fraud or defects discovered subsequent to purchase. . . .

The servile population, adapted to the most varied uses, was infinitely subdivided. A large part remained on the fields, since the extensive cultivation which was gradually being developed called for enormous numbers of hands. As the science of improving the soil was hardly yet known, yields remained mediocre with the consequence that there was a continual endeavour to increase the arable acreage of the domains, and the exploitation . . . [of the larger] . . . of them called for compact masses of workers. . . .

The slaves employed in domestic service properly so-called—that is to say in the upkeep of the house, the preparation of meals or personal service, were, in the houses of the more wealthy citizens, under the orders of a sort of major-domo: . . . it must not be forgotten that in spite of the beginning or the development of independent industries many objects continued to be produced in the house. Thus, even after the opening of the first bakeries in the second century, the great preferred to eat bread baked in their own houses. Slaves were also called upon to weave and spin for the whole house although it was possible to purchase fabrics ready made. . . .

The rich were not satisfied with having their spinning, weaving and dyeing done in the household; their slaves also produced for sale outside it. They kept—either in their sumptuous dwellings in which special annexes

Female household slaves surround their mistress as they help her dress. One adjusts her hair as another holds a mirror. This third-century bas-relief was discovered near the Moselle River in what is now West Germany.

were reserved for the purpose, or in the suburbs or villages near the town—potters, smiths, armourers, gold and silversmiths, tailors, and carpenters in varying numbers. All trades were invaded to some extent by this servile population which worked for the benefit of its masters. Those of the [nobles] who did not wish to be obliged to set up workshops hired their slaves to third persons. Crassus, whose large fortune was notorious, was able to employ hundreds of captive workmen in every branch of production and to derive enormous profit from their exertions. Cato gave to his *servi* special education in order that they should acquire value as craftsmen and then hired them at a fixed tariff or sold them at a profit. . . .

It is certain that this expansion of the slave system, and above all of the role assigned to the captives was bound to lead to a progressive transformation of the law. The legal enactments evolved as the ruling class found it more advantageous in their own interest to increase the capacity of the slave. . . .

The slave system was thus gradually remodelled whilst at the same time the treatment accorded to a section of these unfortunates was modified. It must not, however, be believed that the improvement was general, that liberal precepts of humanity were prevalent in the first century B.C., or that from that time the way was paved to a statute giving slaves the rights of real persons by conferring upon them some guarantee for the safety of their lives, at least, or affording safeguards against corporal punishment and torture. When the law brought alleviation, it was not for the sake of the slaves but for the benefit of the master who thought it profitable to revise the system of exploitation. . . .

If we study the condition of the servile population of vast areas of the Roman world, we shall understand why on numerous occasions they attempted to break their chains. . . . The very increase in the number of slaves, which tended to approach that of free men, constituted a permanent danger and was a measure of the imprudence and the imperiousness of the men at the head of the State and of the avidity of the publicans who incessantly bought at Delos, Athens, and elsewhere fresh hands to serve in the development of their exploitations.

A characteristic and also very logical fact was that these slave risings—the importance of which cannot be exaggerated and which took on the aspect of inevitable social upheavals—broke out above all in those parts of Italy in which large holdings were preponderant and where the [tax collectors] had been granted immense domains. The extreme concentration which, in our days, leads to the organization of labour led two thousand years ago to revolts on the part of the slaves. . . .

A redoubtable [example] was the rising of gladiators of Spartacus in the year 73 B.C. It will be remembered that the rich citizens kept professional combatants either for the purpose of providing spectacles for the public or for hire to new magistrates who wished to celebrate their assumption of office. A certain number of these gladiators rose at Capua near Naples—a very large town and a centre of both industry and luxury—and defied the first troops sent against them. The land slaves of Samnium and of Campania, whose numbers were great in that country of *latifundia,* and the drovers and shepherds of the Apennines, joined them. Thereupon the government of Rome, learning that Spartacus was preparing to march against the capital, was terror-struck and sent a strong army with the consuls: they were, however, defeated. Licinius Crassus also suffered at first the general fate and it was not until the year 71 that Spartacus was killed and his bands dispersed. He had in vain appealed for help to the Sicilians with whom he was not able to communicate directly, but Rome had once more felt the perils of the slave system, which she then attempted to consolidate by crucifying 6,000 of the conquered. This sacrifice of human lives was little felt, for the markets of Europe and Asia were still able to provide all the hands which might be needed.

# Howard Fast: Spartacus Sends a Message to the Senate

Spare and occasionally conflicting reports of Spartacus' uprising in 73–71 B.C. are found in the writings of Roman historians. In a historical novel, *Spartacus* (1951), the American writer Howard Fast offers a moving account of Spartacus' vision of a social order based on justice. Spartacus' speech was made following the annihilation of 3000 Roman soldiers surprised in their encampment by the slaves. Only one soldier was spared to bring Spartacus' message to the Roman Senate. As proof of the victory he was given the carved ivory baton, the symbol of Roman military authority, that had been taken from the slain commander. From *Spartacus* by Howard Fast. 

"Go back to the Senate (said Spartacus) and give them the ivory rod. I make you legate. Go back and tell them what you saw here. Tell them that they sent their cohorts against us, and that we destroyed their cohorts. Tell them that we are slaves—what they call the *instrumentum vocale.* The tool with a voice. Tell them what our voice says. We say that the world is tired of them, tired of your rotten Senate and your rotten Rome. The world is tired of the wealth and splendor that you have squeezed out of our blood and bone. The world is tired of the song of the whip. It is the only song the noble Romans know. But we don't want to hear that song any more. In the beginning, all men were alike and they lived in peace and they shared among them what they had. But now there are two kinds of men, the master and the slave. But there are more of us than there are of you, many more. And we are stronger than you, better than you. All that is good in mankind belongs to us. We cherish our women and stand next to them and fight beside them. But you turn your women into whores and our women into cattle. We weep when our children are torn from us and we hide our children among the sheep, so that we may have them a little longer; but you raise your children like you raise cattle. You breed children from our women, and you sell them in the slave market to the highest bidder. You turn men into dogs, and send them into the arena to tear themselves to pieces for your pleasure, and as your noble Roman ladies watch us kill each other, they fondle dogs in their laps and feed them precious tidbits. What a foul crew you are and what a filthy mess you have made of life! You have made a mockery of all men dream of, of the work of a man's hands and the sweat of a man's brow. Your own citizens live on the dole and spend their days in the circus and the arena. You have made a travesty of human life and robbed it of all its worth. You kill for the sake of killing, and your gentle amusement is to watch blood flow. You put little children into your mines and work them to death in a few months. And you have built your grandeur by being a thief to the whole world. Well, it is finished. Tell your Senate that it is all finished. That is the voice of the tool. Tell the Senate to send their armies against us, and we will destroy those armies as we destroyed this one, and we will arm ourselves with the weapons of the armies you send against us. The whole world will hear the voice of the tool—and to the slaves of the world, we will cry out, Rise up and cast off your chains! We will move through Italy, and wherever we go, the slaves will join us—and then, one day, we will come against your eternal city. It will not be eternal then. Tell your Senate that. Tell them that we will let them know when we are coming. Then we will tear down the walls of Rome. Then we will come to the house where your Senate sits, and we will drag them out of their high and mighty seats, and we will tear off their robes so that they may stand naked and be judged as we have always been judged. But we will judge them fairly and we will hand them a full measure of justice. Every crime they have committed will be held against them, and they will make a full accounting. Tell them that, so that they may have time to prepare themselves and to examine themselves. They will be called to bear witness, and we have long memories. Then, when justice has been done, we will build better cities, clean, beautiful cities without walls—where mankind can live together in peace and in happiness. There is the whole message for the Senate. Bear it to them. Tell them it comes from a slave called Spartacus. . . ."

# David B. Davis: Opposition to Slavery

In his study of the problem of slavery in Western culture, Professor Davis analyzed the response to slavery in Western thought, beginning with what he termed "the ancient legacy." He was struck by the ambivalent attitude toward slavery among the Greeks and Romans and sought to explain the sources of this ambivalence. Reprinted from David B. Davis: *The Problem of Slavery in Western Culture*. Copyright © 1966 by Cornell University. Used by permission of Cornell University Press.

The Sophists were apparently the first to conclude that since slavery was a product of human convention, it had no basis in the objective and unchanging law of nature. . . . Antisthenes, who was the crucial link between Socrates and the Stoics, was said to have written a treatise, "Of Freedom and Slavery," which may have been a source of later Stoic doctrine. Believing that virtue was a matter of individual commitment and independence, this founder of the Cynic school also strove to shock public opinion in a way that anticipated later reformers. He not only set himself off with a beard and peculiar garb, but attacked the state, marriage, and private property. The emblem of the Cynics, who bore a certain resemblance to the bohemians and beatniks of later ages, was the dog.

The pattern of demonstrative contempt for accepted values was most pronounced in Antisthenes's famous pupil, Diogenes of Sinope. Striving for a life of perfect simplicity, he lived in a tub, walked barefoot in snow, and threw his cup away in shame after seeing a child drink from its hands. Though he favored abolishing marriage and holding wives in common, there is no report of his having denounced slavery. Yet a defiant disregard for the conventional distinction between slave and freeman was part of his quest for virtue as an inner freedom and independence. "It would be absurd," he said, when his own slave had run away, "if Manes can live without Diogenes, but Diogenes cannot get on without Manes." When he was captured by pirates on a voyage to Aegina and taken to a slave market in Crete, he pointed to a spectator wearing purple robes, and said, "Sell me to this man; he needs a master." He called the friends who wished to redeem him simpletons. Lions, he said, were not the slaves of those who fed them, "for fear is the mark of the slave, whereas wild beasts make men afraid of them." Whether these tales are true, they illustrate a pattern of thought that gave rise to the first explicit questioning of slavery. For if freedom is conceived as a liberation of the individual from the norms and institutions of society, as well as from the desires of the flesh, external distinctions lose all importance. According to Bion, a pupil of Crates, "Good slaves are free, but evil men are slaves, desiring many things." . . .

And while the Stoics measured the evils of society against the absolute standard of nature, and held that the philosopher-saint must persevere in exercising his virtue, they found no difficulty in accepting as inevitable the many imperfections of the world. The wise man's virtue lay not in good works but in decisions that revealed an inner purity and self-control. Since the world had fallen irretrievably from a former Golden Age, he could not regard poverty, disgrace, slavery, or even death as evils in themselves, any more than he could consider their opposites as intrinsic goods. The only thing that mattered was the way one responded to the vicissitudes of fortune. True freedom meant self-transcendence, a disengagement of the ego from one's surroundings; and thus the environment of the slave was no more dangerous than any other to the well-being of the soul. It might, indeed, afford greater security against distracting stimuli. Epictetus, who had been a slave himself in his early life, used the bondsman's desire for immediate liberty as an example of the illusions of worldly expectations. After describing the plight of the hungry, homeless freedman, Epictetus observed that even if the ex-slave should ultimately enjoy material success, he would have no knowledge of virtue, and would only become a slave to love, to desire, or to political faction. The philosopher pictured the disenchanted freedman looking back with nostalgia to a time when his physical needs were limited and cared for by a master.

But the Stoics' indifference to society and history should not blind us to the fact that they associated slavery with the imperfections of the world, and sin with a special kind of slavery. These associations would have a different meaning if combined with the belief that a particular place or a particular time was marked for the redemption of humanity. Even in the Roman world of the first and second centuries A.D. the Stoic doctrines led to what Westermann has aptly termed a "frigid sympathy" for the slave. Though Cicero believed that subjection was beneficial for some men, he saw slavery as the result of greed and ignorance. Plutarch and Juvenal sharply criticized the cruelty of certain masters. Epictetus suggested that slaveholders could not attain true freedom and virtue, since the owner of a slave could not help but become a slave himself. And Seneca developed the theory that only the body of the slave was at the mercy of his master, for "that inner part cannot be delivered into bondage." Because the slave's soul was untouched by his condition, he had the capacity to do more for his master than required. Such beneficient service might provide the basis for a relationship transcending external condition. The same idea had been rejected by Aristotle but affirmed long before by Euripides. For Seneca, it was essential that masters treat their slaves as they would be treated by their own superiors: "They are slaves," people declare. Nay, rather they are men. . . . "Slaves!" No, they are our fellow-slaves, if one reflects that Fortune has equal rights over slaves and free men alike."

TOPIC 14

# THE BEGINNINGS OF CHRISTIANITY

Jesus was born in Bethlehem in Judaea during the eventful reign of Augustus Caesar. But the antecedents of Christianity reach back far beyond the establishment of the Roman Empire. They find their roots in the longing that prevailed in the Hellenistic Age for comfort and inspiration in a comfortless world and in the promise and anger of the prophetic tradition of the Hebrews. The readings examine the religious background of Christianity and the nature of the Christian appeal.

**Reading 69**

# Erwin Goodenough: The Religious Heritage of Christianity

Erwin Goodenough (1893– ), a respected authority in Hebrew and early Church history who taught for many years at Yale University, prefaced the work from which this reading is taken by noting that it is the job of the historian to tell a story based on historically verifiable facts and to avoid value judgments. But he also emphasized that "any man is free to go on and believe much more about early Christianity than we feel we can assert historically." The reading reflects Goodenough's hypothesis that Christianity was "in at least one respect like all other religions, namely that it was summation of various religious ideas of the environment inherited from the past, with some new added force to give it distinction." From *The Church in the Roman Empire* by Erwin Goodenough. Copyright 1931 by Holt, Rinehart and Winston, Inc. Copyright © 1959 by Erwin Goodenough. Reprinted by permission of Holt, Rinehart and Winston, Inc.

I

### The Appeal of Mystery Religions in the Hellenistic Age

By the beginning of the first century before Christ a great mass of men were finding increasing help in the teaching of those who confessed the inability of man, as he naturally is, to keep his passions and desires always subject to his reason, and who sought to discover in some form of religion a door to a larger life, in which his reasoning faculty, too weak to control his life, might be enlarged and strengthened. For the various philosophies which were monotheistic had taught that the mind or reason of man was a bit of God living in him. Why not then appeal to God to give more of Himself, to make the reason fragment in man larger and stronger? If such an addition to one's natural powers could be achieved, that would be truly salvation, as the age called it, by which was meant an assurance of safety in the vicissitudes of this world, as well as in that next world to which all men were looking with restless expectation. . . .

The first important religion of this type in the Greek world was Orphism, which . . . taught the uselessness of this life, man's sinfulness and need of redemption because of his inability to save himself without divine help; and it solved its own problem in an elaborate ritual in which the believer became "enthusiastic," that is, filled with the saving deity. . . . Other religions, that of the saving Mithra from Persia, and of Isis, Mother of Heaven and the Gods from Egypt, were making a deep mark upon the life of the entire civilized world, for the devotees of both insisted that in their rites, scriptures, and passwords the desire of the Hellenistic Age for a saving revelation of deity had been met. . . .

Each of these religions, as well as many others, had its special appeal. Orphism offered the Spirit through ancient rites and enthusiasm. The beautiful Sun-God Mithra had his atoning slaughter of a sacred bull, by which his devotees might be benefited. In the ceremony of initiation into another mystery, that of Cybele, a bull was butchered in such a way that its blood streamed down over the initiate, making him a partaker in the very life and spirit of the god himself. These mysteries, then, released for men the purifying and saving forces of the universe. Isis, the lovely distraught mother, who found and collected the scattered pieces of her beloved's slaughtered body, and brought him back to life, represented the deeply desired compassion and love of God for men . . . which would heal their broken lives and assure them a happy life after death. Demeter, seeking her daughter Persephone, was the saving *mater dolorosa* of antiquity. And Jews, who had the most magnificent body of revealed writing of any religion, had with it an ability to dominate the material environment which excited the envy of those who ridiculed them for their peculiarities. Yet all these religions by their ritual and moral discipline rather led the initiate up to deity than brought the deity down to men. Or perhaps the two might be regarded as meeting half-way. But the deity did not come down and dwell with men in any permanently accessible form. He or she remained remote, approachable only by mystery and rite, and, as a result of the expense of initiation, frequently accessible not at all to the poor. If, then, there should come a religion which would offer such Scriptures and moral achievement as Judaism, such enthusiasm as Orphism, such vividly enacted dispensation of spiritual rebirth as Cybele and Eleusis, such passionate yearning love in deity as Demeter and Isis, together with magnificent ritual in which the lower classes might participate, it would be a great religion indeed. But if to these it could add a concreteness of conviction, a belief that deity, in his love of men, had actually come down in the flesh and lived with men, loved the poor, helped the suffering, and then had died an agonizing death for mankind, but had conquered that death by coming back to life afterwards; and that now, having gone back to reign with God as before, he was acting as mediator and helper for men; and that he had left behind on earth his Spirit in which men could be reborn and live, die and rise again: could such a story be told by men who could say "I saw him with my own eyes, touched him with my own hands," then the religious need of the age would be met. The story of early Christianity is the story of the rise and conquest of a religion which offered just this appeal.

## Jesus

The early years of Christianity by no means suggested its tremendous future. At the beginning of the Christian Era the Jews who lived in Palestine were one of the few nations of the Roman Empire who were rebellious against Roman domination, for their religious beliefs were completely at variance with the presence of Roman soldiers and rulers in the holy city of Jerusalem. At least an active minority among them believed that their God was to lead them to victory, that the Jews were the chosen people of the world, and the fact that they and their religion must be under the control of heathen outsiders horrified them as the very height of blasphemy against God. Their rage at such a situation could find relief only in ardent hope that some leader would come to cast off the Roman yoke, and lead Israel not only to freedom but even to domination of those who now were ruling over them. Josephus, the Jewish historian, suggests that there was a succession of individuals, each of whom thought that he could play the part of this deliverer. Each stirred up a mob of excited followers, and each in turn was overthrown, until finally Jerusalem and all Jewish national life perished with them.

In the midst of this age of hatred for the Romans, there appeared a preacher in Palestine, about 28 A.D. He was a young carpenter from the north country of Galilee, of whose past we know nothing except that his home was in Nazareth, and that his family consisted of his mother Miriam, or Mary, her husband Joseph and several other children. His own name was Joshua, or in the Greek form, Jesus. Jesus too turned men's faces forward to a time of coming happiness for the Jews, which would be ushered in by the advent of the promised deliverer. At first Jesus apparently did not identify himself with this coming Messiah, as the deliverer was usually called by the Jews, though after he had been preaching for some time, he did so identify himself, at least to his chosen circle. His conception of the blessed future condition he was preaching is variously interpreted, but seems to have been two-fold: he believed that it was not yet here, and was going to be ushered in by a demonstration of power from God, when the heavens would be opened and God be fully revealed; yet he also taught that in a sense the "kingdom of God," the usual term for this state of ideal social happiness, was already here in the hearts of men who were living true and upright lives. Consequently, while he turned men's faces toward the future, at the same time, like the great Jewish prophets of old, he turned their eyes inward, and showed them that true goodness was not a matter of what man did, so much as what he wanted to do. The only foundation for a right life, he taught, was an attitude toward all men of self-forgetting love. He insisted that man should live with man not in hatred and self-seeking, but in genuine loving kindness. He denounced the use of force between men to settle any dispute whatever. If people want ever to beat or rob you, he said, let them do with you as they please. Personal ambition, love of money, pride, narrow patriotism which expresses itself in hatred of one's national foes, indeed most of the qualities ordinarily respected by men, Jesus denounced, and told men to live improvidently like the birds and flowers, and unselfishly and lovingly together.

While Jesus thus denounced the qualities which most men admire, he turned upon all the respectable classes of the Jews. With the people of learning, the scholars, the professional religious classes, with rich men, he would have nothing whatever to do unless they met him upon his own ground. Since this rarely happened he sought companionship among the outcasts of society, for he found a congeniality with such people which he did not find with the respectable classes of Palestine. For followers he chose not young men from good families, but for the most part workers in the humblest occupations and trades in the social scale. . . .

How long Jesus preached we do not know, but probably not more than three years, perhaps only one. At one time he seemed to be very popular, so that the Jewish crowds, who were impressed by his character without understanding his ideas, wanted to compel him to become their general against the Romans. To escape such a contradiction of his hopes, Jesus retired to lonely or remote places for a time with his special followers, and only returned, finally, to attend at Jerusalem, with all good Jews, the great annual feast of the Passover.

Up to this time, Jesus had apparently avoided attracting attention to himself personally, in his endeavor to center men's attention upon his teachings. Now he strangely changed his methods, and deliberately provoked the crowd to hail him on his entry into Jerusalem as the long-expected king and deliverer of the Jewish people. He so well succeeded that his entry was a magnificent triumph, with shouting crowds following and acclaiming him the long-desired leader. But Jesus did not do as the crowd expected. His first move was popular with the crowd, but a challenge to mortal combat with the priestly factions. For instead of using his new authority to attack the Roman governors, as his followers had expected, Jesus turned against those who were profiteering in the Temple, that is, against the Jewish hierarchy itself. With kingly majesty (but without any record of violence) Jesus ordered the people making money from the Jewish sacrificial rites to leave the Temple, and no greater tribute to his personal power could be paid than was done when these profiteers meekly obeyed his command. In the space they had occupied, Jesus now gathered his new following, to denounce the Jewish hierarchy and teach the strange principles of his kingdom.

The members of no upper class are tolerant when approached by a successful insurgent from the classes beneath them, who proposes to ruin their business, and who openly proclaims what seem to them to be libelous absurdities about their characters. . . . [Jesus] was secretly captured, and at once publicly condemned and crucified. . . . [The execution was carried out by Roman authorities.]

But the little group of simple people who constituted Jesus' inner circle of friends could not dismiss him from their minds. The light of their lives, for which they had deserted even their wives and children, had gone out, and the darkness of their despair was abysmal. They had been much changed by the life with their strangely powerful leader, and to go back to the old ways of living seemed a hopeless prospect. In grief they turned their faces from all their hopes to go the long journey back home to the lake of Galilee.

What happened historians do not know. It would seem that on the way, or shortly after their arrival, first Peter and then the others were transfixed at seeing Jesus apparently risen from the dead. Whatever the nature of their vision had been, their conviction that they had actually seen him turned into the most overwhelming religious experience. They rushed back to Jerusalem where the women of the party, who had remained in the city, shared their vision and the religious rapture it brought, until a large company, probably several hundred, were united in that most intense of all excitements, the excitement of a common religious experience. The origin of the Christian Church is quite unintelligible without taking account of this experience. . . .

### The Spread of Christianity

The company of about a hundred "enthusiastic" people, as they may well be called, who formed the first group of Christians in Jerusalem soon grew into a community of their own. They expected momentarily that Jesus would return to them from the skies, when he was going to recast all human society, and inaugurate the "Kingdom of God" on earth. In such an expectation possessions meant nothing to them; they pooled their money and goods, and lived all alike at a common table, from which baskets of food were carried to persons too ill or old to attend the common meal.

In Jerusalem there were found also Jews of another sort who had been regarding their scriptures and religion as the Way to the Spirit, in the Hellenistic sense already described. . . . At least one of them, Paul, . . . came to the epochal conclusion that Jesus was that very Spirit of God which a great number of men of the time have just been described as seeking. The Spirit, it seemed to Paul, had come down as the man Jesus to reveal the love and mercy of God; he had now returned to be with God and help men who wanted to be saved. . . . Freedom, the freedom of conformity to the Law of Nature or of God, which was the Spirit ruling this world, such freedom was no longer a dream but was actually to be had for the asking. So in the revelation of truth in Christ the problem of the late philosophy of Greece and Rome might be considered as having found a solution. . . .

Members of the new faith had from the first been very active in trying to make converts. Convinced that the end of the age was imminent, they thought of nothing but to prepare themselves for the great event of Christ's return, and to get as many people ready along with themselves as possible. Missionaries went out in all directions. The most famous was Paul himself, who, sometimes with assistants, sometimes alone, travelled on the great open roads of the Empire from one metropolis to another. When he came to a city he would visit first the Jewish synagogue; then after the inevitable quarrel of the conservatives with those who were convinced by him he took most of the Gentile, that is, non-Jewish, visitors at the synagogue with his few Jewish converts and started a new group. As one such group became sufficiently grounded in the essentials of his message he pushed on to another city, there to repeat the same struggle. His adventures form one of the most thrilling odysseys of history, until at last he reached Rome itself, in chains, soon, if we may believe tradition, to be executed, but still confident, aggressive, dynamic. Paul was only one of the many, and in a surprisingly short time, thanks alike to Christian zeal and the ease of travel under the Roman administration, there were little Christian groups in every important center of the Empire. These groups, made up for the most part of Gentiles who had been interested in Judaism, were all regarded as hated outcasts by the Jews, and felt themselves not at all dependent upon the Jews. Their teaching was full of ideas which they had taken over from Judaism, but their faces were turned toward the great pagan body of the Empire, as they brought a message that promised to solve the problems of the Gentile world.

## II

## The Relation of Christianity to Judaism and Hellenic Philosophy

Christianity took over several priceless characteristics from its original environment. It had the Jewish scriptures, of course, that superhuman source of truth. With these, like the Hellenized Judaism it had supplanted, it proposed to meet the Greek longing for salvation by a mystical knowledge. Accordingly the early Christians found that the most appealing argument they could adduce either to Jews or Greeks consisted in quoting the Jewish Bible, and then by ingenious explanation demonstrating that the old books had accurately foretold details of the life of Jesus. Further, Christianity took over from the Jewish religion its deep moral purpose, combined with the lofty ethical teaching of the Stoics. Were the Greeks teaching that man should so school himself that he would ask little of life, and be happy under any misfortune? The Christians took them at their word, and amazed the Roman world by being able to live out such a doctrine, until, not an occasional individual, but groups of scores or hundreds at a time, sang hymns of joy in the terrible mines and prisons of the Romans, and even before the lions. It was a Jewish-Greek morality, Jewish in its patient steadfastness, Greek in its flouting of external goods, but still uniquely Christian in its emphasis upon love and humility, and in the abandoned enthusiasm with which it was practised.

And one other great thing Christianity had from Judaism: it had what has recently been called the sense of having a "cause" for which to live and die. Even at its height Graeco-Roman philosophy was never optimistic that the world could be much improved; it encouraged the individual to live by high moral standards, but no charge was ever looked for as a result in general social conditions. The buoyant clamor of the social reformer began with Christianity's new version of the Messianic social expectation of the Jews. For the Christian, like Christ, lived and died not for himself, but for the good of the world, to prepare society for the coming again of Christ when he should rule all men in a new kingdom of righteousness. It is in Christian literature that the word "hope" first, outside the Messianic writing of Jews, became social in its scope. And even when the earlier Jewish form of expectation of Christ's return began to fade into the indefinite future, Christians still believed that but for them the world would be destroyed by a wrathful God, that they were a leaven in the world, and that by their message the ills of humanity might definitely be removed. While schools of philosophy had been only for the intelligent and scorned the multitude, while the mysteries had salvation exclusively for selected groups, Christianity had a message of eternal hope which it wanted to give to all men, high and low alike.

To plain people the simple Jesus who was also the savior Christ, and who was soon associated with his beautifully idealized mother, made a direct appeal of the sort they could understand. To the philosophic mind the identification of Christ with the Spirit opened infinite possibilities of a spiritual philosophy, while it relieved men of the necessity of following that philosophy through intellectually, when, as often, they wanted to leap immediately to their goal. Thus by loyalty to Christ men of all sorts seemed to find the solution of their problems here and hereafter to all eternity. The longing of the Hellenistic Age had been satisfied. . . .

# The Sermon on the Mount

The Sermon on the Mount, as told in the Gospel of Matthew, is perhaps the best expression of the philosophy of Jesus of Nazareth. A comparison of its style with that of the rest of the Gospel has led many scholars to conclude that it might well be a close facsimile of Jesus' actual words. Matthew 5–8:3, *The Holy Bible.* The Scripture quotations in this publication are from the Revised Standard Version of the Bible, copyrighted 1946 and 1952 by the Division of Christian Education of the National Council of the Churches of Christ in the U.S.A., and used by permission.

## I

Seeing the crowds, he went up on the mountain, and when he sat down his disciples came to him. And he opened his mouth and taught them saying:

"Blessed are the poor in spirit, for theirs is the kingdom of heaven.

"Blessed are those who mourn, for they shall be comforted.

"Blessed are the meek, for they shall inherit the earth.

"Blessed are those who hunger and thirst for righteousness, for they shall be satisfied.

"Blessed are the merciful, for they shall obtain mercy.

"Blessed are the pure in heart, for they shall see God.

"Blessed are the peacemakers, for they shall be called sons of God.

"Blessed are those who are persecuted for righteousness' sake, for theirs is the kingdom of heaven.

"Blessed are you when men revile you and persecute you and utter all kinds of evil against you falsely on my account. Rejoice and be glad, for your reward is great in heaven, for so men persecuted the prophets who were before you.

"You are the salt of the earth; but if the salt has lost its taste, how can its saltiness be restored? It is no longer good for anything except to be thrown out and trodden under foot by men.

"You are the light of the world. A city set on a hill cannot be hid. Nor do men light a lamp and put it under a bushel, but on a stand, and it gives light to all in the house. Let your light so shine before men, that they may see your good works and give glory to your Father who is in heaven. . . .

"You have heard that it was said, 'You shall not commit adultery.' But I say to you that every one who looks at a woman lustfully has already committed adultery with her in his heart. If your right eye causes you to sin, pluck it out and throw it away; it is better that you lose one of your members than that your whole body be thrown into hell. And if your right hand causes you to sin, cut it off and throw it away; it is better that you lose one of your members than that your whole body go into hell.

"It was also said, 'Whoever divorces his wife, let him give her a certificate of divorce.' But I say to you that every one who divorces his wife, except on the ground of unchastity, makes her an adulteress; and whoever marries a divorced woman commits adultery.

"Again you have heard that it was said to the men of old, 'You shall not swear falsely, but shall perform to the Lord what you have sworn.' But I say to you, do not swear at all, either by heaven, for it is the throne of God, or by the earth, for it is his footstool, or by Jerusalem, for it is the city of the great King. And do not swear by your head, for you cannot make one hair white or black. Let what you say be simply 'Yes' or 'No'; anything more than this comes from evil.

"You have heard it was said, 'An eye for an eye and a tooth for a tooth.' But I say to you, Do not resist one who is evil. But if any one strikes you on the right cheek, turn to him the other also; and if any one would sue you and take your coat, let him have your cloak as well; and if any one forces you to go one mile, go with him two miles. Give to him who begs from you, and do not refuse him who would borrow from you.

"You have heard it was said, 'You shall love your neighbor and hate your enemy.' But I say to you, Love your enemies and pray for those who persecute you, so that you may be sons of your Father who is in heaven; for he makes his sun rise on the evil and on the good, and sends rain on the just and on the unjust. For if you love those who love you, what reward have you? Do not even the tax collectors do the same? And if you salute only your brethren, what more are you doing than others? Do not even the Gentiles do the same? You, therefore, must be perfect, as your heavenly Father is perfect.

"Beware of practicing your piety before men in order to be seen by them; for then you will have no reward from your Father who is in heaven. Thus, when you give alms, sound no trumpet before you, as the hypocrites do in the synagogues and in the streets, that they may be praised by men. Truly, I say to you, they have their reward. But when you give alms, do not let your left hand know what your right hand is doing, so that your alms may be in secret; and your Father who sees in secret will reward you.

"And when you pray, you must not be like the hypocrites; for they love to stand and pray in the synagogues and at the street corners, that they may be seen by men. Truly, I say to you, they have their reward. But when you pray, go into your room and shut the door and pray to your Father who is in secret; and your Father who sees in secret will reward you.

"And in praying do not heap up empty phrases as the Gentiles do; for they think that they will be heard for their many words. Do not be like them, for your Father knows what you need before you ask him. Pray then like this:

Our Father who art in heaven,
Hallowed be thy name.
Thy kingdom come,
Thy will be done,
On earth as it is in heaven.
Give us this day our daily bread;
And forgive us our debts,
As we also have forgiven our debtors;
And lead us not into temptation.
But deliver us from evil.

"For if you forgive men their trespasses, your heavenly Father also will forgive you; but if you do not forgive men their trespasses, neither will your Father forgive your trespasses. . . .

"Do not lay up for yourselves treasures on earth, where moth and rust consume and where thieves break in and steal, but lay up for yourselves treasures in heaven, where neither moth nor rust consumes and where thieves do not break in and steal; for where your treasure is, there will your heart be also.

## II

"The eye is the lamp of the body. So, if your eye is sound, your whole body will be full of light; but if your eye is not sound, your whole body will be full of darkness. If then the light in you is darkness, how great is the darkness!

"No one can serve two masters; for either he will hate the one and love the other, or he will be devoted to the one and despise the other. You cannot serve God and mammon.

"Therefore I tell you, do not be anxious about your life, what you shall eat or what you shall drink, nor about your body, what you shall put on. Is not life more than food, and the body more than the clothing? Look at the birds of the air: they neither sow nor reap nor gather into barns, and yet your heavenly Father feeds them. Are you not of more value than they? And which of you by being anxious can add one cubit to his span of life? and why be anxious about clothing? Consider the lilies of the field, how they grow; they neither toil nor spin; yet I tell you, even Solomon in all his glory was not arrayed like one of these. But if God so clothes the grass of the field, which today is alive and tomorrow is thrown into the oven, will he not much more clothe you, O men of little faith? Therefore do not be anxious, saying, 'What shall we eat?' or 'What shall we drink?' or 'What shall we wear?' For the Gentiles seek all these things; and your heavenly Father knows that you need them all. But seek first his kingdom and his righteousness, and all these things shall be yours as well.

"Therefore do not be anxious about tomorrow, for tomorrow will be anxious for itself. Let the day's own trouble be sufficient for the day.

"Judge not, that you be not judged. For with the judgment you pronounce you will be judged, and the measure you give will be the measure you get. Why do you see the speck that is in your brother's eye, but do not notice the log that is in your own eye? Or how can you say to your brother, 'Let me take the speck out of your eye,' when there is the log in your own eye? you hypocrite, first take the log out of your own eye, and then you will see clearly to take the speck out of your brother's eye. . . .

"Not every one who says to me, 'Lord, Lord,' shall enter the kingdom of heaven, but he who does the will of my Father who is in heaven. On that day many will say to me,

'Lord, Lord, did we not prophesy in your name, and cast out demons in your name, and do many mighty works in your name?' And then will I declare to them, 'I never knew you; depart from me, you evil-doers.'

"Every one then who hears these words of mine and does them will be like a wise man who built his house upon the rock; and the rain fell, and the floods came, and the winds blew and beat upon that house, but it did not fall, because it had been founded on the rock. And everyone who hears these words of mine and does not do them will be like a foolish man who built his house upon the sand; and the rain fell, and the floods came, and the winds blew and beat against the house, and it fell; and great was the fall of it."

And when Jesus finished these sayings, the crowds were astonished at his teaching, for he taught them as one who had authority, and not as their scribes. When he came down from the mountain, great crowds followed him; and behold, a leper came to him and knelt before him, saying, "Lord, if you will, you can make me clean." And he stretched out his hand and touched him, saying, "I will; be clean." And immediately his leprosy was cleansed.

# The Early Church Appeals to the Hellenized World

The earliest history of the growth of Christianity is found in the New Testament book, Acts of the Apostles. Here the story of the transformation of Christianity from a Jewish sect to a predominantly non-Jewish religion is told by a man who obviously admired Paul's efforts to spread Christianity among the Gentiles (most scholars identify him as a non-Jewish physician, author of the Gospel of Luke). The first reading describes an important conference held in Jerusalem in 49 A.D. to determine whether non-Jewish converts to Christianity must follow Jewish ritual and law. The second reading describes the methods adopted by Paul when on his missionary journeys. The last readings contain excerpts of letters from Paul to the early Christian communities he had established in Corinth and Rome. In them he gets at the core of the Christian message to humanity. (I) Acts: 27–15:3, 5–15, 19, 22–31. (II) Acts 17:16–34. (III) I Corinthians 12:12–13, 12:27–13:13. (IV) Romans 8:2–11. From *The Holy Bible.* The Scripture quotations in this publication are from the Revised Standard Version of the Bible, copyrighted 1946 and 1952 by the Division of Christian Education of the National Council of the Churches of Christ in the U.S.A., and used by permission.

## I. A CONFERENCE AT JERUSALEM DEBATES RITUAL REQUIREMENTS FOR NON-JEWISH CHRISTIANS

And when [Paul and Barnabas arrived in Antioch] they gathered the church together and declared all that God had done with them, and how he had opened a door of faith to the Gentiles. And they remained no little time with the disciples.

But some men came down from Judea and were teaching the brethren, "Unless you are circumcised according to the custom of Moses, you cannot be saved." And when Paul and Barnabas had no small dissension and debate with them Paul and Barnabas and some of the others were appointed to go up to Jerusalem to the apostles and the elders about this question. . . . When they came to Jerusalem, they were welcomed by the church and the apostles and the elders, and they declared all that God had done with them. But some believers who belonged to the party of the Pharisees rose up, and said, "It is necessary to circumcise them, and to charge them to keep the law of Moses."

The apostles and the elders were gathered together to consider this matter. And after there had been much debate, Peter rose and said to them, "Brethren, you know that in the early days God made choice among you, that by my mouth the Gentiles should hear the word of the gospel and believe. And God who knows the heart bore witness to them, giving them the Holy Spirit just as he did to us; and he made no distinction between us and them, but cleansed their hearts by faith. Now therefore why do you make trial of God by putting a yoke upon the neck of the disciples which neither our fathers nor we have been able to bear? But we believe that we shall be saved through the grace of the Lord Jesus, just as they will."

And all the assembly kept silence; and they listened to Barnabas and Paul as they related what signs and wonders God had done through them among the Gentiles. After they finished speaking, James replied, "Brethren, listen to me. [Peter] has related how God first visited the Gentiles, to take out of them a people for his name. And with this the words of the prophets agree. . . .

Therefore my judgment is that we should not trouble those of the Gentiles who turn to God. . . . Then it seemed good to the apostles and the elders, with the whole church, to choose men from among them and send them to Antioch with Paul and Barnabas. They sent Judas called Barsabbas, and Silas, leading men among the brethren, with the following letter: "The brethren, both the apostles and the elders, to the brethren who are the Gentiles in Antioch and Syria and Cilicia, greeting. Since we have heard that some persons from us have troubled you with words, unsettling your minds, although we gave them no instructions, it has seemed good to us in assembly to choose men and send them to you with our beloved Barnabas and Paul, men who have risked their lives for the sake of our Lord Jesus Christ. We have therefore sent Judas and Silas, who themselves will tell you the same things by word of mouth. For it has seemed good to the Holy Spirit and to us to lay upon you no greater burden than these necessary things: that you abstain from what has been sacrificed to idols and from blood and from what is strangled and from unchastity. If you keep yourselves from these, you will do well. Farewell."

So when they were sent off, they went down to Antioch; and having gathered the congregation together, they delivered the letter. And when they read it, they rejoiced at the exhortation.

## II. PAUL PREACHES TO THE ATHENIANS

Now while Paul was waiting . . . at Athens, his spirit was provoked within him as he saw that the city was full of idols. So he argued in the synagogue with the Jews and the devout persons, and in the market place every day with those who chanced to be there. So also the Epicurean and Stoic philosophers met him. And some said, "What would this babbler say?" Others said, "He seems to be a preacher of foreign divinities"—because he preached Jesus and the resurrection. And they took hold of him and brought him to the Areopagus [High Court], saying, "May we know what this new teaching is which you present? For you bring some strange things to our ears; we wish to know therefore what these things mean."

Now all the Athenians and the foreigners who lived there spent their time in nothing except telling or hearing something new. So Paul, standing in the middle of the Areopagus said: "Men of Athens, I perceive that in every way you are very religious. For as I passed along, and observed the objects of your worship, I found also an altar with this inscription, 'To an unknown god.' What therefore you worship as unknown, this I proclaim to you.

"The God who made the world and everything in it, being Lord of heaven and earth, does not live in shrines made by man, nor is he served by human hands, as though he needed anything, since he himself gives to all men life and breath and everything. And he made from one [whole] every nation of men to live on all the face of the earth, having determined allotted periods and the boundaries of their habitation, that they should seek God, in the hope that they might feel after him and find him. Yet he is not far from each one of us, for—

> 'In him we live and move and have our being';

as even some of your poets have said,

> 'For we are indeed his offspring.'

"Being then God's offspring, we ought not to think that the Deity is like gold, or silver, or stone, a representation by the art and imagination of man. The times of ignorance God overlooked, but now he commands all men everywhere to repent, because he has fixed a day on which he will judge the world in righteousness by a man whom he has appointed, and of this he has given assurance to all men by raising him from the dead."

Now when they heard of the resurrection of the dead, some mocked; but others said, "We will hear you again about this." So Paul went out from among them. But some men joined him and believed. . . .

## III. PAUL DESCRIBES THE NATURE OF A CHRISTIAN TO THE CORINTHIANS

Just as the body is one and has many members, and all the members of the body, though many, are one body, so it is with Christ. For by one Spirit we were all baptized into one body—Jews or Greeks, slaves or free—and all were made to drink of one Spirit. . . .

Now you are the body of Christ and individually members of it. And God has appointed in the church first apostles, second prophets, third teachers, then workers of miracles, then healers, helpers, administrators, speakers in various kinds of tongues. Are all apostles? Are all prophets? Are all teachers? Do all work miracles? Do all possess gifts of healing? Do all speak with tongues? Do all interpret? But [all] earnestly desire the higher gifts. And I will show you a still more excellent way.

If I speak in the tongues of men and of angels, but have not love, I am a noisy gong or a clanging cymbal. And if I have prophetic powers, and understand all mysteries and all knowledge, and if I have all faith, so as to remove mountains, but have not love, I am nothing. If I give away all I have, and if I deliver my body to be burned, but have not love, I gain nothing.

Love is patient and kind; love is not jealous or boastful; it is not arrogant or rude. Love does not insist on its own way; it is not irritable or resentful; it does not rejoice at wrong, but rejoices in the right. Love bears all things, believes all things, hopes all things, endures all things.

Love never ends; as for prophecies, they will pass away; as for tongues, they will cease; as for knowledge, it will pass away. For our knowledge is imperfect and our prophecy is imperfect; but when the perfect comes, the imperfect will pass away. When I was a child, I thought like a child, I reasoned like a child; when I became a man, I gave up childish ways. For now we see in a mirror dimly, but then face to face. Now I know in part; then I shall understand fully, even as I have been fully understood. So faith, hope, love abide, these three; but the greatest of these is love.

## IV. PAUL EXPLAINS TO THE ROMANS THE MEANING OF CHRIST TO MANKIND

The law of the Spirit of life in Christ Jesus has set me free from the law of sin and death. For God has done what the law, weakened by the flesh, could not do: sending his own Son in the likeness of sinful flesh and for sin, he condemned sin in the flesh, in order that the just requirement of the law might be fulfilled in us, who walk not according to the flesh but according to the Spirit. For those who live according to the flesh set their minds on the things of the flesh, but those who live according to the Spirit set their minds on the things of the Spirit. To set the mind on the flesh is death, but to set the mind on the Spirit is life and peace. For the mind that is set on the flesh is hostile to God; it does not submit to God's law, indeed it cannot; and those who are in the flesh cannot please God.

But you are not in the flesh, you are in the Spirit, if the Spirit of God really dwells in you. Anyone who does not have the Spirit of Christ does not belong to him. But if Christ is in you, although your bodies are dead because of sin, your spirits are alive because of righteousness. If the Spirit of him who raised Jesus from the dead dwells in you, he who raised Christ Jesus from the dead will give life to your mortal bodies also through his Spirit which dwells in you.

TOPIC 15

# THE STRUGGLE OVER CHRISTIAN AND ROMAN VALUES

Christianity began as the faith of a tiny band of followers of Jesus of Nazareth. Three centuries later it had become the official religion of the Roman Empire and its membership numbered millions. The years of growth, however, entailed bitter struggle and persecution as Christian values clashed with those of the Roman world. The readings provide insight into both value systems, in an effort to explain the ultimate Christian victory.

**Reading 72**

## Christopher Dawson: The Dying World

Christopher Dawson (1889– ), noted Catholic historian, has brought his Christian perspective to his many books on history and culture. His belief that the period of late Rome and the early Middle Ages was the most creative age in Western history, since it witnessed the shaping of that combination of values that compose modern culture, underlies his survey of the age of St. Augustine, from which this reading is taken. Christopher Dawson, "St. Augustine and His Age" from *A Monument to Saint Augustine* edited by M. C. D'Arcy, published by Sheed & Ward Inc., New York, pp. 17–21, 23–24.

Rome had won her world empire by her genius for military and political organization, but her positive contribution to culture was comparatively small. She was rather an agent in the expansion of culture than its creator. Her part was that of the soldier and engineer who cleared the way and built the roads for the advance of civilization. The cosmopolitan culture which became common to the whole Roman Empire was itself mainly the creation of the Hellenic genius. It had its origins in the life of the Greek city-state and had already acquired the character of a world civilization in the great states of the Hellenistic world. Alexander the Great and his successors had made it their mission to spread this civilization throughout the lands that they had conquered. All over the East, from the Mediterranean and the Black Sea to the Oxus and the Indus, countless cities sprang up which in their constitution, their social life, and their buildings were modelled on the pattern of the Greek city. And each of these cities became a centre of diffusion for Western culture. The peasants no doubt continued to live their own life and served their new masters as they had served so many conquerors in the past, but the upper and middle classes were by degrees drawn into the privileged society and were either completely Hellenized or at least acquired a superficial veneer of Greek manners and culture. A single type of urban civilization gradually came to prevail throughout the Hellenistic world.

Rome in her turn took on this inheritance from the great Hellenistic monarchies and carried on their work. But she did so in a strictly practical and utilitarian spirit. At first, indeed, her attitude was entirely selfish, and she organized the world only to exploit it. Roman capitalists, moneylenders, slave-dealers and tax-gatherers descended on the East like a swarm of locusts and sucked the life out of the dependent communities. Every Roman, from the aristocratic capitalist like Brutus or Lucullus down to the meanest agent of the great financial corporations, had his share in the plunder.* The age of the Republic

*It is characteristic that Brutus, who was regarded in later times as a model of republican virtue, quarrelled with Cicero because the latter was forced to reduce the interest on Brutus's loans to the impoverished cities of Cilicia from forty-eight percent to a beggarly twelve percent!

culminated in an orgy of economic exploitation which ruined the prosperity of the subject peoples and brought Rome herself to the verge of destruction.

The crisis was averted by the foundation of the Empire. Julius Caesar and Augustus put an end to the misrule of the capitalist oligarchy and the tyranny of military adventurers and returned to the Hellenistic ideal of an enlightened monarchy. The provinces recovered their prosperity, and alike in the Hellenistic East and the Latin West there was a fresh expansion of urban civilization. For two centuries the ancient world enjoyed an age of continuous material progress.

Everywhere from Britain to Arabia and from Morocco to Armenia wealth and prosperity were spreading, new cities were being founded, and the more backward peoples were adopting a higher form of civilization. And nowhere was this process more striking than in Africa, where even to-day the stately ruins of so many Roman cities still remain to impress the modern tourist with their evidence of vanished civilization. Even a comparatively remote and unimportant town like Timgad, in North Africa, possessed public buildings and monuments finer than those of many a modern city of vastly superior wealth and population. It had its theatres and amphitheatres in which free spectacles were provided for the entertainment of the people. It had porticoes and basilicas where the citizens could attend to business or idle away leisure time. It had baths and gymnasia, libraries and lecture halls, and temples which were not, like our churches, destined solely for religious worship, but were the centre of civic ceremonials and public festivities. There has probably never been an age in which the opportunities for living an enjoyable and civilized existence were so widely diffused. For the ancient city was not, like the average modern town, a factory or a place of business; it existed for the enjoyment of its citizens and it was the centre of an active communal life, lived in public and at the public expense.

This was most strikingly exemplified at Rome itself, where the Greek democratic principle of the right of the citizen to be fed and amused at the expense of the state had been carried to its extreme conclusions. These rights were the only remaining privilege of the Roman democracy, which had completely lost all share in the government of the Empire, but, so far from disappearing with the loss of political rights, they continued to expand down to the last period of the Empire. The corn dole had been limited by Augustus to some 200,000 citizens, but even so it involved a vast organization, the traces of which are to be seen in the remains of the great public corn *dépôts* at Ostia, and the setting aside for the use of the capitol of the chief corn-growing areas of the Mediterranean world—Egypt and Sicily. Moreover, in the course of time the free distribution of other articles such as oil, wine and bacon were added to the corn dole. Gifts of money had been common even in republican times, and during the reign of Augustus no less than six distributions of between £2 and £3 10s. per head were made to between 200,000 and 320,000 persons.

No less important was the amusement of the people. The games of the circus and the amphitheatre involved enormous expenditure and occupied a considerable part of the year. Apart from the special festivals, which might last as long as a hundred days on end, the regular games took up sixty-six days a year in the time of Augustus, and had increased to a hundred and seventy-five days by the fourth century.

Finally, vast sums of public money were absorbed by the public buildings. To some extent this expenditure served ends of real value, above all in the case of the great aqueducts which ensured to Rome a better water supply than that of most modern capitals. For the most part, however, it was entirely unproductive. The Coliseum—which has stood for eighteen centuries as a symbol of the material power of imperial Rome—was created to serve the brutal amusements of the Roman populace. The imperial palaces and fora, with their temples and libraries and porticoes, provided a sumptuous background for the social life of the Court and the capital. But the most characteristic monuments of the imperial period are the thermae, which continued to increase in size and splendour down to the age of Diocletian and Constantine. They were not mere public baths in our sense of the word, but true palaces for the people, of vast size, containing baths and gymnasia, lecture-rooms and libraries, and adorned with the masterpieces of Greek and Hellenistic art. Public building on such a scale far surpassed anything that the modern world has yet seen. Imperial Rome became a city of gold and marble, a worthy incarnation of the *Dea Roma* whom her subjects worshipped. And the same ideal was pursued by all the cities of the Empire according to their capacity. Each tried to surpass its neighbour in the splendour of its public buildings and the number of its games and festivals. Not only millionaires, like Herodes Atticus, but every citizen of moderate wealth, used his money unstintingly in the service of his native city, either by building baths, theatres and porticoes, or by providing public spectacles or endowments for educational and charitable purposes.

All this testifies to a high level of material culture and to an admirable development of public spirit on the part of the citizen class, but from the moral and spiritual point of view it was less satisfactory. All the vast development of material prosperity and external display had no spiritual purpose behind it. Its ultimate end was the satisfaction of corporate selfishness. The religious element in ancient culture, which had been the inspiration of civic patriotism in the fifth and sixth centuries B.C., had almost disappeared from the cosmopolitan civilization of the imperial age. The temples and the gods remained, but they had lost their spiritual significance and had become little more than an ornamental appendage to public life and an occasion for civic ceremonial. For the educated, the only real religion was philosophy—a philosophy which provided high moral ideas for the *élite*, but which was incapable of influencing the mass of society.

The true religion of society was . . . the cult of material pleasure and success. . . . The real Antichrist was not Apollo, but Belial, "the prince of this world." And this is recognized by the majority of Christian writers from the time of St. Paul down to the fifth century. . . .

The mystery religions and the tendency towards mysticism and asceticism are a proof of the religious bankruptcy of society which drove the religious-minded to seek spiritual life outside the life of the city and of society in an esoteric ideal of individual salvation. Even Stoicism, the one sect of the time which inculcated a disinterested ideal of social duty, was fundamentally an unsocial and individualistic creed. The reigning culture had become almost completely secularized, and the religious and the social instincts were becoming opposed to one another.

The one exception to this tendency is to be found in the Jewish tradition, and that was the one religious tradition which had preserved its independence in face of the cosmopolitan Hellenistic culture. . . . The Jews remained a people apart, and refused to submit to the dominant culture or to share in the life of the city. The primitive Church inherited this tradition. The Christians claimed, no less than the Jews, to be a people apart —"a chosen race, a royal priesthood, a holy nation." But this claim no longer involved any political aspirations. Throughout the centuries of persecution the Christians remained faithful to the teachings of St. Peter and St. Paul and submitted to the imperial government as a power ordained of God. . . .

But this political loyalty to the Empire as a state only throws into stronger relief the irreconcilable hostility of Christianity to the imperial culture. The Church was to a great extent an alternative and a substitute for the communal life of the city-state. It appealed to all those elements which failed to find satisfaction in the material prosperity of the dominant culture—the unprivileged classes, the poor and the oppressed, the subject oriental populations, and above all those who were dissatisfied with the materialism and sensuality of pagan society and who felt the need for a living religion on which to base their lives.

Consequently, it was inevitable that Christianity should come into conflict with the pagan government and society. To the ordinary man the Christian was an anti-social atheist, "an enemy of the human race," who cut himself off from everything that made life worth living. To the authorities he was a centre of passive disaffection, a disloyal subject who would not take his share of the public service or pay homage to the emperor. The Christian, on his part, regarded the official worship of the emperor as a supreme act of blasphemy—the deification of material power and the setting up of the creature in place of the Creator. So long as the Empire confined itself to its secular function as the guardian of peace and order, the Church was ready to recognize it as the representative of God, but as soon as it claimed an exclusive allegiance and attempted to dominate the souls as well as the bodies of its subjects, the church condemned it as the representative of Antichrist.

# Nero Persecutes the Christians (64 A.D.)

Tacitus (c. 55–c. 117 A.D.) described the first large-scale persecution of the Christians. By the middle of the first century, Christianity had spread to most of the Mediterranean cities. Rome, as capital of the empire, had a sizeable Christian community. In 64 A.D. Emperor Nero (54–68), who thought himself an all-round artistic genius, was suspected of having set fire to Rome in that year in order to rebuild more grandly. To turn aside Roman upper-class outrage over the damage to their property, Nero promptly blamed the unpopular Christians. Tacitus' comments on the fire are especially interesting. A Roman of the old school, he despised Nero and preached a return to earlier Roman virtues in his writings and was highly critical of contemporary

Roman values. From *Annals of Tacitus,* trans. A. Church and W. Brodribb (London, 1869), pp. 304–305.

But all the endeavors of men, all the emperor's largesse and the propitiations of the gods, did not suffice to allay the scandal or banish the belief that the fire had been ordered. And so, to get rid of this rumor, Nero set up as the culprits and punished with the utmost refinement of cruelty a class hated for their abominations, who are commonly called Christians. Christus, from whom their name is derived, was executed at the hands of the procurator Pontius Pilate in the reign of Tiberius. Checked for the moment, this pernicious superstition again broke out, not only in Judaea, the source of the evil, but even in Rome, that receptacle for everything that is sordid and degrading from every quarter of the globe, which there finds a following. Accordingly, arrest was first made of those who confessed to being Christians; then, on their evidence, an immense multitude was convicted, not so much on the charge of arson as because of hatred of the human race. Besides being put to death they were made to serve as objects of amusement; they were clad in the hides of beasts and torn to death by dogs; others were crucified, others set on fire to serve to illuminate the night when daylight failed. Nero had thrown open his grounds for the display, and was putting on a show in the circus, where he mingled with the people in the dress of charioteer or drove about in his chariot. All this gave rise to a feeling of pity, even towards men whose guilt merited the most exemplary punishment; for it was felt that they were being destroyed not for the public good but to gratify the cruelty of an individual.

# Trajan's Policy Toward the Christians (112 A.D.)

Pliny the Younger, while governor of Bithynia, wrote in 112 A.D. to Emperor Trajan (98–117) about the problems he was experiencing with the Christians in his district. From *The Letters of the Younger Pliny,* ed. I. D. Lewis (London, 1879), pp. 377–380.

## PLINY TO TRAJAN

It is my rule, Sire, to refer to you in matters where I am uncertain. For who can better direct my hesitation or instruct my ignorance? I was never present at any trial of Christians; therefore I do not know what are the customary penalties or investigations, and what limits are observed. I have hesitated a great deal on the question whether there should be any distinction of ages; whether the weak should have the same treatment as the more robust; whether those who recant should be pardoned, or whether a man who has ever been a Christian should gain nothing by ceasing to be such; whether the name itself, even if innocent of crime, should be punished, or only the crimes attaching to that name.

Meanwhile, this is the course that I have adopted in the case of those brought before me as Christians. I ask if they are Christians. If they admit it I repeat the question a second and third time, threatening capital punishment; if they persist I sentence them to death. For I do not doubt that, whatever kind of crime it may be to which they have confessed, their pertinacity and inflexible obstinacy should certainly be punished. There were others who displayed a like madness and whom I reserved to be sent to Rome, since they were Roman citizens.

Thereupon the usual result followed; the very fact of my dealing with the question led to a wider spread of the charge and a great variety of cases were brought before me. An anonymous pamphlet was issued, containing many names. All who denied that they were or had been Christians I considered should be discharged, because they called upon the gods at my dictation and did reverence, with incense and wine, to your image which I had ordered to be brought forward for this purpose, together with the statues of the deities; and especially because they cursed Christ, a thing which, it is said, genuine Christians cannot be induced to do.

Others named by the informer first said that they were Christians and then denied it; declaring that they had been but were so no longer, some having recanted three years or more before and one or two as long ago as twenty years. They all worshipped your image and the statues of the gods and cursed Christ. But they declared that the sum of their guilt or error had amounted only to this, that on an appointed day they had been accustomed to meet before daybreak, and to recite a hymn . . . to Christ, as to a god, and to bind themselves by an oath, not for the commission of any crime but to abstain from theft, robbery, adultery, and breach of faith. . . . After the conclusion of this ceremony it was their custom to depart and meet again to take food; but it was ordinary and harmless food, and they had ceased this practice after my edict in which, in accordance wih your orders, I had forbidden secret societies. I thought it the more necessary, therefore, to find out what truth there was in this by applying torture to two maidservants, who were called

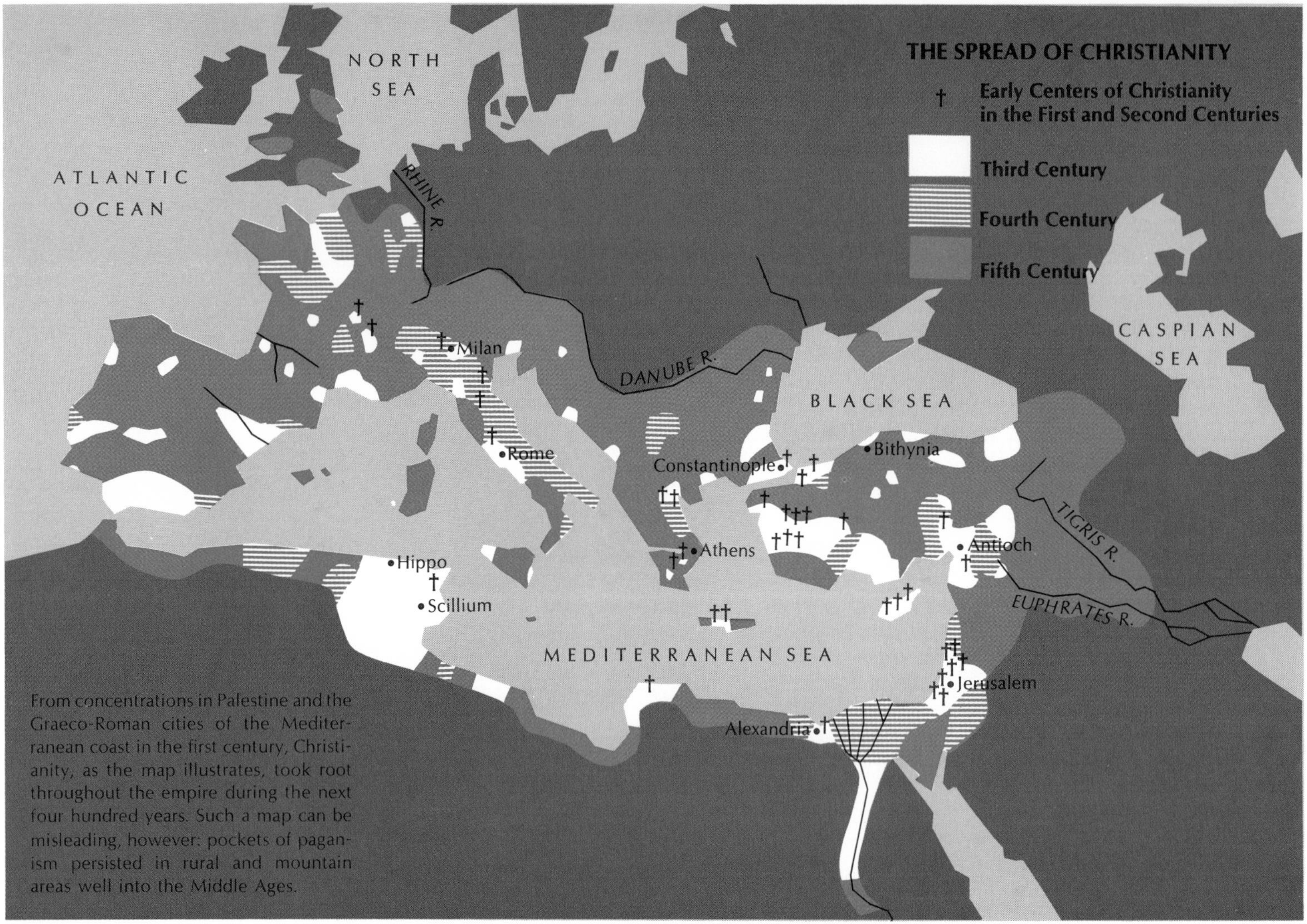


From concentrations in Palestine and the Graeco-Roman cities of the Mediterranean coast in the first century, Christianity, as the map illustrates, took root throughout the empire during the next four hundred years. Such a map can be misleading, however: pockets of paganism persisted in rural and mountain areas well into the Middle Ages.

deaconesses. But I found nothing but a depraved and extravagant superstition, and I therefore postponed my examination and had recourse to you for consultation.

The matter seemed to me to justify my consulting you, especially on account of the number of those imperiled; for many persons of all ages and classes and of both sexes are being put in peril by accusation, and this will go on. The contagion of this superstition has spread not only in the cities, but in the villages and rural districts as well; yet it seems capable of being checked and set right. There is no shadow of doubt that the temples, which have been almost deserted, are beginning to be frequented once more, that the sacred rites which have been long neglected are being renewed, and that sacrificial victims are for sale everywhere, whereas, till recently, a buyer was rarely to be found. From this it is easy to imagine what a host of men could be set right, were they given a chance of recantation.

### TRAJAN TO PLINY

You have taken the right line, my dear Pliny, in examining the cases of those denounced to you as Christians, for no hard and fast rule can be laid down, of universal application. They are not to be sought out; if they are informed against, and the charge is proved, they are to be punished, with this reservation—that if anyone denies that he is a Christian, and actually proves it, that is by worshipping our gods, he shall be pardoned as a result of his recantation, however suspect he may have been with respect to the past. Pamphlets published anonymously should carry no weight in any charge whatsoever. They constitute a very bad precedent, and are also out of keeping with this age.

# The Scillitan Martyrs

**(180 A.D.)**

This account of a trial of a group of North African Christians (from the city of Scillium, near Carthage) in 180 is taken from Roman court records. From E. C. E. Owen, *Some Authentic Acts of the Early Martyrs,* by permission of the Clarendon Press, Oxford, pp. 71–73.

In the consulship of Praesens, then consul for the second time, and Claudian, on the 17th of July, Speratus, Nartzalus and Cittinus, Donata, Secunda, Vestia were brought to trial at Carthage in the council-chamber. The proconsul Saturninus said to them: "You may merit the indulgence of our Lord the Emperor, if you return to a right mind."

Speratus said: "We have never done harm to any, we have never lent ourselves to wickedness; we have never spoken ill of any, but have given thanks when ill-treated, because we hold our own Emperor in honour."

The proconsul Saturninus said: "We also are religious people, and our religion is simple, and we swear by the genius of our Lord the Emperor, and pray for his safety, as you also ought to do."

Speratus said: "If you will give me a quiet hearing, I will tell you the mystery of simplicity."

Saturninus said: "If you begin to speak evil of our sacred rites, I will give you no hearing; but swear rather by the genius of our Lord the Emperor."

Speratus said: "I do not recognize the empire of this world, but rather I serve that God, whom no man has seen nor can see. I have not stolen, but if I buy anything, I pay the tax, because I recognize my Lord, the King of kings and Emperor of all peoples."

The proconsul said to the rest: "Cease to be of this persuasion."

Speratus said: "The persuasion that we should do murder, or bear false witness, that is evil."

The proconsul Saturninus said: "Have no part in this madness."

Cittinus said: "We have none other to fear save the Lord our God who is in heaven."

Donata said: "Give honour to Caesar as unto Caesar, but fear to God."

Vestia said: "I am a Christian."

Secunda said: "I wish to be none other than what I am."

The proconsul Saturninus said to Speratus: "Do you persist in remaining a Christian?"

Speratus said: "I am a Christian." And all consented thereto.

The proconsul Saturninus said: "Do you desire any space for consideration?"

Speratus said: "When the right is so clear, there is nothing to consider."

The proconsul Saturninus said: "What have you in your case?"

Speratus said: "The Books, and the letters of a just man, one Paul."

The proconsul Saturninus said: "Take a reprieve of thirty days and think it over."

Speratus again said: "I am a Christian," And all were of one mind with him.

The proconsul Saturninus read out the sentence from his notebook: "Whereas Speratus, Nartzalus, Cittinus, Donata, Vestia, Secunda and the rest have confessed that they live in accordance with the religious rites of the Christians, and, when an opportunity was given them of returning to the usage of the Romans, persevered in their obstinacy, it is our pleasure that they should suffer by the sword."

Speratus said: "Thanks be to God!"

Nartzalus said: "To-day we are martyrs in heaven: thanks to God!"

The proconsul Saturninus commanded that proclamation be made by the herald: "I have commanded that Speratus, Nartzalus, Cittinus, Veturius, Felix, Aquilinus, Laetantius, Januaria, Generosa, Vestia, Donata, Secunda be led forth to execution."

They all said: "Thanks be to God. . . ."

# A Pagan Finds the Christians Objects of Pity (Late 2d Century)

Minicius Felix, the author of this reading, was a late second-century Roman lawyer who had been converted to Christianity and lost his right to practice law in consequence. Felix wrote a defense of Christian beliefs in the form of a debate between a pagan and a Christian. The pagan arguments were undoubtedly drawn from his own experiences and accurately reflect the pagan point of view, which the Christian in a later section of the book effectively refutes. Reprinted by permission of the publishers and The Loeb Classical Library from Minicius Felix, *Octavius,* Cambridge, Mass.: Harvard University Press, 1931.

"Much I purposely pass over; I have said more than enough of things most or all of which are true, as is shown by the secrecy of this depraved religion. Why make such efforts to obscure and conceal whatever is the object of their worship, when things honourable always rejoice in publicity, while guilt loves secrecy? Why have they no altars, no temples, no recognized images? Why do they never speak in public, never meet in the open, if it be not that the object of their worship and their concealment is either criminal or shameful?

"Whence, who, or where is He, the One and only God, solitary, forlorn, whom no free nation, no kingdom, no superstition known to Rome has knowledge of? The miserable Jewish nationality did indeed worship one God, but even so openly, in temples, with altars, victims, and ceremonies; yet one so strengthless and powerless that he and his dear tribe with him are in captivity to Rome. And yet again what monstrous absurdities these Christians invent about this God of theirs, whom they can neither show nor see! that he searches diligently into the ways and deeds of all men, yea even their words and hidden thoughts, hurrying to and fro, ubiquitously; they make him out a troublesome, restless, shameless and interfering being, who has a hand in everything that is done, interlopes at every turn, and can neither attend to particulars because he is distracted with the whole, nor to the whole because he is engaged with particulars.

"Further, they threaten the whole world and the universe and its stars with destruction by fire, as though the eternal order of nature established by laws divine could be put to confusion, or as though the bonds of all the elements could be broken, the framework of heaven be split in twain, and the containing and surrounding mass be brought down in ruin. Not content with this insane idea, they embellish and embroider it with old wives' tales; say that they are born anew after death from the cinders and the ashes, and with a strange unaccountable confidence believe in one another's lies: you might suppose they had already come to life again. One perversion and folly matches the other. Against heaven and the stars, which we leave even as we found them, they denounce destruction; for themselves when dead and gone, creatures born to perish, the promise of eternity! Hence no doubt their denunciation of funeral pyres and of cremation, just as though the body, even though spared the flame, would not in the course of years and ages be resolved into dust; and just as though it mattered whether it is torn to pieces by wild beasts or drowned in the sea, or buried in the ground, or consumed in the flame; for corpses, if they have sensation, must find all interment painful; while if they have not, speed of dispatch is the best treatment. Under this delusion they promise themselves, as virtuous, a life of never-ending bliss after death; to all others, as evil-doers, everlasting punishment. . . .

"You do not anyhow allow your experiences of the present to undeceive your vain desires of promissory expectation. Let present life, poor fools, be your gauge of what happens after death. See how some part of you, the greater and the better part, as you say, suffer want, cold, toil, hunger; and yet your God permits and seems to overlook it; he is unwilling or unable to help his own; consequently he is either powerless or unjust. You dream of posthumous immortality; when unnerved by danger, when parched with fever, when racked with pain, can you not be sensible of your condition? recognize your feebleness? against your will, poor fool, you are convicted of weakness, and yet will not admit it!

"Things, however, common to all I pass over: but for you there stand in wait punishments, tortures, crosses (crosses not for adoration, but for endurance), yes and the flames which you foretell and fear; where is the God who will succour you in the next life, but in this life cannot? Have not the Romans without your God empire and rule, do they not enjoy the whole world, and lord it over you? Meanwhile in anxious doubt you deny yourselves wholesome pleasures; you do not attend the shows; you take no part in the processions; fight shy of public banquets; abhor the sacred games, meats from the victims, drinks poured in libation on the altars. So frightened are you of the gods whom you deny! You twine no blossoms for the head, grace the body with no perfumes; you reserve your unguents for funerals; refuse garlands even to the grave, pale, trembling creatures, objects for pity—but the pity of our gods! Poor wretches, for whom there is no life hereafter, yet who live not for to-day.

# The State Reacts to the Rapid Growth of Christianity

From Henry Bettensen, ed. *Documents of the Christian Church* (New York: Oxford University Press, 1947), pp. 23-24, 25, 27.

### I. PERSECUTION UNDER DIOCLETIAN (303-304)

IX. x.8 . . . It was enacted by [his] majesty Diocletian that the meetings of Christians should be abolished.

VII. ii.4. March 303 . . . Imperial edicts were published everywhere ordering that the churches be razed to the ground, that the Scriptures be destroyed by fire, that those holding office be deposed and they of the household [imperial court] be deprived of freedom, if they persisted in the profession of Christianity.

5 . . . This was the first edict against us. But not long after other decrees were issued, which enjoined that the rulers of the churches in every place be first imprisoned, and thereafter every means be used to compel them to sacrifice.



April 304 . . . Imperial edicts were issued, in which, by a general decree, it was ordered that all the people without exception should sacrifice in the several cities and offer libations to the idols.

### II. ATTEMPT TO RESTORE PAGANISM UNDER MAXIMIN (308-311)

Therefore a host of letters from Maximin was issued everywhere throughout every province. The governors, and also the military commander, by edicts, letters and public ordinances pressed the magistrates, generals and notaries to implement the imperial decree which ordered that the idols' ruins be rebuilt with all speed; that all without exception—men, women, slaves, and children, even infants in arms—should sacrifice and offer oblations. . . .

Maximin . . . ordered temples to be erected in every city, and the sacred groves to be speedily restored, which had fallen into ruin through lapse of time. He set idol-priests in every place and city, and over them he appointed in each province a high priest, one of the officials who had specially distinguished himself in all kinds of service, giving him a body of troops and a personal guard. . . .

# Constantine Legalizes Christianity (313 A.D.)

The pressures of the third century led to increasingly oppressive and arbitrary government in the Empire. Barbarian tribes pushed at the frontiers; generals vied for imperial power; the economy suffered from growing taxes and inflexible policies. Repression of Christians by the government intensified. Persecution reached its apex under Diocletian (284-305). Eight years later, however, the Christian religion was abruptly legalized by Emperor Constantine (306-337). The background for this action is described by Lactantius, tutor of Constantine's son. It occurred in the wake of a struggle for power among various contenders for Diocletian's throne—Constantine, Maxentius, and Licinius. Constantine became a Christian and quickly assumed the role of arbiter of church affairs. From A. Roberts, J. Donaldson, and A. C. Coxe, ed. *The Ante-Nicean Fathers: Translations of the Writings of the Fathers Down to A.D. 325.* (New York, 1899). First series, VII, pp. 318-320.

And now a civil war (311) broke out between Constantine and Maxentius. Although Maxentius kept himself within Rome, because the soothsayers had foretold that if he went out of it he should perish, yet he conducted the military operations by able generals. In forces he exceeded his adversary; for he had not only his father's army, which deserted from Severus, but also his own, which he had lately drawn together out of Mauritania and Italy. They fought, and the troops of Maxentius prevailed. At length Constantine, with steady courage and a mind prepared for every event, led his whole forces to the neighbourhood of Rome, and encamped them opposite to the Milvian bridge. The anniversary of the reign of Maxentius approached, that is, the sixth of the kalends of November, and the fifth year of his reign was drawing to an end.

Constantine was directed in a dream to cause *the heavenly sign* to be delineated on the shields of his soldiers, and so to proceed to battle. He did as he had been commanded, and he marked on their shields the letter X, with a perpendicular line drawn through it and turned round thus at the top, being the cipher of Christ. Having this sign, his troops stood to arms. The enemies advanced, but without their emperor, and they crossed the bridge. The armies met, and fought with the utmost exertions of valour, and firmly maintained their ground. In the meantime a sedition arose at Rome, and Maxentius was reviled as one who had abandoned all concern for the safety of the commonweal; and suddenly, while he exhibited the Circensian games on the anniversary of his reign, the people cried with one voice, "Constantine cannot be overcome!" Dismayed at this, Maxentius burst from the assembly, and having called some senators together, ordered the Sibylline books to be searched. In them it was found that:—

> *On the same day the enemy of the Romans should perish.*

Led by this response to the hopes of victory, he went to the field. The bridge in his rear was broken down. At sight of that the battle grew hotter. The hand of the Lord prevailed, and the forces of Maxentius were routed. He fled towards the broken bridge; but the multitude pressing on him, he was driven headlong into the Tiber.

This destructive war being ended, Constantine was acknowledged as emperor, with great rejoicings, by the senate and people of Rome. . . .

The conversion of Constantine. Constantine appears at the Milvian bridge with a cross on his shield. From a ninth-century Graeco-Byzantine manuscript.

. . . [O]n the ides of June, [313] while . . . [Licinius] and Constantine were consuls for the third time, he commanded the following edict for the restoration of the Church, directed to the president of the province, to be promulgated:—

"When we, Constantine and Licinius, emperors, had an interview at Milan, and conferred together with respect to the good and security of the commonweal, it seemed to us that, amongst those things that are profitable to mankind in general, the reverence paid to the Divinity merited our first and chief attention, and that it was proper that the Christians and all others should have liberty to follow that mode of religion which to each of them appeared best; so that that God, who is seated in heaven, might be benign and propitious to us, and to every one under our government. And therefore, we judged it a salutary measure, and one highly consonant to right reason, that no man should be denied leave of attaching himself to the rites of the Christians, or to whatever other religion his mind directed him, that thus the supreme Divinity, to whose worship we freely devote ourselves, might continue to vouchsafe His favour and beneficience to us. And accordingly we give you to know that, without regard to any provisos in our former orders to you concerning the Christians, all who choose that religion are to be permitted, freely and absolutely, to remain in it, and not to be disturbed any ways, or molested. And we thought fit to be thus special in the things committed to your charge, that you might understand that the indulgence which we have granted in matters of religion to the Christians is ample and unconditional; and perceive at the same time that the open and free exercise of their respective religions is granted to all others, as well as to the Christians. For it befits the well-ordered state and the tranquillity of our times that each individual be allowed, according to his own choice, to worship the Divinity; and we mean not to derogate aught from the honour due to any religion or its votaries. . . .

In furthering all which things for the behoof of the Christians, you are to use your utmost diligence, to the end that our orders be speedily obeyed, and our gracious purpose in securing the public tranquillity promoted. So shall that divine favour which, in affairs of the mightiest importance, we have already experienced, continue to give success to us, and in our successes make the commonweal happy. And that the tenor of this our gracious ordinance may be made known unto all, we will that you cause it by your authority to be published everywhere."

# Theodosius Outlaws Paganism (392)

Christianity grew rapidly in numbers and power during the fourth century. Most emperors were Christian and pagans, instead of the Christians, now became the persecuted. Emperor Theodosius (379–395), last emperor of both east and west, prohibited pagan worship in 392. From the *Codex Theodosianus,* XVI, 10, 12 in Maude Huttmann, *The Establishment of Christianity and the Proscription of Paganism* (New York: Columbia University Press, 1914) pp. 216–217.

No official or dignitary of whatsoever class or rank among men, whether he be powerful by fortune of birth or humble in the condition of his family, shall in any place or in any city slay an innocent victim for sacrifice to senseless idols. . . .

But if any one in order to make a sacrifice dares to offer a victim or to consult the quivering entrails, let any man be free to accuse him and let him receive as one guilty of lese majesty a fitting punishment for an example, even if he has sought nothing contrary to, or involving the welfare of, the authorities. For it is . . . a crime to wish to undo nature's laws and to investigate what is forbidden; to lay bare secrets, to handle things prohibited, to look for the end of another's prosperity or to predict another's ruin.

But if any one worship with incense idols made by human toil and enduring for a generation, and foolishly fearing on a sudden his own handiwork, seeks to do reverence to vain images, winding a tree with fillets or erecting an altar . . . (for although the worth of the gift be slight, yet the injury to religion is great) let him be judged a violator of religion and a fine be levied on the house or the estate in which he is proved to have committed the deed of heathen superstition. For every place where the smoke of incense has ascended, provided that these places are proved in law to be the property of those who offered the incense, shall be appropriated to the fisc.

But if any one has sought to make such a sacrifice in public temples or shrines or in buildings or in fields belonging to some one else—if it be proved that the place was used without the owner's knowledge, he shall pay a fine of twenty-five pounds of gold; and the same penalty for the man who connives at this crime or who makes the sacrifice.

This statute we wish to be observed by judges, defensors and curials of every city, so that offenses discovered by the latter may be reported to the courts and there punished by the former. But if they think anything may be concealed by favor or passed over by negligence, let them be subjected to judicial action; but if the former being warned, postpone giving sentence and dissimilate, they shall be fined thirty pounds of gold, and members of their court shall be subjected to a like penalty.



# St. Augustine Champions the Heavenly City

Augustine (354–430), a Roman convert to Christianity, and Bishop of Hippo in North Africa, took upon himself the burden of explaining why Christians should continue to believe in their God after the Roman Empire had suffered so much. Indeed, in 410 A.D. just a few years before *The City of God* was written, Alaric's Goths had sacked the city of Rome, and at the time of Augustine's death, the Vandals had invaded North Africa and were beseiging Hippo. His view of the "two cities" owed much to the experiences of the earlier Christian martyrs, and to the conflicts within himself that had to be resolved before his conversion. Christian and worldly values could never be the same. In Augustine's view, however, Christians have a way of accepting worldly authority without compromising their religious ideals. Augustine's work is an important contribution to the history of the tension between Church and State in the

West. From Saint Augustine, *The City of God*, trans. G. Wilson (Book IV), J. Smith (Book V), and M. Dods (Book XIV), (New York: Random House, Inc., 1950) pp. 111-113, 165-168, 477.

## I

I should like first to inquire for a little what reason, what prudence, there is in wishing to glory in the greatness and extent of the [Roman] empire, when you cannot point out the happiness of men who are always rolling, with dark fear and cruel lust, in warlike slaughters and in blood, which, whether shed in civil or foreign war, is still human blood; so that their joy may be compared to glass in its fragile splendour, of which one is horribly afraid lest it should be suddenly broken in pieces. That this may be more easily discerned, let us not come to nought by being carried away with empty boasting, or blunt the edge of our attention by loud-sounding names of things, when we hear of peoples, kingdoms, provinces.

But let us suppose a case of two men; for each individual man, like one letter in a language, is as it were the element of a city or kingdom, however far-spreading in its occupation of the earth. Of these two men let us suppose that one is poor, or rather of middling circumstances; the other very rich. But the rich man is anxious with fears, pining with discontent, burning with covetousness, never secure, always uneasy, panting from the perpetual strife of his enemies, adding to his patrimony indeed by these miseries to an immense degree, and by these additions also heaping up most bitter cares. But that other man of moderate wealth is contented with a small and compact estate, most dear to his own family, enjoying the sweetest peace with his kindred, neighbours, and friends, in piety religious, benignant in mind, healthy in body, in life frugal, in manners chaste, in conscience secure. I know not whether any one can be such a fool, that he dare hesitate which to prefer.

As, therefore, in the case of these two men, so in two families, in two nations, in two kingdoms, this test of tranquillity holds good, and if we apply it vigilantly and without prejudice, we shall quite easily see where the mere show of happiness dwells, and where real felicity. Wherefore if the true God is worshipped, and if He is served with genuine rites and true virtue, it is advantageous that good men should long reign both far and wide. Nor is this advantageous so much to themselves as to those over whom they reign. For, so far as concerns themselves, their piety and probity, which are great gifts of God, suffice to give them true felicity, enabling them to live well the life that now is, and afterwards to receive that which is eternal.

In this world, therefore, the dominion of good men is profitable, not so much for themselves as for human affairs. But the dominion of bad men is hurtful chiefly to themselves who rule, for they destroy their own souls by greater licence in wickedness; while those who are put under them in service are not hurt except by their own iniquity. For to the just all the evils imposed on them by unjust rulers are not the punishment of crime, but the test of virtue. Therefore the good man, although he is a slave, is free; but the bad man, even if he reigns, is a slave, and that not of one man, but, what is far more grievous, of as many masters as he has vices; of which vices when the divine Scripture treats, it says, "For of whom any man is overcome, to the same he is also the bond-slave."

Justice being taken away, then, what are kingdoms but great robberies? For what are robberies themselves, but little kingdoms? The band itself is made up of men; it is ruled by the authority of a prince, it is knit together by the pact of the confederacy; the booty is divided by the law agreed on. If, by the admittance of abandoned men, this evil increases to such a degree that it holds places, fixes abodes, takes possession of cities, and subdues peoples, it assumes the more plainly the name of a kingdom, because the reality is now manifestly conferred on it, not by the removal of covetousness, but by the addition of impunity. Indeed, that was an apt and true reply which was given to Alexander the Great by a pirate who had been seized. For when that king had asked the man what he meant by keeping hostile possession of the sea, he answered with bold pride, "What thou meanest by seizing the whole earth; but because I do it with a petty ship, I am called a robber, whilst thou who dost it with a great fleet art styled emperor." . . .

## II

[The Romans] were honoured among almost all nations; they imposed the laws of their empire upon many nations; and at this day, both in literature and history, they are glorious among almost all nations. There is no reason why they should complain against the justice of the supreme and true God—"they have received their reward."

But the reward of the saints is far different, who even here endured reproaches for that city of God which is hateful to the lovers of this world. That city is eternal. There none are born, for none die. There is true and full felicity—not a goddess, but a gift of God. Thence we receive the pledge of faith, whilst

1 Dignity, restraint, and proportion characterize Roman sculpture of the early Empire: one of the greatest works of the period, the altar of the Augustan Peace, was erected by order of the Senate on the Campus Martius to commemorate Augustus' return from Gaul in 24 B.C. A section of the frieze is shown here. The classically composed and calm figure of the emperor is followed by figures of members of his family—Julia his daughter, his stepson and heir Tiberius, and his grandson Lucius. Typical of early Roman art is the highly stylized fall of the draperies.

## Six Centuries of Roman Art

The art of the Romans was heavily influenced by that of the Greeks, even though it achieved its own distinctive character. Roman control over the Greek settlers of southern Italy and Sicily was well established by the third century B.C., and from this contact came a developing taste for the art of the conquered. The influence of the Greeks grew ever larger, though in different styles, for when the expanding Empire eventually occupied the entire Mediterranean world, its rulers found the cultures of the area already dominated by Hellenistic artistic values. Roman adherence to classical standards reached its apogee during the first century A.D. and thereafter gradually shifted under the pressure of deteriorating conditions and a changing sense of identity to a more abstract and stylized way of viewing the world. The examples of six centuries of Roman art and architecture on the next pages attempt to show these transitions and to indicate the shaping elements in the Christian artistic tradition of medieval Europe.

1

2

3

4

The taste for portraiture developed during the Hellenistic Age was carried to remarkable heights by the Romans. These aristocrats—(**1**) Marcus Brutus, (**2**) Gaius Marius, (**3**) an unidentified lady, and (**4**) a couple purported to be Cato the Elder and his wife—embody the Roman virtues of stalwart individualism. Concern with the here-and-now is visible in the great attention given to realistic appearance. Note the detail of wrinkles, skin texture, and hair.

5 Bacchus, the god of wine, is accompanied by his female attendants, the maenads, in a Tunisian mosaic of the first century A.D. that clearly reveals its Hellenistic heritage.

1 By the second century A.D., Roman art had begun to abandon the strict proportions of the classical tradition, as a comparison of this work with the frieze on the Augustan altar on the first page of this portfolio will indicate. This detail from Trajan's column in Rome (erected 106–113) shows the soldier-emperor who expanded the empire's boundaries to their greatest extent as he accepts the surrender of the Dacian (Rumanian) ruler. The soldiers in the lower right are assembling timber fortifications.

2 The movement away from classical standards is even more obvious in these fourth-century figures at the left of Diocletian and the co-rulers he chose to administer a troubled and turbulent empire. Diocletian in the foreground embraces his fellow Augustus, Maximian, while the two Caesars, Constantius and Galerius, follow suit. All four keep their free hands upon their sword hilts. The figures are highly stylized and their eyes have an abstract look, far different from the realistic expressions of earlier Roman portraiture.

3 A colossal head of Constantine, Diocletian's successor and the first Christian emperor, testifies to the changing standards in Roman sculpture. Early fourth century.

1 The shortened figures, magnified eyes and generally nonclassical proportions and feelings that were a hallmark of later Roman art are apparent in this scene carved on a fifth-century ivory casket, which illustrates an episode from the Passion of Christ. Note the beardless Christ figure.

2 The art of the early Christian era reflected the qualities of Roman art as this wall painting from the catacomb of Saint Priscilla in Rome demonstrates. Probably depicting Mary and the Infant Jesus, it belongs to the late third century, to the reign of Diocletian when the Rome authorities had initiated a concerted persecution of Christians.

3 The earliest Christians gathered for worship in private homes or, in periods of persecution, in underground burial tunnels called catacombs. The legalization of Christianity under Constantine and the rapid growth in Church membership encouraged the construction of formal churches, many of which were modeled on the Roman basilica. This building, a rectangular, timber-roofed hall, often with an apse, a semi-circular protrusion at one end, served as a market house, a court of law, or a military drill hall. The Roman practice of placing within the apse an image of the emperor, before which religious ceremonies were held, provided a sacred function in the public use of the building that blurred the hall's secular origins. Thus it was not illogical that the Christians should choose the basilica as a place where large congregations could gather and where, in the apse, religious services could be performed. The interior view is of another fourth-century Roman church, St. Paul's Outside the Walls (c.386). The building was severely damaged by fire in 1823 but has been painstakingly restored. Its elaborate decoration of gold, marble, prophyry, and mosaic attests to the material affluence of the Church once Christianity had become a legal religion. The columns are possibly spoils taken from a pagan temple. Above is the renovated interior of St. Paul's Outside the Walls.

1 One of the high points of later Christian, more properly Byzantine art, was its sophisticated use of mosaic. The representation of the Emperor Justinian (ruled 527–565) and his suite in the church of San Vitale in Ravenna shows static figures with very long, nonclassical proportions, but some attempt at portraiture has been made in the case of the emperor (center) and Bishop Maximianus. The abstract play of colors and patterns delights the eye.

on our pilgrimage we sign for its beauty. There rises not the sun on the good and the evil, but the Sun of Righteousness protects the good alone. . . .

For I do not see what it makes for the safety, good morals, and certainly not for the dignity, of men, that some have conquered and others have been conquered, except that it yields them that most insane pomp of human glory, in which "they have received their reward," who burned with excessive desire of it, and carried on most eager wars. . . . But let us avail ourselves even in these things of the kindness of God. Let us consider how great things they despised, how great things they endured, what lusts they subdued for the sake of human glory, who merited that glory, as it were, in reward for such virtues; and let this be useful to us even in suppressing pride, so that, as that city in which it has been promised us to reign as far surpasses this one as heaven is distant from the earth, as eternal life surpasses temporal joy, solid glory empty praise, or the society of angels the society of mortals, or the glory of Him who made the sun and moon the light of the sun and moon, the citizens of so great a country may not seem to themselves to have done anything very great, if in order to obtain it, they have done some good works or endured some evils, when those men for this terrestrial country already obtained, did such great things, suffered such great things. . . .

What great thing, therefore, is it for that eternal and celestial city to despise all the charms of this world, however pleasant, if for the sake of this terrestrial city Brutus* could even put to death his son—a sacrifice which the heavenly city compels no one to make? But certainly it is more difficult to put to death one's sons, than to do what is required to be done for the heavenly country, even to distribute to the poor those things which were looked upon as things to be amassed and laid up for one's children, or to let them, go, if there arise any temptation which compels us to do so, for the sake of faith and righteousness. For it is not earthly riches which make us or our sons happy; for they must either be lost by us in our lifetime, or be possessed when we are dead, by whom we know not, or perhaps by whom we would not. But it is God who makes us happy, who is the true riches of minds. . . .

Accordingly, two cities have been formed by two loves: the earthly by the love of self, even to the contempt of God; the heavenly by the love of God, even to the contempt of self. The former, in a word, glories in itself, the latter in the Lord. For the one seeks glory from men; but the greatest glory of the other is God, the witness of conscience. The one lifts up its head in its own glory; the other says to its God, "Thou art my glory, and the lifter up of mine head." In the one, the princes and the subjects serve one another in love, the latter obeying, while the former takes thought for all. The one delights in its own strength, represented in the persons of its rulers; the other says to its God, "I will love Thee, O Lord, my strength."

And therefore the wise men of the one city, living according to man, have sought for profit to their own bodies or souls, or both and those who have known God "glorified Him not as God, neither were thankful, but became vain in their imaginations, and their foolish heart was darkened; professing themselves to be wise"—that is, glorying in their own wisdom, and being possessed by pride—"they became fools, and changed the glory of the incorruptible God into an image made like to corruptible man, and to birds, and four-footed beasts, and creeping things." For they were either leaders or followers of the people in adoring images, "and worshipped and served the creature more than the Creator, who is blessed for ever." But in the other city there is no human wisdom, but only godliness, which offers due worship to the true God, and looks for its reward in the society of the saints, of holy angels as well as holy men, "that God may be all in all."

*Lucius Junius Brutus, known as "father of the Roman Republic," led the successful revolt in 510 B.C. that ended the Etruscan overlordship. In an act of supreme patriotism, he executed his two sons who were involved in a conspiracy with the enemy —Eds.

# Chapter 3

## Transition: Romans, Barbarians, and Christians

In the fifth century, the West was little more than the western portion of the Roman Empire. It was no longer the seat of a great civilization. The price of Rome's efforts to extend and maintain an empire had been paid at home. Economic crisis, social disintegration, and a sense of drift all marked the late Empire. Territorial and cultural identity were themselves sacrificed when the eastern and western portions, into which the Empire had been divided for purposes of administration, moved even further apart. After 476, no further emperors were chosen in the West, which was ruled from Constantinople or by Germanic invaders. The late Empire, because of these changes, has often been considered a period of decline. From the perspective of what was to follow, however, it was a period of transition.

Within the fading Empire, Christian administrators and missionaries joined with the leaders of some of the Germanic tribes to work for the survival of the old learning and the injection of new energy. The German institution of kingship, in particular, offered hope of restoring the notion of a public good and a stable political order to the feudal anarchy of the West. It was the activity of the Church, however, in education, administration, and conversion that made the later revival possible.

Even with this ferment in the late Roman world, the West was sadly lacking in the wealth, organization, and cultural unity which distinguished the imposing Islamic and Byzantine civilizations developing to the East. No one could have guessed, from the perspective of the fifth century, that a civilization would once more flourish. In these readings the despair and the hope of the fifth through the tenth centuries in the West become apparent.

TOPIC 16

# THE ECONOMIC DECLINE OF ROME

The third and fourth centuries A.D. marked a clear decline in the prosperity and stability of the Roman Empire. Increasing pressure on the extended frontiers from Germanic tribes and a revived Persian Empire led to domination by the military and a growing tax burden. Strong emperors such as Diocletian (284–305) and Constantine (306–337) reorganized the imperial administrative system and established strict controls over most aspects of economic life, but the slow ebbing of life in the cities could not be arrested. Political power passed into the hands of the holders of the great landed estates, the *latifundia,* firmly fixing the rural base of later medieval society. The readings are concerned with the reasons for and the effects of this economic decline.

**Reading 81**

## Ferdinand Lot: The Failure of Capitalism To Develop in the Roman World

Ferdinand Lot (1866–1952) in this now classic work tried to establish the characteristics of the Roman world in its decline. In so doing, the French medievalist had to plumb the culture, political organization, and economy of late Roman society. In this reading Lot describes the internal weakness of the Roman imperial economy from the prospective of modern Western capitalist development. Lot utilizes the essential features of capitalism—investment of capital in industry and agriculture, production for a large market, division of labor, and a commercial spirit—to set up a standard by which to judge Roman practices. From *The End of the Ancient World and the Beginnings of the Middle Ages,* by Ferdinand Lot. Copyright 1931 by Alfred A. Knopf, Inc. Reprinted by permission of the publisher.

### I

We are now faced with a problem of the highest importance. How can we explain the fact that the Roman world, economically prosperous at the end of the Republic and during the first two centuries of the Empire, was irreparably ruined? The storm of the third century was terrible in its political consequences, and the monetary system suffered serious upheavals. But Aurelian, Diocletian and Constantine set the Roman world on its feet once more, refounded the administration, improved the financial system, and the currency again became nearly as good as in the first century. Nevertheless, nothing could stop the downfall, which only became more marked in the course of the fourth and the fifth centuries.

This is a very surprising phenomenon to us, who are accustomed to an ever-growing prosperity. A commercial crisis or a war may interrupt this prosperity but we are convinced that after a more or less long period of arrest, business will recover and that the production of wealth will never stop. Why do we have this conviction? Because we live under the capitalist system, under which all the forces of society are bent on the production of [goods] which are sold in wider and wider markets.

Was it the same with Antiquity? In other words, had Antiquity any knowledge of a real capitalist system? . . .

Let us see whether at Rome capital was "invested," as is asserted, in industry and commerce, in which case the existence of capitalism could not be called in question.

### Capital and Industry

From a very early period of Roman history, the crafts became freed from the household, or from domestic economy, to be at the service of the public. Specialization in the crafts and the division of labour were far advanced from the third and second centuries B.C. onwards. Crafts and trades, sometimes organized into "colleges," tended to gather in particular streets. The town dweller could find bakers from whom to purchase bread, shops where fried fish was sold, inns, barbers' and clothiers' shops. But even this does not imply any industrial capitalist production. . . .

In fact capital, which was so plentiful at the end of the Republic and the beginning of the Empire, was not applied or was applied only to a small extent to industry. This already constitutes a profound and essential difference between Roman and modern or contemporary economics.

Why was no attempt made to invest money in industry?

In the first place because of the obstacle of domestic economy. The latter was deeply rooted in the prevailing habits. Every great *villa* possessed not merely its hand-mills, bake-houses, workshops for agricultural requirements (a forge, a carpenter's shop), but also workshops for weaving and clothes, entrusted to the women and slaves. The aristocracy kept embroiderers, gilders, chasers, goldsmiths, painters, architects, sculptors, hairdressers, who were either slaves or freedmen. "Rich families felt a kind of vainglory in being able to say that all the needs of the house could be satisfied by the work within the house itself; thus everything was manufactured in the house, even articles of luxury." To buy things outside was considered a kind of disgrace.

On the other hand, modern capitalism has succeeded, at least in Western Europe, in entirely breaking down domestic industry, by making use of progress in technique. Now it is a significant fact that the technique of the crafts does not seem to have made any appreciable progress amongst the Romans.

We have here a very important special case of the phenomenon of the paralysis of invention which shows itself in all the spheres of human activity, art, literature, science and philosophy, in Greece as early as the second century B.C., in Rome in the second century A.D.

In the absence of technical improvement, capital was not required for investment in industry, while the inventive spirit, in its turn, was not stimulated by the prospect of the profits to be brought to it by capital from applying itself to the improvement of industrial technique. These reciprocal actions and reactions of the inventive spirit and of capitalism, so marked in Europe as early as the eighteenth century and even before, did not exist in the Roman world.

But in the absence of machines and improved tools, could not the employment of human hands at a low or at a minimum price, the employment of slaves, attract capital? Only for a moment. There have been some important enterprises started with slaves.

At Rome also some attempts were made. Contractors and capitalists thought they would do good business by making profits by the work of slaves trained to practise crafts. But the profits soon showed themselves very slender. In the first place money had to be spent on buying the slave, or else, if he was already in the house, on training him, teaching him his craft. If a crisis arises, the slave has still to be kept, however inadequately.

Above all, his working capacity and his yield are very inferior to those of the free man, the margin being so small that the master's profits may vanish altogether. If people kept gangs of slaves (and they did this only up to about the second century) it was from vanity and for show, rather than for any very tangible advantages. Finally, as the master wishes to use his slaves for everything, for labours of the field as well as for town crafts, he cannot carry the division of labour very far. Thus the economics of slavery are proved to be essentially anti-capitalist. . . .

### Urban Market

Was Rome a market? In a certain sense it was, and even a world market as we should say, all the products of nature and art flowing there. But Rome sold nothing in return, since practically nothing was produced there. The populace, kept in semi-idleness by the distributions of provisions and the superabundance of shows, yielded very little in return. Rome, which made the provinces send her everything, never re-imbursed them except with the money from the taxes, that is to say, with the very sums with which these provinces had provided her. Her so-called commerce was thus only indirect robbery. The capital, being an unproductive city, was truly an "octopus."

The new capital, Constantinople [from 325 A.D.], partly deserves the reproaches applied to the old. But only partly; for it was to become the emporium of the Eastern Mediterranean and of the Black Sea. But its commercial rise would need time, as would the increase of its population.

What much more than Rome resembled a great modern city was Alexandria, and to a certain extent Antioch. Extending 5 kilometres by 2, covering an area of 920 hectares, and populated by 300,000 inhabitants, Alexandria remained for a long time "the world's greatest mart." This will not astonish us, if we remember that its hinterland was Egypt, the country with the densest population in Antiquity; it reached 7,500,000 inhabitants.

Speaking generally, the towns were very sparsely populated. Even in the time of the Empire's greatest prosperity, the largest towns in Gaul, Nimes, Toulouse, Autun and Treves, can never have numbered more than 50,000 inhabitants. . . . Famous towns like Marseilles, Milan, Verona, Aquileia and Naples had at all times been small. Still more was this the case when, in consequence of the disasters of the third century and of the resulting depopulation, the towns had to contract, occupying now only a quarter, a tenth or sometimes even a twentieth part of their former area. . . .

Not only was the population not dense, but its buying capacity was poor. The men of Antiquity, if they did not live in opulence, had few needs. Their food was simple and frugal, as is still that of the men of the South [Mediterranean] in our days. The lower classes lived on wheaten bread and paste (the other cereals being despised) and on vegetables. The use of meat was not common, except pork and kid, whence our word "butcher," which means one who sells kid's flesh. Butter was a barbarian article of food and oil was preferred to it. Wine was drunk but little; even the army which was so carefully looked after, had it only every other day. Under these conditions, the trades in foodstuffs could not be thriving.

It was the same with clothing. Clothes were simple and rarely renewed. There was no real linen. Thus there was no development in the clothing industry. It did not succeed in going beyond the stage of production in private workshops, until the extension of the wool trade and the drapery industry, when the shirt of German origin ceased to be an outer garment and came to be made of real linen; this means that these changes took place only at an advanced stage of the history of the Middle Ages. Living, heating and lighting arrangements thus remained stationary.

The population of the large towns was crowded into rented houses divided into mutually independent stories (*insulae*). They were gloomy dwellings with insufficient or no heating, even in winter, except by means of *braseros*. For lighting a primitive oil lamp was used, a mere wick floating in oil. The furniture was very perfunctory, consisting of a bed (a tressel with cushions thrown on it), chests, tables and chairs. The citizen lived as little as possible inside his gloomy dwelling; when his work was over, if he worked, he walked in the streets, under the porticos, in the forum, or frequented the circuses, the theatre and the baths where he was forced to bathe frequently, owing to the lack of linen. Speaking generally, the psychology of the man of Antiquity differed appreciably from ours. He had few wants and his tastes were very stable. Fashion scarcely existed, and it exercised its influence only on the upper classes and not on the whole of society, as it does in our day. Moreover it changed very slowly. Dress, dwelling houses, furniture, objects of art, all tended to become stereotyped into almost unchangeable forms. Whence the monotonous and boring character of Roman civilization.

This simplicity of life and absence of needs and of comfort are most unfavourable to the development of industry. The *aurea mediocritas* [golden mean], so dear to the Romans,. . . is a conception incompatible with a materially advanced civilization.

It is true that in the Roman world were to be found dazzling and colossal fortunes—in comparison with the Middle Ages or the dawn of modern times. But in the ordinary routine of their life, the rich, even in the town, lived on the products of their country estates and bought almost nothing. An exception must be made for articles of luxury which were imported from the four corners of the globe. But modern economics have taught us that the commerce in luxuries, which concerns only a small number of rich men, is absolutely inadequate to produce, stimulate and maintain a thriving industry: "When wealth is concentrated at one pole, luxury breaks up the equilibrium of production by diminishing the manufacture of articles of use and increasing that of articles of luxury." Industry prospers in societies in which wealth is distributed over a great number of persons and descends from the richest to the poorest by graded stages: "the more wealth is divided, the more consumption and consequently production increase."

Unfortunately, except in a very small number of towns in the East, no such gradation is found in the Roman Empire. There was little or no middle class. Between extreme luxury and resigned or snarling poverty, there was nothing. At Rome, the richest and most splendid of all the towns, over against the 1,800 *domus* (palaces) there were 46,600 apartments swarming with a starving population. People of good birth, without any means, lived on *sportulae*. Rome was a town of beggars and remained so almost up to contemporary times.

Further, there was a profound difference between ancient and modern urban life. The modern town lives above all on industry and commerce, wherein lies its peculiar function.

It was not necessarily the same with the ancient town, above all when it was the capital of the State. People of good birth there lived on the produce of their land. Industry and commerce might thrive in addition, but they did not constitute the primary function of the town. The latter did not radiate over the neighbouring territory to fertilize, enrich and civilize it, but sucked in its means of subsistence; it was "tentacular," to use a contemporary expression.

Hence, the towns were not centres of industry connected with each other through interest or even competition. Thus there was no real industrial bourgeoisie in Antiquity, because, strictly speaking, there was no large or middle-scale industry. We will not call by the name of "large-scale industry" the enterprises started under the control of the State, for the provisioning of the capitals and the army. The general stores at Ostia, the two hundred and fifty enormous bakeries at Rome, and the Imperial factories of arms and textiles, certainly necessitated much money, manual labour, and a numerous staff. But this was not large-scale industry; these establishments were confined to the warehousing of commodities for the Roman people, or to producing articles intended for the Emperor and his Court and not for the public. They were kept up only by dint of privileges, exemptions and compulsion. . . .

## Commerce

Though commerce was regarded more favourably than industry, it never reached any very great volume. Producing little, the Roman world carried little and sold little. It came up against deserts in the South, the barbarians in the North, and the economically backward Persian civilization in the East, while its relations with India and China were exceedingly rare. Hence, in the absence of industry in the Roman world, commerce could not convey the products of a foreign industry. Commerce on a large scale could only concern itself with objects of luxury, the high price of which makes it possible to recover the expenses of transport. But about luxury trade we may repeat the observations concerning luxury industry. It is at bottom unproductive. Further, articles of luxury and of art came chiefly from the East, and large-scale commerce is fed only by articles having a large consumption and not by articles of luxury, the sale of which is capricious and may even stop completely, bringing about serious disturbances. Navigation could not thrive on the transport of purple and commodities even from the Far East (silks from China, aromatics, spices, etc.). Lastly, in this traffic, the balance was unfavourable for Rome and the West, which paid in money and sold nothing or practically nothing by way of merchandise. Gold and silver were thus drained towards the East and Far East.

The deep underlying cause of this languid life of business is to be sought in the psychology of the Romans. Unlike the Greeks of the Athenian and of the Hellenistic period, they were not deeply or for a long time interested in trade; they showed "little commercial jealousy" and in spite of what has been asserted, Rome never had a commercial policy. The "Italian" merchants, found to some extent everywhere from Gaul to the East, at the end of the Roman Republic and at the beginning of the Empire, were not inhabitants of Rome, but people from Southern Italy. A number of them were only traffickers who swooped down like the traders in new colonies today to make their fortune quickly by any possible means, and then were off. This class of people disappeared and were absorbed in the Hellenistic world. Trade became the monopoly of the Orientals, especially of Syrians and Jews, as early as the reign of Tiberius and it was still so after the disappearance of the Empire, in Merovingian times. In navigation, the Romans played no part; the crews were Greek, Illyrian or Egyptian.

The upper classes of society (the senatorial and equestrian classes) were turned away from commerce by prejudice and even by law. These classes, which were yet so grasping, did not possess the capitalist spirit of enterprise. Large business did not get from them the help of capital which they alone possessed and the class of real business men, with experience and enterprise, useful and respected, without which there is no real capitalist system, was not formed. . . .

## Agriculture

In default of industry and commerce, could not capital be employed in agriculture? Whether capital is applied to industry or agriculture, it has been said, is a secondary consideration.

The historians who entertain these opinions have especially in view the *latifundia* [large estates] worked by means of slaves on what are maintained to be capitalist lines.

It is certain that at the end of the Republic and under the Empire, sustained efforts were made to apply to agriculture the plentiful capital which was at the disposal of the upper classes. For a man of low birth, who had made his wealth by commerce, the only means of making people forget this stain was to buy land. Small business was "sordid"; but the merchant who retired and employed his fortune in agriculture was worthy of praise.

Custom, legislation, Imperial favour, and fashion even, encouraged men to invest money in the purchase and working of large landed estates.

But the results were not proportionate to these efforts. The capitalist exploitation of the soil ended in complete failure.

The reason is that exploitation by means of slaves not only ties up large capital sums, but requires at least two other conditions in order to be remunerative, a rich soil and densely populated areas in the neighbourhood. But the most fertile parts of Italy, Gaul, etc., remained for a long time fallow; in the absence of scientific knowledge, which is of very recent growth, and also in the absence of large cattle, the greater part of the soil was soon exhausted, especially under the system of biennial rotation. The towns were very poor markets. The majority were, as we have seen, small, sparsely populated, and what was worse, far from each other, conditions which militated against their being profitable markets. There remained Rome; but being provisioned by the "annona"* from Africa, Sicily, etc., the capital was economically like a foreign city in relation to Italy.

Let us remember that the consuming power of the population of the towns was very limited, neither meat nor wine being in demand. The transport of wine, oil, etc. (by means of earthenware vases or wine-skins) was moreover inconvenient, and that of fruits more difficult still.

Hence the large slave-worked estates knew only extensive exploitation, chiefly pasturing. They produced not so much for the market as for the upkeep of the owner, his family and clients. The *latifundia* come under domestic economy. They herald and prepare the way for feudal economy, it may be, but not at all for the capitalist system.

*The annona was a tax on agricultural production and was paid in food (grain, livestock, and so on) —Eds.

Thus, wherever this was possible, the landowner came to divide his estates into plots assigned to [workers called] *coloni.*

Were these *coloni* farmers in the modern sense, that is to say small capitalist owners of cattle, agricultural implements and movable stock? Certainly not. The free *colonus* had only his hands and his family to help him, but no capital; and this no doubt explains the ease with which he became bound to the soil under the Latin Empire. . . .

Thus, capitalism, when applied to agriculture, was unable to change its character of natural economy and nothing is less like capitalist economy than the agriculture of the Roman Empire. . . .

## Investment and Usury

Of the landed investments we have already spoken. They were scarcely, if at all, productive. Their aim was social and snobbish and they were of small economic value. First and foremost usury flourished. . . . Usury on a large scale was approved of and it was not considered shameful to engage in it. And what usury! Knights and Senators lent money to Kings in the East, then to towns, corporations and private individuals, at incredible rates of interest. The rule was 4 per cent per month; some lent only at 75 per cent or 100 per cent; Atticus, for example, who was looked upon by his contemporaries as the King of the Knights. As he was a patron of men of letters, he has, in spite of this, left behind him the reputation of a gentleman. Brutus lent at 48 per cent. "All the great names in Roman history are connected with transactions of usury." So much for the provinces.

In Italy, even in settled times the rate of 12 per cent was legal. "Rome's great industry was usury." Money went neither to the land, nor to commerce, nor to industry. The capital of the Roman world did not feed enterprise. Being applied to usury, capital even dried up the spirit of enterprise, and by attacking the sources of wealth, it discouraged production. "Usury was at Rome, as it will always be in countries in which there is little commercial industry, an exorbitant tax exacted from the poor and needy by capitalists, a cause of ruin for the people. The less trade there is, the more excessive is usury." There is nothing more barren or harmful than usury. It only thrives in countries and times in which real credit does not exist, in other words, when the mind has not yet risen to the capitalistic conception of business.

This usurious, idle, and by no means capitalistic aristocracy was in addition horribly spendthrift. The luxury of the higher classes may have been exaggerated; but it remains nevertheless certain that at the end of the Roman Republic and the beginning of the Empire, senseless acts of prodigality, involving a wholesale destruction of wealth, were indulged in. This wealth had been created not by Rome but by the Hellenistic world. Rome's industry in the second and first centuries B.C. had been war and spoliation of the vanquished. Drained at Rome, without being fed by a real spirit of enterprise, capital, the product of long centuries of work of the Mediterranean world, soon dried up. "The fruits of conquest were dissipated in a century." The time of the greatest luxury extends from the middle of the first century B.C. to the death of Nero. Already under Vespasian [69–79 A.D.], the senatorial and equestrian order had almost been annihilated in consequence of the political persecutions, but also because of the dissipation of their fortunes. Vespasian was obliged to found a new nobility with provincial families. From this time onward, no fortune lasted for more than three or four generations.

Finally, it should be observed that the Ancients had no sound conception of the nature of productive capital. . . . Roman "capitalism" had been but a thin layer swept away by the breath of the storm, and the underlying rock of natural economy very quickly came to the surface.

This return to natural economy, after the arrest of monetary economy, already marks the economic Middle Ages. Politically and socially, it is the introduction to the Middle Ages.

### General Decline

With the material prosperity and stage of civilization reached by Ancient Society was bound up the stability of the Imperial regime. The economic system being in process of marked retrogression, the expenses ought to have been reduced. But to this men could not resign themselves. The Roman State, from the end of the third century, was like a ruined landlord who wants to keep up the same establishment as in the days of his prosperity. These attempts were all in vain. The army was badly recruited; the decurion fled from the *curia,* the peasant from the land and the artisan from his *collegium.* The State saw only one way of salvation; to bind every man by force to his occupation, to chain him and his descendants to the same post, and it established a real caste system. The reforms of Diocletian, Constantine and their successors betray the desperate struggle of an organism refusing to die, with natural economic forces which will not allow society to maintain with very reduced means a large and complex State. . . .

# R. F. Arragon: The Growth of Landed Estates

Reginald Arragon (1891-     ), American cultural historian, finds that the shift from urban to rural living was one of the marks of the movement from the Roman to the medieval world. From *The Transition from the Ancient to the Medieval World* by R. F. Arragon. 

## PEASANT FARMING AND THE COLONATE

The simpler economic order meant the predominance of agriculture over manufacture and commerce. The self-sufficient communities were in immediate contact with fields and flocks, and the products of these were worked up directly by the handicrafts for local use. Agriculture itself was transformed. Large-scale farming with central management, scientific methods, slave labor and a marketable surplus disappeared. Peasant farming took its place. This change was not accompanied by the break-up of the large estates. Indeed they became larger, at the same time that the scale of operations became smaller. The cultivators were tenants. Their equipment was simpler, their crops less specialized and their methods cruder, and their production was chiefly for consumption on the estate. This system was less productive but more practical or convenient in the condition of the later empire than the treatment of cultivation as a business enterprise.

Tenant-farming had been known in the late republic. On the estates of Pompey were tenants who were at once free peasants and clients. In this way the farming of the peasant landowner of the early republic was adapted to the estate of the great landowner. It was the spread of tenancy under the principate that marked the decline of slavery in agriculture. Peasant tenancy prevailed as early as the second century on the vast imperial estates (known as *saltus*) of Africa, from which there is direct evidence. Signs of a like tenure elsewhere are confirmed by the legislation of the fourth century. Great privately-owned properties were organized like those of the emperors. These estates centered in villas or countryhouses where lived the private magnate or the imperial agent (the chief farmer, or *conductor,* who was in effect the chief tenant). Aside from the chief farm connected directly with the villa, the estate was divided into the small farms of the tenants, and, already in the second century, at least on some imperial estates, the tenants owed a number of days of labor to the chief farmer as a condition of their tenantry. Dues in produce and in labor were the characteristic return for these peasant leases. This system of cultivation came to be dominant throughout the Mediterranean world, and in the disorders that accompanied and followed the disappearance of the empire in the West such peasant free-holdings as had survived the rise of the slave *latifundia* tended to become tenancies under the protection of great proprietors.

The status of the tenants is known as the colonate. The term implies more than the rental of land, for the status made the tenant a dependent of the landlord and obligated him to remain on the estate. He was not a slave nor usually a freedman. He was most likely to be a descendant of peasants, Italians, Gauls, Iberians, Berbers or others, and himself a freeman before the law. Yet the *coloni* became bound to the soil as were their successors, the serfs of the Middle Ages. There has been much dispute as to how this came about. The term *colonus* descended the social scale from the settler and soldier in the "colonies" of the early republic, and then to the soil-bound peasant on great landed properties of the empire.

Servile tenancy had age-old precedents, in Egypt and the East, in Lacedaemonia and Thessaly, at Carthage and Syracuse and perhaps in the pre-Roman Gaul. Certain forms of land-tenure recognized by the laws of the principate for furthering the use of waste lands may have encouraged it. Essentially however it was the result of the economic and social inferiority of the tenant combined with basic importance for the revenues of the landlord and of the state. Tenantry became bondage through the weakness of the peasants in the face of the agents of the emperors and of private magnates, amid political conditions which emphasized the obligations of the weak to the strong. The tenant was the "client" of the landlord proprietor, who as patron represented him at law and treated him as a dependent inferior. He had normally no means of livelihood save his tenancy, to which he was tied, moreover, by obligations in money, produce and labor for rent and other dues. If he were a freedman who had leased a ground-plot from his master, his ties were still closer. The tenant had little defense against the arbitrary demands of a chief farmer or other imperial officials or of private landlords. Irregular exactions and other oppression on imperial estates in the second and third centuries are revealed by the appeals of groups of *coloni* to the emperor over the heads of his agents, but occasional redress of grievances provided no general remedy for local tyranny.

Imperial policy tended, on the contrary, to strengthen the bondage, for more rigorous taxation increased the obligations placed upon the *coloni* and the importance of keeping them on the land. Landlords and imperial agents could not permit *coloni* to escape from land with which they had been counted in the assessment. Nor could the fiscal needs of the government allow it. Constantine in a law of 322 forbade their flight, and similar more drastic laws followed in the late fourth century and after. Legislation joined the landlords' pressure in creating of the *coloni* a case of cultivators. They and their descendants were attached to the land as a part of the estates without freedom of movement and occupation and even without the Roman slave's expectation of manumission. They were above the status of the slave in that they could not legally be deprived of their use of the land. This assured them a combination of hereditary tenancy and bondage, the serfdom which characterized a large part of the agricultural workers of the Middle Ages.

## THE VILLA

The significance of the great estates was not simply in the development of the colonate. They became the self-sufficient economic and social units of the society that was losing its wider ties. Such were the imperial estates in Africa, which dated from the early principate and in some cases were as extensive as principalities. Such too were private properties of the fourth and fifth centuries in Gaul. Similar holdings were to be found in the other provinces. Imperial *saltus* were rivaled by the estates surrounding the villas of great officials and of favorites of the emperors. Private magnates as well as imperial procurators and *conductores* were made responsible for the maintenance of law and order as for the taxes of their lands. They gained a personal jurisdiction and immunity from interference in the domestic affairs of their villas that has already been discussed in connection with political decentralization. They were the forerunners of the feudal lords, and their estates became medieval manors.

The development of these great landed properties not only was in contrast with the organization of agriculture under the municipal system at the height of its prosperity but was at its expense. The cities, as we have seen, leaned heavily upon the land, and the spread of cities had meant a spread of territory under municipal control. The estates just described were independent of this control, and their growth was a reversal of the urban trend. Some large tracts of fertile and populated land, chiefly in the possession of the emperors, had never been incorporated in the territories of cities, and others were withdrawn from this jurisdiction by the influence and position of their owners. Before the end of the fourth century, the government legalized the independence of the great landlords from the tax-jurisdiction of the cities. While the tax-burden of the municipal aristocracies became more oppressive, their revenues were being impaired by shrinking territories as well as by changing agricultural methods. This was linked with the "flight" of the *curiales* (into the class of great landlords and even into tenancy under these) and the repeated efforts of the government to stop it, which were dealt with in the first chapter. Thus the city was, in a sense, supplanted by the villa or manor, since the center of social gravity shifted from one to the other. In such a change institutions are created as well as destroyed. Here we see again how the social organization of the late empire furnished essential and constructive elements for medieval society. . . .

# Diocletian Decrees Price Controls (301)

Emperor Diocletian (284-305) attempted to meet the crisis facing the empire by reorganizing the government. The Edict of 301 is representative of his endeavor to restore stability and prosperity by recourse to law. From Tenney Frank, trans. and ed., *An Economic Survey of Ancient Rome* (Baltimore: Johns Hopkins Press, 1940), V, pp. 313-316.

Who is so insensitive and so devoid of human feeling that he . . . has not perceived that in the commerce carried on in the markets or involved in the daily life of cities immoderate prices are so widespread that the uncurbed passion for gain is lessened neither by abundant supplies nor by fruitful years. . . . Men whose aim is always to profit even from the generosity of the gods, to restrain general prosperity, and furthermore to use a poor year to traffic in harvest losses and agents' services —men who, individually abounding in great riches which could completely satisfy whole nations, try to capture smaller fortunes and strive after ruinous percentages—concern for humanity in general persuades us to set a limit . . . to the avarice of such men. . . .

Who does not know that insolence, covertly attacking the public welfare—wherever the public safety demands that our armies be directed, not in villages or towns only, but on every road—comes to the mind of the profiteer to extort prices for merchandise, not fourfold or eightfold, but such that human speech is incapable of describing either the price or the act; and finally that sometimes in a single purchase a soldier is deprived of his bonus and salary, and that the contribution of the whole world to support the armies falls to the abominable profits of thieves. . . .

Aroused justly and rightfully by all the facts which are detailed above, and with mankind itself now appearing to be praying for release, we have decreed that there be established, not the prices of articles for sale—for such an act would be unjust when many provinces occasionally rejoice in the good fortune of wished-for low prices and, so to speak, the privilege of prosperity—but a maximum, so that when the violence of high prices appears anywhere—may the gods avert such a calamity!—avarice which, as if in immense open areas, could not be restrained, might be checked by the limits of our statute or by the boundaries of a regulatory law. It is our pleasure, therefore, that the prices listed in the subjoined summary be observed in the whole of our empire in such fashion that every man may know that while permission to exceed them has been forbidden him, the blessing of low prices has in no case been restricted in those places where supplies are seen to abound, since special provision is made for these when avarice is definitely quieted. Moreover, among buyers and sellers who customarily visit ports and foreign provinces this universal decree should be a check so that, when they too know that in the time of high prices there is no possibility of transcending the determined prices for commodities, such a reckoning of places, transportation, and the whole business may be made at the time of sale that the justice of our decree forbidding those who transport merchandise to sell anywhere at higher prices may be evident.

Since, therefore, it is agreed that even in the time of our ancestors it was customary in passing laws to restrain insolence by attaching a prescribed penalty—since it is indeed rare for a situation tending to the good of humanity to be embraced spontaneously, and since, as a guide, fear is always found the most influential preceptor in the performance of duty—it is our pleasure that anyone who shall have resisted the form of this statute shall for his daring be subject to a capital penalty. And let no one consider the penalty harsh since there is at hand a means of avoiding the danger by the observance of moderation. . . .



# Constantine Supports the Landlords (332)

The landless peasantry of the late Roman Empire were known as *coloni.* In many cases they, or their fathers, had once owned land and had transferred it to a local landlord in exchange for protection and employment. The Decree of Constantine (306-337) was later published in a collection of Roman laws and the "interpretation" added by Latin jurists. From *The*

*Theodosian Code and Novels and The Sirmondian Constitutions,* trans. by Clyde Pharr (Copyright 1952 by Clyde Pharr, published by Princeton University Press). Reprinted by permission of Princeton University Press.

Emperor Constantine Augustus to the Provincials.

Any person in whose possession a colonus that belongs to another is found not only shall restore the aforesaid colonus to his first status but also shall assume the capitation [head] tax for this man for the time that he was with him.

(1) Coloni also who meditate flight must be bound with chains and reduced to a servile condition, so that by virtue of their condemnation to slaves they shall be compelled to fulfill the duties that befit freemen. . . .

*Interpretation:* If any person should knowingly retain in his own household a colonus that belongs to another, he shall first restore the man himself to his owner and he shall be compelled to pay his tribute for as long a time as the man was with him. But the colonus himself who was unwilling to be what he had been born shall be reduced to slavery.

# The Emperors Try To Legislate Stability

### (Fourth Century)

The crisis of the late Empire affected the urban classes as well as the peasantry. The burdens on the former self-governing towns became so great that the affluent tried to escape office and even their occupations in order to avert financial ruin. The government reacted by tying men to their jobs and civic responsibilities. Hard hit were the urban elite, the decurion class, which had been accountable for managing the public finances, overseeing public construction, and providing relief and entertainment to the poor. The decrees in this reading stem from various reigns. From *The Theodosian Code and Novels and The Sirmondian Constitutions,* trans. by Clyde Pharr (Copyright 1952 by Clyde Pharr, published by Princeton University Press). Reprinted by permission of Princeton University Press.

XII, 1, 13 (326). Since we have learned that the municipal councils are being left desolate by those persons who are obligated to them through birth status and who are requesting imperial service for themselves through supplications to the Emperor and are running away to the legions and various governmental offices, we order all municipal councils to be admonished that if they should apprehend any persons with less than twenty terms of service in governmental offices . . . they shall drag such persons back to the municipal councils. . . .

XIII, 4, 2 (337). We command that artisans who dwell in each city and who practice the skills included in the appended list shall be free from all compulsory public services, since indeed their leisure should be spent in learning these skills whereby they may desire the more to become more proficient themselves and to instruct their children.

(Appended list.) Architects, makers of paneled ceilings, plasterers, carpenters, physicians, stonecutters, silversmiths, builders, veterinarians, stonemasons, gilders of arms, step-makers, painters, sculptors, engravers, joiners, statuaries, workers in mosaics, coppersmiths, blacksmiths, marblemasons, gilders, founders, dyers in purple, layers of tessellated stones, goldsmiths, mirror-makers, carriage-makers, directors of the distribution of the water supply, glass workers, workers in ivory, fullers, potters, plumbers, furriers.

XII, 1, 62 (364). If a decurion should steal into a guild of artisans for the purpose of evading other duties, he shall be restored to his pristine status, and in the future no person who derives his birth status from decurions shall dare to aspire to the duties of such a guild.

XIV, 3, 8 (365). The office of Your Sincerity shall be on guard that if any man should once and for all be assigned to the guild of breadmakers, he shall not be granted the opportunity and power in any way to withdraw, even if the assent of all the breadmakers should strive to obtain his release. . . . Not even this privilege shall be granted to any breadmaker, namely, that he may pass from one breadmaking establishment to another.

V, 14, 30 (382, 389). If any person should cultivate and equip waste land which belongs to the imperial patrimonial domain and should make it fertile and useful, he may defend his right to hold it by perpetual and private ownership, but subject to the patrimonial fixed land tax thereon, he may hold it for himself, and he may leave it to his descendants, just as though it were a family estate, acquired by succession from his ancestors.

XII, 1, 133 (393). If any . . . plebeians, in the presence of the senate of any municipality, should be proved to be suitable because of the ownership of farms and money, he shall be added to those persons that are obligated to the performance of the compulsory public services of decurions.

XII, 1, 146 (395). We observe that many men are hiding under the shadow of powerful men, in order that they may defraud their municipalities of the services which they owe. Therefore, a fine must be established to the effect that if any man should violate the general rule of the prescribed law, he shall be forced to pay to Our fisc five pounds of gold for each decurion and one pound each for each member of a guild.

XV, 3, 6 (423). Far be it from Us that We should [call] the construction of public roads and bridges and the work on pavements dedicated by the titles of great Emperors as compulsory public services of a menial nature. Therefore, no class of men, by merit of any high rank or veneration, shall be exempt from the construction and repair of roads and bridges. . . . The judges of all the provinces shall be notified of this law, so that they may know that what antiquity decreed should be assigned to the public roads must be furnished without the exception of any person on the grounds of reverence or high rank.

## TOPIC 17

# THE ROMANS AND THE BARBARIANS

The primitive Germanic tribes with whom the Romans came in contact across the cultural and military frontiers established on the Rhine and Danube Rivers did not share the Roman attitude toward the state, urban living, and law. Nonetheless these tribes that poured into the Empire in ever greater numbers from the fourth century onward seldom rejected Roman ways completely. The readings examine the contrast between Germanic and Roman behavior and the contribution of the German tribes to Western institutions and values.

**Reading 86**

# The Barbarian Invasions



Throughout its long life the Empire had been surrounded on almost all sides by barbarians, wild Celts in Wales and Scotland, Germans in the heart of Europe, Persians or Parthians in the East ("barbarian" only in the ancient sense of speaking neither Greek nor Latin), and, in the southeast, the Arabs. (In the South the Empire simply faded off into the Sahara.) These barbarians, always with the exception of Persia, had never been brought within the pale of ancient civilization. They remained illiterate, unsettled, townless, more or less nomadic, and frequently bellicose. Somewhat like the Chinese, who about 200 B.C. built the Great Wall to solve the same problem, the Romans simply drew a line beyond which they themselves rarely ventured, and would not allow the barbarians to pass. Nevertheless generals recruited bands of them to serve in the Roman armies. Their service over, they would receive farmlands, settle down, marry and mingle with the population. By the fourth and fifth centuries a good many individuals of barbarian birth were even reaching high positions of state. At the same time, in the West, for reasons that are not fully understood, the activity of the Roman cities began to falter, commerce began to decay, local governments became paralyzed, taxes became more ruinous, and free farmers were bound to the soil. The army seated and unseated emperors. Rival generals fought with each other. Gradually the West fell into decrepitude and an internal barbarization so that the old line between the Roman provinces and the barbarian world made less and less difference.

The barbarians themselves, after some centuries of relative stability, rather suddenly began to move. Sometimes they first sought peaceable access to the Empire, pushed by other peoples from behind, or attracted by the warmer Mediterranean climate, or desiring with a child-like eagerness to share in the advantages of Roman civilization. More often, tribes consisting of a few tens of thousands, men, women, and children, moved swiftly and by force, plundering, fighting, and killing as they went. At first most of the barbarians threatening the Empire were Germanic, going under many names. The Angles and Saxons overran Britain about 450, the Franks invaded Gaul at the same time, the Vandals reached as far as Roman Africa in 429, the East Goths appeared in Asia Minor in 382 and in Italy in 393, the West Goths lunged toward Constantinople about 380, tore through Greece in 396, sacked Rome itself in 410, and reached Spain about the year 420. In 476 the last Roman Emperor in the West was deposed by a barbarian chieftain. Sometimes in the general upheaval wild Turkman peoples fresh from Asia were intermixed. Of these the most famous were the Huns, who cut through central Europe and France about 450 under their leader Attila, the "scourge of God"—and then disappeared. . . .

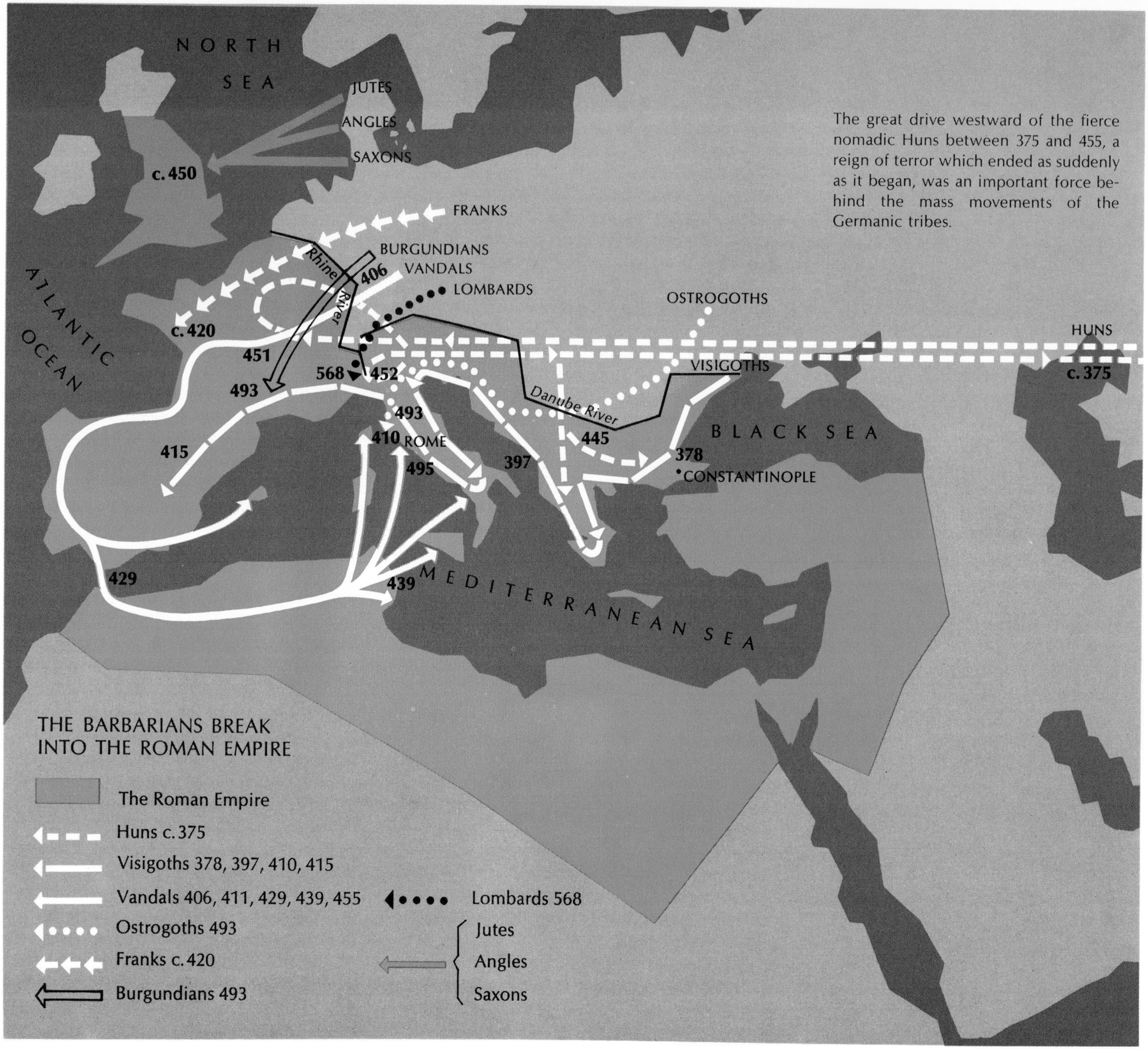
NORTH SEA
JUTES
ANGLES
SAXONS
c. 450
FRANKS
BURGUNDIANS
VANDALS
LOMBARDS
ATLANTIC OCEAN
Rhine River
406
c. 420
451
568
452
493
OSTROGOTHS
HUNS
VISIGOTHS
c. 375
Danube River
493
410 ROME
495
415
397
445
BLACK SEA
378
CONSTANTINOPLE
429
439
MEDITERRANEAN SEA
The great drive westward of the fierce nomadic Huns between 375 and 455, a reign of terror which ended as suddenly as it began, was an important force behind the mass movements of the Germanic tribes.
THE BARBARIANS BREAK INTO THE ROMAN EMPIRE
The Roman Empire
Huns c. 375
Visigoths 378, 397, 410, 415
Vandals 406, 411, 429, 439, 455
Ostrogoths 493
Franks c. 420
Burgundians 493
Lombards 568
Jutes
Angles
Saxons

# Tacitus Describes the Early German Tribes

## (98 A.D.)

Tacitus (c. 55–117 A.D.) enjoyed a long career as Roman senator, consul, and finally governor of Asia. He is better remembered, however, for his literary works and his histories. *On Germany* (written in 98 A.D.) was one of his first published works and has survived as a major source on which later historians have had to rely for their knowledge of early German life. In its day, *On Germany* attracted much interest because Roman troops had long been engaged in a stalemated struggle with German tribes along the Rhine and Danube Rivers. Through their resistance, the Germans established the rough limits of Roman occupation and settlement in western and central Europe. Tacitus found much to admire in German life and did not keep his opinions out of this account. It is possible that he never traveled among the Germans, although he was able to use the eye-witness accounts of returning soldiers and merchants. This is, nonetheless, a very valuable source for the social and political customs of the German tribes before the barbarian invasions. From *Tacitus on Britain and Germany*, H. Mattingly, trans. (London: Penguin Books, 1948), pp. 101–102, 103–107, 109–123.

### I

The Germans themselves, I am inclined to think, are natives of the soil and extremely little affected by immigration or friendly intercourse with other nations. For, in ancient times, if you wished to change your habitat, you travelled by sea and not by land; and the vast ocean that lies beyond and, so to speak, defies intruders, is seldom visited by ships from our world. Besides—to say nothing of the perils of a wild and unknown sea—who would leave Asia, Africa or Italy to visit Germany, with its unlovely scenery, its bitter climate, its general dreariness to sense and eye, unless it were his home? . . .

The physical type, if one may generalize at all about so vast a population, is everywhere the same—wild, blue eyes, reddish hair and huge frames that excel only in violent effort. They have no corresponding power to endure hard work and exertion, and have little capacity to bear thirst and heat; but their climate and soil *have* taught them to bear cold and hunger.

The country in general, while varying somewhat in character, either bristles with woods or festers with swamps. It is wetter where it faces Gaul, windier where it faces Noricum and Pannonia. Though fertile in grain crops, it is unkind to fruit trees. It is rich in flocks, but they are for the most part undersized. Even the cattle lack the splendid brows that are their natural glory. It is numbers that please, numbers that constitute their only, their darling, form of wealth. Heaven has denied them gold and silver—shall I say in mercy or in wrath? But I would not go so far as to assert that Germany has not lodes of silver and gold. Who has ever prospected for them? The Germans take less than the normal pleasure in owning and using them. One may see among them silver vessels, which have been given as presents to their envoys and chiefs, as lightly esteemed as earthenware. The Germans nearest us do, however, value gold and silver for their use in trade, and recognize and prefer certain types of Roman money. The peoples of the interior, truer to the plain old ways, employ barter. They like money that is old and familiar, denarii with the notched edge and the type of the two-horse chariot. Another point is that they try to get silver in preference to gold. They have no predilection for the metal, but find plenty of silver change more serviceable in buying cheap and common goods.

There is not even any great abundance of iron, as may be inferred from the character of their weapons. Only a very few use swords or lances. The spears that they carry—*frameae* is the native word—have short and narrow heads, but are so sharp and easy to handle, that the same weapon serves at need for close or distant fighting. The horseman asks no more than his shield and spear, but the infantry have also javelins to shower, several per man, and can hurl them to a great distance; for they are either naked or only lightly clad in their cloaks. There is nothing ostentatious in their turn-out. Only the shields are picked out with carefully selected colours. Few have breastplates; only here and there will you see a helmet of metal or hide. Their horses are not distinguished either for beauty or for speed, nor are they trained in Roman fashion to execute various turns. They ride them straight ahead or with a single swing to the right, keeping the wheeling line so perfect that no one drops behind the rest. On a general survey, their strength is seen to lie rather in their infantry, and that is why they combine the two arms in battle. The men whom they select from the whole force and station in the van are fleet of foot and fit admirably into cavalry action.

The number of these select men is exactly fixed. A hundred are drawn from each district, and 'the hundred' is the name they bear at home. What began as a mere number ends as a title of distinction. The line is made up of wedge formations. To retreat, provided that you return to the attack, is considered crafty rather than cowardly. They bring in the bodies of the fallen even when the battle hangs in the balance. To throw away one's shield is the supreme disgrace; the guilty wretch is debarred from sacrifice or council. Men have often survived battle only to end their shame by hanging themselves.

They choose their kings for their noble birth, their leaders for their valour. The power even of the kings is not absolute or arbitrary. As for the leaders, it is their example rather than their authority that wins them special admiration—for their energy, their distinction, or their presence in the van of fight. Capital punishment, imprisonment and even flogging are allowed to none but the priests, and are not inflicted merely as punishments or on the leaders' orders, but in obedience to the god whom they believe to preside over battle. They also carry into the fray figures and emblems taken from their sacred groves. Not chance or the accident of mustering makes the troop or wedge, but family and friendship, and this is a very powerful incitement to valour. A man's dearest possessions are at hand; he can hear close to him the laments of his women and the wailing of his children. These are the witnesses that a man reverences most, to them he looks for his highest praise. The men take their wounds to their mothers and wives, and the latter are not afraid of counting and examining the blows, and bring food and encouragement to the fighting men.

It stands on record that armies wavering on the point of collapse have been restored by the women. They have pleaded heroically with their men, thrusting their bosoms before them and forcing them to realize the imminent prospect of their enslavement—a fate which they fear more desperately for their women than for themselves. It is even found that you can secure a surer hold on a state if you demand among the hostages girls of noble family. More than this, they believe that there resides in women an element of holiness and prophecy, and so they do not scorn to ask their advice or lightly disregard their replies. . . .

On matters of minor importance only the chiefs debate, on major affairs the whole community; but, even where the commons have the decision, the case is carefully considered in advance by the chiefs. Except in case of accident or emergency they assemble on fixed days, when the moon is either crescent or nearing her full orb. These, they hold, are the most auspicious times for embarking on any new enterprise. They count, not like us, by days, but by nights. It is by nights that they fix dates or make appointments. Night is regarded as ushering in the day.

It is a defect of their freedom that they do not assemble at once or in obedience to orders, but waste two or three days in their dilatory gathering. When the mass so decide, they take their seats fully armed. Silence is then demanded by the priests, who on that occasion have also power to enforce obedience. Then such hearing is given to the king or chief as age, rank, military distinction or eloquence can secure; but it is rather their prestige as counsellors than their authority that tells. If a proposal displeases them, the people roar out their dissent; if they approve, they clash their spears. No form of approval can carry more honour than praise expressed by arms.

One can launch an accusation before the Council or bring a capital charge. The punishment varies to suit the crime. The traitor and deserter are hanged on trees, the coward, the shirker and the unnaturally vicious are drowned in miry swamps under a cover of wattled hurdles. The distinction in the punishment implies that deeds of violence should be paid for in the full glare of publicity, but that deeds of shame should be suppressed. Even for lighter offences the punishment varies. The man who is found guilty is fined so and so many horses or cattle. Part of the fine is paid to the King or State, part to the injured man or his relatives. In the same councils are elected the chiefs, who dispense justice through the country districts and villages. Each of them is attended by a hundred companions, drawn from the commons, both to advise him and to add weight to his decisions.

No business, public or private, is transacted except in arms. But it is the rule that no one shall take up his arms until the State has attested that he is likely to make good. When that time comes, one of the chiefs or the father or a kinsman equips the young warrior with shield and spear in the public council. This with the Germans is the equivalent of our *toga*—the first public distinction of youth. They cease to rank merely as members of the household and are now members of the state. Conspicuous ancestry or great services rendered by their fathers can win the rank of chief for boys still in their teens. They are attached to the other chiefs, who are more mature in strength and longer approved in valor, and no one blushes to be seen thus in the ranks of the companions. This order of companions has even its different grades, as determined by the leader, and there is intense rivalry among the companions for the first place by the chief, among the chiefs for the most numerous and enthusiastic companions. Dignity and power alike consist in being continually attended by a corps of chosen youths. This gives you consideration in peace-time and security in war. Nor is it only in a man's own nation that he can win name and fame by the superior number and quality of his companions, but in neighbouring states as well. Chiefs are courted by embassies and complimented by gifts, and they often virtually decide wars by the mere weight of their reputation.

On the field of battle it is a disgrace to the chief to be surpassed in valour by his companions, to the companions not to come up to the valour of their chief. As for leaving a battle alive after your chief has fallen, *that* means lifelong infamy and shame. To defend and protect him, to put down one's own acts of heroism to his credit—that is what they really mean by 'allegiance.' The chiefs fight for victory, the companions for their chief. Many noble youths, if the land of their birth is stagnating in a protracted peace, deliberately seek out other tribes, where some war is afoot. The Germans have no taste for peace; renown is easier won among perils, and you cannot maintain a large body of companions except by violence and war. The companions are prodigal in their demands on the generosity of their chiefs. It is always 'give me that war-horse' or 'give me that bloody and victorious spear.' As for meals with their plentiful, if homely, fare, they count simply as pay. Such open-handedness must have war and plunder to feed it. You will find it harder to persuade a German to plough the land and to await its annual produce with patience than to challenge a foe and earn the prize of wounds. He thinks it spiritless and slack to gain by sweat what he can buy with blood.

## II

When not engaged in warfare, they spend some little time in hunting, but more in idling, abandoned to sleep and gluttony. All the heroes and grim warriors dawdle their time away, while the care of house, hearth and fields is left to the women, old men and weaklings of the family. The warriors themselves lose their edge. They are so strangely inconsistent. They love indolence, but they hate peace. It is usual for states to make voluntary and individual contributions of cattle or agricultural produce to the chiefs. These are accepted as a token of honour, but serve also to relieve essential needs. The chiefs take peculiar pleasure in gifts from neighbouring states, such as are sent not only by individuals, but by the community as well—choice horses, splendid arms, metal discs and collars; the practice of accepting money payments they have now learnt—from us.

It is a well-known fact that the peoples of Germany never live in cities, and will not even have their houses set close together. They live apart, dotted here and there, where spring, plain or grove has taken their fancy. Their villages are not laid out in Roman style, with buildings adjacent or interlocked. Every man leaves an open space round his house, perhaps as a precaution against the risk of fire, perhaps because they are such inexpert builders. They do not even make any use of little stone blocks or tiles; what serves their every purpose is ugly timber, both unimpressive and unattractive. They smear over some parts of their houses with an earth that is so pure and brilliant that it looks like painting or coloured mosaics. They have also the habit of hollowing out caves underground and heaping masses of refuse on the top. In these they can escape the winter's cold and store their produce. In such shelters they take the edge off the bitter frosts; and, should an invader come, he ravages the open country, but the secret and buried stores may pass altogether unnoticed or escape detection, simply because they have to be looked for.

The universal dress is the short cloak, fastened with a brooch or, failing that, a thorn. They pass whole days by the hearth fire wearing no garment but this. The richest are not distinguished, like the Persians and Sarmatians, by a long flowing robe, but by a tight one that shows the shape of every limb. They also wear the pelts of wild animals, the tribes near the Rhine without regard to appearance, the more distant peoples with some refinement of taste, for there is no other finery that they can buy. These latter peoples make careful choice of animal, then strip off the pelt and mottle it with patches of the spotted skins of the beasts that live in the outer ocean and the unknown sea. The dress of the women differs from that of the men in two respects only. The women often wear undergarments of linen, embroidered with purple, and, as the upper part does not extend to sleeves, forearms and upper arms are bare. Even the breast, where it comes nearest the shoulder, is exposed too.

For all that, marriage in Germany is austere, and there is no feature in their morality that deserves higher praise. They are almost unique among barbarians in being satisfied with one wife each. The exceptions, which are exceedingly rare, are of men who receive offers of many wives because of their rank; there is no question of sexual passion. The

Tacitus gained much of his information about the Germanic tribes from Roman soldiers stationed on the frontier. This scene from a column commemorating the deeds of the emperor Marcus Aurelius (162–180) records the sacking of a German village.

dowry is brought by husband to wife, not by wife to husband. Parents and kinsmen attend and approve of the gifts, gifts not chosen to please a woman's whim or gaily deck a young bride, but oxen, horse with reins, shield, spear and sword. For such gifts a man gets his wife, and she in turn brings some present of arms to her husband. In this interchange of gifts they recognize the supreme bond, the holy mysteries, the presiding deities of marriage. A woman must not imagine herself free to neglect the manly virtues or immune from the hazards of war. That is why she is reminded, in the very ceremonies which bless her marriage at its outset, that she is coming to share a man's toils and dangers, that she is to be his partner in all his sufferings and adventures, whether in peace or war. That is the meaning of the team of oxen, of the horse ready for its rider, of the gift of arms. On these terms she must live her life and bear her children. She is receiving something that she must hand over unspoilt and treasured to her children, for her son's wives to receive in their turn and pass on to the grandchildren.

Thus it is that the German women live in a chastity that is impregnable, uncorrupted by the temptations of public shows or the excitements of banquets. Clandestine love-letters are unknown to men and women alike. Adultery in that populous nation is rare in the extreme, and punishment is summary and left to the husband. He shaves off his wife's hair, strips her in the presence of kinsmen, thrusts her from his house and flogs her through the whole village. They have, in fact, no mercy on a woman who prostitutes her chastity. Neither beauty, youth nor wealth can find the sinner a husband. No one in Germany finds vice amusing, or calls it 'up-to-date' to debauch and be debauched. It is still better with those states in which only virgins marry, and the hopes and prayers of a wife are settled once and for all. They take one husband, like the one body or life that they possess. No thought or desire must stray beyond him. They must not love the husband so much as the married state. To restrict the number of children or to put to death any born after the heir is considered criminal. Good morality is more effective in Germany than good laws in some places that we know.

The children grow up in every home, naked and dirty, to that strength of limb and size of body which excite our admiration. Every mother feeds her child at the breast and does not depute the task to maids and nurses. The master is not to be distinguished from the slave by any pampering in his upbringing. They grow up together among the same flocks and on the same ground, until maturity sets apart the free and the spirit of valour claims them as her own. The young men are slow to mate, and their powers, therefore, are never exhausted. The girls, too, are not hurried into marriage. As old and full-grown as the men, they match their mates in age and strength, and the children reproduce the might of their parents. The sons of sisters are as highly honoured by their uncles as by their own fathers. Some even go so far as to regard this tie of blood as peculiarly close and sacred, and, in taking hostages, insist on having them of this class; they think that this gives them a firmer grip on men's hearts and a wider hold on the family. However, a man's heirs and successors are his own children, and there is no such thing as a will; where there are no children, the next to succeed are, first, brothers, and then uncles, first on the father's, then on the mother's side. The larger a man's kin and the greater the number of his relations by marriage, the stronger is his influence when he is old. Childlessness in Germany is not a paying profession.

A man is bound to take up the feuds as well as the friendships of father or kinsman. But feuds do not continue unreconciled. Even homicide can be atoned for by a fixed number of cattle or sheep, and the satisfaction is received by the whole family. This is much to the advantage of the community, for private feuds are peculiarly dangerous side by side with liberty.

No nation abandons itself more completely to banqueting and entertainment than the German. It is accounted a sin to turn any man away from your door. The host welcomes his guest with the best meal that his means allow. When supplies run out, the host takes on a fresh role; he directs and escorts his guest to a new hostelry. The two go on, uninvited, to the nearest house. It makes no difference; they are welcomed just as warmly. No distinction is ever made between acquaintance and stranger as far as the right to hospitality is concerned. As the guest takes his leave, it is usual to let him have anything he asks for; the host, too, is no more shy in asking. They take delight in presents, but ask no credit for giving them and admit no obligation in receiving them. There is a pleasant courtesy in the relations between host and guest.

As soon as they rise from their sleep, which is often protracted well into the day, they wash in water that is usually warm; can one wonder, where winter holds such sway? After washing, they breakfast; each has his special place and his special table. Then they sally forth in arms to business or, as often as not, to banquets. Drinking bouts, lasting a day and night, are not considered in any way disgraceful. Such quarrels as inevitably arise over the cups are seldom settled by mere hard words, more often by blows and wounds. Nonetheless, they often make banquets an occasion for discussing such serious affairs as the reconciliation of enemies, the forming of marriage alliances, the adoption of new chiefs, and even the choice of peace or war. At no other time, they feel, is the heart so open to frank suggestions or so quick to warm to a great appeal. The Germans are neither canny nor cunning, and take advantage of the occasion to unbosom themselves of their most secret thoughts; every soul is naked and exposed. The next day, comes reconsideration, and so due account is taken of both occasions. They debate at a time which cuts out pretence, they decide at a time that precludes mistake.

For drink they extract a juice from barley or grain, which is fermented to make something not unlike wine. The Germans who live nearest the Rhine can actually get wine in the market. Their food is plain—wild fruit, fresh game or curdled milk. They satisfy their hunger without any elaborate service or appetizers. But they show no corresponding self-control in drinking. You have only to indulge their intemperance by supplying all that they crave, and you will gain as easy a victory through their vices as through your own arms.

They have only one form of public show, which is the same wherever they foregather. Naked youths, trained to the sport, dance among swords and spears that are levelled at them. Practice begets skill, and skill grace, but they are not professionals or paid. However adventurous the play, their only reward is the pleasure they give the spectators. But they go in for dicing, if you can believe it, in all seriousness and in their sober hours, and are so recklessly keen about winning or losing that, when everything else is gone, they stake their personal liberty on the last decisive throw. The loser goes into slavery without complaint; younger or stronger he may be, but he suffers himself to be bound. Such is their perverse persistence, or, to use their own word, their honour. Slaves of this sort are sold and passed on, so that the winner may be clear of the shame that even he feels in his victory.

Slaves in general are not allotted, as we allot them, to special duties in the establishment. Each has control of his own house and home. The master imposes a fixed charge of grain, cattle or clothing, as he would on a tenant, and up to this point the slave will obey; but domestic tasks, as a whole, are performed by a man's wife and children. It is seldom that they flog a slave or punish him with imprisonment or forced labour; but they often put one to death, in no spirit of stern discipline, but in a fit of passion, as they might an enemy—only they have not to pay for it. Freedmen rank little higher than slaves; they have seldom any serious influence in the household, never in the State, excepting only in nations under the rule of kings. There they mount high above free men and nobles. With the rest the inferiority of freedmen is the hallmark of liberty.

The practice of usury and compound interest is simply unknown. Ignorance here is a surer defence than any ban. Lands are taken into occupation, turn and turn about, by whole villages in proportion to the number of cultivators, and are then alloted in order of rank. The distribution is made easy by the vast extent of open land. They change their plough-lands yearly, and still there is ground to spare. The fact is that their soil is fertile and plentiful, but they refuse to give it the labour it deserves. They plant no orchards, fence off no meadows, water no gardens; the only levy on the earth is the corn crop. Hence it comes that they divide the year into fewer seasons than we do. Winter, spring and summer are familiar to them both as ideas and as names, but autumn is as unknown to them, as are the gifts she has to bring.

There is no pomp about their funerals. The one rule observed is that the bodies of famous men are burned with special kinds of wood. When they have heaped up the fire they do not throw robes or spices on the top; but only a man's arms, and sometimes his horse, too, are cast into the flames. The tomb is a raised mound of turf. They disdain to show honour by laboriously rearing high monuments of stone; they would only lie heavy on the dead. Weeping and wailing are soon abandoned—sorrow and mourning not so soon. A woman may decently express her grief in public; a man should nurse his in his heart.

Such is the general account that we find given of the origin and customs of the Germans as a whole. . . .

# Norman Cantor: Political and Social Institutions of the Germans

Norman Cantor (1929– ), an American medievalist, here seeks to limn Germanic society at the time of the invasions of the Roman Empire. In it he finds elements of contemporary democratic processes. Reprinted with permission of The Macmillan Company from *Medieval History, The Life and Death of a Civilization* by Norman F. Cantor. Copyright © by The Macmillan Company, 1968.

## I

The word "barbarian" was borrowed by the Romans from the Greeks, who used it to designate an alien, and therefore, by definition, someone inferior in culture to a Hellene. The Romans applied the word "barbarian" in the pejorative sense to the people who came to live along the Rhine-Danube frontier. The Romans also generically termed these people *Germani,* which was originally the name of only one of the tribes living beyond the Roman frontier. Another tribe was called the *Allemanni,* which later became the root of the French and Spanish terms for "German." The Germans referred to themselves with a word which has become the root of the modern *Deutsch* and Teuton, that is, *Theut,* which simply means "the folk" or "people."

Who were the Germans? Where did they come from and why? What were their political and social institutions? These important questions exercised the energy and imagination of many historians, particularly in Germany where naturally the study of the *Völkerwanderungen,* or the migration of the peoples, has been encouraged by nationalist feeling. The literary sources, however, are extremely meager, and all we know about the Germans before the first century B.C. has been derived from archeological research. These studies reveal that the German invaders of the Roman empire originally came from Scandinavia. Therefore, the later Vikings, whose migrations and invasions of western Europe came during the ninth century A.D., were ethnically the same people as the ones whom the Romans called the Germans. About 1000 B.C. the Germans began to move southward from their original homes in Denmark and southern Norway and Sweden. By 100 or so B.C. spreading south and west, they had reached the Rhine river, and somewhat later, perhaps in the first century A.D., they migrated into the Danube basin as well.

As the Germans began to press across the Rhine, they had an easy time pushing back the Celts, who were peaceful people given to agriculture, poetry, and song. The Germans would have conquered Gaul, as they later were to conquer Britain and push the Celts into the Welsh mountains, had it not been for the arrival on the scene in the middle of the first century B.C. of Julius Caesar and the Roman legions. After hard fighting, Caesar pushed the Germans back beyond the Rhine, and the Romans extensively colonized the southern half of Gaul. The Germans temporarily crossed the Rhine in the middle of the third century, during the period of transitory imperial breakdown, but the Rhine frontier was soon reconstructed. Until the final collapse of the Rhine frontier in 406 A.D. the only Germans who crossed the great river into Roman territory were the tribes who were allowed to become federates or mercenaries in the imperial army. . . .

There is no positive evidence as to the causes of the *Völkerwanderungen.* We can only surmise the causation a priori. The Germans left Scandinavia partly because of a shortage in food supply due to population growth and partly because of continual wars between the tribes, in which the losers were driven from their homeland to seek a new place to live in the south. As the Germans approached the frontier of the empire, they came in contact with the wealth, advanced technology, and pleasant climate of the Mediterranean. They sought to get into the empire not to destroy it, but rather to participate in its higher standard of living. . . .

From the limited written and archeological evidence that we have about the development of Germanic society from the time the Germans came to settle along the Rhine-Danube frontier to the establishment of the Germanic kingdoms in western Europe—let us say from 100 B.C. to 500 A.D.—two fundamental facts emerge which must be realized if we are to understand correctly the Germanic society in the time of the invasions. The first fact is that the degree to which the Germanic peoples across the Rhine-Danube frontier had been influenced by Roman civilization differed markedly from one tribe to another. Some had reached a stage of civilization about the same as that which they saw across the frontier along the border of the empire. They devoted themselves to agriculture, engaged in extensive commerce with Roman merchants, and accepted Christianity. . . . Such Germans only wanted to enter the empire as federates and participate in the life of the Mediterranean world. They greatly respected Roman power and had no intention of bringing harm to it. This level of civilization was reached especially among the Goths living in the Danube basin. They were in contact with the richest and most heavily populated part of the empire.

On the other hand, it appears evident that other Germanic peoples had been little affected by Romanization and were fierce, ignorant, and barbarian in every sense of the word. Most, though not all, of the Germans who invaded the empire from across the Rhine appear to belong to this category. The reasons for this are not very clear. It would seem, however, that the Germans here remained in closer contact with their Scandinavian homeland, which was, of course, closer. Here, too, there were a greater number of German peoples stacked up against the Rhine frontier, so that those who were further back from the frontier tended to be progressively less affected by contact with the empire. Thus the Franks were more violent and less civilized than some of the early invaders, such as the Burgundians. And the Anglo-Saxons, who came directly from the North Sea area, were untouched by Romanization.

Thus it is not easy to generalize about the Germanic peoples. Some were at a social and cultural level equivalent to the peasants of the empire; others indeed impress us as primitives, in spite of attempts by modern German historians to portray them as quite civilized.

The second fundamental fact which should be borne in mind in regard to the Germans of the period of the great invasions is that their political and social institutions did not remain static over the period between 100 B.C. and 500 A.D., but underwent profound changes. Like many primitive peoples Germanic society was at first organized according to blood ties—the family and kindred. While these ties were to a considerable extent preserved up to and through the period of the invasions (as shown by the blood feud in criminal cases), another form of social organization was slowly emerging, and it became central in the period of the invasions (400–600). During this period the bonds of kinship were weakened, a process which shows itself in the prevalence of strife between relatives. The binding force formerly possessed by kinship was increasingly transferred to the relationship between "lord" and "man," between whom no bond of blood relationship was necessary, only the bond of loyalty. Thus during this period there is a decrease in importance of kinship and a great increase in the use of the bond of allegiance or loyalty.

This great change in social organization went along with, and facilitated, a change in political organization, the growth of an irresponsible type of kingship resting not upon the folk but upon military prestige. To the war leader who could provide booty went the allegiance of his followers, but these followers might not even belong to the same kindred or folk as their "king."

Thus, during the period of the Germanic invasions, and at least partly the result of the circumstances of a people on the move and engaging in conquest, there is a great social and political transformation within Germanic society itself. Many of the able-bodied fighters were emancipating themselves from the tribal obligations and bonds by which a society of primitive peoples is usually governed. Furthermore, the princes who emerged among the Germans during this period were freeing themselves, to a large extent, from any public control on the part of the tribe or community. As long as they could feed and enrich their soldiers, they retained the allegiance of these warriors, and neither the king nor war band had any social or political obligation to the folk as a whole. We shall see this situation appear many times among Germans during the Germanic invasions; the Frankish kingdom of the sixth century arises out of this social and political context.

The basic German political institution at the end of the fourth century can therefore be said to be the *comitatus,* or *gefolge,* consisting of the chief or king and his war band, who accorded him their loyal service in return for his protection and largess. A chief who reigned for a long time or who achieved great military success was able to create a royal dynasty. The dynasty would claim descent from Woden, put on sacred airs, and possess the kingship as its private property. But succession to the kingship could not be by primogeniture; this was not an early Germanic idea and was restricted by the original power of the war band to give or refuse loyalty. At the death of the king, the leaders of the folk would come together and choose that member of the royal family who was most "throne-worthy," that is, the best fighter. While strict hereditary succession appeared very rapidly in the new Germanic kingdoms of the fifth and sixth centuries, the right of election by the folk remained a strong medieval political tradition for many centuries, especially in areas where the original Germanic institutions remained influential. The election of the king by the leaders of the community was operative in England in the later ninth century in the case of the elevation of the famous king Alfred to the English throne, and as late as 1199 the infamous king John owed his crown in part to the electoral principle. The Germanic electoral principle played havoc with dynastic continuity in the medieval German empire and, in fact, survived to the nineteenth century. The perpetuation of this aspect of early German institutions was due at least in part to the fact that it found favor with the church, which recognized in the principle of throne-worthiness a way of exercising a veto on royal accessions.

The *comitatus* was an extremely weak nucleus for the medieval state. In fact, it can be said that the Germans had no concept of a state, no idea of public authority, and no understanding of loyalty other than the personal loyalty to a chieftain. With some exaggeration, it may be said that the Germanic political theory was not above the level of that held today by marauding street gangs. The distance from the sophisticated Roman idea of public authority and office and of loyalty to an impersonal emperor who represents the state was vast, and the decline in the level of political thinking was precipitous. To understand the disastrous histories of all early medieval kingdoms, it must be remembered that the medieval state had to develop from this abysmal and crude level. Early medieval political construction was constantly challenged and inhibited by the inability of the Germans to conceive of public, as distinct from personal, loyalty. It is not surprising, therefore, that the medieval state did not begin to take shape until the eighth and ninth centuries and did not experience its first era of greatness until the middle years of the eleventh century. And even this late and partial success was only made possible by the addition of ecclesiastical (in part, Roman) conceptions of authority and loyalty to the primitive Germanic political tradition.

The original Germanic legal conceptions were scarcely more advanced than their political ideas. The purpose of the Germanic law courts and forms of procedure was not to establish justice, which the Germans had no way of determining or even of defining, but simply to stop a fight. The aim of Germanic legal process was to inhibit the blood feud, to find an alternative for an aggrieved kin or family seeking vengeance. There were various ways of doing this, and the purpose of the law courts was simply to put these alternatives to the blood feud into operation. The first of these was the payment of *wergeld* (man money), a monetary compensation to a family for the killing of one of its members, or a smaller payment to an individual who had been maimed. The so-called Germanic law code consisted mostly of tables of *wergeld:* so much to be paid for the slaying of a nobleman, so much for a freeman, so much for a serf, so much for an arm, so much for an eye, etc. The compensation required was often very heavy, and even then the aggrieved kinsmen or individual need not always accept it, and might prefer to gain satisfaction by vengeance. It was the court's duty to convince the plaintiff to take the *wergeld* and thereby preclude the outbreak of a blood feud. Nevertheless, blood feuds were frequent in early Germanic society. We know of such a feud in England as late as 1060 which decimated whole families. Anyone who reads early medieval legal records knows that life then was nasty, brutish, and short. It was a violent society in which drunken brawls ending in homicide were extremely common, and the resulting blood feuds a constant possibility.

## II

Early medieval men did not think of a brawl resulting in homicide as murder. Their legal conception resembled that of the American frontier, at least as represented in popular literature and entertainment. To kill a man in a fair fight meant that you had to reckon with his kinsmen, but it was not murder. Murder was killing someone by stealth; murder was a homicide in which the killer was not certainly known. Such a situation put heavy pressure on the Germanic law court, for if the court did not designate the murderer, the slain man's kin would take justice into their own hands and exact vengeance from whomever they suspected. It was therefore necessary to hold a trial and prove the guilt or innocence of the suspect. But neither the methods of proof and assessment of evidence devised by Roman law, which involved a thorough inquiry by a panel of judges, nor the later common-law jury system were available to the Germanic law court. The leaders of the Germanic court would not have known how to assess the evidence even if it were presented to them. This left two methods of proof; the ordeal, involving divine decision, and compurgation, involving the swearing of oaths.

In proof by ordeal the odds were weighted heavily against the defendant. In the ordeal of hot iron the defendant was required to grasp a red-hot piece of metal. His hand was then bandaged, and if after three days the burns had healed, the defendant was innocent; otherwise he was guilty. The ordeal of hot water worked similarly: the defendant was made to put his arm into a caldron of boiling water and lift a stone from the bottom; his arm was then bandaged and in three days it was inspected to decide guilt or innocence. The ordeal of cold water was a favorite in England, where there were numerous rivers and brooks. The defendant was tied hand and foot and thrown into the water; if he sank he was innocent, and if he floated he was guilty, on the premise that water, a divine element, would not receive a guilty person. In the feudal period an additional ordeal, trial by combat between the accuser and the defendant or their "champions" (representatives), was instituted. Because guilt or innocence was decided by the strength of the champion, trial by combat did not leave the question sufficiently to divine judgment; a wealthy man could hire the biggest thug in the country and systematically get rid of his enemies through the bringing

The hand of God hovers over the ordeal by fire of Kunigunde, wife of the devout Emperor Henry II (1002–1024). Legend had it that the Empress, accused of marital unfaithfulness, proved her fidelity by emerging uninjured after walking barefoot over a glowing grate. This illustration from a twelfth-century life of the royal couple depicts Henry watching his wife, her hands held by two bishops, undergo the ordeal.

of false accusations. Hence, trial by combat was severely limited by the powerful monarchies of the twelfth century, although technically this method of proof was not abolished in England until 1819. While the three common ordeals were rough on the defendant, it must be emphasized that they were intended to be biased in this direction. For the defendant who was put to the ordeal—in England this was called "making his law"—was either someone who was reputed to be a criminal by the opinion of his neighbors or was a person of low social status. A wealthy or highborn person of good reputation in his community was very seldom put to the ordeal. The ordeal, therefore, was a method of providing divine support for popular prejudice. Through the ordeal each folk court was able to cleanse the community of the ill-famed, who sooner or later were bound to be accused of a crime and put to the ordeal.

The church was initially hostile to the Germanic ordeal; but if it was to influence early medieval legal process, it had to accept this common method of proof. After the Germans were converted, the church imposed a religious sanction on the ordeal: before going to the ordeal the defendant appeared in church and swore on the Bible or a holy relic that he was innocent, while the priest admonished him to confess his guilt in order not to damn his soul and lose eternal as well as mortal life. We think that in many cases this brainwashing resulted in confession and that thereby an element of rationality was added to the crude legal process. A defendant convicted by the ordeal was hanged on the spot, hanging being one of the Germanic contributions to civilization. At times in the early middle ages the church succeeded in having kings substitute maiming for the death penalty. Medieval medicine being what it was, the loss of a limb frequently amounted to a slow death in any case. It is also very doubtful that the community courts followed these humanitarian pronouncements.

Compurgation was a privilege of a defendant who had popular opinion on his side, and this usually meant that he was wealthy or highborn. Compurgation greatly favored the defendant, for by this method of proof the defendant simply denied his guilt under oath and produced a certain number of oath-helpers, preferably of high social status, to swear that his oath was a true and good, or "clean" one. While the church warned about the perils of perjury, we know that this was very common in proof by compurgation. A guilty man who had important relatives or a powerful lord who were willing to lie for him would never be convicted. The conditions of compurgation further attest the underlying fact that Germanic criminal process was very class-biased. The poor, the unfree, the lordless were lucky if they did not end on the gallows, and on the contrary, the rich and well-connected could only come to this end through the most flagrant and repeated crimes, and even then usually only when their victim was himself from the upper strata of society.

It is apparent that very little can be said in favor of early Germanic process. Yet German law made one great contribution to western civilization. It was enormously inferior to Roman law except in the instance of its political implications. Roman law found its origin in the will of the despotic emperor and favored political absolutism. The king had no control over Germanic law; his only legal function was to see that the community courts met and decided cases, and even in this regard his contribution was often negligible. Germanic law was based on the principle that law resided in the folk, that law was the custom of the community, and that the king could not change this law without the assent of the community. Because of this difference between Germanic and Roman law, and because England, even in the high middle ages, remained relatively untouched by Roman law, the Victorian historians found the origin of English parliamentary institutions and the idea of the rule of law in the forests of Germany. While it has been fashionable among twentieth-century writers to scoff at this interpretation, there is an element of truth in it. The Victorians, with their organic conception of institutional development, erred in thinking that the great oak of English liberalism grew *inevitably* out of the acorn of German law. There was nothing inevitable about this development; in 1200 England appeared to be going in the direction of absolutism, and it took centuries of experience and political strife before the legislative supremacy of Parliament triumphed. But it is true that from Germanic law England received a heritage of the legal supremacy of the community over the king. All western European countries could have drawn upon the same legal tradition. But after 1100 the Roman law principle of legal absolutism slowly won out on the continent, whereas England alone preserved the early Germanic idea that law resides in the folk rather than in the will of the king. . . .

# Jordanes Relates the Conquest of the Visigoths

### (Early 5th Century)

The Visigoths were a German tribe that entered the Empire in 376 in flight from the Huns. They wanted to share the benefits of Roman civilization but the emperors preferred to try to get rid of them. The following account by the German Christian historian Jordanes shows the impact the invasion of such barbarians had on the stability of the Roman Empire. From *The Gothic History of Jordanes,* trans. C. Mierow (Princeton: Princeton University Press, 1915), pp. 92–96.

Now when this Alaric was made king, he took counsel with his men and persuaded them to seek a kingdom of their own exertions rather than serve others in idleness. In the consulship of Stilicho and Aurelian he raised an army and entered Italy, which seemed to be bare of defenders, and came through Pannonia and Sirmium along the right side. Without meeting any resistance, he reached the bridge of the river Candidianus at the third milestone from the royal city of Ravenna. This city lies amid the streams of the Po between swamps and the sea, and is accessible only on one side. . . .

When the army of the Visigoths had come into the neighborhood of this city, they sent an embassy to the Emperor Honorius [ruled 395–423], who dwelt within. They said that if he would permit the Goths to settle peaceably in Italy, they would so live with the Roman people that men might believe them both to be of one race; but if not, whoever prevailed in war should drive out the other, and victor should henceforth rule unmolested. But the Emperor Honorius feared to make either promise. So he took counsel with his senate and considered how he might drive them from the Italian borders. He finally decided that Alaric and his race, if they were able to do so, should be allowed to seize for their own home the provinces farthest away, namely Gaul and Spain. For at this time he had almost lost them, and moreover they had been devastated by the invasion of Gaiseric, king of the Vandals. The grant was confirmed by an imperial rescript, and the Goths, consenting to the arrangement, set out for the country given them.

When they had gone away without doing any harm in Italy, Stilicho, the Patrician and father-in-law of the Emperor Honorius—for the Emperor had married both his daughters, Maria and Thermantia, in succession, but God called both from this world in their virgin purity—this Stilicho, I say, treacherously hurried to Pollentia, a city in the Cottian Alps. There he fell upon the unsuspecting Goths in battle, to the ruin of all Italy and his own disgrace. When the Goths suddenly beheld him, at first they were terrified. Soon regaining their courage and arousing each other by brave shouting, as is their custom, they turned to fight the entire army of Stilicho and almost exterminated it. Then forsaking the journey they had undertaken, the Goths with hearts full of rage returned again to Liguria whence they had set out. When they had plundered and spoiled it, they also laid waste Aemilia, and then hastened toward the city of Rome along the Flaminian Way, which runs between Picenum and Tuscia, taking as booty whatever they found on either hand. When they finally entered Rome [410] by Alaric's express command they merely sacked it, and did not set the city on fire, as wild peoples usually do, nor did they permit serious damage to be done to the holy places. Thence they departed to bring like ruin upon Campania and Lucania, and then came to Bruttii. Here they remained a long time and planned to go to Sicily and thence to the countries of Africa.

Now the land of the Bruttii is at the extreme southern bound of Italy, and a corner of it marks the beginning of the Apennine mountains. It stretches out like a tongue into the Adriatic Sea and separates it from the Tyrrhenian waters. It chanced to receive its name in ancient times from a Queen Bruttia. To this place came Alaric, king of the Visigoths, with the wealth of all Italy which he had taken as spoil, and from there, as we have said, he intended to cross over by way of Sicily to the quiet land of Africa. But since man is not free to do anything he wishes without the will of God, that dread strait sunk several of his ships and threw all into confusion. Alaric was cast down by his reverse and, while deliberating what he should do, was suddenly overtaken by an untimely death and departed from human cares. His people mourned for him with the utmost affection. Then turning from its course the river Busentius near the city of Consentia—for the stream flows with its wholesome waters from the foot of a mountain near that city—they led a band of captives into the midst of its bed to dig out a place for his grave. In the depths of this pit they buried Alaric, together with many treasures, and then turned the waters back into their channel. And that none might ever know the place, they put to death all the diggers. They bestowed the kingdom of the Visigoths on Athavulf his kinsman, a man of imposing beauty and great spirit; for though not tall of stature, he was distinguished for beauty of face and form.

When Athavulf became king, he returned again to Rome, and whatever had escaped the first sack his Goths stripped bare like locusts, not merely despoiling Italy of its private wealth, but even of its public resources. The Emperor Honorius was powerless to resist even when his sister Placidia, the daughter of the Emperor Theodosius by his second wife, was led away captive from the city. But Athavulf was attracted by her nobility, beauty and chaste purity, and so he took her to wife in lawful marriage at Forum Julii, a city of Aemilia. When the barbarians learned of this alliance, they were the more effectually terrified, since the Empire and the Goths now seemed to be made one. Then Athavulf set out for Gaul [412], leaving Honorius Augustus stripped of his wealth, to be sure, yet pleased at heart because he was now a sort of kinsman of his. Upon his arrival the neighboring tribes who had long made cruel raids into Gaul—Franks, and Burgundians alike—were terrified and began to keep within their own borders. Now the Vandals and the Alani, as we have said before, had been dwelling in both Pannonias by permission of the Roman Emperors. Yet fearing they would not be safe even here if the Goths should return, they crossed over into Gaul. But no long time after they had taken possession of Gaul they fled thence and shut themselves up in Spain, for they still remembered from the tales of their forefathers what ruin Geberich, king of the Goths, had long ago brought on their race, and how by his valor he had driven them from their native land. And thus it happened that Gaul lay open to Athavulf when he came. Now when the Goth had established his kingdom in Gaul, he began to grieve for the plight of the Spaniards and planned to save them from the attacks of the Vandals. So Athavulf left with a few faithful men at Barcelona his treasures and those who were unfit for war, and entered the interior of Spain [415]. Here he fought frequently with the Vandals and, in this third year after he had subdued Gaul and Spain, fell pierced through the groin by the sword of Euervulf, a man whose short stature he had been wont to mock.

TOPIC 18

# THE CONTRAST BETWEEN MOHAMMEDANS AND FRANKS

The wave of Germanic invasion that washed over Europe resulted in a dilution of Roman civilization in the West. In the seventh century new eruptions burst upon the Graeco-Roman world from the East where the Arab followers of the prophet Mohammed in a surprisingly short time conquered much of the remaining territory of the Empire and subdued the neighboring Persians as well. The resulting Moslem civilization, in contrast to developments in the West, preserved and extended many of the significant achievements of antiquity. The readings compare life in the Germanic kingdom of the Franks with that in the Mohammedan centers of Baghdad and Cordova.

**Reading 90**

## The End of Mediterranean Unity



The slow decay of the Roman Empire did not at first affect the unity of Mediterranean civilization. There had been growing dissatisfaction with that civilization, but it had endured so long that it was not easy to conceive of an alternative way of life. The Germanic kingdoms of the West clung to the old forms as well as they could; they were not very civilized, but what scraps of civilization they possessed were Roman. The East was still united under the emperor at Constantinople, who governed through the old Roman bureaucracy under the forms of Roman law. . . . Western Europe was more provincial than it had been in the great days of Rome, but it was still part of the Mediterranean world, not the seat of an independent civilization.

Yet within the Mediterranean unity, separatist tendencies were developing, and these tendencies were strongest in the East. The Germans had lowered the level of Roman civilization, but they had no rival civilization to set in its place. In the East there were rival civilizations, long suppressed but strangely potent. The Greeks and the Romans had ruled Syria and Egypt for over seven hundred years, and yet Graeco-Roman civilization had not stifled the old native cultures. It had formed a thin hard crust on top of a fermenting mass of old beliefs and institutions, and as the crust cracked under the strains of the third and fourth centuries the obscure folk-ways of the native populations began to bubble out into sight. Every student of the Late Roman Empire has noticed the revival of oriental forms and beliefs—in government, in religion, in art and literature. At first it was possible to absorb these oriental ideas into the dominant Graeco-Roman culture. The emperors assumed some of the trappings and many of the powers of an oriental despot; the most popular religions were modified versions of oriental faiths; the prevailing art-forms showed the influence of oriental motifs. But as the movement continued it became impossible to fit it into the old pattern of Mediterranean civilization. The Latin West would accept only a minimum of oriental influence, and would not abandon its old traditions entirely. Egypt and Syria, where the oriental revival was strongest, either had to compromise or drop out of the orbit of Graeco-Roman civilization. . . .

The latent hostility of the Oriental peoples to Graeco-Roman supremacy crystallized around the Arab Empire and permanently separated the southern and eastern shores of the Mediterranean from the civilizations of the north and northeast.

The Arabs, like the Germans, were a small, rather poorly organized group of peoples, who had raided the Empire intermittently for centuries without constituting a real military danger. Nothing shows the weakness of the old Mediterranean civilization in its last days quite so clearly as the fact that these weak border peoples could change the fate of

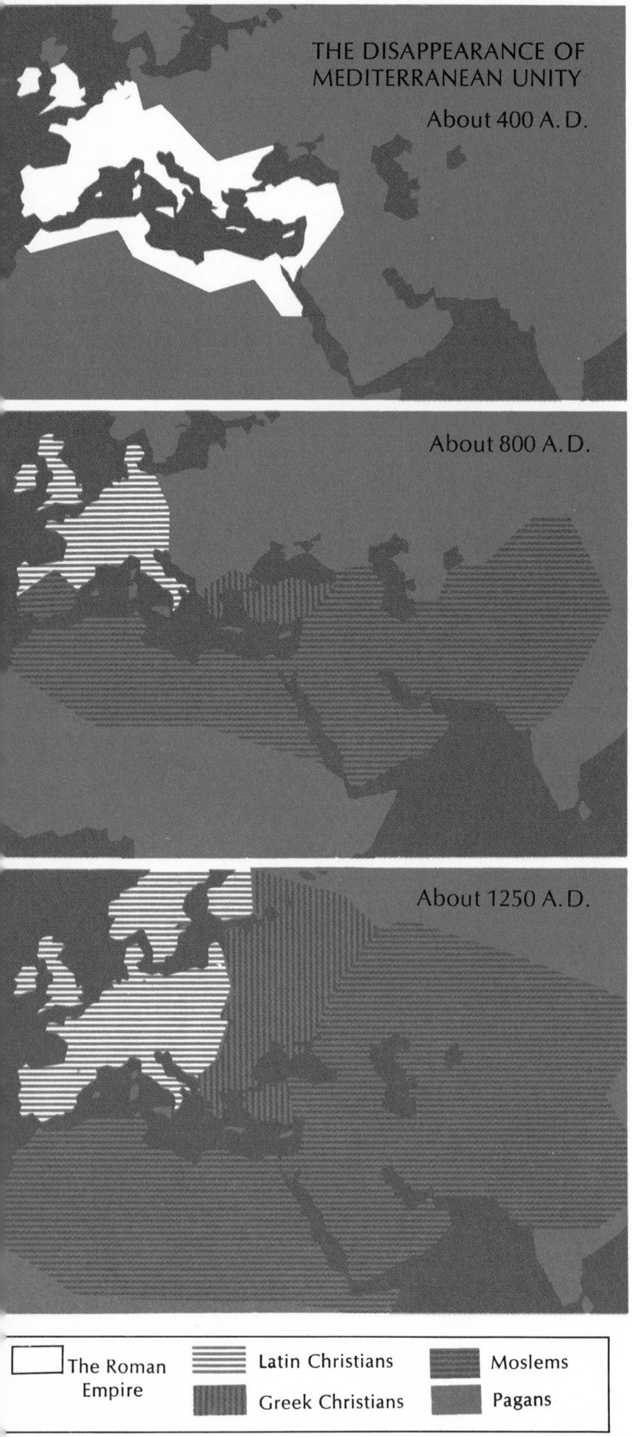


millions with only a slight effort. The results are out of all proportion to the cause unless we realize that the invaders, German or Arab, merely set off a reaction which was already prepared. They were the detonators, but the explosives were already stored up in the Mediterranean basin. The Arabs had probably grown in numbers during the sixth century, and Mohammed gave them a better organization than they had ever had before, but the whole population of Arabia was less than that of many imperial provinces. Once more the Empire was to lose wide territories because there was no real interest in preserving its authority, no common loyalty to hold its people together.

Mohammed was a man of great ability and it was only through his efforts that the Arabs were able to take advantage of the opportunities on their northern frontiers. Like many of his countrymen, he was dissatisfied with the rather crude religion of Arabia, which often was not better than fetish-worship. He had heard fragments of the Christian story; he had met Arabic-speaking Jews who told him some of their traditions; he was familiar with Arabic legends which were not unlike the stories of the Hebrew prophets. Brooding over this material, he became convinced that God had chosen him as the last and greatest of the prophets, as the bearer of the final revelation to man. The new doctrine, as it finally emerged in Mohammed's sermons and conversation, had enough familiar elements in it to be acceptable to many of the peoples of the East. He taught that there was one all-powerful God, the creator of the world, the protector and judge of mankind; that God had revealed His will to men through a series of prophets, of whom the greatest were Abraham, Jesus, and Mohammed; that those who believed His prophets and obeyed His commandments would enjoy Paradise whereas the wicked were to suffer endlessly. After a discouraging start, Mohammed began to gain followers and eventually converted most of the tribes of northern and central Arabia. His original concept of his role seems to have been that of a purely religious leader, but he soon learned that he could spread his faith only by becoming head of a political organization which would protect his followers from the unenlightened, and suppress family and tribal feuds among the faithful. At his death in 632 he was ruler of a large part of the Arabian peninsula. There were still tribes which had not accepted his political and religious leadership, but they were too weak to form an effective opposition.

Mohammed had given the Arabs their first effective political organization, and his immediate successors profited more from this than they did from his promulgation of a new faith. Like all new religions, Mohammedanism was slow to sink into the minds and hearts of the people. The Arabs and their neighbors did not become fanatical Mohammedans overnight, and the great Arab conquests of the seventh century were the result of political, not religious imperialism. Mohammed's successors, the Caliphs, could not claim to be prophets, and the only way in which they could maintain their position of leadership was by military success. They sent out raiding parties against the nearest imperial provinces and were amazed to find little resistance. Almost without planning it, they became involved in a conquest of Syria and Egypt. The native populations were not alarmed by the change of rulers; in fact, often preferred the tolerant Arabs to the Greeks who had been accusing them of heresy. The old Persian kingdom, even weaker than the remnants of the Roman Empire, was also overrun by the Arabs, and the Caliphs soon found themselves masters of the whole Middle East. With this solid block of territory at their disposal, it was easy for them to push along the North African coast, and in 711 to cross into Spain. By 720 the Arab Empire stretched from the borders of India to the Pyrenees and Arab raiders were plunging deep into the heart of Gaul.

As a result of the Arab conquests, the last remnants of Mediterranean unity were destroyed, and three sharply contrasted civilizations arose within the old Graeco-Roman sphere of influence. The growth of Mohammedan sea power soon made it difficult, though not impossible, for the Christians to use the Mediterranean. Land travel between East and West had always been slow and expensive. Religious differences emphasized the physical difficulties of communication. . . .

In this shattering of Mediterranean unity it was Western Europe which had the most to lose. The Mohammedans had inherited much of the learning of the Greeks, and to this they added significant material from Persia and India. On these extensive foundations they were able to build a great structure of philosophical and scientific thought which made them leaders in these fields for centuries. They occupied the key position on the ancient trade-route between East and West and made the most of their opportunity by building up an active commerce and thriving industries. Even when, in the ninth century, the Arab Empire broke up into smaller states, Mohammedan civilization retained its essential unity and ideas and goods moved easily from India to Spain. At a time when the largest Western towns were mere fortified villages, when the most learned men of the West were painfully studying commentaries and encyclopedias, the Mohammedans had great commercial cities and scholars who were making original contributions in almost every field of science.

The Eastern Roman Empire was not quite so impressive as the Arab Empire, but it was still an important center of civilization. The wealth of Constantinople, the manpower of Asia Minor, and a sophisticated diplomatic and military tradition gave it unusual strength and resilience. With its rich heritage of Greek and Christian culture it developed a remarkable civilization—conservative but not decadent, orientalized but not oriental, profoundly Christian but not theocratic. It could no longer claim to be a universal empire, and though it kept the name of Rome in official documents, it was the Empire of the Greeks, of Constantinople, or of Byzantium to most outsiders. Its political boundaries were contracted, but its sphere of influence spread far beyond the narrow limits of the Byzantine provinces. The Slavic peoples of the Balkans usually admitted the hegemony of the emperor and took their basic concepts of religion, art, and literature from Constantinople. The Russians were converted by the Greek Orthodox Church and so the stream of Byzantine culture flowed into the great plains of Eastern Europe. Thus the division between East and West, which had begun in the last days of the old Roman Empire, was extended far beyond the limits of the Mediterranean basin. . . .

Western Europe was the weakest and poorest of the three areas which emerged from the old Mediterranean world. It had always been backward, both economically and intellectually, but in the classical period it had been able to draw on the East both for supplies and ideas. Now it had to face its own deficiencies without outside aid. The southern shores of the Mediterranean had become, and were to remain, a completely foreign region, while mutual suspicion between Westerners and Byzantines made it impossible to rely on Constantinople for leadership. The dangers of . . . travel reinforced the psychological obstacles and threw the West back on its own resources.

These resources were not very great. On the material side, the West was an almost exclusively agricultural region. It contained some of the best farming land in the world, but much of this land was not yet cleared, and the part which was used was cultivated by inefficient methods. A few Italian towns, such as Venice and Amalfi, kept up a hazardous trade with the East, and the Scandinavians managed to import some oriental luxuries across the plains of Russia; otherwise there was little commerce. Industry was at an even lower level; few craftsmen produced for more than a limited, local market. As a result the population was thin, poor, and scattered. The governments of the Germanic kingdoms were weak and unstable, unable to prevent disorder at home or to ward off attacks from the outside. Intellectually and spiritually the situation was almost as bad. The West had retained only part of its legacy from Rome, which at best was only part of the whole body of classical learning, and even this small fraction of the classical heritage was not yet fully understood. The Roman version of Christianity had no serious rivals in the West, but it had not yet made much of an impression on the people. They were Christian because they could be nothing else, but the Church in the West was too disorganized, and in many places too corrupt, to give them much leadership. Altogether, the situation of Western Europe in the seventh century was not promising. It had a rudimentary economic system, and an even more rudimentary political organization; it had inherited a few ideas about government and law, and a somewhat larger body of philosophical and literary material from Rome; it had accepted Christianity but had not yet developed either a well-organized Church or wide-spread individual piety. Western Europe was now on its own, but no one in the seventh century could have predicted that it would develop a civilization which would rival those of Bagdad and Byzantium.

# Gregory of Tours Writes a History of the Franks

Gregory, Bishop of Tours (b. 538), came from an established Gallo-Roman family that had contributed bishops to the Roman Church in Gaul for at least four generations. In his *History of the Franks* he set out to describe the line of Frankish Kings who, since the fifth century, had asserted their authority over the territory of what is now largely France. Gregory noted how far the conduct of the Germanic tribes fell from the level prescribed by the Church. At the same time, he indicated in his writings the popular beliefs of his age, the state of literacy and learning, and the notion of government and justice which prevailed. Because of the information which Gregory revealed, intentionally and unintentionally, his is considered a major source on sixth-century life in the barbarian West. From Gregory of Tours, *History of the Franks,* trans. Ernest Brehaut (New York: Columbia University Press, 1916), pp. 1, 37-38, 39-41, 47-48, 80-82, 130, 165-166.

I

## Preface

With liberal culture on the wane, or rather perishing in the Gaulic cities, there were many deeds being done both good and evil: the heathens were raging fiercely; kings were growing more cruel; the church, attacked by heretics, was defended by Catholics; while the Christian faith was in general devoutly cherished, among some it was growing cold; the churches also were enriched by the faithful or plundered by traitors—and no grammarian skilled in the dialectic art could be found to describe these matters either in prose or verse; and many were lamenting and saying: "Woe to our day, since the pursuit of letters has perished from among us and no one can be found among the people who can set forth the deeds of the present on the written page." Hearing continually these complaints and others like them I (have undertaken) to commemorate the past, in order that it may come to the knowledge of the future; and although my speech is rude, I have been unable to be silent as to the struggles between the wicked and the upright; and I have been especially encouraged because, to my surprise, it has often been said by men of our day, that few understand the learned words of the rhetorician but many the rude language of the common people. . . .

## Career of Clovis (King of the Franks, A.D. 481-511)

After these events Childeric died and Clovis his son reigned in his stead. . . . At that time many churches were despoiled by Clovis's army, since he was as yet involved in heathen error. Now the army had taken from a certain church a vase of wonderful size and beauty, along with the remainder of the utensils for the service of the church. And the bishop of the church sent messengers to the king asking that the vase at least be returned, if he could not get back any more of the sacred dishes. On hearing this the king said to the messenger: "Follow us as far as Soissons, because all that has been taken is to be divided there and when the lot assigns me that dish I will do what the father asks." Then when they came to Soissons and all the booty was set in their midst, the king said, "I ask of you, brave warriors, not to refuse to grant me in addition to my share, yonder dish," that is, he was speaking of the vase just mentioned. In answer to the speech of the king those of more sense replied: "Glorious king, all that we see is yours, and we ourselves are subject to your rule. Now do what seems well-pleasing to you; for no one is able to resist your power." When they said this a foolish, envious and excitable fellow lifted his battle-ax and struck the vase, and cried in a loud voice: "You shall get nothing here except what the lot fairly bestows on you." At this all were stupefied, but the king endured the insult with the gentleness of patience, and taking the vase he handed it over to the messenger of the church, nursing the wound deep in his heart. And at the end of the year he ordered the whole army to come with their equipment of armor, to show the brightness of their arms on the field of March. And when he was reviewing them all carefully, he came to the man who struck the vase, and said to him: "No one has brought armor so carelessly kept as you; for neither your spear nor sword nor ax is in serviceable condition." And seizing his ax he cast it to the earth, and when the other had bent over somewhat to pick it up, the king raised his hands and drove his own ax into the man's head. "This," said he, "is what you did at Soissons to the vase." Upon the death of this man, he ordered the rest to depart, raising great dread of himself by this action. He made many wars and gained many victories. . . .

The queen, Clotilda, a Christian, did not cease to urge him to recognize the true God and cease worshipping idols. But he could not be influenced in any way to this belief, until at last a war arose with the Alamanni, in which he was driven by necessity to confess what before he had of his free will denied. It came about that as the two armies were fighting fiercely, there was much slaughter, and Clovis's army began to be in danger of destruction. He saw it and raised his eyes to heaven, and with remorse in his heart he burst into tears and cried: "Jesus Christ, whom Clotilda asserts to be the son of the living God, who art said to give aid to those in distress, and to bestow victory on those who hope in thee, I beseech the glory of thy aid, with the vow that if thou wilt grant me victory over these enemies, and I shall know that power which she says that people dedicated in thy name have had from thee, I will believe in thee and be baptized in thy name. For I have invoked my own gods, but, as I find, they have withdrawn from aiding me; and therefore I believe that they possess no power, since they do not help those who obey them. I now call upon thee, I desire to believe thee, only let me be rescued from my adversaries." And when he said this, the Alamanni turned their backs, and began to disperse in flight. And when they saw that their king was killed, they submitted to the dominion of Clovis, saying: "Let not the people perish further, we pray; we are yours now." And he stopped the fighting, and after encouraging his men, retired in peace and told the queen how he had had merit to win the victory by calling on the name of Christ. This happened in the fifteenth year of his reign. [496 A.D.]

Then the queen asked Saint Remi, bishop of Rheims, to summon Clovis secretly and began to urge him to believe in the true God, maker of heaven and earth, and to cease worshipping idols, which could help neither themselves nor any one else. But the king said: "I gladly hear you, most holy father; but there remains one thing: the people who follow me cannot endure to abandon their gods; but I shall go and speak to them according to your words." He met with his followers, but before he could speak the power of God anticipated him, and all the people cried out together: "O pious king, we reject

The baptism of Clovis, as seen in a thirteenth-century manuscript, *La vie de Saint-Denis.*

our mortal gods, and we are ready to follow the immortal God whom Remi preaches." . . . And so the king confessed all-powerful God in the Trinity, and was baptized in the name of the Father, Son, and Holy Spirit, and was anointed with the holy ointment with the sign of the cross of Christ. And of his army more than 3000 were baptized. . . .

### Clovis, The Christian King

When King Clovis was dwelling at Paris [c. 507], he sent secretly to the son of Sigibert saying: "Behold your father has become an old man and limps in his weak foot. If he should die," said he, "of due right his kingdom would be yours together with our friendship." Led on by greed the son plotted to kill his father. And when his father went out from the city of Cologne and crossed the Rhine and was intending to journey through the wood Buchaw, as he slept at midday in his tent his son sent assassins in against him, and killed him there, in the idea that he would get his kingdom. But by God's judgment he walked into the pit that he had cruelly dug for his father. He sent messengers to king Clovis to tell about his father's death, and to say: "My father is dead, and I have his treasures in my possession, and also his kingdom. Send men to me, and I shall gladly transmit to you from his treasures whatever pleases you." And Clovis replied: "I thank you for your good will, and I ask that you show the treasures to my men who come, and after that you shall possess all yourself." When they came, he showed his father's treasures. And when they were looking at the different things he said: "It was in this little chest that my father used to put his gold coins." "Thrust in your hand," said they, "to the bottom, and uncover the whole." When he did so, and was much bent over, one of them lifted his hand and dashed his battle-ax against his head, and so in a shameful manner he incurred the death which he had brought on his father. Clovis heard that Sigibert and his son had been slain, and came to the place and summoned all the people, saying: "Hear what has happened. When I," said he, "was sailing down the river Scheldt, Cloderic, son of my kinsman, was in pursuit of his own father, asserting that I wished him killed. And when his father was fleeing through the forest of Buchaw, he set highwaymen upon him, and gave him over to death, and slew him. And when he was opening the treasures, he was slain himself by some one or other. Now I know nothing at all of these matters. For I cannot shed the blood of my own kinsmen, which it is a crime to do. But since this has happened, I give you my advice, if it seems acceptable; turn to me, that you may be under my protection." They listened to this, and giving applause with both shields and voices, they raised him on a shield, and made him king over them. He received Sigibert's kingdom with his treasures, and placed people, too, under his rule. For God was laying his enemies low every day under his hand, and was increasing his kingdom, because he walked with an upright heart before him, and did what was pleasing in his eyes. . . .

## II

### King Chilperic (575–584)

In these days king Chilperic was very sick. When he got well his younger son, who was not yet reborn of water and the Holy Spirit, fell ill, and when they saw he was in danger they baptized him. He was doing a little better when his older brother named Clodobert was attacked by the same disease. Their mother Fredegunda saw they were in danger of death and she repented too late, and said to the king: "The divine goodness has long borne with our bad actions; it has often rebuked us with fevers and other evils but repentance did not follow and now we are losing our sons. It is the tears of the poor, the outcries of widows and the sighs of orphans that are destroying them. We have no hope left now in gathering wealth. We get riches and we do not know for whom. Our treasures will be left without an owner, full of violence and curses. Our storehouses are full of wine and our barns of grain, and our treasuries are full of gold, silver, precious stones, necklaces, and all the wealth of rulers. But we are losing what we held more dear. Come, please, let us burn all the wicked tax lists and let what sufficed for your father king Clothar, suffice for your treasury." So the queen spoke, beating her breast with her fists, and she ordered the [tax] books to be brought out that had been brought from her cities, . . . and when she had thrown them in the fire she said to the king: "Why do you delay; do what you see me do, so that if we have lost our dear children we may at least escape eternal punishment." Then the king repented and burned all the tax books and when they were burned he sent men to stop future taxes. [Despite the king's actions,] the younger child wasted away in great pain and died. They carried him with great grief from Braine to Paris and buried him in the church of St. Denis. Clodobert they placed on a litter and took him to St. Medard's church in Soissons, and threw themselves down at the holy tomb and made vows for him, but being already breathless and weak he died at midnight. They buried him in the holy church of the martyrs Crispin and Crispinian. There was much lamenting among all the people; for men and women followed this funeral sadly wearing the mourning clothes that are customary when a husband or wife dies. After this king Chilperic was generous to cathedrals and churches and the poor. . . .

III

## An Unworthy Bishop (c. 550)

Now Cautinus on taking up the duties of bishop of Clermont became greatly addicted to wine, and proved to be of such a character that he was loathed by all. He was often so befuddled by drink that four men could hardly take him away after dinner. Because of this habit he became an epileptic later on—a disease which frequently showed itself in public. He was also so avaricious that if he could not get some part of the possessions of those whose boundaries touched him he thought it was ruin for him. He took from the stronger with quarrels and abuse, and violently plundered the weaker. . . .

There was at that time a priest Anastasius, of free birth, who held some property secured by deeds of queen Clotilda, [wife of Clovis], of glorious memory. Usually when he met him the bishop would entreat him to give him the deeds of the queen mentioned above, and place the property under his charge. And when Anastasius postponed complying with the will of his bishop, the latter would try now to coax him with kind words and now to terrify him with threats. When he continued unwilling to the end, he ordered him to be brought to the city and there shamelessly detained, and unless he surrendered the deeds, he was to be loaded with insults and starved to death. But the other made a spirited resistance and never surrendered the deeds, saying it was better for him to waste away with hunger for a time than to leave his children in misery. Then by the bishop's command he was given over to the guards with instructions to starve him to death if he did not surrender these documents. Now there was in the church of St. Cassius the martyr a very old and remote crypt, in which was a great tomb of parian marble wherein it seems the body of a certain man of long ago had been placed. In this tomb upon the dead body the living priest was placed and the tomb was covered with the stone with which it had been covered before, and guards were placed at the entrance. But the faithful guards seeing that he was shut in by a stone as it was winter lit a fire and under the influence of hot wine fell asleep.

But the priest like a new Jonah prayed insistently to the Lord to pity him from the interior of the tomb as from the belly of hell, and the tomb being large, as we have said, he was able to extend his hands freely wherever he wished although he could not turn his whole body. There came from the bones of the dead, as he used to relate, a killing stench, which made him shudder not only outwardly but in his inward parts as well. While he held his robe tightly against his nose and could hold his breath his feelings were not the worst, but when he thought that he was suffocating and held the robe a little away from his face he drank in the deadly smell not merely through mouth and nose but even, so to speak, through his very ears. Why make too long a story! When he had suffered, as I suppose, like the Divine Nature, he stretched out his right hand to the side of the sarcophagus and found a crowbar which had been left between the cover and the edge of the tomb when the cover sank into place. Moving this by degrees he found that with God's help the stone could be moved, and when it had been moved so far that the priest could get his head out he made a larger opening with greater ease and so came out bodily. Meanwhile the darkness of night was overspreading the day though it had not spread everywhere as yet. So he hastened to another entrance to the crypt. This was closed with the strongest bars and bolts, but was not so smoothly fitted that a man could not see between the planks. The priest placed his head close to this entrance and saw a man go by. He called to him in a low voice. The other heard, and having an ax in his hand he at once cut the wooden pieces by which the bars were held and opened the way for the priest. And he went off in the darkness and hastened home after vigorously urging the man to say nothing of the matter to any one.

He entered his home and finding the deeds which the queen mentioned before had given him took them to king Clothar, informing him at the same time how he had been committed to a living burial by his own bishop. All were amazed and said that never had Nero or Herod done such a deed as to place a live man in the grave. Then bishop Cautinus appeared before king Clothar but upon the priest's accusation he retreated in defeat and confusion. The priest, according to directions received from the king, maintained his property as he pleased and kept possession of it, and left it to his children. In Cautinus there was no holiness, no quality to be esteemed. He was absolutely without knowledge of letters both ecclesiastical and secular. . . .

## Saints and Miracles

I will relate what happened at that time in a certain monastery, but I do not wish to give the name of the monk, who is still alive, for fear that when this account comes to him he may become vainglorious and lose merit. A young man came to the monastery and presented himself to the abbot with the proposal to pass his life in God's service. The abbot made many objections, explaining that the service there was hard, and he could never accomplish what was required of him. But he promised that he would call on the Lord's name and accomplish it all. And so he was admitted by the abbot. After a few days during which he proved to all that he was humble and holy, it happened that the monks threw out of the granary about three *chori* of grain and left it to dry in the sun and appointed this monk to guard it. And while the others were taking refreshment and he was left to guard the grain, the sky suddenly became overcast, and a heavy rain with roaring wind came swiftly in the direction of the heap of grain. Upon seeing it the monk knew not how to act or what to do. He thought however that even if he called the rest considering the great quantity of grain they would not be able to store it in the granary before the rain, and so giving up everything else he devoted himself to prayer, beseeching the Lord not to allow a drop of the rain to fall on the wheat. And when he threw himself on the ground and prayed, the cloud was divided, and although there was a heavy downpour all around, if it is right to say so, it did not dampen a single grain of the wheat. And when the other monks and the abbot became aware of the coming storm they came quickly to take the grain within, and saw this miracle, and looking for the man in charge of the grain they found him close by stretched out on the sand praying. The abbot on seeing this prostrated himself close to him, and when the rain had passed and the prayer was finished he called to him to arise, and gave orders to seize him and punish him with stripes, saying: "My son, you must grow in the fear and service of God with humility, and not be puffed up with prodigies and miracles." He ordered him to remain shut up in his cell seven days, and to fast as if he were at fault, in order to keep vainglory from forming an obstacle before him. At the present, as we learn from men of the faith, the same monk is so abstemious that he eats no bread in the forty days of Lent and drinks only a cup of barley-water every third day. . . .

# Philip Hitti: Arab Civilization

Philip Hitti (1886- ) was born in Lebanon and was for many years professor in Semitic Literature at Princeton University. In this reading from his history of the Arabs, he provides evidence to back his assertion that "no people in the early Middle Ages contributed to human progress so much as did the Arabs." From Philip Hitti, *The Arabs: A Short History* (New York: St. Martin's Press, Inc., 1965), pp. 84–86, 87–89, 124, 129–132.

## I

### Baghdad: Peerless City

Though less than half a century old, Baghdad (the Arab capital), by the time of Harun, 786–809, had grown from nothingness to a world center of prodigious wealth and international significance, standing alone as the rival of Byzantium. Its splendor had kept pace with the prosperity of the empire of which it was the capital. It had become "a city with no peer throughout the whole world."

The royal palace with its many annexes for harems, eunuchs and special functionaries occupied one-third of the Round City. Particularly impressive was its audience chamber with its rugs, curtains and cushions, the best the Orient could produce. The caliph's cousin-wife, Zubaydah, who in tradition shares with her husband the halo of glory and distinction bestowed by later generations, would tolerate at her table no vessels not made of gold or silver and studded with gems. She was the first to ornament her shoes with precious stones. On one holy pilgrimage she is reported to have spent three million dinars, which included the expense of furnishing the city of Mecca with water from a stream twenty-five miles away. . . .

Especially on ceremonial occasions, such as the installation of the caliph, weddings, pilgrimages and receptions for foreign envoys, did the courtly wealth and magnificence make its fullest display. The marriage ceremony of the caliph al-Mamun to the eighteen-year-old Buran, daughter of his vizir, was celebrated in 825 with such fabulous expenditure of money that it has lived in Arabic literature as one of the unforgetable extravaganzas of the age. At the nuptials a thousand pearls of unique size, we are told, were showered from a gold tray upon the couple who stood on a golden mat studded with pearls and sapphires. A two-hundred-rotl candle of ambergris turned the night into day. Balls of musk, each containing a ticket naming an estate or a slave or some such gift, were showered on the royal princes and dignitaries. In 917 the caliph al-Muqtadir received in his palace with great ceremony and pomp the envoys of the young Constantine VII, whose mission evidently involved the exchange and ransom of prisoners. The caliphal array included 160,000 cavalry and footmen, 7,000 black and white eunuchs and 700 chamberlains. In the parade a hundred lions marched, and in the caliphal palace hung 38,000 curtains of which 12,500 were gilded, besides 22,000 rugs. The envoys were so struck with awe and admiration that they first mistook the chamberlain's office and then the vizir's for the royal audience chamber. Especially impressed were they with the Hall of the Tree which housed an artificial tree of gold and silver weighing 500,000 drams, in the branches of which were lodged and automated singing birds of the same precious metals. In the garden they marveled at the artificially dwarfed palm trees which by skilled cultivation yielded dates of rare varieties. . . .

Along Baghdad's miles of wharves lay hundreds of vessels, including ships of war and pleasure craft and varying from Chinese junks to native rafts of inflated sheepskins, not unlike those of our present day, which were floated down from Mosul. Into the bazars of the city came porcelain, silk and musk from China; spices, minerals and dyes from India and the Malay Archipelago; rubies, lapis lazuli, fabrics and slaves from the lands of the Turks in Central Asia; honey, wax, furs and white slaves from eastern Africa. Chinese wares had a special bazar devoted to their sale. The provinces of the empire itself sent by caravan or sea their domestic products; rice, grain and linen from Egypt; glass, metalware and fruits from Syria; brocade, pearls and weapons from Arabia; silks, perfumes and vegetables from Persia.

From Baghdad and other export centers, Arab merchants shipped to the Far East, Europe and Africa fabrics, jewelry, metal mirrors, glass beads and spices. The hoards of Arab coins recently found in places as far north as Russia, Finland, Sweden and Germany testify to the worldwide commercial activity of the Moslems of this and the later period. The adventures of Sinbad the Sailor, which form one of the best-known tales in *The Thousand and One Nights,* have long been recognized as based upon actual reports of voyages made by Moslem merchants.

## II

Merchants played a leading part in the Baghdad community. Members of each craft and trade had their shops in the same market as in the present day. The monotony of street life was interrupted from time to time by the occasional passage of a wedding or circumcision procession. Professional men—physicians, lawyers, teachers, writers and the like—began to occupy a conspicuous place. A biographer has left us a picture of the daily routine of a member of the learned fraternity, which indicated that scholarship had a considerable market value in those days. We are first shown this man of learning after his daily ride, at the public bath, where attendants poured water over him. On emerging he put on a lounging-robe, sipped a drink, ate a biscuit and lay down, sometimes falling asleep. The siesta over, he burned perfume to fumigate his person and ordered a dinner which generally consisted of soup, chicken and bread. Then he resumed his sleep and on waking drank four rotls of old wine, to which he might add quinces and Syrian apples.

The luxurious scale of living made this period popular in history and in fiction, but what has rendered it especially illustrious in world annals is the fact that it witnessed the most momentous intellectual awakening in the history of Islam and one of the most significant in the whole history of thought and culture. The awakening was due in large measure to foreign influences, partly Indo-Persian and Syrian but mainly Hellenic, and was marked by translations into Arabic from Persian, Sanskrit, Syriac and Greek. Starting with very little science, philosophy or literature of his own, the Arabian Moslem, who brought with him from the desert a keen sense of intellectual curiosity and many latent faculties, soon became, as we have learned before, the beneficiary and heir of the older and more cultured peoples whom he conquered or encountered. Just as in Syria he adopted the existing Aramaic civilization, itself influenced by the later Greek, so did he in Iraq adopt the same civilization influenced by the Persian. Three-quarters of a century after the establishment of Baghdad the Arabic-reading world was in possession of the chief philosophical works of Aristotle, of the leading Neo-Platonic commentators, and of most of the medical writings of Galen, as well as of Persian and Indian scientific works. In only a few decades the Arabs assimilated what had taken the Greeks centuries to develop. In absorbing the main features of both Hellenic and Persian cultures, Islam lost most of its own original character, which breathed the spirit of the desert and bore the stamp of Arabian nationalism, but thereby took an important place in the medieval cultural unit which linked southern Europe with the Near East. This culture, it should be remembered, was fed by a single stream, a stream with sources in ancient Egypt, Babylonia, Phoenicia and Judea, all flowing to Greece and now returning to the East in the form of Hellenism. . . .

## Cordova: Jewel of the World

While the eastern branch of the Moslem empire was reaching its golden day, the far-western branch in Spain was enjoying a period of corresponding splendour. It was a time of even greater importance to us, for it was chiefly from Moslem Spain that Arab culture advanced to interpenetrate the Christian culture of the early Middle Ages to produce the civilization which we inherited. The climax of this western Moslem civilization came between the ninth and eleventh centuries. . . .

In this period, roughly the tenth century, the Umayyad capital of Cordova took its place as the most cultured city in Europe and, with Constantinople and Baghdad, as one of the three cultural centres of the world. With its one hundred and thirteen thousand homes, twenty-one suburbs, seventy libraries and numerous bookshops, mosques and palaces, it acquired international fame and inspired awe and admiration in the hearts of travellers. It enjoyed miles of paved streets illuminated by lights from the bordering houses, whereas "seven hundred years after this time there was not so much as one public lamp in London," and "in Paris, centuries subsequently, whoever stepped over his threshold on a rainy day stepped up to his ankles in mud."

The Arab attitude toward the Nordic barbarians found expression in the words of the learned Toledan judge Said, who thought that "because the sun does not shed its rays directly over their heads, their climate is cold and atmosphere clouded. Consequently their temperaments have become cold and their humours rude, while their bodies have grown large, their complexion light and their hair long. They lack withal sharpness of wit and penetration of intellect, while stupidity and folly prevail among them." Whenever the rulers of Leon, Navarre or Barcelona needed a surgeon, an architect, a master singer, or a dressmaker, it was to Cordova that they applied. The fame of the Moslem capital penetrated distant Germany, where a Saxon nun styled it "the jewel of the world."

Spain under the caliphate was one of the wealthiest and most thickly populated lands of Europe. The capital boasted some thirteen thousand weavers and a flourishing leather industry. From Spain the art of tanning and embossing leather was carried to Morocco and from these two lands it was brought to France and England, as the terms cordovan, cordwainer and morocco indicate. Wool and silk were woven not only in Cordova but in Malaga, Almeria and other centres. The raising

Garden of the Generalife, from the Arabic *jannat-al-árif,* "the inspector's paradise." The Moorish villa and gardens are part of the Alhambra palace, designed and constructed for the Moorish rulers of Southern Spain in the thirteenth and fourteenth centuries.

Frankish and Arab nobles at a game of chess. Invented in India, chess was introduced to medieval Westerners by the Moslems. Twelfth-century illuminated manuscript.

of silkworms, originally a monopoly of the Chinese, was introduced by Moslems into Spain, where it thrived. Almeria also produced glassware and brasswork. Paterna in Valencia was the home of pottery. Jaen and Algarve were noted for their mines of gold and silver, Cordova for its iron and lead, and Malaga for its rubies. Toledo, like Damascus, was famous all over the world for its swords. The art of inlaying steel and other metals with gold and silver and decorating them with flower patterns, which was introduced from Damascus, flourished in several Spanish and other European centres and left a linguistic heritage in such words as damascene and damaskeen.

The Spanish Arabs introduced agricultural methods practised in Western Asia. They dug canals, cultivated grapes and introduced, among other plants and fruits, rice, apricots, peaches, pomegranates, oranges, sugar cane, cotton and saffron. The south-eastern plains of the peninsula, especially favoured by climate and soil, developed important centres of rural and urban activity. Here wheat and other grains, as well as olives and sundry fruits, were raised by a peasantry who worked the soil on shares with the owners. . . .

The industrial and agricultural products of Moslem Spain were more than sufficient for domestic consumption. Seville, one of the greatest of its river ports, exported cotton, olives and oil; it imported cloth and slaves from Egypt and singing girls from Europe and Asia. The exports of Malaga and Jaen included saffron, figs, marble and sugar. Through Alexandria and Constantinople Spanish products found markets as far away as India and Central Asia. Especially active was the trade with Damascus, Baghdad and Mecca. The international nautical vocabulary of the modern world contains not a few words which testify to the former Arab supremacy on the seas—admiral, arsenal, average, cable, shallop.

The government maintained a regular postal service. It modelled its coinage on Eastern patterns, with the dinar as the gold unit and the dirham as the silver unit. Arab money was in use in the Christian kingdoms of the north, which for nearly four hundred years had no coinage other than Arabic or French.

The real glory of this period, however, lies in fields other than political. Al-Hakam, Abd-al-Rahman III's successor, was himself a scholar and patronized learning. He granted munificent bounties to scholars and established twenty-seven free schools in the capital. Under him the University of Cordova, founded in the principal mosque by Abd-al-Rahman III, rose to a place of pre-eminence among the educational institutions of the world. It preceded both al-Azhar of Cairo and the Nizamiyah of Baghdad, and attracted students, Christian and Moslem, not only from Spain but from other parts of Europe, Africa and Asia. Al-Hakam enlarged the mosque which housed the university, conducted water to it in lead pipes and decorated it with mosaics brought by Byzantine artists. He invited professors from the East to the university and set aside endowments for their salaries.

In addition to the university the capital housed a library of first magnitude. Al-Hakam was a bibliophile; his agents ransacked the bookshops of Alexandria, Damascus and Baghdad with a view to buying or copying manuscripts. The books thus gathered are said to have numbered 400,000, their titles filling a catalogue of forty-four volumes, in each one of which twenty sheets were devoted to poetical works alone. Al-Hakam, probably the best scholar among Moslem caliphs, personally used several of these works; his marginal notes on certain manuscripts rendered them highly prized by later collectors. In order to secure the first copy of the *Aghani,* which al-Isbahani, a descendant of the Umayyads, was then composing in Iraq, al-Hakam sent the author a thousand dinars. The general state of culture in Andalusia reached such a high level at this time that the distinguished Dutch scholar Dozy went so far as to declare enthusiastically that "nearly everyone could read and write"—all this when in Christian Europe only the rudiments of learning were known, and that chiefly by a few churchmen.

TOPIC 19

# HOPE FOR REVIVAL

In the great disorganization of Western life during the sixth and seventh centuries, pockets of the Church remained centers of literacy, order, and human cooperation. Out of the monasteries dominated by the Benedictine rule came the discipline that would vitalize the organization of Western Christianity and spread its faith to other peoples. From the bishop of Rome came the authority and direction that would preserve the institution of the Church and the values on which it was based. The readings examine the origins of monasticism and the independent papacy and their contribution to sustaining and regenerating Western life.

**Reading 93**

## The Church Provides Leadership in the West

I. Reprinted from *Western Civilizations, Their History and Their Cultures,* Seventh Edition by Edward McNall Burns. By permission of W. W. Norton & Company, Inc. Copyright © 1968 by W. W. Norton & Company, Inc., pp. 248–249. II. Reprinted with permission of the Macmillan Company from *Medieval History, The Life and Death of a Civilization* by Norman F. Cantor. Copyright © 1968 by The Macmillan Company.

### I. EVOLUTION OF CHURCH ORGANIZATION

The growth of Christian organization was one of the most important developments of the whole medieval era. Even during the first few centuries of that period the church and its related institutions evolved into an elaborate structure which ultimately became the principal framework of society itself. As the Roman Empire in the West decayed, the church took over many of its functions and helped to preserve order amid the deepening chaos. That anything at all was saved out of the wreckage was due in large part to the stabilizing influence of the organized church. It aided in civilizing the barbarians, in promoting ideals of social justice, and in preserving and transmitting the antique learning.

The organization of the church was at first very simple. The early Christian congregations met in the homes of their members and listened to the spiritual testimony of various of the brethren who were believed to have been in direct communication with the Holy Ghost. No distinction between laymen and clergy was recognized. Each independent church had a number of officers, generally known as bishops and elders, whose functions were to preside at the services, discipline members, and dispense charity. Gradually, under the influence of the pagan mystery religions, the ritual of Christianity increased to such a stage of complexity that a professional priesthood seemed to become necessary. The need for defense against persecution and the desire to attain uniformity of belief also favored the development of ecclesiastical organization. The consequence was that about the beginning of the second century one bishop in each important city came to be recognized as supreme over all the clergy in that vicinity. The sphere of his jurisdiction corresponded to the *civitas,* the smallest administrative unit of the Roman state. As the number of congregations multiplied, and as the influence of the church increased due to the adoption of Christianity as the official religion of Rome, distinctions of rank among the bishops themselves began to appear. Those who had their headquarters in the larger cities came to be called metropolitans, with authority over the clergy of an entire province. In the fourth century the still higher dignity of the patriarch was created to designate those bishops who ruled over the oldest and largest of Christian communities—such cities as Rome, Constantinople, Antioch, and Alexandria with their surrounding districts. Thus the Christian clergy by 400 A.D. had come to embrace a definite hierarchy of patriarchs, metropolitans, bishops, and priests.

The climax of all this development was the growth of the primacy of the bishop of Rome, or in other words the rise of the papacy. For several reasons the bishop of Rome enjoyed a pre-eminence over the other patriarchs of the church. The city in which he ruled was venerated by the faithful as a scene of the missionary activities of the Apostles Peter and Paul. The tradition was widely accepted that Peter had founded the bishopric of Rome, and that therefore all of his successors were heirs of his authority and prestige. This tradition was supplemented by the theory that Peter had been commissioned by the Christ as his vicar on earth and had been given the keys of the kingdom of heaven with power to punish men for their sins and even to absolve them from guilt.* This theory, known as the doctrine of the Petrine Succession, has been used by Popes ever since as a basis for their claims to authority over the church. The bishops of Rome had an advantage also in the fact that after the transfer of the imperial capital to Constantinople there was seldom any emperor with effective sovereignty in the West. Finally, in 455 the Emperor Valentinian III issued a decree commanding all Western bishops to submit to the jurisdiction of the Pope. It must not be supposed, however, that the church was yet under a monarchical form of government. The patriarchs in the East regarded the extreme assertions of the papal claims as a brazen effrontery, and even many bishops in the West continued to ignore them for some time.

*"Thou art Peter, and upon this rock (Greek *petra*) I will build my church; and the gates of hell shall not prevail against it. And I will give thee the keys to the kingdom of heaven, and whatsoever thou shalt bind on earth shall be bound in heaven; and whatsoever thou shalt loose on earth shall be loosed in heaven." Matthew 16: 18–19.

The leadership which was so badly needed by the disorganized western society of the sixth century could come initially only from the church, which had in its ranks almost all the literate men in Europe and the strongest institutions of the age. The church, however, had also suffered severely from the Germanic invasions. The bishops identified their interests with those of the lay nobility and in fact were often relatives of kings and the more powerful aristocrats; the secular clergy in general was ignorant, corrupt, and unable to deal with the problem of Christianizing a society which remained intensely heathen in spite of formal conversion of masses of Germanic warriors to Christianity. The grossest heathen superstitions were grafted onto Latin Christianity; the religiosity of the sixth and seventh centuries was infected with devils, magic, the crudest kind of relic worship, the importation of local nature deities into Christianity in the guise of saints, and a general debasement of the Latin faith by religious primitivism. There was no parish churchman who could go out into the countryside and counter these crudities; at most, a member of the cathedral clergy would occasionally journey out from the episcopal see to administer the sacraments. The secular clergy were neither interested in nor capable of undertaking extensive missionary work. No one even cared about attempting the formal conversion of the German tribes within the Merovingian kingdom who lived east of the Rhine, and they remained heathens until the eighth century. By the beginning of the seventh century church discipline in Gaul was in a state of chaos, and the problem was the most basic one of preserving the sufficient rudiments of literacy to perpetuate the liturgy and doctrines of Latin Christianity. Many priests literally did not know what they were saying at church services, but uttered a mumbo-jumbo which vaguely resembled Latin as a magical incantation in order to impress their near-savage parishioners.

The Latin church was preserved from extinction, and European civilization with it, by the two ecclesiastical institutions which alone had the strength and efficiency to withstand the impress of the surrounding barbarism; the regular clergy [that is, the monks] and the papacy. Of all the institutions in western Europe, only monasticism and the papacy were able to provide leadership for European society, and out of their joint efforts was eventually to come the amelioration of Germanic kingship and its transformation into an additional creative force in early medieval society. But while the papacy and Germanic kingship were ultimately to provide the most dramatic and effective direction to the people of western Europe, it was the monks who were the most continuous force for education, organization, and social amelioration between the sixth and twelfth centuries and a determining factor of the most fundamental kind in the formation of medieval civilization. How did the regular clergy, that is, the clergy living under monastic rule, come to assume these indispensable social obligations? The structure of the new civilization which was created in the early middle ages was determined by the answer to this question. . . .

The figure of the hermit-saint was a particularly prominent and popular one in the Greek church, and Greek monasticism never entirely overcame the pattern established by its anchoritic origins. The ideal hermit type was established by Athanasius' *Life of St. Antony,* the most famous of the fourth-century desert fathers. Greek anchoritism (solitary living) was liable to go to extremes as the populace confused holiness with extreme physical privation. Such was the case with the early fifth-century Syrian saint, Simeon Stylites, who was reputed to have spent the last thirty years of his life sitting on top of a pillar seventy feet high. The more sensitive and cultured minds in the Greek church discouraged such extreme asceticism. The great fourth-century Christian humanist and Greek church father, St. Basil, contended that the monks ought to obey the commandment to love one's neighbor as well as God. St. Basil was the leader in the creation of a communal type of monasticism in the Greek church which gradually came to predominate over the old anchoritic form. But the Greek cenobitic [communal] form of ascetic life remained loose, and the individual monk retained most of his independence. The characteristic Greek monastery was a large community where monks lived together for convenience, but the abbot (*abbas,* father) had very little control over them; he was merely a revered and senior religious. . . .

By the end of the ninth century the basic rule for all western monasteries, with the exception of those in Ireland, was the one set down by St. Benedict of Nursia (d. 543) for his own monastery of Monte Cassino near Naples. Western monasticism became identified with the Benedictine order, and because of the indispensable contributions of the black monks (as they were called from the color of their habit) to religion, education, government, and economy, the period from 550 to 1150 has often been called the Benedictine centuries. St. Benedict certainly did not intend to establish an institution which would provide leadership in medieval society. There is even some debate as to whether he intended his rule to be applied universally to all Latin monasteries, but assuredly he hoped that others would imitate the form of the religious life he established at Monte Cassino. He arrived at the final form of his *Rule for Monks* only after many years of careful consideration of the ideal religious life and some painful experiments. St. Benedict was a member of the old Roman aristocracy, and he brought to the monastic life the Roman corporate sense of order, discipline, and authority. He turned in revulsion from the school at Rome to which his parents had sent him and fled to a wild region to become a hermit, but he found the lonely anchoritic life unsatisfactory and psychologically dangerous. He then became the abbot in a prevailing Greek kind of loose cenobitic community, but he was chagrined by the laxity and disorder he found there. Out of these experiences he derived the severe criticisms of the older forms of monasticism which he presented in the introduction to his *Rule.*

The purpose of the Benedictine community was to assure salvation for the souls of its members. It was a completely self-contained community, economically and politically as well as spiritually, and was not to rely upon the world for anything, except in the extreme case of the notorious corruption of the monastic community. Only when the abbot and the monks were obviously living scandalous lives was there a provision in the Benedictine Rule for outside interference; only then were the bishop or pious laymen of the neighborhood expected to intervene and restore regular life. With the exception of this unusual situation, the Benedictine monastery was to be a completely self-contained, self-supporting, and self-governing world of its own. . . .

The self-contained nature of the Benedictine monastery made it an institutional unit which was eminently suited to the circumstances of the early middle ages. Only actual physical destruction could disperse the self-supporting and self-governed Benedictine community. In the new world that was coming into being after the Germanic invasions, social and political life was atomized, and the local units in society were the most effective ones. The estate, the village, the province were rapidly replacing the state and the city as the centers of civilization. The Benedictine monastery fitted in completely with the tendency toward localism, and because of its efficiency and self-perpetuating nature it came to assume several important functions: educational, religious, economic, and political. . . .

# Life with an Eastern Hermit (5th Century)

It was often considered good training by early Christians to spend a period of time with holy hermits. The following account, written by Palladius, a bishop in Asia Minor, describes one such experience. From W. K. L. Clarke, *The Lausiac History of Palladius* (London, 1908), pp. 48–50.

Handing me over to Dorotheus, a Theban ascetic who was spending the sixtieth year in his cave, [the priest] ordered me to complete three years with him in order to tame my passions—for he knew that the old man lived a life of great austerity—bidding me return to him afterwards for spiritual instruction. But being unable to complete the three years owing to a breakdown in health, I left Dorotheus before the three years were up,

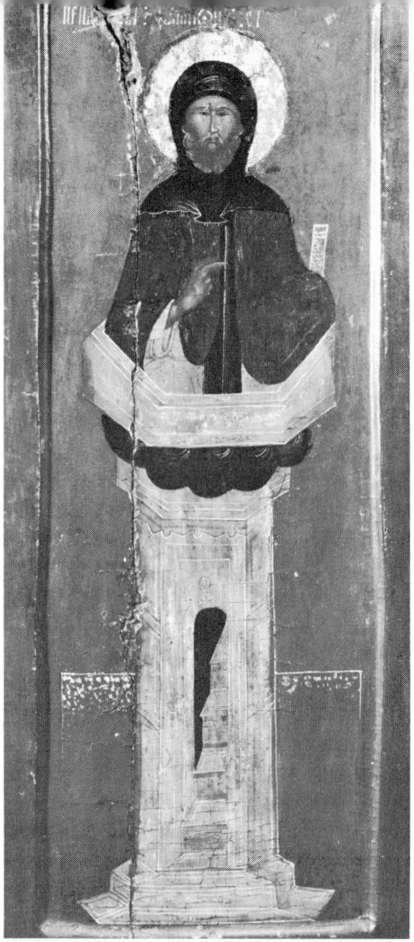

Three views of the medieval religious: **a)** a fourteenth-century Tuscan view of the isolated life of the hermits of Thebes (Egypt) who lived on the banks of the Nile River near modern Luxor; **b)** a sixteenth-century Russian ikon depicting St. Simeon Stylites sitting on his pillar; **c)** an illustration in an early manuscript of an abbot and monks in procession.

for living with him one got parched and all dried-up. For all day long in the burning heat he would collect stones in the desert by the sea and build with them continually and make cells, and then he would retire in favour of those who could not build for themselves. Each year he completed one cell. And once when I said to him: "What do you mean, father, at your great age by trying to kill your poor body in these heats?" he answered thus: "It kills me, I kill it." For he used to eat daily six ounces of bread and a bunch of herbs, and drink water in proportion. God is my witness, I never knew him to stretch his legs and go to sleep on a rush mat, or on a bed. But he would sit up all night long and weave ropes of palm leaves to provide himself with food. Then, supposing that he did this for my benefit, I made careful inquiries also from other disciples of his, who lived by themselves, and ascertained that this had been his manner of life from a youth, and that he had never deliberately gone to sleep, only when working or eating he closed his eyes overcome by sleep, so that often the piece of food fell from his mouth at the moment of eating, so great was his drowsiness. Once when I tried to constrain him to rest a little on the mat, he was annoyed and said: "If you can persuade angels to sleep, you will also persuade the zealous man." . . .

# The Rule of St. Benedict

From Abbot Justin McCann, ed. and trans., *The Rule of Saint Benedict* (New York: Paulist Newman Press, 1952). 

## I

### Chapter 2. What Kind of Man the Abbot Should Be

An abbot who is worthy to rule a monastery should always remember what he is called and realize in his actions the name of a superior. For he is believed to be the representative of Christ in the monastery. . . . Therefore the abbot ought not to teach, or ordain, or command anything which is against the law of the Lord; on the contrary, his commands and teaching should be infused into the minds of his disciples like the leaven of divine justice. Let the abbot remember always that at the dread Judgement of God there will be an examination of both these matters, of his teaching and of the obedience of his disciples. . . .

Let him not make any distinction of persons in the monastery. Let him not love one more than another, unless he find him better in good works and obedience. Let not a freeborn monk be put before one that was a slave, unless there be some other reasonable ground for it. But if the abbot, for just reason, think fit so to do, let him fix anyone's order as he will; otherwise let them keep their due places; because, whether slaves or freemen, we are all one in Christ, and have to serve alike in the army of the same Lord. *For there is no respect of persons with God.* In this regard only are we distinguished in his sight, if we be found better than others in good works and humility. Therefore let the abbot show an equal love to all, and let the same discipline be imposed on all in accordance with their deserts. . . .

Above all let him not have great solicitude for fleeting, earthly, and perishable things, and so overlook or undervalue the salvation of the souls committed to him; but let him always remember that he has undertaken the government of souls and will have to give an account of them. And if he be tempted to complain of lack of means, let him remember the words: *Seek ye first the kingdom of God and his approval, and all these things shall be yours without the asking.* And again: *Those that fear him never go wanting.* And let him know that he who has undertaken the government of souls, must prepare himself to render an account of them. And whatever number of brethren he knows he has under his care, let him regard it as certain that he will have to give the Lord an account of all these souls on the Day of Judgement, and certainly of his own soul also. And thus, fearing always the examination which the shepherd will have to face for the sheep entrusted to him, and anxious regarding the account which will have to be given for others, he is made solicitous for his own sake also; and while by his admonitions helping others to amend, he himself is cleansed of his faults.

### Chapter 33. Whether Monks Should Have Anything of Their Own

This vice especially ought to be utterly rooted out of the monastery. Let no one presume to give or receive anything without the abbot's leave, or to have anything as his own, anything whatever, whether book or tablets or pen or whatever it may be; for monks should not have even their bodies and wills at their own disposal. But let them look to the father of the monastery for all that they require, and let it be unlawful to have anything which the abbot has not given or allowed. And, as the Scripture saith, *let all things be common to all, nor let anyone say that anything is his own* or claim it for him-

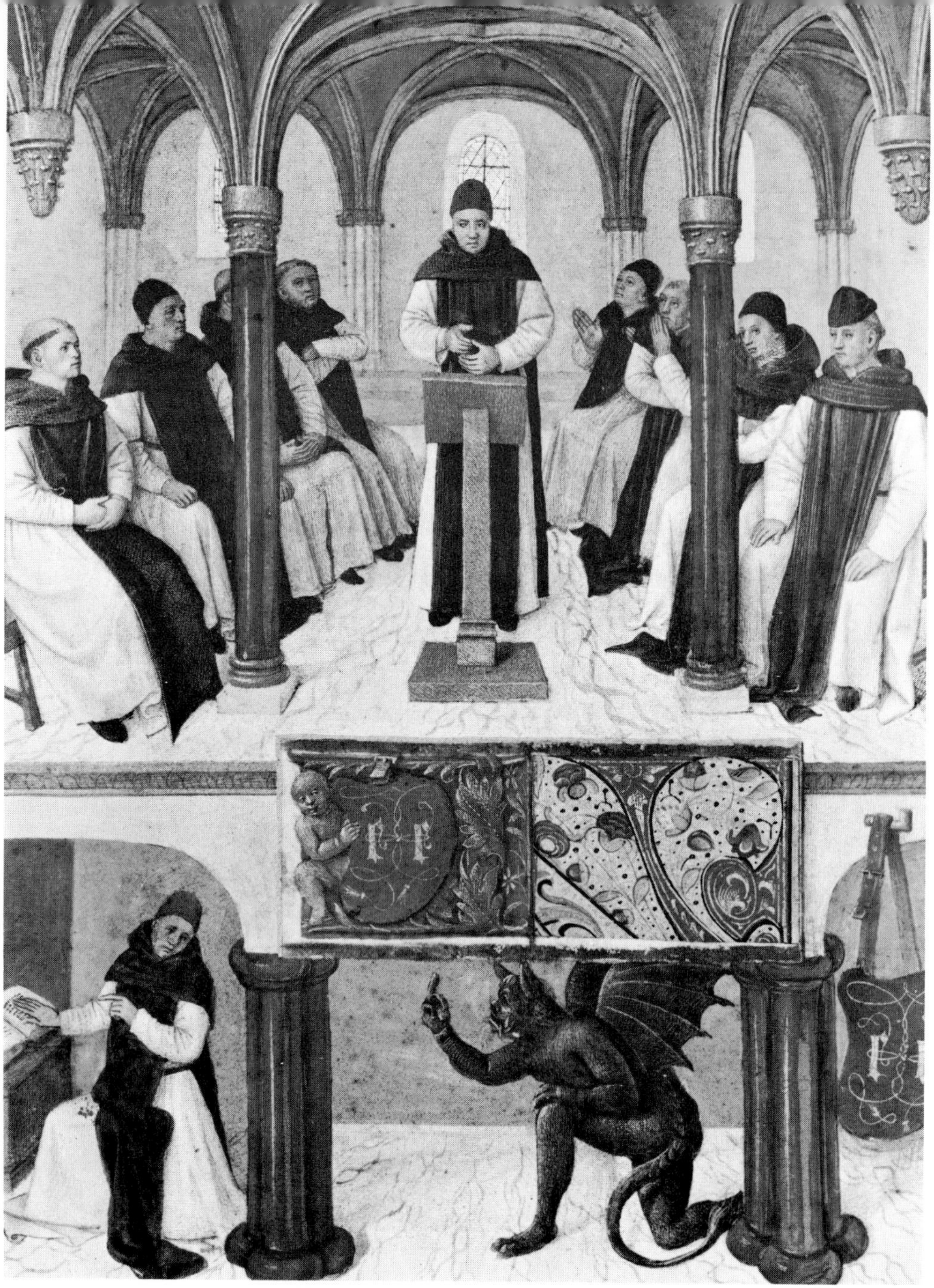

self. But if anyone shall be found to indulge in this most wicked vice, let him be admonished once and a second time; if he do not amend, let him undergo punishment.

## Chapter 48. Of the Daily Manual Labour

Idleness is the enemy of the soul. The brethren, therefore, must be occupied at stated hours in manual labour, and again at other hours in sacred reading. To this end we think that the times for each may be determined in the following manner. From Easter until September the 14th, the brethren shall start work in the morning and from the first hour until about the fourth do the tasks that have to be done. From the fourth hour until about the sixth let them apply themselves to reading. After the sixth hour, having left the table, let them rest on their beds in perfect silence; or if anyone wishes to read by himself let him read so as not to disturb the others. Let None [prayers] be said early, at the middle of the eighth hour; and let them again do what work has to be done until Vespers. But if the circumstances of the place or their proverty require them to gather the harvest themselves, let them not be discontented; for then are they truly monks when they live by the labour of their hands, like our fathers and the apostles. Yet let all things be done in moderation on account of the faint-hearted.

On Sundays likewise all shall apply themselves to reading, except those who are assigned to various duties. But if there be anyone so careless and slothful that he will not

St. Bernard of Clairvaux (1091–1153), who used the simplicity of the Benedictine rule to reform many of the monasteries in the twelfth century, preaches to the monks at Cîteaux in France. Below, the saint resists the temptations of the devil.

Vignettes of the monastic life, eighth to fourteenth centuries: **a)** harvesting wheat; **b)** splitting wood; **c)** reading; **d)** in the wine cellar.

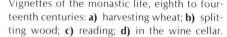

or cannot study or read, let him be given some work to perform, so that he may not be idle. Sick or delicate brethren should be assigned a task or craft of such a kind that on the one hand they be not idle, and on the other be not overborne by excessive toil and driven away from the monastery. The abbot should have consideration for their weakness.

II

## Chapter 55. The Clothes and Shoes of the Brethren

Let clothing be given to the brethren according to the nature of the locality in which they dwell and its climate; for in cold districts they will need more clothing, and in warm districts less. It is the abbot's business to take thought for this matter. But we believe that in ordinary places the following dress is sufficient for each monk: a tunic, a cowl (thick and woolly in winter, but thin or worn in summer), a belt for work, and for the feet shoes and stockings. And let not the monks complain of the colour or coarseness of any of these things, but be content with what is to be found in the district where they live and can be purchased cheaply.

Let the abbot see to the size of the garments, that they be not too short for their wearers, but of the proper fit. When the brethren receive new clothes, let them always return the old ones at once, that they may be stored in the clothesroom for the poor. For it is sufficient if a monk have two tunics and two cowls, to allow for a change at night and for the washing of these garments; more than that is superfluity and should be curtailed. And let them return their stockings, and anything else that is old, when they receive new ones. Those who are sent on a journey shall receive drawers from the clothesroom, which they shall wash and restore when they return. And let their cowls and tunics be somewhat better than the ones they wear usually. They shall receive them from the clothesroom when they are starting on their journey and restore them when they return.

For bedding let this suffice: a mattress, a blanket, a coverlet, and a pillow. The beds should be examined frequently by the abbot, lest any private property be concealed in them. If any brother be found to have anything that he has not received from the abbot, let him undergo the strictest punishment. And in order that this evil or private ownership may be rooted out utterly, let the abbot provide all things that are necessary: that is, cowl, tunic, stockings, shoes, belt, knife, pen, needle, handkerchief, and tablets; so that all pretext of need may be taken away. Yet let the abbot always consider those words of the Acts of the Apostles: *Distribution was made to everyone according as he had need.* So too let the abbot consider the weaknesses of the needy, and not the ill-will of the jealous. But in all his decisions let him think upon the retribution of God.

## Chapter 65. If a Brother Be Commanded To Do Impossible Things

If it happen that something hard or impossible be laid upon any brother, let him receive the command of his superior with all docility and obedience. But if he see that the weight of the burden altogether exceeds the measure of his strength, let him explain the reasons of his incapacity to his superior calmly and in due season, without pride, obstinacy, or contentiousness. If after his representations the superior still persist in his decision and command, let the subject know that it is expedient for him, and let him obey out of love, trusting in the assistance of God.

## Chapter 71. That the Brethren Be Obedient to One Another

Not only shall the virtue of obedience be practised by all towards the abbot, but the brethren shall also obey one another, knowing that by this road of obedience will they go to God. The commands of the abbot or of the superiors appointed by him must rank first, and no unofficial commands take precedence of them; but, for the rest, let all the juniors obey their seniors with all love and diligence. If anyone be found quarrelsome, let him be corrected. And if any brother, for however trifling a reason, be corrected in any way by the abbot, or any of his seniors, or if he perceive that any senior, in however small a degree, is displeased or angry with him, let him at once without delay cast himself on the ground at his feet, and lie there making reparation, until that displeasure is appeased and he bless him. But if anyone should disdain to do this, let him either undergo corporal punishment, or, if he be stubborn, let him be expelled from the monastery.

## Chapter 72. Of the Good Zeal Which Monks Ought To Have

Just as there is an evil zeal of bitterness which separates from God and leads to hell, so is there a good zeal which separates from evil and leads to God and life everlasting. Let monks, therefore, exercise this zeal with the most fervent love. . . . Let them bear with the greatest patience one another's infirmities, whether of body or character. Let them vie in paying obedience one to another. Let none follow what seems good for himself, but rather what is good for another. Let them practise fraternal charity with a pure love. Let them fear God. Let them love their abbot with a sincere and humble affection. Let them prefer nothing whatever to Christ. And may he bring us all alike to life everlasting.

# R. H. C. Davis: Pope Gregory the Great

**(590-604)**

English historian R. H. C. Davis (1918- ) credits Pope Gregory I with saving the Church from the deterioration of the Roman state. A Roman by birth and inclination, Gregory more or less took over the function of emperor in the West. He revitalized the Church further by organizing an extensive missionary campaign to convert the pagans of England and Germany to Christianity. The papacy, at his death, had gained an independent position it was never to lose. From R. H. C. Davis, *A History of Medieval Europe* (New York: David McKay Company, 1957), pp. 79-86, 87-88.

## I

### Pope Gregory the Great (590-604)

In the pontificate of Gregory I (590-604) the Papacy begins to emerge in its medieval form. In it the first steps taken towards the organization of an ordered hierarchy of the Western Church under the direct control of the Pope,* and the first developments that led to the creation of a Papal State, were to be seen. Paradoxically, however, Gregory the Great was essentially a conservative man, embodying in himself all the diverse traditions of *Romania*. *Romania* was a word which came into use in the fourth century to express the Roman as opposed to the barbarian way of life. Exponents of its traditions included Augustine who was an African, Cassiodorus who was a Roman, Justinian who was an Illyrian, and the Christian Church which had its roots in Judaism. Each represented, no matter how much he might differ from the others, a way of life that was foreign to the barbarian world. Pope Gregory the Great represented them all.

He was by birth a Roman of good senatorial family, and his great-great-grandfather had been Pope Felix III (483-492). His father had a large house on the *Clivus Scauri* in Rome, and he himself was *praefectus urbis* in 573. But the city in which he had held this once-glorious office had lost its splendour and was falling into ruins. Quite apart from the disasters of the fifth century, it had been besieged and captured three times in Justinian's Gothic War, during which Gregory himself had been born (c. 540).

> She that once appeared the mistress of the world (wrote Gregory), we have seen what has become of her, shattered by everything that she has suffered from immense and manifold misfortunes—the desolation of her inhabitants and the menace of her enemies. Ruins on ruins. . . Where is the senate? Where the people? All the pomp of secular dignities has been destroyed. . . . And we, the few that we are who remain, every day we are menaced by scourges and innumerable trials. . . . No more senate, no more people, but for that which still survives, sorrows and groanings, multiplied every day. Rome is deserted and in flames, and as for her buildings we see them fall down of their own accord.

One of the main reasons for his pessimism was that the imperial power in Italy was declining rapidly. In 568, only fourteen years after the end of the Gothic War, the Lombards invaded Italy under their king Alboin. They crossed the Alps with their families, goods, and chattels and within ten years had occupied large parts of Italy and had completely disrupted the imperial administration. But neither they nor the imperial forces were strong enough to win a decisive victory. Though some Lombard forces made their settlements as far south as Spoleto and Benevento, the emperor's representative, the exarch, was able to maintain a tenuous control over a strip of territory that stretched across Italy from Venice and Ravenna on the east coast to Rome and Naples on the west. It was exposed to attack from both north and south, its lines of communication were often cut, and its permanent defence was impossible. It was a pitiable remnant of imperial power. Gregory compared it to an eagle that had gone bald.

> Man has only his head that is bald; but the eagle becomes bald all over its body, and when it grows old it loses all its feathers, including those of its wings.

In Gregory's opinion, the decay of imperial power, of *Romania*, and of civilization all betokened that the world was rapidly drawing to its end. The Kingdom of Heaven was at hand. . . . Gregory became a monk. He founded six monasteries on the estates he had inherited in Sicily, and himself entered a sev-

*The word "pope" is a translation of *papa*, father. In the first four centuries bishops were commonly known as *papa*, and in Greece the word is used to this day in addressing an ordinary priest. The word began to be used as the special designation of the Bishop of Rome in the fifth century.—Eds.

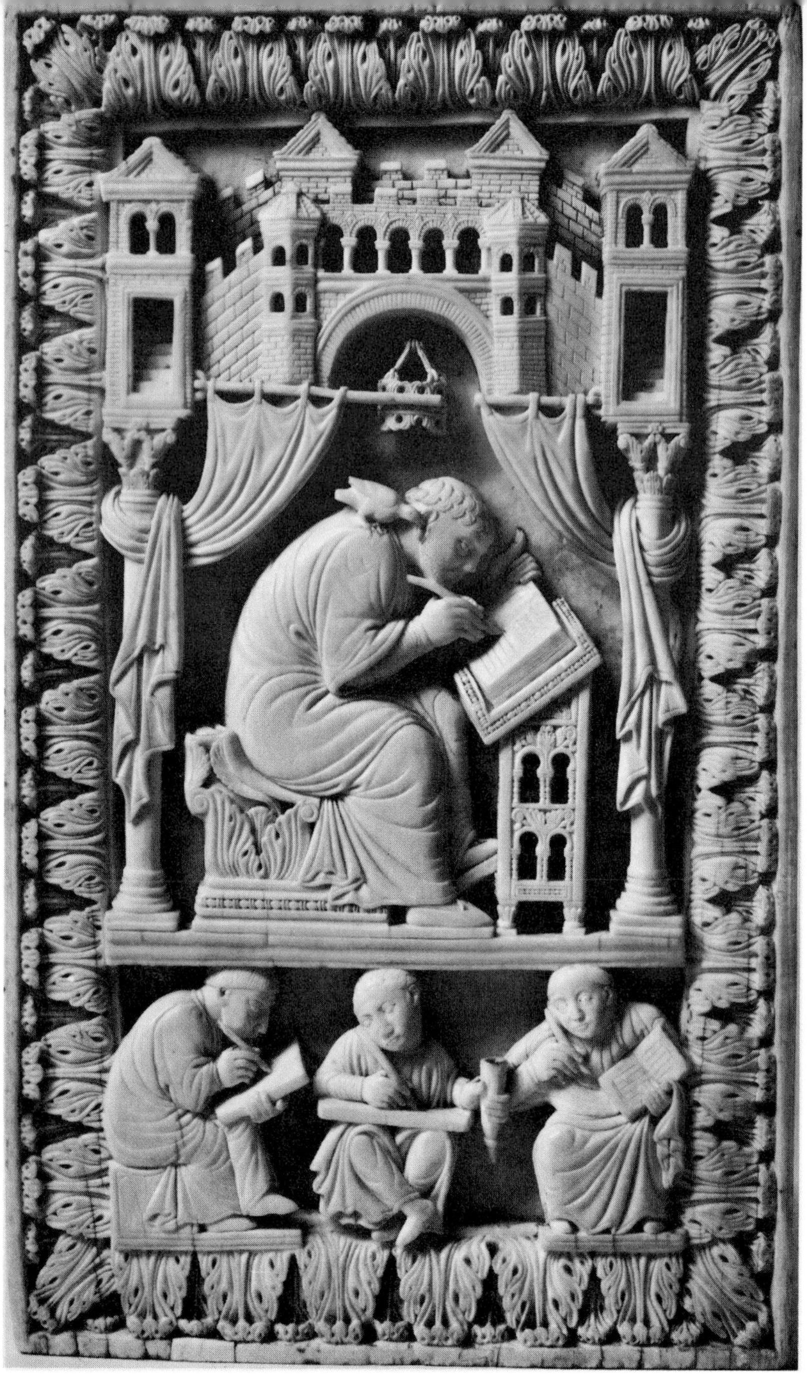

Gregory the Great is inspired by the Holy Spirit depicted as a dove perched upon his shoulder. Ivory relief.

enth, dedicated to St. Andrew, which he had founded in his father's house on the *Clivus Scauri* in Rome. What was important, however, was that he became a monk of the Benedictine type. He was, as Professor Knowles puts it, 'saturated with the traditions of St. Benedict's life', and accepted his ruling-principles wholeheartedly; the monk was to be humble, obedient, and a member of a community—'he must know that he has henceforth no power even over his own body'. . . .

In 590 Pope Pelagius II died and the Roman people elected Gregory to succeed him, though he was not consecrated till the imperial consent had been received from Constantinople. He was at first unwilling to accept the office, and attempted to escape from the city, but in the *Regula Pastoralis* he later made it clear that he would have considered that he had failed in his duty to God if he had refused consecration, even for the sake of the contemplative life. He scorned the ambition that sought high office for its own sake, but declared that humility was not genuine when it resisted the command of God. He accepted the Papacy and endeavoured to serve God's Church with the same obedience that he would have given to his abbot as a monk. His official title was *servus servorum Dei,* servant of the servants of God.

His attitude to his office is best seen in his attitude to the Church's property, St. Peter's patrimony. He supervised its administration with care and efficiency, but considered that he held the wealth derived from it in trust for the whole community. When a beggar died of hunger in the streets of Rome, Gregory held himself responsible and suspended himself from his priestly functions. He is even said to have had a register drawn up to show the names of persons of every age, sex, and profession who were in receipt of regular allowances from his treasury. Previously such distributions of bread or money had been the responsibility of the emperor. But the imperial administration had broken down, and the need was great. Just as an abbot ruled his monastery in all things both spiritual and temporal, so Gregory cared for all the needs of the people of Rome, who were his flock. He was able to do so, because the patrimony of St. Peter was large and included many estates in Sicily, which was still at peace, not having been invaded by the Lombards.

The wealth of the Church was, indeed, increasing. In many cities, landowners who found it impossible to pay their taxes surrendered their land to the bishop. In this way the bishops, whose bishoprics were in any case coincident with the administrative districts of the 'cities', found themselves shouldering the responsibilities of the city's *curia* [municipal council]; they might be responsible for the maintenance of the town walls, the aqueducts, or other public buildings. Gregory himself found that he was even acting as the emperor's banker, advancing the wages for the imperial troops, or the money to be paid as tribute to the Lombards. As the administration of the Empire broke down, so the Church stepped in to save as much as could be saved of *Romania*. . . .

## II

Amongst the most immediate of the secular responsibilities that fell on Gregory was the defence of Rome. The emperor was in Constantinople and could spare no reinforcements, and the exarch was preoccupied with the defence of Ravenna. In moments of emergency Gregory found it necessary not only to protest when the exarch moved troops away from Rome, but to appoint military commanders. When all else failed, he would write to the local bishop asking him to see that the citizens were compelled to do their turns of guard-duty on the walls of the town. Nobody thought that he was thereby usurping the imperial prerogative. His actions were not questioned until he began to formulate a policy that was contrary to that of the emperor. This was that peace would have to be made with the Lombards. There was no doubt that he would have preferred to continue the fight if there had been any chance of success. But if the emperor was unable to send reinforcements, success was impossible. The only way he had been able to save Rome from being sacked had been by entering into negotiations with the Lombard Duke of Spoleto whom he described as 'the unspeakable Ariulf'. When the emperor blamed him for his 'simplicity' in pursuing such a policy, Gregory replied in a letter that was full of indignation:

> My pious lord may think all the evil he wants of me, provided that, for the sake of the usefulness of the Republic and for the cause of Italy's deliverance, he will not listen to every one who comes along, but will deign to believe *facts* rather than *words*.

Roman, imperialist, and conservative though he was, Gregory saw that he was living in a new world. It was no use lamenting the past. It was no use, even, to retreat to a monastery if it was only to shut one's eyes to what was happening in the world. The barbarians had come to stay. The Roman Empire in the West, at any rate in the form in which Gregory knew it, was in the last stages of decrepitude. If the Pope, as St. Peter's successor, was to guard the interests of the Church, and to see that the Faith survived in its purity, it was obviously his duty to convert the barbarians. They might be 'unspeakable' and unclean; they might represent everything that was repugnant to the conception of *Romania;* but Gregory accepted with due humility the fact that God must have willed that these barbarians should overcome the Empire, and that it was his duty as Pope to watch over their Faith.

This was no easy matter. Previously the Church had relied to a very large extent on the assistance of the imperial government for the summoning of Church councils and the enforcing of their decisions. . . . But at the end of the sixth century there were few parts of the West in which the imperial authorities were capable of helping the Church. . . . What Gregory did was to make use of the officials who were charged with the administration of the lands of St. Peter's patrimony. . . . As they were scattered all over Italy and Sicily it was only natural for the Pope to use them as his agents in all matters. They were all directly under his control, and he frequently wrote to them as often as once a month. They kept him informed on all matters that concerned the Church, and consequently Gregory's supervision of the Church in Italy was effective.

. . . It was no longer sufficient for the Papacy to claim the 'primacy' of the Church; it had to govern it, and to control even the remotest parts of the Church by its own central authority. The first steps towards such a central control were taken by Gregory in the organization of his mission to England. His original plan had been to buy young English slaves, educate them in the monasteries of

Gaul, and then send them back to England to convert their heathen countrymen. But in the event he abandoned this plan in favour of another which ensured direct papal control of the mission. The man he sent out, Augustine, was not English, knew nothing of the country, and could not speak a word of the language. He had very few, if any, of the conventional qualities of a missionary, but he was a monk, and what was more, he was Gregory's monk from his own monastery. He had the virtue of obedience. He obeyed the instructions that the Pope had given him and, when confronted with unforseen difficulties, wrote back to Rome for further advice, his questions, and Gregory's answers, being preserved in Bede's *Ecclesiastical History.* The conversion of the English was therefore Gregory's own achievement, even though he worked through the agency of Augustine. . . .

'I know of no bishop', wrote Gregory, 'who is not subject to the Apostolic See when a fault has been committed.' He felt himself to be the head of the Church and responsible for its good order. None the less, he was sufficiently conservative to respect the rights of other bishops, and even of the other patriarchs. He firmly rejected the title of 'universal bishop', not only because it had been usurped by the Bishop of Constantinople, but also because he thought that any bishop who desired such a title must be 'the forerunner of Antichrist'.

> I do not wish [he wrote] for an honour that would be conferred upon me at the expense of the honour of my brothers [i.e. other bishops]. My honour is that of the universal Church. It is also the solid authority of my brothers. I am honoured when the honour due to my brothers is refused to none of them. If Your Holiness treats me as *papa universalis,* you disqualify your own rank as bishop, by assuming that I am universal.

It is difficult to say which is the more impressive, the evident modesty of the words or the grandeur of the central assumption.

There is, of course, much more that could be said of Gregory's pontificate, and of his relations with the great sees of the East and the other churches of the West. But it is hoped that enough has been said to show why he was regarded as the very type of what a Pope should be. It was not simply that he was a particularly virtuous and religious man, nor simply that he was renowned throughout the Middle Ages as the author of the *Regula Pastoralis* which was the standard handbook on the duties of a bishop to his flock. What made him so specially great was that, at a time when the imperial power was crumbling and when the world seemed to be coming to an end, Gregory undertook the task of saving the Church. But for him it might easily have decayed like the Empire: in Italy it might have become nothing more than a landed interest, and in the kingdom of the Franks a royal possession. Gregory reformed it, organized it, and gave it an independent existence. He translated the theory of papal *principatus* into the practical terms of papal supremacy. Even if the Moslems had not obliterated the rival churches of Alexandria and Antioch, the Papacy would almost certainly have enjoyed the position which it subsequently held in Christendom, for it alone had given to the Church an organization that was independent of the Empire or any other lay power. That was the achievement of Gregory the Great.

# The Conversion of England

The Angles, Jutes, and Saxons from Northern Germany invaded the British isle after it had been abandoned by Roman forces in the fifth century. The barbarians slaughtered most of the native British population and established a number of little pagan kingdoms. About a hundred and fifty years later, in 597, Pope Gregory I sent the monk Augustine (not to be confused with the author of the *City of God,* who died in 430) to bring the Anglo-Saxons to the Christian faith. The story of Augustine's missionary activities was paralleled by similar efforts in Holland and Germany. From J. H. Robinson, *Readings in European History* (Boston, 1904) I, pp. 97–101.

## A. POPE GREGORY SENDS AUGUSTINE TO CONVERT THE ANGLO-SAXONS

In the year of our Lord 582, Maurice, the fifty-fourth emperor from Augustus, ascended the throne and reigned twenty-one years. In the tenth year of his reign, Gregory, a man renowned for learning and behavior, was promoted to the apostolic see of Rome, and presided over it thirteen years, six months, and ten days. He being moved by divine inspiration, about the one hundred and fiftieth year after the coming of the English into Britain, sent the servant of God, Augustine, and with him several other monks who feared the Lord, to preach the word of God to the English nation. . . .

[Augustine, with his companions, arrived in Britain.]

Some days later the king came into the island and, sitting in the open air, ordered Augustine and his companions to be brought into his presence. For he had taken precaution that they should not come to him in any house, lest, according to an ancient superstition, if they practiced any magical arts they might impose upon him, and so get the better of him. But they came furnished with divine, not with magic, power, bearing a silver cross for their banner, and the image of our Lord and Saviour painted on a board; and singing the litany, they offered up their prayers to the Lord for the eternal salvation both of themselves and of those to whom they came. . . .

As soon as they entered the dwelling place assigned them, they began to imitate the course of life practiced in the primitive church: applying themselves to frequent prayer, watching, and fasting; preaching the word of life to as many as they could; despising all worldly things, as not belonging to them; receiving only their necessary food from those they taught; living themselves in all respects conformably to what they prescribed to others, and being always disposed to suffer any adversity, and even to die for that truth which they preached. In short, several believed and were baptized, admiring the simplicity of their innocent life and the sweetness of their heavenly doctrine.

There was on the east side of the city a church dedicated to St. Martin, built whilst the Romans were still in the island, wherein the queen, who, as has been said before, was a Christian, used to pray. In this they first began to meet, to sing, to pray, to say mass, to preach, and to baptize, till the king, being converted to the faith, allowed them to preach openly and to build or repair churches in all places.

When he among the rest, induced by the unspotted life of these holy men and their delightful promises, which, by many miracles, they proved to be most certain, believed and was baptized, greater numbers began daily to flock together to hear the word and, forsaking their heathen rites, to associate themselves, by believing, to the unity of the Church of Christ.

## B. POPE GREGORY'S INSTRUCTIONS TO THE MISSIONARIES IN ENGLAND

When Almighty God shall bring you to the most reverend Bishop Augustine, our brother, tell him what I have, after mature deliberation on the affairs of the English, determined upon, namely, that the temples of the idols in that nation ought not to be destroyed; let holy water be made and sprinkled in the said temples; let altars be erected, and relics placed. For if those temples are well built, it is requisite that they be converted from the worship of devils to the service of the true God; that the nation, seeing that their temples are not destroyed, may remove error from their hearts and, knowing and adoring the true God, may . . . resort to the places to which they have been accustomed.

And because they have been used to slaughter many oxen in the sacrifices to devils, some solemnity must be substituted for them on this account, as, for instance, that on the day of the dedication, or of the nativities of the holy martyrs whose relics are there deposited, they may build themselves huts of the boughs of trees about those churches which have been turned to that use from temples, and celebrate the solemnity with religious feasting, no more offering beasts to the devil, but killing cattle to the praise of God in their eating, and returning thanks to the Giver of all things for their sustenance; to the end that, whilst some outward gratifications are permitted them, they may the more easily consent to the inward consolations of the grace of God.

For there is no doubt that it is impossible to efface everything at once from their obdurate minds, because he who endeavors to ascend to the highest place rises by degrees or steps and not by leaps. Thus the Lord made himself known to the people of Israel in Egypt; and yet he allowed them to use the sacrifices which they were wont to offer to the devil in his own worship, commanding them in his sacrifice to kill beasts to the end that, changing their hearts, they might lay aside one part of the sacrifice, whilst they retained another; that whilst they offered the same beasts which they were wont to offer, they should offer them to God, and not to idols, and thus they would no longer be the same sacrifices.

TOPIC 20

# BYZANTIUM AND THE CAROLINGIAN WEST

The Roman Empire continued in the East for a thousand years after the deposition of the last Western emperor. Not until 1453 were the remaining territories about the capital city of Constantinople conquered by the Ottoman Turks. Roman in name, the Empire was Greek in spirit and is often referred to as Byzantium, the original Greek name for the city of Constantine. In the West division and anarchy were temporarily halted by the rise of the powerful Frankish Carolingian family, the greatest of whom, Charlemagne, resurrected the Western Empire in 800. The readings compare the state of civilization in the East and West in the ninth and tenth centuries.

Reading 98

## Robert Wolff: The Byzantine Empire

The greatest beneficiary of the break-up of the Roman Empire was Byzantium. From the capital at Constantinople the Eastern emperor looked down upon both Latin peoples and Germanic tribes in the West. As Christians the Easterners claimed the most direct and continuous association with the centers of the apostolic Church; as Greeks the most direct ties to the ancient Hellenic and Hellenistic civilizations. Professor Robert Wolff, a noted Byzantinist and professor of history at Harvard University, here examines the civilization which maintained its authority while the West struggled through a period of transition. Crane Brinton, John B. Christopher, and Robert Lee Wolff, *A History of Civilization, Volume One: Prehistory to 1715,* 2nd ed., © 1960. Reprinted by permission of Prentice-Hall, Inc., Englewood Cliffs, New Jersey.

Quite apart from its cultural achievements, . . . Byzantium's military and economic achievements are so striking that any student of civilization needs to appreciate them. After the barbarian invasions of the fourth and fifth centuries, which shattered imperial unity in the West, Europe was repeatedly threatened by other waves of invaders moving north and west from Asia. So the Persians in the seventh century, the Arabs from the seventh century on, and the Turks beginning in the eleventh century, beat against the Byzantine frontiers in an effort to break into Europe.

The Byzantine Empire was often shaken by these blows: the eastern Roman provinces of Syria and Egypt were lost forever in the seventh century as a result of the impact of Persians and Arabs. And western Europe was not entirely spared the effects of these invasions. The Arab expansion brought waves of Moslems into Sicily and southern Italy, and across the Straits of Gibraltar into Spain, whence a small force even challenged the Franks at Tours in 732. But Charles Martel's victory at Tours was a far less significant achievement in checking the Moslem tide at high-water mark than the victory of the Byzantine Emperor Leo III the Isaurian, who had repelled a major Arab attack on Byzantium itself in 717, fifteen years before.

We ought to ask: What might have been the fate of western Europe had not the Byzantines succeeded, with great losses and at great expense, in containing these Persian and Arab and Turkish attacks, down to the end of the eleventh century? During this entire period the western Europeans might well have proved unable to take care of themselves. The answer is clear: Had it not been for Byzantium, we might all be Moslems.

Byzantium thus served as a buffer that absorbed the heaviest shock of eastern invasions and cushioned the West against them. . . .

### ECONOMIC PROSPERITY

Good armies and navies and shrewd diplomacy are expensive, and depend directly upon the economic strength of the state that creates and uses them. Byzantium was enormously rich. In fact, the city was a great center of trade, to which came vessels from every

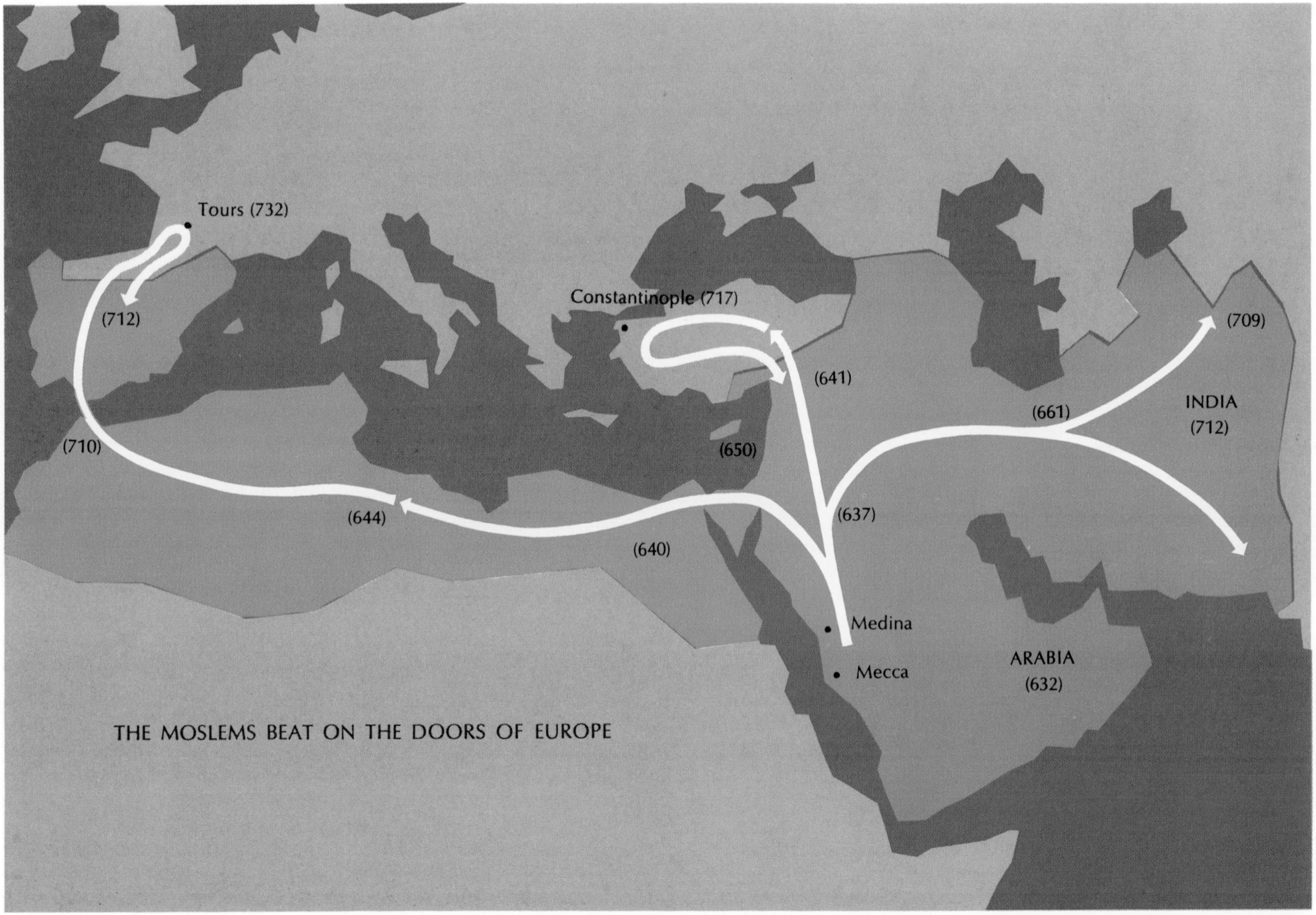


Moslem expansion into Europe was stopped for centuries by defeat at Constantinople and in Central France in the eighth century.

quarter of the compass. From the countries around the shore of the Black Sea came furs and hides, grain, slate, and wine, and slaves from the Caucasus. From India, Ceylon, Syria, and Arabia came spices, precious stones, and silk; from Africa, slaves and ivory; from the West, especially Italy, merchants eager to buy the products sold in Constantinople, often the products of the imperial industries.

The Byzantine emperors themselves were able for a time to maintain a monopoly of the manufacture and sale of silk textiles, purple dye, and gold embroidery, which were not then merely luxuries, but absolute necessities for the dignitaries of church and state in the West as in the East. For long a closely guarded secret of the Persians, silk manufacture came to Byzantium in the middle of the sixth century, when two monks explained to the emperor that the mysterious cloth was the product of silkworms. Later—so the story goes—bribed by the promise of a great reward, they actually brought back silkworms' eggs hidden in a hollow cane. They taught the emperor that the worms must be fed mulberry leaves; great plantations of mulberries were established, especially in Syria; and a mighty enterprise was under way.

The power that was derived from the control over the manufacture and sale of silk has rightly been compared with modern controls over strategic materials like coal, oil, and iron. But it was not only the imperial treasury that profited: the rich were able to embellish their persons and their homes; many middle-class merchants and craftsmen found a livelihood in the industry; and the flow of revenue into the imperial treasuries made it possible for the emperors to tax the lower classes less than would otherwise have been necessary for national defense and other official expenses. An elaborate system of control over manufacture (which was in the hands of carefully regulated imperial guilds) and over sales (which were permitted only in official salesrooms) safely secured the monopoly down to the eleventh century.

Besides controlling silk, the emperor forbade the export of gold, a measure obviously designed to prevent the depletion of reserves. In fact, one of the unmistakable signs of enduring Byzantine prosperity during the whole period from the fourth to the eleventh century is the Byzantine gold coinage. The *nomisma,* as the Byzantine gold coin was called, was standard all over the Mediterranean and even in the East. Until the late eleventh century it was almost never debased, and even then only under the impact of crisis brought about by civil strife and foreign invasion, and only gradually. But for eight hundred years this money was stable.

The wealth of Byzantium was noticed and envied by all visitors to the Empire, especially by visitors from the West, whose own largely rural society and meager way of life contrasted so strikingly with the urban glitter and sophistication of the imperial capital. This was not merely a matter of splendid silken garments embroidered with gold, of palaces and churches aglow with mosaics and richly carved columns of semi-precious stones imported at great expense from distant lands, of treasures of jewelry and gold and ivory worn by the wealthy citizens and displayed in their houses. The impression created by these superficial externals was dazzling indeed. But beneath the splendor and the show lay the hard economic realities that preserved the state for centuries. These were a thriving commerce and industry and a substantial revenue. . . .

## THE EMPEROR

Deeply conscious of the ties that bound them to Rome, the Byzantine emperors believed in the divine mission of their empire. After Constantine had become a Christian, the Christian empire only slightly modified the old pagan tradition of the god-emperor. The emperor was no longer God, but he was ordained of God to rule, and his power was divine. There was but one God in heaven, so there could be but one emperor on earth. Though there were still nations left to conquer, it was the destiny of the Roman Empire to conquer them. . . .

Once chosen, the Byzantine emperor received a collar and was raised aloft on a shield as a sign of army approval. This ceremony made him *imperator,* or commander in chief. By the mid-fifth century he was also formally crowned by the highest dignitary of the Church, the patriarch. This was a Christian ceremony, which, by the seventh century, took place in Santa Sophia. At his coronation the emperor swore to defend the Christian faith. Besides the crown, the insignia of empire included a pair of high purple boots and a purple robe. . . .

The emperor was an absolute ruler. Though now only the servant of the Christian God, he was still hedged by the old divinity. God bestowed his position upon him; God lent victory to his arms. Since the state was founded on the favor of heaven, there could be no need for change. Although the individual autocrat might be overthrown by the conspiracy of a rival, autocracy as such was never challenged. And of course these divinely awarded powers entailed immense earthly responsibilities: the "Imperial power," says an eighth-century text, "is legal authority established for the good of all subjects. When it strikes a blow, it is not through favoritism; but like the referee in a fight, it awards to each man the recompense he deserves." . . .

The emperor was bound by an elaborate and rigid code of etiquette that governed every movement he made every day of the year. So complex were the rules of his life that entire treatises were written to describe them. Silence in his presence was the rule. He spoke and gave his commands through simple, brief, and established formulas. When he gave gifts, his subjects hid their hands beneath their cloaks, a Persian ritual gesture implying that the touch of a mere human hand would soil his. As Liudprand reported, a person admitted to audience with the emperor was required to approach him with an official holding him by the arm on either side. When he came near to the divine presence, the suppliant fell on his face and made obeisance. On public occasions the emperor was acclaimed in song, to the sound of silver trumpets.

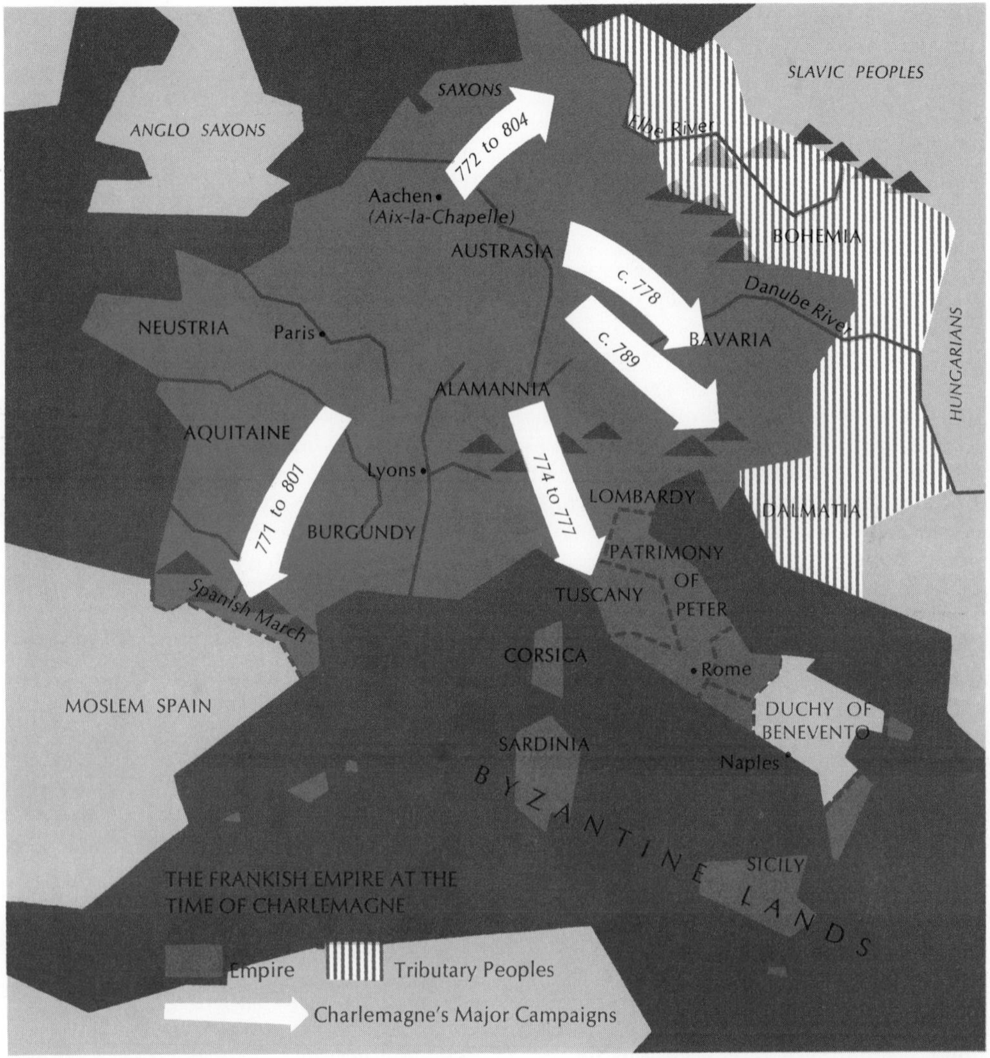


# Europe in the Ninth and Tenth Centuries



## THE EMPIRE OF CHARLEMAGNE, A.D. 800

Among the Franks, in what is now northern France and the German Rhineland, there had meanwhile arisen a line of capable rulers of whom the greatest was Charlemagne, [768–814]. The Frankish kings made it their policy to cooperate with the pope. The pope needed a protector against depredations by his barbarian neighbors, and against the political claims of the Byzantine Empire upon the city of Rome. The Frankish kings, in return for protection thus offered, won papal support to their side. This made it easier for them to control their own bishops, who were more often seen on horseback than in the episcopal chair, and was of use in pacifying their own domains and in wars of conquest against the heathen. In the year 800, in Rome, the pope crowned Charlemagne as Emperor of the West. Frankish king and Roman bishop both believed that if only the Roman Empire could be restored peace and order might once more reign. Church and Empire, the spirit and the state, were to be as two mighty swords employed in the same holy cause.

Charlemagne crossed the Pyrenees and won back the northeastern corner of Spain to Christian rule. He overthrew and subordinated the barbarian kings who had set themselves up in Italy. He sent forces down the Danube, penetrated into Bohemia, and proceeded against some of the still heathern Germans (the Saxons) who lived along the river Elbe, and whom he either massacred or converted to Christianity. All these regions he brought within his new empire. Except for England and Ireland, which remained outside, the borders of his empire were coextensive with those of the Latin Christian world.

Once more, to a degree, the West was united. But a momentous change had occurred. Its capital was now not Rome, and did not lie in the ancient world of the Mediterranean. Its capital was at Aix-la-Chapelle, or Aachen, near the mouth of the Rhine. Its ruler, Charlemagne, was a German of an ethnical group which ancient civilization had left outside. Its people were Germans, French, and Italians, or the ancestors from whom these nationalities were to be developed. In the Greco-Roman world the north had always been at best provincial. Now the north became a center in its own right. Charlemagne dispatched embassies to the emperor at Constantinople, and to Harun al-Rashid, the great caliph at Bagdad. In intellectual matters, too, the north now became a capital. Centuries of violence and confusion had left ignorance very widespread. Charlemagne himself, though he understood Latin, could barely read and never learned to write. He used his authority to revive the all but forgotten ancient learning and to spread education at least among the clergy. To his palace school came scholars from England, Germany, France, Italy, Spain. They wrote and spoke Latin, the only Western language in which any complicated ideas could at the time be expressed. Disintegrating ancient manuscripts were copied, and then again copied to assure a more abundant supply for study—always by hand, but in a more rapid script than had before been used, the so-called Carolingian minuscule, from which come the small letters of the modern western alphabet, only the capitals being Roman. Commerce also, which had virtually disappeared, Charlemagne undertook to foster. He created a new and more reliable coinage, which was based on silver, the gold coins of the Roman Empire having long since vanished. A pound of silver was divided into 20 *solidi* and 240 pennies. This scheme of values, though long used in many parts of Europe, survives today only in the country that remained outside Charlemagne's empire, namely England, in its pound sterling of 20 shillings each containing twelve pence. . . .

Meanwhile West and East continued to drift apart. The refusal of Greek patriarchs at Constantinople to recognize the claims to primacy of the bishop of Rome, whom they regarded as a kind of western barbarian, and the refusal of the Roman pontiff to acknowledge the political pretensions of the Byzantine empire, led to the Great Schism of East and West. This schism, after developing for three centuries, became definite in 1054. It divided the Christian world into the Latin or Roman Catholic and the Greek Orthodox Churches. It was from Constantinople that Christianity reached the peoples of Russia. The Russians, like the Balkan peoples, remained out of contact with the West during the centuries when spiritual and intellectual contacts were carried through the clergy. They believed, indeed, that the Latin West was evil, heretical, contumacious, and unholy. The Latin West, at the same time, by the schism, cut one more of its ties with antiquity, and emerged the more clearly as an independent center of its own civilization.

By the year 1000, or soon thereafter, the entity that we call Europe had been brought into existence. From the turbulence that followed the collapse of the Greco-Roman civilization had issued the peoples and the countries of modern Europe. A kingdom of France was in being, adjoining the great ill-defined bulk of Germany to the east. There were small Christian kingdoms in northern Spain and a number of city-states in the Italian peninsula. In the north there were now a kingdom of England and a kingdom of Scotland, and Denmark, Norway, and Sweden had taken form. In the east rose the three great kingdoms of Poland, Bohemia, and Hungary, the first two predominantly Slavic, Hungary predominantly Magyar, but all Latin and Catholic in culture and religion, and western in orientation. The east Slavs, or Russians, and the Slavs and other peoples of the Balkan peninsula, also formed kingdoms of their own. Their way was diverging from the West. Christianized by Byzantine missionaries, they were Greek and Orthodox in culture and religion, and oriented towards Constantinople.

The civilization of the West, in the year 1000, was still not much to boast of in the more polished circles of Byzantium or Bagdad. It might still seem that the West would suffer more than the East from their separation. But the West began at this time to experience a remarkable activity, ushering in the European civilization of the High Middle Ages.

# Einhard Writes about the Life and Reign of Charlemagne

The Frankish scholar Einhard (c. 775–840) used royal records and his own recollections to write this penetrating biography of the great Charles. The historic setting for Charlemagne's accomplishments and details on Einhard's own life are provided by the late Sidney Painter, a respected medievalist, in a foreword to the *Life*. From Einhard, *The Life of Charlemagne* (Ann Arbor: University of Michigan Press, 1960), pp. 5–10, 30–32, 50–58.

## I

### Foreword to Einhard's Life of Charlemagne

Charlemagne or Charles the Great who is counted as Charles I in the conventional lists of kings of France was one of the truly imposing figures of history. At the height of his power he ruled all the Christian lands of Western Europe except the British Isles and southern Italy and Sicily under the titles of king of the Franks and the Lombards and Roman emperor. He held this vast realm in a grip of iron and cowed its foes on every frontier. He also initiated and encouraged a revival of learning which is sometimes called the Carolingian Renaissance. While this was a brief flash of light in a dark age, it left sparks which made the succeeding period less gloomy and supplied the beginnings of a permanent revival in the twelfth century.

In order to understand the magnitude of Charlemagne's achievement it is necessary to know something of the world into which he was born. In the fifth and sixth centuries after Christ, Germanic invaders overran the western provinces of the Roman Empire. In the year 700 most of England was ruled by a number of Anglo-Saxon kings, Spain by Visigothic monarchs, and northern and central Italy by the kings of the Lombards. The lands covered today by France and Belgium and the part of Germany known in the Middle Ages as Franconia formed the Frankish state ruled by the kings of the Merovingian line. In 711 Moslems from North Africa overwhelmed the Visigothic kingdom and occupied Spain. Along the eastern frontier of the Frankish state were such Germanic peoples as the Saxons and Bavarians. The plains of the Danube Valley were occupied by a Turkish people called Avars. Southern Italy, Sicily, and a few isolated districts such as Rome and Ravenna recognized the sovereignty of the Byzantine emperor in Constantinople, the successor to the Roman emperors.

Roman civilization had gradually disappeared under the rule of the Germanic kings. Except for Ireland where a few monks still cherished the ancient learning and Northumbria where both Irish and Roman missionaries had fostered a brief revival, Western Europe knew little of bare literacy and practically nothing of real learning. In the Frankish state even the bishops were barely literate.

The economic system of the Roman Empire had also decayed. The Germanic kings had no interest in keeping up roads and bridges and less in policing the trade routes. Overland trade had largely disappeared. The Mediterranean which had formed the heart of the Roman system of communications was harassed by Moslem fleets. As trade declined, the circulation of money grew less and less. By 700 Western Europe was essentially a region of localized agricultural economy. The farmer raised his own raw material and made the crude goods his family needed. The nobles lived on the rents collected from men who farmed their land.

In 700 the Merovingian state was weak and disorganized. The kings were mere figureheads, and the land was ruled by cliques of nobles who fought each other fiercely for power. Its armies were half-armed mobs of little effectiveness in war. While the realm was officially Christian and kings and nobles made generous gifts to churches and monasteries, the clergy were hard to distinguish in life and thought from the secular lords. Christian ethics had as yet had little effect on the ways of the Germans.

Charlemagne's grandfather, Charles Martel, was the head of a victorious noble group. As mayor of the palace, or as he usually called himself *dux* or leader of the Franks, he organized an effective military force by seizing church lands and using them to support soldiers who would serve him as heavily armed cavalry. He repulsed a Moslem invasion and conquered part of Saxony. His successor, Pepin, reorganized the Frankish church with the aid of the great Anglo-Saxon missionary, St. Boniface of Crediton. Pepin removed the last Merovingian king and was himself crowned king, first by St. Boniface and later by Pope Stephen. He drove the Lombards from the vicinity of Rome and gave the government of that region to the pope. This was the origin of the later states of the Church.

Einhard's biography will tell you what Charlemagne accomplished, but it is important to remember the difficulties he faced which Einhard does not mention because he took them for granted. Charlemagne had no revenue in money. He and his court lived on the produce of the royal estates. He supported his officials and his cavalry by giving them land and the labor to farm it. The rest of his army was a general levy of infantry from his subjects. How he succeeded in mustering large armies at a distant frontier and supplying them during long and strenuous campaigns is almost incomprehensible. Just as difficult to understand is how he procured the obedience of his officials scattered over his vast realm. The only possible answer seems to be that he was a man of amazing ability and force of character. We do not need Einhard to show us that Charlemagne was a great man—the chronicles of his reign and the official documents which are still preserved show that. But Einhard gives us a picture of the man and his way of life.

Einhard was born in the ancient Frankish homeland in the valley of the River Main about 775. He was brought up in the monastery of Fulda, which was the chief center of learning in the Frankish lands. In 791 or 792 his abbot persuaded Charlemagne to take him into his court. Early in his reign Charlemagne had gathered men of learning about him and established a palace school headed by a Northumbrian scholar named Alcuin. Soon after Einhard's arrival Alcuin retired to a monastery near Tours. When in 799 Charlemagne asked Alcuin a question about the classics, he told him to consult Einhard. Although Einhard clearly was on intimate terms with Charlemagne and carried out a number of errands for him on affairs of state, he never achieved high office during his reign. But after Charlemagne's death in 814 his son and successor Louis the Pious made Einhard his private secretary and loaded him with honors and benefices. He retired from court in 828, when the quarrels between Louis and his sons grew acute, and lived in a quiet retreat until 840. . . .

This bronze statue of Charlemagne on horseback is said to be of the ninth century.

## II

### Einhard: Life of Charlemagne

Charles was large and strong, and of lofty stature, though not disproportionately tall (his height is well known to have been seven times the length of his foot); the upper part of his head was round, his eyes very large and animated, nose a little long, hair fair, and face laughing and merry. Thus his appearance was always stately and dignified, whether he was standing or sitting; although his neck was thick and somewhat short, and his belly rather prominent; but the symmetry of the rest of his body concealed these defects. His gait was firm, his whole carriage manly, and his voice clear, but not so strong as his size led one to expect. His health was excellent, except during the four years preceding his death, when he was subject to frequent fevers; at the last he even limped a little with one foot. Even in those years he consulted rather his own inclinations than the advice of physicians, who were almost hateful to him, because they wanted him to give up roasts, to which he was accustomed, and to eat boiled meat instead. In accordance with the national custom, he took frequent exercise on horseback and in the chase, accomplishments in which scarcely any people in the world can equal the Franks. He enjoyed the exhalations from natural warm springs, and often practiced swimming, in which he was such an adept that none could surpass him; and hence it was that he built his palace at Aix-la-Chapelle, and lived there . . . during his latter years until his death. He used not only to invite his sons to his bath, but his nobles and friends, and now and then a troop of his retinue or body guard, so that a hundred or more persons sometimes bathed with him.

He used to wear the national, that is to say, the Frank, dress—next to his skin, linen breeches, and above these a tunic fringed with silk; while hose fastened by bands covered his lower limbs, and shoes his feet, and he protected his shoulders and chest in winter by a close-fitting coat of otter or marten skins. Over all he flung a blue cloak, and he always had a sword girt about him, usually one with a gold or silver hilt and belt; he sometimes carried a jeweled sword, but only on great feast days or at the reception of ambassadors from foreign nations. . . .

Charles was temperate in eating, and particularly so in drinking, for he abominated drunkenness in anybody, much more in himself and those of his household; but he could not easily abstain from food, and often complained that fasts injured his health. He very rarely gave entertainments, only on great feast days, and then to large numbers of people. His meals ordinarily consisted of four courses, not counting the roast, which his huntsmen used to bring in on the spit; he was more fond of this than of any other dish. While at table, he listened to reading or music. The subjects of the readings were the stories and deeds of olden time: he was fond, too, of St. Augustine's books, and especially of the one entitled "The City of God." He was so moderate in the use of wine and all sorts of drink that he rarely allowed himself more than three cups in the course of a meal. In summer, after the midday meal, he would eat some fruit, drain a single cup, put off his clothes and shoes, just as he did for the night, and rest for two or three hours. He was in the habit of awaking and rising from bed four or five times during the night. While he was dressing and putting on his shoes, he not only gave audience to his friends, but if the Count of the Palace told him of any suit in which his judgment was necessary, he had the parties brought before him forthwith, took cognizance of the case, and gave his decision, just as if he were sitting on the judgment seat. This was not the only business that he transacted at this time, but he performed any duty of the day whatever, whether he had to attend to the matter himself, or to give commands concerning it to his officers.

Charles had the gift of ready and fluent speech, and could express whatever he had to say with the utmost clearness. He was not satisfied with command of his native language merely, but gave attention to the study of foreign ones, and in particular was such a master of Latin that he could speak it as well as his native tongue; but he could understand Greek better than he could speak it. He was so eloquent, indeed, that he might have passed for a teacher of eloquence. He most zealously cultivated the liberal arts, held those who taught them in great esteem, and conferred great honors upon them. He took lessons in grammar of the deacon Peter of Pisa, at that time an aged man. Another deacon, Albin of Britain, surnamed Alcuin, a man of Saxon extraction, who was the greatest scholar of the day, was his teacher in other branches of learning. The King spent much time and labor with him studying rhetoric, dialectics, and especially astronomy; he learned to reckon, and used to investigate the motions of the heavenly bodies most curiously, with an intelligent scrutiny. He also tried to write, and used to keep tablets and blanks in bed under his pillow, that at leisure hours he might accustom his hand to form the letters; however, as he did not begin his efforts in due season, but late in life, they met with ill success.

He cherished with the greatest fervor and devotion the principles of the Christian religion, which had been instilled into him from infancy. Hence it was that he built the beautiful basilica at Aix-la-Chapelle, which he adorned with gold and with rails and doors of solid brass. He had the columns and marbles for this structure brought from Rome and Ravenna, for he could not find such as were suitable elsewhere. He was a constant worshipper at this church as long as his health permitted, going morning and evening, even after nightfall, besides attending mass; and he took care that all the services there conducted should be administered with the utmost possible propriety, very often warning the sextons not to let any improper or unclean thing be brought into the building or remain in it. . . .

He cherished the Church of St. Peter the Apostle at Rome above all other holy and sacred places, and heaped its treasury with a vast wealth of gold, silver, and precious stones. He sent great and countless gifts to the popes, and throughout his whole reign the wish that he had nearest at heart was to reestablish the ancient authority of the city of Rome under his care and by his influence, and to defend and protect the Church of St. Peter, and to beautify and enrich it out of his own store above all other churches. Although he held it in such veneration, he only repaired to Rome to pay his vows and made his supplications four times during the whole forty-seven years that he reigned.

When he made his last journey thither, he had also other ends in view. The Romans had inflicted many injuries upon the Pontiff Leo, tearing out his eyes and cutting out his tongue, so that he had been compelled to call upon the King for help. Charles accordingly went to Rome, to set in order the affairs of the Church, which were in great confusion, and passed the whole winter there. It was then that he received the title of Emperor and Augustus, to which he at first had such an aversion that he declared that he would not have set foot in the Church the day that they were conferred, although it was a great feast day, if he could have foreseen the design of the Pope. He bore very patiently with the jealousy which the Roman emperors showed upon his assuming these titles, for they took this step very ill; and by dint of frequent embassies and letters, in which he addressed them as brothers, he made their haughtiness yield to his magnanimity, a quality in which he was unquestionably much their superior.

It was after he had received the imperial name that, finding the laws of his people very defective (the Franks have two sets of laws, very different in many particulars), he determined to add what was wanting, to reconcile the discrepancies, and to correct what was vicious and wrongly cited in them. However, he went no further in this matter than to supplement the laws by a few capitularies, and those imperfect ones; but he caused the unwritten laws of all the tribes that came under his rule to be compiled and reduced to writing. He also had the old rude songs that celebrate the deeds and wars of the ancient kings written out for transmission to posterity. He began a grammar of his native language. He gave the months names in his own tongue, in place of the Latin and barbarous names by which they were formerly known among the Franks. He likewise designated the winds by twelve appropriate names. . . .

## III

No war ever undertaken by the Frank nation was carried on with such persistence and bitterness, or cost so much labor (as did the Saxon war), because the Saxons, like almost all the tribes of Germany, were a fierce people, given to the worship of devils, and hostile to our religion, and did not consider it dishonorable to transgress and violate all law, human and divine. Then there were peculiar circumstances that tended to cause a breach of peace every day. Except in a few places, where large forests or mountain ridges intervened and made the bounds certain, the line between ourselves and the Saxons passed almost in its whole extent through an open country, so that there was no end to the murders, thefts, and arsons on both sides. In this way the Franks became so embittered that they at last resolved to make reprisals no longer, but to come to open war with the Saxons. Accordingly war was begun against them, and was waged for thirty-three successive years with great fury; more, however, to the disadvantage of the Saxons than of the Franks. It could doubtless have been brought to an end sooner, had it not been for the faithlessness of the Saxons. It is hard to say how often they were conquered, and, humbly submitting to the King, promised to do what was enjoined upon them, gave without hesitation the required hostages, and received the officers sent them from the King. They were sometimes so much weakened and reduced that they promised to renounce the worship of devils, and to adopt Christianity, but they were no less ready to violate these terms than prompt to accept them, so that it is impossible to tell which came easier to them to do; scarcely a year passed from the beginning of the war without such changes on their part. But the King did not suffer his high purpose and steadfastness—firm alike in good and evil fortune—to be wearied by any fickleness on their part, or to be turned from the task that he had undertaken; on the contrary, he never allowed their faithless behavior to go unpunished, but either took the field against them in person, or sent his counts with an army to wreak vengeance and exact righteous satisfaction. At last, after conquering and subduing all who had offered resistance, he took ten thousand of those that lived on the banks of the Elbe, and settled them, with their wives and children, in many different bodies here and there in Gaul and Germany. The war that had lasted so many years was at length ended by their acceding to the terms offered by the King; which were renunciation of their national religious customs and the worship of devils, acceptance of the sacraments of the Christian faith and religion, and union with the Franks to form one people. . . .

# Saxon Capitulary

**(782)**

The following record contains some of the peace terms imposed by Charlemagne on his fiercest enemies, the Saxons. They reveal Charles' role in furthering the spread of Christianity eastward into Europe. From D.C. Munro, ed. and trans., *Translations and Reprints from the Original Sources of European History.* (Philadelphia: University of Pennsylvania, n.d.) VI, pp. 2–4.

2. If any one shall have fled to a church for refuge, let no one presume to expel him from the church by violence, but he shall be left in peace until he shall be brought to the judicial assemblage; and on account of the honor due to God and the saints, and the reverence due to the church itself, let his life and all his members be granted to him. Moreover, let him plead his cause as best he can and he shall be judged; and so let him be led to the presence of the lord king, and the latter shall send him where it shall have seemed fitting to his clemency.

3. If any one shall have entered a church by violence and shall have carried off anything in it by force or theft, or shall have burned the church itself, let him be punished by death.

4. If any one, out of contempt for Christianity, shall have despised the holy Lenten fast and shall have eaten flesh, let him be punished by death. But, nevertheless, let it be taken into consideration by a priest, lest perchance any one from necessity has been led to eat flesh. . . .

6. If any one deceived by the devil shall have believed, after the manner of the pagans, that any man or woman is a witch and eats men, and on this account shall have burned the person, or shall have given the person's flesh to others to eat, or shall have eaten it himself, let him be punished by a capital sentence.

7. If any one, in accordance with pagan rites, shall have caused the body of a dead man to be burned and shall have reduced his bones to ashes, let him be punished capitally.

8. If any one of the race of the Saxons hereafter concealed among them shall have wished to hide himself unbaptized, and shall have scorned to come to baptism and shall have wished to remain a pagan, let him be punished by death.

9. If any one shall have sacrificed a man to the devil, and after the manner of the pagans shall have presented him as a victim to the demons, let him be punished by death.

10. If any one shall have formed a conspiracy with the pagans against the Christians, or shall have wished to join with them in opposition to the Christians, let him be punished by death; and whosoever shall have consented to this same fraudulently against the king and the Christian people, let him be punished by death. . . .

17. Likewise, in accordance with the mandate of God, we command that all shall give a tithe of their property and labor to the churches and priests; let the nobles as well as the freemen, and likewise the *liti,* according to that which God shall have given to each Christian, return a part to God.

18. That on the Lord's day no meetings and public judicial assemblages shall be held, unless perchance in a case of great necessity or when war compels it, but all shall go to the church to hear the word of God, and shall be free for prayers or good works. Likewise, also, on the especial festivals they shall devote themselves to God and to the services of the church, and shall refrain from secular assemblies.

19. Likewise, it has been pleasing to insert in these decrees that all infants shall be baptized within a year; and we have decreed this, that if any one shall have despised to bring his infant to baptism within the course of a year, without the advice or permission of the priest, if he is a noble he shall pay 120 *solidi* to the treasury, if a freeman 60. . . .

# Charlemagne's Administration of Justice (802)

The records of Charlemagne's orders to his representatives, the *missi,* provide a key to the powers which the emperor sought to exercise. The following record, a capitulary, or civil ordinance, indicates the kind of law the emperor tried to impose on his kingdom. From Oliver Thatcher and Edgar McNeal, eds., *A Sourcebook for Medieval History* (New York, 1905), pp. 49–51.

Concerning the representatives sent out by the emperor. The most serene and Christian emperor, Karl, chose certain of the ablest and wisest men among his nobles, archbishops, bishops, abbots, and pious laymen, and sent them out through his realm, and through these, his representatives, he gave his people rules to guide them in living justly. He ordered these men to investigate and to report to him any inequality or injustice that might appear in the law as then constituted, that he might undertake its correction. He ordered that no one should dare to change the prescribed law by any trickery or fraud, or to pervert the course of justice for his own ends, as many were wont to do, or to deal unjustly with the churches of God, with the poor or the widows and orphans, or with any Christian man. . . . And he ordered his *missi,* as they desired to win the favor of Almighty God and keep the faith which they had promised him, to inquire diligently into every case where any man complained that he had been dealt with unjustly by anyone, and in the fear of God to render justice to all, to the holy churches of God, to the poor, to widows and orphans, and to the whole people. And if any case arises which they can not correct and bring to justice with the aid of the local counts, they are to make a clear report of it to the emperor. They are not to be hindered in the doing of justice by the flattery or bribery of anyone, by their partiality for their own friends, or by the fear of powerful men. . . . He has also commanded that every man in his kingdom, clergyman or layman, who has already taken the oath of fidelity to him as king, shall now renew it to him as emperor; and that all persons over twelve years of age who have not yet taken the oath shall do so now.



# Liutprand Reports on His Mission to Constantinople

Archbishop Liutprand of Cremona was sent in 968 as envoy to the Byzantine court by Emperor Otto I (ruled 936–973), a successor (in Germany and Italy) to Charlemagne. Liutprand's mission was to arrange a marriage between Otto's son and the Byzantine princess Theophano in the expectation that her dowry would include areas in southern Italy held by the East Romans and desired by Otto. The negotiations assumed that Otto and Byzantine Emperor Nicephorus (ruled 963–969) could deal with one another as equals. Questions of status, territorial jurisdiction, and power complicated the Western envoy's task, as his report from which these excerpts were taken indicates. From "Liutprand's Report of His Mission to Constantinople" in *Select Historical Documents of the Middle Ages,* ed. and trans. Ernest Henderson, London: G. Bell & Sons, Ltd. Reprinted by Bilbo & Tannen, Inc., 1963.

## I

On the day before the Nones of June (June 4) we came to Constantinople, and there, as a mark of disrespect to yourselves, being shamefully received, we were harshly and shamefully treated. We were shut up in a palace large enough, indeed, but uncovered, neither keeping out the cold nor warding off the heat. Armed soldiers were made to stand guard who were to prevent all of my companions from going out and all others from coming in. This dwelling, into which we alone who were shut up could pass, was so far removed from the palace that our breath was taken away when we walked there—we did not ride. . . .

As stated above, we arrived at Constantinople before the Carian gate and waited with our horses, in no slight rain, until the eleventh hour. But at the eleventh hour, [Emperor] Nicephorus, not regarding us, who had been so distinguished by your mercy, as worthy to ride, ordered us to approach; and we were led to the aforesaid hated, waterless, open marble house. But on the eighth day before the Ides (June 6), on the Saturday before Pentecost, I was led into the presence of his brother Leo, the marshal of the court, and chancellor; and there we wearied ourselves out in a great discussion concerning your imperial title. For he called ye not emperor, which is Basileus in his tongue, but, to insult ye, Rex, which is king in ours. And when I told him that the thing signified was the same although the terms used to signify it were different, he said that I had come not to make peace but to excite discord; and thus angrily rising he received your letters, truly insultingly, not in his own hand, but through an interpreter. . . .

## II

On [June 7 the Emperor] ordered me to be his guest. Not thinking me worthy, however, to be placed above any of his nobles, I sat in the fifteenth place from him, and without a tablecloth. Not only did no one of my suite sit at table, but not one of them saw even the house in which I was a guest. During which disgusting and foul meal, which was washed down with oil after the manner of drunkards, and moistened also with a certain other exceedingly bad fish liquor, he asked me many questions concerning your power, many concerning your dominions and your army. And when I had replied to him consequently and truly, "Thou liest," he said, "the soldiers of thy master do not know how to ride, nor do they know how to fight on foot; the size of their shields, the weight of their breast-plates, the length of their swords, and the burden of their helms permits them to fight in neither one way nor the other." Then he added, smiling: "their gluttony also impedes them, for their God is their belly, their courage but wind, their bravery drunkenness. Their fasting means dissolution, their sobriety panic. Nor has thy master a number of fleets on the sea. I alone have a force of navigators; I will attack him with my ships, I will overrun his maritime cities with war, and those which are near the rivers I will reduce to ashes. . . .

When I wished to reply to him and to give forth an answer worthy of his boasting, he did not permit me; but added as if to scoff at me: "You are not Romans but Lombards [i.e. Germans]." When he wished to speak further and was waving his hand to impose silence upon me, I said in anger: "History teaches that the fratricide Romulus, from whom also the Romans are named, was born in adultery; and that he made an asylum for himself in which he received insolvent debtors, fugitive slaves, homicides, and those who were worthy of death for their deeds. And he called to himself a certain number of such and called them Romans. From such nobility those are descended whom you call world-rulers, that is, emperors; whom we, namely the Lombards, Saxons, Franks, Lotharingians, Bavarians, Swabians, Burgundians, so despise, that when angry we can call our enemies nothing more scornful than Roman—comprehending in this one thing, that is in the name of the Romans, whatever there is of contemptibility, of timidity, of avarice, of luxury, of lying: in a word, of viciousness. But because thou dost maintain that we are unwarlike and ignorant of horsemanship, if the sins of the Christians shall merit that thou shalt remain in this hard-heartedness: the next battle will show what you are, and how warlike we." . . .

## III

[Liutprand's mission bogged down amidst mutual recriminations. The envoy tried to leave the city but was detained a virtual prisoner by the Byzantines. In September a new peril threatened.]

On the fifteenth day before the Calends of October (Sept. 17), as much dead as alive, I was summoned to the palace. . . . Their discourse began as follows: "The pallor in thy face, the emaciation of thy whole body, thy long hair, and thy beard—flowing, contrary to thy custom—show that there is immense grief in thy heart because the date of thy return to thy master has been delayed. But, we pray thee, be not angry with the holy emperor nor with us. For we will tell thee the cause of the delay. The Roman pope—if indeed he is to be called pope who has held communion and worked together with the son of Alberic the apostate, with an adulterer and unhallowed person—has sent letters to our most holy emperor, worthy of himself, unworthy of Nicephorus, calling him the emperor 'of the Greeks,' and not 'of the Romans.' Which thing beyond a doubt has been done by the advice of thy master."

"What do I hear?" I said to myself. "I am lost; there is no doubt but what I shall go by the shortest way to the judgment-seat."

"Now listen," they continued, "we know thou wilt say that the pope is the simplest of men; thou wilt say it, and we acknowledge it." "But," I answered, "I do not say it."

"Hear then! The stupid silly pope does not know that the holy Constantine transferred hither the imperial sceptre, the senate, and all the Roman knighthood, and left in Rome nothing but vile minions—fishers, namely, pedlars, bird catchers, bastards, plebeians, slaves. He would never have written this unless at the suggestion of thy king; how dangerous this will be to both—the immediate future, unless they come to their senses, will show." "But the pope," I said, "whose simplicity is his title to renown, thought he was writing this to the honour of the emperor, not to his shame. We know, of course, that Constantine, the Roman emperor, came hither with the Roman knighthood, and founded this city in his name; but because you changed your language, your customs, and

Compare the dress of the Frankish king Charles II, grandson of Charlemagne, shown at his coronation, with the eleventh-century depiction of the Eastern Emperor Nicephorus Botaniates.

your dress, the most holy pope thought that the name of the Romans as well as their dress would displease you. He will show this, if he lives, in his future letters; for they shall be addressed as follows: 'John, the Roman pope, to Nicephorus, Constantine, Basileus, the great and august emperors of the Romans!" And now mark, I beg, why I said this.

Nicephorus came to the throne through perjury and adultery. And since the salvation of all Christians pertains to the care of the Roman pope, let the lord pope send to Nicephorus an epistle altogether like to those [coffins] which without are whited, within are full of dead men's bones; within let him show to him how through perjury and adultery he has obtained the rule over his masters; let him invite Nicephorus to a synod, and, if he do not come, let him hurl the anathema at him. But if the address be not as I have said, it will never reach him.

But to return to the matter in hand. When the princes . . . heard from me the aforesaid promise concerning the address, not suspecting any guile: "We thank thee," they said, "oh bishop. It is worthy of thy wisdom to act as mediator in so great a matter. Thou art the only one of the Franks whom we now love; but when at thy behest they shall have corrected what is evil, they also shall be loved. And when thou hast come to us again thou shalt not go away unrewarded."

I said to myself: "If I ever come back here again, may Nicephorus present me with a crown and a golden sceptre!" . . .

## IV

[The negotiations ended in failure; Liutprand threatened the Byzantines with Otto's anger.]

"If he attempts it," they said, "we will not say Italy, but not even the poor Saxony where he was born—where the inhabitants wear the skins of wild beasts—will protect him. With our money, which gives us our power, we will arouse all the nations against him; and we will break him in pieces like a potter's vessel, which, when broken can not be brought into shape again. And as we imagine that thou, in his honour, hast bought some costly garments, we order thee to bring them before us. What are fit for thee shall be marked with a leaden seal and left to thee; but those which are prohibited to all nations except to us Romans, shall be taken away and the price returned."

When this had been done they took away from me five most costly purple stuffs; considering yourselves and all the Italians, Saxons, Franks, Bavarians, Swabians—nay, all nations—as unworthy to be adorned with such vestments. How unworthy, how shameful it is, that these soft, effeminate, long-sleeved, hooded, veiled, lying, neutral-gendered, idle creatures should go clad in purple, while you heroes—strong men, namely, skilled in war, full of faith and love, reverencing God, full of virtues—may not! What is this, if it be not contumely? "But where," I said, "is the word of your emperor, where the imperial promise? For when I said farewell to him, I asked him up to what price he would permit me to buy vestments in honour of my church. And he said: 'Buy whatever ones and as many as thou dost wish;' and in thus designating the quantity and the quality, he clearly did not make a distinction as if he had said 'excepting this and this.' . . .

"But," they said, "these things are prohibited; and when the emperor spoke as thou sayest he did, he could not imagine that thou would'st even dream of such things as these. For, as we surpass other nations in wealth and wisdom, so also we ought to surpass them in dress; so that those who are singularly endowed with virtue, should have garments unique in beauty."

[Finally, on October 2, his mission unaccomplished, Liutprand was permitted to return to Italy.]

TOPIC 21

# FEUDAL RELATIONS IN AN AGE OF DISORDER

The invasions of the ninth and tenth centuries revealed the political and military weakness of the West and exposed its population to grave physical danger. Attacked by Norsemen, Muslims, Mongols, and Slavs, Western Europe generally turned for its defense to the countryside, where new men capable of defending their territory became the local and regional leaders. These warriors gradually developed ties of mutual loyalty and through these ties kept the West from complete anarchy. The readings examine the factors that led to the development of the feudal system and then attempt to define its nature.

Reading 104

## New Invasions Strengthen Localism

From Robert S. Lopez, *The Birth of Europe*, 

Between the middle of the ninth century and middle of the tenth, Christendom was ravaged throughout by the most brutal enemies it had ever met with since the fall of the Roman Empire in the West. The suffering was the more cruel since the new invaders had neither the means nor even the intention of undertaking the thorough conquest of Europe and thus at least, through servitude, of restoring peace.

### EUROPE TORN TO PIECES

On the islands of the Aegean, at the gates of Rome, even on the Côte d'Azur, Mohammedans set up their numerous robber strongholds and pirate lairs. From the Côte d'Azur they pressed forward as far as the passes of the Swiss Alps, killing or holding to ransom, plundering and destroying everything that fell into their hands. They were indeed the dregs of Arab society, miserable representatives of the great Muslim civilization. As a matter of fact, the central Caliphate of Baghdad had been partitioned at the same time as the Empire of Charlemagne and successor states were racked with quarrels among themselves and internal problems. The only believers left to carry on Islam's Holy War against the Infidels were greedy adventurers, 'evil-doers, rebels, rabble of many nations, panders, contemptible men', to use the obviously biased comments of a learned Baghdadi.

The Scandinavians plundered their way down the Atlantic coast and into the Mediterranean, penetrating into the heart of France both by land and water and landing on the coast of Tuscany to sack the town of Luni, which they mistook for Rome. By way of the Russian rivers they reached the Black Sea and the outskirts of Constantinople. Ever since the Bronze Age they had built up a material civilization of some splendour and originality but they had scarcely improved upon it in the following centuries. Despite their frequent contact with more advanced peoples both east and west of them, they retained some prehistoric customs. They did not show respect for their chiefs, or for their parents. Sometimes they would offer human sacrifices to Odin, their highest god, but again sometimes they refused all worship because . . . 'they believed only in their own strength.' One might add that this strength consisted almost as much of guile as of physical force.

As for the Hungarians whom the Eastern Roman emperors had called up from the steppes to make life harder for their Bulgarian neighbours, they turned on the Danubian plain, but recently evacuated by the Avars, like an embodiment of the horsemen of the Apocalypse. From there they raided as far as Aquitaine and the outskirts of Rome. They may have been less wild than other non-Indo-European peoples who before them had forced their way into Europe, such as the

Huns, the Avars and the Bulgarians. Nevertheless, it was their name that became a word to frighten children: 'Ogres'.

Swallowed by the Ogres, young and promising Moravia, the first organized state of the Western Slavs, disappeared. Farther north, Slavic tribes of various strains broke through the weak defences of the *Respublica Christiana,* into the lands of the Bavarians and the Saxons. Other Slavs, strengthened perhaps by Scandinavian elements, raided the Adriatic shores.

All of these pressures, added to family strife and personal inadequacy, made the burden of the Carolingians impossible to bear. Though there continued to be claimants to the imperial title, after 887 no descendant of Charlemagne was able to bring together, through talent or luck, the dismembered fragments of the empire. Ironically, the Roman Empire, prepared by mythical Romulus and inaugurated by Augustus, had ended five centuries of rule in the West with the deposition of the child emperor Romulus Augustus. No less ironically, the Carolingian Empire, started by Charles 'the Great', went down with the deposition of Charles 'the Fat.'

## RESISTANCE ON THE LOCAL SCALE

The network of communications and command being so slack throughout Europe, resistance was but slowly organized. It was only at the eastern end in the Byzantine Empire and at the western end in the Caliphate of Cordova that regular fleets, standing armies and frontiers garrisoned or at least patrolled by professional troops existed. The border marches established by the Carolingians and their successors to act as buffers were too weakly held to absorb the initial shock. Inland vassals showed no undue haste in leaving their fief in answer to the call of the sovereign to whom they owed military service. In Britain and in northern Italy, there was not even a recognized ruler of the whole country who might have co-ordinated defensive efforts.

But if it was impossible to stop the invaders—and buying their withdrawal served

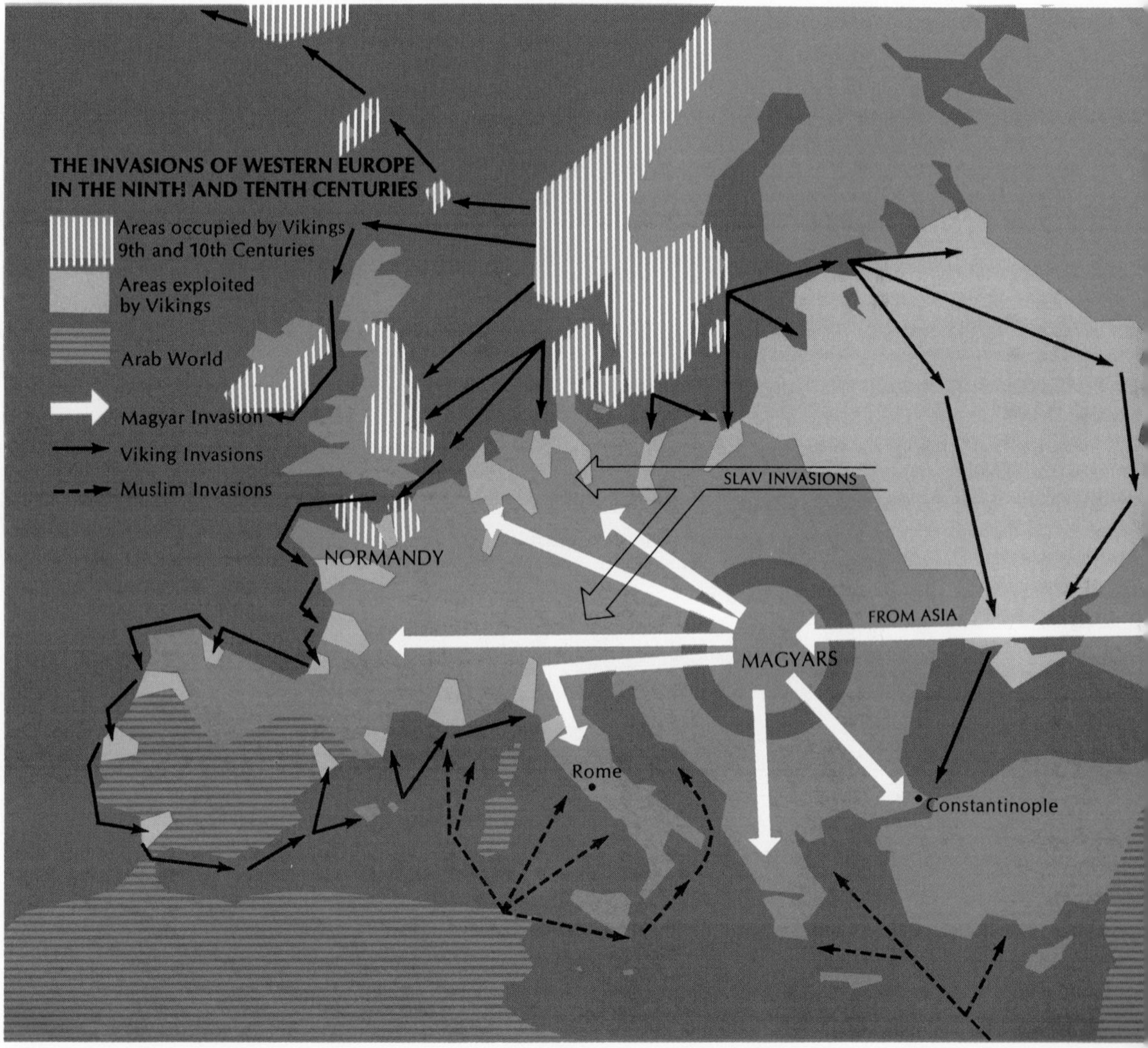

only to invite further extortion—the prudent course was to conceal one's most precious possessions, seek shelter, and watch for an opportunity to fall upon columns weighed down by their booty. Towns and monasteries which had at first been taken unawares and sacked, began to build strong fortifications. Castles rose up on every hilltop and on the banks of every river. Kings, popes, leagues of nobles or townspeople organized a local resistance which gradually stiffened and ultimately brought victory. Occasionally there was a pitched battle, the most notable being the severe defeat which Otto 'the Great', duke of Saxony and king of the Germans, inflicted on the Hungarians in 955.

Still it was above all thanks to her lack of centralization and the poverty of her land that the spineless Europe of the tenth century withstood the invasions better than the Roman Empire of the fifth century had done. Nowhere was there a vital centre, main road or economic node whose loss could cause the downfall of a whole province, but self-supporting villages and almost self-supporting towns were countless. To destroy one by one those minute cells would have required a plan of action and a steadfastness of purpose which the aggressors by no means possessed.

## EUROPE ENLARGED

Worn out by their very effort, thrown back here and there, softened, moreover, by their contacts with settled people, the invaders finally became attached to the soil in the territories they had wrested from the old states of Catholic Europe and even in their native lands. This made them more accessible to the influence of their neighbours, whose warlike nobility and poverty-stricken peasantry differed from theirs in degree of development more than in kind. After a while most of them embraced the political and religious institutions of the older nations and set up a Christian church and state of their own. In this way the area of the Christian community known to Charlemagne was almost doubled, and the family of European peoples that we know today was nearly completed.

Assimilation was fairly easy for the Scandinavians, both in the many bridgeheads they established in the British Isles and Normandy and in their home countries, soon to be consolidated as the three Catholic kingdoms of Denmark, Norway and Sweden. It was harder for the Hungarians, the only people not of Indo-European stock that took root in the heart of medieval Europe without losing their language and identity. Yet even . . . they became a Catholic kingdom. . . .

Similarly, the evangelization and political education of the Slavs, which had already produced results in the Balkans and in Moravia in the ninth century, were almost completed in the course of the tenth under the influence of rival religious and diplomatic missions sent from Byzantium and the West. All along the frontier between Orthodox and Catholic Europe certain groups of Slav tribes formed kingdoms: Poland, Russia, Bohemia, Croatia, to which must be added their elder sister Bulgaria, founded by Hunnic tribes but deeply influenced by the Slavs in the course of the centuries. After much hesitation Bulgaria and Russia joined the political and religious family of Byzantium. The other Slavic states ended by choosing the West, as did Hungary and the Scandinavian states, but tried to emphasize their obedience to the Roman pope in order to escape the heavy overlordship of the German kings. . . .

## EUROPE SHIELDED: THE TRIUMPH OF LOCALISM

The emergence of fairly orderly Christian states in the northern and eastern periphery of Catholic Europe, at the very moment when a general recovery was at long last possible, is an event of capital importance. In the tenth century for the first time in history, the older core of Europe was protected by an outer bulwark against which the invasions of successive centuries wore themselves out.

It had not been improper to describe the *Respublica Romana* as an immense fortress besieged by barbarians howling at its walls; the *Respublica Christiana* of the Catholic faith, shielded in the south by the unfriendly but civilized power of Islam, sheltered in the south-east by the inconvenient but familiar presence of the Byzantine Empire, cushioned in the north and north-east by the very peoples who had up to then been a constant threat, no longer had any direct contact with untamed 'barbarians'. More fortunate than Asia, Africa or even Orthodox Europe, which continued to be exposed to the attacks of nomadic people, Catholic Europe has for the last thousand years developed her civilization without intrusion of unpredictable assailants.

Had the decisive turning point arrived a hundred years earlier, it might have given a new lease of life to the Carolingian Empire and started new-born Europe on a uniform basis. Whatever its shortcomings, the central government in the ninth century was a more active driving force than the local units. But in the tenth century the material strength of the empire had melted away, while the beginning demographic and economic revival aroused each cell of the European tissue from its torpor. Localism became the dominant factor in the history of Europe. . . .

# The Vikings Invade Western Europe

The account of the Viking invasions is from the "Annals of Saint-Bertin," a manuscript of the eighth and ninth centuries found in a French monastery. It is clearly the work of more than one author, but the portion of the work quoted here, dealing with years 845–859, has been attributed to Prudence, Bishop of Troyes. The description of the siege of Paris is from a contemporary account written by a monk. From Frederick Ogg, ed., *A Source Book of Medieval History* (New York, 1907), pp. 166–171.

## I. EUROPE IS PLUNDERED BY THE NORTHMEN (845–859)

The Northmen with a hundred ships entered the Seine on the twentieth of March and, after ravaging first one bank and then the other, came without meeting any resistance to Paris. [The king] resolved to hold out against them; but seeing the impossibility of gaining a victory, he made with them a certain agreement and by a gift of 7,000 livres he bought them off from advancing farther and persuaded them to return.

Euric, king of the Northmen, advanced, with six hundred vessels, along the course of the River Elbe to attack Louis of Germany. The Saxons prepared to meet him, gave battle, and with the aid of our Lord Jesus Christ won the victory.

Northmen invading England. This scene of Danish Vikings preparing to land on England's North Sea coast appears in the "Miracles of Saint Edmund," an illuminated manuscript of the twelfth century.

The Northmen returned [from Paris] down the Seine and coming to the ocean pillaged, destroyed, and burned all the regions to the coast.

The Danish pirates landed in Frisia. They were able to force from the people whatever contributions they wished and, being victors in battle, they remained masters of almost the entire province.

The Northmen made their appearance in the part of Gaul inhabited by the Britons and won three victories. . . .

On the eighteenth of April, the Danish pirates came to the city of Orleans, pillaged it, and went away without meeting opposition. Other Danish pirates came into the Seine about the middle of August and, after plundering and ruining the towns on the two banks of the river, and even the monasteries and villages further back, came to a well located place near the Seine called Jeufosse, and, there quietly passed the winter.

The Danish pirates having made a long sea-voyage (for they had sailed between Spain and Africa) entered the Rhone, where they pillaged many cities and monasteries and established themselves on the island called Camargue. . . . They devastated everything before them as far as the city of Valence [180 miles from the coast]. Then after ravaging all these regions they returned to the island where they had fixed their habitation. Thence they went on toward Italy, capturing and plundering Pisa and other cities.

## II. THE SIEGE OF PARIS (885–886)

The Northmen came to Paris with 700 sailing ships, not counting those of smaller size which are commonly called barques. At one stretch the Seine was lined with the vessels for more than two leagues, so that one might ask in astonishment in what cavern the river had been swallowed up, since it was not to be seen. The second day after the fleet of Northmen arrived under the walls of the city, Siegfred, who . . . was in command of the expedition, came to the dwelling of the illustrious bishop. He bowed his head and said: "Gauzelin, have compassion of yourself and on your flock. We beseech you to listen to us, in order that you may escape death. Allow us only the freedom of the city. We will do no harm and we will see to it that whatever belongs either to you or to Odo shall be strictly respected." Count Odo, who later became king, was then the defender of the city. The bishop replied to Siegfred, "Paris has been entrusted to us by the Emperor Charles [the Fat], who, after God, king and lord of the powerful, rules over almost all the world. He has put it in our care, not at all that the kingdom may be ruined by our misconduct, but that he may keep it and be assured of its peace. If, like us, you had been given the duty of defending these walls, and if you should have done that which you ask us to do, what treatment do you think you would deserve?" Siegfred replied, "I should deserve that my head be cut off and thrown to the dogs. Nevertheless, if you do not listen to my demand, on the morrow our war-machines will destroy you with poisoned arrows. You will be the prey of famine and pestilence and these evils will renew themselves perpetually every year." So saying he departed and gathered together his comrades.

In the morning the Northmen, boarding their ships, approached the tower and attacked it. They shook it with their engines and stormed it with arrows. The city resounded with clamor, the people were aroused, the bridges trembled. All came together to defend the tower. There Odo, his brother Robert, and the Count Ragenar distinguished themselves for bravery; likewise the courageous Abbot Ebolus, the nephew of the bishop. A keen arrow wounded the prelate, while at his side the young warrior Frederick was struck by a sword. Frederick died, but the old man, thanks to God, survived. There perished many Franks; after receiving wounds they were lavish of life. At last the enemy withdrew, carrying off their dead. The evening came. The tower had been sorely tried, but its foundations were still solid, as were also the narrow *baies* [bays] which surmounted them. The people spent the night repairing it with boards. By the next day, on the old citadel had been erected a new tower of wood, a half higher than the former one. At sunrise the Danes caught their first glimpse of it. Once more the latter engaged with the Christians in violent combat. On every side arrows sped and blood flowed. With the arrows mingled the stones hurled by slings and war-machines; the air was filled with them. The tower which had been built during the night groaned under the strokes of the darts, the city shook with the struggle, the people ran hither and thither, the bells jangled. The warriors rushed together to defend the tottering tower and to repel the fierce assault. Among these warriors two, a count and an abbot [Ebolus], surpassed all the rest in courage. The former was the redoubtable Odo who never experienced defeat and who continually revived the spirits of the worn-out defenders. He ran along the ramparts and hurled back the enemy. On those who were secreting themselves so as to undermine the tower he poured oil, wax, and pitch, which, being mixed and heated, burned the Danes and tore off their scalps. Some of them died;

others threw themselves into the river to escape the awful substance.

Meanwhile Paris was suffering not only from the sword outside but also from a pestilence within which brought death to many noble men. Within the walls there was not ground in which to bury the dead. . . . Odo, the future king, was sent to Charles, emperor of the Franks, to implore help for the stricken city. . . .

# The Emergence of Local Leaders

Since the established political authorities in the West proved unable to stem the Scandinavian attacks, men turned to capable local figures for protection. The decentralized political order created by these "new men" is described in this reading. The first selection is from pp. 5–7, *Life on a Medieval Barony* by William Stearns Davis, Copyright 1923 by Harper & Brothers; renewed 1950 by Alice Redfield Davis. The second selection is from R. W. Southern, *The Making of the Middle Ages* (New Haven, Conn.: Yale University Press, 1953), pp. 80–83, 86–88.

## I. WILLIAM S. DAVIS: THE BARONY OF ST. ALIQUIS

Very uncertain is the ancestry of the redoubtable warrior Heribert, who about A.D. 875 seized the rocky triangle at the mouth of the Rapide, and built the first castle of St. Aliquis. Perhaps he was descended from one of Charlemagne's famous Frankish "counts." He did, indeed, only what was then being done everywhere to check the Scandinavian hordes: he built a castle and organized the levies of the region, hitherto footmen, into an effective cavalry force. This castle was anything save the later majestic fortress. It was merely a great square tower of rough masonry, perched on the crag above the streams. Around it was a palisade of heavy timbers, strengthened on the landward side by a ditch. Inside this compound were huts for refugees, storehouses for fodder, and rude stalls for the cattle. To stop passage up the Claire a heavy chain of iron was stretched across the river and stone piers were sunk at shallow places, thus forcing boats to pass close under the fortress in range of descending missiles. Where the chain was landed there was built another smaller stone tower. All the crossing

Bodiam Castle in Sussex, England.

then had to be by skiffs, although somewhat later an unsteady bridge was thrown over the stream.

The second expedition of vikings found that these precautions had ruined their adventure. They lost many men and a dragon ship when they tried to force the iron chain. Heribert's new cavalry cut off their raiding parties. Finally they departed with thinned numbers and scant spoils. Heribert was hailed as savior of the region, just as other champions, notably the great Count Odo at the siege of Paris, won similar successes elsewhere on a larger scale. The vikings had departed, but Heribert's tower remained. So began the castle of St. Aliquis.

Heribert had taken possession ostensibly as the king's "man," claiming some royal commission, but as the power of Charlemagne's feeble rulers dwindled, Heribert's heirs presently forgot almost all their allegiance to their distant royal "master." This was merely as seemed the case about A.D. 900 all through the region then coming to be called "France." Castles were rising everywhere, sometimes to repel the vikings, sometimes merely to strengthen the power of some local chief. Once erected, the lords of those castles were really little princes, able to defy the very weak central authority. To capture a considerably less formidable fortalice than St. Aliquis implied a tedious siege, such as few kings would undertake save in an emergency.

The result was that ere A.D. 1000 Heribert's great-grandsons had almost ceased to trouble about the king. The person they genuinely feared was the local Duke of Quelqueparte, another feudal seigneur with more followers and more castles than they. Partly from prudence, partly from necessity, they had "done homage" to him, become "his men," and as his vassals rode to his wars. The dukes, in turn, full of their own problems, and realizing the strength of St. Aliquis, seldom interfered in the fief, save on very serious occasions. The barons of St. Aliquis therefore acted very nearly like sovereign princes. They, of course, had their own gallows with power of life and death, waged their own personal wars, made treaties of peace, and even coined a little ill-shapen money with their own superscription. "Barons by the Grace of God," they boasted themselves, which meant that they obeyed the duke and *his* suzerain, the king, very little, and, we fear, God not a great deal.

In the recent centuries, however, the barony had changed hands several times. About 1070 the lord had the folly to refuse his ordinary feudal duty to the Duke of Quelqueparte. The latter roused himself, enlisted outside aid, and blockaded and starved out the castle of St. Aliquis. The unfortunate baron—duly adjudged "traitor and felon" by his "peers," his fellow vassals—was beheaded. The duke then bestowed the fief, with the hand of the late owner's niece, upon Sire Rainulf, a younger son of a south-country viscount, who had visited the duke's court, bringing with him an effective battle-ax and fifty sturdy followers. Sire Rainulf, however, died while in the First Crusade. The reigning duke next tried to give the barony to another favorite warrior, but the son of the late baron proved himself of sturdy stuff. He fought off his suzerain and enlisted allies from Burgundy. The duke was forced, therefore, to leave him in peace.

## II. R. W. SOUTHERN: THE COUNTS OF ANJOU

Politically, the great question in the tenth century, outside Germany, was how far the disintegration of authority would go. The immediate cause of the disintegration was lack of loyalty, and with lack of loyalty to persons went a decay and confusion of the ideas for which the persons stood. It was a time when claims of allegiance and duty, however well founded in law or in history, counted for nothing when they went beyond the bounds of effective personal power. It was easy for the Count of Anjou to throw off his obligations to the King of France. Would it prove equally possible for the lord of Loches or of any of the castles of the Loire to throw off the authority of the Count of Anjou? How far would the process go? . . .

Perhaps more simply than anywhere else in Europe, the shaping of a new political order may be seen in the valley of the river Loire. There was here so clean a sweep of ancient institutions, title deeds and boundaries, that the emergence of new forms of loyalty and authority was facilitated. Elsewhere the same processes are to be observed, men have the same objects in view, but they work towards them less directly and less swiftly. We shall observe the ambitions, and the restraints imposed on the wills, of some of the most powerful personalities of their time, in studying the emergence of one of the strongest new political units of the eleventh century in the Loire valley.

### The County of Anjou

The history of this county from the late tenth to the mid-twelfth century provides a rich portrait gallery of the makers of a medieval "state." Like other families, the counts took a great interest in their past; they were proud of it, and in the course of years they left a large collection of documents, which illuminate their history. Towards the end of the eleventh century, there was a historically minded Count, Fulk Rechin, who set himself to record the traditions of the family and his own recollections of his predecessors. Looking back from the eminence which the family had attained in his time, he could dimly perceive the origins of their good fortune in the career of an ancestor two hundred years earlier. Nothing was clearly reported about this ancestor except that his name was Ingelgarius, nor was much known about his descendants for nearly another hundred years; but the later panegyrists of the family were able to fill this gap by proclaiming that Ingelgarius was descended from an ancient Romano-British family of high rank. No amount of research or invention could discover how the family had lived in the intervening period since the fall of Rome, but it was concluded that "the matter is unimportant for we often read that senators have lived on the land and emperors have been snatched from the plough." This classical background was a twelfth-century addition to the history of the family—it reveals the romantic prejudices of that period—but in essentials the historians of the family were right. They saw that the effective origins of the family were to be sought in the later years of the ninth century—a time when, as one of them remarked, "the men in established positions relied on the merits of their ancestors and not on their own," and allowed themselves to be elbowed out of the way by new men pushing their way to the front by superior energy and military effectiveness.

The family of Ingelgarius were among these new men. War made them conspicuous, grants of land established their position, marriage consolidated it, and the acquisition of ancient titles of honour cloaked their usurpations. Ingelgarius gained the first foothold in the valley of the Loire, but it was his son Fulk the Red—with a name and physical characteristic which kept reappearing in his descendants—who made the family a power to be reckoned with in the neighborhood: marriage added to his possessions, force held them together, and the commital rights (for what they were worth), which had previously been shared, were not acquired outright. Two more generations, covering the period from 941 to 987, gave the family a place in legend and in general repute, establishing them in a subtle way in men's minds as well as in their physical experience. The time of Fulk the Good (941 to c.960) was looked back to as a period of growth, though it was not a time of territorial expansion: it was now that the unnatural fertility of the soil—the fruit of long years of depopulation—was discovered, and prodigious crops rewarded the labours of new settlers. The prize of the Loire valley, the capital city of Tours, still lay outside the range of the count's authority, but the family had great claims to the gratitude of the church in that city. It was said that Ingelgarius had restored to it by force of arms the relics of its patron saint, thus starting the family tradition of goodwill towards the church of Tours. Fulk's reputation in this respect was of a more scholarly kind. It was reported that he delighted to take part in the choir services with the canons and that he was the author of a famous rebuke to a king who ridiculed his clerical tastes. The story is exceedingly improbable, but it illustrates the way in which the family was adding to itself fame of a more than military kind. Fulk's son, Geoffrey Greymantle, who was Count from about 960 to 987, added to this legendary reputation: he was one of the select band of tenth-century heroes whose names were handed down to form part of the stock-in-trade of twelfth-century poetic memory. He was pictured as the standard bearer of Charlemagne in the *Song of Roland,* and in his own right he was the hero of various stories, in which his prowess and counsel saved the kingdom from its enemies.

By 987 the family was ready to emerge from its legendary and epic age on to the stage of history. At this moment there appeared one of those powerful figures, who combined all the qualities and ferocity of his race and consolidated the achievements of the last four generations: Fulk Nerra, the Black, Count of Anjou from 987 to 1040. We cannot do better than look at him through the eyes of his grandson, Count Fulk Rechin. This is what he records of Fulk Nerra:

1. He built thirteen castles, which he can name, and many more besides.
2. He won two pitched battles, against his neighbours to East and West.
3. He built two abbeys, one at Angers and the other near Loches, the great outpost of his power in the South East.
4. He went twice to Jerusalem (this is an understatement: it is almost certain that he went three times); and he died on his way home during his last journey.

Each one of these items, properly considered, stamps him as a man of note: taken together they convey a vivid impression of a pioneer in the art of feudal government. In the first place, the castles: they were the guarantee of the stability of the regime. Fulk was a pioneer in the building of stone keeps, and one formidable example of his handiwork still survives at Langeais. The inexpugnable fortresses solved at once the problem of defence and of government—they made loyalty easy. The battles were more speculative—brilliant gambles based on the solid capital of defensive positions. It was a time when he who committed himself to open battle, committed his fortune to the winds. But the reward of successful enterprise was great, as befitted the uncertainty of the outcome; and the battle of Conquereuil in 992 against the Count of Brittany was one of the foundations of Angevin greatness. . . .

His life-time brings us to an age of serious, expansive wars waged by well-organized and strongly fortified territorial lords. The confused warfare, haphazard battles and obscure acts of force of the first hundred years of the family's history had turned scattered and precarious rights into a complex, but geographically compact and militarily impregnable association, dependent on the Count. The process was directed by an instinctive feeling for strategic advantage, which perhaps lends to the history of these years an appearance of consistency greater than in fact it possessed. The methods were not refined, but they were practised with a consistency of purpose which inspires a certain respect. The swallowing of an important strong point might be preceded by many years of steady encroachment. It was necessary, first, to get established at some point within the territory to be threatened—an operation carried out by a careful marriage, a purchase which the documents represent as a gift, or an act of force or fraud. Then a castle was built as a base of operations. After that, watchfulness: a minority, the chance offered by the enemy's engagement elsewhere, or a lucky battle, might complete the circle. . . .

But by the middle of the eleventh century, easy progress by these familiar methods was no longer possible. The weak had been made dependent, the strongholds of intruding neighbours had been taken and, by the same token, distant claims of the Counts outside their own territory had been abandoned. To the west stood Brittany, to the east Blois, to the north—across the still debatable land of Maine—Normandy, to the south Poitou. They faced each other as equals. Although the armed peace was often broken, the chief interest of the next hundred and fifty years lies in the emergence of stable political institutions and the elaboration of a new system of law. The swashbuckling days were over, and the regimes which had emerged began to clothe themselves in habits of respectability. Up to this point, St. Augustine's dictum that secular governments are nothing but large-scale robbery seemed to be abundantly justified by the facts: but slowly something more complex, more sensitive to the positive merits of organized society, seemed to be required. Government became something more than a system of exactions from a conquered countryside, and there developed a routine for the peaceful exploitation of resources and for the administering of justice. . . .

# Zoë Oldenbourg: The Feudal System

Russian-born Zoë Oldenbourg (1916– ) has written both history and accomplished historical novels. The introductory chapter to her history of the crusades provides the reader with an overview of the conditions of life in the Europe of the time and a deft sketch of the relationship of land, loyalty, and warfare in the feudal system. From *The Crusades,* by Zoë Oldenbourg. 

## I

Throughout the Middle Ages, and especially at the time of the Crusades, the nobility was the ruling class and the only class to wield real and undisputed power: the power of arms. . . .

These nobles were, for the most part, of Frankish or Germanic origin. Four centuries after the Germanic peoples first appeared in Gaul, Spain, and northern Italy, the descendants of the invaders still formed the aristocracy of the conquered lands. The mingling of the various races took place quite smoothly but very slowly, since the Germanic peoples had not arrived as conquering armies but in nomadic tribes, bringing their wives and children with them. The barbarians were gradually assimilated, but they remained the dominant race and the word "Frank" became synonymous with "free," which the non-Franks, in theory, were not. Over the centuries, the descendants of the Franks, Visigoths, Burgundians, and the rest lost all memory of their former religions and languages, but they still formed a kind of military aristocracy; and although the idea of national differences had disappeared and the great Frankish families were actually more anxious to trace Roman ancestry for themselves than to boast of their barbarian origin, the European nobles remained in blood, and still more in mind, more Germanic than Latin. They had inherited the proud, unstable temperament of the old nomadic German conquerors and, in particular, their cult of honor, which was linked to a strong sense of military solidarity. Their history as a ruling race gave them a strong caste pride, and even when latinized and converted to Christianity they remained, in spite of everything, very little affected by outside influences.

The Norse invasions of the ninth and tenth centuries represented a peril which had a galvanizing effect on this Frankish nobility. The Northmen, who settled on the coast on either side of the English Channel, were a powerful stimulant to the warlike nobles. The Northman very soon ceased to be an enemy and was accepted as a relative in blood and spirit, and before long a complicated system of intermarriage had injected Scandinavian blood into most of the great families of Western Europe.

This Scandinavian element—which by the eleventh century was already thoroughly assimilated—coupled with the still more ancient Germanic one, was clearly not so important that we have to regard European nobility as a kind of ruling class of foreign origin. Racial memory is short, especially among illiterate peoples, and it is language and religion rather than racial stock which define a nation. Even the most purebred Franks were incontestably Latins, while their neighbors across the Rhine had remained Teutons, but they were Latins with a short past and therefore with a comparatively meager intellectual and emotional background.

Nevertheless, theirs was a strong society, overflowing with vitality and strong in other ways than the mere possession of military strength. It was strong because it was fully conscious of its own worth, and had its own ethic and its own tried and tested concept of life.

The feudal system was already an ancient institution. It had grown and developed gradually according to the needs of the time until by the eleventh century it had become the only imaginable social system, and was so generally recognized throughout Western Europe that men conceived even their relations to God in terms of feudal laws. These laws bound man to man by a personal and, in principle, indissoluble tie, and they were based much more on the idea of the individual than on more abstract concepts of state, justice, or the public good.

In fact, the feudal system recognized two basic values: man and land. In these exclusively agricultural countries, land ultimately meant wealth. "No lord without land and no land without its lord." Beginning as a system of reciprocal contracts between a sovereign and the subject to whom he entrusted the

A vassal kneels bareheaded before his lord, paying hommage in the ceremony of investiture. From a fifteenth-century Italian manuscript.

administration of certain lands, by the tenth century feudalism had come to be almost entirely based on the laws of heredity. The fief which the suzerain granted to his vassal became, in effect, the inalienable property of the latter's family. In the case of a province or a very large domain, this fief might be further divided into smaller and likewise hereditary fiefs held by the vassal's vassals. The great baron who was nominal lord of all the lands held by his vassals and his vassals' vassals could actually enjoy only those lands which formed his personal inheritance, and might often have vassals who were richer and more powerful than himself.

A vassal's obligations to his overlord were not extensive. They were confined to: (1) Military service. This was generally a fixed number of days in any year (usually forty). In the case of liege service, the period was for the duration of the war the overlord was engaged in, but as we shall see, there were good reasons why such wars could not be allowed to drag on indefinitely at the whim of the suzerain. (2) Financial assistance on certain clearly defined occasions. These included wars, the knighting of the lord's eldest son, the marriage of his eldest daughter, and the payment of ransom should the lord be taken prisoner. (3) Attendance at councils, parliaments, and possibly court sessions. In other words, the vassal was obliged to be present two or three times a year at a general reunion of all his suzerain's vassals, to assist him in dealing with matters of general concern such as wars or building operations, to administer justice, or merely to increase the overlord's prestige at banquets and state occasions. (4) Offering his suzerain hospitality should he happen to pass through the vassal's domain.

Beyond these four obligations the vassal was, for all practical purposes, independent. Indeed, since the suzerain was bound to defend his vassals in the event of injury or attack, the feudal system seems to have been designed for the express purpose of providing the nobles with the maximum freedom combined with the maximum security possible in these conditions.

When he could grant no more fiefs without leaving himself completely landless, the prince or great baron possessed only a symbolic authority, dependent on the goodwill of his principal vassals, who in their turn had not always the means to make their own vassals obey them. In practice, power was so effectively divided that the feudal system should be regarded as organized anarchy rather than as a social order. The multiplication of fiefs led inevitably to administrative complications. Only the lords of the great provinces had the right to coin money, but even their subsidiary vassals possessed the right to administer high justice (that involving the death penalty). Furthermore, since the same lord might have a hereditary title to a number of fiefs held from different overlords, circumstances could arise in which he found himself fighting for one suzerain against another. Only a leader who was gifted with an exceptionally powerful personality could boast of being able to rule effectively, and in fact, no prince was able to make a decision of any importance without his vassals' consent. The fact that their interests rarely coincided made it difficult to arrive at any decision at all.

But if there was anarchy, at least it was indisputably "organized." The oath of allegiance was no mere formality. It was taken very seriously—and this in spite of exceptions so numerous that they cannot even be said to prove the rule. On the lowest level, that binding the small *vavasseur* (the vassal of a vassal) to his immediate overlord, it was nearly always regarded as a sacred obligation, as was perfectly natural. The bond generally becomes increasingly lax as one travels up the social scale, and it is quite clear that the king of France, as suzerain of the count of Toulouse, the duke of Guyenne, and the king of England, no longer received from them anything but the most nominal homage. On the level of provinces, dioceses, and cantons, loyalty to an overlord was frequently bound up with clan solidarity, and the most faithful vassals were obviously those united to their overlords by ties of propinquity, kinship, or friendship, and especially those whom the overlord had knighted with his own hand. But the oath of allegiance or investiture was above all else a mystical and symbolical act whose force was universally acknowledged.

Although in practice this system of contracts for mutual assistance led to situations of inextricable complexity, the principle on which it was based was simple enough and had in fact resulted in the formation of a remarkably homogeneous society with a strong sense of caste solidarity, a kind of international brotherhood so real that later centuries were to regard it as an actual order of chivalry.

## II

The concept of chivalry did not exactly coincide with the idea of nobility, or with the profession of arms. In present-day terms, it corresponds more accurately to the idea of the officer class, but the title applied equally to a commander in chief and to the youngest subaltern. It was simultaneously a title, a rank, and a virtue, and to say that a man was "a good knight" was the highest possible praise. Young or old, rich or poor, a model of virtue or a sink of iniquity, a soldier of noble birth was judged first and foremost on his qualities as a knight. In the eleventh century the concept of chivalry certainly involved no moral values beyond courage in battle, although knights were expected to refrain from too violently infringing current notions of morality. . . .

However, the obligations imposed by the profession of arms were many, complex, and strictly honored, and constituted a moral code which had all the force of law. There was no written manual laying down the qualities of the perfect knight—and even if there had been, not many knights were able to read—but there was an unwritten law which was universally recognized. This was something like a professional qualification, and concerned the use of arms and all the technical knowledge expected of a knight. With so little in the way of mechanical tools, a knight needed quick wits and considerable ingenuity as well as an ability to turn his hand to a variety of tasks: he must be able in case of need to direct the building of siege engines; to become, at a moment's notice, engineer, architect, general (even if only on a small scale), doctor (or sick nurse, at least), or veterinarian; and also must possess some rudimentary knowledge of ballistics, mechanics, and even accounting, all of which were necessary to the profession of soldiering.

Loyalty to his suzerain and the duty of protecting the soldiers under his command figured largely among a knight's obligations. The concept of military discipline as such did not exist, except in the most elementary form, so that the knight's personal initiative counted for a good deal. Intelligence was one of the knightly virtues, especially the kind of practical intelligence which consists in the ability to adapt readily to unexpected situations and turn them to the best advantage.

Evidently a good knight was not an ignoramus, but he lived in an age and environment when the average man thought no more of reading or writing than most people today think of learning to ride or fence: these were luxury occupations, expensive and without much practical application in everyday life. The learned clerk's academic knowledge was valued according to its usefulness, and in war it was not vital.

Feudal nobility was, by definition, almost exclusively military. The nobles were soldiers by profession and vocation, and though it is not easy to see how a relatively numerous ruling class could be one with the life of the country and yet solely taken up with fighting, they were so well trained and educated for war that in the end they had no other aim in life. The time of the great invasions was past. Even the struggles against the Moors in Spain and the Slavonic and Lithuanian pagans in the north of Germany had become merely spasmodic local outbreaks. The Norman advance had ceased to be a menace to the West, and there was no longer a powerful aggressor to be driven back or new lands to conquer. The West was discovering its own internal balance. This was, admittedly, precarious. There were bitter struggles between pope and emperor for the domination of Italy, uprisings among the great feudal lords in Germany and the great vassals of the French crown, the quarrels of Saxons and Normans in England, and the Christians' fight against the Moors in Spain, but none of this could prevent Europe from becoming gradually what it still is: a collection of peoples belonging to one civilization, the product of Western Feudalism and of the Catholic religion. The feudal system was the life and soul of this new civilization, but feudal society was essentially warlike, and the West no longer offered sufficient scope for military aggression.

# John of Toul Makes Known the Obligations of a Vassal

This declaration from the eleventh century reveals some of the complexities of the lord-vassal relationship. A vassal receiving fiefs from two different lords for the performance of military services was in a difficult position when the two lords went to war with one another. From Oliver Thatcher and Edgar McNeal, eds., *A Source Book for Medieval History* (New York, 1905), pp. 364–365.

I, John of Toul, make known that I am the liege man of the Lady Beatrice, countess of Troyes, and of her son Theobald, count of Champagne, against every creature, living or dead, saving my allegiance to lord Enjorand of Coucy, lord John of Arcis, and the count of Grandpré. If it should happen that the count of Grandpré should be at war with the countess and count of Champagne on his own quarrel, I will aid the count of Grandpré in my own person, and I will send to the count and the countess of Champagne the knights whose service I owe to them for the fief which I hold of them. But if the count of Grandpré shall make war on the countess and the count of Champagne on behalf of his friends and not in his own quarrel, I will aid in my own person the countess and count of Champagne, and will send one knight to the count of Grandpré for the service which I owe him for the fief which I hold of him, but I will not go myself into the territory of the count of Grandpré to make war on him.

# Marc Bloch: The Profession of Arms in Feudal Times

In his great work *Feudal Society,* French historian Marc Bloch (1886–1944) treated feudalism as a living force in the society of medieval Europe. In this reading he analyzes the connection between fighting and political authority. From Marc Bloch, *Feudal Society,* trans. L.A. Manyon (University of Chicago, 1961), pp. 289–292.

It was not only vassals, of course, who had the capacity or the duty to fight; nor were they the only ones with a love of fighting in that first feudal age [roughly 850–1050 A.D.],

This illustration of a knight and foot soldiers represents a scene from the life of St. Aubin, a sixth-century bishop of Angers in France. The dress and weapons, however, are faithful to the ninth century, when the illustration was made.

when society from top to bottom was imbued with the taste for violence or the fear of it. The laws which attempted to restrict or prohibit the bearing of arms by members of the lower classes did not make their appearance before the second half of the twelfth century, and they coincided both with the progress of legal differentiation between classes and with a relative abatement of disorder. . . .

He [the knight] fought on horseback; and though he might on occasion dismount during the battle, he always moved about on horseback. Moreover, he fought fully equipped; his offensive weapons were the lance and the sword, occasionally the mace, while for defence he wore a helmet and a garment made wholly or partly of metal, and he carried a round or triangular shield. Strictly speaking, it was not the horse alone which made the knight; his humbler companion, the squire, whose duty it was to look after the horses and arrange the change of mounts along the road, was also mounted. Sometimes in addition to the heavy cavalry of the knights, armies included the more lightly equipped horsemen usually known as 'serjeants'. The distinguishing mark of the highest class of fighting-man was the combination of horse and complete equipment.

The improvements introduced in the warrior's equipment from the Frankish period onwards had made it more costly (and also more difficult to handle), with the result that it became less and less possible for anyone who was not a rich man—or the vassal of a rich man—to take part in this form of warfare. As the logical consequence of the adoption, about the tenth century, of the stirrup, the short spear of former days, brandished at arm's length like a javelin, was abandoned and replaced by the long and heavy lance, which the warrior, in close combat, held under his armpit and, when at rest, supported on the stirrup itself. To the helmet was added the nasal and later the visor. Finally, the *broigne,* a sort of garment of leather or cloth, on which were sewn iron rings or plates, gave place to the hauberk, perhaps copied from the Arabs; completely woven of metal rings, it was of much more delicate workmanship, and might have to be imported. By degrees moreover, the class monopoly, which had at first been imposed by mere practical necessity, began to pass into law. In their effort to keep their manorial officials in a state of relative inferiority, the monks of Beaulieu, shortly after 970, forbade them to carry the shield and sword; those of St. Gall, at about the same time, reproached the stewards of their estates with possessing arms of excessively fine quality.

Imagine a military force of the period. It presents a dual aspect. On the one hand there is a body of infantry as ill-equipped for attack as for defence, slow in advancing to the assault and slow in flight, and quickly exhausted by long marches on wretched tracks or across-country. On the other hand, looking down from their chargers on the poor wretches who, 'shamefully' as one court romance puts it, drag their feet in the dust and mire, are stalwart soldiers, proud of being able to fight and manoeuvre swiftly, skilfully, effectively—the only force, indeed, in the opinion of the Cid's biographer, which it is worth the trouble of counting when assessing the numerical strength of an army. In a civilization where war was an everyday matter, there was no more vital contrast than this. The word 'knight', which had become almost synonymous with vassal, became also the equivalent of 'noble'. Conversely, more than one text in applying to the lower orders the contemptuous designation of *pedones,* 'foot-soldiers'—or rather perhaps 'foot-sloggers'—raised it almost to the status of a legal term. Among the Franks, said the Arab emir Ousama, 'all pre-eminence belongs to the horsemen. They are in truth the only men who count. Theirs it is to give counsel; theirs to render justice.'

Now is it surprising that in the eyes of generations which had good reasons for exalting force in its crudest form the fighting-man *par excellence* should have been the most feared, the most sought-after and the most respected of men? A theory at that time very widely current represented the human community as being divided into three 'orders': those who prayed, those who fought, and those who worked. It was unanimously agreed that the second should be placed much higher than the third. But the evidence of the epic goes farther still, showing that the soldier had little hesitation in rating his mission even higher than that of the specialist in prayer. Pride is one of the essential ingredients of all class-consciousness. That of the 'nobles' of the feudal era was, above all, the pride of the warrior.

Moreover, fighting was for them not merely an occasional duty to be performed for the sake of their lord, or king, or family. It represented much more—their whole purpose in life.

# Chapter 4

## The Middle Ages: A Christian Traditional Society

Lord and land were the determining elements in the feudal society that arose in the beleaguered West of the ninth and tenth centuries. Roman-Christian and Germanic cultures accommodated themselves to this static landed society but also provided means for its regeneration—such as the creation of feudal monarchy, forerunner of the national state. The usual outlook was a traditional one, hostile to change, fostered by the defense of the lord's interest and the low level of economic activity. The economy continued to remain basically rural throughout the Middle Ages, although the end of centuries of invasion, improved agricultural techniques, and population growth did promote the gradual growth of towns. These did not, nonetheless, constitute a challenge to the traditional way of life in Europe. For the country village remained the natural home of the vast majority of the Western population.

The Middle Ages mirrored a traditional society but one with a special Christian imprint. The role of medieval Church leaders was critical. Without them the construction of the remarkable Latin Christian civilization, at its height in the twelfth and thirteenth centuries, would never have occurred. The Church itself, however, was bound by the power of lord and land and the enveloping feudal system against which it struggled. Moreover, a traditional society by its nature imposes limits upon future growth. Medieval intellectual achievements were constrained by the subordination of reason to revelation. As medieval civilization became more advanced, the answers that had satisfied a simpler society were found insufficient by ever larger numbers of men. The overwrought emotionalism of the flagellants and the dance of death took the place of the sturdier passion of the monastic movement and the Crusades. New doors had to be opened if Western Civilization was to fulfill its destiny.

TOPIC 22

# THE AGRICULTURAL BASIS FOR MEDIEVAL LIFE

The manorial economy, the agricultural basis for medieval life, provided a firm foundation for feudal society. Even after the weakening of feudal ties, it continued to supply the understructure for an aristocratic social order that survived in some parts of the Western world into the twentieth century. The distinction between free and unfree, between lord and serf, had its concrete expression in the privileges and obligations assumed by each on the land. The customary way of doing things on the manor expressed the social relationships of a traditional society. The readings are concerned with this pattern of life.



## Rural Life in the Middle Ages



In the eleventh century life in the West, and in the countries of Western Europe in particular, was very hard compared with today, but even so it was much less harsh than in certain parts of South America and the Far East in the twentieth century. Western Europe was comparatively sparsely populated, but it was not so in proportion to the acreage of cultivable land. More than half the land was covered by forests, and hunting and clearing new ground were still tasks of the utmost importance, while wolves, deer, and wild boars were a constant threat to fields, flocks, and men.

The fields were plowed by hand, sown one year in every two or three, and the rest of the time allowed to lie fallow and unfertilized. The yield per acre was only half what it would be today, and produce was not enough to feed the population. Nearly all the peasants were serfs, who were compelled to give up half their harvest to their masters, while what remained was not enough to last them the year. Moreover, the population was increasing appreciably faster than the amount of arable land. . . .

The rich—the nobility, that is—lived in stone-built castles and measured their wealth by the thickness of their walls and the strength of their outer fortifications. Peasants built themselves huts of mud and wattle and though these burned down from time to time, they could be rebuilt almost at once without their owner suffering any great loss in the catastrophe beyond a few clay pots and blankets of skins. But if the village's reserve stocks of grain were burned, it meant starvation, and to prevent this the sacks were frequently buried underground. Townsmen's houses were still built largely of wood rather than stone, and in the densely-packed alleys inside city walls, fire was an ever-present menace.

There were no sewers nor any system of drainage for surplus water, and a spell of wet weather turned castle courtyards and the streets of towns and villages into quagmires. The quantities of dung produced by the large numbers of animals meant that even in the cities and the houses of great lords there was a prevailing smell of ordure, smoke, and damp. Under the tables at great feasts the beggars and dogs fought for the generous scraps of meat and bones flung to them by the guests.

Nevertheless, we must not take too seriously this lack of hygiene and comfort and the promiscuity which resulted from it. All

Daily life on the land. Scenes from the peasants' year: planting, gathering apples, chopping wood for fuel, sowing and harvesting wheat, sharpening a sickle. Flemish, fifteenth century.

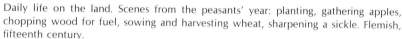

The beating of flax, usually done in November, was necessary to separate wood pith from fiber. The latter was spun into thread. Flemish, fifteenth century.

things considered, the smell of stables is not a great deal more unpleasant than the reek of gasoline fumes, and people from the eleventh century would probably find our own lives hard to bear. When water had to be fetched from a well or spring, fires lit and tended, and the only light came from candles which were precious and expensive or resin torches which provided as much smoke as light, these things were valued at their true worth. People who traveled on foot were rewarded by learning about the country through which they passed. Men were enriched as well as enslaved by having to struggle for the basic necessities of life. . . . Everything had to be made by hand, and even for the very modest demands of the time, the number of master craftsmen—carpenters, smiths, metalworkers, tinsmiths, sculptors in wood or stone, weavers, potters, saddlers, seamstresses, lace-makers, engravers, shoemakers, and others—was proportionately much greater than in our own day. . . .

Man depended on the land to a far greater extent than today, and the land was at once harsher and kinder to him. Fertilizers and irrigation methods were rudimentary, harvests were poor, livestock more difficult to feed, periodically decimated by epidemics, and comparatively speaking more numerous.

Horses, donkeys, mules, and oxen did the work of trains, cars, and machines, and provided raw materials as well as motive power. Cement for building was manufactured from a basis of bull's blood, and in time of war the flayed skins of hundreds of bulls served men for protection under fire. The creatures' hides, intestines, sinews, and horns were in daily domestic use and were among the most necessary raw materials. Sheep were everywhere, providing wool for clothes. Fields of flax and hemp lay alongside the fields of wheat and barley, and the peasants spun and wove, and bleached linen and woolen stuffs in their own meadows. The fabric was hard to make but it was very strong, and one dress might last an entire lifetime. In the absence of soap, people washed with ashes, and that only rarely. As far as the poor were concerned, minstrels claim that they never washed at all, except in the rain. The poor . . . had no shirts and the rich did not always wear them either. Children up to the age of six or seven ran about stark naked when the weather was not too cold, and adults' clothes were simple and roughly made, though they preserved a rigorous decency.

For lighting there was tallow, wood dipped in resin, oil, and wax, but people rose and went to bed with the sun rather than waste their store of illumination. The fields and meadows provided mattresses and floor coverings as well as bread and fodder; people slept on palliasses and strewed their floors of wood or beaten earth with straw. Poultry was plentiful and supplied the rich with feathers for covers and cushions, and the horns of slaughtered animals were used for cups and drinking horns.

With the multiplication of the human race and the gradual disappearance of the great forests, varieties of wild animals are vanishing so fast today that we are being compelled to restock what is left of our forests artificially, and it is hard for us to imagine the abundance of game that existed eight or even four hundred years ago; forests, scrub, and heathland seething with earths and nests, woods filled with the clamor of birdsong every morning, and the sky black with clouds of migrating birds in spring and autumn. Herds of deer browsed in the clearings and would even come into the fields around the village. Wild boars ravaged the harvests, to say nothing of the damage done by hares and rabbits, and foxes and wolves preyed constantly on the poultry and cattle. Man bitterly defended the soil he had conquered against the depredations of wild beasts.

Medieval man's passion for the chase had undoubtedly very little in common with the kind of enthusiasm people feel for it in the twentieth century. Hunting was not a luxury or a pastime; it was a serious job of work, though one that contained elements of sport, war, and holiday, and its object was usually the daily nourishment of the hunter and his family. . . . Meat, even when dried in the sun or smoked in the great chimneys, did not keep well and supplies had to be frequently replenished. There was never enough of the salt and pepper which were indispensable for preserving perishable foodstuffs and also for making them more palatable.

Trees were felled in countless numbers to provide for fuel and building. The poor made do with twigs and brushwood, but the rich consumed hundreds of trees in constructing palisades, bridges, and fortifications for their castles, which were periodically destroyed by fire. Wherever they happened to be, they would use the wood they found on the spot to build siege engines, drawbridges, barrels, grandstands, boats, gibbets, ladders, and a host of other things. Wood at that time was the most basic raw material, and it still seemed a gift as freely given as the air men breathed and was squandered with total disregard. At this stage, men were still having to struggle against the encroaching trees, clearing and deforesting to make cultivable land. Even so, there was all too little available because men had to work too hard to wrest a living from the existing fields and vineyards to undertake the immense labor of clearing the woods. In the eleventh century, man had not yet tamed his land and he regarded it as an apparently inexhaustible source of wealth which he had to conquer by the unceasing sweat of his brow. . . .

## THE NOBILITY

Socially the feudal lord was an oppressor. Nevertheless the people had their rights, and peasants would not compromise over the raising of the dues they paid to their overlord or the amount of time they devoted to his service. Once a custom had become established, the people would tolerate no infringement. Social relations were based on a system of joint contracts, in general respected by both parties. But for the bulk of the people, for the small farmers, nearly all of whom were serfs, the terms of this contract were singularly harsh. The lord was supposed to protect the peasants and this, within the limits of his means, he did because it was in his interest to do so, but he also exploited them severely. Not content with taking his share of their produce, which might be a half or more according to the region, and exacting his days of free labor, he also retained a monopoly over such essential items as the

Christ separates men into the saved and the damned in this twelfth-century Last Judgment on the central facade portal of Autun Cathedral in France.

mill, wine press, and bread ovens and made the peasant pay for the right to use them.

The rights of the people were paltry compared with those of the nobility, but they existed, and the notion of law existed, and this in itself was a good deal. The spirit of revolt also existed naturally enough in every peasant, although it rarely took the form of action because the punishments for rebellion were terrible.

The Christian Church proclaimed that all men were equal, at least in the sight of God. Pictures of the Last Judgment showed kings and bishops among the first ranks of the damned. But it was understood that the poor must wait for the end of the world and the life hereafter before they could contemplate any such reversal of values. On earth, it was the rich who ruled. If things are still very much the same today, it is only fair to point out that in the Middle Ages this state of affairs was accepted with cynical realism. Moreover, community of religion on the one hand and low economic and cultural standards on the other made the gulf between rich and poor, comparatively speaking, smaller than it is in our own times.

The noble, like the peasant, ate with his fingers, frequently slept on straw, shivered with cold or stifled in smoke-filled rooms in winter, tramped through the mud, and bathed in lakes and rivers. Like the peasant he studied the sky, because he too depended on the fields for his livelihood, and hunted himself the venison he ate. For lack of spacious halls and splendid palaces, even the greatest lords entertained their guests in "flowery meadows" and voluntarily camped out in the open air, taking with them wherever they went what little they possessed in the way of carpets, plates, chests of clothes, and caskets of jewels. They were not above sitting on the grass and weaving themselves crowns of field flowers, or decorating their tents, banqueting halls, and lists with garlands of foliage.

A nobleman's chief wealth was in his lands and therefore in the peasants who worked them. The peasants were serfs, that is to say they were attached to the land. Over and above what they owed to their lord, they paid a tithe, or tax, to the Church of a tenth of all their income. Forests and rivers were reserved, almost exclusively, for the lord's hunting and fishing; common land on which the peasants could graze their cattle was not extensive, and they had to pay for the right to pasture their animals on the lord's meadows. The same was true of wood, a basic necessity for heating as well as for making tools.

Small landowners were entitled to dispense low justice for crimes involving penalties of corporal punishment, fines, or imprisonment. High justice, dealing with crimes punishable by mutilation or death, was the prerogative of the wealthy lord, the suzerain of vast domains. For the common people, such crimes were numerous: a man could be hanged for stealing a horse, an ox, or a sum of money, especially if the person from whom he stole them happened to be of noble birth; and the lords were tempted to extend their rights of high justice to such derelictions as poaching. . . .

Those of the common people who had to come into direct contact with their lord, such as his servants, were completely at his mercy and he was free to beat them or abuse them with no risk of interference from the law. At most he incurred the disapproval of the Church, which at one time found itself obliged to issue a formal reminder to noblewomen that it was a sin to beat their servants to death. . . .

In fact, the nobles were often above the law, and for one very good reason: the force of arms. Even a small landowner, if he possessed a well-fortified castle, could either fail to turn up at his trial or declare himself dissatisfied with the verdict; and once he was behind his own walls, there was every chance that the law would tire of pursuing him, especially since, in the absence of an official police force, it was up to the plaintiff to prosecute the miscreant. Strong power was needed to enforce the law, and at that time a man like Hugh of Puiset could barricade himself in his castle a few miles outside Paris and defy even the king himself. . . .

# Sidney Painter: The Manorial Economy

Sidney Painter (1902–1960) of Johns Hopkins University was a knowledgeable commentator on medieval society. In this reading he described the agricultural economic patterns that determined the shape of medieval life. Reprinted from Sidney Painter: *Mediaeval Society*. 

I

### Two- and Three-Field System

Each village had two or three arable fields that were cultivated in rotation. Thus in a village with two fields one would be planted and the other lie fallow. Where there were three fields, one would grow winter grain, one spring, and the third would be fallow. There is some evidence that originally all villages used the two-field system and that the three-field arrangement was an improvement developed in the more fertile districts. In addition to its arable land each village would have its waste, land almost useless, its pasture, usually fair land to steep for the plow, its meadow, and its woods. The land in the arable fields was divided into long, narrow strips. It is possible that at one time these strips were distributed each year by lot; this was often done with the meadow in the Middle Ages. But as soon as we have any adequate evidence we find the strips in the fields permanently assigned to certain tenements. A tenement would consist of a hut in the village, a fenced garden plot with perhaps a few fruit trees, an equal amount of land in each arable field, and a right to share in any use that would be made of waste, pasture, meadow, and woods. In actual practice tenements varied greatly in size, but there is reason to believe that the normal one had about a *virgate,* or thirty acres, of land in the arable fields.

The basic agricultural instrument was the heavy plow that could turn over the heavy soils of northern Europe. Apparently at first it was drawn by eight oxen, but by the twelfth century four ox teams seem to have been usual. . . . These oxen consumed great quantities of fodder, and one of the chief problems

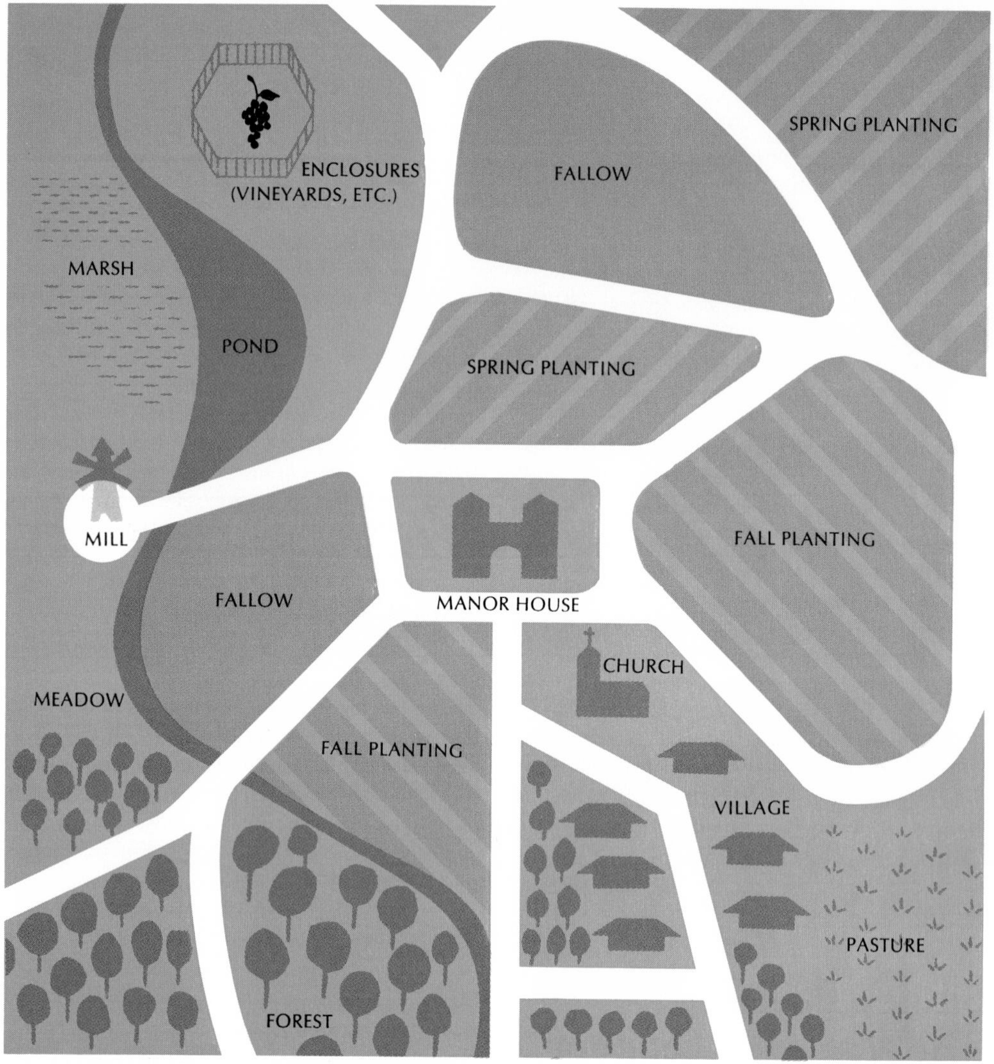


Diagonal lines in each of the fields mark the scattered holdings of the Lord and each of his tenants. The scattering among different fields offered wider access to good land. Strips were long so that a heavy plow would not have to be turned too frequently. The heavy plow, used widely in Northern Europe, required several draft animals to pull it and encouraged cooperation among the villagers. The fields were generally unenclosed so that cattle could graze after the harvest and manure the soil.

of mediaeval agriculture was to keep enough land under grass to supply them with pasture in the summer and hay in the winter.

## Agricultural Productivity

Agricultural productivity was in general extremely low. Seed was sown broadcast to the great delight of the birds. Although by the thirteenth century it was known that seed from another district produced better results, most villages could not get it and simply used part of their own crop. The value of manure was understood, but no effective use was made of what little was available. When a crop was harvested, the cattle were turned into the field and kept on it while it lay fallow, but manuring by that method was extremely casual. And in general no village could support enough cattle to supply adequate manure. All the land that could be put under the plow was needed to supply grain for bread. Since a village had to keep enough meadow to feed its plow teams over the winter, there was little hay left over for other animals. Thus the cows lived in summer on the sparse pasture land and starved in winter. All animals not needed for breeding were usually slaughtered in the fall. The cows supplied milk that was usually turned into cheese. The sheep gave wool to make the necessary clothing. Both cows and sheep were eaten when they were slaughtered, but such occasions were rare. Moreover, the hard, rangy animals fed on the common pasture were thin and tough. A fifteenth-century writer stated that if he were forced to choose between eating a cow or its hide he would choose the hide. The most important food-producing animal was the pig. He could fend for himself winter and summer. Villages that had oak or beech woods were peculiarly fortunate because the nuts and acorns fed the swine. In England the area of a village's woodland was usually expressed in terms of the number of pigs it could feed.

Experts have calculated that a family with thirty acres in the fields and its share in wood, pasture, and meadow could probably feed itself reasonably well in good years. But the margin between the peasant and hunger was never wide, and in poor years everyone starved. The peasant's food consisted primarily of bread. To this was added some fruit and vegetables from his garden plot. Fish and chicken were rare luxuries and meat, with the exception of pork, rarer still. The well-known fat back of the southern tenant farmer was the usual meat of his mediaeval predecessor.

Until the twelfth century at least the village was essentially self-sufficient economically. It grew its own food and drink. The wool from its sheep was made into cloth by the village women. The absolutely essential craftsmen, the smith and the miller, were villagers who worked part time at those trades. The village could exist without any exchange of goods with the world beyond its borders. Although it seems likely that there was always some exchange of produce by barter, let us say one village's surplus pigs for another's surplus chickens, in general there was no market for agricultural products and hence the village had no means with which to purchase outside goods.

## The Village Economy

It is important to realize that the village was far more than a group of huts surrounded by arable land, meadow, pasture, waste, and woods: it was a corporation for the exploitation of the land. The cultivation of the land was governed by the villagers as a whole. They decided when to plant, when to weed, when to harvest, what crops to grow, and what seed to use. Certain villagers were assigned specific tasks. There was a general executive to see that the common decisions were carried out. There was a hay warden who looked after the meadow and cowherds and swineherds to watch the animals in the common pasture. There was always some kind of village court to settle disputes over tenements and punish those who failed to perform their tasks.

The village was also a social and religious unit. The villagers had their festivals and celebrations. As a rule their sons and daughters married within the group. When the rural parish system was developed in the ninth and tenth centuries, the village usually became a parish with its church and priest. A group of the village elders, usually called churchwardens, looked after . . . the church and cared for the cemetery. In short, the village was the basic unit in mediaeval rural life. . . .

II

## The Seignorial System

Essentially the seignorial system [another term to describe manorial society] was a set of institutions through which the nonproductive classes, nobles and clergy, drew their support from the agricultural workers. . . . By the twelfth century most villages were under the domination of a lord, and the lords exploited their villages by rather similar means. Scholars have debated at length as to whether these villages ruled by lords were originally great Roman estates worked by slaves or villages of free German farmers that had in some way fallen under the domination of lords. Recent research has shown that both these theories are valid. The Roman imperial estates in Gaul passed into the hands of the Frankish kings or were given by them to the church or to their followers. Many of the great senatorial estates survived either in the hands of

AGRICULTURAL PRODUCTIVITY

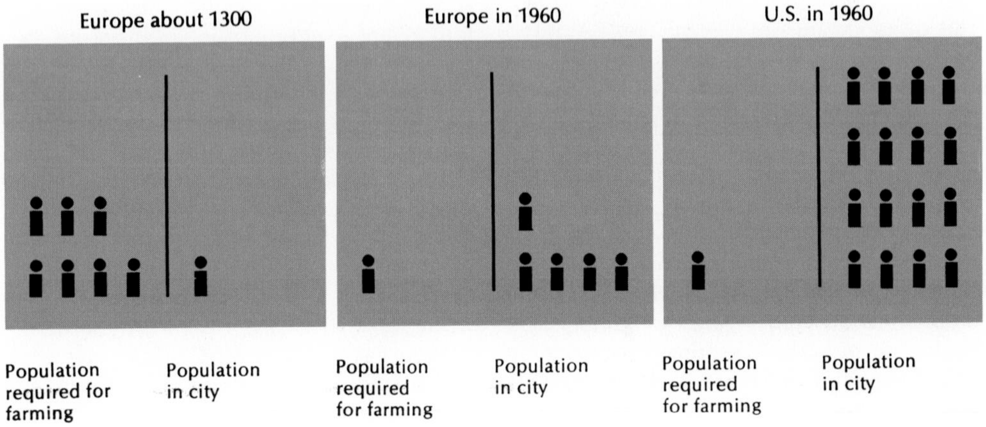

the descendants of their Roman owners or in those of Frankish nobles. In the late days of the empire cultivation by slaves had largely given place to cultivation by *coloni.* [See Reading 84] The *colonus* had a cottage and a small piece of land for his own use, but most of his time was devoted to working on the land reserved by the estate owner. He would not leave the estate without the owner's permission. In short, he was a semi-free tenant who paid his rent for his house and plot of land by working for his lord. He was the most obvious ancestor of the mediaeval serf.

In Carolingian times we find great estates of both Roman and Frankish origin cultivated on much this same system. There is a village of tenants, and they have small plots of ground for their own use, but the major part of the land is reserved for the lord and cultivated for him by the tenants. Yet it seems clear that there were also free villages where there was no lord. Free farmers lived together and cultivated their fields in co-operation. Such villages are found in parts of England as late as the eleventh century, and they were predominant in parts of Germany. In France they probably disappeared somewhat earlier. This disappearance of free villages is not too hard to explain. In periods of violence and disorder the peasants were helpless against the knights. A village lying near a castle had little choice but to submit to the lord of the castle. If it did so, he protected it from other knights, and if it did not, he plundered it himself. Thus in times of general disorder small free farmers had only two choices: to become knights themselves or to seek the protection of a knight. And the number who could muster the resources to acquire knightly equipment must have been fairly small. Once a knight took over a village, he set up the institutions that were most effective for its exploitation, and they may well have been derived from those of the estates that had once been Roman villas.

III

## The Lord's Rights

Throughout most of the region of villages the seignorial system followed a common general pattern. A part of the land in the arable fields was reserved for the lord. This part, which was likely to be about a third of the total arable land, was called the demesne. The lord also reserved for himself a part of the meadow. The villagers worked the demesne for the lord: they sowed, cultivated, and harvested his grain, cut his hay, and did any other necessary work. The village herdsmen looked after the lord's cattle and swine as well as those of the villagers. If the lord wanted a moat dug for his castle or a fence built to keep deer in part of the woodland, the villagers were obliged to do it. In general, they devoted three days of the week to working for the lord, but he could require more on special occasions. Then the villagers paid the lord as rent a set proportion of the crops they grew on their own land. In addition they owed him a wide variety of payments for the use of the resources of the village lands. For pasturing their cattle they paid the lord cheeses; for letting their swine roam in the woods they paid a certain number of pigs. When the villagers fished in the stream or pond, the lord got part of the catch—usually the larger fish. In most parts of France the pike was a fish that always went to the lord.

The villagers paid rent for their tenements by working for the lord on his demesne and by paying a wide variety of miscellaneous dues for various privileges. Then the lord usually had certain profitable monopolies. Thus usually the lord owned the mill, and the villagers were compelled to have their grain ground there. The possession of a hand mill was a serious crime. In return for grinding the grain the lord took a part of the flour. Then the lord controlled the ovens where the bread was baked and took his fee for that. In most parts of France only the lord could keep doves. They fed on the peasants' crops and were themselves eaten by the lord. Finally, the lord had a court where offenses against the rules of the village were punished. If a man tried to dodge doing the work owed the lord, if a swineherd went to sleep and lost the swine, if a villager stole apples from the lord's orchard, or if anyone was caught using a hand mill, he was tried and punished in this court. . . .

## The Serf

By the eleventh century most of the people who lived in the villages were unfree. A villager could not leave his lord's land without his consent. He could not own any personal property; everything he possessed belonged to his lord. He could not marry the tenant of another lord. His lord could increase the services and rents due from the villager whenever he saw fit. But he was not a slave in the usual sense. His lord could not sell him or give him away unless he gave his tenement with him. His lord could not legally beat him or maltreat him physically. In England this distinction was very clear. The unfree villager could not bring any civil suit against his lord; he had no property rights against him. But he could carry a criminal charge against his lord to the royal courts. In France, where the lord often had full rights of jurisdiction, this distinction was probably more theoretical than practical, but it always existed. When a French baron hanged his unfree tenant, he did so as the king's delegate, not as a manorial lord. Nevertheless, the tenant had no economic rights against his lord and could be exploited at the lord's will. But here again practice probably did not follow theory too closely. The Middle Ages was a time when custom had enormous weight, and most lords probably continued to collect the same services and dues as had their ancestors, even though they had the right to increase them. Moreover, much increase was likely to be impractical. The villagers were the lord's labor force, and his land was useless to him unless they were alive and able to work.

Contemporary writers used many different terms to describe the unfree villager, and the meaning of these terms varied from region to region. Perhaps the most common was *villain,* which meant simply villager. Another was *rusticus* or countryman. . . .

The word used in France to describe the unfree—and the unfree only—was *servus* or serf. . . .

# A Survey of the Demesne of the Abbey of St. Germain

Much of our knowledge of medieval rural conditions comes from the surveys made of their estates by landowners who wanted to keep a record of their holdings and of their incomes. The survey from which the following excerpts were taken was made for the great abbey of St. Germain near Paris in the ninth century. The survey began with an account of the abbey's holding (demesne) at Palaiseau and then detailed the obligations of the tenants, free and unfree, living on the property. Reprinted with permission from White's (trans.), "Polyptyque de L'Abbe Irminon" in *Medieval History: A Source Book,* Donald White, ed. (Homewood, Ill.: The Dorsey Press) pp. 280–282.

In Palaiseau there is a demesne manse [portion of land reserved for the estate owner] with a house and other sufficient buildings. There are six fields of arable land containing 287 *bunuaria* (992.65 acres) where 1300 *modios* (about 2250 bushels) of wheat can be sown. There are 127 *aripennos* (127 acres) of vine which provide 800 *modios* (11,088 gallons) of wine.

It has 100 *aripennos* (100 acres) of meadow which provide 150 cartloads of hay.

The woodland measures as a whole one league in circumference and can fatten 50 pigs.

It has three mills which pay a rent of 153 *modios* (about 2580 bushels). . . .

It also has a church in Gito held by the priest Warodus. Seven tenants belong to it. They work one day a week with food and owe one hen, 5 eggs and 3 *denarios.* It also demands, in gift, one horse.

Walafredus, a *colonus* and mayor, and his wife, a *colona* . . . , dependents (*homines*) of St. Germain; they have 2 children. . . . He holds 2 free manses having 7 *bunuaria* (about 24 acres) of arable land, 6 acres of vine and 4 of meadow. He owes for each manse a cow one year, a pig the next, 4 *denarios* for the right to use the wood, 2 *modios* of wine (almost 28 gallons) for the right to use the pasture, a ewe and a lamb. He plows 4 perches ($\frac{1}{3}$ of an acre?) for winter wheat, 2 perches for spring wheat. He owes *corvées,* cartage, manual labor, tree-felling when ordered, 3 hens and 15 eggs. . . .

Ebrulfus, a *colonus,* and his wife, a slave, . . . dependants of St. Germain; they have 4 children. Ermenoldus, a slave, and his wife, a *colona,* . . . dependents of St. Germain; they have 4 children. . . . Teutgardis, slave of St. Germain; she has one child. . . . These three hold a free manse having 4 *bunuaria* and one *antsingam* (?) of arable land, 4 acres of vine and 2 of meadow. They work 8 acres (of the lord's) vine. They owe 2 *modios* (almost 28 gallons) of wine for right of pasture and 2 *sestarios* ($1\frac{1}{2}$ gallons?) of mustard. . . .

Maurus, a slave, and his wife, a freedwoman, . . . dependents of St. Germain; they have 2 children. . . . Guntoldus, a *colonus* of St. Germain. These two hold one servile manse, having 2 *bunuaria* (about 7 acres) of arable land, $2\frac{1}{2}$ acres of vine and $1\frac{1}{2}$ of meadow. They work 8 acres (of the lord's) vine and owe 4 *modios* (about $55\frac{1}{2}$ gallons) of wine for right of pasture; 2 *sestarios* ($1\frac{1}{2}$ gallons?) of mustard, three hens and 15 eggs; also manual labor, corvées and cartage.

Leodarus, freedman of St. Germain, holds a quarter of a manse, having 2 *bunuaria* (about 7 acres) of arable land and $\frac{1}{2}$ acre of vine. He works 4 acres (of the lord's) vine. He owes 1 *modius* (almost 14 gallons) of wine for right of pasture, one *sestarios* ($\frac{3}{4}$ gallon?) of mustard, one hen and five eggs.

Nadalfredus, a slave, and his wife, a *colona,* . . . dependents of St. Germain; they have 3 children. . . . Electulfs, a slave, and his wife, a *colona,* dependents of St. Germain; they have 3 children. . . . Todoinus, a slave, and his wife, a *colona*, . . . dependents of St. Germain. These three hold one servile manse having 1 *bunuaria* (about $2\frac{1}{3}$ acres) of arable land, 1 acre of vine and $\frac{1}{2}$ acre of meadow. They work 8 acres (of the lord's) vine. They owe 3 *modios* ($41\frac{1}{2}$ gallons) of wine for right of pasture and 3 *sestarios* (about 2 gallons) of mustard.

# George C. Homans: The Medieval Peasant as a Farmer

In his study of the English villagers of the thirteenth century, Harvard sociologist George C. Homans (1910– ) attempted to describe a social order of the past by examining the villagers' skills at making a living from the soil and how they lived and worked together. Reprinted by permission of the publishers from George C. Homans, *English Villagers of the Thirteenth Century*, Cambridge, Mass.: Harvard University Press, Copyright 1941 by the President and Fellows of Harvard College; 1969 by George Caspar Homans. pp. 39–42, 51.

The husbandman of the Middle Ages, Piers Plowman, was a subsistence farmer, to use an American phrase. He raised crops not so much to be sold in the market as to be consumed by himself, his household, and his stock. And his subsistence was largely of grain, with peas and beans, baked into bread, boiled into puddings, or brewed into ale. Some leeks or cabbages he may have grown in his garden. He kept a few tough, razor-backed hogs, either running half-wild in the woods and battening on the mast of English oaks and beeches, or about the village, ringed or yoked to prevent their rooting up the turf. Swine flesh, salted or smoked, was the flesh Piers commonly ate. He kept hens and geese, too, and sometimes slaughtered a sheep, a cow, or one of his plow oxen. But he cannot have supped every evening on a dish of meat. Bread, throughout the Middle Ages, was the staff of life. . . .

The first man who cultivated grains must have been cast from self-satisfaction to despair when he found that his plot yielded every year smaller and smaller crops. Perhaps it is not right to say that husbandmen have known ever since that fields cannot be cropped continuously without becoming exhausted. It is not a question of exhaustion in the sense that the fields will eventually bear no crop at all, unless as a result of cultivation the top-soil has washed or blown away, something which has happened in parts of the United States. But they will bear much poorer crops than they might otherwise have borne. Piers Plowman knew at least three means by which the fertility of fields which had been under crop could be restored or improved. The first was the simplest of all. He knew that if fields were simply let alone for a time they would bear better crops. This method he called fallowing. The second method was marling. In many parts of England he could dig marl, a soil of clay combined with carbonate of lime, and spread it on the fields. Marl was a fertilizer. The third method was dunging. He could fold his sheep systematically on the fields. Or he could spread on the fields the manure of his cattle, commonly as mixed with straw in the form of compost. In some countries a cow or an ox is more important as a machine for producing dung than it is for any other purpose. Since Piers seldom could get marl in large quantities and never had vast dunghills because of faults in his technique which will appear presently, he was reduced to fallowing as the only means of bringing any large part of his land back into good heart.

So far Piers Plowman possessed a respectable understanding of agriculture. The great gap in his skill was that he did not know turnips or the grasses, such as the clovers and alfalfa, as field crops. Modern farmers employ the grasses in ways which serve either directly or indirectly to keep the soil rich. Directly, a crop like alfalfa grown on a piece of worn-out land and plowed in will restore to the soil the nitrogen it needs to produce grain. Indirectly, grass can be grown as a fodder for cattle; the cattle produce manure, and the manure is spread on the fields. Using the judicious combinations of these means, a modern farmer can almost manufacture the kind of soil he requires. The artificial grasses and turnips do not seem to have been introduced into England much before the second half of the seventeenth century and were not in common use until a century later. The introduction of new methods is called the Agricultural Revolution, which is less spoken of but hardly less important than the Industrial Revolution which took place at the same time. But it is better to put the matter in this way: the important thing the Agricultural Revolution brought in was not any specific method but an idea—the idea that all methods of agriculture could be studied and improved, the idea of a rational agriculture. This idea was new in Europe, at least since Roman times. In the Middle Ages, agriculture was customary. Men farmed as their fathers had farmed and did not dream of anything better.

Piers Plowman did not know the grasses as field crops. He did not know anything about sowing them in worn-out fields in order to bring the land back into good heart. He had only fallowing as a means of making any large part of his land once more able to bear crops, and thus no matter how hard he worked he was limited by the original qualities of the soil. More important, he did not sow the grasses for fodder for his cattle. The greatest difference between medieval agriculture and modern is in this humble but vital matter of hay. The men of the Middle Ages knew nothing of hay deliberately sown as a crop. This notion is a hard one for us to get used to, but it seems to be true. This does not mean that Piers Plowman had no hay. But the hay he had was only such as grew naturally and luxuriantly in the river bottoms and other low, wet places. Again, this does not mean strictly that it grew without any cultivation. Piers' forefathers had to reclaim the meadows from swamp, and Piers himself had to mow them every year and see that the ditches were clean. But he did not sow grass-seed as he sowed corn. Unhappily the amount of water meadow in England is limited, and in the Middle Ages an acre of meadow was worth something like three times as much as an acre of arable land. Piers' hay crop was small, and since it was small his cattle were few. During the summer they could graze in the pastures, but in the winter they had to be fed on hay, together with as much of the spring-corn crop as Piers used for fodder. And since his cattle were few, the amount of dung Piers had to spread on his fields was small also. Husbandry is full of such vicious circles. In still another way, then, Piers was brought back to fallowing as his only large-scale means of restoring the qualities of the soil. From time to time, he simply had to leave the soil alone. . . .

Such were some of the important skills, techniques of husbandry known to Piers Plowman in the thirteenth century. So far they have been described simply as available knowledge: there has been little to say in detail about the ways in which they were actually put into effect. Conceivably the possible ways of putting them into effect were many. This we can appreciate from the history of the present time. Americans and Russians today know approximately the same techniques of farming. The Russians are making, as fast as they can, tractors just like the American ones. But the human group which puts the techniques into effect is in the United States what is called the individual farm, in the Union of Soviet Socialist Republics what is called the collective farm. The lesson to be read is that the particular application of any set of skills is determined not only by the skills themselves and by the physical environment in which they are used but also by the sentiments, traditions, ideals of the people who use them. . . .

# Lynn White: Technology and Invention in the Middle Ages

A common misconception of the Middle Ages holds that they were an ignorant and static era. In this reading Professor Lynn White, Jr. (1907–      ), for many years president of Mills College, collected evidence to show that medieval men were open to change when it had relevance to their direct concerns.

Reprinted from Lynn White, "Technology, and Invention in The Middle Ages," *Speculum,* XV, 2 (April 1940), published by The Mediaeval Academy of America. Reprinted with permission. Pp. 149, 151–155.

The Dark Ages doubtless deserve their name: political disintegration, economic depression, the debasement of religion and the collapse of literature surely made the barbarian kingdoms in some ways unimaginably dismal. Yet because many aspects of civilization were in decay we should not assume too quickly that everything was backsliding. . . .

The basic occupation was, of course, agriculture. We have passed through at least two agricultural revolutions: that which began . . . in the early eighteenth century, and another, equally important, in the Dark Ages.

The problem of the development and diffusion of the northern wheeled plow, equipped with colter, horizontal share and moldboard, is too thorny to be discussed here. Experts seem generally agreed: (1) that the new plow greatly increased production by making possible the tillage of rich, heavy, badly-drained river-bottom soils; (2) that it saved labor by making cross-plowing superfluous, and thus produced the typical northern strip-system of land division, as distinct from the older block-system dictated by the cross-plowing necessary with the lighter Mediterranean plow; (3) most important of all, that the heavy plow needed such power that peasants pooled their oxen and plowed together, thus laying the basis for the mediaeval cooperative agricultural community, the manor. But whatever may be the date and origin of the fully developed heavy plow, its effects were supplemented and greatly enhanced in the later eighth century by the invention of the three-field system, an improved rotation of crops and fallow which greatly increased the efficiency of agricultural labor. For example, by switching 600 acres from the two-field to the three-field system, . . . peasants could plant 100 acres more in crops each year with 100 acres less of plowing. Since fallow land was plowed twice to keep down the weeds, the old plan required three acres of plowing for every acre in crops, whereas the new plan required only two acres of plowing for every productive acre. . . .

In ways less immediately significant the Dark Ages likewise made ingenious improvements. . . . Perhaps the most successful amateur student of early mediaeval technology was the Commandant Lefebvre des Noëttes, who after his retirement from active service in the French cavalry, devoted himself to his hobby, the history of horses. . . . From his investigations Lefebvre des Noëttes concluded that the use of animal power in antiquity was unbelievably inefficient. The ancients did not use nailed shoes on their animals, and broken hooves often rendered beasts useless. Besides, they knew only the

Old and new harnesses are seen in these eleventh-century illustrations. The choking effect of the old harness on a team of oxen is apparent. Below, the new stiff collar resting upon the shoulders allowed the animal to breathe freely. This is the example of a horse being used for harrowing in the Bayeux Tapestry mentioned by Professor White.

yoke-system of harness. While this was adequate for oxen, it was most unsatisfactory for the more rapid horse. The yoke rested on the withers of a team. From each end of the yoke ran two flexible straps: one a girth behind the forelegs, the other circling the horse's neck. As soon as the horse began to pull, the flexible front strap pressed on his windpipe, and the harder he pulled the closer he came to strangulation. Moreover the ancient harness was mechanically defective: the yoke was too high to permit the horse to exert his full force in pulling by flinging his body-weight into the task. Finally, the ancients were unable to harness one animal in front of another. Thus all great weights had to be drawn by gangs of slaves, since animal power was not technically available in sufficient quantities.

According to Lefebvre des Noëttes this condition remained unchanged until the later ninth or early tenth century when, almost simultaneously, three major inventions appear: the modern horse-collar, the tandem harness, and the horseshoe. The modern harness, consisting of a rigid horse-collar resting on the shoulders of the beast, permitted him to breathe freely. This was connected to the load by lateral traces which enabled the horse to throw his whole body into pulling. It has been shown experimentally that this new apparatus so greatly increased the effective animal power that a team which can pull only about one thousand pounds with the antique yoke can pull three or four times that weight when equipped with the new harness. Equally important was the extension of the traces so that tandem harnessing was possible, thus providing an indefinite amount of animal power for the transport of great weights. Finally, the introduction of the nailed horseshoe improved traction and greatly increased the endurance of the newly available animal power. Taken together these three inventions suddenly gave Europe a new supply of nonhuman power, at no increase of expense or labor. They did for the eleventh and twelfth centuries what the steam-engine did for the nineteenth. Lefebvre des Noëttes has therefore offered an unexpected and plausible solution for the most puzzling problem of the Middle Ages: the sudden upswing of European vitality after the year 1000.

However, Lefebvre des Noëttes failed to point out the relation between this access of energy and the contemporary agricultural revolution. He noted that the new harness made the horse available for agricultural labor: the first picture of a horse so engaged is found in the Bayeux Tapestry. But while the horse is a rapid and efficient power-engine, it burns an expensive fuel—grain—as compared with the slower, but cheaper, hay-burning ox. Under the two-field system the peasant's margin of production was insufficient to support a work-horse; under the three-field system the horse gradually displaced the ox as the normal plow and draft animal of the northern plains. By the later Middle Ages there is a clear correlation on the one hand between the horse and the three-field system and on the other between the ox and the two-field system. The contrast is essentially one between the standards of living and of labor-productivity of the northern and the southern peasantry: the ox saves food; the horse saves man-hours. The new agriculture, therefore, enabled the north to exploit the new power more effectively than the Mediterranean regions could, and thereby the northerners increased their prosperity still further. . . .

TOPIC 23

# KINGSHIP AND THE FEUDAL STATE

Feudalism resulted from the inability of central authority to carry out the functions of government. During the invasions that engulfed Europe, these functions were taken over by local chieftains who served for all practical purposes as petty kings. As a result, with the exception of outstanding personalities such as Charlemagne, few monarchs in the early feudal era exercised much real authority. By the twelfth and thirteenth centuries, however, ambitious kings proved able to fashion loyalties out of feudal ties that strengthened the powers of a new "feudal monarchy." Such powers accumulated through the timeless mystique of kingship itself, the aid of the Church which saw kingship as a buttress to its religious objectives, the calculated use of force, and the steady labor of the kings' servants. In administration, justice, and military organization the new monarchy planted the seeds of the modern state. The readings examine the growing exercise of royal authority within the feudal state.

Reading 115

## The Growth of National Monarchies

From *A History of the Modern World,* by Robert R. Palmer and Joel Colton. Copyright 1950, © 1956, 1965 by Alfred A. Knopf, Inc. Reprinted by permission of the publisher.

About A.D. 1000, there began to be more security of life and limb [in Europe]. The farmer could plant with more confidence that he would reap. A man could build a house and expect to live his life in it and pass it on to his children. Hence there was more planting and building. One reason for the new personal security was that, after the Norse and Magyar inroads, Europe was spared the assaults of barbarians. Moreover, the church persuaded warring nobles to moderate their quarrelsome habits. In the Peace of God, instituted in the eleventh century, the bishops and magnates of a locality joined together to repress violence and levied fines on offenders. Thirdly, peace and personal security were advanced by the growth of institutions that we know as "feudalism."

Feudalism . . . a means of carrying on some kind of government on a local basis where no organized state existed. After the collapse of Charlemagne's empire the real authority fell into the hands of persons who were most often called "counts." The count was the most important man of a region covering a few hundred square miles. To build up his own position, and strengthen himself for war against other counts, he tried to keep the peace and maintain control over the lesser lords in his country, those whose possessions extended over a few hundred or a few thousand acres. These lesser lords accepted or were forced to accept his protection. They became his vassals, and he became their "lord." . . .

This feudal scheme . . . gradually spread. Lords at the level of counts became in turn the vassals of dukes. In the year 987 the great lords of France chose Hugh Capet as their king, and became his vassals. The kings of France enjoyed little real power for another two hundred years, but the descendants of Hugh occupied their throne for eight centuries, until the French Revolution. Similarly the magnates of Germany elected a king in 911; in 962 the German king was crowned Emperor, as Charlemagne had been before him; thus originated the Holy Roman Empire. . . .

To England, in these formative centuries, it was not given to choose a king by election. England was conquered in 1066 by the Duke of Normandy, William. The Normans (the old Norsemen re-shaped by a century of Christian and French influence) imposed upon England a centralized and efficient type of feudalism which they had developed in Normandy. In England, from an early date, the king and his central officials therefore had considerable power. In England there was more civil peace and personal security than on the Continent. Within its strong monarchy self-governing institutions could eventually develop with a minimum of disorder.

The notable feature of feudalism was its mutual or reciprocal character. In this it differed from the old Roman imperial principle, by which the emperor had been a majestic and all-powerful sovereign. Under feudalism no one was sovereign. King and people, lord and vassal, were joined in a kind of contract. Each owed something to the other. If one defaulted, the obligation ceased. If a vassal refused his due services, the king had the right to enforce compliance. If the king violated the rights of the vassal, the vassals could join together against him. The king was supposed to act with the advice of the vassals, who formed his council or court. If the vassals believed the king to be exceeding his lawful powers, they could impose terms upon him. It was out of this mutual or contractual character of feudalism that ideas of constitutional government later developed. . . .

Meanwhile the kings were busy, each trying to build his kingdom into an organized monarchy that would outlast his life. Monarchy became hereditary; the king inherited his position like any other feudal lord or possessor of an estate. Inheritance of the crown made for peace and order, for elections under the conditions of the time were usually turbulent and disputed, and where the older Germanic principle of elective monarchy remained alive, as in the Holy Roman Empire, there was periodic commotion. The kings sent out executive officers to supervise their interests throughout their kingdoms. The kings of England sent a sheriff into each of the forty shires; the kings of France created similar officers who were called bailiffs. The kings likewise instituted royal courts, under royal justices, to decide property disputes and repress crime. This assertion of legal jurisdiction, together with the military force to enforce judgments upon obstinate nobles, became a main pillar of the royal power. In England especially, and in lesser degree elsewhere, the kings required local inhabitants to assist royal judges in the discovery of relevant facts in particular cases. They put men on oath to declare what they knew of events in their own neighborhood. It is from this enforced association of private persons with royal officers that the jury developed.

The kings needed money to pay for their governmental machinery or to carry on war with other kings. Taxation, as known in the Roman Empire, was quite unknown to the Germanic and feudal tradition. In the feudal scheme each person was responsible only for the customary fees which arose on stated occasions. The king, like other lords, was supposed to live on his own income—on the revenue of manors that he owned himself, the proceeds of estates temporarily under his wardship, or the occasional fees paid to him by his vassals. No king, even for the best of reasons, could simply decree a new tax and collect it. At the same time, as the use of money became more common, the kings had to assure themselves of a money income. In England, in the twelfth century, the customary obligation of the vassal to render military service to the king was converted into a money payment, called "scutage" or shield money. As the towns grew up, with a new kind of wealth and a new source of money income, they agreed to make certain payments in return for their royal charters.

The royal demands for money, the royal claims to exercise jurisdiction, were regarded as innovations. They were constantly growing and sometimes were a source of abuse. They met with frequent resistance in all countries. A famous case historically (though somewhat commonplace in its own day) was that of Magna Carta in England in 1215, when the English lords and high churchmen, joined by representatives of the city of London, required King John to confirm and guarantee their historic liberties.

The king, as has been said, like any lord, was supposed to act in council or "court" with his vassals. The royal council became the egg out of which departments of government were hatched—such as the royal judiciary, exchequer, and military command. From it also was hatched the institution of parliaments. The kings had always, in a rough sort of way, held great parleys or "talks" (the Latin *parliamentum* meant simply a "talking") with their chief retainers. In the twelfth and thirteenth centuries the growth of towns added a new element to European life. To the lords and bishops was now added a burgher class, which, if of far inferior dignity, was too stubborn, free-spirited, and well furnished with money to be overlooked. When representatives of the towns began to be normally summoned to the king's great "talks," along with lords and clergy, parliaments may be said to have come into being.

Parliaments, in this sense, sprouted all over Europe in the thirteenth century. Nothing shows better the similarity of institutions in Latin Christendom, or the inadequacy of tracing the history of any one country by itself. The new assemblies were called *cortes* in Spain, diets in Germany, estates-general in France, parliaments in the British Isles. Usually they are referred to generically as "estates," the word "parliament" being reserved for Britain, but in origin they were all essentially the same.

The kings called these assemblies as a means of publicizing and strengthening the royal rule. They found it more convenient to explain their policies, or to ask for money, to a large gathering brought together for that purpose than to have a hundred officials make

## Reading 116

Charles the Bald, grandson of Charlemagne, holds a council. From Count Vivian's Bible, Tours, 843–851.

local explanations and strike local bargains in a hundred different places. The kings did not recognize, nor did the assemblies claim, any right of the parliament to dictate to the king and his government. But usually the king invited the parliament to state grievances; his action upon them was the beginning of parliamentary legislation.

The parliaments were considered to represent not the "nation" nor "people" nor yet the individual citizen, but the "estates of the realm," the great collective interests of the country. The first and highest estate was the clergy, the second the landed or noble class; to these older ruling groups were added, as a "third estate," the burghers of the chartered towns. Quite commonly these three types of people sat separately as three distinct chambers. But the pattern varied from country to country. . . .

# William the Conqueror's Power as King

The author, a monk in William's day, contributed this description of the Norman conqueror of Anglo-Saxon England to a longer account known as *The Saxon Chronicle*. From Frederic A. Ogg, *A Source Book of Medieval History* (New York, 1907), pp. 241–244.

If any one would know what manner of man King William was, the glory that he obtained, and of how many lands he was lord, then will we describe him as we have known him, we who have looked upon him and who once lived at his court. This King William, of whom we are speaking, was a very wise and a great man, and more honored and more powerful than any of his predecessors. He was mild to those good men who loved God, but severe beyond measure towards those who withstood his will. He founded a noble monastery on the spot where God permitted him to conquer England, and he established monks in it, and he made it very rich. In his days the great monastery at Canterbury was built, and many others also throughout England; moreover, this land was filled with monks who lived after the rule of St. Benedict; and such was the state of religion in his days that all who would, might observe that which was prescribed by their respective orders.

King William was also held in much reverence. He wore his crown three times every year when he was in England: at Easter he wore it at Winchester, at Pentecost at Westminster, and at Christmas at Gloucester. And at these times all the men of England were with him, archbishops, bishops, abbots and earls, thanes and knights. So also was he a very stern and a wrathful man, so that none durst do anything against his will, and he kept in prison those earls who acted against his pleasure. He removed bishops from their sees and abbots from their offices, and he imprisoned thanes, and at length he spared not his own brother Odo. This Odo was a very powerful bishop in Normandy. His see was that of Bayeux, and he was foremost to serve the king. He had an earldom in England, and when William was in Normandy he [Odo] was the first man in this country [England], and him did William cast into prison.

Amongst other things, the good order that William established is not to be forgotten. It was such that any man, who was himself aught, might travel over the kingdom with a bosom full of gold unmolested; and no man durst kill another, however great the injury he might have received from him. He reigned over England, and being sharp-sighted to his own interest, he surveyed the kingdom so thoroughly that there was not a single hide of land throughout the whole of which he knew not the possessor, and how much it was worth, and this he afterwards entered in his register. The land of the Britons [Wales] was under his sway, and he built castles therein; moreover he had full dominion over the Isle of Man; Scotland also was subject to him, from his great strength; the land of Normandy was his by inheritance, and he possessed the earldom of Maine; and had he lived two years longer, he would have subdued Ireland by his prowess, and that without a battle.

Truly there was much trouble in these times, and very great distress. He caused castles to be built and oppressed the poor. The king was also of great sternness, and he took from his subjects many marks of gold, and many hundred pounds of silver, and this, whether with or without right, and with little need. He was given to avarice, and greedily loved gain. He made large forests for the deer, and enacted laws therewith, so that whoever killed a hart or a hind should be blinded. As he forbade killing the deer, so also the boars; and he loved the tall stags as if he were their father. He also commanded concerning the hares, that they should go free. The rich complained and the poor murmured, but he was so sturdy that he recked nought of them; they must will all that the king willed, if they would live, or would keep their lands, or would hold their possessions, or would be maintained in their rights. Alas that any man should so exalt himself, and carry himself in his pride over all! We have written concerning him these things, both good and bad, that virtuous men may follow after the good, and wholly avoid the evil, and may go in the way that leadeth to the kingdom of heaven.

# Magna Carta, the Feudal Struggle against the English Monarchy

William the Conqueror and his descendants were kings of England, but they retained extensive land holdings in France for which, in name at any rate, they were vassals of the king of France. The existence of such a powerful vassal, whose holdings were actually greater in extent than that of the French kings, created a threat that the latter attempted to remove as soon as they were strong enough to do so. While the struggle for control of the Norman lands was going on in the first decade of the thirteenth century, King John of England found himself confronting a rebellion among his nobles at home who were dissatisfied with his attempts to increase the prerogatives of the crown. The first reading describes the sequence of events leading to King John's granting of the charter (1215). The second contains excerpts from the Charter. In it John accepted the demands of the rebels. The *Magna Carta* influenced the course of later English constitutional development. It showed the potential within the English feudal monarchy for the evolution of limited government under law. Later movements for political rights in England would find support in this guarantee of feudal liberties. I. From Guy C. Lee, *Source Book of English History,* Second Edition (New York, 1909), pp. 167–169. II. From Edward P. Cheyney, ed., "English Constitutional Documents of the Middle Ages," in *Translations and Reprints from the Original Sources of European History,* edited by Department of History of the University of Pennsylvania (Philadelphia, 1897), I, No. 6, pp. 6–17.

## I. THE BACKGROUND OF MAGNA CARTA

### Demands of the Barons

In Easter week of this same year [1215], the above-mentioned nobles assembled at Stamford, with horses and arms; for they had now induced almost all the nobility of the whole kingdom to join them, and constituted a very large army; for in their army there were computed to be two thousand knights, besides horse soldiers, attendants, and foot soldiers, who were variously equipped . . . all of these being united by oath, were supported by the concurrence of Stephen archbishop of Canterbury, who was at their head. The king at this time was awaiting the arrival of his nobles at Oxford. On the Monday next after the octave of Easter, the said barons assembled in the town of Brackley; and when the king learned this, he sent the archbishop of Canterbury, and William Marshal earl of Pembroke, with some other prudent men, to them to inquire what the laws and liberties were which they demanded. The barons then delivered to the messengers a paper, containing in great measure the laws and ancient customs of the kingdom, and declared that, unless the king immediately granted them and confirmed them under his own seal, they would, by taking possession of his fortresses, force him to give them sufficient satisfaction as to their beforenamed demands. The archbishop with his fellow messengers then carried the paper to the king, and read to him the heads of the paper one by one throughout. The king when he heard the purport of these heads, derisively said, with the greatest indignation, "Why, amongst these unjust demands, did not the barons ask for my kingdom also? Their demands are vain and visionary, and are unsupported by any plea of reason whatever." And at length he angrily declared with an oath, that he would never grant them such liberties as would render him their slave. . . .

As the archbishop and William Marshal could not by any persuasions induce the king to agree to their demands, they returned by the king's order to the barons, and duly reported all they had heard from the king to them; and when the nobles heard what John said, they appointed Robert FitzWalter commander of their soldiers, giving him the title of "Marshal of the army of God and the holy church," and then, one and all flying to arms, they directed their forces towards Northampton.

### London Given Up to the Barons

When the army of the barons arrived at Bedford, they were received with all respect by William de Beauchamp. There also came to them there messengers from the city of London, secretly telling them, if they wished to get into that city, to come there immediately. The barons, inspirited by the arrival of this agreeable message, immediately moved their camp and arrived at Ware; after this they marched the whole night, and arrived early in the morning at the city of London, and, finding the gates open, they, on the 24th of May, which was the Sunday next before our Lord's ascension, entered the city without any tumult whilst the inhabitants were performing divine service; for the rich citizens were favourable to the barons, and the poor ones were afraid to murmur against them. The barons having thus got into the city, placed their own guards in charge of each of the gates, and then arranged all matters in the city at will. They then took security from the citizens, and sent letters throughout England to those earls, barons, and knights, who appeared to be still faithful to the king, though they only pretended to be so, and advised them with threats, as they regarded the safety of all their property and possessions, to abandon a king who was perjured and who warred against his barons, and together with them to stand firm and fight against the king for their rights and for peace; and that, if they refused to do this, they, the barons, would make war against them all, as against open enemies, and would destroy their castles, burn their houses and other buildings, and destroy their warrens, parks, and orchards. . . . The pleas of the exchequer and of the sheriff's courts ceased throughout England, because there was no one to make a valuation for the king or to obey him in any thing.

### Meeting at Runnymede

King John, when he saw that he was deserted by almost all, so that out of his regal superabundance of followers he scarcely retained seven knights, was much alarmed lest the barons would attack his castles and reduce them without difficulty, as they would find no obstacle to their so doing; and he deceitfully pretended to make peace for a time with the aforesaid barons, and sent William Marshal earl of Pembroke, with other trustworthy messengers, to them, and told them that, for the sake of peace, and for the exaltation and honour of the kingdom, he would willingly grant them the laws and liberties they required; he also sent word to the barons by these same messengers, to appoint a fitting day and place to meet and carry all these matters into effect. The king's messengers then came in all haste to London, and without deceit reported to the barons all that had been deceitfully imposed on them; they in their great joy appointed the fifteenth of June for the king to meet them, at a field lying between Staines and Windsor. Accordingly, at the time and place pre-agreed on, the king and nobles came to the appointed conference, and when each party had stationed themselves apart from the other, they began a long discussion about terms of peace and the aforesaid liberties. . . . At length, after various points on both sides had been discussed, king John, seeing that he was inferior in strength to the barons, without raising any difficulty granted the underwritten laws and liberties, and confirmed them by his charter as follows:—

## II. MAGNA CARTA

John, by the grace of God, king of England, lord of Ireland, duke of Normandy and Aquitaine, count of Anjou, to the archbishops, bishops, abbots, earls, barons, justiciars, foresters, sheriffs, reeves, servants, and all bailiffs and his faithful people greeting. Know that by the inspiration of God and for the good of our soul and those of all our predecessors and of our heirs, to the honour of God and the exaltation of holy church, and the improvement of our kingdom. . . .

1. We have granted . . . to all free men of our kingdom for us and our heirs forever all the liberties written below, to be had and holden by themselves and their heirs from us and our heirs.

2. If any of our earls or barons, or others holding from us in chief by military service shall have died, and when he has died his heir shall be of full age and owe relief [inheritance tax], he shall have his inheritance by the ancient relief. . . .

8. No widow shall be compelled to marry so long as she prefers to live without a husband, provided she gives security that she will not marry without our consent, if she holds from us, or without the consent of her lord from whom she holds, if she holds from another.

9. Neither we nor our bailiffs will seize any land or rent for any debt so long as the chattels [movable property] of the debtor are sufficient for the payment of the debt. . . .

12. No scutage or aid shall be imposed in our kingdom except by the common council of our kingdom, except for the ransoming of our body, for the making of our oldest son a knight, and for once marrying our oldest daughter, and for these purposes it shall be only a reasonable aid; in the same way it shall be done concerning the aids of the city of London.

13. And the city of London shall have all its ancient liberties and free customs, as well by land as by water. Moreover, we will and grant that all other cities and boroughs and villages and ports shall have all their liberties and free customs.

20. A free man shall not be fined for a small offense, except in proportion to the measure of the offense; and for a great offense, saving his freehold; and a merchant in the same way, saving his merchandise; and the villein shall be fined in the same way, saving his wainage [harvested crops for seed and estate needs], if he shall be at our mercy; and none of the above fines shall be imposed except by the oaths of honest men of the neighborhood.

21. Earls and barons shall be fined only by their peers, and only in proportion to their offense.

23. No manor or man shall be compelled to make bridges over the rivers except those which ought to do it of old and rightfully.

28. No constable or other bailiff of ours shall take anyone's grain or other chattels, without immediately paying for them in money, unless he is able to obtain a postponement at the good will of the seller.

30. No sheriff or bailiff of ours or anyone else shall take horses or wagons of any free man for carrying purposes except on the permission of that free man.

31. Neither we nor our bailiffs will take the wood of another man for castles, or for anything else which we are doing, except by permission of him to whom the wood belongs.

39. No free man shall be taken or imprisoned or dispossessed, or outlawed, or banished, or in any way destroyed, nor will we go upon him, nor send upon him, except by the legal judgment of his peers or by the law of the land.

40. To no one will we sell, to no one will we deny, or delay right or justice.

41. All merchants shall be safe and secure in going from England and coming into England and in remaining and going through England, as well by land as by water, for buying and selling, free from all evil tolls, by the

ancient and rightful customs, except in time of war, and if they are of a land at war with us. . . .

42. It is allowed henceforth to any one to go out from our kingdom, and to return, safely and securely, by land and by water, saving their fidelity to us, except in time of war and for some short time, for the common good of the kingdom. . . .

55. All fines which have been imposed unjustly and against the law of the land, and all penalties imposed unjustly and against the law of the land are altogether excused, or will be on the judgment of the twenty-five barons of whom mention is made below in connection with the security of the peace, or on the judgment of the majority of them. . . .

60. Moreover, all those customs and franchises mentioned above which we have conceded in our kingdom, and which are to be fulfilled, as far as pertains to us, in respect to our men; all men of our kingdom as well clergy as laymen, shall observe as far as pertains to them, in respect to their men.

61. Since, moreover, for the sake of God, and for the improvement of our kingdom, and for the better quieting of the hostility sprung up lately between us and our barons, we have made all these concessions; wishing them to enjoy these in a complete and firm stability forever, we make and concede to them the security described below; that is to say, that they shall elect twenty-five barons of the kingdom, whom they will, who ought with all their power to observe, hold, and cause to be observed, the peace and liberties which we have conceded to them, and by this our present charter confirmed to them, in this manner, that if we or our justiciar, or our bailiffs, or any of our servants shall have done wrong in any way towards any one, or shall have transgressed any of the articles of peace or security; and the wrong shall have been shown to four barons of the aforesaid twenty-five barons, let those four barons come to us or to our justiciar, if we are out of the kingdom, laying before us the transgression, and let them ask that we cause that transgression to be corrected without delay. And if we shall not have corrected the transgression or, if we shall be out of the kingdom, if our justiciar shall not have corrected it within a period of forty days . . . the aforesaid four barons shall refer the matter to the remainder of the twenty-five barons, and let these twenty-five barons with the whole community of the country distress and injure us in every way they can; that is to say by the seizure of our castles, lands, possessions, and in such other ways as they can until it shall have been corrected according to their judgment, saving our person and that of our queen, and those of our children; and when the correction has been made, let them devote themselves to us as they did before. . . .

Given by our hand in the meadow which is called Runnymede, between Windsor and Staines, on the fifteenth day of June, in the seventeenth year of our reign.

# The French King Supervises the Governing of the Kingdom

The medieval French monarchy was at its height under Louis IX (1226–1270). He perfected the system of administration by non-noble officials (seneschals and bailiffs) and enhanced the image of the king as dispenser of justice and protector of Christian values. Louis often personalized his role by hearing cases out of doors, seated under a big tree with the people around him. But he also set up rules for the behavior of his distant officials as these excerpts from his orders on governing the kingdom show. From *The Medieval World and Its Transformations* by G. Straka. (New York: McGraw-Hill Book Co., 1967). Used with permission of McGraw-Hill Book Co.

## ORDERS FOR THE ADMINISTRATION OF THE KINGDOM

1. We order that all our seneschals, bailiffs and all others, whatever their office, shall swear that as long as they shall hold said offices, they shall deal justly with all, making no exceptions, with poor as with rich, with stranger as with friend, and that they shall keep the good and tested customs of the region. And should it happen that they [break] their oath and are caught, we want them to be punished by fine and imprisonment, in accordance with their misdeeds.

3. They will swear not to accept, either directly or through others, any gift, gold or silver, or any material or spiritual benefit or anything else, unless it be fruit or wine or other gifts valued at no more than 10 sols in any one week.

5. All our officials will swear that they [the bailiffs and seneschals] will not seek to profit by selling or marketing any of our revenues, provostships, bailiwicks, [control] over our waters, forests, mints, nor of any other of our holdings, nor of anything belonging to us;

and they will faithfully turn over to us the amount of taxes they collect in our name, and when they sell our property or lease other of our sources of revenue they will sell or lease them at the best possible price, as faithfully, suitably and profitably as they can.

6. They will swear that if they know of any officials or sergeants under their authority who are disloyal, robbers, usurers, or having other vices which should result in their dismissal from our service, they [the higher officials] will not aid and abet them by way of gifts, promises, personal intervention, nor by any other means, but rather will they force them to make reparation for their misdeeds.

8. And in order that these oaths be more firmly kept, we want them to be sworn in the public square before all clerics and laymen, even if such oaths have already been taken before ourselves, so that the oath-taker may fear to incur the vice of perjury not only before God and ourselves, but for fear of being shamed before the people.

9. We further desire and order that all our seneschals, bailiffs, and all our other officials and servants, of whatever estate or condition they may be, refrain from uttering words disrespectful of God, of our Blessed Lady Mary, and of all the saints, and stay away from dice games, brothels, and taverns.

10. Let the making of dice be forbidden and outlawed throughout our kingdom. Any man who will be found playing at dice or who is known to be a habitual frequenter of taverns and brothels, shall be reputed infamous and disqualified from bearing witness.

11. Let all tarts and common whores be expelled from all of our good towns and cities. In particular, let them be kept off the streets of said good towns, to be forced to dwell outside the city walls, as well as far away from any holy places such as churches and cemeteries. And whosoever in such cities, good towns and other charted municipalities should rent any house to prostitutes, or receive them in his own house, shall have to pay one year's rent to the municipality by our order.

17. We forbid any seneschal, bailiff, or other officer in our service, whoever he may be, to oppress our subjects unjustly or to imprison them for any outstanding debt, unless the debt [owed] be to ourselves.

23. We forbid them to deprive any person of any possession without just cause or without special orders from us. Nor are they to oppress our subjects by new exactions of the *taille* [the basic tax on property held by commoners] and by novel taxes; nor are they to order anyone to call a [feudal] levy for monetary gain [by means of exemption payments]. No one should be obliged to appear in person with the host [the feudal army] unless there be a reasonable and necessary cause. Those who do appear in person should not be constrained to buy their way out with money.

25. After they leave office, we want all our seneschals, bailiffs, and other officials to remain for a period of forty days within the region which they had administered either personally or through delegates, so that they are answerable to those whom they may have wronged and who may want to bring suit against them before the new seneschals, bailiffs, or other officials in charge.

26. And in all these things that we have ordained for the peace and tranquility of our subjects and our kingdom, in behalf of our [royal] prerogative we retain the power to proclaim, to add, to amend, and to diminish as we see fit. Proclaimed in Paris in the year 1256.

# Herbert Luethy: The Growth of Centralized Administration in France

From Herbert Luethy, *France Against Herself*, trans. Eric Mosbacher (New York: Frederick A. Praeger, Inc., 1955), pp. 5–9, 14.

When the Christians of the West took up arms in the first crusade the fact that the King of France remained at home remained unnoticed, and nobody missed him. In the eleventh century France clothed herself with cathedrals, and the first notes of European poetry were sounded at her chivalrous courts; Norman French kingdoms were set up in England and Sicily; and the flower of the French nobility took up the cross in answer to the call of a French Pope at Clermont and ringed the eastern shore of the Mediterranean with French feudal states. But this tremendous century represented a point in the history of the French monarchy so low that it approximated to zero. No place in the *Gesta Dei per Francos* was found for Philip I, the fourth King of the House of Capet to occupy the throne of the western Franks, and the great events of his century seem to have affected him once only; he exploited the shortage of money of one of his vassals who desired to go to the Holy Land to buy his jurisdiction over Bourges, and thus established a first foothold for the royal dominions south of the Loire.

The clergy, who monopolised the writing of history, covered his reign of a half-a-century with obloquy; we see him sitting in his court like a leper, abandoned by his lords and barons, living in open adultery, scorned and excommunicated, perjured towards his vassals, to whom he hired out his services like a mercenary, hawking the episcopal sees that remained to him in shameless simony, a minor brigand who plundered travelling merchants. Apart from the monarch's personal characteristics, the picture presented by his kingdom was pitiful enough. Even within the narrow limits of the royal dominions in the northerly Ile de France to which his power and reputation were confined, he was scarcely able to move with safety outside his tiny city of Paris; a fortress or robber baron's castle on the road to Senlis, Orleans or Corbeil was sufficient to hold the King of France in check; and in 1081, when he bestirred himself to undertake the biggest military enterprise of his career, an expedition against the petty lords of Puiset, he suffered a disgraceful defeat outside the gates of Orleans at the hands of a minor vassal. The royal mantle had fallen on the shoulders of a scarecrow. . . .

[Philip] was mean and lazy, and with his resigned withdrawal into his own domains the character of the kingdom began to alter: a more-or-less nomadic monarchy with a retinue of turbulent vassals began to develop into a firmly anchored and organised institution. The court settled down. Paris became and remained the capital, the king's permanent retinue assumed the functions of the royal council, which should in theory have consisted of all the spiritual and temporal lords of the realm, and these functions shrank into the prosaic administration of the royal domains. The royal archives of Philip the Slothful plainly show the depopulation of the court. The chaos of signatures and seals of barons and magnates of the realm accidentally present at court disappears and gradually gives way to those of the great court officials. System is introduced, and in two legal documents at the end of this entirely lustreless reign the signatures of these officials appear alone. A haphazard medley of nobles has given way to a sharply defined body of advisers, much more like a Cabinet. The introduction of this element of permanence was as important an event in the history of the mediaeval state as was the transition to static settlements and agriculture in the history of humanity. . . .

After this there were periods of marking time, of confusion, and even of retreat; nevertheless developments followed their own inherent law and continued without a break. A century after the impotent reign of Philip the Slothful, his great-grandson Philip II could be given the additional appellation of Augustus without exciting ridicule, and at his court there had plainly crystallised out of those institutions whose unremitting and impersonal operation assured the permanence of the state even when the ruler was incapable or took up the cross, as three kings now did in succession; namely the royal council, the present-day successor of which is the Council of State, and the Treasury, which still reigns supreme over the whole state administration. When Philip Augustus set out for the Third Crusade he entrusted the keys of his Treasury and the royal seal, not to a feudal regency council, but to a court official and a council of six citizens of his city of Paris with names as revealing as Theobald the Rich and Ebroin the Money-Changer; and in his will he called on "all the men of Paris" to safeguard his treasure for his son. Most important of all, his will shows that the *baillis* [bailiffs] were already fully functioning. These officials remained the most effective instrument of the monarchy until the seventeenth century; their present-day successors are the prefects, the delegates of the central administration who supervise the work of the local authorities, proclaim the king's law monthly within their respective domains, and three times yearly give an account of their stewardship in Paris.

The century-long process of welding France into a state in the modern sense of the word began with the daily guerrilla warfare waged by these officials against all special rights and privileges, their unremitting efforts to widen the area within which all power belonged to the king, their zeal in never allowing a royal claim to drop, even if for the time being they were powerless to enforce it, and their vigour in exploiting every opportunity of establishing a precedent which might one day be used for making good a royal claim; and, while this mole-like labour went on remorselessly in every corner of the country, royal jurists like Fontaine and Beaumanoir transformed *le droit du plus fort* [the right of the stronger] of early feudalism into the rigid, hierarchical, legal framework of the later feudal state. This led irresistibly to the conception that the Crown was the source of all power and privilege and that all land was held directly or indirectly in fee from the king; an imposing idea which overcame the disorders of early feudalism with its own inherent logic and ended by identifying France with the royal demesne. His kingdom might have fallen to pieces, but in gathering the fragments together again and welding them into a whole the king was only "re-entering into his own" and relying on the feudal duties which his vassals had never denied that they owed him. True, before the monarchy could put these legal claims into practice, it had first to establish itself on a firm basis of power and forge suitable instruments with which to exercise it; but the king's rights were "as clear as the day", and it was this that gave his claims priority over all others, and in the long run made the mole-like labour of his officials and jurists irresistible. The most powerful instrument in the century-long process by which France was turned into a nation—far more effective, enduring and irresistible in its effect than warfare, alliances and dynamic politics—was the patient, legalistic labour, concerned here with a right of way, a mill, a castle, an impost, a question of local jurisdiction, and there with a county or a dukedom. . . .

Thus the history of France might be written as the history of an administration; an anonymous, prosaic, tremendously persistent, and in the deepest sense of the word non-political administration. The secret of the continuity of French history lies in this administration, and not in any particular far-sightedness on the part of her rulers and statesmen. . . .

# Wallace Ferguson: The Kings Recover Control of Armed Force

Wallace Ferguson (1902–       ), Canadian-born specialist in Renaissance history, here tells how the medieval kings regained control of military organization in their kingdoms, a function that had been taken over by the landholding nobility along with the administration of justice and the collection of taxes. From Wallace R. Ferguson, "Toward the Modern State," in *The Renaissance* (New York: Metropolitan Museum of Art, 1953), pp. 10–12, 14–15.

Along with the administration of justice and the maintenance of law and order, an equally important function of government is the defense of the state against the attacks of enemies from without or rebellion from within; and we can scarcely conceive of a state in which the central government does not assume full responsibility for the organization, equipment, and pay of the country's armed forces. Nor can we easily envisage a state in which all able-bodied citizens are not liable for military service. Yet in the early feudal state the king neither paid nor equipped an army, and he could do little to shape or control its organization. All he could do was call upon his vassals-in-chief to do the military service they owed—forty days or so a year—accompanied by such of their vassals as they could force to abandon their private feuds for a few weeks to serve the state. For all practical purposes, only the nobles were liable for military service, and they made up the only effective branch of the army, the heavy cavalry composed of armored knights. The majority of the population in the early feudal period consisted of serfs, who were not expected to fight. In a national emergency the king could call upon burghers and other freemen to serve as infantry, but these militia forces were poorly armed and poorly trained. Altogether, feudal armies were generally small, unreliable, undisciplined, and unmanageable on the field of battle. They were fit only for the local warfare that was the normal state of feudal society. For war on a national scale they were totally inadequate.

With increasing revenue, the kings of the twelfth and thirteenth centuries made some improvement in this situation by hiring foreign mercenaries and by paying a small permanent force, as well as by offering partial pay to vassals or commons who served beyond the customary time. The first decisive step toward the formation of a really national army did not, however, come until the last years of the thirteenth century. . . .

Regular payment of wages on a graduated scale was an essential part of the new military organization. This made it possible to hold the army together for long campaigns. It also made possible the organization of the army into companies under royal officers who could impose discipline. Without pay, too, it would have been difficult, if not impossible, for many knights to bear the rapidly rising cost of armor in this period when heavy plate was beginning to replace the simpler chain mail of the crusading era. Fully equipped knights were, of course, expensive, and the king of a relatively poor country like England could not afford many of them.

Obviously, the substitution of a royal army for the more or less voluntary service of noble vassals was a triumph for the monarchy and a blow to both the prestige and the real power of the feudal lords. Obviously, too, the emergence of the infantry as an effective branch of the army was a blow to the nobles' monopoly of military force, on which their political power and independence had long rested securely. But there was more than this involved in the change. Infantry were effective only if well trained and well equipped and when used in fairly large bodies. That meant a permanent, paid force, which only a government supported by state taxation

This thirteenth-century fighting scene illustrates the weapons and tactics of the time—the catapult, bow and arrow, sword, axe, armor, used in siege warfare and man-to-man combat that the development of new weapons and military organization altered.

could afford. The introduction of firearms during the fifteenth century added further to the cost of maintaining infantry, and, incidentally, forced the knights to adopt heavier and heavier armor until it became a crushing burden in both the physical and financial sense. Finally, the development of artillery, chiefly as siege weapons, gave to state governments, which alone could afford such expensive pieces, the means by which to batter down the castles of rebellious nobles. Warfare, in short, was becoming a big business, too expensive to be indulged in as a private sport, as it had been during the feudal age. . . .

TOPIC 24

# THE CHURCH IN THE FEUDAL WORLD

In a traditional society authority customarily rests upon a working alliance between chieftains and priests, or those who provide society with protection and government and those who offer moral structure and a key to the unknown. Far from being clear-cut, the role of each within the alliance has frequently overlapped. Such an arrangement and such a befogging of responsibilities were strikingly manifest in the Middle Ages. Although the Christian Church exercised sweeping spiritual authority, the structure of feudalism threatened the very survival of an independent Christian voice. What Romans and barbarians had been unable to still was nearly suffocated by the temptations and obligations created by lay influence over clerical offices. The great Christian reformers of the tenth through the twelfth centuries nonetheless found ways of freeing the Church from its secular bondage, enlarging the authority of the Papacy and reasserting the power of the Christian conscience. These readings are concerned with the consequences of the feudalization of the Church.

**Reading 121**

## The Medieval Church

From *Civilization Past and Present* by T. Walter Wallbank, Alastair M. Taylor, Nels M. Bailkey. Copyright © 1965 by Scott, Foresman and Company.

It is important to keep in mind that, although the Church was an institution, it was not an extraneous body imposed upon Christianity and consisting solely of a clerical hierarchy and a set of ceremonies. St. Paul's description of the Church as "the body of Christ" was interpreted to mean that the Church included all of Christian society itself. Every baptized child of Christian parents automatically began life within the ranks of the Church; almost all western Europeans, therefore, were subject to its authority. Obedience to the Church was enforced by all political as well as religious rulers in western Christendom.

The nature and process of salvation were set forth in theology—the field of study which deals with the nature of God and His relations to the universe and man. According to the theology of the Church, Adam had bequeathed the taint of original sin to his descendants, so that all the human race was displeasing in the sight of God. But He did not leave man without hope. Jesus, the Son of God, had sacrificed Himself upon the cross to atone for mankind's sins, and through His sacrifice God gave man an opportunity to earn salvation. This opportunity was bestowed only on those who believed in redemption through Christ's atonement and who followed His precepts. But salvation itself was won only with the grace of God. Since man could perform no act worthy of salvation without divine grace, how was this to be earned? The theologians taught that God bestowed His grace on man by means of sacraments through the Church and its officials.

The problems of theology attracted the attention primarily of the intellectuals. The majority of the people then, as today, accepted the current beliefs without very much questioning. To the unlettered, the following points constituted the essentials of the Christian faith: (1) the creation and fall of Adam, (2) the Birth and Crucifixion of Christ, (3) the Last Judgment, (4) the horrors of hell, (5) the eternal bliss of heaven, and (6) the usefulness of the sacraments in helping them win salvation.

## THE SACRAMENTS

The sacraments have been defined as outward or visible signs instituted by Christ to signify and to give grace. By the twelfth century seven sacraments had been recognized, a number made official by a papal announcement in 1438. The seven sacraments were Baptism, Confirmation, Holy Eucharist, Penance, Extreme Unction, Holy Orders, and Matrimony.

In Baptism the taint of original sin was washed away and the person given a Christian name, hence "christening." Confirmation strengthened the character of the recipient, especially in his formative years. The sacrament of Matrimony was instituted to give the married couple spiritual help—although celibacy was prescribed for those who entered the Church as a career. Holy Orders, or ordination into the priesthood, was administered by the bishop. This sacrament conferred the power and grace to perform the sacred duties of the clergy; the ordained priest was capable of administering all sacraments except Confirmation and Holy Orders. Penance enabled sins committed after Baptism to be forgiven through the absolution of the priest. Extreme Unction was administered when death appeared imminent; it forgave remaining sins and bestowed grace and spiritual strength on the dying Christian.

Perhaps the most important sacrament was the Holy Eucharist, defined as "both a sacrament and a sacrifice; in it Our Savior, Jesus Christ, body and blood, soul and divinity, under the appearance of bread and wine, is contained, offered, and received." The significance of this sacrament can be fully appreciated only when the doctrine of transubstantiation is understood. According to this doctrine, when the priest performing the Mass pronounces over the bread and wine the words Christ used at the Last Supper, "This is My Body. . . . This is the chalice of My Blood. . . ," a miracle takes place. To all outward appearances, the bread and wine remain unchanged, but in "substance" they have been transformed into the very body and blood of the Savior.

## ENFORCING BELIEF

The Church was in advance of secular states in emerging out of feudal decentralization and developing its own legal system of canon law and Church courts to enforce its teachings and commands. Canon law was based on the Scriptures, writings of the Church Fathers, and decrees of Church councils and popes. In the twelfth century the Church issued its official body of canon law, the ecclesiastical counterpart of the Justinian Code. Canon law guided the Church courts in judging perjury, blasphemy, sorcery, usury (for the medieval Church denounced moneylending), and heresy. Heresy was the most horrible of all crimes in medieval eyes. A murder was a crime against a fellow man, but the heretic's disbelief in the teachings of Christ or His Church was considered a crime against God himself.

Although the medieval Church sometimes resorted to physical punishment, the chief weapons to support clerical authority were spiritual penalties. The most powerful of these was excommunication, which meant exclusion from the Church. The seriousness of this penalty lay in the denial of the sacraments and therefore the endangering of salvation.

The wording of the excommunication service had a terrifying ring to it, as may be seen in the concluding lines of a thirteenth-century Scottish excommunication directed against enemies of the Church:

> Accursed be all the forenamed persons; cursed by they without and within, from the sole of the foot even to the crown of the head. . . . May their days be few and their offices let others take; may their children be orphans . . . may the lights [of their lives] be extinguished before the face of Him who liveth for ever and ever; and may their souls be plunged in hell unless they repent and amend their ways and make satisfaction. So be it! So be it! Amen!

Interdict, which has been termed "an ecclesiastical lockout," was likewise a powerful instrument. Whereas excommunication was directed against individuals, interdict punished whole groups of people, such as the inhabitants of an entire area. In the area thus penalized, Church services were withheld, along with all sacraments other than Baptism, Penance, Confirmation, and Extreme Unction.

## THE PAPACY

The influence of the medieval Church was felt by every inhabitant of every hamlet throughout western Europe. The universality and power of the Church rested not only upon a systematized, uniform creed but also upon the most highly organized administrative system in the West.

At the head was the pope, or bishop of Rome. The geographical extent and the vast membership of the Church required that the pope have administrative assistance. This was provided by the *Curia,* originally the papal court, which in the course of time developed an intricate administrative system. Judicial and secretarial problems were handled by the papal *Chancery,* financial matters by the *Camera,* and disciplinary questions by the *Penitentiary.* From 1059 on, the leading ecclesiastics of the *Curia* formed the College of Cardinals, which elected the new pope; this method has continued to the present day.

## THE HIGHER CLERGY

Europe was divided into a number of ecclesiastical provinces, each administered by an archbishop. A province comprised in turn several dioceses. The archbishop was a powerful prelate, who summoned provincial councils, occasionally visited dioceses and monastic houses, announced papal decrees of general import, and handled all affairs in his own diocese. Sometimes an archbishop would play a leading part in the council of the king.

While the archbishop was responsible for a diocese of his own, called an arch-diocese, the other dioceses in each province were managed by bishops. A diocese was made up of many parishes and numerous religious houses. The bishop's court held a wide jurisdiction over both clergy and laity. Because the claims of lay courts challenged the bishop's domain, especially on such matters as wills and dowries, which had both a spiritual and a secular character, the scope of his administrative and disciplinary powers was a very controversial issue.

The bishop had his headquarters in the city where his cathedral stood. (The word *cathedral* comes from *cathedra,* which means "bishop's throne.") Outside the city he had other houses and estates, where he lived from time to time. Often, though not necessarily, of high social origin, the bishop was an exalted person; whether haughty or humble, he had to maintain an elaborate household. As a rule, the bishop did not come into close personal contact with the common people, even on his diocesan visits or on occasions when he confirmed the young, ordained deacons and priests, or dedicated churches.

## THE PRIEST IN HIS PARISH

The real foundation on which the medieval Church rested was the ordinary people in the parishes. In the last analysis the Church's strength depended upon the ability of the parish priest to administer the sacraments, attend the sick, hear confessions, supervise the morals of the parish, and hold the respect of his parishioners. Although the priest was very likely of humble birth and little education, he was father confessor, social worker, policeman, and recreation director, all rolled into one. . . .

The parish priest gave his charges their religious instruction mainly during the sermon. He painted the terrors of hell—how the damned are thrust from the flames into icy water so they do not know which is worse, and how:

> . . . to increase their pains the loathsome hellworms, toads, and frogs that eat out their eyes and nostrils, and adders and water-frogs, not like those here, but a hundred times more horrible, sneak in and out of the mouth, ears, eyes, naval, and at the hollow of the breast, as maggots in putrid flesh. . . .

Heaven was pictured to be just as desirable as hell was hateful, and the Church assured the parishioner of heaven as the reward for his prayers and supplications. The priest would also upbraid his parishioners for their lax attendance at church, their addiction to the joys of the tavern, their squabbling and fighting, their laziness or gluttony. He made every person, high or low, supremely aware of the vividness, and omnipresence, and the reality of religion. . . .

## THE CHURCH-STATE RIVALRY

Medieval political theory begins with the concept of a universal community divided into two spheres—the spiritual and the temporal. As Pope Gelasius I declared in the fifth century, God had entrusted spiritual and temporal powers to two authorities—the Church and the State—each supreme in its own sphere. At first the question of ultimate superiority between these authorities did not arise. However, the issue could not be permanently shelved; a fight for supremacy was inevitable.

When Pepin and later Charlemagne were crowned by the pope, the temporal prestige and authority of the head of the Church rose.

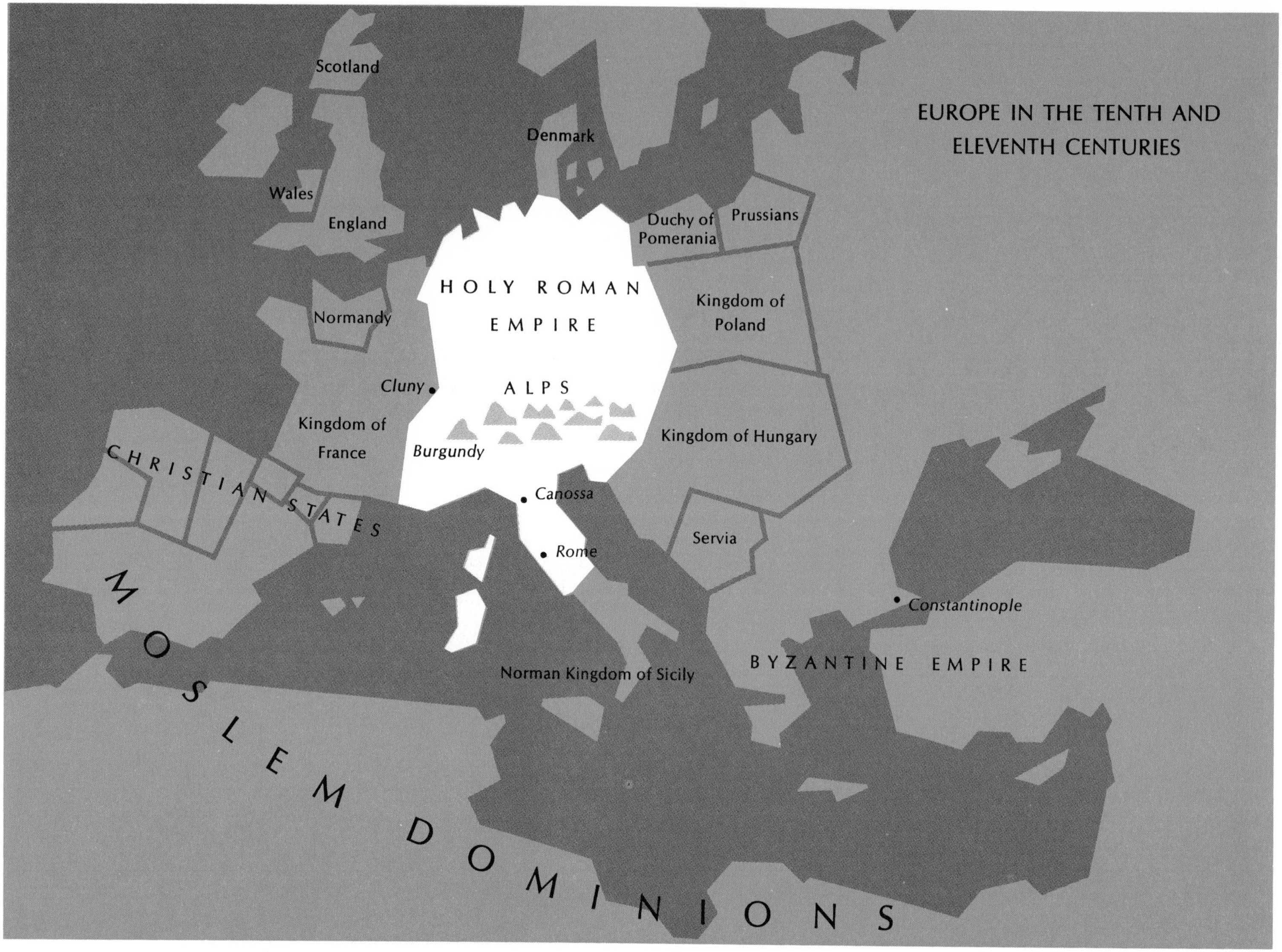


In sheer size the Holy Roman Empire dominated medieval Europe. The potential power of the emperors was diluted, however, by the difficulty of maintaining imperial authority south of the Alps which straddled the empire.

From the ecclesiastical point of view these coronations could be interpreted to signify the supremacy of the pope over secular rulers. On the other hand, Charlemagne's imperial authority threatened the Popes. There was always the danger that the pope would come under the domination of the western emperor, just as the patriarch of Constantinople had gradually fallen subservient to the Byzantine ruler.

The Holy Roman Empire was created in 962 when the German king, Otto the Great, was crowned in Rome. This act reemphasized the concept of the dual leadership of pope and emperor. The empire, it was said, was the legitimate successor of the old Roman empire. Universal authority was claimed for it, though its actual power was confined to Germany and Italy. At first the papacy looked to the German king for protection against feudal abuses and the unruly Italian nobles and Roman mobs. From the Church's viewpoint, however, this arrangement soon had its drawbacks, for the German kings continued to interfere in ecclesiastical affairs—even in the election of popes—to serve royal purposes.

Another aspect of the controversy between Church and State centered around the problem of lay investiture. Theoretically, a bishop or abbot on assuming his office was subject to two investitures. His spiritual authority was bestowed by an ecclesiastical official and his feudal or civil authority by the king or a noble. In Germany, the monarch came to control both the appointment and the installation of bishops.

The king and nobles had granted many of the Church lands to the higher clergy, who became their vassals. The new bishop had to do them homage for his fief and received from them his ring and pastoral staff, the symbols

The medieval ideal of harmonious cooperation between spiritual and temporal authorities is reflected in this scene of Pope Nicholas I (858–867) and Emperor Louis II (855–875), a great-grandson of Charlemagne. In the Emperor's left arm nestles the royal scepter; his right hand is on the Bible.

of his spiritual office. Furthermore, the nobility were given control over Church property during the vacancy between the death of one incumbent and the selection of his successor, which meant that powerful laymen had an important stake in the election to Church offices. Thus "to all intents and purposes the German Church was a state Church."

For his part, the king was anxious to have a faithful vassal in each bishop's throne for a number of reasons. The most important need was to have the vast Church lands furnish loyal feudal troops for the royal armies. Many German bishops proved to be valiant warriors. Faithful bishops were also the most reliable and best-educated men to counsel a king and administer the royal government and finances.

The pope, therefore, had reason to complain about his bishops on spiritual and temporal grounds alike. The papacy was rescued from its plight, however, by a great religious revival and the advent of Pope Gregory VII and his powerful successors.

## THE CLUNIAC REFORM

Beginning in the tenth century and reaching full force in the next, the religious revival affected all classes. Plagues, famines, and chaos had turned the common people increasingly toward religion at the same time that Church officials recognized the deplorable conditions within the feudalized Church.

The most far-reaching force of the revival was the new monastic order of Cluny, founded in 910. From the original monastery in Burgandy and its many daughter houses all over western Europe, there radiated a tremendous impulse for reform. The Cluniac

Bishop Adalbert of Gniesen is invested with his bishop's staff by Emperor Otto II (973-983). Bronze relief from the Cathedral of Gniezno, Poland.

program called for enforcement of clerical celibacy and the abolition of simony, whereby an ecclesiastical office was sold to the highest bidder or was acquired by bribery. (The term comes from Simon the magician, who tried to buy the gift of the Holy Spirit from the apostles.) The success of reform depended on freeing the Church from secular control and subjecting it to papal authority. In 1059 the papacy itself was freed from secular influence by the creation of the College of Cardinals.

## GREGORY VII

The most ambitious proponent of the Cluniac reform was Gregory VII (1073–1085), who raised the papacy to unprecedented heights. Short-legged, fat, inclined to stammer, and possessed of little formal learning, this seemingly unimpressive individual overshadowed monarchs with his zeal and magnetic power. Gregory held as his ideal the creation of an international government under papal control. Instead of conceding equality between the ecclesiastical and secular powers, Gregory VII maintained that the Church was supreme. Until his death in 1085, he devoted his extraordinary energy to breaking all resistance to the Church.

Outstanding among Gregory's attempts at reforms—and certainly the most difficult to enforce—were his efforts to suppress simony and lay investiture. He interpreted simony to include lay investiture because he felt that this practice weakened the authority of the papacy and the Church.

## THE QUARREL WITH HENRY IV

In 1075 Gregory VII formally prohibited lay investiture and threatened to excommunicate any layman who performed it and any ecclesiastic who submitted to it. This drastic act was the same as declaring war against Europe's rulers, since almost all of them practiced lay investiture. The climax to the struggle occurred in Gregory's clash with the emperor Henry IV. The latter was accused of simony in appointing his own choice to the archbishopric of Milan and was summoned to Rome to explain his conduct. Henry's answer was to convene a synod of German clergy in 1076 and to depose the pope. In retaliation, Gregory excommunicated Henry and deposed him in turn, absolving his subjects from their oaths of allegiance.

At last, driven by a revolt among his barons to make peace with the pontiff, Henry appeared in January 1077 before Gregory at Canossa, a castle in the Apennines. Here, garbed as a penitent, the emperor stood barefoot in the snow of the courtyard and begged

On his way to Canossa, Henry IV (kneeling) pleaded with Abbot Hugh of the reform monastery of Cluny and with the powerful Countess Mathilda of Tuscany to intercede for him with Pope Gregory.

forgiveness for three days until, in Gregory's words:

> We loosed the chain of the anathema and at length received him into the favor of communion and into the lap of the Holy Mother Church. . . .

Controversy between the Church and the State is a recurring theme in history. In modern times totalitarian states have claimed jurisdiction over religious problems. Even in states where the individual's religion is accorded the greatest respect, clashes occur between religious and governmental aims. For example, the views of pacifists and conscientious objectors in our own society are sometimes difficult to mesh with the goals of the government. It is not always simple to "Render to Caesar the things that are Caesar's, and to God the things that are God's. ". . .

# The Punishment of Heretics

Heresy, or disbelief in the teaching of the Church, was the most serious crime possible in the Middle Ages. A definition of heresy by Thomas Aquinas (1225–1274), a leading churchman and philosopher, explaining why punishment of heretics was so severe is followed by examples of excommunication and interdict. In the latter instance Pope Innocent III (1198–1216) refused to sanction the action of Philip II of France, whose bishops had permitted him to divorce Ingeborg, his Danish wife, and marry a beautiful French noblewoman. The pope would not recognize the legality of this second marriage and used the interdict to force the king to return to Ingeborg. Philip was able to hold out for less than a year after the interdict was imposed on France. I. From Joseph Rickaby, *Aquinas Ethicus: or, The Moral Teaching of St. Thomas* (London, 1896), Vol. II, pp. 332–333. II. From O. Thatcher and E. McNeal, eds., *A Source Book for Medieval History* (New York, 1905), pp. 309–310. III. From E. B. Krehbiel, *The Interdict* (Washington, 1909), pp. 114–115.

## I. ST. THOMAS AQUINAS DEFINES HERESY (THIRTEENTH CENTURY)

With regard to heretics two elements are to be considered, one element on their side, and the other on the part of the Church. On their side is the sin whereby they have deserved, not only to be separated from the Church by excommunication, but also to be banished from the world by death. For it is a much heavier offense to corrupt the faith, whereby the life of the soul is sustained, than to tamper with the coinage, which is an aid to temporal life. Hence if coiners or other malefactors are at once handed over by secular princes to a just death, much more may heretics, immediately they are convicted of heresy, be not only excommunicated, but also justly doomed to die. But on the part of the Church is mercy in view of the conversion of them that err; and therefore she does not condemn at once, but "after the first and second admonition," as the Apostle teaches. After that, however, if the man is still found pertinacious, the Church having no hope of his conversion, provides for the safety of others, cutting him off from the Church by the sentence of excommunication; and further she leaves him to the secular tribunal to be exterminated from the world by death.

## II. POPE NICHOLAS III EXCOMMUNICATES HERETICS (1280)

We hereby excommunicate, and anathematize all heretics, . . . by whatever name they may be called. When condemned by the Church, they shall be given over to the secular judge to be punished. Clergymen shall be degraded before being punished. If any, after being seized, repent and wish to do proper penance, they shall be imprisoned for life. We condemn as heretics all who believe the errors of heretics. We decree that all who receive, defend, or aid heretics, shall be excommunicated. . . . Those who associate with the excommunicated shall themselves be excommunicated and properly punished. If those who are suspected of heresy can not prove their innocence, they shall be excommunicated. If they remain under the ban of excommunication a year, they shall be condemned as heretics. They shall have no right of appeal. If judges, advocates, or notaries serve them in an official way, they shall be deprived of their office. The clergy shall not administer to them the sacraments, nor give them a part of the alms. If they do, they shall be deprived of their office and they can never be restored to it without the special permission of the pope. Whoever grants them Christian burial shall be excommunicated until he makes proper satisfaction. He shall not be absolved until he has with his own hands publicly dug up their bodies and cast them forth, and no one shall ever be buried in the same place. . . .

### III. POPE INNOCENT III IMPOSES AN INTERDICT ON FRANCE (1200)

All churches shall be closed, and no one shall be admitted to them unless it is to baptize infants, nor shall they be opened for any other purpose than for the care of the lights, or when the priest must get the host and holy water for the consecration of the host needed for the sick, but only one clerk may be present to assist the priest. . . . They shall not permit bodies to be buried, or to be placed unburied, in cemeteries. . . . The priests shall forbid parishioners to enter open churches in the land of the king; they shall not bless the wallets of pilgrims, unless it be outside of the church. In passion-week they shall not celebrate; on Easter-day they may celebrate privately, but only one clerk may be admitted, as has been stated above; no one shall commune even on Easter, unless he is sick and at the point of death. Either on Palm Sunday or during passion-week the people shall be told to gather before the church on the morning of Easter, where they will be given the privilege of eating the blessed bread and meat of the day. Clerks positively may not admit women into the church for purification; they shall advise them to gather with their neighbors on the day of churching, and to pray outside of the church; women who are to be purified may not enter the church even for the purpose of raising children to the sacred font for baptism; even after the interdict, they may not enter the church until they are invited to do so by the priest. The confession of all who seek it shall be heard by the priests in the vestibule of the church; and, if the church has no vestibule, the confession may be heard on the threshold of the outermost door, which the inclemency of wind or rain permits to be opened, but nowhere else; all must be excluded except the person who wished to confess, but the voices must be so loud that the priest and the person confessing can be heard by those who chance to be outside of the church. If the weather is mild, confession shall be heard before closed church-doors. Receptacles with holy water shall not be placed outside of the church; nor shall clerks use holy water anywhere, since it is understood that all ecclesiastical sacraments are prohibited but those two which are excepted. Extreme Unction, which is the last sacrament, may not be given.

# Feudalization of the Clergy



### I. Reprinted from Marshall W. Baldwin. *The Medieval Church.* Copyright 1953 by Cornell University. Used by permission of The Cornell University Press. II. Reprinted from *An Introduction to Medieval Europe 300–500* by James Westfall Thompson and Edgar Nathaniel Johnson. By permission of W. W. Norton & Company, Inc. Copyright 1937, by W. W. Norton & Company, Inc. Copyright renewed 1965 by Edgar Nathaniel Johnson, pp. 359–361.

TEMPORAL RESPONSIBILITIES ENCROACH UPON THE BISHOP'S RELIGIOUS DUTIES

The period roughly included between the years 900 and 1150 was predominantly feudal, and feudalism, it will be recalled, developed to meet certain adverse conditions—weak central government, limited commerce, invasion. Since feudalism implied decentralization, life tended to become localized. Communications were inadequate. Violence and insecurity were common. As a consequence, orderly ecclesiastical administration—and the same was true of secular government—was gravely endangered. All this threw a heavy responsibility upon ecclesiastical individuals, for their duties had all too often to be fulfilled in isolation. . . .

Bishops stood at the summit of the ecclesiastical hierarchy because bishops were in the mind of the church the successors of Christ's apostles. The prospective candidate for the episcopate became a bishop through the sacrament of holy orders. The most solemn moment in the bishop's consecration was when three other bishops placed their hands on the candidate's head and pronounced the words, "Receive the Holy Spirit (*Accipe Sanctum Spiritum*)." Only a bishop could confer holy orders on a priest. Even the supremacy of the pope rested on the fact that he was bishop of Rome, a see founded by St. Peter, chief of the apostles.

Exacting as were a bishop's ecclesiastical obligations, they were not, in the Middle Ages, his sole concern, for bishops had many temporal responsibilities as well. His church was the center of a domain which, in addition to dwellings for himself and his clergy, comprised manors, vineyards, and even fiscal rights such as income from tolls. All this, the res ecclesiae, was held to be not secular property, but the patrimony of the patron saint. Actually, of course, the bishop administered this collection of properties, privileges, and responsibilities. Thus he became identified with the bishopric, much as the count, originally a royal functionary, became identified with the county.

Various concessions by kings who granted immunities, tolls, or customs rights, occasionally even the right of coinage, furthered this secularization of the bishopric. Moreover, as the power of the king's official, normally the count, was thus diminished, the judicial responsibility of the bishop within his diocese was enhanced. In certain cases, bishops were given political authority over all or part of a county. Such a policy appealed particularly to the kings of Germany. Since no one could legitimately inherit the bishop's authority, German rulers fortified the secular power of bishops as a counterweight to the great lay feudatories. In short, the bishopric, like the county, gradually took its position in the feudal hierarchy.

The consequences of feudalism for the bishopric are clear. As a lord and administrator of landed property, the bishop had to supervise the affairs of his own vassals. Much of this could be delegated to subordinates, but the ultimate responsibility was his. As a vassal the bishop was expected to take an oath of allegiance, homage commonly not being required of an ecclesiastic. He must supply men-at-arms and attend the feudal court. Indeed, certain rulers demanded that bishops appear with their feudal military levy in person.

To a conscientious cleric, anxious to fulfill his churchly duties, these obligations must have seemed a real burden, as indeed they were. But to some, attendance at a king's court was exciting, a welcome break in the routine of ecclesiastical activity. Such, no doubt, must have been the attitude of the more worldly bishops, especially those who had entered the Church, or been forced to enter by ambitious relatives, in the hope of social or political advancement. The prospective revenues of a wealthy bishopric could be a source of temptation to a feudal family oversupplied with younger sons. And simony, the purchase or sale of ecclesiastical preferment, was unfortunately not uncommon in the tenth and eleventh centuries.

Such considerations go far toward explaining why a number of bishops—enough to have attracted the attention of comtemporary chroniclers—behaved, after their installment, with something less than episcopal dignity. An extreme case, which caused one of the great scandals of the early Middle Ages, was the bishop who was so inordinately fond of hunting that he moved the altar and furnishings to the porch of his church and stabled his horses and dogs in the nave. Happily such cases were rare. More common were the bishops who interpreted their feudal military obligation in a literal manner. Some, deferring to the canonical injunction which forbids any cleric to shed blood, swung a heavy mace. Others were less squeamish. . . .

## II. THE GERMAN EMPERORS USE BISHOPS AS ADMINISTRATORS

What Otto I [Holy Roman Emperor, 936–973] and his successors established was their own system of ecclesiastical feudalism, of which the king was the actual, not merely the theoretical, head. They did with the Church what the dukes of Normandy and the Norman kings of England did with the secular nobility: kept it tied to the crown. Bishops and archbishops in Germany were in effect appointed by the king. To be sure, the formalities of canon law providing for the election of a bishop by the clergy and people were complied with, but the candidate elected was usually the king's nominee. Indeed, the right of free election was a special privilege granted by the king. Frequently the king's nominees came from the royal chancellery or chapel, where they had been trained in state affairs and become personally known to the king. In time the relationship between king and bishop became strictly feudal: the bishop as vassal performed homage and took the oath of fealty to the king as lord. He received his lands and privileges and his spiritual office as a fief from the hands of the king in an actual ceremony of investiture. Before the twelfth century no clear distinction was made between his lands and privileges and his spiritual functions, the ring symbolizing the bishop's marriage to the Church and the staff or crozier his position as shepherd of his flock. According to canon law these two symbols were to be turned over to the newly elected bishop by his archbishop, but the actual practice was for ring and staff to be carried to court immediately upon the death of a bishop and for the king to confer them on his newly elected successor. In this way it was made clear that an episcopal office was a royal office; to all intents and purposes the German Church was a state church.

The services that the bishops rendered the crown were largely the ordinary feudal services of a vassal. The one most important service was their military aid, which filled perhaps the king's greatest single need. The armies of the Ottonians were composed mostly of episcopal contingents, contributed by each bishop according to his means. It was not unusual for a bishop to lead his troops in person. Bishop Michael of Regensburg lost an ear fighting against the Magyars, and if Udalrich of Augsburg did not actually fight, he certainly paced the walls of his city directing the defense against them. The art of war became an essential episcopal accomplishment. Bishops were held to attendance at court when the court was near, and on important occasions were held to attendance no matter where it was. The kings claimed the feudal *droit de gite* from the Church. When in the course of its perambulations the court had to leave the royal manors, it resorted to monasteries, or preferably to episcopal towns, for food, lodging, and entertainment. But the kings relied upon the bishops for many necessary services for which they could never have trusted feudal nobles at all. Bishops administered royal lands. They were the tutors of princes and counsellors of kings. The chief officials of the chancellery and chapel were bishops, the Archbishop of Mainz ordinarily being ex-officio archchancellor and archchaplain. Bishops acted as regents and were left in complete charge of the government when the king was absent in Italy. For what we would call diplomatic service the kings used bishops. They even entrusted rebels to them for custody.

Under these circumstances the German Church became almost thoroughly secularized. German bishops acquired such a reputation that other kings envied the German kings their hard-fighting episcopal warriors; and later writers remarked that, if there was one thing certain, it was that a German bishop could not be pious. Megingaud, Bishop of Eichstätt in the reign of Henry II (whose kinsman he was), being about to start out on a journey to Rome, secured permission from his chapter to swear one hundred times, but this meager supply was so soon exhausted that he had to send back for several supplementary hundreds. Especially during Lent he suffered from what he called "the impatience of his belly," so, as an incentive to his chapter to speed through the services, he had placed before them in the middle of the choir a good-sized fish; the prolonged Easter Mass he simplified by starting different parts of the service at the same time. . . .

The career of Otto I's younger brother Bruno is perhaps more representative of the alliance between Church and state, and at the same time typical of the tenth-century Church at its best. Bruno felt himself "begotten for the State," in whose service he wore himself out at the early age of forty. While he was Archbishop of Cologne and archchancellor of the realm, an illegitimate son of Otto was Archbishop of Mainz and another kinsman of Trier, so that all three of the very important Rhenish archbishoprics belonged to members of the family. When Otto was faced with the revolt of 953–55, in which the Duke of Lorraine participated, he simply made Bruno Duke of Lorraine for a while. As a side line Bruno acted as a kind of regent for the young Carolingians of France, whose uncle he was, and as mediator in the quarrels between them and the rising Capetian house, to which he was also related. After the king he was the most important man in the kingdom. . . .

# Founding Charter of Cluny (910)

The terms of the Charter granted by Duke William the Pious of Aquitaine to the Benedictine monastery at Cluny in Burgundy (in Southeastern France) provided a model for the liberation of other monasteries from feudal control. The abbots of Cluny became leaders in the reform movement of the tenth and eleventh centuries. From *Monastic Life at Cluny* by Joan Evans, Published by Oxford University Press.

I will provide at my expense for men living together under monastic vows, with this faith and hope that if I cannot myself despise all the things of this world, at least by sustaining those who despise the world, those whom I believe to be righteous in the eyes of God, I may myself receive the reward of the righteous.

To all those who live in the unity of the faith and who implore the mercy of Christ, to all who shall succeed them and shall be living so long as the world endures, I make known that for the love of God and of our Saviour Christ Jesus I give and deliver to the Apostles Peter and Paul the village of Cluny, on the river Grosne, with its curtilage and its house, with the Chapel that is dedicated in honour of St. Mary Mother of God and of St. Peter, Prince of the Apostles, with all the property that depends thereon, cottages, chapels, serfs both men and women, vines, fields, meadows, forests, water and watercourses, mills, crops and revenues, land tilled and untilled, with no reservations. All these things are situate in the country of Macon or near it, each enclosed within its bounds. I, William, with my wife Ingelberge, give these things to the aforesaid Apostles, first for the love of God, then for the soul of my lord and King Eudes, for the souls of my father and mother, for me and my wife, that is for the salvation of our souls and bodies, for the soul of Ava my sister who left me these properties by will, for the souls of our brothers and sisters, our nephews and of all our kindred, men and women, for our faithful servants, and

Pope Urban II (left) dedicates the high altar of the new church at Cluny in 1095. At the right of the altar stands Abbot Hugh who headed the monastery for sixty years.

for the maintenance and integrity of the Catholic faith. Finally, since as Christians we are all bound together by the bonds of our faith and charity, may this gift be made also for the faithful of times past, present and to come.

I give on condition that a Regular Monastery be established at Cluny in honor of the Apostles Peter and Paul; that monks shall form a congregation there living under the rule of St. Benedict; that they shall for ever possess, hold and order the property given in such wise that this honourable house shall be unceasingly full of vows and prayers, that men shall seek there with a lively desire and an inner fervour the sweetness of converse with Heaven, and that prayers and supplications shall be addressed thence without ceasing to God, both for me and for those persons commemorated above.

We ordain that our foundation shall serve forever as a refuge for those who having renounced the world as poor men bring nothing with them but their good will, and we desire that our superfluity shall become their abundance. May the monks and all the aforesaid possessions be under the power and dominion of Abbot Berno, who shall rule according to his knowledge and power so long as he shall live. After his death may the monks have the power and liberty to elect as abbot and ruler the monk of their order whom they shall prefer, according to the good pleasure of God and the rule laid down by St. Benedict, with no contradiction or impediment of this election by our power or that of any man. Nevertheless every five years they shall pay to Rome twelve pieces of gold for the upkeep of the candles of the Church of the Apostles. May they have as protectors the Apostles themselves, and for defender the Pontiff of Rome. Out of the fullness of their hearts and souls may they themselves build a monastery in this place, according to their knowledge and capacity. We also desire that in our time and in the time of our successors, as much at least as the circumstances of the time and the situation of the place admit, they may each day perform with fervent zeal works of mercy to the poor, to beggars, strangers and travellers.

It has pleased us to set forth in this testament that from this day forward the monks united in congregation of Cluny shall be wholly freed from our power, from that of our kindred, and from the jurisdiction of royal greatness, and shall never submit to the yoke of any earthly power. I beg and pray that no secular Prince, no Count, no Bishop, no Pontiff of the Roman Church, by God and through God and all his saints, under threat of the awful day of judgment, may ever invade the possessions of these servants of God. Let him not sell, nor diminish, nor exchange, nor take any thing which is theirs; let him set up no ruler over them against their will. That this prohibition may bind the bold and evil with straiter bonds, once again I say it, and add: I conjure you, ye Holy Apostles and glorious Princes of the Earth, Peter and Paul; and thou, Pontiff of Pontiffs of the Apostolic See, do ye cut off from the communion of the Holy Catholic Church and from life eternal, by the canonical and apostolic authority received from God, those who steal, invade or sell these things which I give to you with eager wish and a joyful heart. Be yet the guardians and defenders of Cluny and of the servants of God who shall dwell there, and of their goods that are destined for the giving of alms, for the imitation of the loving-kindness and mercy of our most Holy Redeemer. . . .

# The Buying of a Bishopric Demonstrates the Evils of Simony

Berengar, a nobleman, made this complaint against Archbishop Wifred of Toulouse before a church council gathered at Toulouse in Southern France in 1056. From Brian Tierney, *The Crisis of Church and State, 1050–1300,* © 1964. Reprinted by permission of Prentice-Hall, Inc., Englewood Cliffs, New Jersey.

I Berengar, consul of the city of Narbonne, declare plainly before all of you this great complaint that I have against your brother, my metropolitan. The archbishopric of Narbonne used to belong to my uncle, Archbishop Ermengaud, and in his day it was one of the best bishoprics between Rome and Spain, richly endowed with manors and castles, with estates and allodial lands. The church, filled with books and adorned with gilded pictures, caskets and crucifixes, was resplendent with golden crowns and precious stones. The voices of many canons were heard at regular hours, prayers were offered, and all good works increased. . . .

But, when the aforementioned archbishop of holy memory died, Count Wifred of Cerdana, to whom my wife was a kinswoman, came to Narbonne and approached both my parents and myself to obtain the archbishopric for his son, our bishop mentioned above, who was only ten years old at the time; and he offered a great gift of a hundred thousand *solidi* to my father and the count of Rodez. But my father and mother would not agree. I, however, moved by regard for his kinship and deceived by his pretence of friendship, broke with my parents over this matter and declared that I would destroy them if they did not give way to me. My father, seeing me so moved and so hostile to him acceded to my wishes and to the requests of Wifred, and, having received a hundred thousand *solidi* for ourselves and the count of Rodez as the price of the bishopric, we gave it to Wifred's son, our bishop. Calling God to witness and swearing an oath, he gave his firm word and pledged his faith that if he was to be our bishop, as he was and is, no injury would be done to us or ours or to the bishopric.

I was confident that when he was enthroned in the cathedral and grew in years and honor he would be a protection to me and a shield against the spears of all my enemies, that he would remember his kinship to my wife and how I had helped to place him in a position of such honor, and that, as he had declared, he would help me to have and to hold my honor. But then, arrogant as a devil, he unexpectedly provoked me to anger and harassed me and built castles against me and made cruel war on me with a vast army, so that on account of him almost a thousand men were slaughtered on both sides. Then he snatched away from God and his ministers the castles and manors, estates and possessions of the aforesaid church, together with the revenues and possessions of the canons and what they held in common, and gave them to the devil and his servants. . . .



# Pope Leo IX Attacks Simony (1049)

Leo IX (1049–1054), a strong believer in the objectives of the Cluniac movement, determined to use the potential inherent in the papal office to reform the Church. Although a relative of the German emperor Henry III and although he received his appointment as Pope with the emperor's assistance, Leo insisted upon going through the regular process of election in Rome. The first move in his reform campaign took place at the Council of Rheims in France. This reading is based on an account of Leo's procedure in Rheims by a monk in the monastery of St. Remigius. Remigius was known as "the apostle of the Franks" for his connection with the conversion of Clovis in 496. From R. W. Southern, *The Making of the Middle Ages* (New Haven, Conn.: Yale University Press, 1953), pp. 125–127.

The Feast of St. Remigius, 1 October [1049], had been fixed for the ceremony of translation, and the Pope [Leo IX] arrived in Rheims

A pope presides over a council. Here Boniface VIII (1294–1303) opens a meeting of the College of Cardinals.

on 29 September. The King of France had refused to be present, and he was largely responsible for the poor attendance of bishops. But the vast concourse of people who filled the town formed a striking and instructive contrast to the sparse gathering of notabilities. The 30 September was spent in rest; then, on the appointed day, amid scenes of immense popular enthusiasm and excitement, the bones of St. Remigius were carried round the town. The time had now arrived for the Pope to place them in their new resting place, but instead of doing so, he had them laid on the high altar of the church in which the Council was to be opened on the following day. The awful presence of the apostle of the Franks [St. Remigius] appeared from that moment to dominate the meeting. When the Council opened, the Pope—through the mouth of his chancellor, the cardinal deacon Peter, who was in charge of the business—made an unusual demand: before proceeding to the business of the meeting, each bishop and abbot was enjoined to rise and declare whether he had paid any money to obtain his office. The proposal caused considerable consternation. The Archbishop of Rheims asked for a personal interview with the Pope; the Bishops of Langres, Nevers, Coutances and Nantes remained silent. Of the abbots, only a few seem to have made the necessary declaration: the silence of the remainder expressed their embarrassment or guilt. Apparently the case against the abbots was allowed to drop; but during the remaining two days of the Council, in the intervals of the humdrum business of ecclesiastical disputes, the Papal Chancellor relentlessly pressed the bishops who had not dared to make the required declaration. The position of the Archbishop of Rheims, who was the host, was delicate: he was spared to the extent of being ordered to appear at Rome in the following year to make his explanation at the Council to be held in the middle of April. The full weight of the Chancellor's attack fell on the Bishop of Langres, a somewhat learned man, who, we notice, had just written a pamphlet against the heresy of Berengar of Tours. He asked for counsel: two archbishops undertook his defence, but one of them (the archbishop of Besançon) found some difficulty in speaking when his turn came, and the other (the archbishop of Lyons) made a partial admission of guilt on behalf of his client. The matter was adjourned, and came to a climax on the following day. The Bishop of Langres was found to have disappeared in the night. He was excommunicated; and his counsel, the archbishop of Besançon, revealed that he himself had been struck dumb on the previous day when he attempted a defence of his guilty colleague. The assembly felt the influence of the awful presence on the altar, and a wave of excitement ran through the church. The Pope rose with the name of St. Remigius on his lips, and the business was interrupted while they all sang the antiphon *Sancte Remigi.* After these excitements, the case against the other bishops was quickly disposed of. The Bishop of Nevers confessed that his parents had paid a high price for his bishopric, but declared that he was ignorant of this at the time. He laid down his pastoral staff at the Pope's feet, and the Pope restored him to office, giving him (the symbolism is significant) another staff. The Bishop of

Coutances then said that his bishopric had been bought for him by his brother without his knowledge; and that when, on discovering the transaction, he had tried to flee, he had been brought back and forcibly invested with the bishopric. He was declared innocent and he lived to be one of the builders of the Anglo-Norman State and one of the most magnificent prelates of his age. The Bishop of Nantes fared worse: he confessed that his father, who had been bishop before him, had obtained for him from the count the reversion of the bishopric, and that he himself had been obliged to pay a large sum to enter into his inheritance. He was deprived of his episcopal ring and staff, and allowed only to retain the status of a priest.

The business of the Council was now rapidly brought to an end. Various excommunications were pronounced against absent or contumacious bishops, decrees were promulgated which were long remembered for their disciplinary vigour, and a number of sentences and prohibitions were directed against laymen. On the day after the dissolution of the Council, the Pope raised the body of St. Remigius from the high altar and bore it on his own shoulders to its new resting place. He had been in Rheims just a week, and during this time, he had left a mark on the affairs of the Church which would not easily be effaced. The Pope had appeared in a more commanding position than at any time in living memory; out of the handful of bishops present at the Council, a quarter had confessed to simony, and had been judged as if they had committed a crime; an archbishop had been summoned to Rome. The promptings of conscience of men like Reginald of Liege were being stiffened by the sterner voice of authority.

# Reform Decrees of 1059

These sweeping reforms were made at the Lateran Synod during the pontificate of Nicholas II (1058–1061). Most importantly, by establishing the College of Cardinals to represent the clergy and people of Rome, the power of secular rulers to determine the selections of popes was cut drastically. From Brian Tierney, *The Crisis of Church and State 1050–1300*, 

Nicholas, bishop, servant of the servants of God, to all Catholic bishops and to all the clergy and people, affectionate greetings and apostolic benediction.

Since we must be diligently solicitous for all men with the vigilance that pertains to our universal rule, taking heed for your salvation, we are carefully sending to you the decrees that were canonically enacted in a synod recently held at Rome in the presence of one hundred and thirteen bishops and, despite our unworthiness, under our presidency; for we desire that you give effect to them for your salvation, and by apostolic authority we command this.

1. Firstly it was enacted in the sight of God that the election of the Roman pontiff should be in the power of the cardinal bishops, so that anyone who is enthroned without their previous agreement and canonical election and without the subsequent consent of the other orders of clergy and of the people shall not be held for a pope and an apostle, but rather for an apostate.
2. That when the bishop of Rome or of any city dies no one shall dare to plunder their possessions, but these shall be preserved intact for their successors.
3. That no one shall hear the mass of a priest who, he knows for certain, keeps a concubine or has a woman living with him. . . .
4. And we firmly decree that those of the above-mentioned orders who, in obedience to our predecessors, have remained chaste shall sleep and eat together near the church to which they have been ordained as is fitting for pious clergy and that they shall hold in common whatever revenues come to them from the church, and we urge them especially that they strive to attain the apostolic way of life, which is a life in common.
5. Further, that tenths and first fruits and gifts of living or dead persons be faithfully handed over to the church by lay folk and that they be at the disposal of the bishop. Any who keep them back are cut off from the communion of holy church.
6. That no cleric or priest shall receive a church from laymen in any fashion, whether freely or at a price.
7. That no one shall receive the habit of a monk in the hope or with the promise of becoming an abbot.
8. Nor shall any priest hold two churches at the same time.
9. That no one shall be ordained or promoted to any ecclesiastical office by simoniacal heresy. . . .

# The Church Proclaims a Truce of God To Cut Down Violence

Church reform also took the practical shape of attempting to cope with the almost continuous violence in the feudal era that grew from the absence of overall authority. The French clergy in the tenth century preached the merits of the so-called Peace of God, forbidding attacks on defenseless people. This was later expanded into the Truce of God, a North German example (1083) of which appears in this reading. From Dana C. Munro, trans., *Translations and Reprints from the Original Sources of European History* (Philadelphia: University of Pennsylvania, n.d.), I, No. 2, pp. 9-11.

1. From the first day of the Advent of our Lord [four Sundays before Christmas] through Epiphany [January 6] and from the beginning of Septuagesima [third Sunday before Lent] to the eighth day after Pentecost and through that whole day, and throughout the year on every Sunday, Friday and Saturday, and on the fast days of the four seasons, and on the eve and the day of all the apostles, and on all days canonically set apart—or which shall in the future be set apart—for fasts or feasts, this decree of peace shall be observed; so that both those who travel and those who remain at home may enjoy security and the most entire peace, so that no one may commit murder, arson, robbery or assault, no one may injure another with a sword, club or any kind of weapon. . . . If it shall happen that any castle is besieged during the days which are included within the peace, the besiegers shall cease from attack unless they are set upon by the besieged and compelled to beat the latter back. . . .

3. It is not an infringement of the peace, if any one orders his delinquent slave, pupil or any one in any way under his charge to be chastised with rods or cudgels. It is also an exception to this constitution of peace, if the Lord King publicly orders an expedition to attack the enemies of the kingdom or is pleased to hold a council to judge the enemies of justice. The peace is not violated if, during the time, the duke or other counts advocates or their substitutes hold courts and inflict punishment legally on thieves, robbers and other criminals. . . .

5. If any one attempts to oppose this pious institution and is unwilling to promise peace to God with the others or to observe it, no priest in our diocese shall presume to say a mass for him or shall take any care for his salvation; if he is sick, no Christian shall dare to visit him; on his death-bed he shall not receive the Eucharist, unless he repents. The supreme authority of the peace promised to God and commonly extolled by all will be so great that it will be observed not only in our times, but forever among our posterity, because if any one shall presume to infringe, destroy or violate it, either now or ages hence, at the end of the world, he is irrevocably excommunicated by us.

TOPIC 25

# THE CHARACTER OF MEDIEVAL LEARNING

Intellectual activity in a traditional society is concerned with confirming the inherited beliefs that give the society its unity. Limitations are thus placed upon the conclusions attainable by the human mind but not necessarily upon the techniques of reasoning. Thus the simple level of learning found amidst the chaos and anarchy that followed the decline of Roman civilization was transformed into a comprehensive intellectual system during the centuries of stability that composed the High Middle Ages (1100–1350). Universities, created to assume educational tasks beyond the capacity of the monasteries, produced scholars trained in Aristotelian logic and philosophy. Environment and training led such scholars to wrestle with the relationship between revealed religion and human reason, whose conclusions frequently seemed incompatible. The readings examine the medieval educational system and the way in which educated people approached the big questions of existence.

Reading 129

## The Development of Universities

From *A Survey of European Civilization*, Copyright © 1962 by Wallace K. Ferguson and Geoffrey Bruun. Reprinted by permission of the publisher, Houghton Mifflin Company.

During the High Middle Ages, in every field of human endeavor, the peoples of the West emerged from the darker ages into the full light of medieval civilization. The great revival of learning, which took place during that period, was the intellectual counterpart of the economic and social energy that produced the new trade and town life, of the religious force that built the great structure of the medieval church, and of the tendency toward social stability that was gradually imposing order upon feudal chaos. The inspiration for the new learning came largely from the Greek and Moslem East, partly through the crusades, partly through Italy, but still more from Mohammedan Spain. The scientific and philosophical works of Aristotle, the writings of the ancient Greek mathematicians and physicians, usually from the translations and commentaries made by Arabic scholars, were now eagerly studied. . . .

The old monastery and cathedral schools were no longer adequate to cope with the demands of this enlarged curriculum. They gave way gradually before the rising universities.

The twelfth century was the period in which the earliest universities took shape. By the end of the century those of Bologna, Paris, Montpellier, and Oxford, at least, were well established. We do not know just when to date their beginnings, for they simply grew, evolving slowly from the need for protection of students and teachers and from the natural tendency of men with common interests to organize themselves and to form institutions. The official charters granted by king and pope in the early years of the thirteenth century were merely the recognition of an accomplished fact. The University of Paris served as a model for all northern universities, including Oxford, which owed its origin to the recall of English students from Paris about 1167; Cambridge, founded by a migration from Oxford in 1209; and the German universities which sprang up in the fourteenth and fifteenth centuries. Early in the twelfth century, Paris became a famous center of learning, drawing students and teachers from all parts of Europe. The fame of the brilliant young philosopher, Peter Abelard, attracted hundreds of students, and after his departure the theologian, Peter Lombard, and scores of other teachers maintained the reputation of the city. Originally, these teachers had given private courses independently. But for a variety of reasons this proved unsatisfactory to both students and teachers. Some form of organization was obviously necessary.

The formation of a university as a guild of teachers and students was the logical solution of the problem. In order to prevent unqualified men from teaching, the chancellor of the cathedral was empowered to grant licenses to those who had passed a satisfactory examination, which, of course, necessitated the fixing of a curriculum of studies so that the candidates would know on what material they were to be examined. Those who were granted licenses were called masters of arts and formed the governing body of the university, the faculty of arts. Following the analogy of the guild, the students may be considered as the apprentices, and the bachelors as the journeymen with a limited license who were permitted to teach in certain elementary courses. The master's degree was accepted as a guaranty of proficiency, sought by all, even though all did not intend to use it for active teaching. After becoming a master of arts, if the student wished specialized training in one of the professions, he might pursue a further course of study leading to the degree of doctor and admittance to the faculties of theology, medicine, or law. The University of Bologna, famous for its law school, was organized somewhat differently, for there the governing body was the society or university of students, who had first organized for mutual protection against teachers and townspeople alike. The faculties were there subordinate to the students. Most of the southern universities followed this model rather than that of Paris.

The universities were essentially clerical institutions. Both teachers and students were classed as clerics, and so were exempt from ordinary civil jurisdiction. The charter granted to the University of Paris by Philip Augustus in 1200 recognized this exemption from the jurisdiction of royal or municipal courts. Further independence of local authority was acquired shortly after the papal edict. The university, as a corporation, was freed from the jurisdiction of the bishop, and disciplinary powers were vested in the faculty, subject only to the pope. The same arrangement was also made in regard to the other universities, thus giving them a remarkable degree of corporate independence.

The jurisdictional authority of the university was important, for the students were a riotous lot at times. The medieval university provided no organized sports or student activities to serve as an outlet for youthful energy and high spirits, and it was an age when men resorted easily to physical violence. Despite all prohibitions, many a student carried a knife concealed under his gown, and used it on the slightest provocation. Contemporary preachers raised their hands in horror at the drunkenness, violence, and immorality of the students, all the more because they were legally clerics; and the student poems and songs, which celebrate the less respectable joys of life in charming but unclassical Latin, bear out the indictment. Undoubtedly the medieval students were more undisciplined than those of modern times, but otherwise they were very much like students in all ages. In the letters and records that have survived, we can find all the recognizable types—students rich and poor, diligent and lazy, those who were earnestly laying the foundations of a career, and those who were merely enjoying a vacation from home. Letters written home for more funds to meet unexpected expenses, none too well itemized, were evidently as common then as now. So were letters from parents complaining that their sons were wasting their time and their parents' hard-earned money in irresponsible pleasures.

The medieval university had very little of the physical equipment that seems so important in its modern counterpart. In the twelfth and thirteenth centuries it had no buildings, except an occasional residential college for poor students, no laboratories, no library, and even no regular classrooms. A staff of teachers was all that the university possessed. Classes were held in a room in the professor's house or in a hired hall. In Paris, the students sat on the floor, which was covered with straw, while the professor lectured from a platform with a desk to hold his notes. The classes were long, beginning often at daybreak, and the rooms must have been cold and uncomfortable. The sole method of instruction was the lecture, based on a definite textbook. Medieval scholars had great respect for authoritative books, of which there were still relatively few, and the business of the professor was to explain and comment on the authorities in his field. Books were scarce and expensive, since all had to be copied by hand. Few students could afford to own their texts, though they could often rent them. As a rule, however, the method of lecturing made the possession of texts by all the students unnecessary. Taking the text passage by passage, the professor read it slowly so that the students could copy it verbatim. He then expounded it sentence by sentence, drawing upon his knowledge of the subject for a possible ray of light that could be shed upon its meaning. At the end of the course, the student's notes, if he were diligent, would comprise a complete copy of the text with the lecturer's gloss or explanation.

The course in the faculty of arts leading to the M. A. degree, normally a six-year course with the bachelor's degree somewhere along the way, was the essential part of the university curriculum. It was taken by all students, including those who intended to enter the higher faculties later. . . .

In the first half of the twelfth century, there had been a considerable revival of interest in classical Latin literature; but the introduction

Impressions of a medieval classroom. The professor lectures from a desk raised above the students who exhibit various degrees of attentiveness. This fourteenth-century German miniature appeared in an edition of Aristotle's *Nicomachean Ethics.*

of Aristotle's *Logic* at about the same time and of his *Metaphysics* in the early years of the thirteenth century turned the attention of scholars more and more to logic and philosophy, while grammar and rhetoric sank back into second place. They became merely a means to the end of teaching Latin, the language in which all texts were written and all lectures delivered. The Latin of the medieval universities was strictly utilitarian. It was used to convey information and hence remained a living tongue, changing and adapting itself to fit the needs of the age in a way that would have been impossible had it remained bound to classical precedent. Logic and philosophy were also used for practical purposes, furnishing a method of study that could be applied to theology, medicine, law, and science. They were the universal tools of the medieval scholar, who was more given to close, hard reasoning from authoritative texts and to metaphysical speculation than to experiment or to observation of natural phenomena.

# Letter of a University Student

**(14th Century)**

From G. G. Coulton, *A Medieval Garner* (London, 1910), pp. 559–560.

Well-beloved father, I have not a penny, nor can I get any save through you, for all things at the University are so dear: nor can I study in my Code or my Digest, for they are all tattered. Moreover, I owe ten crowns in dues to the Provost, and can find no man to lend them to me; I send you word of greetings and of money.

The Student hath need of many things if he will profit here; his father and his kin must needs supply him freely, that he be not compelled to pawn his books, but have ready money in his purse, with gowns and furs and decent clothing, or he will be damned for a beggar; wherefore, that men may not take me for a beast, I send you word of greetings and of money.

Wines are dear, and hostels, and other good things; I owe in every street, and am hard bested to free myself from such snares. Dear father, deign to help me! I fear to be excommunicated; already have I been cited, and there is not even a dry bone in my larder. If I find not the money before this feast of Easter, the church door will be shut in my face: wherefore grant my supplication, for I send you word of greetings and of money.

# Medieval Scholars Look at the Universe

Medieval science revolved chiefly around the interpretation of Scripture. Experimentation was largely absent and the observation of natural phenomena served largely as a factor that needed to be explained away when it obtruded. The first reading, taken from a tenth-century English document, describes the common medieval concept of the universe. The second reading is from the *Natural Questions* of Adelard of Bath, a twelfth-century English scholar. From James H. Robinson, ed., *Readings in European History* (Boston, 1904), I, p. 441. Simplified by John M. Good. II. From Adelard of Bath, "Quaestiones Naturales," in John M. Good, *The Shaping of Western Society* (New York: Holt, Rinehart and Winston, 1968), pp. 169–170.

## I. A TENTH-CENTURY VIEW OF THE ORGANIZATION OF THE UNIVERSE

On the second day, God made the heaven. It is visible, but can never be closely examined, since it is so high, the clouds are so thick, and our eyes are so weak. Heaven surrounds the whole world, and turns about the world faster than any mill wheel. It is as deep under the earth as it is above. It is round and studded with stars.

Truly the sun follows God's commands, going above the earth by day and below the earth by night. The sun is forever running around the earth, and so it shines under the earth at night as it does above our heads by day. The sun is very large. From what the books say, it is as broad as the entire earth. Yet it appears to be very small, since it is very far away. The farther anything is from us the smaller it appears. The moon and all of the stars receive their light from the great sun. The sun is typical of our savior, Jesus Christ, who is the sun of righteousness. Good Christians are like the stars. They shine because Christ has let his light fall upon them.

## II. A MEDIEVAL SCIENTIST EXPLAINS NATURAL PHENOMENA (TWELFTH CENTURY)

[Nephew] Why is seawater bitter and salty?

[Adelard] I believe that the heat of the sun and the planets causes the saltiness. The ocean flows through the hot zone of the earth near the equator. The planets overhead also have their course through the same zone. The great heat of the stars heats the sea and it becomes salty. One fact which supports this theory is that seawater when it is dried by the sun on the rocks near the ocean turns into salt. . . .

[Nephew] If, as the common people believe, all rivers flow into the sea, then why do they not increase the size of the ocean?

[Adelard] If you follow the common people you will tumble into a pit. They understand nature so poorly that they are like men in a dream, and when they talk about nature they positively snore. It is not true that all rivers

A favorite medieval study was alchemy, which sought a way of transforming base metals like lead or copper into silver and gold. Here a German alchemist ponders his next step while his assistant works at the furnace.

run into the sea, though many do. But just as some run into it, some run out of it. The sea gives as well as receives, and, therefore, does not increase in size. In fact, since so many underground streams flow out of the ocean and the stars evaporate so much of its water, some people have asked why the ocean does not decrease in size.

[Nephew] Lo! I am confused again. If rivers run from the sea, why are they not salty when they reach us?

[Adelard] They lose their salt on the route to us. Though they were salty when they started, the rivers were strained in their passage through the center of the earth and leave their saltiness there. . . .

# The Significance of Aristotle in the Middle Ages

The work of the Greek philosopher Aristotle had an extraordinary impact on medieval thought. This impact is shown in the readings, the first of which comes from the pen of Averroës (1126–1198), a Moslem lawyer, physician, and philosopher of Spain, influential in spreading interest in Aristotle's writings. The second reading presents a list of the books students at the University of Paris had to master in the thirteenth century in order to get a degree. The third reading is taken from a series of University lectures by Columbia philosopher Paul Kristeller in which he analyzed the influence of classical thinking on Western thought between 1300 and 1600 A.D.

I and II. From *Readings in the History of Education.* Copyright 1947, by Helen Cubberly. Reprinted by permission of the publisher, Houghton Mifflin Company, Pp. 136–137, 168–169. III. Reprinted by permission of the publisher from Paul Kristeller, *The Classics and Renaissance Thought,* Cambridge, Mass: Harvard University Press, Copyright 1955 by the Board of Trustees of Oberlin College, Pp. 9–13, 18–21, 25, 27–28, 30–34.

## I. AVERROËS ON ARISTOTLE

Aristotle was the wisest of the Greeks and constituted and completed logic, physics, and metaphysics. I say that he constituted these sciences, because all the works on these subjects previous to him do not deserve to be mentioned and were completely eclipsed by his writings. I say that he put the finishing touches on these sciences, because none of those who have succeeded him up to our time, to wit, during nearly fifteen hundred years, have been able to add anything to his writings or to find in them any error of any importance. Now that all this should be found in one man is a strange and miraculous thing, and this privileged being deserves to be called divine rather than human.

## II. BOOKS REQUIRED AT PARIS FOR THE ARTS DEGREE, 1254

The following books were prescribed for the A.B. and A.M. degrees at Paris by the Statutes of 1254. The list does not distinguish the books required for the baccalaureate degree only, but gives them for both degrees together. . . .

The great preponderance of Aristotle in the list is noticeable, showing how completely Aristotle had been adopted by this time as the great authority of mediaeval Europe. In addition to having heard lectures on these subjects, the candidate must also have taken part in a number of disputations.

A The "Old" Logic.
1. Introduction to the Categories of Aristotle (Isagoge), Porphyry.
2. Categories, and On Interpretation, Aristotle.
3. Divisions, and Topics except Bk. IV, Boethius.

B The "New" Logic.
1. Prior and Posterior Analytics, Aristotle.
2. Sophistical Refutations, Aristotle.
3. Topics, Aristotle.

C Moral Philosophy.
1. Ethics, 4 Bks., Aristotle.

D Natural Philosophy.
1. Physics, Aristotle.
2. On the Heavens and the Earth, Aristotle.
3. Meteorics, Aristotle.
4. On Animals, Aristotle.
5. On the Soul, Aristotle.
6. On Generation, Aristotle.
7. On Sense and Sensible Things, Aristotle.
8. Sleep and Waking, Aristotle.
9. Memory and Recollection, Aristotle.
10. On Life and Death, Aristotle.
11. On Plants, Aristotle (?)

E Metaphysics.
1. Metaphysics, Aristotle

F Other Books.
1. On the Six Principles, Gilbert de la Porree.
2. Barbarismus (Bk. 3, Larger Grammar), Donatus.
3. Grammar (Major and Minor), Priscian.

4. On Causes, Costa ben Luca.
5. On the Differences of Spirit and Soul (another translation of On Causes).

## III. PAUL KRISTELLER: THE ARISTOTELIAN TRADITION

If we want to understand the impact of Aristotle upon later thought, we must remember some curious facts connected with the transmission of his writings. When Aristotle died in 322 B.C., he left a very extensive body of writings which consisted of two completely different groups. On the one hand, there was a large group of dialogues and other popular treatises which had been published during his lifetime, and which continued to be widely read through many centuries until they were finally lost towards the end of antiquity. These popular writings . . . were praised for their literary elegance, and apparently the most famous . . . were composed in Aristotle's earlier years and were comparatively close to Plato in their philosophical opinions. The second group of Aristotle's writings, which is the one that has come down to us, represents a collection of the lecture courses which he delivered in his school in Athens. These courses served no literary purpose, but in turn they are highly technical in character, very detailed in their reasoning and in the information supplied, and fairly systematic in their over-all arrangement, forming a vast encyclopaedia of philosophical and scientific knowledge.

When the Arabs began to translate the works of Greek literature that interested them, they largely omitted the Greek poets, orators, and historians, and centered their efforts on astronomy, medicine, astrology and alchemy, and philosophy. The translated Greek works provided the nucleus of subject matter in these disciplines, to which the Arabs subsequently added their own contributions. . . . Aristotle attained among the Arabs an authority and doctrinal preponderance that he had never possessed in Greek antiquity to the very end. . . . The Aristotelian corpus, supplemented by medicine and mathematics, seemed to represent a complete encyclopaedia of learning whose various writings coincided with the branches of knowledge as such. The authority of Aristotle was probably further enhanced by that of Galen, who was strongly influenced by Aristotelian philosophy and exercised a similar influence upon Arabic medicine, especially since some of the most important Arabic thinkers combined philosophy and medicine in their work. Thus the major Arabic philosophers, such as Avicenna and Averroës, were commentators and followers of Aristotle. . . .

During the early Middle Ages, the Latin West was largely cut off from the richer Greek tradition and reduced to the indigenous resources of Roman literature, which was weak in philosophy, as we have noticed. The body of secular learning provided in the monastic and cathedral schools of the period was limited to the elementary encyclopaedia of the seven liberal arts, that is, grammar, rhetoric, dialectic, arithmetic, geometry, astronomy, and music. In this scheme, which prevailed to the eleventh century, grammar was the leading subject, which included at times the study of the Latin poets. Philosophy was represented only by dialectic, that is, elementary logic, and this subject was largely based on the Aristotelian treatises translated by Boethius. Philosophy in the broad sense of the word as known to the ancient Greeks was almost forgotten, and the only author who made a genuine contribution to philosophical thought in that period, Scotus Eriugena, was an isolated figure distinguished for his acquaintance with Greek Neoplatonism.

This situation was completely changed through the remarkable rise of philosophical, theological, and scientific studies that began during the second half of the eleventh century and culminated in the thirteenth. During that period, the body of learning expanded steadily until it surpassed the traditional limits of the seven arts. A large amount of writings on philosophy, on the sciences and the pseudo sciences was translated from Arabic and from Greek that introduced precious material previously unavailable in Latin and tended to stimulate and transform Western thought. Among the philosophical authors thus translated, Proclus and other Neoplatonic authors were well represented, but the most extensive and most important body of literature consisted of the nearly complete corpus of Aristotle, accompanied by a few Greek commentaries, and by a much larger body of Arabic commentaries, especially by Avicenna and Averroës. The writings of Aristotle and of his Greek commentators as well as of Proclus were in part translated from the original text, to be sure, but the selection of subjects and of authors clearly reflects the Arabic rather than the ancient Greek tradition of philosophy. At the same time, new institutions of higher learning developed, the universities, which differed considerably from the earlier schools in their curriculum, textbooks, and methods of instruction. The instruction centered around the *lectura,* the continuous reading and exposition of a standard text, and the *disputatio,* the public discussion of a proposed thesis with the help of formalized arguments. These forms of instruction produced the two main types of mediaeval scholarly literature, the commentary and the question. The subject matter of university instruction was fixed during the thirteenth century at Paris and the other Northern universities in the system of four faculties, theology, law, medicine, and arts or philosophy. Whereas the teaching of theology was based on the Bible and on Peter Lombard's *Sentences,* and that of law on the *Corpus Juris* of Justinian and on Gratian's *Decretum,* the instruction in medicine and in philosophy came to be based on some of the new translations from the Greek and Arabic. The philosophical disciplines thus became for the first time in the Latin world subjects of separate instruction, and the texts adopted for this instruction, after some resistance, were the writings of Aristotle along with those of Averroës and of other commentators. The chief subjects were logic and natural philosophy, whereas ethics and metaphysics attained the status of elective courses only. Thus the writings of Aristotle had become by the middle of the thirteenth century the basis of philosophical instruction at the universities. They owed this position not merely to Arabic precedent, but also to the solidity of their content and to their systematic and encyclopaedic character. Aristotle was not studied as a "great book," but as a textbook that was the starting point for commentaries and questions and supplied a frame of reference for all trained philosophical thinkers even when they ventured to reinterpret him, or to depart from his doctrine, according to their own opinions. The Aristotelianism of the later Middle Ages was characterized not so much by a common system of ideas as by a common source material, a common terminology, a common set of definitions and problems, and a common method of discussing these problems. . . .

It has been my intention to show how Aristotle had become by the early fourteenth century "the master of those who know," in order to emphasize the additional fact, which is less widely known, that this Aristotelian tradition, though exposed to attacks and subject to transformations, continued strongly and vigorously to the end of the sixteenth century and even later. The failure to appreciate this fact is due to various reasons. Historians, like journalists, are apt to concentrate on news and to forget that there is a complex and broad situation which remained unaffected by the events of the moment. They also have for some time been more interested in the origins rather than in the continuations of intellectual and other developments. More specifically, many historians of thought have been sympathetic to the opponents of Aristotelianism in the Renaissance, whereas most of the defenders of mediaeval philosophy have limited their efforts to its earlier phases before the end of the thirteenth century, and have sacrificed the late scholastics to the critique of their contemporary and modern adversaries. Yet we have learned through recent studies that the chief progress made during the later fourteenth century in the fields of logic and natural philosophy was due to the Aristotelian . . . school at Paris and Oxford. During the fifteenth and sixteenth centuries, university instruction in the philosophical disciplines continued everywhere to be based on the works of Aristotle; consequently, most professional teachers of philosophy followed the Aristotelian tradition, used its terminology and method, discussed its problems, and composed commentaries and questions on Aristotle. . . .

# Sources and Objectives of Medieval Philosophy

From John Stipp, C. Warren Hollister, Allen W. Birrim, *The Rise and Development of Western Civilization* (New York: John Wiley & Sons, Inc., 1967), Vol. I, pp. 437–439.

The high medieval philosophers drew nourishment from five earlier sources: (1) From the Greeks they inherited the great philosophical systems of Plato and Aristotle. At first these two Greek masters were known in the West only through a handful of translations and commentaries dating from late Roman times. By the thirteenth century, however, new and far more complete translations were coming into Christendom from Spain and Sicily, and Aristotelian philosophy became a matter of intense interest and controversy in Europe's universities. (2) From the Islamic world came a flood of Greek scientific and philosophical works which had long before been translated from Greek to Arabic and were now translated from Arabic into Latin. These works came into Europe accompanied by extensive commentaries and original writings of Arab philosophers and scientists, for the Arabs had come to grips with Greek learning long before the advent of the High Middle Ages. Islamic thought made its own distinctive contribution to European science; in philosophy it was important chiefly as an agency for the transmission and interpretation of Greek thought. (3) The early Church fathers, particularly the Latin Doctors, had been a dominant influence on the thought of the Early Middle Ages and their authority remained strong in the twelfth and thirteenth centuries. St. Augustine retained his singular significance, and was, indeed, the chief vessel of Platonic and Neoplatonic thought in the medieval universities. No philosopher of the High Middle Ages could ignore him, and some of the most distinguished of them were conscious and devoted Augustinians. (4) The early medieval scholars themselves contributed significantly to the high medieval intellectual revival. Gregory the Great [and others] . . . were all studied seriously in the new universities. The original intellectual contributions of these men were less important, however, than the fact that they and their contemporaries had kept learning alive, fostered and perpetuated the classical tradition in Europe, and created an intellectual climate that made possible the reawakening of philosophical speculation in the eleventh century. Although stimulated by contacts with other civilizations, the intellectual surge of the High Middle Ages was fundamentally an internal phenomenon with roots in Ottonian, Carolingian, and pre-Carolingian Europe. (5) The high-medieval philosophers looked back beyond the scholars of the Early Middle Ages, beyond the fathers of the early Church, to the Hebrew and primitive Christian religious traditions as recorded in Scripture. Among medieval theologians the Bible, the chief written source of divine revelation, was quite naturally the fundamental text and the ultimate authority.

## NATURE OF SCHOLASTICISM

Such were the chief elements—Greek, Islamic, Patristic, early medieval, and scriptural—which underlay the thought of the scholastic philosophers of the High Middle Ages. Narrowly defined, "scholasticism" is simply the philosophical movement associated with the high medieval schools—the cathedral and monastic schools, and later the universities. More basically it was a movement concerned above all with exploring the relationship between rationalism and theism—reason and revelation. All medieval scholastics were theists, all were committed, to some degree, to the life of reason. Many of them were immensely enthusiastic over the intellectual possibilities inherent in the careful application of Aristotelian logic to basic human and religious problems. Some believed that the syllogism* was the master key to a thousand doors, and that with sufficient methodological rigor, with sufficient exactness in the use of words, the potentialities of human knowledge were all but limitless.

The scholastics applied their logical method to a vast number of problems. They were concerned chiefly, however, with matters of basic significance to human existence: the nature of man, the purpose of human life, the existence and attributes of God, the fundamentals of human morality, the ethical imperatives of social and political life, the relationship between God and man.

It would be hard to deny that these are the most profound sorts of questions that philosophers can ask, although many thinkers of our own day are inclined to reject them as unanswerable. Perhaps they are, but the scholastics, standing near the beginning of Europe's long intellectual journey and lacking the modern sense of disillusionment, were determined to make the attempt.

*The *syllogism* is an exercise in logic that consists of a major and a minor premise and a conclusion. *Example:* Only God is immortal. Man is not God. Therefore, man is not immortal—Eds.

## RELATIONSHIP OF FAITH AND REASON

The issue of faith *versus* reason was perhaps the most farreaching of the diverse investigations and conflicting opinions of the medieval thinkers. Ever since Tertullian in the third century, there had been Christian writers who insisted that God so transcended reason that any attempt to approach him intellectually was useless and, indeed, blasphemous. It was the mystic who knew God, not the theologian. Tertullian had posed the rhetorical questions,

> What has Athens to do with Jersusalem? What concord is there between the Academy and the Church? . . . Let us have done with all attempts to produce a bastard Christianity of Stoic, Platonic, and dialectic composition! We desire no curious disputation after possessing Christ Jesus, no inquisition after enjoying the Gospel!

Tertullian had many followers in the Middle Ages. St. Peter Damiani, standing at the fountainhead of the new medieval piety, rejected the intellectual road to God in favor of the mystical. Damiani had insisted that God, whose power is limitless, cannot be bound or even approached by logic. He was followed in this view by such later mystics as St. Bernard, who denounced and hounded his brilliant rationalist contemporary Peter Abelard, and St. Francis, who regarded intellectual speculation as irrelevant and perhaps even dangerous to salvation. A later spiritual Franciscan, Jacopone da Todi, expressed the anti-intellectual position in verse:

Plato and Socrates may oft contend,
And all the breath within their bodies spend,
Engaged in disputations without end.
What's that to me?
For only with a pure and simple mind
Can one the narrow path to heaven find,
And greet the King; while lingers far behind,
Philosophy.

The contrary view was just as old. Third-century theologians such as Clement and Origen in the school of Alexandria had labored to provide Christianity with a sturdy philosophical foundation and did not hesitate to elucidate the faith by means of Greek—and particularly Platonic—thought. The fourth-century Latin Doctors, Ambrose, Jerome, and Augustine, had wrestled with the problem of whether a Christian might properly use elements from the pagan classical tradition in the service of the Faith, and all three ended with affirmative answers. As Augustine expressed it,

> If those who are called philosophers, and especially the Platonists, have said aught that is true and in harmony with our faith, we must not only not shrink from it, but claim it for our own use from those who have unlawful possession of it.

Such is the viewpoint that underlies most of high medieval philosophy—that reason has a valuable role to play as a servant of revelation. St. Anselm, following Augustine, declared, "I believe so that I may know." Faith comes first, reason second; faith rules reason, but reason can perform the useful service of illuminating faith. Indeed, faith and reason are separate avenues to a single body of truth. By their very nature they cannot lead to contradictory conclusions, for truth is one. Should their conclusions ever *appear* to be contradictory, the philosopher can be assured that some flaw exists in his logic. Reason cannot err, but man's use of it can, and revelation must therefore be the criterion against which reason is measured.

This, in general, became the common position of later scholastic philosophers. The intellectual system of St. Thomas Aquinas was built on the conviction that reason and faith were harmonious. Even the archrationalist of the twelfth century, Peter Abelard, wrote: "I do not wish to be a philosopher if it means resisting St. Paul; I do not wish to be Aristotle if it must separate me from Christ." Abelard believed that he could at once be a philosopher and a Christian, but his faith took first priority.

# Peter Abelard Recalls His First Years as a Teacher

Peter Abelard (1079–1142) is best known today for his tragic love affair with Heloise, his pupil, but he deserves to be remembered as one of the quickest minds of the Middle Ages. Philosopher and teacher, he helped found the University of Paris. Abelard was a man who did not hide his light under a bushel and consequently made many enemies among other intellectuals of his day. He began this engaging autobiography, entitled *Historia Calamitatum* (The Story of My Adversities), by describing his education and first teaching.

From *The Story of Abelard's Adversities,* trans. Father J. T. Muckle (Toronto: The Pontifical Institute of Medieval Studies, 1954), pp. 11–18.

To begin, then, I was born in . . . Britanny . . . . I was lighthearted and had talent for letters, characteristics derived from my country and family. My father was a man who had acquired some literary knowledge before he donned the uniform of a soldier and he retained such a liking for learning that he intended to procure for whatever sons he was to have a training in letters before their military service. And he carried out his purpose. As he loved me the more, being his first-born, so he saw to it that I was carefully instructed. The further I went in my studies and the more easily I made progress, the more I became attached to them and came to possess such a love of them that, giving up in favor of my brothers the pomp of military glory along with my right of inheritance and the other prerogatives of primogeniture, I renounced the field of Mars to be brought up at the knee of Minerva. Since I preferred the armor of logic to all the teaching of philosophy, I exchanged all other arms for it and chose the contests of disputation above the trophies of warfare. And so, practising logic I wandered about the various provinces wherever I heard the pursuit of this art was vigorous and became thereby like the peripatetics.

I finally reached Paris where this branch of learning was especially cultivated and enrolled under William of Champeaux, a man who at that time was an outstanding teacher in this branch both in reputation and in fact. I remained under him some little time; at first I was welcome but after a while he found me burdensome as I began to question some of his statements and quite often to argue against his position; sometimes I was apparently the winner in the discussions. Those of my fellow-students who were considered outstanding became the more deeply incensed at my conduct as they looked upon me as younger than they and as having spent less time at books. From this my troubles began and have plagued me to this day; and the more widespread my fame has become, the more has the jealousy of others been enkindled against me.

Finally it came about that with a presumption of ability beyond my years, I formed the ambition, young as I was, to be at the head of a school and to get as a location what was then the renowned town of Melun which was also a royal seat. My above-mentioned master sensed this and in an attempt to have my school far removed from him he slyly used every means in his power before I withdrew from his school to hinder the furtherance of my plans and to deprive me of the place I had now arranged for. But some men of influence there were opposed to him and relying on their help I accomplished my purpose, as his open antipathy gained for me the support of many.

With the establishment of this my first school, my reputation in dialectical skill began to spread so that the fame not only of my former fellow-students but also of my master gradually lessened and went into eclipse. As a result, being more self-confident I transferred my school to Corbeil nearer Paris that I might prove a greater embarrassment and offer more frequent challenges to debate.

But after the lapse of a comparatively short time, owing to the heavy strain of study, I fell sick and was forced to return home; and though absent from France for several years, all those who were anxious for instruction in logic kept eagerly trying to seek me out.

After a few years had passed I was well recovered from my illness. My teacher William, archdeacon of Paris, had changed his state and entered the Order of Regular Clerics for the purpose, it was said, of being considered more pious and thereby of gaining promotion to the rank of a major prelacy, as happened when he was made bishop of Châlons. But his taking the religious habit did not withdraw him from Paris or from his former philosophical pursuits. On the contrary, he immediately conducted a public school as formerly, right in the monastery to which he had gone for a life in religion.

At that time I returned to him to hear him lecturing on rhetoric. Among other essays at discussion I forced him by clear proofs from reasoning to change, yes, to abandon his old stand on universals. For he held the position on the common existence of universals that the same thing exists wholly and essentially in all individuals of a class and that there is no distinction of essence in them but only variety through multiplicity of accidents. . . . Once William had corrected, yes under compulsion had abandoned his position, his lectures bogged down into such carelessness that they could scarcely be called lectures on logic at all, as though the whole art were confined to the problem of universals.

From then on my teaching gained such strength and prestige that those who formerly had somewhat vigorously championed the position of our master and had most forcefully attacked mine now flocked to my school and even he who had taken over the chair of our master in the cathedral school of Paris offered his place to me that along with the other students he might follow my lectures right where our common master had held sway. Within a few days after my taking over the chair of dialectics, envy began to eat the heart out of my master and anguish to seize him to a degree I can hardly express. His seething soul did not long endure the misery which had taken hold of him before he cunningly attempted to depose me. And because there was nothing he could do against me personally, he set out by laying the basest charges to take the school away from him who had turned the chair over to me and to put another, one of my rivals, in that position. I then returned to Melun and once more set up my school there. And the more openly he attacked me in his jealousy, the more prestige he gave me. . . .

# Abelard Raises Questions for Debate

While Peter Abelard (1079–1142) was teaching theology in Paris in the early twelfth century, he prepared a small textbook for his students, which he called *Sic et Non* (Yes and No). He listed a large number of questions about Church doctrine and practices and followed each question with conflicting opinion taken from the New Testament and the writings of the early Church Fathers. Abelard, himself, was careful to draw no conclusions to his questions, leaving this up to his readers. This reading contains the introduction to *Sic et Non,* in which the author explains his objectives and procedure, and representative questions treated in the book. From *Readings in the History of Education.* Copyright, 1947, by Helen Cubberly. Reprinted by permission of the publisher, Houghton Mifflin Company.

### A. FROM THE INTRODUCTION TO *SIC ET NON*

In truth, constant or frequent questioning is the first key to wisdom; and it is, indeed, to the acquiring of this (habit of) questioning with absorbing eagerness that the famous philosopher, Aristotle, the most clear-sighted of all, urges the studious when he says: "It is perhaps difficult to speak confidently in matters of this sort unless they have often been investigated. Indeed, to doubt in special cases will not be without advantage." For through doubting we come to inquiry, and through inquiry we perceive the truth. As the Truth Himself says: "Seek and ye shall find, knock and it shall be opened to you." And He also, instructing us by His own example, about the twelfth year of His life wished to be found sitting in the midst of the doctors, asking them questions, exhibiting to us by His asking of questions the appearance of a pupil, rather than, by preaching, that of a teacher, although there is in Him, nevertheless, the full and perfect wisdom of God.

Now when a number of quotations from (various) writings are introduced they spur on the reader, and allure him into seeking the truth in proportion as the authority of the writing itself is commended. . . .

In accordance, then, with these forecasts it is our pleasure to collect different sayings of the holy Fathers as we planned, just as they have come to mind, suggesting (as they do) some questioning from their apparent disagreement, in order that they may stimulate tender readers to the utmost effort in seeking the truth and may make them keener as the result of their seeking.

### B. TYPES OF QUESTIONS HE RAISED FOR DEBATE

Of the 158 questions he raised and gave evidence on, the following are illustrative.

Should human faith be based on reason, or no?
Is God one, or no?
Is God a substance, or no?
Does the first Psalm refer to Christ, or no?
Is sin pleasing to God, or no?
Is God the author of evil, or no?
Is God all-powerful, or no?
Can God be resisted, or no?
Has God free will, or no?
Was the first man persuaded to sin by the devil, or no?
Was Adam saved, or no?
Did all the apostles have wives except John, or no?
Are the flesh and blood of Christ in very truth and essence present in the sacrament of the altar, or no?
Do we sometimes sin unwillingly, or no?
Does God punish the same sin both here and in the future, or no?
Is it worse to sin openly than secretly, or no?

## St. Thomas Aquinas Uses Reason To Prove That Man's Ultimate Happiness Lies Not in This Life (13th Century)

Like Peter Abelard, the great medieval philosopher St. Thomas Aquinas (1225–1274) collected conflicting opinions on theological questions but, unlike Abelard, he drew conclusions that proved that there was no inherent barrier between faith and reason. Aquinas' *Summa Theologica* (The Complete Theology), a huge collection of philosophical questions, evidence pro and con, and reasoned judgments presented overpowering proof that religion had nothing to fear from correct reasoning which was simply another way of getting at God's truth. The reading is representative of Aquinas' method of interrelating reason and faith. From St. Thomas Aquinas, "Summa contra Gentiles," Book III, Ch. 48, trans. by the Fathers of the English Dominican Province, in *Basic Writings of St. Thomas Aquinas*, ed. by Anton C. Pegis (New York: Random House, Inc., 1945), II, 84–87.

Seeing, then, that man's ultimate happiness does not consist in that knowledge of God whereby He is known by all or many in a vague kind of opinion, nor again in that knowledge of God whereby He is known in the speculative sciences through demonstration, nor in that knowledge whereby He is known through faith, as we have proved above; and seeing that it is not possible in this life to arrive at a higher knowledge of God in His essence, or at least so that we understand other separate substances, and thus know God through that which is nearest to Him, so to say, as we have proved; and since we must place our ultimate happiness in some kind of knowledge of God, as we have shown: —it is impossible for men's happiness to be in this life.

Again. Man's last end is the term of his natural appetite, so that when he has obtained it, he desires nothing more; because if he still has a movement towards something, he has not yet reached an end wherein to be at rest. Now this cannot happen in this life, since the more man understands, the more is the desire to understand increased in him (for this is natural to man), unless perhaps there be someone who understands all things. Now in this life this never did nor can happen to anyone that was a mere man, seeing that in this life we are unable to know separate substances which in themselves are more intelligible, as we have proved. Therefore man's ultimate happiness cannot possibly be in this life.

Besides. Whatever is in motion towards an end has a natural desire to be established and at rest therein. Hence a body does not move away from the place towards which it has a natural movement, except by a violent movement which is contrary to that appetite. Now happiness is the last end which man naturally desires. Therefore it is his natural desire to be established in happiness. Consequently, unless together with happiness he acquires a state of immobility, he is not yet happy, since his natural desire is not yet at rest; so that all agree in conceiving stability as a necessary condition of happiness. Hence the philosopher [Aristotle] says: *We do not look upon the happy man as a kind of chameleon.* Now in this life there is no sure stability, since, however happy a man may be, sickness and misfortune may come upon him, so that he is hindered in the operation, whatever it be, in which happiness consists. Therefore man's ultimate happiness cannot be in this life.

Moreover. It would seem unfitting and unreasonable for a thing to take a long time in becoming, and to have but a short time in being; for it would follow that for a longer duration of time nature would be deprived of its end. Hence we see that animals which live but a short time are perfected in a short time. But if happiness consists in a perfect operation according to perfect virtue [as Aristotle argues], whether intellectual or moral, it cannot possibly come to man except after a long time. This is most evident in speculative matters, wherein man's ultimate happiness consists, as we have proved; for hardly is man able to arrive at perfection in the speculations of science, even though he reach the last stage of life, and then, in the majority of cases, but a short space of life remains to him. Therefore man's ultimate happiness cannot be in this life.

Further. All admit that happiness is a perfect good, or else it would not bring rest to the appetite. Now perfect good is that which is wholly free from any admixture of evil; just as that which is perfectly white is that which is entirely free from any admixture of black. But man cannot be wholly free from evils in this state of life, and not only from evils of the body, such as hunger, thirst, heat, cold, and the like, but also from the evils of the soul. For there is no one who at times is not disturbed by inordinate passions; who sometimes does not go beyond the mean, wherein virtue consists, either in excess or in deficiency; who is not deceived in some thing or another; or who at least is not ignorant of what he would wish to know, or does not feel doubtful about an opinion of which he would like to be certain. Therefore no man is happy in this life.

Again. Man naturally shuns death, and is sad about it, not only shunning it at the moment when he feels its presence, but also when he thinks about it. But man, in this life, cannot obtain not to die. Therefore it is not possible for man to be happy in this life.

Besides. Ultimate happiness consists, not in a habit, but in an operation, since habits are for the sake of actions. But in this life it is impossible to perform any action continuously. Therefore man cannot be entirely happy in this life.

Further. The more a thing is desired and loved, the more does its loss bring sorrow and pain. Now happiness is most desired and loved. Therefore its loss brings the greatest sorrow. But if there be ultimate happiness in this life, it will certainly be lost, at least by death. Nor is it certain that it will last till death, since it is possible for every man in this life to encounter sickness, whereby he is wholly hindered from the operation of virtue, e.g., madness and the like, which hinder the use of reason. Such happiness therefore always has sorrow connected with it, and consequently it will not be perfect happiness. . . .

Again. Natural desire cannot be empty, since *nature does nothing in vain* [as Aristotle insists]. But nature's desire would be empty if it could never be fulfilled. Therefore man's natural desire can be fulfilled. But not in this life, as we have shown. Therefore it must be fulfilled after this life. Therefore man's ultimate happiness is after this life.

Besides. As long as a thing is in motion towards perfection, it has not reached its last end. Now in the knowledge of truth all men are always in motion and tending towards perfection; because those who follow make discoveries in addition to those made by their predecessors, as is also stated in [Aristotle's] *Metaph.ii.* Therefore in the knowledge of truth man is not situated as though he had arrived at his last end. Since, then, as Aristotle himself shows, man's ultimate happiness in this life consists apparently in speculation, whereby he seeks the knowledge of truth, we cannot possibly allow that man obtains his last end in this life. . . .

Averroës held that man's ultimate happiness does not consist in that human knowledge obtained through the speculative sciences, but in that which results from a union with a separate substance, which union they deemed possible to man in this life. But as Aristotle realized that man has no knowledge in this life other than that which he obtains through the speculative sciences, he maintained that man attains to a happiness which is not perfect, but a human one.

Hence it becomes sufficiently clear how these great minds suffered from being so straitened on every side. We, however, shall be freed from these straits if we hold, in accordance with the foregoing arguments, that man is able to reach perfect happiness after this life, since man has an immortal soul; and that in that state his soul will understand in the same way as separate substances understand, as we proved in the Second Book.

Therefore man's ultimate happiness will consist in that knowledge of God which the human mind possesses after this life, a knowledge similar to that by which separate substances know him. Hence our Lord promises us a *reward . . . in heaven* (*Matt. v. 12*) and states (*Matt.* xxii. 30) that the saints shall *be as the angels,* who always see God in heaven (*Matt.* xviii. 10).

TOPIC 26

# THE CHRISTIAN CRUSADE

In the late eleventh century, the medieval European heartland, long the object of attack from without, itself began to expand in the mighty push that was the Christian Crusade. For most, perhaps, the Crusades were a thrust toward reestablishing contact with ancient civilization. Pressed forward by the restlessness of a burgeoning population, inspired by the voices of militant Church leaders, and emboldened by the participation of Europe's military elite, hundreds of thousands marched southeastward under the banners of Western Christianity toward the strongholds of Islamic and Byzantine power. But similar movements, also impelled by militant Christianity, spread south into Spain and Sicily, west into Britain, Iceland, and Greenland, and northeast into the Baltic and Slavic lands of Central Europe. The consequences of the Crusades were the physical extension of Europe, a broadening of European awareness of other ways and other peoples, and a commercial revival that ushered in great changes in the Western economy in the twelfth and thirteenth centuries (changes which will be considered more fully in a later topic). The readings seek to shed light on the conflicting motivations and behavior of the Crusaders and the significance the crusading movement had for medieval civilization.



**Reading 137**

## Hugh Trevor-Roper: Spiritual Conquest and European Expansion

Hugh Trevor-Roper (1914– ), professor of modern history at Oxford, is concerned here with what gave Western society its power of recovery after the nadir that followed the decline of the Roman Empire. How, he asks in the preface to *The Rise of Christian Europe,* was it "that Christendom was able to launch a great counterattack" at the end of the eleventh century against the forces that had almost overwhelmed the West? Excerpted from *The Rise of Christian Europe* by Hugh Trevor-Roper, 

### I

In the eleventh century a great change came over Europe: a change which began north of the Alps. Exactly what that change was we can hardly say. Only one thing is certain in history, and that is that no historical process, or historical change, has a single cause: all depend not on simple mathematical logic but on a complex chemistry of causes. But one element in the chemical change of the eleventh century was undoubtedly a great, though to us unmeasurable, increase in population, and one cause, or at least concomitant, of this increase of population was a series of technical improvements which increased the productivity of the land. . . .

These agricultural innovations could sustain a certain increase of working population. But an increase in population is never nicely calculated, and in fact, in a generation of opportunity, the larger families which survive infant mortality will always, when they grow up, press too heavily even on expanded means of production. In the eleventh century Europe north of the Alps could not sustain the whole increase of its population, and so, on every frontier, the pressure grew. At the same time, those two preservative and aggressive institutions [monasticism and feudalism] which Europe had found for itself discovered a new vitality, a new unity. The reforming zeal . . . was taken over by the monks of Cluny in France, who sought to colonize and, by colonizing, to rescue and control the Church. Where the Benedictine abbeys had been equal, independent foundations, the Cluniac houses were a disciplined, organized system, controlled from the top, from the abbey of Cluny itself, and so capable of a united policy in the Christian world. The institution of feudalism was taken over by the Norman invaders of France who used it to conquer kingdoms and fiefs for themselves and their followers in Italy and England.

It was in Italy that the two forces, always allied in society, met politics. In 1059 the papacy, already influenced by the ideas of Cluny, allied itself with the Norman adventurers in South Italy. Seven years later it was with the blessing of a reforming pope that William of Normandy, with his small band of invincible, horsed, stirruped knights, conquered in one day the un-feudal kingdom of England. A generation later it was the same alliance of a reformed papacy and Norman feudal knights from France, England and South Italy, which sought to create new kingdoms in the East. The pressure of population forced the pace; the new institutions provided the ideology, the technique, the leadership. And in the end the ideology, as always, was adaptable: what was constant was the expansion, the conquest. The crusaders who justified their aggession against the Moslems by their virtuous detestation of the false prophet, Mahomet, did not falter when that pretext failed. The Anglo-Saxons were Christian; so were the Irish; indeed Anglo-Saxons and Irish, in the past, had been among the makers of Christian Europe. That did not save the former from William the Conqueror nor the latter from Strongbow. The Greeks of Constantinople were Christians too. That did not save them from those terrible Franks, that army of land-hungry younger sons and superfluous peasants who swarmed out, to the West as well as to the East, in search of earthly as well as spiritual salvation.

Everywhere it is the same. Let us turn from the eastern to the western Mediterranean, from the north to the south Atlantic coast of Europe. In the ninth and tenth centuries, Moslem Spain, like the rest of Islam, enjoyed its golden age. While the caliph of Córdoba built the magnificent mosque there, the relics of independent Spanish Christendom cowered in northern pockets of the peninsula, worshipping in low, cavernous churches, barrel-vaulted like crypts. But in the next century, here too, we find a new Christian pressure; and once again it comes from outside, from the north. It was the monks of Cluny and the knights from France who gave form and spirit to the movement. It was the monks of Cluny who organized the pilgrimages to the great shrine of Santiago de Compostela on the remote north-west tip of Spain. They turned Santiago—the apostle St. James, the brother of Jesus—into the military, crusading, patron saint of Christian Spain, and made the road to Compostela one of the great pilgrim routes of Europe; and from the beginning it was Frenchmen who ran the hotels along the route. The petty kings of Christian Spain welcomed these enterprising immigrants, gave them lands, made them bishops in Spain. With the monks and the [hotelkeepers] came the feudal knights, Normans and Burgundians, to animate the 'Reconquest'—that is, the war to recover the rest of Spain from its Moorish conquerors. Ten years before the First Crusade, it was with Burgundian soldiers that the Christians had captured Toledo; and a Frenchman was made bishop of it. It was with Norman soldiers that they twice captured the great Aragonese fortress of Barbastro. And other foreigners came too. Fifty years later a party of English and Flemish crusaders, sailing towards the Mediterranean to join the Second Crusade, arrived at the mouth of the river Douro. They were easily persuaded that there was no need to sail farther. There were infidels in Portugal, and lands as rich as any in Palestine. The crusaders agreed. They stayed. Instead of Edessa they captured Lisbon; and having massacred the Moslem inhabitants and installed themselves on their lands, they forgot about the Christian kingdom of Jerusalem and founded—with immense, undreamed-of consequences—that of Portugal.

Italy, England, Palestine, Spain, Portugal: in all directions the frontiers of Christendom are being pushed forward. In Germany, too, we can see it. In the eighth century, the Englishman St. Boniface had converted the Germans by preaching to them, and Charlemagne had converted the Saxons by knocking them on the head; but beyond the Elbe lay the world of the Prussians and the 'Slavs', those conveniently heathen sub-men who hitherto had passed through the pages of history, as they passed through the Christian kingdoms, only as long coffles of marketable eunuchs and slaves, heading for Moslem lands. In the early tenth century we find German colonists and missionaries pressing forward into the land of the Slavs and new bishoprics being founded on the Elbe; but fifty years later the Slavs have risen in revolt and all the work is undone. In the East, as in the West, the effort of Carolingian times cannot be sustained. Advance is followed, at least temporarily, by retreat.

Spanish knights battle Moorish warriors in this thirteenth-century illustration.

Yet, in the next century, the advance is resumed. And, once again, it is barons and churchmen who lead the way, confident that from the pressing population behind them they will always have hands for the task. Soon they will have another instrument too. The Germans who have gone as crusaders to the Holy Land have been formed into a military order, the Order of St. Mary's Hospital at Jerusalem, known as the Teutonic Knights. When opportunities in the Holy Land run short, the Teutonic Knights will be transferred to this northern theatre and will end as a rich, colonial aristocracy, a master race on the shores of the Baltic. The crusading movement is indivisible—against Moslems in the Mediterranean, pagans in eastern Europe, schismatic Christians in Byzantium, heretical Christians in the south-west of France, orthodox Christians in England and Ireland. It is indivisible because the real causes are not religion; religion only consecrated and canalized a great movement of social expansion. . . .

## II

My point is that the Crusades were not just a religious movement—whether we regard them as a heroic movement or an 'epidemical folly'. They were not even, by themselves, the cause of the European break-through. They were part of a much larger, much wider process: a process which can be seen all over Europe and on all the frontiers of western Christendom: beyond the Pyrenees, beyond the Elbe, on the Scottish border, in Ireland. This process is essentially a north European process. It is based on a new population-growth and new techniques, agricultural, social, military. The heavy German iron plough drives the wooden Slav plough before it beyond the Elbe, just as the heavy, stirruped,

Norman knights drive the Anglo-Saxon or Celtic footmen before them in England and Ireland, and the new Cistercian monasteries press forward against the empty wastes of the Welsh and Scottish borders, the Pomeranian plain and the Baltic seashore. The towns, and the rising prices which accompany the growth of trade, do more than the Crusades to dissolve the 'feudal' power of rural knights. Perhaps, as Gibbon wrote, the Crusades were a diversion of this great expansion into the sideline of unprofitable imperialism; perhaps the imperialism was inseparable from the expansion. That is another question.

Moreover, when we look at this movement in the perspective of time, we see another thing. The Crusades were no more isolated in time than in substance. They are not a unique, unrepeatable episode. In particular combination of detail of course they are unrepeatable. No historical situation is ever exactly repeatable. But in general character they are a social phenomenon which has occurred often in history and will occur again, very shortly, even in European history. We only have to look closely to see it. The adventurers who carved out estates for themselves in the Levant, and whose grim castles still dominate the hills of Syria and scowl, impossibly alien, down the romantic valleys of Greece; the sugar plantations which the Venetians and Genoese established in the conquered islands, and the slave-labour by which they worked them; the monopolies thereby created and the spectacular fortunes of the Italian maritime cities which rested thereon —are not all these familiar at another time too?

We think of the later conquest of America. It too was a crusade. Just as the monasteries of Cluny directed the conquest of the Levant, so the great Jeronymite monasteries of Spain directed the conquest of America. For that conquest too was to be a 'spiritual conquest'. Monks and friars would accompany it and animate it, preaching down the false gods, smashing down their temples, and studding the New World with gigantic convents, granaries for the new harvest of souls. If the discovery of the Holy Lance and the True Cross inspired the crusaders in the East, Santiago on his white horse would appear to encourage the conquistadors in the West. He was *'Santiago Matamoros'*—St. James the Moor-killer—but he would do to kill Red Indians too. To America also Spaniards and Portuguese would transplant all the techniques which had been developed four centuries before in the Levant. Hernán Cortés would bring to Mexico the sugar-industry which had been practised since the Crusades in the Venetian and Genoese colonies of the eastern Mediterranean. Slave-labour on the plantations and in the mills, first applied in those Levantine conquests, would become the 'peculiar institution' of the new continent. In many ways the islands of the eastern Mediterranean, now abandoned to the Turks, must have served their purpose as experimental farms for the vaster exploitations in the western hemisphere. And in the two movements, the colonization of the East in the twelfth century and the colonization of the West in the sixteenth, the spiritual and economic motives would be equally mixed. We came to America, wrote Bernal Díaz del Castillo, the companion of Cortés, as he rested on his conquered estates in Guatemala, *'para servir a Dios y hacernos ricos'*—to serve God and become rich. The inducement to the earlier crusades had been exactly the same. Come to the East, cried the Norman conqueror Bohemond, take the cross, save the tottering principality of Edessa for Christ, and get yourselves strong castles and rich cities and lands. And in Germany, at a great gathering at Merseburg in 1108, the same rewards were offered to those who would cross the Elbe and make war on the pagan Slavs: 'the country is excellent, rich in meat, honey, feathered game and flour. Therefore come hither, you Saxons and Franconians, Lorrainers and Flemings, for here two things can be won together: salvation for your souls and settlement on the best lands.' . . .

# Pope Urban II Preaches the Crusade (1095)

In the following account Pope Urban II (1088–1099) sets the first Crusade in motion. Pope Urban's call to war is a key to the motives of the Franks in their drive toward Jerusalem. There were eight major Crusades and countless minor ones, chiefly directed against the Moslems but also aimed at pagans, such as the Slavs and Baltic peoples, at heretics, and even against the Greek Christians of the Eastern Roman Empire. The First Crusade (1096–1099) captured the eastern coast of the Mediterranean including the Holy Land, and established a chain of little Christian kingdoms which gradually fell to the reinvigorated Moslems during the following century. The Second (1147–1149) and Third Crusades (1189–1192; after the fall of Jerusalem to the Moslems in 1187) were attempts to retain this Christian foothold in Asia. The Fourth Crusade (1202–1204) was diverted to an attack on Constantinople. Later Crusades (the last in 1270) were no more successful in extending Western power in the Mohammedan world. From Frederick Ogg, *A Source Book of Medieval History* (New York, 1907), pp. 284–288.

I

In the year of our Lord's Incarnation one thousand and ninety-five, a great council was convened within the bounds of Gaul, in Aubergne, in the city which is called Clermont. Over this Pope Urban II presided, with the Roman bishops and cardinals. This council was a famous one on account of the concourse of both French and German bishops, and of princes as well. Having arranged the matters relating to the Church, the lord Pope went forth into a certain spacious plain, for no building was large enough to hold all the people. The Pope then, with sweet and persuasive eloquence, addressed those present in words something like the following, saying:

"Oh, race of Franks, race beyond the mountains [the Alps], race beloved and chosen by God (as is clear from many of your works), set apart from all other nations by the situation of your country, as well as by your Catholic faith and the honor you render to the holy Church: to you our discourse is addressed, and for you our exhortations are intended. We wish you to know what a serious matter has led us to your country, for it is the imminent peril threatening you and all the faithful that has brought us hither.

"From the confines of Jerusalem and from the city of Constantinople a grievous report has gone forth and has been brought repeatedly to our ears; namely, that a race from the kingdom of the Persians [Turks], an accursed race, a race wholly alienated from God, 'a generation that set not their heart aright, and whose spirit was not steadfast with God' [Ps., lxxviii. 8], has violently invaded the lands of those Christians and has depopulated them by pillage and fire. They have led away a part of the captives into their own country, and a part they have killed by cruel tortures. They have either destroyed the churches of God or appropriated them for the rites of their own religion. They destroy the altars, after having defiled them with their uncleanness. . . . The kingdom of the Greeks [the Eastern Empire] is now dismembered by them and has been deprived of territory so vast in extent that it could not be traversed in two months' time.

"On whom, therefore, rests the labor of avenging these wrongs and of recovering this territory, if not upon you—you, upon whom, above all other nations, God has conferred remarkable glory in arms, great courage, bodily activity, and strength to humble the heads of those who resist you? Let the deeds of your ancestors encourage you and incite your minds to manly achievements—the glory and greatness of King Charlemagne, and of his son Louis [the Pious], and of your other monarchs, who have . . . extended the sway of the holy Church over lands previously pagan. Let the holy sepulcher of our Lord and Saviour, which is possessed by the unclean nations, especially arouse you, and the holy places which are now treated with ignominy and irreverently polluted with the filth of the unclean. Oh most valiant soldiers and descendants of invincible ancestors, do not degenerate, but recall the valor of your ancestors.

"But if you are hindered by love of children, parents, or wife, remember what the Lord says in the Gospel, 'He that loveth father or mother more than me is not worthy of me' [Matt., x. 37]. 'Every one that hath forsaken houses, or brethren, or sisters, or father, or mother, or wife, or children, or lands, for my name's sake, shall receive an hundred-fold, and shall inherit everlasting life' [Matt., xix. 29]. Let none of your possessions restrain you, nor anxiety for your family affairs. For this land which you inhabit, shut in on all sides by the seas and surrounded by the mountain peaks, is too narrow for your large population; nor does it abound in wealth; and it furnishes scarcely food enough for its cultivators. Hence it is that you murder and devour one another, that you wage war, and that very many among you perish in civil strife.

"Let hatred, therefore, depart from among you; let your quarrels end; let wars cease; and let all dissensions and controversies slumber. Enter upon the road of the Holy Sepulcher; wrest that land from the wicked race, and subject it to yourselves. That land which, as the Scripture says, 'floweth with milk and honey' [Num., xiii. 27] was given by God into the power of the children of Israel. Jerusalem is the center of the earth; the land is fruitful above all others, like another paradise of delights. This spot the Redeemer of mankind has made illustrious by His advent, has beautified by His sojourn, has consecrated by His passion, has redeemed by His death, has glorified by His burial.

"This royal city, however, situated at the center of the earth, is now held captive by the enemies of Christ and is subjected, by those who do not know God, to the worship of the heathen. She seeks, therefore, and desires to be liberated, and ceases not to implore you to come to her aid. From you especially she asks succor, because, as we have already said, God has conferred upon you,

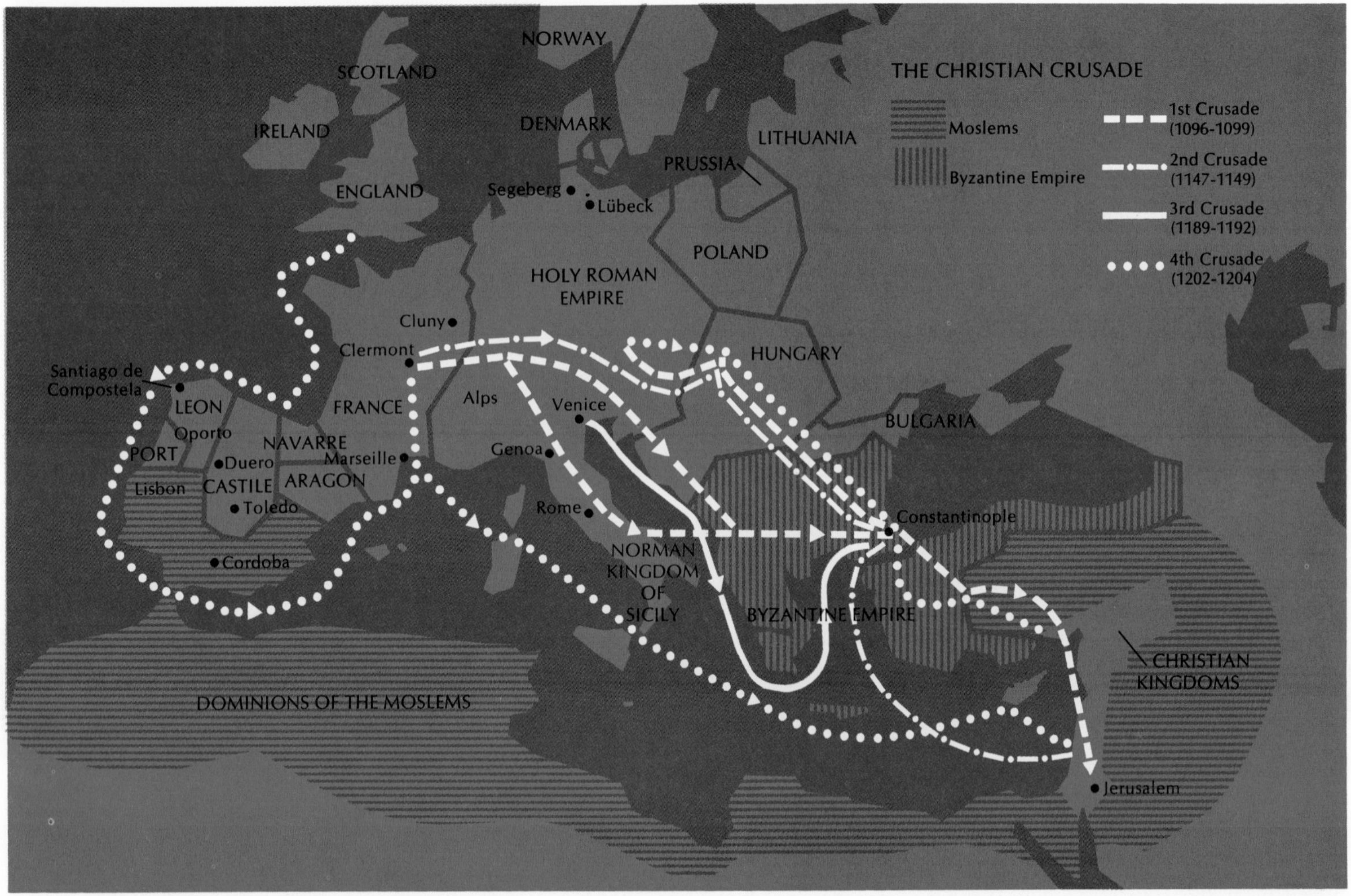


Christian territorial conquests during the Crusades—a strip of land along the coast of the eastern Mediterranean—were almost all regained by the Moslems within a century, but the contact with a wider world opened new horizons for Western Europeans. The main routes of the crusaders, seen on this map, are evidence of the new areas into which westerners pushed.

above all other nations, great glory in arms. Accordingly, undertake this journey eagerly for the remission of your sins, with the assurance of the reward of imperishable glory in the kingdom of heaven."

When Pope Urban had skilfully said these and very many similar things, he so centered in one purpose the desires of all who were present that all cried out, "It is the will of God! It is the will of God!"

II

When the venerable Roman pontiff heard that, with eyes uplifted to heaven, he gave thanks to God and, commanding silence with his hand, said:

Leaders of the First Crusade, responding to the appeal of Urban II at Clermont, attack a Turkish fortification on their expedition to liberate the Holy Land. From a twelfth-century manuscript.

"Most beloved brethren, to-day is manifest in you what the Lord says in the Gospel, 'Where two or three are gathered together in my name, there am I in the midst of them' [Matt., xviii. 20]. For unless God has been present in your spirits, all of you would not have uttered the same cry; since, although the cry issued from numerous mouths, yet the origin of the cry was one. Therefore I say to you that God, who implanted this in your breasts, has drawn it forth from you. Let that, then, be your war cry in battle, because it is given to you by God. When an armed attack is made upon the enemy, let this one cry be raised by all the soldiers of God: 'It is the will of God! It is the will of God!' . . .

"Whoever, therefore, shall decide upon this holy pilgrimage, and shall make his vow to God to that effect, and shall offer himself to Him for sacrifice, as a living victim, holy and acceptable to God, shall wear the sign of the cross of the Lord on his forehead or on his breast. When he shall return from his journey, having fulfilled his vow, let him place the cross on his back between his shoulders. Thus shall ye, indeed, by this twofold action, fulfill the precept of the Lord, as He commands in the Gospel, 'He that taketh not his cross, and followeth after me, is not worthy of me.' " [Luke, xiv. 27].

# Three Contemporaries View the European Push in the Near East

Two accounts are by Crusaders, the third by a Moslem. The first describes the bloody capture of Jerusalem during the First Crusade after a long siege. The second relates the activities of an abbot during the similar pillaging of Constantinople during the Fourth Crusade. The third contains the unfavorable impressions of an Arab noble Usámah (1095–1188), friend of Saladin, concerning the conquerors from the West. I. From *The Portable Medieval Reader* edited by James Bruce Ross and Mary Martin McLaughlin. Copyright 1949 by the Viking Press, Inc. Reprinted by permission of the Viking Press, Inc. II. From Dana C. Munro, ed., *Translations and Reprints from the Original Sources* (Philadelphia, n.d.), Vol. III, No. 1., pp. 16–19. III. From P. K. Hitti, trans., *Memoirs of Usámah,* in *Records of Civilization,* No. 10 (New York: Columbia University Press, 1929), pp. 161–164.

### I. THE SACK OF JERUSALEM (1099)

Entering the city [July 15, 1099], our pilgrims pursued and killed Saracens [Moslems] up to the Temple of Solomon, in which they had

In the picture from a fourteenth-century manuscript to the left, Western knights scale the walls of Jerusalem while a catapult (lower right in the picture) hurls stones against the fortifications. Inside the city the passion of Christ is reenacted, symbolic of the sacredness of the city to Christians. After their conquest Frankish knights established a kingdom in the Holy Land that lasted for fifty years. Above, the ruins of a castle in Caesarea built by crusaders to defend their territories.

assembled and where they gave battle to us furiously for the whole day so that their blood flowed throughout the whole temple. Finally, having overcome the pagans, our knights seized a great number of men and women, and they killed whom they wished and whom they wished they let live. . . . Soon the crusaders ran throughout the city, seizing gold, silver, horses, mules, and houses full of all kinds of goods.

Then rejoicing and weeping from extreme joy our men went to worship at the sepulchre of our Saviour Jesus and thus fulfilled their pledge to Him. . . .

Then, our knights decided in council that each one should give alms with prayers so that God should elect whom He wished to reign over the others and rule the city. They also ordered that all the Saracen dead should be thrown out of the city because of the extreme stench, for the city was almost full of the cadavers. The live Saracens dragged the dead out before the gates and made piles of them, like houses. No one has ever heard of or seen such a slaughter of pagan peoples since pyres were made of them like boundary marks, and no one except God knows their number.

## II. ABBOT MARTIN'S THEFT OF RELICS

While the victors were rapidly plundering the conquered city, which was theirs by right of conquest, the abbot Martin began to cogitate about his own share of the booty, and lest he alone should remain empty-handed while all the others became rich, he resolved to seize upon plunder with his own sacred hands. But, since he thought it not meet to handle any booty of worldly things with those sacred hands, he began to plan how he might secure some portion of the relics of the saints, of which he knew there was a great quantity in the city.

Accordingly, having a presentiment of some great result, he took with him one of his two chaplains and went to a church which was held in great reverence because in it the mother of the most famous emperor Manuel had a noble grave, which seemed of importance to the Greeks, but ours held for naught. There a very great amount of money brought in from all the surrounding country was stored, and also precious relics which the vain hope of security had caused them to bring in from the neighboring churches and monasteries. Those whom the Greeks had driven out, had told us of this before the capture of the city. When many pilgrims broke into this church and some were eagerly engaged in stealing gold and silver, others precious stones, Martin, thinking it unbecoming to commit sacrilege except in a holy cause, sought a more retired spot where the very sanctity of the place seemed to promise that what he desired might be found.

There he found an aged man of agreeable countenance, having a long and hoary beard, a priest, but very unlike our priests in his dress. Thinking him a layman, the abbot, though inwardly calm, threatened him with a very ferocious voice, saying: "Come, perfidious old man, show me the most powerful relics you have, or you shall die immediately." The latter, terrified by the sound rather than the words, since he heard but did not understand what was said, and knowing that Martin could not speak Greek, began in the *Romana lingua,* of which he knew a little, to entreat Martin and by soft words to turn away the latter's wrath, which in truth did not exist. In reply, the abbot succeeded in getting out a few words of the same language, sufficient to make the old man understand what he wanted. The latter . . . opened a chest bound with iron and showed the desired treasure, which was more grateful and pleasing to Martin than all the royal wealth of Greece. The abbot hastily and eagerly thrust in both hands and working quickly, filled with the fruits of the sacrilege both his own and his chaplain's bosom. He wisely concealed what seemed the most valuable and departed without opposition.

Moreover what and how worthy of veneration those relics which the holy robber appropriated were, is told more fully at the end of this work. When he was hastening to his vessel, so stuffed full, if I may use the expression, those who knew and loved him, saw him from their shops as they were themselves hastening to the booty, and inquired joyfully whether he had stolen anything, or with what he was so loaded down as he walked. With a joyful countenance, as always, and with pleasant words he said: "We have done well." To which they replied: "Thanks be to God."

### List of Relics Taken by Abbot Martin

Therefore "Blessed be the Lord God, who only doeth wondrous things," who in His unspeakable kindness and mercy has looked upon and made glorious His church at Paris through certain gifts of His grace, which he deigned to transmit to us through the venerable man, already so frequently mentioned, abbot Martin. In the presence of these the church exults and by their protection any soul faithful to God is aided and assisted. In order that the readers' trust in these may be strengthened, we have determined to give a partial list.

This ornate reliquary in the treasury of the cathedral of Trier, Germany was designed to contain the foot of Saint Andrew.

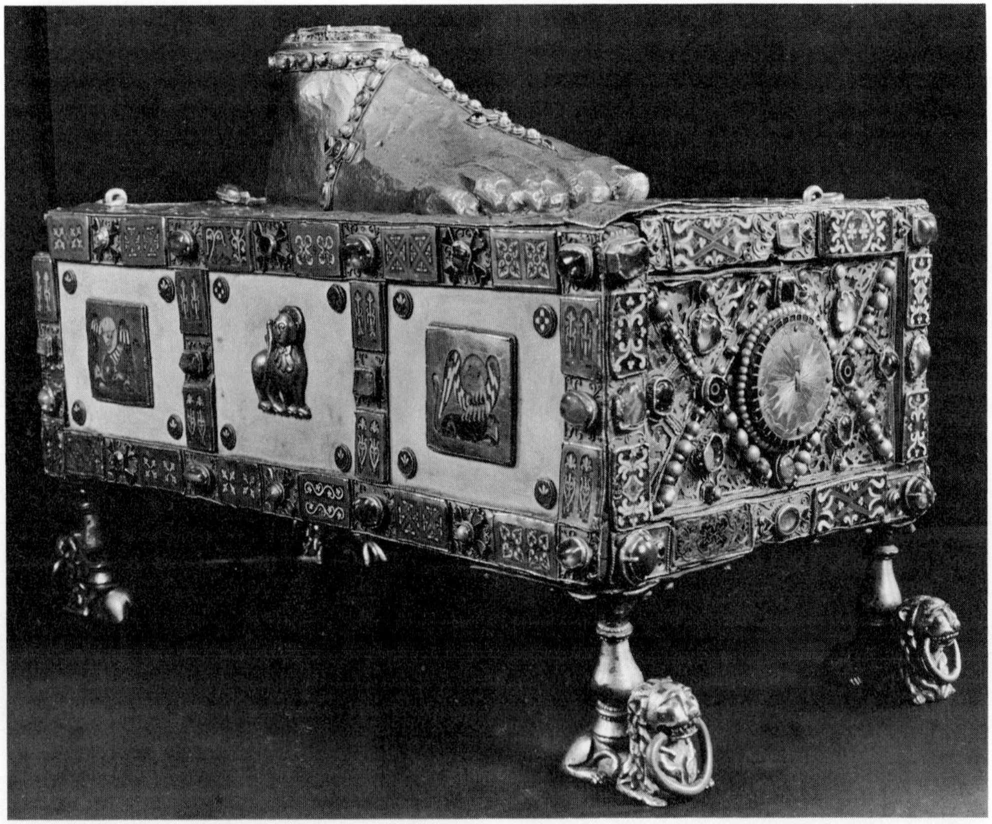

First, of the highest importance and worthy of all veneration: A trace of the blood of our Lord Jesus Christ, which was shed for the redemption of all mankind.

Second, a piece of the cross of our Lord on which the Son of the Father, the new Adam, sacrificed for us, paid the debt of the old Adam.

Third, a not inconsiderable piece of St. John [the Baptist] the fore-runner of our Lord.

Fourth, the arm of St. James, the Apostle, whose memory is venerated by the whole church. . . .

Also relics from the following: the place of the Nativity of our Lord; Calvary; our Lord's sepulchre; the stone rolled away; the place of our Lord's ascension; the stone on which John stood when he baptized the Lord; the spot where Christ raised Lazarus; the stone on which Christ was presented in the temple; the stone on which Jacob slept; the stone where Christ fasted; the stone where Christ prayed; the table on which Christ ate the supper; the place where He was captured; the place where the mother of our Lord died; His grave; the grave of St. Peter, the apostle; the relics of the holy apostles, Andrew and Philip; the place where the Lord gave the law to Moses [etc.]. . . .

## III. AN ARAB WONDERS AT THE MEN OF THE WEST

Mysterious are the works of the Creator, the author of all things! When one comes to recount cases regarding the Franks, he cannot but glorify Allah (exalted is he!) and sanctify him, for he sees them as animals possessing the virtues of courage and fighting, but nothing else; just as animals have only the virtues of strength and carrying loads. I shall now give some instances of their doings and their curious mentality.

In the army of King Fulk, son of Fulk, was a Frankish reverend knight who had just arrived from their land in order to make the holy pilgrimage and then return home. He was of my intimate fellowship and kept such constant company with me that he began to call me "my brother." Between us were mutual bonds of amity and friendship. When he resolved to return by sea to his homeland, he said to me:

My brother, I am leaving for my country and I want thee to send with me thy son (my son, who was then fourteen years old, was at that time in my company) to our country, where he can see the knights and learn wisdom and chivalry. When he returns, he will be like a wise man.

Thus there fell upon my ears words which would never come out of the head of a sensible man; for even if my son were to be taken captive, his captivity could not bring him a worse misfortune than carrying him into the lands of the Franks. However, I said to the man:

By thy life, this has exactly been my idea. But the only thing that prevented me from carrying it out was the fact that his grandmother, my mother, is so fond of him and did not this time let him come out with me until she exacted an oath from me to the effect that I would return him to her.

Thereupon he asked, "Is thy mother still alive?" "Yes." I replied. "Well," said he "disobey her not."

A case illustrating their curious medicine is the following:

The lord of al-Munaytirah wrote to my uncle asking him to dispatch a physician to treat certain sick persons among his people. My uncle sent him a Christian physician named Thābit. Thābit was absent but ten days when he returned. So we said to him, "How quickly has thou healed thy patients!" He said:

They brought before me a knight in whose leg an abscess had grown; and a woman afflicted with imbecility. To the knight I applied a small poultice until the abscess opened and became well; and the woman I put on diet and made her humor wet. Then a Frankish physician came to them and said, "This man knows nothing about treating them." He then said to the knight, "Which wouldst thou prefer, living with one leg or dying with two?" The latter replied, "Living with one leg." The physician said, "Bring me a strong knight and a sharp ax." A knight came with the ax. And I was standing by. Then the physician laid the leg of the patient on a block of wood and bade the knight strike his leg with the ax and chop it off at one blow. Accordingly he struck it—while I was looking on—one blow, but the leg was not severed, He dealt another blow, upon which the marrow of the leg flowed out and the patient died on the spot. He then examined the woman and said, "This is a woman in whose head there is a devil which has possessed her. Shave off her hair." Accordingly they shaved it off and the woman began once more to eat their ordinary diet—garlic and mustard. Her imbecility took a turn for the worse. The

These scenes from Roger of Salerno's *Chirurgia,* a French book of c.1300, illustrate six aspects of medieval surgery. From left to right; the use of hot water to soften broken ribs; the removal of an arrow and a lance from a man's chest; cutting open the chest and abdomen. Below; a wound in the lungs; an operation on the intestines; a man suffering from "phlegmatic abcess."

physician then said, "The devil has penetrated through her head." He therefore took a razor, made a deep cruciform incision on it, peeled off the skin at the middle of the incision until the bone of the skull was exposed and rubbed it with salt. The woman also expired instantly. Thereupon I asked them whether my services were needed any longer, and when they replied in the negative I returned home, having learned of their medicine what I knew not before. . . .

Whenever I visited Jerusalem I always entered the Aqsa Mosque, beside which stood a small mosque which the Franks had converted into a church. When I used to enter the Aqsa Mosque, which was occupied by the Templars, who were my friends, the Templars would evacuate the little adjoining mosque so that I might pray in it. One day I entered this mosque, repeated the first formula, "Allah is great," and stood up in the act of praying, upon which one of the Franks rushed on me, got hold of me and turned my face eastward saying, "This is the way thou shouldst pray!" A group of Templars hastened to him, seized him and repelled him from me. I resumed my prayer. The same man, while the others were otherwise busy, rushed once more on me and turned my face eastward, saying, "This is the way thou shouldst pray!" The Templars again came in to him and expelled him. They apologized to me, saying, "This is a stranger who has only recently arrived from the land of the Franks and he has never before seen anyone praying except eastward." Thereupon I said to myself, "I have had enough prayer." So I went out and have ever been surprised at the conduct of this devil of a man, at the change in the color of his face, his trembling and his sentiment at the sight of one praying towards the [holy city of Mecca]. . . .

# The Germans Expand Eastward

Helmold (c. 1125–after 1177), a Saxon monk, wrote a detailed account of the German efforts to convert the pagan Slavs who lived along the Baltic Sea. The excerpts in this reading focus on the work of a missionary, and later bishop, named Vicelin in the area called Holstein today. From Helmold's *Chronicle of the Slavs,* trans. F. J. Tschan in *Records of Civilization,* No. 21 (New York: Columbia University Press, 1935), pp. 149–150, 160–161, 163–164, 166–167, 168–169.

## VICELIN GOES TO WAGRIA (HOLSTEIN) (1127)

When they had come to the place to which he had been appointed, Vicelin observed the appearance of the locality and the fields, frightful as a wasted and unproductive heath. It was also a boorish and uncultivated folk, having nothing of religion saving only the name of Christianity; for there existed among them the manifold error of groves and springs and other superstitions. In beginning, then, to live "in the midst of a crooked and perverse nation" and "in a desert land, and in the waste howling wilderness" Vicelin commended himself the more entirely to the divine protection, [the more] he was destitute of human solace. The Lord, however, gave him grace and favor in the sight of that folk, for as soon as he began to preach the glory of God and the happiness of the life to come and the resurrection of the body, the boorish people was by a great miracle deeply moved at the novelty of the teaching it had not understood, and the darkness of sin was dispelled by the brightness of the illuminating grace of God. . . . As his sanctity became widely known there came to him many of both clerical and lay estate. Among the first and foremost of these were the venerable priests Ludolph, Eppo, Luthmund, and Volkward, and very many others of whom some are fallen asleep and some still survive. These men, then, banded together by sacred vows and determined to adopt the celibate life, to endure in prayer and fasting, to be diligent in works of piety, to visit the sick, to succor the needy, to be solicitous for their own and for their neighbors' salvation. However, solicitous above all about the conversion of the Slavs, they prayed God to open the door of faith as soon as possible. . . .

## THE BUILDING OF SEGEBERG (1131)

Since the illustrious Caesar [Emperor] Lothar [ruled 1125–1137] and his very worthy consort Richenza were most devoutly solicitous for the divine service, the priest of Christ, Vicelin, went to him while he was tarrying at Bardowiek and suggested to him that he should provide for the Slavic race some means of salvation in keeping with the power that had been bestowed on him by Heaven. Vicelin, moreover, made known to him that there is in the province of Wagria a mountain adapted for the erection of a royal castle for the protection of the land. . . . The emperor attended to the prudent counsel of the priest and sent competent men to determine the fitness of the mountain. On being assured by the reports of the messengers, he crossed the river [Elbe] and went into the land of the Slavs to the place appointed. He ordered all the Nordalbingian people to come together for the building of the castle. In obedience to the emperor, the princes of the Slavs also were present, taking part in the business, but with great sadness, for they discerned that the structure was being erected for their oppression. One prince of the Slavs, therefore, said to another: . . . "Who has prepared this misfortune for us, and who has betrayed this mountain to the king?" The prince replied to him: "Do you see that baldheaded manikin [Vicelin] standing by the king? He has brought all this evil upon us."

The castle was finished and secured with a numerous soldiery and called Segeberg. In charge of the castle the Caesar put Hermann, one of his henchmen. Not content with these arrangements, he ordered the establishment of a new church at the foot of the mountain and set aside, for the maintenance of divine worship and for the support of the brethren to be congregated there, six or more villages, confirming the grant by charters according to usage. Furthermore, he committed the stewardship of that basilica to the lord Vicelin, that he might be the more disposed to push forward the erection of dwellings and bring together clerics. . . . His purpose was, as he himself publicly declared, to subject the whole Slavic race to the divine religion and to make a great bishop of the minister of Christ. . . .

## THE DESTRUCTION OF SEGEBERG AND THE GERMAN REACTION (1137–1139)

[The death of Emperor Lothar in 1137 led to rivalry and rebellion among the German nobles]

While these disturbances were breaking out everywhere in Saxony, Pribislav of Lübeck [a Slavic leader] with the band of robbers that he had brought together seized the opportunity utterly to destroy the suburb of Segeberg and all the surrounding hamlets in which the Saxons dwelt. The new oratory and the recently constructed monastery were then consumed by fire, and Volker, a brother of great simplicity, was pierced through by the sword. The other brethren, who escaped, fled for refuge to the haven of Faldera. . . . They were in a difficult position at a difficult time and in full dread of death. Besides being in want and daily in danger for their lives they were forced to see the chains and the various kinds of torture inflicted on the worshipers of Christ, whom the robber band was wont to capture here and there. . . .

Now Henry, [Duke of Saxony] who governed the county, a man strenuous at arms and impatient of inactivity, secretly brought together an army . . . and invaded Slavia in the winter. Attacking those who were next to hand and who were like thorns piercing the eyes of the Saxons, he made a great slaughter of them in all the territory, to wit, of Plön, Lütjenburg, Oldenburg, and the whole of the country which begins at the River Schwale and is encompassed by the Baltic Sea and the River Trave. In one incursion with plunder and fire they wasted all that region except the cities which were fortified with walls and bars and required the more onerous exertion of a siege. The following summer, spurring one another on, [they] went up to the stronghold Plön. . . . With the help of Divine Providence and contrary to their expectation they took this fortress, which was stronger than the others, and put the Slavs who were in it to the sword. That year they waged a very successful war and in frequent incursions devastated the country of the Slavs. They did to the Slavs what the Slavs had set themselves to do to them: all their land was reduced to a wilderness. . . .

## WAGRIA IS SETTLED BY GERMANIC PEOPLES (1143)

Matters having been arranged in this manner, Adolph began to rebuild the fortress at Segeberg and girded it with a wall. As the land was without inhabitants, he sent messengers into all parts, namely, to Flanders and Holland, to Utrecht, Westphalia, and Frisia, proclaiming that whosoever were in straits for lack of fields should come with their families and receive a very good land,—a spacious land, rich in crops, abounding in fish and flesh and exceeding good pasturage. To them he said:

> Have you not subjugated the land of the Slavs and bought it with the blood of your brothers and fathers? Why, then, are you the last to enter into possession of it? Be the first to go over into a delectable land and inhabit it and partake of its delights, for the best of it is due you who have wrested it from the hands of the enemy.

An innumerable multitude of different peoples rose up at this call and they came with their families and their goods into the land of Wagria to Count Adolph that they might possess the country which he had promised them. . . .

Thus the deserted places of the land of Wagria began to be occupied and the number of its inhabitants was multiplied. Vicelin, the priest, too, on the invitation as well as with the assistance of the count, got back the properties about the fortress of Segeberg which the emperor Lothar had in times past given him for the construction of a monastery and for the support of servants of God.

# Christians Recover Lisbon from the Moslems

The Crusade against Lisbon in 1147 was part of a series of attacks against the Moslem occupiers of Portugal and Spain. The English, Norman, German, and Dutch members of this expedition, the account of which was written by an unknown English participant, swore an oath to divide the spoils of conquest equitably. They would then turn over the land itself to the Christian King of Portugal, who held the area previously wrested from the Moslems to the north of Lisbon. After the capture of the strongly fortified city, part of the expedition continued on to the Near East and participated in the Second Crusade. From "The Conquest of Lisbon," ed. and trans. C. W. Davis in *Records of Civilization,* No. 24 (New York: Columbia University Press, 1936), pp. 115–123, 131–133, 175–179.

## THE CRUSADERS OFFER TERMS OF SURRENDER

It was decided by the common counsel of all [the Crusaders] that commissioners should be sent to parley with the enemy, so that we might not appear to be attacking them except unwillingly. Accordingly, the archbishop of Braga and the bishop of Oporto and a few of our men were sent to the city. After signals had been exchanged as the alcayde [Moslem military commander] stood in person on the wall with the . . . chief men of the city, a truce was mutually ratified in order that on each side they might say what they wished. Then the archbishop made the following speech:

"May the God of peace and love remove the veil of error from your hearts and convert you to himself. And therefore have we come to you to speak of peace. For in concord small things grow great, in discord the greatest go to ruin. But, in order that discord may not forever reign between us, we have come hither to you with a message of conciliation. For Nature so begat us from one and the same principle that, by reason of the common bond of humanity and the chain of harmony derived from the mother of all, one ought not to be unacceptable to another. And, if you will, we have come hither to this city which you possess not to subdue you and drive you out and despoil you. For the inborn kindliness of Christians ever holds to this principle, that, while it seeks its own, it seizes not the property of others. . . .

"You are holding our cities and landed possessions unjustly—and for three hundred and fifty-eight years you have so held them—which before that were held by Christians; Christians whom not the sword of the oppressor compelled to their religion, but whom the preaching of the word caused to be adopted among the sons of God, under our apostle James and his disciples and successors. . . . But since by the spread of your race and uninterrupted occupation you have now held the city for a long time, we are displaying towards you our usual benevolence: only surrender into our hands . . . your castle, and each of you may preserve the liberties which he has hitherto enjoyed; for we do not wish to drive you out from such ancient seats. Let each one live according to his own customs, unless some of you should voluntarily be added to the church of God. . . .

To this one of their elders who were standing by replied in this wise:

"I perceive that you have your words very well under control. You are not transported by your speech, nor has it carried you further than you meant to go. It has been directed to a single end, namely, to the taking of our city. But I cannot wonder enough concerning you, for, while a single forest or a district suffices for many elephants and lions, neither the land nor the sea is enough for you. Verily, it is not the want of possessions but ambition of the mind which drives you on.

"As to what you have advanced above concerning the lot assigned to each, truly, you interfere with our destiny. Labeling your ambition zeal for righteousness, you misrepresent vices as virtues. For your greed has already grown to such proportions that base deeds not only please you but even delight you; and now the opportunity of effecting a cure has almost passed, for the consummate infelicity of your cupidity has almost exceeded the bounds of natural measure. You adjudge us to exile and destitution in order that you may become famous. This kind of vainglorious boasting is defined as crass ambition. But your greed, when it has grown beyond measure, has always been smothered in itself and dwindled away. How many times now within our memory have you come [hither] with pilgrims and barbarians to subdue us and drive us hence? But do your possessions give you no pleasure at all, or have you incurred some blame at home, that you are so often on the move? Surely your frequent going and coming is proof of an innate mental instability, for he who is unable to arrest the flight of the body cannot control the mind.

"Not yet have we decided to hand over our city unconditionally to you or to remain in it and become your subjects. Not yet has our magnanimity advanced to the point where we would give up certainties for uncertainties. For in large affairs decisions must be made with largeness of view. This city did indeed, as I believe, once belong to your people; but now it is ours. In the future it will perhaps be yours. But this shall be in accordance with divine favor. While God willed we have held it; when he shall have willed otherwise, we shall no longer hold it. For there is no wall which is impregnable against the arbitrament of his will. . . .

## THE SIEGE BEGINS

In the meantime, as we kept watch night and day beneath their walls, they derided us and hurled many a taunt at us, adjudging us worthy of a thousand deaths, as men who, forsooth, despising our own possessions as something vile, coveted those of others as something precious; nor did they recall that they had done us any injury, unless in this, that if they had anything in their possession of the very highest quality, we thought it ought to be ours and judged them unworthy to have it. And they taunted us with numerous children about to be born at home in our absence, and said that . . . our wives would not be concerned about our deaths, since they would have bastard progeny enough. And they undertook that if any of us should survive, we would return to our home lands in poverty and misery; and they mocked us and gnashed their teeth against us.

Besides, they constantly attacked the blessed Mary, Mother of the Lord, with coarse insults and abusive and shameful words, declaring it unworthy of us that we should venerate the son of a poor woman with as much reverence as if he were God himself, and should call him both God and the Son of God, although it was well known that there is one God only, by whom all things which have a beginning were begun, and that he has no one coeval with himself and a sharer in his divinity. . . . Besides, they displayed the symbol of the cross before us with mockery; and spitting upon it and wiping the filth from their posteriors with it, and finally making water upon it as something vile, they threw it at us. And Christ was again seen actually blasphemed by unbelievers, saluted with mock genuflections, spat upon by wicked men, afflicted with chains, beaten with staves, and fastened to the opprobrious cross. Out of pity for which it was fitting that we should become more bitter against the enemies of the cross.

And this is just what happened, while divine justice made them blind. How often did we concede them their wealth and possessions, if only they would withdraw from the city and go whithersoever they wished, how often did we propose that everything should remain to them with their rights intact, if only they would surrender to us the fortifications of the city; yet our God never permitted their obstinacy to be ended except in the last and worst disgrace. For God had foreordained especially in these times that vengeance should be wrought upon the enemies of the cross through the most insignificant men. . . .

## THE MOSLEMS SURRENDER AFTER A SIEGE OF SEVENTEEN WEEKS

Oh, what rejoicing there was on the part of all! Oh, what especial pride on the part of all! Oh, what a flow of tears of joy and piety, when to the praise and honor of God and of the most holy Virgin Mary, the ensign of the salvation-bearing cross was beheld by all placed upon the highest tower in token of the subjection of the city, while the archbishop and the bishops together with the clergy and all the people, not without tears, intoned with a wonderful jubilation the *Te Deum laudamus* together with the *Asperges me* and devout prayers! The king, meanwhile, made the circuit of the walls of the upper castle on foot.

Thereupon the men of Cologne and the Flemings, when they saw so many temptations to greed in the city, observed not the bond of their oath or plighted faith. They rushed about hither and thither; they pillaged; they broke open doors; they tore open the innermost parts of every house; they drove out the citizens and treated them with insults, against right and justice; they scattered utensils and clothing; they insulted maidens; they made wrong equal with right; they secretly snatched away all those things which ought to have been made the common property of all the forces. They even slew the aged bishop of the city, against all right and decency, by cutting his throat. They seized the alcayde himself and carried everything out of his house. . . . But finally having come to their senses, they obtained from us by insistent prayers that our men upon the same footing with theirs should peacefully bring together the remainder of the booty of the city with the portions already collected, in order that thus at last after shares had been apportioned to all, they might nullify the insults and the thefts in peace by being prepared to give satisfaction for what they had wrongfully taken in advance.

Accordingly, when the enemy within the city had been despoiled, from early Saturday morning until the following Wednesday so great a multitude of people was seen steadily filing out through three gates that it seemed as if all Spain had flowed together into it. . . .

When the city had been taken after we had besieged it for seventeen weeks, the inhabitants of Cintra surrendered the stronghold of their castle and gave themselves up to the king. And the castle of Palmela, after it had been evacuated by its garrison, was occupied by the king while empty. And so, the strongholds appurtenant to the city in the surrounding country having been taken, the name of the Franks was magnified throughout all parts of Spain, and terror seized upon the Moors [Moslems] among whom tidings of this action were made known. . . .

TOPIC 27

# THE MOLD OF CHRISTIAN CONFORMITY

Not until the High Middle Ages did the organization of Western society allow the Church to reach most of the men, women, and children of Europe. The Church of the eleventh through thirteenth centuries, reflecting the tone of its vast public, shaped its message to fit the more sophisticated needs of a changing society, appealed to emotion and to the senses, and tried to swallow the more manageable critics of its wealth and structure by broadening the dimensions permitted self-expression. For those who deviated too far from the baselines of Christian doctrine, however, formal tolerance gave way to the purge of inquisition and the violence of an internal crusade. Had it not been for the treatment of the religious non-conformists in its midst, Western Christendom might have confirmed, in practice, the universality to which it aspired. Nonetheless, acceptance of a divinely created natural and social order and of man as both a sensual and reasonable being made the fold of conformity a large one for the Christian flock. The readings describe the qualities of the new mass religion as they appeared in literature and life.



**Reading 142**

## Popular Piety and Heresy

From John L. Stipp, C. W. Hollister, and Allen W. Birrim, *The Rise and Development of Western Civilization* (New York: John Wiley & Sons, Inc., 1967), I, pp. 363, 367–372.

### Evolution of Piety

The ever-increasing scope of the Church, together with the rising vigor of the new age, resulted in a deepening of popular piety throughout Europe. The High Middle Ages witnessed a profound shift in religious attitude from the awe and mystery characteristic of earlier Christianity to a new emotionalism and dynamism. This shift is evident in ecclesiastical architecture, as the stolid, earthbound Romanesque style gave way in the later twelfth century to the tense, upward-reaching Gothic. A parallel change is evident in devotional practices as the divine Christ sitting in judgment gave way to the tragic figure of the human Christ suffering on the Cross for man's sins. And it was in the High Middle Ages that the Virgin Mary came into her own as the compassionate intercessor for hopelessly lost souls. No matter how sinful a person might be, he could be redeemed if only he won the sympathy of Mary, for what son could refuse the petition of his mother? Indeed, a legend of the age told of the devil complaining to God that the tender-hearted Queen of Heaven was cheating Hell of its most promising candidates. In this atmosphere of religious romanticism, Christianity became, as never before, a doctrine of love, hope, and compassion. The God of Justice became the merciful, suffering God who died in agony to atone for the sins of men and to bring them everlasting life.

Like all other human institutions, the medieval Church fell far short of its ideals. Corrupt churchmen were in evidence throughout the age, and certain historians have delighted in cataloguing instances of larcenous bishops, gluttonous priests, and licentious nuns. But cases such as these were clearly exceptional. The great shortcoming of the medieval Church was not gross corruption but rather a creeping complacency which resulted sometimes in a shallow, even mechanical attitude toward the Christian religious life. . . .

**Rise of Heresy**

The surge of popular piety also raised serious problems for the Church and society, for it resulted in a flood of criticism against churchmen. It was not that churchmen had grown worse, but rather that laymen had begun to judge them by harsher standards. Popular dissatisfaction toward the workaday Church manifested itself in part in the rush toward the austere twelfth-century monastic orders. Yet the majority of Christians could not become monks, and for them, certain new heretical doctrines began to exert a powerful appeal.

The heresies of the High Middle Ages flourished particularly in the rising towns of Southern Europe. The eleventh-century urban revolution had caught the Church unprepared; whereas the new towns were the real centers of the burgeoning lay piety, the Church, with its roots in the older agrarian feudal order, seemed unable to minister effectively to the vigorous and widely literate new burger class. Too often the urban bishops appeared as political oppressors and enemies of *burghal* independence rather than inspiring spiritual directors. Too often the Church failed to understand the townsmen's problems and aspirations or to anticipate their growing suspicion of ecclesiastical wealth and power. Although the vast majority of medieval townsmen remained loyal to the Church, a troublesome minority, particularly in the south, turned to new, anticlerical sects. . . . One such sect, the Waldensians, was founded by a merchant of Lyons named Peter Waldo who, c. 1173, gave all his possessions to the poor and took up a life of apostolic poverty. He and his followers worked at first within the bounds of orthodoxy, but gradually their anticlericalism and their denial of special priestly powers earned them the condemnation of the Church. Similar groups, some orthodox, some heretical, arose in the communes of Lombardy and were known as the *Humiliati*. Naturally these groups proved exceedingly troublesome and embarrassing to the local ecclesiastical hierarchies, but generally they escaped downright condemnation unless they themselves took the step of denying the authority of the Church. Many of them did take that step, however, and by the thirteenth century heretical, anticlerical sects were spreading across northern Italy and southern France, and even into Spain and Germany.

The most popular and dangerous heresy in southern France was sponsored by a group known as the *Cathari* (the pure) or the Albigensians—after the town of Albi where they were particularly strong. The Albigensians represented a fusion of two traditions: (1) the anticlerical protest against ecclesiastical wealth and power, and (2) an exotic theology derived originally from Persian dualism. The Albigensians recognized two gods: the god of good who reigned over the universe of the spirit, and the god of evil who ruled the world of matter. The Old Testament God, as creator of the material universe, was their god of evil; Christ, who was believed to have been a purely spiritual being with a phantom body, was the god of good. Albigensian morality stressed a rigorous rejection of all material things—of physical appetites, wealth, worldly vanities, and sexual intercourse—in the hope of one day escaping from the prison of the body and ascending to the realm of pure spirit. In reality this severe ethic was practiced only by a small élite known as the *perfecti;* the rank and file, who were called *credentes* (believers), normally begat children, and participated only vicariously in the rejection of the material world—by criticizing the affluence of the Church. Indeed, their opponents accused them of gross licentiousness, and it does seem to be true that certain Provençal noblemen were attracted to the new teaching by the opportunity of appropriating Church property in good conscience.

However this may be, Albigensianism was spreading rapidly as the thirteenth century dawned and was becoming an ominous threat to the unity of Christendom and the authority of the Church. Pope Innocent III, recognizing the extreme gravity of the situation, tried with every means in his power to eradicate Albigensianism. At length, in 1208, he responded to the murder of a papal legate in southern France by summoning a crusade against the Albigensians—the first crusade ever to be called against European Christians. The Albigensian Crusade was a ruthless, savage affair which succeeded in its purpose but only at the cost of ravaging the vibrant civilization of southern France. . . .

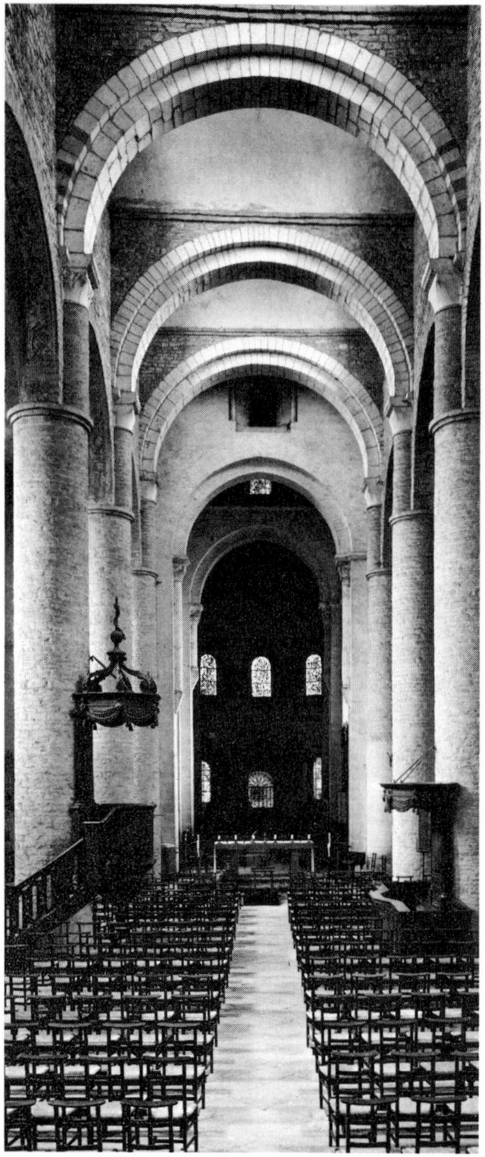

1.

2.

3.

**4.**

**5.**

The movement from the Romanesque to the Gothic is illustrated by this series of church interiors in northern France, eleventh to thirteenth centuries. The soaring Gothic style brought light and grace to structures of a size unknown in the earlier history of Western religious architecture.

**1.** Eglise St. Philibert, Tournus. Work on the nave was begun in the early eleventh century.

**2.** Eglise Ste. Etienne, Abbaye aux Hommes, Caen. Begun in the mid-eleventh century.

**3.** Cathedral of Notre Dame, Paris. The principal construction work on the nave was completed by the end of the twelfth century.

**4.** Cathedral of Chartres. Construction on the nave was carried on between 1194 and 1220.

**5.** Cathedral of Rheims, nave looking toward facade. Construction of this section was begun in 1211 and expresses the pure Gothic style of the early thirteenth century.

Christ, surrounded by the heavenly host, commands the central portal of Notre Dame in Paris (upper left). The dead arise for the Last Judgment. At right the damned are hurled through the jaws of Hell into eternal torment. At left angels direct the saved to their place in Paradise. The Virgin, as Mediatrix, intercedes for the souls (detail). Contrast this view with that of the mortal Christ of the thirteenth century suffering on the cross as the Virgin looks on.

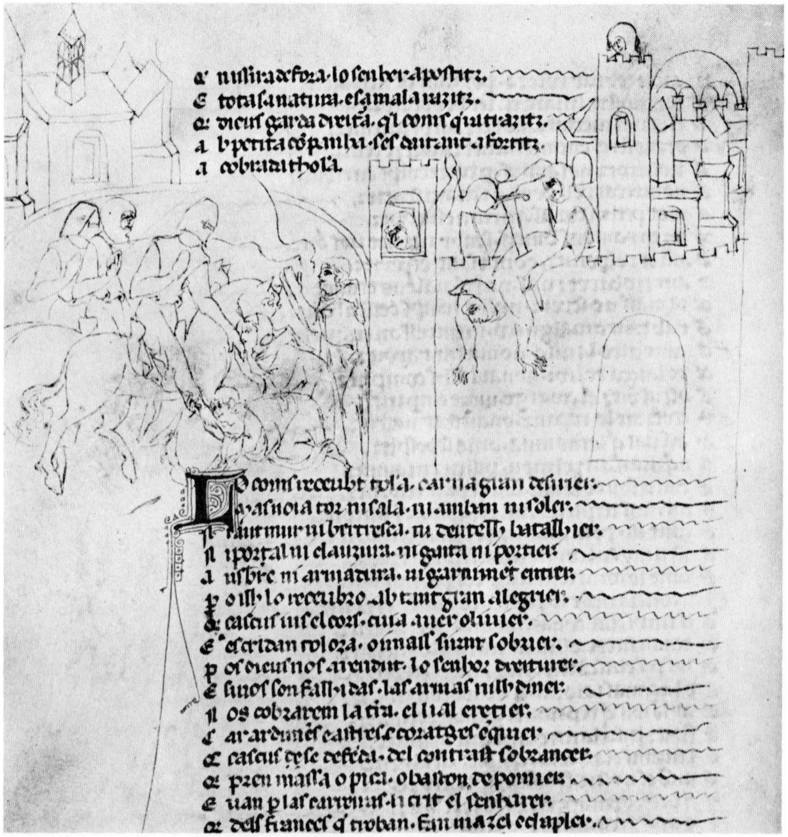

Toulouse in southern France was a center of the Albigensian movement, and hence a prime target for the crusaders. The illustrations in this medieval manuscript show the citizens of the besieged and captured city paying homage to their conquerors (left), who proceed to wreak vengeance on the heretics (right).

In the years immediately following the Albigensian Crusade, there emerged an institution that will always stand as a grim symbol of the medieval Church at its worst: the Inquisition. The Christian persecution of heretics dates from the later fourth century, but it was not until the High Middle Ages that heterodox views presented a serious problem to European society. Traditionally, the problem of converting or punishing heretics was handled at the local level, but in 1233 the papacy established a permanent central tribunal for the purpose of standardizing procedures and increasing efficiency in the suppression of heresies. The methods of the Inquisition included the use of torture, secret testimony, conviction on the testimony of only two witnesses, the denial of legal counsel to the accused, and other procedures offensive to the Anglo-American legal tradition but not times. Indeed, many of these procedures—including torture—were drawn from the customs of Roman Law. In defense of the Inquisition it might be said that convicted heretics might escape death by renouncing their "errors," and that far from establishing a reign of terror, the Inquisition seems to have enjoyed popular support.

Some historians have adduced other arguments in an attempt to defend an indefensible institution. Let us say here merely that the Christian faith was far more important to the people of medieval Europe than national allegiance—that the medieval Church, with its elaborate charitable activities, its hospitals and universities, and its other social services, performed many of the functions of the modern state, and that therefore medieval heresy was analogous to modern treason. To the medieval Christian, heresy was a hateful, repugnant thing, an insult to Christ, and a source of contamination to others. Today, when political and economic doctrines are more important to most people than religious creeds, the closest parallel to medieval Waldensianism or Albigensianism is to be found in the communist and Nazi parties in modern America. In examining popular opposition toward extremist groups such as these, perhaps we can gain an inkling of the state of mind that produced the medieval Inquisition.

St. Dominic presides over the central tribunal of the Inquisition during the Albigensian crusade. Heretics are led to execution below.

## Mendicantism

The thirteenth-century church found an answer to the heretical drift in urban piety which was far more compassionate and effective than the Inquisition. In the opening decades of the century two radically new orders emerged—the Dominican and the Franciscan—which were devoted to a life of poverty, preaching, and charitable deeds. Rejecting the life of the cloister, they dedicated themselves to religious work in the world—particularly in the towns. Benedictines and Cistercians had traditionally taken vows of personal poverty, but the monastic orders themselves could and did acquire great corporate wealth. The Dominicans and Franciscans, on the contrary, were pledged to both personal and corporate poverty, and were therefore known as mendicants (beggars). . . .

## The Dominicans

St. Dominic (1170–1221), a well-educated Spaniard, spent his early manhood as an Augustinian canon at a cathedral in Castile. In his mid-thirties he traveled to Rome, met Pope Innocent III, and followed the Pope's bidding to preach in southern France against the Albigensians. . . . The Dominican order evolved out of a small group of volunteers who joined Dominic in his work among the Albigensians. Gradually, Dominic came to see the possibility of a far greater mission for his followers: to preach and win converts to the faith throughout the world. . . . The Dominican Rule drew freely from the earlier rule of the Augustinian Canons which Dominic had known in his youth, but added new elements and provided a novel direction for the religious life. The order was to be headed by a minister-general, elected for life. . . . The friars themselves belonged not to a particular house or province but to the order, and their place of residence and activity was determined by the minister-general. Their life, strictly regulated and austere, included such rigors as regular midnight services, total abstinence from meat, frequent fasts, and prolonged periods of mandatory silence. And the entire order was strictly bound by the rule of poverty which Dominic had learned from his contemporary, St. Francis. Not only should poverty be the condition of individual Dominicans as it was of individual Benedictines, it was to be the condition of the order itself. The Dominican order was to have no possessions except churches and priories. It was to have no fixed incomes, no manors, but was to subsist through charitable gifts. It was, in short, a mendicant order.

The Dominican order expanded at a phenomenal rate during the course of the thirteenth century. Dominican friars carried their evangelical activities across the length and breadth of Europe and beyond, into the Holy Land, Central Asia, Tartary, Tibet, and China. Joining the faculties of the rising universities they became the leading proponents of Aristotelian philosophy and included in their numbers such notable scholars as St. Albertus Magnus and St. Thomas Aquinas. Dominic himself had insisted that his followers acquire broad educations before undertaking their mission of preaching and that each Dominican priory include a school of theology. Within a few decades after his death his order included some of the most brilliant intellects of the age.

The Dominicans were, above all, preachers, and their particular mission was to preach among heretics and non-Christians. Their contact with heretics brought them into close involvement with the Inquisition, and in later years their reputation was darkened by the fact that they themselves became the leading inquisitors. The grand inquisitor of Spain, for example, was customarily a Dominican. They acquired the ominous nickname *"Domini canes"*—hounds of God—by their willingness to supplement St. Dominic's policy of persuasion with the easier and crueler policy of force. . . .

## The Franciscans

Dominic's remarkable achievement was overshadowed by that of his contemporary, St. Francis (c. 1182–1226)—a warm and appealing man who is widely regarded as Christianity's ideal saint. Francis was a true product of the medieval urban revolution. He was the son of a wealthy cloth merchant of Assisi, a northern Italian town with an influential Albigensian minority. As a youth he was generous, high-spirited, and popular, and in time he became the leader of a boisterous but essentially harmless "teenage gang." He was by no means a rake or a dissolute young man but rather, as one writer has aptly expressed it, he "seems altogether to have been rather a festive figure."

Saint Francis, in his great empathy for all of God's creation, may well have preached to the birds, as in this painting by the famous Renaissance artist, Giotto.

In his early twenties, St. Francis underwent a profound religious conversion which occurred in several steps. It began on the occasion of a banquet which he was giving for some of his friends. After the banquet Francis and his companions went out into the town with torches, singing in the streets. Francis was crowned with garlands as king of the revellers, but after a time he disappeared and was found in a religious trance. Thereafter he devoted himself to solitude, prayer, and service to the poor. He went as a pilgrim to Rome where he is reported to have exchanged clothes with a beggar and spent the day begging with other beggars. Returning to Assisi, he encountered an impoverished leper and, notwithstanding his fear of leprosy, he gave the poor man all the money he was carrying and kissed his hand. Thenceforth he devoted himself to the service of lepers and hospitals.

To the confusion and consternation of his bourgeois father, Francis now went about Assisi dressed in rags, giving to the poor. His former companions pelted him with mud, and his father, fearing that Francis' incessant almsgiving would consume the family fortune, disinherited him. Undaunted, Francis left the family house gaily singing a French song. He spent the next three years of his life in the environs of Assisi, living in abject poverty, ministering to lepers and social outcasts, and continuing to embarrass his family by his unconventional behavior. It was at this time that he began to frequent a crumbling little chapel known as the Porticuncula. One day, in the year 1209, while attending mass there, he was struck by the words of the Gospel which the priest was reading: "Everywhere on your road preach and say, 'The kingdom of God is at hand.' Cure the sick, raise the dead, cleanse the lepers, drive out devils. Freely have you received; freely give. Carry neither gold nor silver nor money in your girdles, nor bag, nor two coats, nor sandals, nor staff, for the workman is worthy of his hire." (Matt. X. 7–10.) Francis at once accepted this injunction as the basis of his vocation and immediately thereafter—even though a layman—began to preach to the poor.

Disciples now joined him, and when he had about a dozen followers he is said to have remarked, "Let us go to our Mother, the Holy Roman Church, and tell the pope what the Lord has begun to do through us and carry it out with his sanction." This may have been a naive approach to the masterful, aristocratic Pope Innocent III, yet when Francis came to Rome in 1210, Innocent sanctioned his work. Doubtless the Pope saw in the Franciscan mission a possible orthodox counterpoise to the Waldensians, Albigensians, and other heretical groups who had been winning masses of converts from the Church by the example of their poverty and simplicity. For here was a man whose loyalty to Catholicism was beyond question and whose own artless simplicity of life might bring erring souls back into the Church. . . .

Pious men of other times have fled the world; the Albigensians renounced it as the epitome of evil. But Francis embraced it joyfully as the handiwork of God. In his "Song of Brother Sun," he expressed poetically his holy commitment to the physical universe:

Praise be to Thee, my Lord, for all thy creatures,
Above all Brother Sun
Who brings us the day, and lends us his light;
Beautiful is he, radiant with great splendor,
And speaks to us of Thee, O most high.
Praise to Thee, my Lord, for Sister Moon and for the stars;
In heaven Thou hast set them, clear and precious and fair.
Praise to Thee, my Lord, for Brother Wind.
For air and clouds, for calm and all weather
By which Thou supportest life in all Thy creatures.
Praise to Thee, my Lord, for Sister Water
Which is so helpful and humble, precious and pure.
Praise to Thee, my Lord, for Brother Fire,
By whom Thou lightest up the night.
And fair is he, and gay and mighty and strong.
Praise to Thee, my Lord, for our sister, Mother Earth,
Who sustains and directs us,
And brings forth varied fruits, and plants and flowers bright. . . .
Praise and bless my Lord, and give Him thanks,
And serve Him with great humility.

# F. M. Powicke: Paganism in the Middle Ages

Sir Frederick Maurice Powicke (1879–1963) was the leading English medievalist of his time. Especially interested in moral and intellectual history, he shows in his writings the admiration he felt for medieval values. In the present reading Powicke is concerned with harmonizing the Christian view of the world with the life and immediate concerns of the ordinary man in the Middle Ages. From F. M. Powicke, "The Christian Life" in *The Legacy of the Middle Ages,* ed. G. C. Crump and E. F. Jacob, by permission of the Clarendon Press, Oxford.

How did it come about that the authority of the Church was so generally accepted as inseparable from the duties and aspirations of the Christian life? We now know enough about what used to be called the 'age of faith' to discount the conception of an obedient society, orderly to a point of unnatural self-suppression in everything relating to the government, the doctrine, the worship, the artistic interests of the Church. We no longer believe in that well-behaved body of the faithful, which, though essentially barbarous and ignorant, was always so sweetly submissive in its attitude to the mysteries of the Christian faith. Paganism in the Middle Ages was as endemic, speculation as bold, speech as pungent, the varieties of religious experience as numerous and as extravagant as at any time in the history of mankind. . . .

By paganism I mean a state of acquiescence, or merely professional activity, unaccompanied by sustained religious experience and inward discipline. It is not a state of vacancy and scepticism. It is confined to no class of persons, and is not hostile to, though it is easily wearied by, religious observance. It accepts what is offered without any sense of responsibility, has no sense of sin, and easily recovers from twinges of conscience. At the same time, it is full of curiosity and is easily moved by what is now called the group-mind. It is sensitive to the activities of the crowd, is often emotional, and can be raised to those moods of passion, superstition, and love of persecution into which religion, on its side, can degenerate. A medieval, like a modern, man remained a Christian because he was born a Christian, and most medieval Christians were probably men of this kind. . . .

The history of the Church is the record of the gradual and mutual adaptation of Christianity and paganism to each other. The complete victory of the former has always been a remote vision. St. Paul's Epistles to the Corinthians show how the attempt to persuade their converts to put away earthly things taxed the patience and energy of the earliest apostles. The task became impossible when every member of any political community which possessed an ecclesiastical organization was supposed to be a follower of Christ. . . . As the Christian faith penetrated the society of the Roman world, it fell under the influence . . . of a variegated paganism which shaded off into those philosophical and mystical refinements so dear to the theologians. . . . From the first the Church was the victim as well as the victor, and as it absorbed the peoples of the Mediterranean in the west and spread eastwards into Persia and India, its spiritual life was shot through and through with the glittering fancies, the antinomianism, the morbid extravagances and the endless subtleties of men. It tried to purify a great sluice into which all the religious, every kind of philosophy, every remedy for the troubles and ennui of life had passed. And from this ordeal it passed on to cope with the mental and spiritual traditions of the great northern peoples. If we imagine that the Church was able to work upon a *tabula rasa,* we cannot understand the development either of its theology, its ritual, or its religious experience. . . .

We must begin by realizing that, although its influence meant much more than this, the Church was the systematic expression of a life which had taken the place of the older religions. It was organized in dioceses of Roman or tribal origin; its ministers were not foreign enthusiasts, but men drawn from feudal and village society. . . .

Life on earth would never be comfortable, or even tolerable, if men had no way of grappling with its mysteries and terrors; and if they require protection against these, they must pay the price. On the whole the medieval pagans paid the price cheerfully. They paid tithes and dues. They allowed the clergy to receive their children into society at baptism, to define the limits within which marriage was permissible, to punish their sexual irregularities, to supervise the disposition of their goods by will, to guide their souls at the hour of death and to bury their bodies. They recognized the obligations of confession, penance, communion. In one form or another much of the discipline was as old as society; there must be initiation, regulation, and ceremonial in human relations if men and women are to live together; and, on the other hand, it was not altogether as though the wide-spreading, penetrating, exotic life of the Church was not largely in their own keeping. It was their own brothers and cousins who crowned and anointed kings, ruled bishoprics and monasteries, and celebrated in their churches—the churches which they themselves had built or helped to maintain. . . . They gibed incessantly at the clergy with their hypocrisy, venality, immorality, yet they had a good deal of sympathy with them, for they were of their own flesh. The real enemies were the cranks and heretics who would not play the game.

What we call abuses or superstition in the medieval Church were part of the price paid for, not obstacles to, its universality. They were due to the attempt of pagans to appropriate a mystery. If the people paid, so did the Church. We distort the facts if we try to separate clergy and laity too sharply, for paganism was common to both. Medieval thinkers and reformers saw this far more clearly than we can, and were never tired of discussing the problem. In the eleventh century Cardinal Peter Damiani pointed out in his lurid way that it was of no use to try to keep the clergy apart from the laity unless strict evangelical poverty were insisted upon for all clergy alike. But Damiani and all the preachers of Apostolic poverty who came after him were entangled on the horns of a dilemma. If it is the function of the Church to drive out sin, it must separate itself from sin; if the Church separates itself from sin, it becomes a clique. The Church took another course. Under the guidance of austere pontiffs like Gregory VII and Innocent III it embarked upon an intensive policy of discipline, whose basis was the very claim to universality. . . .

# Medieval Poets Sing of Love and Death

Poetry mirrors the hopes, beliefs, and anxieties of an age. The four poems in this reading present a hint of the richness of medieval civilization. The first is the work of an anonymous minstrel in southern France, one, probably, of the wandering poets who entertained noble audiences in isolated castles with lyric images and gusty tales of battle. The others were composed by Walther von der Vogelweide (c. 1170–c. 1230), a court poet of the German emperors, whose part he took in the continual sparring between emperors and popes. Walther's poems ranged from poignant memories of romance to moral and idealistic statements of the human condition. I. From "Alba" in *Early Medieval French*

Henry von Veldeke, a German minnesinger (minstrel), rests amidst flowers and birds that announce, like his poetry, the approach of spring.

*Lyrics,* ed. C. C. Abbott (London: Oxford University Press, 1932). II & III. From *The Minnesingers,* ed. and trans. Jethro Bithell (London, 1909). IV. From *I Saw the World,* trans. I. G. Colvin (London: Edward Arnold Ltd., 1938).

### I. LOVE WITHOUT SIN

Anonymous Provençal (12th century)

In orchard where the leaves of hawthorn hide,
The lady holds a lover to her side,
Until the watcher in the dawning cried.
*Ah God, ah God, the dawn! it comes how soon.*

"Ah, would to God that never night must end,
Nor this my lover far from me should wend,
Nor watcher day nor dawning ever send!
*Ah God, ah God, the dawn! it comes how soon.*

"Come let us kiss, dear lover, you and I,
Within the meads where pretty song-birds fly;
We will do all despite the jealous eye:
*Ah God, ah God, the dawn! it comes how soon.*

"Sweet lover come, renew our lovemaking
Within the garden where the light birds sing,
Until the watcher sound the severing.
*Ah God, ah God, the dawn! it comes how soon."* . . .

### II. THE DAY OF JUDGMENT

Walther von der Vogelweide (13th century)

Awake! The day is coming now
That brings the sweat of anguish to the brow
Of Christians, Jews, and Pagans all!
Many a token in the sky
And on the earth shows it is nigh:
Foretold in Holy Writ withal.
The sun no longer shows
His face; and treason sows
His secret seeds that no man can detect;
Fathers by their children are undone;
The brother would the brother cheat;
And the cowled monk is a deceit,
Who should the way to Heaven direct;
Might is right, and justice there is none.
Arise! we slept, nor of the peril recked.

### III. ON THE POPE'S CRUSADE BOX

Walther von der Vogelweide (13th century)

Sir Savings-Box, hath the Pope sent you with his sermons
To enrich himself and beggar all the Germans?
Soon as the heaps of money he shall hold
A fine trick he will play—his trick of old:
He will say the Empire's in a parlous state—
And with our money will again be satiate.
Ah! little of the silver will reach the Holy Land:
Rich treasure seldom gives away priest's hand.
Sir Box, to rob us right and left is your command,
And to cozen all the fools that take the bait.

### IV. MY BROTHER MAN

Walther von der Vogelweide (13th century)

Who fears not, God, Thy gifts to take,
And then Thy ten commandments break,
Lacks that true love which should be his salvation.
For many call Thee Father, who
Will not own me as brother too:
They speak deep words from shallow meditation.
Mankind arises from one origin;
We are alike both outward and within;
Our mouths are sated with the selfsame fare.
And when their bones into confusion fall,
Say ye, who knew the living man by sight,
Which is the villein [serf] now and which the knight,
That worms have gnawed their carcasses so bare?
Christians, Jews, and heathens serve Him all,
And God has all creation in His care.

# Our Lady's Tumbler

**(Thirteenth Century)**

Popular piety was perhaps best expressed in the High Middle Ages by the cult of the Virgin Mary who served medieval men as a compassionate, loving, human mediator before the stern justice of God. The story told in this reading is thought to have been brought home from the Near East by the Crusaders and reshaped to fit the Western image of the Queen of Heaven who helped all men, however sinful, toward salvation. From Alice Kemp-Welch, *Of the Tumbler of Our Lady and Other Miracles* (London, 1903).

In the "Lives of the Fathers," the matter of which is of profit, a story is told, than which I do not say that none more pleasing has been heard, but this one is not so without worth that it may not well be told. Now will I tell and rehearse unto you of that which happened to a minstrel.

So much had he journeyed to and fro in so many places, and so prodigal had he been, that he became a monk of a holy Order, for that he was weary of the world. Therefore he entered this holy profession at Clairvaux.

And when that this tumbler, who was so graceful, and fair, and comely, and well

formed, became a monk, he knew not how to perform any office that fell to be done there. Of a truth, he had lived only to tumble, to turn somersaults, to spring, and to dance. To leap and to jump, this he knew, but naught else, and truly no other learning had he, neither the "Paternoster," nor the "Canticles," nor the "Credo," nor the "Ave Maria," nor aught that could make for his salvation. He was sore affrighted in their midst, for he knew not what to say, or what to do of all that fell to be done there. And because of this, he was very sad and pensive. And everywhere he saw the monks and the novices each one serving God in such office as he held. He saw the priests at the altars, for such was their office, the deacons at the Gospels, and the subdeacons at the epistles. And at the proper time, the acolytes straightway rang the bell at the vigils. One recited a verse, and another a lesson, and the young priests were at the psalter, and the novices at the misereres, and the least experienced were at the paternosters, for in suchwise was their work ordered. And he looked everywhere throughout the offices and the cloisters, and saw hidden in the corners here four, here three, here two, here one. And he observed each one as closely as he was able. One made lamentation, another wept, and another groaned and sighed. And much did he marvel what ailed them.

And at length he said, "Holy Mary, what ails these folk that they deport themselves thus, and make show in this manner of such grief? Much disquieted must they be, it seems to me, when they all with one accord make

An angel hands the Virgin a white cloth with which to fan the faithful tumbler. A thirteenth-century illustration of the tale.

such great dolour!" And then he said, "Ah, miserable being! By the Holy Mary, what have I said? I trow that they pray God's grace. But, unhappy being that I am, what do I here, when that he who, in his calling, serves God with all his might, is thus enslaved? Never shall I render any service here, for naught can I do or say. Very hapless was I when that I became a monk, for I know not how even to pray aright. I look hither and thither, and naught do I, save to waste time and to eat bread to no purpose. If in this I am found out, I shall be utterly undone. I am a lusty villain, and if I do naught here but eat, I shall be turned out into the fields. Very miserable am I in this high office!"

Then he wept to allay his grief, and truly did he desire to be dead. "Holy Mother Mary," said he, "beseech your sovereign Father of His grace to guide me, and to bestow upon me such wisdom that I may be able to serve both Him and you in suchwise as to be worthy of the food which I eat here, for well know I that now I do wrong."

And when he had thus made lament, he went prying about the Church until that he entered a crypt, and he crouched down nigh unto an altar, and hid himself there as best he could. And above the altar was the image of Our Lady, the Holy Mary. And in nowise did it surprise him that he felt in safety there, and he perceived not that it was God, who well knows how to guide His own, who had led him there.

And when he had heard the bell ring for the Mass, he rushed forth from the crypt all trembling. "Ah!" said he, "I am like unto a traitor! Even now each one is saying his response, and here am I a tethered ox, and I do naught here but browse, and waste food in vain. Shall I therefore neither speak nor act? By the Mother of God, this will I do, and never shall I be blamed for it. I will do that which I have learnt, and thus, after mine own manner, will I serve the Mother of God in her Church. The others do service with song, and I will do service with tumbling."

And he took off his habit, and then stripped himself, and laid his garments beside the altar, but so that his body should not be uncovered, he kept on a tunic, the which was very clinging and close fitting. Little better was it than a shift; nevertheless was his body wholly covered. And thus was he fitly clad and equipped, and he girded his tunic, and duly prepared him, and he turned him to the image, and gazed on it very humbly. "Lady," said he, "to your keeping I commend my body and my soul. Gentle Queen and Lady, despise not that which I am acquainted with, for, without ado, I will essay me to serve you in good faith, if so be that God will aid me."

Then he began to turn somersaults, now high, now low, first forwards, then backwards, and then he fell on his knees before the image, and bowed his head. "Ah, very gentle Queen!" said he, "of your pity, and of your generosity, despise not my service." Then he tumbled, and leaped, and turned gaily the somersault of Metz. And he bowed to the image, and worshipped it, for he paid homage to it as much as he was able. And anon he turned the French somersault, and then the somersault of Champagne, and after that, those of Spain and of Brittany, and then that of Lorraine. And he laboured to the utmost of his power.

And after that, he did the Roman somersault, and then he put his hand before his face, and turned him with great grace, and looked very humbly at the image of the Mother of God. "Lady," said he, "I do homage to you with my heart, and my body, and my feet, and my hands, for naught beside this do I understand. Now would I be your gleeman. Yonder they are singing, but I am come here to divert you. Lady, you who can protect me, for God's sake do not despise me." Then he beat his breast, and sighed, and mourned very grievously that he knew not how to do service in other manner. And then he turned a somersault backwards. "Lady," said he, "so help me God, never before have I done this. Lady! How that one would have his utmost desire, who could dwell with you in your right glorious mansion! For God's sake, Lady, receive me there. I do this for your sake, and in nowise for mine own." Then he again turned the somersault of Metz, and tumbled and capered full many a time.

And when he heard the monks celebrating, he began to exert himself, and so long as the Mass dured, he ceased not to dance, and to jump, and to leap, until that he was on the point to faint, and he could not stand up, and thus he fell to the ground, and dropped from sheer fatigue. And like as the grease issues from the spitted meat, so the sweat issued from him all over, from head to foot. "Lady," said he, "no more can I do now, but of a surety I shall come back again."

And he was quite overcome of heat. And he took up his clothing, and when that he was dressed, he took his leave, and he bowed to the image, and went his way. "Farewell, very gentle friend," said he. "For God's sake, grieve not at all, for if that I am able, and it is permitted unto me, I will come back, for each hour would I serve you to the utmost of my power, so gracious are you."

And longwhiles he led this life, and, at each hour precisely he repaired to the image, to render service and homage. Certes, so greatly did it please him, and with such right good will did he do this, that never a day was he so tired that he could not do his very utmost to delight the Mother of God, and never did he desire to do other service.

Well known was it that he went each day into the crypt, but no one, save God, knew what he did there, nor would he, for all the riches of the whole world, that any, save . . . God alone, should know of his doings.

Think you now that God would have prized his service if that he had not loved Him? By no means, however much he tumbled. But He prized it because of his love. Much labour and fatigue, many fasts and vigils, many tears and sighs and groans and prayers, much diligence in discipline, both at Mass and at matins, the bestowal of all that you have and the payment of whatsoever you owe, if you love not God with all your heart, all these are wholly thrown away in such manner, understand well, that they avail naught for true salvation. Of a truth, without love and without pity, before God all counts for naught. God asks not for gold or for silver, but only for true love in the hearts of men, and this one loved God truly. And because of this, God prized his service.

Longwhiles did the good man live thus, but for how long time he so lived contented, I cannot tell unto you, but in the course of time sore trouble came to him, for one of the monks, who in his heart greatly blamed him that he came not to matins, kept watch on him. And he much marvelled what happened, and said that never would he desist until that he knew who he was, and for what he was worth, and in what manner he earned his bread. And so closely did the monk pursue him, and follow him, and keep watch on him, that he distinctly saw him perform his service in a simple manner, even as I have told it unto you. "By my faith," said he, "he has a good time of it, and much greater diversion, it seemeth to me, than we have all together." . . . And he went to the abbot, and rehearsed unto him, from beginning to end, all that he had learnt, even as you have heard it. . . .

And then they went thither quite quietly, and without delay they hid themselves in a covert nook nigh unto the altar, so that he saw them not. And the abbot, watching there, observed all the service of the novice, and the divers somersaults the which he turned, and how that he capered, and danced, and bowed before the image, and jumped, and leaped, until that he was nigh fainting. And so greatly was he overcome of fatigue, that he fell heavily to the ground, and so exhausted was he, that he sweated all over from his efforts, so that the sweat ran all down the middle of the crypt. But in a little, the Mother of God, whom he served all without guile, came to his succour, and well knew she how to aid him.

And anon the abbot looked, and he saw descend from the vaulting so glorious a lady, that never had he seen one so fair or so richly crowned, and never had another so beautiful been created. Her vesture was all wrought with gold and precious stones, and with her were the angels and the archangels from the heavens above, who came around the tumbler, and solaced and sustained him. And when that they were ranged around him, he was wholly comforted, and they made ready to tend him, for they desired to make recompense unto him for the services the which he had rendered unto their Lady, who is so precious a gem. And the sweet and noble Queen took a white cloth, and with it she very gently fanned her minstrel before the altar. And the noble and gracious Lady fanned his neck and body and face to cool him, and greatly did she concern herself to aid him, and gave herself up to the care of him; but of this the good man took no heed, for he neither perceived, nor did he know, that he was in such fair company.

And the holy angels who remained with him, paid him much honour, but the Lady no longer sojourned there, and she made the sign of the cross as she turned away, and the holy angels, who greatly rejoiced to keep watch over their companion, took charge over him, and they did but await the hour when God would take him from this life and they might bear away his soul.

And full four times did the abbot and the monk witness, without hindrance, how that each hour he went there, and how that the Mother of God came there to aid and succour her liegeman, for well knows she how to protect her own. And the abbot had much joy of it, for very desirous had he been to know the truth concerning it. Now had God verily shown unto him that the services which this poor man rendered were pleasing unto Him. And the monk was quite bewildered by it, and from anguish he glowed like fire. "Your mercy, Sire!" said he to the abbot, "this is a holy man whom I see here. If that I have said aught concerning him that is evil, it is right that my body should make amends for it. Therefore ordain me a penance, for without doubt he is altogether an upright man. Verily have we seen all, and no longer can we be mistaken." . . .

And thus passed the time, until that, a little while after, it came to pass that the abbot sent for him who was so good. And when he heard that he was sent for, and that it was the abbot who made enquiry for him, so greatly was he troubled, that he knew not what he should say. "Alas," said he, "I am found out. Never a day passes without distress, or without toil or disgrace, for my service counts for naught. Methinks it is not pleasing unto God. Gentle Lady, Holy Mary, how troubled is my mind! I know not, Lady, from whom to get counsel, so come now to mine aid. And at the first word, anon will they say, 'Away with you!' Woe is me! How shall I be able to make answer when I know not one single word with which to make explanation? But what avails this? It behoves me to go."

And weeping, so that his face was all wet, he came before the abbot, and he knelt before him in tears. "Sire," said he, "for God's sake, have mercy! Would you drive me hence? Tell me all your behests, and all your bidding will I do."

Then said the abbot, "This would I know, and I would that you answer me truly. Longwhiles have you been here, both winter and summer, and I would know by what services, and in what manner, you earn your bread."

"Alas," said he, "well knew I that all would become known, and that when all my doings were known, no longer would any one have to do with me. Sire," said he, "now will I depart hence. Miserable am I, and miserable shall I be, for I never do aught that is right." . . .

Then he straightway unfolded unto him, howsoever grievous it was, his whole life, from beginning to end, in such sort that he left naught unsaid, just as I have told it unto you. And with clasped hands, and weeping, he told and rehearsed unto him everything, and, sighing, he kissed his feet.

And the holy abbot turned to him, and, all weeping, raised him up. And he kissed both his eyes. "Brother," said he, "be silent now, for truly do I promise unto you that you shall be at peace with us. God grant that we may have your fellowship so long as we are deserving of it. Good friends shall we be. Fair, gentle brother, pray for me and I will pray in return for you. And so I beseech and command of you, my sweet friend, that you forthwith render this service openly, just as you have done it, and still better even, if that you know how." . . .

And the holy Fathers have related unto us that it thus befell this minstrel. Now let us pray God, without ceasing, that He may grant unto us so worthily to serve Him, that we may be deserving of His love. The story of the Tumbler is set forth.

# Robert Lopez: The Fate of Nonconformists

Italian-born historian Robert Lopez teaches at Yale University. Seeing the function of the non-conformist "to serve as a touchstone and a warning" to the society in which he lives, Professor Lopez here points out the flaw in medieval civilization which left no room for heretics or nonbelievers. From Robert S. Lopez, *The Birth of Europe*. Copyright © 1962 by Max Leclerc et Cie, Proprietors of Librairie Armand Colin and Copyright © 1966 Translation J. M. Dent & Sons Ltd. and reprinted by permission of the American publisher, M. Evans and Company.

In one way or another, nearly all the inhabitants of Catholic Europe derived some benefit from the economic, intellectual and political awakening of the 12th and 13th centuries. Even those almost unorganised peoples around the Baltic who lost their independence, gained some advantage from association with a more mature civilisation than their own. Only the nonconformists, heretics or Jews experienced the disappearance of the relative security they had enjoyed up to then, despite sporadic bursts of ill-feeling on the part of the people and intermittent persecutions under the law. There was no practical gain which compensated, or could compensate, for the threat of violent death to which they were henceforth constantly exposed.

This change was tragically highlighted in a letter written by the 'Pillars of the World' (as the proud chiefs of the Jewish community in Mainz called themselves) in reply to a circular from the French communities, dated 1096. Stricken with fear at the sight of this new spectacle of hundreds of knights embracing the cross, French Jews had ordered a period of fasting, with the hope of appeasing Divine wrath, and they implored their co-religionists in the Rhenish towns to do the same. As a gesture of solidarity, the Pillars of the World complied with their wishes, but made the point that it could not happen in Mainz, since 'no sword hung over their heads'. Their confidence could not have been more misplaced: the Jews of Mainz were among the first victims of the First Crusade.

The turn of heretics would not be long in coming; not as a side show of expeditions launched with other objects as their primary aim, but as a result of special crusades dedicated wholly to their destruction. The Crusade against the Albigensians, those against the Yugoslav Bogomils, the Crusade waged from 1306–7 against the Adventists of Fra Dolcino in the Alps—every one of these Crusades was more merciless than any undertaken against the Moslems. And while enthusiasm for war in the Holy Land gradually waned, then died out in the course of the 13th century, hostility towards nonconformists relentlessly increased throughout Catholic Europe. Much later, when oversea Crusades had become a thing of the past, it was at home that the West put the torch to the stakes of the *autos da fé*.

## THE RELIGIOUS PROBLEM: TOLERATION OR REPRESSION?

On the surface, the disasters falling upon those who do not conform would seem to be by-products of triumphant religion. As theological thinking became more thorough and more precise, and as the masses moved on from an almost passive observance of ritual to direct spiritual experience and action, inevitably the presence of scabby sheep in the Christian fold would stand out as a shameful blemish. Nevertheless, one might ask: was violence necessary to remove it? Once more, we come face to face with the questions we asked about the Crusades. Saint Bernard of Clairvaux, a pious but stern man, who promoted the Second Crusade and was an implacable enemy of Abelard, definitely opposed this kind of violence: 'The Church,' he wrote, 'can overcome the Jews by convincing them and converting them day by day better than by putting them all to the sword.' As for heretics, 'it is not by force of arms that we must crush them, but by argument . . . by education and persuasion.'

In the 13th century, the policy of persuasion found other eloquent partisans. St. Francis, bearing no arms at all, joined the Crusade of 1219 so that he could preach the Gospel to the Moslems of Egypt, unsuccessfully, it is true. Raymond Lull, shining light of the Franciscan Order, endeavoured to promote mutual understanding by encouraging the study of languages spoken by the Infidels. After a long and brave apostolate in North Africa, he was martyred at Bougie in 1315. Other Franciscans, however, were more fortunate. In Europe they led thousands of heretics peacefully back to the fold. In Asia they set up new dioceses, as a result of which the eastern boundary of the Catholic Church advanced step by step from Syria to China.

St. Dominic of Calahorra also joined the Crusade against the Albigenses as an unarmed preacher. In a moment of stress, however, he gave way to a few words which appeared to favour violence: 'During many years, I have sought in vain to convince you by gentleness, by preaching, by tears, by prayer; but as one of my country's proverbs says, where blessings achieve nothing, blows will succeed. We will summon princes and prelates against you. . . .' His famous disciple, Thomas Aquinas, while disapproving of forced conversions, expressed himself harshly against the Jews and approved extreme measures against heretics as a means to protect the great mass of the faithful from danger of infection. Could he have expressed himself otherwise without running the risk of conflict with his superiors? As early as 1233, Dominicans and Franciscans had been placed in charge of that 'prophylactic' institution—the Inquisition. . . .

Is religious zeal really the main cause of intolerance? Certainly, religion provides a reason or pretext for violence, silencing those who might wish to protect non-conformists. . . . In the eyes of the masses, the worst sin of the non-conformists is that they are different, unassimilable and bound up in some mysterious way with malignant forces from outside—invasions, extortions, epidemics, poor harvests. Characteristically, an Inquisitor points out as probable heretics all those who 'do not kneel down and join their hands like the others when they pray.' They are people who should be kept at arm's length, excluded from political and professional associations and relegated to the odious and unpleasant jobs. If they counterattack, they lay themselves open to vengeance from an infuriated mob. If they shut themselves completely away inside their mountain villages or town ghettos, they incur even more suspicion. If they abandon their beliefs, they are made to denounce and defame their former co-religionists as proof of their sincerity.

In the view of the authorities, the nonconformists are guilty of every fault ascribed to them by the masses, plus that of being stubborn rebels to whom the normal provisions of the law cannot be applied. This does not alter the fact that it is sometimes expedient to protect them in order to exploit them. This, of course, is a dangerous game when it comes to heretics, for these people have no right even to existence; governments who wish to make use of their talents must pretend that they are good Christians and treat them as such. As for Jews, civil and religious law concedes them a right to live, as witnesses of the Truth revealed in Holy Scripture, but condemns them to bondage as the people responsible for the Crucifixion. Kings, princes and prelates take advantage of the situation to make use of the Jews in some way as both a sponge and a filter. The filter serves to trap all the resentments and complaints of the people, and it can be discarded when it has fulfilled its purpose. The sponge absorbs the wealth of the nation and squeezes it back into the royal coffers. . . .

TOPIC 28

# AUTUMN OF A TRADITIONAL SOCIETY

By the late fourteenth century the equilibrium achieved by the medieval system was crumbling. The years that followed were on the whole ones of political, economic, and social instability and insecurity. Feudalism was declining, the economy in general receding, and the dominant tone of life dissatisfied and aimless. It is this era of fading and decay that Professor Johan Huizinga captured in his suggestive image, "the autumn of the Middle Ages." The readings are concerned with the signs of a waning civilization.

**Reading 147**

## The Decay of Manorialism and Feudalism

Excerpted from *Europe in the Middle Ages*, Second Edition, by Robert S. Hoyt, © 1957, 1966 by Harcourt, Brace & World, Inc. and reprinted with their permission.

I

The fourteenth and fifteenth centuries witnessed a general economic recession. The full effects were not felt in some areas until c. 1350, and other areas were well on the way to recovery c. 1450, but stagnation set in earlier and lasted later in many places. Not all economic activities suffered, but medieval agriculture, trade, and industry as a whole were contracting. Enterprise was no longer so rewarding as in the high Middle Ages, a period of expanding economy. For this general condition there were many interacting causes which were also in turn the results of other causes. Perhaps the basic factor was a slow decline in total population, a decline that diminished both the supply of labor and the market for goods produced. . . .

### Agrarian Unrest

The economic position of the nobility was based on control of land, and land continued to be the most important form of wealth. We have already seen how the nobility, enjoying a rising standard of living in the twelfth and thirteenth centuries, exploited their landed wealth for the money income it would provide. The two ways of extracting profits from the land were by renting part or all of the manor to peasants, and by exploiting the manor directly by employing peasant labor on the demesne, that part of the manor reserved for the lord's own occupation. In an age of rising prices the latter method was generally more successful. Then in the fourteenth century prices of agricultural products began to decline. This situation was aggravated by the fact that prices of non-agricultural commodities tended to hold firm or even to increase. Thus the landholding class was caught between lower prices for what was sold and steady or higher prices for what was bought.

Except in especially favorable circumstances for direct exploitation—as when a manor was very productive and located near a good market—many lords were willing to convert their manorial rights into a money income. The demesnes were let out to the peasants, whose services were commuted for money payments to the lords. From the lords' point of view this system was satisfactory if rents held up, but the peasants were now squeezed between high rents and declining prices. The old bonds that held the manorial population together were being dissolved by the new cash nexus between landlord and tenant, the result being a relatively greater freedom of movement for the peasants. Hence lords found it difficult to hold their tenants to their contractual obligations. Some peasants moved to more prosperous regions where they found opportunity to work for wages, others went to the towns to hire out their labor. Manorial lords were therefore under increasing pressure to lower rents. In some cases the manorial population declined to the point where tenements were actually deserted. To keep their land in production some lords turned to hiring labor for wages. This system had the advantage of flexibility. Instead of adapting the operations of a manor to the labor supply on hand, lords could hire as much labor as was needed at a particular time, for example during spring plowing or for harvesting. These generalizations apply to many regions north of the Pyrenees and the Alps, but the economic picture of rural Europe in the fourteenth century was extremely complex and exceptional conditions were found everywhere: exceptionally prosperous and exceptionally depressed localities, depending mainly on fluctuations in local production and prices.

Then in 1348 the Black Death struck Europe. It moved slowly westward from the Far East, carried along the trade routes. This was by far the worst "invasion" from Asia since Attila the Hun. All the wars of the Middle Ages did not cause such loss of life as the first onslaught and the successive waves of bubonic plague during the second half of the fourteenth century. The disease was spread by fleas infected by plague-stricken rats. In an age wholly ignorant of sanitation there was no defense against what seemed to be the wrath of God: to the destruction of life was added the horror and uncertainty in which men lived. The economic results must therefore be measured not only by the loss of population but also by the disruption of normal existence. Men fled from stricken areas, deserting their jobs and spreading the plague to new regions. Some people squandered their money in one last fling; others abandoned their wealth and worldly goods in a last desperate effort to earn salvation by a life of asceticism and penance before death overtook them. [The mortality has been variously estimated, ranging from a fifth to a third of the total population. . . .]

The immediate results of the Black Death were deceptive. The mortality produced a labor shortage and a sudden increase in the amount of money per capita. Employers, both urban and rural, could therefore pay higher wages, while producers could demand higher prices. The result was an apparent prosperity. Peasants migrated to the towns to replace urban workers who had died, and the shortage of rural labor made possible not only higher wages for peasants but also the purchase of freedom from the manorial obligations of serfdom. For a few years everyone had more money and prices increased sharply. Then the reaction set in. Prosperity had been based on inflation, not on an expanding market. Production of agricultural and industrial commodities was soon able to meet the now diminished demand, and employers sought to cut their costs by rolling back wages to the level of 1348. . . .

The workers and peasants had no legal means for improving their lot. Many peasants were still unfree and subject to the jurisdic-

Survivors bury the dead in mass graves in this Flemish scene of 1352. The artist has captured a sense of pervading death and despair.

tion of their lord's manorial court. Those who were free from the customary services were restive under legislation which favored the propertied classes by fixing wages and prices. . . . The result of these economic grievances was a series of revolts and uprisings during the second half of the fourteenth century [such as] the Peasants' Revolt in England in 1381, the sporadic risings of the *Jacquerie* in France, and the Ciompi rising in Florence in 1378. . . .

II

## The Decay of Feudalism

Later medieval society still contained feudal elements. . . . But these survivals obviously do not explain the nature of modern society. Less obviously, the continuity of feudal institutions in the later Middle Ages does not reveal the real nature of the society of that period. There were still lords and vassals, but their relations had changed. There were still fiefs and feudal incidents, feudal jurisdictions and feudal privileges, but their nature had changed and their effectiveness had been circumscribed. In two ways feudal institutions were no longer the real framework of later medieval society. First, the obligations of the noble to the lord from whom he held his fief were no longer so important as his obligations to the territorial ruler. Within the aristocracy the vassal-lord relationship was less immediate and binding than the subject-ruler relationship. Second, the economic position of the aristocracy was no longer assured merely by the possession of landed wealth. Nobles who could not make their manors pay a profit in an age of uncertain markets, declining agricultural prices, and depreciated currency were no longer able to maintain their status.

Ladies and gentlemen of the court of Philip the Good (Duke of Burgundy, 1419–1467) on a falcon hunt. Contrast these rather unwarlike aristocrats with the knights on the following page.

Many of the lesser nobles sank into an economic and social condition hardly superior to that of their peasants. . . .

The political role of the aristocracy also declined during the thirteenth century, when the western monarchies were building governments that employed professional civil servants and no longer needed to depend so much on the cooperation of the nobles. In central Europe no central government was strong enough to subordinate the nobility, but the tendency toward disintegration or particularism resulted in the multiplication of petty principalities. The power of the nobles as a whole, as an estate, increased; but the power of individual nobles declined as the territories and populations which the majority of nobles ruled grew smaller. Two different tendencies are therefore apparent. In the western monarchies the aristocracy struggled to regain its lost political power; in central Europe the aristocracy was jealous to preserve its rights of local political autonomy against any assertion of authority by the emperor or by the greater princes of the Empire or, in Italy, by the pope. . . .

The main constitutional significance of these later medieval struggles among factions of the aristocracy lies in the fact that they were simply struggles for power. There was no thought of political theories or principles. All the nobles contended for was control of the government, in contrast with earlier baronial opposition to the crown that appealed to the medieval principle that all government should be limited by law. The political ambitions of the nobility achieved few constructive results, but they did teach contemporaries an important lesson. A nearly universal complaint throughout western Europe was that overmighty subjects must be

Medieval knights in chain mail and armor from the facade of Rheims Cathedral.

forced to obey the laws and keep the peace. Therefore the strong monarchies in France and England, under Louis XI and Edward IV, enjoyed the support of a large majority of the people. The obvious cure for disorder and faction seemed to be the establishment of a central government so powerful that no group of nobles dared to defy it. Hence the tendencies toward absolute monarchy which characterize the transition from medieval to early modern Europe were successful because they were popular. . . .

In the economic sphere the confusion of ideals and realities in the decadent feudal society of the later Middle Ages is a striking feature. Just as the noble was ideally supposed to maintain the peace and repress tyranny, but often spent his time fighting civil wars or oppressing the weak and defenseless, he was also supposed to promote the general welfare of the people, but actually devoted his energies to exploiting or simply robbing whatever poor peasants or wealthy merchants came within his reach. The "robber-barons" of Germany are appropriately so called. . . .

As the realities of feudal society gave way to a new social order, in its military, political, and economic aspects, the ideals and values of feudalism were asserted even more strongly. People seemed unwilling to recognize the changes that were shaping a new Europe. The age that witnessed the triumph of the foot soldier over the mounted knight, the relative rise of both peasants and townsmen to a greater share in the total wealth of Europe, and the advent of strong monarchies in the west and power politics in all regions, was also the age in which the ideals of chivalry were expressed most extravagantly. The vogue of the "new chivalry" reached its climax in the foundation of several new knightly orders. Edward III, for example, founded the Order of the Garter; John the Good of France established his Order of the Star; and Duke Philip the Good instituted the Order of the Golden Fleece. The overt aims of these orders may be indicated by a contemporary explanation of the high purpose of the Order of the Golden Fleece:

Not at all for play or pastime,
But to the end that praise be given
First to God above all,
And also glory and high renown to good men.

Actually, these orders were sponsored by the courts almost exclusively for courtiers, noble politicians, and foreign nobles whose political support was coveted. They had an elaborate and artificial ceremonial, complete with special offices, titles, and chivalrous vows, and they were very popular with the aristocracy, or at least with those who had social and political ambitions. In contrast with . . . earlier times, these latter-day orders of chivalry performed no military, social, or economic function of immediate practical value. They provided a kind of organized social dream world for the nobles who made good in the later Middle Ages.

# Disaster Strikes France in the Mid-Fourteenth Century

The decay of medieval economic and social institutions in France stands out in the chronicle of the years 1340 to 1368 written by Jean de Venette, a Parisian friar and champion of old French values. In the excerpts in this reading Venette describes the consequences of the Black Death, the unrest and uncertainty of rulers, upper classes, and peasantry alike, and finally the great peasant uprising in 1358 (the *Jacquerie,* derived from the derisive term "Jacques Bonhomme," or simple fellow, applied by the nobles to the peasants). To add to the internal difficulties of France, a bitter struggle between the French and English went on throughout the period covered by the chronicle and kept large areas of France in turmoil (Hundred Years' War, 1338–1453). From trans. Jean Birdsall, *The Chronicle of Jean de Venette,* ed. Richard Newhall in Records of Civilization, No. 50 (New York: Columbia University Press, 1953), pp. 48–50, 52, 62–63, 67, 76–77.

## THE BLACK DEATH

In A.D. 1348, the people of France and of almost the whole world were struck by a blow other than war. For in addition to the famine which I described in the beginning and to the wars which I described in the course of this narrative, pestilence and its attendant tribulations appeared again in various parts of the world. In the month of August, 1348, after Vespers when the sun was beginning to set, a big and very bright star appeared above Paris, toward the west. . . . At length, when night had come, this big star, to the amazement of all of us who were watching, broke into many different rays and, as it shed these rays over Paris toward the east, totally disappeared and was completely annihilated. Whether it was a comet or not, whether it was composed of airy exhalations and was finally resolved into vapor, I leave to the decision of astronomers. It is, however, possible that it was a presage of the amazing pestilence to come, which, in fact, followed very shortly in Paris and throughout France and elsewhere, as I shall tell. All this year and the next, the mortality of men and women, of the young even more than of the old, in Paris and in the kingdom of France, and also, it is said, in other parts of the world, was so great that it was almost impossible to bury the dead. People lay ill little more than two or three days and died suddenly, as it were in full health. He who was well one day was dead the next and being carried to his grave. Swellings appeared suddenly in the armpit or in the groin—in many cases both—and they were infallible signs of death. This sickness or pestilence was called an epidemic by the doctors. Nothing like the great numbers who died in the years 1348 and 1349 has been heard of or seen or read of in times past. This plague and disease came from association and contagion, for if a well man visited the sick he only rarely evaded the risk of death. Wherefore in many towns timid priests withdrew, leaving the exercise of their ministry to such of the religious as were more daring. In many places not two out of twenty remained alive. . . .

This plague, it is said, began among the unbelievers, came to Italy, and then crossing the Alps reached Avignon, where it attacked several cardinals and took from them their whole household. Then it spread, unforeseen, to France, through Gascony and Spain, little by little, from town to town, from village to village, from house to house, and finally from person to person. It even crossed over to Germany, though it was not so bad there as with us. During the epidemic, God of His accustomed goodness deigned to grant this grace, that however suddenly men died, almost all awaited death joyfully. Nor was there anyone who died without confessing his sins and receiving the holy viaticum. To the even greater benefit of the dying, Pope Clement VI through their confessors mercifully gave and granted absolution from penalty to the dying in many cities and fortified towns. Men died the more willingly for this and left many inheritances and temporal goods to churches and monastic orders, for in many cases they had seen their close heirs and children die before them.

Some said that this pestilence was caused by infection of the air and waters, since there was at this time no famine nor lack of food supplies, but on the contrary great abundance. As a result of this theory of infected water and air as the source of the plague the Jews were suddenly and violently charged with infecting wells and water and corrupting the air. The whole world rose up against them cruelly on this account. In Germany and other parts of the world where Jews lived, they were massacred and slaughtered by Christians, and many thousands were burned everywhere, indiscriminately. The unshaken, if fatuous, constancy of the men and their wives was remarkable. For mothers hurled their children first into the fire that they might not be bap-

This woodcut of the Jews of the Rhenish city of Cologne being burned alive was included in a chronicle *Liber Chronicarum mundi* published in Nürnberg in 1493.

The same chronicle offered a description of flagellant sects, with this as accompanying illustration.

tized and then leaped in after them to burn with their husbands and children. It is said that many bad Christians were found who in a like manner put poison into wells. But in truth, such poisonings, granted that they actually were perpetrated, could not have caused so great a plague nor have infected so many people. There were other causes; for example, the will of God and the corrupt humors and evil inherent in air and earth. . . .

### THE FLAGELLANTS

In the year 1349, while the plague was still active and spreading from town to town, men in Germany, Flanders, Hainaut, and Lorraine uprose and began a new sect on their own authority. Stripped to the waist, they gathered in large groups and bands and marched in procession through the crossroads and squares of cities and good towns. There they formed circles and beat upon their backs with weighted scourges, rejoicing as they did so in loud voices and singing hymns suitable to their rite and newly composed for it. Thus for thirty-three days they marched through many towns doing their penance and affording a great spectacle to the wondering people. They flogged their shoulders and arms with scourges tipped with iron points so zealously as to draw blood. . . .

### THE DISSOLUTENESS OF THE NOBILITY

In the year 1356 the luxury and dissoluteness of many of the nobles and the knights became still more deeply rooted. I have described above the far too brief and scanty garments which they had already adopted. Now they began to disfigure themselves in a still more extravagant way. They wore pearls on their hoods or on their gilded and silver girdles and elaborately adorned themselves from head to foot with gems and precious stones. So assiduously did all men, from the least to the greatest, cover themselves with these luxuries that pearls and other precious stones were sold for high prices and could hardly be found at all in Paris. . . . Men also began to wear the plumes of birds fastened on their hats. By night they devoted themselves immoderately to the pleasures of the flesh or to games of dice; by day, to ball or tennis. Wherefore the common people had reason to lament, and did lament greatly, that the taxes levied on them for the war were uselessly spent on such sports and converted to such uses. It was at this time that

The cult of luxury is seen in this detail of the wedding of children of two wealthy Florentine families in the fifteenth century.

the nobles in derision called peasants and simple folk Jacques Bonhomme. . . .

### THE GOVERNMENT IS PARALYZED

In A.D. 1357, while King John [John (1350–1364) had been captured in the battle of Poitiers in 1356] was in England, misfortune was added to misfortune, as I have said, in France and about Paris. For enemies multiplied throughout the land, and robbers increased to such a degree that they despoiled the inhabitants of country villages in their own houses. Yet Charles, duke of Normandy, the king's eldest son, who was bound by hereditary right to defend the realm and to rule the state, applied no remedy. Wherefore a large proportion of the rural population, unable to stay longer in their villages, began at this time to hasten for protection to Paris with their wives and children and other goods. The enemy seized many castles and fortresses and captured the men who dwelt round about. Some they held for ransom; some they slaughtered miserably. Nor did they spare the religious. Therefore monks and nuns abandoned their monasteries and took refuge as best they could with their friends in Paris and elsewhere. . . . Though this situation aroused no slight wonder and amazement among the people, nothing was done to remedy it. . . .

### THE JACQUERIE

While, then, these cities and the city of Paris were being ill treated and little defended, there befell near Paris something hitherto unheard of. In the summer of 1358, the peasants living near Saint-Leu-d'Essérent and Clermont in the diocese of Beauvais, seeing the wrongs and oppression inflicted on them on every side and seeing that the nobles gave them no protection but rather oppressed them as heavily as the enemy, rose and took arms against the nobles of France. . . . Going forth with their arms and standards, they overran the countryside. They killed, slaughtered and massacred without mercy all the nobles whom they could find, even their own lords. Not only this: they leveled the houses and fortresses of the nobles to the ground, and, what is still more lamentable, they delivered the noble ladies and their little children upon whom they came to an atrocious death. Thus, they destroyed the castle of Ermenonville, then the strongest in France, and slew many noble men and women who were in hiding there. This tribulation increased in strength until it reached even to Paris. A noble hardly dared appear outside his stronghold, for if he had been seen by the peasants or had fallen into their hands, he would either have been killed or would have escaped only after rough handling. The number of peasants eager to extirpate the nobles and their wives and children and to destroy their manor houses grew until it was estimated at five thousand. Therefore the nobles kept themselves in seclusion and did not appear abroad as they had before. But this monstrous business did not long endure. For, since the peasants had begun it entirely of themselves, not of God nor of due authority such as that of an overlord, all their desire suddenly failed and came to an end. Those who had begun with a zeal for justice, as it had seemed to them, since their lords were not defending them but rather oppressing them, turned themselves to base and execrable deeds. It is said that they subjected noble ladies to their vile lust, slew their innocent little children, as I have said, and carried off such property as they found, wherewith they clothed themselves and their peasant wives luxuriously. What was so ill done could not long endure, nor was it fitting that it should. . . . For the knights and nobles recovered their strength and, eager to avenge themselves, united in force. Overrunning many country villages, they set most of them on fire and slew miserably all the peasants, not merely those whom they believed to have done them harm, but all they found, whether in their houses or digging in the vineyards or in the fields. . . .

# Consequences of the Black Death in England

As did France, England too suffered economically and socially in the fourteenth century. The ravages caused by the Black Death created a labor shortage and forced landowners to raise wages and prices. King Edward III tried to meet the resulting inflation by setting both back at the 1348 level (Statute of Laborers, 1351), but the impossibility of enforcing such legislation and the continuing costs of the Hundred Years' War intensified peasant unrest which culminated in violent rebellion in 1381. King at the time was Edward's grandson Richard II, a youth of fourteen, who with luck and cunning managed to restore a semblance of order. I. From ed. Elizabeth Kendall, *Source-Book of English History* (New York, 1900), pp. 105–106. II. From ed. Edward Cheyney, *Readings in English History* (New York, 1908), pp. 261–265.

## I. A CONTEMPORARY DESCRIBES THE ECONOMIC EFFECTS IN ENGLAND (AFTER 1351)

Meanwhile the king sent proclamation into all the countries that reapers and other labourers should not take more than they had been accustomed to take, under the penalty appointed by statute. But the labourers were so lifted up and obstinate that they would not listen to the king's command, but if anyone wished to have them he had to give them what they wanted, and either lose his fruit and crops, or satisfy the lofty and covetous wishes of the workmen. And when it was known to the king that they had not observed his command, and had given greater wages to the labourers, he levied heavy fines upon abbots, priors, knights, greater and lesser, and other great folk and small folk of the realm. . . . And afterwards the king had many labourers arrested, and sent them to prison; many withdrew themselves and went into the forests and woods; and those who were taken were heavily fined. Their ringleaders were made to swear that they would not take daily wages beyond the ancient custom, and then were freed from prison. And in like manner was done with the other craftsmen in the boroughs and villages. . . . After the aforesaid pestilence, many buildings, great and small, fell into ruins in every city, borough, and village for lack of inhabitants, likewise many villages and hamlets became desolate, not a house being left in them, all having died who dwelt there; and it was probable that many such villages would never be inhabited. In the winter following there was such a want of servants in work of all kinds, that one would scarcely believe that in times past there had been such a lack. . . . And so all necessaries became so much dearer that what in times past had been worth a penny, was then worth 4d. or 5d.

## II. THE ENGLISH PEASANTS RISE IN REVOLT (1381)

In the year 1381, the second of the reign of King Richard Second, during the month of May, on Wednesday, the fourth day after the feast of Trinity, that impious band began to assemble from Kent, from Surrey, and from many other surrounding places. Apprentices also, leaving their masters, rushed to join these. And so they gathered on Blackheath, where, forgetting themselves in their multitude, and neither contented with their former cause nor appeased by smaller crimes, they unmercifully planned greater and worse evils and determined not to desist from their wicked undertaking until they should have entirely extirpated the nobles and great men of the kingdom. . . .

On the Friday following the feast of the Consecration they came over the bridge to London; here no one resisted them, although, as was said, the citizens of London knew of their advance a long time before; and so they directed their way to the Tower where the king was surrounded by a great throng of knights, esquires, and others. . . . The people had determined to kill the archbishop and others. . . . The king, however, desired to free the archbishop and his friends from the jaws of the wolves, so he sent to the people a command to assemble outside the city, at a place called Mile End, in order to speak with the king and to treat with him concerning their designs. The soldiers who were to go forward, consumed with folly, lost heart, and gave up, on the way, their boldness of purpose. Nor did they dare to advance, but, unfortunately, struck as they were by fear, like women, kept themselves within the Tower.

But the king advanced to the assigned place, while many of the wicked mob kept following him. . . . More, however, remained where they were. When the others had come to the king they complained that they had been seriously oppressed by many hardships and that their condition of servitude was unbearable, and that they neither could nor would endure it longer. The king, for the sake of peace, and on account of the violence of the times, yielding to their petition, granted to them a charter with the great seal, to the effect that all men in the kingdom of England should be free and of free condition, and should remain both for themselves and their heirs free from all kinds of servitude and villeinage forever. This charter was rejected and decided to be null and void by the king and the great men of the kingdom in the parliament held at Westminster in the same year, after the feast of St. Michael.

[While the conference at Mile End was going on, the part of the mob which had stayed in the city murdered the Archbishop of Canterbury and many royal officials.]

On the following day, which was Saturday, [the rebels] gathered in Smithfield, where there came to them in the morning the king, who although only a youth in years yet was

Richard II faces the rebelling peasantry (right) at Smithfield in 1381; at left Wat Tyler is killed. The fifteenth-century artist took several liberties with the actual details.

in wisdom already well versed. Their leader, whose real name was Wat Tyler, approached him; already they were calling him by the other name of Jack Straw. He kept close to the king, addressing him for the rest. He carried in his hand an unsheathed weapon which they call a dagger, and, as if in childish play, kept tossing it from one hand to the other in order that he might seize the opportunity, if the king should refuse his requests, to strike the king suddenly (as was commonly believed); and from this thing the greatest fear arose among those about the king as to what might be the outcome.

They begged from the king that all the warrens, and as well waters as park and wood, should be common to all, so that a poor man as well as a rich should be able freely to hunt animals everywhere in the kingdom. . . . When the king hesitated about granting this concession Jack Straw came nearer, and, speaking threatening words, seized with his hand the bridle of the horse of the king very daringly. When John de Walworth, a citizen of London, saw this, thinking that death threatened the king, he seized a sword and pierced Jack Straw in the neck. . . . He sank back, slowly letting go with his hands and feet, and then died. A great cry and much mourning arose: "Our leader is slain." When this dead man had been meanly dragged along by the hands and feet into the church of St. Bartholomew, which was near by, many withdrew from the band, and, vanishing, betook themselves to flight, to the number it is believed of ten thousand. . . .

After these things had happened and quiet had been restored the time came when the king caused the offenders to be punished. So Lord Robert Tresillian, one of the judges, was sent by order of the king to inquire into the uprisings against the peace and to punish the guilty. Wherever he came he spared no one, but caused great slaughter. . . . For whoever was accused before him in this said cause, whether justly or as a matter of spite, he immediately passed upon him the sentence of death. He ordered some to be beheaded, others to be hanged, still others to be dragged through the city and hanged in four different parts thereof; others to be disemboweled, and the entrails to be burned before them while they were still alive, and afterwards to be decapitated, quartered, and hanged in four parts of the city according to the greatness of the crime and its desert. . . .

# J. Huizinga: The Emotional Character of Late Medieval Life

Johan Huizinga (1872–1945), Dutch historian and philosopher, regarded the history of the fourteenth and fifteenth centuries as a period of termination. Rather than viewing the late Middle Ages as a prelude to the Renaissance, as was commonly done, he saw instead the end of a unique civilization. This reading, which contains the opening pages of his provocative work on the ebbing years of medieval society, is evidence of Huizinga's conviction that history should be presented in all its complexity, as a social reality and a state of mind. From J. Huizinga, *The Waning of the Middle Ages* (London: Edward Arnold, Ltd., 1924), pp. 1–6.

To the world when it was half a thousand years younger, the outlines of all things seemed more clearly marked than to us. The contrast between suffering and joy, between adversity and happiness, appeared more striking. All experience had yet to the minds of men the directness and absoluteness of the pleasure and pain of child-life. Every event, every action, was still embodied in expressive and solemn forms, which raised them to the dignity of a ritual. For it was not merely the great facts of birth, marriage and death which, by the sacredness of the sacrament, were raised to the rank of mysteries; incidents of less importance, like a journey, a task, a visit, were equally attended by a thousand formalities: benedictions, ceremonies, formulae.

Calamities and indigence were more afflicting than at present; it was more difficult to guard against them, and to find solace. Illness and health presented a more striking contrast; the cold and darkness of winter were more real evils. Honours and riches were relished with greater avidity and contrasted more vividly with surrounding misery. We, at the present day, can hardly understand the keenness with which a fur coat, a good fire on the hearth, a soft bed, a glass of wine, were formerly enjoyed.

Then, again, all things in life were of a proud or cruel publicity. Lepers sounded their rattles and went about in processions, beggars exhibited their deformity and their misery in churches. Every order and estate, every rank and profession, was distinguished by its costume. The great lords never moved about without a glorious display of arms and liveries, exciting fear and envy. Executions and other public acts of justice, hawking, marriages and funerals, were all announced by cries and processions, songs and music. The lover wore the colours of his lady; companions the emblem of their confraternity; parties and servants the badges or blazon of their lords. Between town and country, too, the contrast was very marked. A medieval town did not lose itself in extensive suburbs of factories and villas; girded by its walls, it stood forth as a compact whole, bristling with innumerable turrets. However tall and threatening the houses of noblemen or merchants might be, in the aspect of the town the lofty mass of the churches always remained dominant. . . .

All things presenting themselves to the mind in violent contrasts and impressive forms, lent a tone of excitement and of passion to everyday life and tended to produce that perpetual oscillation between despair and distracted joy, between cruelty and pious tenderness which characterize life in the Middle Ages.

One sound rose ceaselessly above the noises of busy life and lifted all things unto a sphere of order and serenity: the sound of bells. The bells were in daily life like good spirits, which by their familiar voices, now called upon the citizens to mourn and now to rejoice, now warned them of danger, now exhorted them to piety. They were known by their names: big Jacqueline, or the bell Roland. Every one knew the difference in meaning of the various ways of ringing. However continuous the ringing of the bells, people would seem not to have become blunted to the effect of their sound.

Throughout the famous judicial duel between two citizens of Valenciennes, in 1455, the big bell, "which is hideous to hear," says Chastellain, never stopped ringing. What intoxication the pealing of the bells of all the churches, and of all the monasteries of Paris, must have produced, sounding from morning till evening, and even during the night, when a peace was concluded or a pope elected.

The frequent processions, too, were a continual source of pious agitation. When the times were evil, as they often were, processions were seen winding along, day after day, for weeks on end. In 1412 daily processions were ordered in Paris, to implore victory for the king, who had taken up the oriflamme against the Armagnacs. They lasted from May to July, and were formed by ever-varying orders and corporations, going always by new roads, and always carrying different relics. The Burgher of Paris calls them "the most touching processions in the memory of men." People looked on or followed, "weeping piteously, with many tears, in great devotion." All went barefooted and fasting, councillors of the Parlement as well as the poorer citizens. Those who could afford it, carried a torch or a taper. A great many small children were always among them. Poor country-people of the environs of Paris came barefooted from afar to join the procession. And nearly every day the rain came down in torrents.

Then there were the entries of princes, arranged with all the resources of art and luxury belonging to the age. And, lastly, most frequent of all, one might almost say, uninterrupted, the executions. The cruel excitement and coarse compassion raised by an execution formed an important item in the spiritual food of the common people. They were spectacular plays with a moral. For horrible crimes the law invented atrocious punishments. At Brussels a young incendiary and murderer is placed in the centre of a circle of burning fagots and straw, and made fast to a stake by means of a chain running round an iron ring. He addresses touching words to the spectators, "and he so softened their hearts that every one burst into tears and his death was commended as the finest that was ever seen." During the Burgundian terror in Paris in 1411, one of the victims, Messire Mansart du Bois, being requested by the hangman, according to custom, to forgive him, is not only ready to do so with all his heart, but begs the executioner to embrace him. "There was a great multitude of people, who nearly all wept hot tears." . . .

Rarer than processions and executions were the sermons of itinerant preachers, coming to shake people by their eloquence. The modern reader of newspapers can no longer conceive the violence of impression caused by the spoken word on an ignorant mind lacking mental food. The Franciscan friar Richard preached in Paris in 1429 during ten consecutive days. He began at five in the morning and spoke without a break till ten or eleven, for the most part in the cemetery of the Innocents. When, at the close of his tenth sermon, he announced that it was to be his last, because he had no permission to preach more, "great and small wept as touchingly and as bitterly as if they were watching their best friends being buried; and so did he." Thinking that he would preach once more at Saint Denis on the Sunday, the people flocked thither on Saturday evening, and passed the night in the open, to secure good seats.

Another Minorite friar, Antoine Fradin, whom the magistrate of Paris had forbidden to preach, because he inveighed against the bad government, is guarded night and day in the Cordeliers monastery, by women posted around the building, armed with ashes and stones. In all the towns where the famous Dominican preacher Vincent Ferrer is expected, the people, the magistrates, the lower clergy, and even prelates and bishops, set out to greet him with joyous songs. He journeys with a numerous and ever-increasing following of adherents, who every night make a circuit of the town in procession, with chants and flagellations. Officials are appointed to take charge of lodging and feeding these multitudes. A large number of priests of various religious orders accompany him everywhere, to assist him in celebrating mass and in confessing the faithful. Also several notaries, to draw up, on the spot, deeds embodying the reconciliations which this holy preacher everywhere brings about. His pulpit has to be protected by a fence against the pressure of the congregation which wants to kiss his hand or habit. Work is at a stand-still all the time he preaches. He rarely fails to move his auditors to tears. When he spoke of the Last Judgment, of Hell, or of the Passion, both he and his hearers wept so copiously that he had to suspend his sermon till the sobbing had ceased. Malefactors threw themselves at his feet, before every one, confessing their great sins. One day, while he was preaching, he saw two persons, who had been condemned to death—a man and a woman—being led to execution. He begged to have the execution delayed, had them both placed under the pulpit, and went on with his sermon, preaching about their sins. After the sermon, only some bones were found in the place they had occupied, and the people were convinced that the word of the saint had consumed and saved them at the same time. . . .

The diatribes of the preachers against dissoluteness and luxury produced violent excitement which was translated into action. Long before Savonarola started bonfires of

The burning of vanities. St. Dominic watches as worldly books are thrown to the flames.

"vanities" at Florence, to the irreparable loss of art, the custom of these holocausts of articles of luxury and amusement was prevalent both in France and in Italy. At the summons of a famous preacher, men and women would hasten to bring cards, dice, finery, ornaments, and burn them with great pomp. Renunciation of the sin of vanity in this way had taken a fixed and solemn form of public manifestation, in accordance with the tendency of the age to invent a style of everything. All this general facility of emotions, of tears and spiritual upheavals, must be borne in mind in order to conceive fully how violent and high-strung was life at that period. . . .

# William Langer: Psychological Aspects of the Black Death

William Langer (1896– ) has had a distinguished career as a scholar and advisor to government. His range of interest in the historical spectrum is wide, as indicated by these excerpts from his presidential address to the American Historical Association in 1957. Examining the effect of the Black Death on the European psyche, he made an appeal that psychological factors in history be more closely examined. From William L. Langer, "The Next Assignment," *The American Historical Review* (Washington, 1958), Vol. LXIII, No. 2, Jan. 1958, pp. 292–300. Reprinted by permission of the author.

Western Europe seems to have been relatively free from major epidemics in the period from the sixth to the fourteenth century and it may well be that the revival of trade and the growth of towns, with their congestion and lack of sanitation, had much to do with the spread and establishment of the great mortal diseases like plague, typhus, syphilis, and influenza. At any rate, the Black Death was worse than anything experienced prior to that time and was, in all probability, the greatest single disaster that has ever befallen European mankind. In most localities a third or even a half of the population was lost within the space of a few months, and it is important to remember that the great visitation of 1348–1349 was only the beginning of a period of pandemic disease with a continuing frightful drain of population. It is hardly an exaggeration to say that for three hundred years Europe was ravaged by one disease or another, or more usually by several simultaneously, the serious outbreaks coming generally at intervals of five to ten years. . . .

The extensive records of the Black Death have been long and carefully studied, not only with reference to their medical aspects, but also in connection with the economic and social effects of so sudden and substantial a loss of population. The English population is estimated to have fallen from 3,700,000 in 1348 to 2,100,000 in 1400, the mortality rates of the period 1348–1375 far exceeding those of modern India. While the figures for continental countries are less complete, the available data suggests that the losses were comparable. Cities and towns suffered particularly, but in some areas as many as 40 per cent of the villages and hamlets were abandoned, the survivors joining with those of other settlements or moving to the depopulated towns where opportunity beckoned. Although a generation ago there was a tendency. . . to minimize the social effects of the Black Death, more recent writers . . . acknowledge that the great epidemic, if it did not evoke entirely new forces, did vastly accelerate those already operative. The economic progress of Europe, which had been phenomenal in the thirteenth century, came to a halt and was soon followed by a prolonged depression lasting until the mid-fifteenth century and in a sense even into the seventeenth.

I make only the most fleeting reference to these questions, because my chief concern, as I have said, is to determine, if possible, what the long-term psychological effects of this age of disease may have been. The immediate horrors of great epidemics have been vividly described by eminent writers from Thucydides to Albert Camus and have been pictured on canvas by famous artists like Raphael and Delacroix. At news of the approach of the disease a haunting terror seizes the population, in the Middle Ages leading on the one hand to great upsurges of repentance in the form of flagellant processions and on the other to a mad search for scapegoats, eventuating in large-scale pogroms of the Jews. The most striking feature of such visitations has always been the precipitate flight from the cities, in which not only the wealthier classes but also town officials, professors and teachers, clergy, and even physicians took part. The majority of the population, taking the disaster as an expression of God's wrath, devoted itself to penitential exercises, to merciful occupations, and to such good works as the repair of churches and the founding of religious houses. On the other hand, the horror and confusion in many places brought general demoralization and social breakdown. Criminal elements were quick to take over, looting the deserted

Three fifteenth-century versions of the Dance of Death. In the first, skeletal figures play a lively tune while others move gaily about. The caption reads (freely translated):

Now gentlemen here's our decree:
Jump about lively, for whipped you'll be.
Handsome or ugly, young and gray,
You must all in this dance for your sins pay.

In the second woodcut, Death, using a church organ as accompaniment, pulls along a priest who still clutches his moneybag. The third, by Hans Holbein the Elder (1460–1524), finds Death taking command of a poor plowman's team.

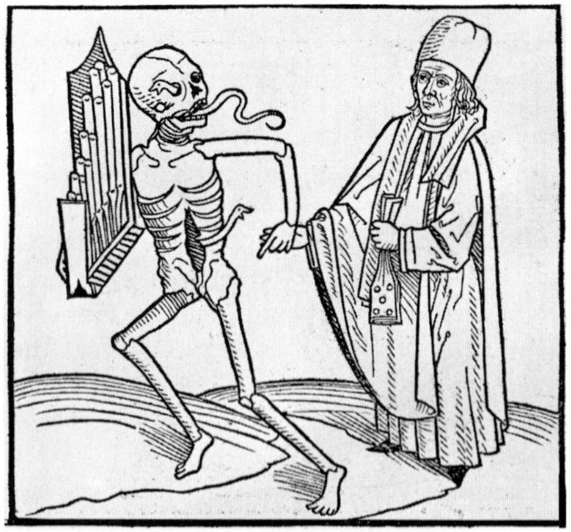

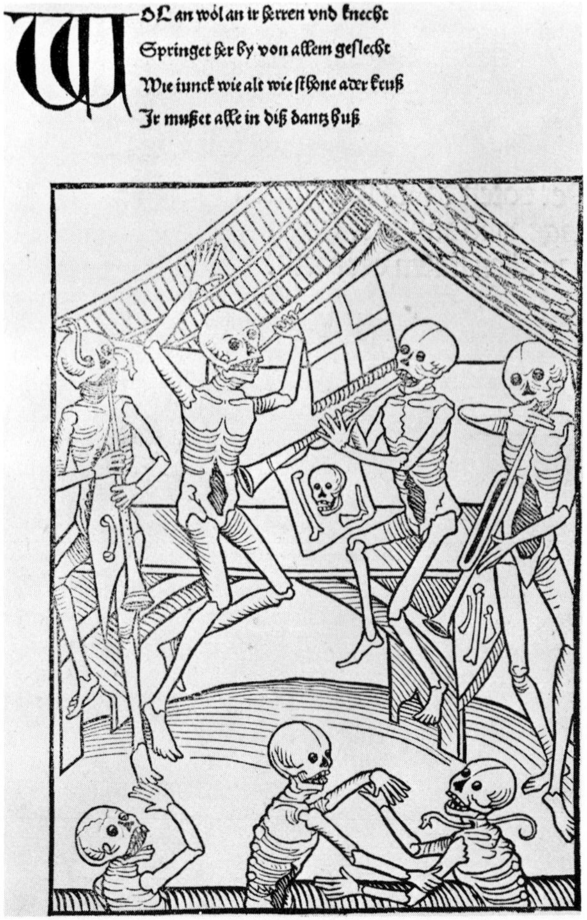

houses and even murdering the sick in order to rob them of their jewels. Many, despairing of the goodness and mercy of God, gave themselves over to riotous living, resolved, as Thucydides says, "to get out of life the pleasures which could be had speedily and which would satisfy their lusts, regarding their bodies and their wealth alike as transitory." Drunkenness and sexual immorality were the order of the day. "In one house," reported an observer of the London plague of 1665, "you might hear them roaring under the pangs of death, in the next tippling, whoring and belching out blasphemies against God." . . .

That unusual [psychological] forces were operative in the later Middle Ages seems highly probable. Indeed, a number of eminent historians have in recent years expatiated on the special character of this period. I will not attempt even to summarize the various interpretations of the temper of that age which have been advanced on one side or the other. None of the commentators, so far as I can see, have traced or determined the connection between the great and constantly recurring epidemics and the state of mind of much of Europe at that time. Yet this relationship would seem to leap to the eye. The age was marked, as all admit, by a mood of misery, depression, and anxiety, and by a general sense of impending doom. Numerous writers in widely varying fields have commented on the morbid preoccupation with death, the macabre interest in tombs, the gruesome predilection for the human corpse. Among painters the favorite themes were Christ's passion, the terrors of the Last Judgment, and the tortures of Hell, all depicted with ruthless realism and with an almost loving devotion to each repulsive detail. Altogether characteristic was the immense popularity of the Dance of Death woodcuts and murals, with appropriate verses, which appeared soon after the Black Death and which, it is agreed, expressed the sense of the immediacy of death and the dread of dying unshriven. Throughout the fifteenth and sixteenth centuries these pitilessly naturalistic pictures ensured man's constant realization of his imminent fate.

The origins of the Dance of Death theme have been generally traced to the Black Death and subsequent epidemics, culminating in the terror brought on by the outbreak of syphilis at the end of the fifteenth century. Is it unreasonable, then, to suppose that many of the other phenomena I have mentioned might be explained, at least in part, in the same way? We all recognize the late Middle Ages as a period of popular religious excitement or overexcitement, of pilgrimages and penitential processions, of mass preaching, of veneration of relics and adoration of saints, of lay piety and popular mysticism. It was apparently also a period of unusual immorality and shockingly loose living, which we must take as the continuation of the "devil-may-care" attitude of one part of the population. This the psychologists explain as the repression of unbearable feelings by accentuating the value of a diametrically opposed set of feelings and then behaving as though the latter were the real feelings. But the most striking feature of the age was an exceptionally strong sense of guilt and a truly dreadful fear of retribution, seeking expression in a passionate longing for effective intercession and in a craving for direct, personal experience of the Diety, as well as in a corresponding dissatisfaction with the Church and with the mechanization of the means of salvation as reflected, for example, in the traffic in indulgences.

These attitudes, along with the great interest in astrology, the increased resort to magic, and the startling spread of witchcraft and Satanism in the fifteenth century were, according to the precepts of modern psychology, normal reactions to the sufferings to which mankind in that period was subjected. It must be remembered that the Middle Ages, ignoring the teachings of the Greek physicians and relying entirely upon Scripture and the writings of the Church fathers, considered disease the scourge of God upon a sinful people. All men, as individuals, carry within themselves a burden of unconscious guilt and a fear of retribution which apparently go back to the curbing and repression of sexual and aggressive drives in childhood and the emergence of death wishes directed against the parents. This sense of sin, which is fundamental to all religion, is naturally enhanced by the impact of vast unaccountable and uncontrollable forces threatening the existence of each and every one. Whether or not there is also a primordial racial sense of guilt, as Freud argued in his *Totem and Taboo* (1913), it is perfectly clear that disaster and death threatening the entire community will bring on a mass emotional disturbance, based on a feeling of helpless exposure, disorientation, and common guilt. Furthermore, it seems altogether plausible to suppose that children, having experienced the terror of their parents and the panic of the community, will react to succeeding crises in a similar but even more intense manner. In other words, the anxiety and fear are transmitted from one generation to another, constantly aggravated.

Now it has long been recognized by psychologists that man, when crushed by unfathomable powers, tends to regress to infantile concepts and that, like his predecessor in primitive times, he has recourse to magic in his efforts to ward off evil and appease the angry deity. It is generally agreed that magic and religion are closely related, both deriving from fear of unknown forces and especially of death, and both reflecting an effort to ensure the preservation of the individual and the community from disease and other afflictions. Death-dealing epidemics like those of the late Middle Ages were bound to produce a religious revival, the more so as the established Church was proving itself ever less able to satisfy the yearning for more effective intercession and for a more personal relationship to God. . . .

# Chapter 5

## The Brink of the Modern World

With the waning of the Middle Ages came the breakdown of traditional Latin Christendom, tied to the soil, locked in European frontiers, united in a common faith, and organized in a single Church. Beyond the specific breakdown of medieval values, however, the period of the thirteenth through sixteenth centuries witnessed a great onslaught upon the structure of traditional society itself.

It was not a period that can be neatly labelled. "Commercial Revolution," "Renaissance," and "Reformation" touch upon its perimeter but do not catch the spirit of the whole. It was a time of bridging between what had been and what was to come, as is true in a sense of all historical time, but, in this case, what had been was the traditional world and what was to come, the modern.

As such, it was an age of marked contradictions. Towns grew up and capitalism developed, but the vast masses of society remained in rural isolation. Vestiges of feudalism contrasted with the efforts of kings to extend royal authority. Popes upheld the universality of the Church, while religious dissidents multiplied. On the one hand there was a marked striving for a renewal of religious values and a return to an earlier sense of community; on the other, materialism and individualism, grown from the affluence of the commercial revival and the subsequent loosening of traditional ties, had ever growing impact.

Capitalism, the growth of national states, the recoupling of links with ancient civilization, the "discovery" of man, and the rise of religious questioning are all hallmarks of these years, as well as that strong urge to exploit the non-Western world for the benefit of European interests, which we call the "Age of Discovery." Western man was thus developing an awareness of how he might move beyond the traditional Christian society but was still restrained by the limitations of the old world-view. He had been brought in his consciousness to the brink of the modern world.

TOPIC 29

# THE REEMERGENCE OF COMMERCE AND TOWNS

The first great crack in the wall of medieval traditionalism had been the revival of urban living in the eleventh and twelfth centuries. Fortified areas and trading centers multiplied, older Roman cities were revitalized, and many new towns were laid out, challenging the rigid social division of the feudal system. The serfs who fled their servile status and other persons who migrated to the towns expected to be treated as free men and resented existing feudal restraints on their movement and livelihood. That they were still without an acknowledged place in the social order was particularly galling to the growing number of merchants, whose material affluence often exceeded that of nobles dependent on the manorial economy. The readings trace the growth of the merchant class, the development of towns, and the aspirations for self-rule on the part of their inhabitants. The final readings shift to China, where, in the reportage of Marco Polo, a man typical of the traders who restlessly pushed out beyond the bounds of the known world, a glimpse is caught of the attraction to wealth and power that motivated the new class.

**Reading 152**

## Henri Pirenne: The Origins of the Merchant Class

Henri Pirenne (1862–1935), pioneering Belgian medieval historian, emphasized in his writing the historical role of the capitalist class. His theme is apparent in this reading which concerns the emergence of the medieval merchants and their efforts to win status within the feudal order. From *Medieval Cities* by Henri Pirenne (Copyright 1925, 1952 Princeton University Press; Princeton Paperback, 1969). Reprinted by permission of Princeton University Press.

### I

In certain countries, trade appears as an original and spontaneous phenomenon. This was the case, for example, at the dawn of history in Greece and Scandinavia. There, navigation was at least as old as agriculture. Everything led men to engage in it: the deep conformation of the coast-lines, the abundance of harbors, and the subtle attraction of those islands and low-lying shores which were visible on the horizon and which made a sea-faring life seem the more tempting because there was so little to be hoped for from a soil as barren as was that of the homeland. The proximity of older and poorly defended civilizations held out, in addition, the lure of rich plunder. Piracy was the initiator of maritime trade among the Greeks of the Homeric era, as among the Norse vikings; for a long time the two vocations developed in concert.

Nothing of the sort, however, was to be found in the Middle Ages. There was no sign of that heroic and barbarian occupation. The Germanic tribes that invaded the Roman provinces in the fifth century were complete strangers to a maritime life. They contented themselves with appropriating the soil, and the shipping of the Mediterranean continued, as in the past, to fill the peaceful role which had fallen to it under the Empire.

The Moslem invasion which caused its ruin and closed the sea provoked no reaction. The situation was taken for granted, and the continent of Europe, deprived of its traditional markets, remained an essentially rural civilization. The sporadic trade which Jews, peddlers and occasional merchants still carried on during the Carolingian era was too feeble and was too effectively discouraged by the invasions of the Norsemen and Saracens to lend support to the belief that it was the precursor of the commercial revival whose first symptoms were visible in the tenth century.

It would seem natural to suppose, at first glance, that a merchant class grew up little by little in the midst of the agricultural masses. Nothing, however, gives credence to that theory. In the social organization of the late Middle Ages, where each family from father to son was bound to the soil, it is hard to see what possibly could have induced men to exchange, for a livelihood made sure by the possession of the soil, the precarious livelihood of the trader. The love of gain and the desire to ameliorate one's condition must have carried, at best, very little weight with a population accustomed to a traditional way of living, having no contact with the outside world, in which no novelty, no curiosity stirred the imagination, and in which the spirit of initiative was probably completely lacking. Though they frequented the small local markets the peasants never made enough money out of them to be inspired with the desire for, or even to be inclined to envisage the possibility of, a manner of life based on trade. Theirs must have seemed to them merely a normal and customary occupation. The idea of selling one's land in order to procure liquid assets certainly did not occur to any of them. The state of society and the general outlook on life was entirely opposed to it. . . .

It was in the course of the tenth century that there reappeared in continental Europe a class of professional merchants whose progress, very slow at first, gathered speed as the following century moved forward. The increase in population, which began to be manifest at the same era, is certainly in direct relation to this phenomenon. It had as a result the detaching from the land an increasingly important number of individuals and committing them to that roving and hazardous existence which, in every agricultural civilization, is the lot of those who no longer find themselves with their roots in the soil. It multiplied the crowd of vagabonds drifting about all through society, living from day to day, by alms from the monasteries, hiring themselves out at harvest-time, enlisting in the armies in time of war and holding back from neither rapine nor pillage when occasion presented. It is among this crowd of foot-loose adventurers that the first adepts of trade must, without any doubt, be looked for.

Their manner of life naturally drove them towards all those localities where the affluence of the inhabitants gave them the hope of gain or offered some fortunate opening. If they assiduously took part in pilgrimages, they were certainly no less drawn by the ports, the markets, and the fairs. There they hired themselves out as sailors, as boatmen, as stevedores or porters. Energetic characters, tempered by the experience of a life full of the unexpected, must have abounded among them. Many knew foreign languages and were conversant with the customs and needs of divers lands. Let a lucky chance present itself—and heaven knows that chances are numerous in the life of a vagabond—they were remarkably well equipped to profit thereby. And a small profit, with skill and intelligence, can always be turned into a big profit. This must have been particularly true in an era when the insufficiency of communications and the relative rarity of merchandise offered for sale must have naturally kept prices at a very high level. Famines were multiplied throughout Europe, sometimes in one province and sometimes in another, by that inadequate system of communications, and increased still more the opportunities, for those who knew how to make use of them, of getting rich. A few timely sacks of wheat, transported to the right spot, sufficed for the realizing of huge profits. For a man, adroit and sparing no pains, Fortune then held out the prospect of fruitful operations. . . .

The nobility never had anything but disdain for these upstarts come from no one knew where, and whose insolent good fortune they could not bear. They were infuriated to see them better supplied with money than themselves; they were humiliated by being obliged to have recourse, in time of trouble, to the purse of these newly rich. Save in Italy, where aristocratic families did not hesitate to augment their fortunes by having an interest in commercial operations in the capacity of money-lender, the prejudice that it was degrading to engage in business remained deep-rooted in the heart of the feudal caste up to the time of the French Revolution.

As to the clergy, their attitude in regard to merchants was still more unfavorable. In the eyes of the Church, commercial life was dangerous to the safety of the soul. "The merchant," says a text attributed to St. Jerome, "can please God only with difficulty." Trade seemed to the canonists to be a form of usury. They condemned profit-seeking, which they confounded with avarice. . . . Every form of speculation seemed to them a sin. And this severity was not entirely caused by the strict interpretation of Christian morality. Very likely, it should also be attributed to the conditions under which the Church existed. The subsistence of the Church, in fact, depended exclusively on that [manorial] organization which, as has been seen above, was so foreign to the idea of enterprise and profit. If to this be added the ideal of poverty which Clunisian mysticism gave to religious fervor, it can be readily understood why the Church took a defiant and hostile attitude toward the commercial revival which must, from the very first, have seemed to it a thing of shame and a cause of anxiety.

We must admit, however, that this attitude was not without its benefits. It certainly resulted in preventing the passion for gain from spreading without limit; it protected, in a certain measure, the poor from the rich, debtors from creditors. The scourge of debts, which in Greek and Roman antiquity so sorely afflicted the people, was spared the social order of the Middle Ages, and it may well be that the Church contributed largely to that happy result. The universal prestige it enjoyed served as a moral check-rein. If it was not strong enough to subject the traders to the doctrine of "fair price," it was strong enough to restrain them from giving way entirely to greediness for profits. They were certainly very uneasy over the peril to which their way of living exposed their eternal salvation. The fear of the future life tormented their conscience. Many there were who, on their death beds, founded by their wills charitable institutions or appropriated a part of their wealth to reimburse sums unjustly acquired. . . .

## II

The legal status of the merchants eventually gave them a thoroughly singular place in that society which they astonished in so many respects. By virtue of the wandering existence they led, they were everywhere regarded as foreigners. No one knew the origins of these eternal travellers. Certainly the majority among them were born of non-free parents, from whom they had early taken leave in order to launch upon adventures. But serfdom was not to be presumed: it had to be proven. The law necessarily treated as a free man one who could not be ascribed to a master. It therefore came about that it was necessary to treat the merchants, most of whom were without doubt the sons of serfs, as if they had always enjoyed freedom. In detaching themselves from their natal soil they had freed themselves in fact. In the midst of a social organization where the populace was attached to the land and where everyone was dependent upon a liege lord, they presented the strange picture of circulating everywhere without being claimed by anyone. They did not demand freedom; it was conceded to them because no one could prove that they did not already enjoy it. They acquired it, so to speak, by usage and limitation. In short, just as agrarian civilization had made of the peasant a man whose normal state was servitude, trade made of the merchant a man whose normal condition was liberty. From that time on, in place of being subject to seignorial and demesnial jurisdiction, he was answerable only to public jurisdiction. Alone competent to try him were the tribunals which still kept, above the multitude of private courts, the old framework of the judicial constitution of the Frankish State.

Public authority at the same time took him under its protection. The local princes whose task it was to preserve, in their territories, peace and public order—to which pertained the policing of the highways and the safeguarding of travellers—extended their tutelage over the merchants. In doing so they did nothing more than to continue the tradition of the State, the powers of which they had usurped. In that agricultural empire of his, Charlemagne himself had given careful attention to the maintenance of the freedom of circulation. He had issued edicts in favor of pilgrims and traders, Jew or Christian, and the capitularies of his successors attest to the fact that they remained faithful to that policy. The emperors of the House of Saxony followed suit in Germany, and the kings of France, after they came into power, did likewise. The princes had, furthermore, every interest in attracting numerous merchants to their countries, whither they brought a new animation and where they augmented bountifully the revenues from the market-tolls. The counts early took active measures against highwaymen, watching over the good conduct of the fairs and the security of the routes of communication. In the eleventh century great progress had been made and the chroniclers state that there were regions where one could travel with a sack full of gold without running the risk of being despoiled. On its part, the Church punished highwaymen with excommunication, and the Truces of God, in which it took the initiative in the tenth century, protected the merchants in particular.

But it was not enough that merchants be placed under the safeguard and the jurisdiction of the public authority. The novelty of their profession had further consequences. It forced a law, made for a civilization based on agriculture, to become more flexible and to adapt itself to the fundamental needs which this novelty imposed upon it. Judicial procedure, with its rigid and traditional formalism, with its delays, with its methods of proof as primitive as the duel, with its abuse of the absolutory oath, with its "ordeals" which left to chance the outcome of a trial, was for the merchants a perpetual nuisance. They needed a simpler legal system, more expeditious and more equitable. At the fairs and markets they elaborated among themselves a commercial code (*jus mercatorum*) of which the oldest traces may be noted by the beginning of the eleventh century. Most probably it was introduced very early into the legal practice, at least for suits between merchants. It must have constituted for them a sort of personal law, the benefits of which the judges had no motive for refusing them. The contemporary texts which make allusion to it unfortunately do not make clear its terms. There is, however, no doubt but that it was a collection of usages born of business experience and which spread from place to place commensurately with the spread of trade itself. The great fairs whither came, periodically, merchants from divers countries and which had a special tribunal charged with the rendering of speedy justice, must have seen from the very first the elaboration of a sort of commercial jurisprudence, the same everywhere despite the differences in country, language, and national laws.

The merchant thus seems to have been not only a free man but a privileged man to boot. Like the cleric and the noble, he enjoyed a law of exception. Like them, he escaped the demesnial and seignorial authority which continued to bear down upon the peasants.

# The Rise of Towns

From *Economic History of Europe*, 3d ed., by S. B. Clough & C. W. Cole. Copyright ©, 1952, by D. C. Heath & Co., a Division of Raytheon Education Co., Boston, Mass.

It was indeed in the Italian towns that the commerce of medieval western Europe came to life, and it was a commerce born of, based on, and carried on by towns. In every country the rise of towns and cities was one of the most important phenomena of the middle ages. It can be explained only by the fact that the rebirth of commerce, local and distant, necessitated the creation of trade centers and gave them the opportunity to engage in industrial production for a market which slowly grew larger and larger.

In Italy many of the Roman towns never disappeared, and it required only the stimulus of the increasing trade to reawaken them into vigorous life. Rome, Naples, Ravenna, Florence, Milan, Verona, Lucca, Pisa, Genoa, among others, enjoyed some sort of continuous existence from Roman times on into the middle ages. Venice, probably no more than a fishing village in Roman days, was gradually peopled after the fifth century by refugees who fled from the mainland during the invasions. In other lands, too, Roman cities, towns, villages, and camps, and even the early non-Roman towns of the Germans, were inhabited continuously, and were ready to grow and flourish when opportunity offered.

## THE BURG

Outside of Italy many towns owed their origin not to Roman survivals but to medieval conditions. During the troublous times of local wars and invasion by Saracens or Norsemen, some kind of fortified retreat was almost essential for a locality. A stockade with a moat around it and a fortified tower inside was a crude but effective safeguard against marauding bands. Such a place was most often called a *burgus,* and in one form or another the word has survived in many modern town names (Edinburgh, Hamburg, Peterborough, Luxembourg, Bourg-en-Bresse, etc.). Often such a burg would be the home of a bishop or a count or a prince. Gradually from his needs, his tax collections, trade sprang up and the burg might become a market center to which the neighborhood sent its surplus produce. Indeed, the needs of trade and the needs of defense were the twin origins of many towns. A town might grow up under the wing of a castle or a monastery that offered some protection, but it might also rise at the crossing of two roads or trade routes, at the head of navigation on a stream, at the junction of two rivers, or on a good harbor. There were thousands of burgs or villages clustered beside strongholds. Those that grew to be important usually had some advantage of site or general location. . . .

The process by which a burg, castle, monastery, shrine, or church grew into a town was varied. Often the presence of a lord or church-

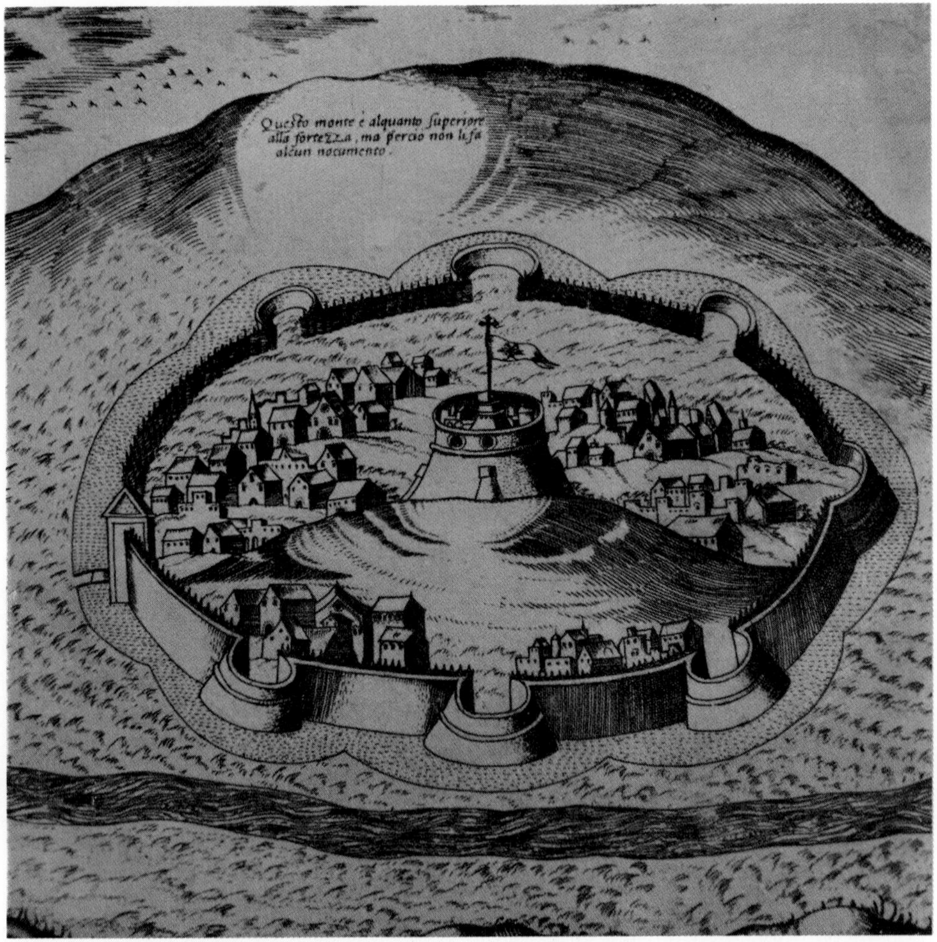
Questo monte è alquanto superiore alla fortezza, ma percio non li fa alcun nocumento.

The fortified town of Agria in Hungary (1368) provides a good example of a medieval burg. Moat and wall surround a central tower on a hill about which the houses cluster.

Medieval streets are still found in the old quarters of European cities today.

men encouraged the creation of a small but regular market, or perhaps merely stimulated a little local market which had had some sort of existence for centuries. Slowly traders gathered and built their huts in the shadow of the wall while the lord smiled on them, for from them he collected tolls and dues. The presence of traders, even though some of them might be peddlers who returned only from time to time, attracted other residents—people to supply them with food and clothing, drink and lodging. . . .

Because most medieval towns were within walls—first of palisades and earthwork, later of stone—they were crowded, huddled together as if they remembered, in fear, the times of invasion and war. The streets were narrow, often only six or eight feet wide. To gain more floor space, the upper stories of the houses projected over the street until they nearly met in the middle. Pigs ran in the streets and were the chief means of garbage disposal. There were no street lights. There were only open sewers (if any) awaiting the next rainfall for a flushing. Cows and horses were stabled in sheds built into or on to the houses. Stores opened directly on the streets, each with a wooden window of which half was raised to make a canopy, and half was lowered to make a counter. The population was often as dense as in a modern city with much taller buildings. The medieval town was a hustling, lusty, dirty, crowded place. Some chroniclers report that such a town could be smelled from more than a mile away.

From a modern point of view, medieval towns and cities were never very large in population. In the fourteenth century it is likely that only Paris, Palermo, Venice, and Florence had as many as 100,000 inhabitants. A few more, such as London and Milan, had about 50,000. But a town of 20,000 was considered good-sized, and many important centers were much smaller.

Despite its walls, the medieval town was not cut off so distinctly from the surrounding countryside as is a twentieth century city. As a town grew, peasants from round about moved in for protection and for social life, but continued to cultivate their fields. Towns that grew out of villages retained their old common fields and pastures, and some of the townsmen would fare forth each day to work in them. Villagers from neighboring manors brought their produce into the town once a week to sell in the market, and stayed a while to gossip, drink a cup of wine, or buy some needed article. It is easy to forget this rural side of town life, but it was important. Cambridge was still girt about by common fields in the seventeenth century. At Norwich, in the sixteenth century, the weavers had to stop work each year to help with the harvest. Even in London the Husting Court was suspended in harvest time. One of the chief thoroughfares in Ghent is still called Field Street.

Yet in the feúdal countryside the slowly growing towns were in some ways alien. In the earlier stages, the feudal lords tended to treat them like overgrown manors. They taxed them, subjected them to the feudal courts, and preserved the banalities, endeavoring on the one hand to fit them into the existing order of things, and on the other to get as much revenue from them as possible. Indeed, a town was so profitable to its lord that many a noble and churchman encouraged the founding of new towns (villes neuves, etc.) on his lands. In the course of time, however, as the towns grew in size and strength the feudal bonds irked them more and more. Gradually they shook themselves loose from the more burdensome forms of control. In some areas, especially in England and France, towns developing on royal lands gained considerable freedom early, for the kings saw in these rising centers a power which could be set against the overweening authority of the great nobles; but for most towns the acquisition of freedom was the fruit of a long, hard struggle.

From early days, most of the merchants were freemen; even if serfs by birth, since they traveled far from home, they were not likely to be recaptured by their lords. But the artisans, laborers, and other workers who came in from the neighborhood were usually serfs still within reach of their lords. Furthermore, the children of a free merchant and a serf wife were apt to be considered serfs. What the towns wanted was, first, personal freedom for the inhabitants, second, their own court which would enforce town, merchant law, not feudal land law; and third, exemption from the feudal dues, taxes, and restrictions. In the eleventh century the towns began to be strong enough to gain their demands, though the merchants of Venice won power even earlier (976). The Italian cities led the way. Milan revolted against its lord, the archbishop, in 1057 and eventually secured the right to have its own magistrates, who were called consuls. Lucca had a city court by 1068. Before many years Cremona, Bologna, Florence, Genoa, Pavia, and other towns had gained some degree of self-government.

From Italy the movement spread northward. Marseilles had consuls by 1128, as did Nimes and Arles shortly after. In Flanders the movement was almost contemporaneous with that in Italy. Cambrai revolted against its bishop in 1077 and formed a *commune* or municipal government, and before the middle of the twelfth century other cities of the Low Countries and northern France had followed suit. Many towns, especially in England, bought their way to freedom. For the varied feudal dues they were able to substitute a single payment (*firma burgi*) which they raised themselves by municipal taxes, thus excluding the tax agents of the lord. Many a noble anxious to raise money for a crusade sold municipal rights or privileges to a town on his land for a lump sum and annual payments thereafter. In other instances, from Italy to Germany, the winning of town freedom was the result of a long and often bloody struggle between the commune desirous of the new freedom and the lord anxious to maintain his old rights. By the thirteenth century many towns had won from their overlords charters granting them the right to have their own institutions, and it was generally conceded that the town air made men free. A serf who stayed in a town for a year and a day without being reclaimed by his lord was considered a freeman. The towns were largely self-governing even though they might give dues or allegiance to king or noble; and the burgher owed his first loyalty, his patriotism, to his town. It was his home, his country. The townsman was free. He was to a large degree outside the feudal system. He belonged to a new and growing class—the middle class, the burghers, the *bourgeoisie,* which was to increase in importance until at last it overthrew the old feudal system. . . .

Gildsmen in their shops in a late fourteenth-century town scene. From left to right are tailors, furriers, a barber, and a druggist.

To protect their interests and preserve their local monopoly the merchants and tradesmen of a town from the early days joined together in an organization usually called a gild merchant or merchant gild. This gild was often older than the town charter. In fact, it was frequently the merchant gild which waged the fight or raised the funds that secured a charter from the overlord. The gild did not include all townsmen but was composed rather of the merchants and tradesmen to the exclusion of nobles, serfs, ecclesiastics, and ordinary workmen. In Saint-Omer there was a merchant gild by 1050, with a head to enforce discipline, with regular meetings for eating, drinking, and deliberation, with funds for community purposes and the assistance of sick members, and with a gildhall in which to meet. Other towns of Flanders probably had similar organizations, and during the next century and a half merchant gilds were organized in most of the important towns of France, Flanders, England, and Germany.

Because a gild merchant included all the important businessmen of a town, it was able to maintain a real monopoly which it relaxed only on the occasions of markets and fairs. Ordinarily only a gildsman could buy, sell, or manufacture goods in a town. An outsider could do business only with gildsmen. Certain goods could be exported only by gild members. A foreigner passing through might be forced to sell his wares to gildsmen. The merchant gilds negotiated with the overlord on behalf of the town. They dominated the town government. In England, for example, the municipal government and the merchant gild became so interlocked that it was sometimes

One of the primary functions of the gild was to maintain standards. Here a regal figure, symbolic of the spirit of the gild, oversees the work of a stone-mason chiseling a capital for a column, perhaps intended for a church, and of a carpenter drilling with an auger.

impossible to distinguish between them. The merchant gild carried on negotiations and made treaties with towns near-by and in distant countries, often getting special and important privileges. If a member got into trouble on his travels, the gild paid his fine, or bargained for his release, or paid his debts. If a town treated visiting merchants unfairly, their home gilds retaliated by seizing merchants or goods from the offending place. The gild had a chapel in the local church and took part in religious ceremonies. It provided impressive funerals for its deceased members and took care of their widows. It supervised the regulations for markets, business, weights, measures, and quality. In short, until it declined in importance after the thirteenth century, the merchant gild functioned as the organization that took care of all the interests of the businessmen of the town.

# Helmar Krueger: Impact of the Crusades on Commerce

Helmar Krueger (1904–      ), specialist in medieval economic history, here points out the role played by Italian townsmen and merchants in exploiting the commercial possibilities of a Mediterranean reopened in the wake of the Crusades. From Helmar C. Krueger, "Economic Aspects of Expanding Europe" in *Twelfth-Century Europe and the Foundations of Modern Society,* ed. Marshall Clagett, Gaines Post, and Robert Reynolds (Madison, Wis.: University of Wisconsin Press, 1961), pp. 71–73.

To the Italian merchants the Crusades always appeared to be extraordinary economic opportunities. From the very start the Italians gained financial rewards. Their ships carried the crusaders and their equipment, even their horses, to the Holy Land, and then supplied the Crusaders with food, drink, and, on occasion, with timber, manpower, and siege machinery. Genoa and Pisa commandeered all possible ships in their domains for transport purposes and ordered the construction of more and larger vessels. The transport services were a source of immediate income for the communes, merchants, and shipowners. . . .

In at least a dozen coastal towns of the Levant the Italians possessed throughout most of the twelfth century residential and commercial quarters, from which they gained an income from rentals, leases, harbor dues, and court fines. In these centers the Italian merchants carried on their trade with the European colonists and feudal residents, with Arab traders, and with their associates and agents who worked in the area. The Italian quarters of the Levant became the centers of exchange for Oriental and European goods and markets for the western imports that increased as the century wore on. The Oriental trade was highly profitable and another source of capital in the new money economy of the period. The Crusades were the strongest influence on the development of medieval trade and industry.

Something needs to be said about the Crusades and the general structure of medieval business and capitalism. First of all, the Crusades created a situation in which capital appeared and circulated. Feudal, clerical, and royal participants mortgaged and sold their holdings to obtain money to buy equipment, hire soldiers, and pay for passage. In some instances they melted down their plate and jewelry. . . . Guibert de Nogent wrote: "As everyone hastened to take the road of God, each hurried to change into money everything that was not of use for the journey, and the price was fixed not by the seller, but by the buyer." Generally, as already indicated, this capital went to the Italian merchants and shippers for transportation or other services connected with the venture. Eventually, numerous other people received jobs and wages, including armorers, shipbuilders, ropemakers, and vintners. Obviously, much of the capital paid to the Italians covered the cost of materials and labor, but a considerable part was profit and gain. In turn, much of the profit was reinvested in the Levantine trade, which also was extremely lucrative. The Crusades had promoted the capitalistic cycle of capital, investment, profit, and reinvestment of profit for further profit and capital. The Crusades, cities, and commerce initiated a money economy which threatened and certainly modified the older land economy of western Europe.

Another capitalistic instrument given impetus by the Crusades was credit. Credit, after all, was based on the expectancy of income and profit by the borrower. Many participants in the Crusades bought their equipment or obtained loans on credit, expecting to profit from the material rewards which Urban had promised. In the Holy Land many again resorted to loans from the Templars and Hospitallers, hoping to repay from their ventures in the Near East or from their properties in western Europe. The rulers of course, could expect to pay their loans from tax receipts or new crusade aids. . . .

Similarly, the Crusades gave to commerce an international aspect. They again opened up the entire Mediterranean Sea to Christian ships and trade and provided an entry into the trade with the Near and Far East. The crusaders' acquaintance with Arab and Moslem customs created a demand for Oriental goods in Christian Europe, so that dyes, spices, pearls, and alum became regular western imports from the Italian quarters in the East. Henry of Champagne acknowledged some gifts of Saladin with: "You know that your robes and turbans are far from being held in scorn among us. I will certainly wear your gifts." At the same time the growing industries of the West gave the Italian merchants the chance to carry western goods, especially cloths, eastward to exchange them for the Levantine goods, and the continued residence of westerners in the East created a demand for those western wares. . . .

# List of Rules for the Spurriers' Gild (1345)

This list of rules for the London craftsmen who made spurs for horsemen is typical of medieval gild regulations. From James H. Robinson, *Readings in European History* (Boston, 1904), Vol. I, pp. 409–411.

Be it remembered, that on Tuesday, the morrow of St. Peter's bonds, in the nineteenth year of the reign of King Edward III, the articles underwritten were read before John Hammond, mayor, Roger de Depham, recorder, and the other aldermen; and seeing that the same were deemed befitting, they were accepted and enrolled in these words.

In the first place, that no one of the trade of spurriers shall work longer than from the beginning of the day until curfew rings out at the church of St. Sepulcher, without Newgate; by reason that no man can work so neatly by night as by day. And many persons of the said trade, who compass how to practice deception in their work, desire to work by night rather than by day; and then they introduce false iron, and iron that has been cracked, for tin, and also they put gilt on false copper, and cracked.

And further, many of the said trade are wandering about all day, without working at all at their trade; and then, when they have become drunk and frantic, they take to their work, to the annoyance of the sick, and all their neighborhood as well, by reason of the broils that arise between them and the strange folk who are dwelling among them. And then they blow up their fires so vigorously, that their forges begin all at once to blaze, to the great peril of themselves and of all the neighborhood around. And then, too, all the neighbors are much in dread of the sparks, which so vigorously issue forth in all directions from the mouths of the chimneys in their forges.

By reason thereof it seems unto them that working by night should be put an end to, in order to avoid such false work and such perils; and therefore the mayor and the aldermen do will, by the assent of the good folk of the said trade and for the common profit, that from henceforth such time for working, and such false work made in the trade, shall be forbidden. And if any person shall be found in the said trade to do the contrary hereof, let him be amerced [fined], the first time in forty pence, one half to go to the use of the Chamber of the Guildhall of London, and the other half to the use of the said trade; the second time, in half a mark; and the third time, in ten shillings, to the use of the same Chamber and trade; and the fourth time, let him forswear the trade forever.

Also that no one of the said trade shall hang his spurs out on Sundays, or on any other days that are double feasts; but only a sign indicating his business; and such spurs as they shall so sell, they are to show and sell within their shops, without exposing them without or opening the doors or windows of their shops, on the pain aforesaid.

Also, that no one of the said trade shall keep a house or shop to carry on his business, unless he is free of the city; and that no one shall cause to be sold, or exposed for sale, any manner of old spurs for new ones, or shall garnish them or change them for new ones.

Also, that no one of the said trade shall take an apprentice for a less term than seven years, and such apprentice shall be enrolled according to the usages of the said city. . . .

Also, that no alien of another country, or foreigner of this country, shall follow or use the said trade, unless he is enfranchised before the mayor, aldermen, and chamberlain; and that, by witness and surety of the good folk of the said trade, who will go surety for him, as to his loyalty and his good behavior.

Also, that no one of the said trade shall work on Saturdays, after *nones* has been rung out in the city; and not from that hour until the Monday morning following.

# Merchants Riot in Cologne (1074)

The rebellion described in this reading is an example of the reaction to the pretensions of the lords that usually led to the gaining of self-government for the cities. Such rebellions frequently began with merchant discontent. Cologne was one of the three major episcopal cities in Germany and an important Rhine shipping center. The reference to Worms at the end of the reading concerns a similar uprising in a neighboring episcopal city. From the *Annals of Lambert of Hersfeld*, V, pp. 211 ff. in Oliver Thatcher & E. H. McNeal, *A Source Book for Medieval History* (New York, 1905), pp. 585–586.

The archbishop spent Easter in Cologne with his friend, the bishop of Münster, whom he had invited to celebrate this festival with him. When the bishop was ready to go home, the archbishop ordered his servants to get a suitable boat ready for him. They looked all about, and finally found a good boat which belonged to a rich merchant of the city, and demanded it for the archbishop's use. They ordered it to be got ready at once and threw out all the merchandise with which it was loaded. The merchant's servants, who had charge of the boat, resisted, but the archbishop's men threatened them with violence unless they immediately obeyed. The merchant's servants hastily ran to their lord and told him what had happened to the boat, and asked him what they should do. The merchant had a son who was both bold and strong. He was related to the great families of the city, and, because of his character, very popular. He hastily collected his servants and as many of the young men of the city as he could, rushed to the boat, ordered the servants of the archbishop to get out of it, and violently ejected them from it. The advocate of the city was called in, but his arrival only increased the tumult, and the merchant's son drove him off and put him to flight. The friends of both parties seized their arms and came to their aid, and it looked as if there were going to be a great battle fought in the city. The news of the struggle was carried to the archbishop, who immediately sent men to quell the riot, and being very angry, he threatened the rebellious young men with dire punishment in the next session of court. Now the archbishop was endowed with all virtues, and his uprightness in all matters, both of the state and of the church, had often been proved. But he had one vice. When he became angry, he could not control his tongue, but overwhelmed everybody, without distinction, with bitter upbraidings and violent vituperation. When his anger had passed, he regretted his fault and reproached himself for it. The riot in the city was finally quieted a little, but the young man, who was very angry as well as elated over his first success, kept on making all the disturbance he could. He went about the city making speeches to the people about the harsh government of the archbishop, and accused him of laying unjust burdens on the people, of depriving innocent persons of their property, and of insulting honorable citizens with his violent and offensive words. . . . It was not difficult for him to raise a mob. . . . Besides, they all regarded it as a great and glorious deed on the part of the people of Worms that they had driven out their bishop because he was governing them too rigidly. And since they were more numerous and wealthy than the people of Worms, and had arms, they disliked to have it thought that they were not equal to the people of Worms in courage, and it seemed to them a disgrace to submit like women to the rule of the archbishop, who was governing them in a tyrannical manner. . . .

# Marco Polo Tells Tales of Cathay

Marco Polo (1254–1324) was born in Venice and in 1271 accompanied his merchant father and uncle to the vast Asian empire of the Mongol conqueror Kublai Khan. There the Polos stayed for twenty-four years and rose high in the esteem of the emperor whom they served on various public missions that carried them across China. Finally they returned in 1295 to Venice (after traveling for three years), where they amazed their skeptical friends and relatives with sumptuous silks and precious stones carried back with them to Europe. Even more amazing were the fanciful tales of fabulous Cathay (as China then was called) which Marco Polo told. When a few years later he was captured in a naval battle between Venice and Genoa and imprisoned for several months, he utilized the opportunity to write down his adventures, excerpts from which form this reading. The account of the riches to be had in far-away places served as a spur to generations of adventurers and businessmen who dreamed of excitement and easy wealth. For did not Polo himself on his deathbed, when begged to retract some of his more extreme descriptions, sigh, "I have not told half of what I saw." From *The Book of Ser Marco Polo the Venetian concerning the Kingdoms and Marvels of the East,* trans. and ed. Henry Yule (London, 1875).

## I

You must know that for three months of the year, to wit December, January, and February, the Great Khan resides in the capital city of Cathay, which is called Cambaluc and which is at the north-eastern extremity of the country. In that city stands his great palace, and now I will tell you what it is like. . . .

The hall of the palace is so large that it could easily dine 6000 people; and it is quite a marvel to see how many rooms there are besides. The building is altogether so vast, so rich, and so beautiful, that no man on earth could design anything superior to it. The outside of the roof also is all coloured with vermilion and yellow and green and blue and other hues, which are fixed with a varnish so fine and exquisite that they shine like crystal, and lend a resplendent lustre to the palace as seen for a great way round. This roof is made, too, with such strength and solidity that it is fit to last for ever.

On the interior side of the palace are large buildings with halls and chambers, where the Emperor's private property is placed, such as his treasures of gold, silver, gems, pearls, and gold plate, and in which reside the ladies and concubines. There he occupies himself at his own convenience, and no one else has access. . . .

You must know that the City of Cambaluc hath such a multitude of houses, and such a vast population inside the walls and outside, that it seems quite past all possibility. There is a suburb outside each of the gates, which are twelve in number; and these suburbs are so great that they contain more people than the city itself, for the suburb of one gate spreads in width till it meets the suburb of the next, whilst they extend in length some three or four miles. In those suburbs lodge the foreign merchants and travellers, of whom there are always great numbers who have come to bring presents to the Emperor, or to sell articles at Court, or because the city affords so good a mart to attract traders. There

are in each of the suburbs, to a distance of a mile from the city, numerous fine hostelries for the lodgment of merchants from different parts of the world, and a special hostelry is assigned to each description of people, as if we should say there is one for the Lombards, another for the Germans, and a third for the Frenchmen. And thus there are as many good houses outside of the city as inside, without

The wealth and magnificence of China during the Western Middle Ages can be seen in these two works of art. The thirteenth-century ink drawing depicts the imperial palace at Loyang. The procession of courtiers at a New Year's reception was painted in the eleventh century.

counting those that belong to the great lords and barons, which are very numerous.

You must know that it is forbidden to bury any dead body inside the city. If the body be that of an Idolater it is carried out beyond the city and suburbs to a remote place assigned for the purpose, to be burnt. And if it be of one belonging to a religion the custom of which is to bury, such as the Christian, the Saracen, or what not, it is also carried out beyond the suburbs to a distant place assigned for the purpose. And thus the city is preserved in a better and more healthy state.

Moreover, no public woman resides inside the city, but all such abide outside in the suburbs. And 'tis wonderful what a vast number of these there are for the foreigners; it is a certain fact that there are more than twenty thousand of them living by prostitution. And that so many can live in this way will show you how vast is the population.

Guards patrol the city every night in parties of thirty or forty, looking out for any persons who may be abroad at unseasonable hours, i.e. after the great bell hath stricken thrice. If they find any such person he is immediately taken to prison, and examined next morning by the proper officers. If these find him guilty of any misdemeanour they order him a proportionate beating with the stick. Under this punishment people sometimes die; but they adopt it in order to eschew bloodshed; for their Bacsis say that it is an evil thing to shed man's blood.

To this city also are brought articles of greater cost and rarity and in greater abundance of all kinds than to any other city in the world. For people of every description and from every region bring things (including all the costly wares of India, as well as the fine and precious goods of Cathay itself with its provinces), some for the sovereign, some for the court, some for the city which is so great, some for the crowds of barons and knights, some for the great hosts of the Emperor which are quartered round about; and thus between court and city the quantity brought in is endless.

As a sample, I tell you, no day in the year passes that there do not enter the city a thousand cart-loads of silk alone, from which are made quantities of cloth of silk and gold, and of other goods. And this is not to be wondered at; for in all the countries round about there is no flax, so that everything has to be made of silk. It is true, indeed, that in some parts of the country there is cotton and hemp, but not sufficient for their wants. This, however, is not of much consequence, because silk is so abundant and cheap, and is a more valuable substance than either flax or cotton.

Round about this great city of Cambaluc there are some two hundred other cities at various distances, from which traders come to sell their goods and buy others for their lords; and all find means to make their sales and purchases, so that the traffic of the city is passing great. . . .

## II

All merchants arriving from India or other countries, and bringing with them gold or silver or gems and pearls, are prohibited from selling to anyone but the Emperor. He has twelve experts chosen for this business, men of shrewdness and experience in such affairs; these appraise the articles, and the Emperor then pays a liberal price for them in those pieces of paper. The merchants accept his price readily, for in the first place they would not get so good an one from anybody else, and secondly they are paid without any delay. And with this paper-money they can buy what they like anywhere over the Empire, whilst it is also vastly lighter to carry about on their journeys. And it is a truth that the merchants will several times in the year bring wares to the amount of 400,000 bezants, and the Grand Sire pays for all in that paper. So he buys such a quantity of those precious things every year that his treasure is endless, whilst all the time the money he pays away costs him nothing at all. Moreover several times in the year proclamation is made through the city that any one who may have gold or silver or gems or pearls, by taking them to the Mint shall get a handsome price for them. And the owners are glad to do this, because they would find no other purchaser to give so large a price. Thus the quantity they bring in is marvellous, though those who do not choose to do so may let it alone. Still, in this way, nearly all the valuables in the country come into the Khan's possession.

When any of those pieces of paper are spoilt—not that they are so very flimsy neither—the owner carries them to the Mint, and by paying three per cent on the value he gets new pieces in exchange. And if any baron, or any one else soever, hath need of gold or silver or gems or pearls in order to make plate or girdles or the like, he goes to the Mint and buys as much as he list, paying in this paper-money. . . .

It is a fact that all over the country of Cathay there is a kind of black stones existing in beds in the mountains, which they dig out and burn like firewood. If you supply the fire with them at night, and see that they are well kindled, you will find them still alight in the morning; and they make such capital fuel that no other is used throughout the country. It is true that they have plenty of wood also, but they do not burn it, because those stones burn better and cost less.

Moreover with that vast number of people, and the number of hot-baths that they maintain—for every one has such a bath at least three times a week, and in winter if possible every day, whilst every nobleman and man of wealth has a private bath for his own use—the wood would not suffice for the purpose.

You must know that when the Emperor sees that corn is cheap and abundant, he buys up large quantities, and has it stored in all his provinces in great granaries, where it is so well looked after that it will keep for three or four years.

And this applies, let me tell you, to all kinds of corn, whether wheat, barley, millet, rice, panic, or what not, and when there is any scarcity of a particular kind of corn he causes that to be issued. And if the price of the corn is at one bezant the measure, he lets them have it at a bezant for four measures, or at whatever price will produce general cheapness; and every one can have food in this way. And by this providence of the Emperor's, his people can never suffer from dearth. He does the same over his whole Empire; causing these supplies to be stored everywhere according to calculation of the wants and necessities of the people.

# Nathaniel Peffer: The West Reestablishes Contact with the East

Professor Peffer holds that history is a study in comparative culture of the relationship between one form of life and another. Here he describes the sparse and intermittent interrelations between the Western world and the Far East to the end of the Middle Ages, a time when Chinese civilization was vastly superior to that in the West. From Nathaniel Peffer, *The Far East: A Modern History* (Ann Arbor, Mich.: The University of Michigan Press, 1958), pp. 42–44.

Eastern Asia and Europe were first joined, literally, by a silken thread. It used to be written with poetic flourish that the togas of the Caesars were woven with silk spun from worms that fed on the mulberry trees of China. This is true as well as poetic. Both by caravan, on the land route from the China coast across Central Asia to Eastern Europe—called the Silk Road to this day—and by ship, along the coast of Asia through the South China Sea, Indian Ocean, Persian Gulf, Red Sea, and Mediterranean, Chinese silk was borne to Rome. The lure of the luxuries and riches of the East, it will be seen, began to exercise its pull early in European history. Its attraction has grown with the centuries.

There was trade, too, with the Arabs very early, a colony of Arab traders having settled in Canton in the fourth century. Also the first Christians began to arrive as early as the seventh century, when the Nestorians made their way from Persia. They were hospitably received and for at least two hundred years well treated. Likewise small companies of Jews arrived, though exactly when is not certain. They, too, were well treated and have been entirely absorbed by the Chinese, now being indistinguishable from Chinese although until after the beginning of the present century they were conscious of themselves as a different people and the last synagogue was still standing in Kaifeng, in Central China. It is interesting to observe, in parenthesis, that the Chinese are the only people to have fully absorbed the Jews. They are also the only people to have treated them without discrimination. There may or may not be a cause and effect relation here. It may be that the physical and cultural vitality of the Chinese gives them greater assimilative power than other peoples or it may be that the Jews were willing to assimilate when well treated. In any case the fact is worth noting.

Beyond this, however, there was little intercourse between East and West until the Middle Ages. About the thirteenth century Europe began to take a more active interest in the East, perhaps as a by-product of the Crusades. A number of travelers, emissaries either of the Church or of European monarchies, attempted the perilous journey across Asia, not all of them getting as far as China. But they learned enough about the mighty Asian empire to whet Europe's interest. So in the same way did another historic travel exploit, though one of another order and not exactly representing East-West intercourse. This was the prodigious sweep of the Mongol hordes across the Eurasian continent from the shores of the Pacific to the Hungarian plains, first under Genghis Khan and then under his grandson Kublai Khan, who brought China under his sway in the thirteenth century and established the Yuan dynasty, destined to last a hundred years. By making a kind of bridge between East and West, though a bridge of corpses and ruins, the Mongols added to Europe's awareness of the East, especially China.

In the thirteenth century also came the most famous visitation of all, that which was really to open Europe's eyes to China and help to generate the eagerness and curiosity that produced the great explorers who opened the unknown world. This was the legendary journey of Marco Polo, who came to China, traveled all over the country, and became an official under Kublai Khan. After a second journey to China he went back to Europe and wrote his famous book reporting on his experiences—probably the most remarkable travel book in history. Marco Polo made an immeasurable and lasting impression on the Western world in his time and after. His book is a glowing account of wonders to behold. He came, it must be remembered, from Venice when Venice was at its height and exemplified what was best in European culture at the time. And coming from Venice he was astounded by the marvels that he found in China—cities of unparalleled magnificence, impressive public works, law and order, efficient government, lavish wealth, luxury, an atmosphere of culture and refinement, elegance in houses and private grounds, in costume and manners. He might well have been. Compared with Hangchow, Soochow, and Canton, the cities of Europe were provincial, if not backward. The Europeans were somewhat incredulous but also dazzled and, still more, tempted.

It is in the light of this attitude of Europe that one must try to understand China's state of mind and actions later. The comparison was one of which the Chinese, too, became conscious, and if later they were to manifest airs of superiority to the West, manifest them openly and even with contempt, it was not only out of conceit and arrogance. There was arrogance no doubt, but it also had some basis. When East and West first came together, the East really was superior in all the things by which excellence is measured—culture, wealth, refinement, efficiency, public order, good government, technological grasp. Unfortunately the Chinese assumed that the world was static and immutable and were so indurated in certitude and complacency that 500 years later they could not perceive that the balance had shifted, and they still bore themselves to the white man as if Europe were still the Europe of the thirteenth century. . . .

TOPIC 30

# THE NEW WORLD OF BUSINESS

By the thirteenth and fourteenth century ways of conducting business had developed that can be called capitalistic. Merchants accumulated and reinvested capital, organized business partnerships, and introduced sophisticated methods of financial exchange and bookkeeping. The need for money and credit called into being an intricate banking system, far removed from the ancient services of money changers and money lenders. Merchants and bankers made and lost fortunes that outdid the incomes of kings. The Church raised moral objections to the new emphasis on profit-making but was itself too involved in business enterprise to combat consistently the trend of the times. The readings describe the new men and business techniques which were challenging the structure of feudal society.

**Reading 159**

## The Beginnings of Capitalism

From *Economic History of Europe*, 3d ed., by S. B. Clough & C. W. Cole. Copyright ©, 1952, by D. C. Heath & Co., a Division of Raytheon Education Co., Boston, Mass.

### I

### Money-Making in Medieval Society

Many people talk about capitalism, but nobody seems to know exactly what it is. . . . To talk intelligently about capitalism and its development, however, we must have a . . . definite notion as to its chief characteristics, which are many. . . . But for the sake of simplicity we can focus our attention, in describing the rise of capitalism, on three main features: (1) the growth of the capitalist spirit—that is, the desire for profits as a dominating motive in life; (2) the accumulation of capital—that is, the heaping up of money which is then used in business for the purpose of making profits (more money); (3) the development of capitalist techniques—that is, methods by which capital can be built up, handled, transferred, and used in business so as to make profits. . . . It is evident that the early middle ages were not capitalistic. In the twelfth century, for example, the desire for profits was not the most powerful or even an important motive in men's lives. There were no large accumulations of capital. Capital was not generally used in any fashion to make profits. . . .

The medieval thinker had a functional idea of society. To him, society was an organic whole. Each man belonged to a class. Each class had its function. The priests, monks, and nuns were to pray. The nobles were to fight and protect. The rest were to work. Each was doing his bit not for himself but for all men. The monk's prayers, the knight's battles, the peasant's plowing, represented a contribution to the welfare of everybody. Each person was expected to try to do the work appropriate to his station in life. He was born to a station and he should remain in it, contentedly doing his part and thinking of his reward in heaven. For a man to want to raise himself to a higher class betokened selfishness of some sort.

It was therefore wrong for a man to try to earn more than was necessary to keep him comfortably in the station of life to which he was born. The peasant should live like a peasant, the artisan like an artisan, the merchant like a merchant. To try to climb the economic or social ladder was wrong, and the worst way to rise was by heaping up wealth. The middle ages distrusted wealth. Jesus had told the rich man to take all that he had and give it to the poor, and He had indicated that it would be difficult if not impossible for a rich man to get into heaven. If a man got rich, it was suspected that he had obtained his wealth at the expense of his fellows. Certainly he had not given enough to charity or he would not be rich. . . .

Of the ways of making money, that of the merchant or trader was to the middle ages particularly dangerous and suspect. If the merchant worked on the goods he sold and took a fair reward for his labors, or even if he was content to earn by his efforts just enough to keep him comfortably in his station of life, his activities could be justified. But the trader was tempted to cheat and to seek profits. He risked his immortal soul in every transaction, for he might give way to avarice or greed. To the strictest view, any profits from pure trade were wrong. Gratian, an Italian monk of the twelfth century, wrote:

> Whosoever buys a thing, not that he may sell it whole and unchanged, but that it may be material for fashioning something, he is no merchant. But the man who buys it in order that he may gain by selling it again unchanged and as he bought it, that man is of the buyers and sellers who are cast forth from God's temple.

Thomas Aquinas, the greatest of the medieval philosophers, showed how strongly ethics influenced his views on trade when he insisted that a person knowingly selling an article with a defect in it was committing a sin and was morally bound to make restitution. It was a sin not to tell a buyer of a concealed defect in the goods. It was even a sin, according to Thomas, to trade with gain as the primary object, though it was legitimate for the merchant to seek moderate gains with which to support his family or to aid charity.

The medieval point of view is clearly seen in two economic doctrines on which there was substantial agreement—that of the *just price* and that of the *prohibition of usury.* The idea underlying the just price was that it was wrong to sell a thing for more than it was worth. What it was worth could be determined roughly in several ways. First, it was worth just enough to give to each person who helped to produce it a sum sufficient to reward him for his labor and keep him in his station in life. Second, it was worth what "common estimation" held it to be worth—that is, what well-informed people would say it was worth if they were consulted. Finally, it might be worth what the city, or state, or Church said it was worth in an ordinance or law issued to protect the consumer. Thomas Aquinas held that, "to sell dearer or buy cheaper than a thing is worth is in itself unjust and unlawful," though he admitted that, since "the just price of things is not absolutely definite but depends rather upon a kind of estimate," slight variations from the just price could be permitted.

The prohibition of usury was more complicated. Usury to the middle ages meant any charge purely for the use of money loaned or advanced. What we should call interest on borrowed money would then have been called usury. The belief that usury was wrong was based partly on a number of passages in the Bible which forbade taking it . . . .

> If thou lend to any of my people that is poor by thee, thou shalt not be to him as a usurer, neither shalt thou lay upon him usury. [Exodus, 22:25.]
>
> Take thou no usury of him or increase. [Leviticus, 25:36.]
>
> Lend hoping for nothing again. [Luke, 6:35.]

Aside from the Biblical injunctions, there was a general feeling that money was sterile. If you lent a man a field, he could raise crops on it. If you lent him a horse, he could ride it. If you lent him a house, he could live in it. But if you lent him money, he could only spend it. Money could not breed money. Aristotle, the most respected of the ancient philosophers, had been of this opinion. . . .

In the world of business between 1300 and 1500, many ways were evolved by which a loan at interest could be made to look like something else—a sale, a lease, an exchange transaction, a partnership. High profits might be immoral, but it seems that many a medieval merchant sought them with the utmost avidity. In the realm of ideas, the same period saw a weakening of the moral stand of the earlier day. Teachers, preachers, and writers began to justify usury and profits, from a dozen different angles. It was early held that if the lender suffered a loss by lending he might charge interest as compensation. Before long some people were maintaining that if by lending money a man missed a chance to make profits, it was proper to take interest. Gradually the very word *usury* took on its modern meaning of excessive charges for loans, while *interest* or some other pleasing word was used for moderate charges. The same gradual weakening took place in regard to the doctrine of the just price. By the fifteenth century a churchman so holy that he was later made a saint (Saint Antoninus, 1389–1459) was arguing that it was sometimes permissible for a seller to charge as much as 50 per cent more than the fixed price.

The development can be summed up briefly. In the centuries following the twelfth, with the rise of commerce and business, there grew up a class of merchants, traders, and financiers who sought profits and in many cases took usury as a normal part of their business life. As they became more and more important and as the Church, itself wealthy, became involved in the financial and business mechanisms of the times, the ideas of the Church and the public slowly readjusted themselves toward the acceptance of the capitalist spirit. The process was not complete

A Flemish moneylender weighs a coin as his wife watches. Fifteenth century.

by 1500, since more than a century later usury was still being denounced by churchmen, rulers, and publicists; but by the end of the middle ages the change was well under way. . . .

II

### The New Bankers in Italy

During the thirteenth century a new kind of banking was built up by a series of Italian firms, usually partnerships of the family type. These new bankers were no mere pawnbrokers sitting behind tables and making small loans in the Lombard Street of some European city. They were wealthy financiers who participated in trade and moneylending on a big scale. Such Italian bankers were loaning money to German churchmen at the fairs of Champagne as early as 1213. In 1233 bankers from Siena were acting as financial agents of the papacy. These bankers sought out profit in any line of work that seemed to promise it. They dealt in wheat, spices, cloth, and wine. They financed ships and trading voyages. They transferred money from city to city. They loaned money to needy rulers and ambitious merchants alike.

Two factors that helped the Italian banking firms to become important were the kings and the papacy. The kings of France, England, and Castile were gradually consolidating their territories and slowly organizing them into more unified states. Continually involved in wars, they needed money to pay for troops, supplies, and fortifications, to bribe their enemies, or to keep up a kingly luxury. When they had used up all the income from taxes and feudal dues, they frequently had to resort to borrowing, paying the bankers who could supply the cash they needed handsome rates of interest that ranged from 10 per cent to 40 per cent or more.

The papacy was even more important. It collected taxes, dues, fees, Peter's pence, or the like, from almost every land in Europe. These moneys had to be collected. They had to be sent to Rome or elsewhere.They had to be held till they were needed. Sometimes, despite its wealth, the papacy had to borrow money to meet a temporary need. All the financial machinery thus required was gradually converted into a highly organized working system during the course of the thirteenth century. In this process the Italian bankers played a great part as fiscal agents, collectors, lenders, transferrers, and holders of deposits.

The towns and cities were also active in financial affairs. They borrowed money to build walls, wage wars, make public improvements, or buy grain in famine times. It was in connection with municipal debts and financial transactions that the first public banks of deposit were founded—in Barcelona in 1401, in Valencia in 1407, and in Genoa (Bank of St. George, which carried on deposit banking from 1407 to 1445 and again after 1586). These banks were created and controlled by the cities to facilitate the handling of their debts and money affairs. But many towns with large debts were dependent on private bankers, often the big Italian firms. . . .

The Bardi, one of the most successful of the Florentine houses, may serve as an example. Their prosperity began in 1294 when they began to deal with the King of Naples, who was also Count of Provence (in southern France). They lent him money to finance his wars and in return got the exclusive right to control the exports of grain, fruit, and dairy products from Apulia (southern Italy) and grain from Provence. Later they traded extensively in French textiles and scarlet cloth from Ypres. In 1303 they became one of the firms active in banking for the pope, and in his behalf they transferred funds in Europe, to Cyprus, and even as far as Armenia. They helped to collect Peter's pence in England for the pope, and used the proceeds to buy wool which they sent to Florence to be manufactured into fine cloth. By 1310 the Bardi had surpassed their chief rivals, the Acciaiuoli and Peruzzi. Already in 1300 their interests in northern Europe were so extensive that none of the fifteen partners was residing in Florence. In 1320 the capital of the firm was

The offices of a Genoese banker in the late fourteenth century: at top, the bankers are counting coins and taking money from a strong box; at bottom, customers await service while the bankers refer to their account book.

149,796 livres of Paris. From 1310 to 1330 its annual profits averaged about 20 percent. But troubles lay ahead. Joanna of Naples repudiated half the debt owed to the Bardi by her kingdom. English mobs rioted against the foreign usurers. Finally in 1345–1346 Edward III of England was unable to pay the huge sums he had borrowed from the Bardi. This catastrophe threw the Bardi into bankruptcy and they paid their creditors only "forty-eight cents on the dollar." It was probably little comfort to them that the Peruzzi were involved in the same crisis and likewise went bankrupt.

A number of firms survived the crash of the mid-fourteenth century, but the financial leadership in Florence in the fifteenth century went to a relatively new family, the Medici, whose coat of arms (red balls on a gold field) gave rise to the modern pawnbroker's sign. In the early fifteenth century, the Medici banking firm had branches in Paris, London, Bruges, Lyons, Venice, Rome, Genoa, Naples, and eight other cities as well as the home office in Florence. Mixing politics with finance, the Medici made themselves actual rulers of the city-state of Florence. They used their great fortune for diplomatic as well as business ends, and also beautified Florence with churches, paintings, and sculpture. Cosimo de' Medici (1389–1464) spent more than $10,000,000 (1940 dollars) on such patronage of art and religion. At the time of his death, the income of his family was more than $3,000,000 a year. The most famous of the Medici, Lorenzo the Magnificent, ruled Florence in splendor from 1469 to 1492. Though the political power of the family waned after the end of the middle ages, they remained important. They gave the Church a number of cardinals and two popes, and France two queens (Catherine and Marie). Branches of the family were princes and dukes down into the eighteenth century. . . .

An important point to notice in connection with most of these early capitalists is the combination of commercial and financial activities, of trade and banking. The type of capitalism which was growing up in Europe in the middle ages and was well established by 1500 was predominantly of this sort. There were examples of purely financial capitalism in the early Jewish or Lombard moneylenders, and there were rich merchants who did little banking and much trade. But as wealth accumulated and the capitalist's desire for profits grew, it was normal for a firm to use its money in the way that seemed to promise the quickest, surest, and largest return, whether that involved investing in shipping, loaning money to merchants, churchmen, and rulers, or dealing directly in goods. For the most part the production of goods was still carried on in a small way, on the basis of handicraft work. . . .

III

## The Fuggers of Germany

Though there were many family firms of bankers in the sixteenth century, none achieved quite the position of the Fuggers. A brief account of their history will serve to illustrate many things—the accumulation of capital, the connection between banking and commerce, the relationship between state finance and the rise of capitalists, the organization of a family partnership, the power of the capitalist. The first Fugger known to history is Hans, a weaver by trade, who came to Augsburg in southern Germany from the village of Graben about 1380. In his new home he built up a considerable business. He made and sold fustians (a fabric made of linen and cotton). He imported cotton from Venice, for himself and probably for his fellow weavers as well. He may have dealt in other goods. At his death he left a small fortune of 3,000 gold gulden (the equivalent of something like $100,000 today).

The business passed to his son Jacob I, who, before his death in 1469, increased the family fortune from the cloth trade. Jacob's widow managed the business for a while, then passed it on to her oldest sons, Ulrich and George. They dealt in silks, damasks, and brocades as well as woolens, linens, and fustians; and in spices, fruit, saffron, and jewels as well as textiles. They established commercial connections with Italy, the Netherlands, Silesia, Poland, and Hungary. In 1473 the Fugger brothers began selling textiles to the Habsburgs, the ruling house of Austria, and about the same time they began to do financial work for the pope, transferring money for him from Scandinavia to Rome. The main interests of the Fuggers were still commercial, the wholesale and retail trade in textiles and other goods, but they were commencing to lend money and deal in bills of exchange. Before long they were loaning money to the Habsburgs as well as selling them goods.

Ulrich and George Fugger had a younger brother named Jacob II (1459–1525), later called Jacob the Rich. He had intended to enter the priesthood but in 1478 he gave up that idea, went into the business, and spent some time in Venice studying bookkeeping and business methods. Back in Augsburg he quickly became the most active member of the firm. Even before the death of his brothers (1506 and 1510) he was the dominant figure in it, and from 1510 to 1525 he shaped all its policies. This family enterprise was organized and reorganized several times, but the articles of agreement of 1502 were typical. They provided that only Fuggers in the direct line should be members of the firm. No outsiders, not even relatives by marriage, were to be admitted. The brothers were to run the business until only one was left alive. The survivor was to train up a son or nephew to succeed him as head of the firm. The bulk of the capital was to be left in the business, and the part called the "preferred share" was never to be taken out of it.

Jacob II was shrewd, fearless, able, a business genius typical of the new capitalism. One of his favorite sayings was "Business is business." On one occasion, when he was urged to abandon a risky mining venture, he sounded the keynote of the new capitalist age by replying, "I am of quite a different point of view and wish to continue making a profit as long as I can." Jacob brought to the firm the best business methods of the day. He built up an elaborate news service by which agents in every port and city kept him informed of each turn of the markets, of wars, piracy, and political rumors. He used the most up-to-date bookkeeping techniques. He got security for every loan, took his profits while he still had them, and skillfully cut his losses when they were unavoidable. He had branches, agencies, or agents for trade and banking operations in almost every important commercial city of Europe.

Under Jacob II the Fuggers' old cloth and merchandise business became secondary. On the one hand, he engaged heavily in mining ventures. He lent money to the Habsburgs on the security of the royalties coming to them from the copper and silver mines of the Tyrol and after 1522 rapidly acquired extensive holdings there for his firm. In alliance with a family of mine experts and managers named Thurzo he came to control the copper, silver, and lead mines of Hungary. By 1525 the Fuggers had made 1,500,000 gold gulden out of Hungarian minerals. At one point they controlled so much copper that they joined with some other firms in an unsuccessful attempt to corner the market and raise the price.

On the other hand, Jacob II engaged in finance. The greatest private banker of his time, he transferred money for kings, popes, and merchants. He accepted deposits and bought, sold, and issued bills of exchange and letters of credit. At some periods business preferred bills on the Fuggers to gold coin. Most important, he loaned money, financing merchants, bishops, cities, and kings. Especially close were his relations with the Habsburgs. Charles V won his election as Holy Roman Emperor through bribes financed by Jacob Fugger. Jacob the Rich had his finger in almost every financial pie in Europe. Luther's great revolt against the Church was initiated in part as a protest against the high pressure salesmanship of a certain indulgence hawker named Tetzel. On his travels, Tetzel was accompanied by a Fugger agent, who took charge of all the money collected, of which part went to pay debts owed to the Fuggers.

Jacob II was popular in Augsburg. He gave plays, dances, and skating parties, and lived in splendor. For the poor of the city he built a walled garden suburb called the Fuggerei, where rents were very low. But many people in Germany denounced him as a usurer, a grasping monopolist, a ruthless seeker after wealth. Indeed, so strong was the feeling that Fugger became a term of abuse. The capital of the Fugger firm had been 54,385 gold gulden in 1494. At Jacob's death in 1525 it amounted to about 2,000,000 gold gulden, probably the largest sum that had ever up till then been under the control of a single business firm. . . .

Jacob Fugger (seated) discusses business with his chief bookkeeper Matthäus Schwartz, who painted this watercolor sketch (1516). The drawers in the background designate branch offices of the Fugger bank—Rome, Venice, Cracow, Lisbon, etc.

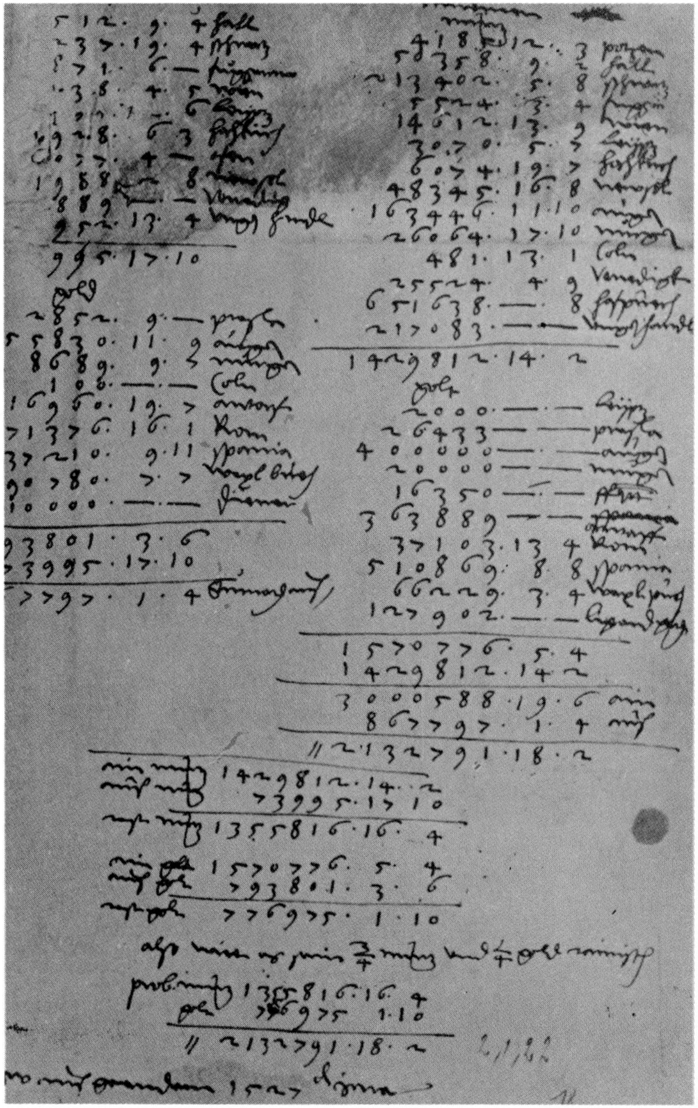

An idea of the Fugger riches can be gained from this page reproduced from their account books of 1527, two years after Jacob Fugger's death. The balance 2,132,791.18 gulden is equivalent to well over $50,000,000 today.

# The Merchant of Prato, a Fourteenth-Century Man of Wealth

In her biography of Francesco di Marco Datini, the Italian historian Iris Origo explored the mind and accomplishments of a successful fourteenth-century international merchant. Like all good biography, the account of the merchant of Prato brings the reader closer both to the man and to the world of his experience. From *The Merchant of Prato,* by Iris Origo. © Copyright 1957 by Iris Origo. Reprinted by permission of Alfred A. Knopf, Inc. This is published in Canada by Jonathan Cape Limited.

In the square of the busy little city of Prato, beneath the faded brick walls of the Palazzo Comunale in which he sat as a councillor, stands the statue of a merchant. Clothed in the round biretta and sweeping robes of the fourteenth century, he holds in his hand a sheaf of bills of exchange. This is the man to whom Prato owes the foundation of her riches: Francesco di Marco Datini [1335–1410].

The story of the rise of his trading-houses in Avignon, Prato and Florence, in Pisa and Genoa, in Spain and Majorca, is as remarkable as the success-story of a modern millionaire, and quite as fully recorded. His fellow citizens to this day pride themselves on it and dwell, above all, on the charity which bequeathed to the poor of Prato not only his whole fortune of 70,000 gold florins, but the very house in which he lived, and in it, his greatest gift to posterity, his papers. During his lifetime he himself collected every letter and business document he received, telling the managers of all his branches to do the same, and in his will he left instructions for all these papers to be collected and preserved in his own house in Prato.

These instructions were carried out somewhat carelessly, for although there is a record in 1560 that Francesco di Marco's ledgers and papers had been carefully put away in cupboards in his own house, they were found three hundred years later in sacks in a dusty recess under the stairs. But in the long run this neglect may not prove to have been entirely unfortunate. *"Bene qui latuit, bene vixit."* A few of these pages were nibbled by mice or worms; but at least thieves and fools remained unaware of their existence—and when in 1870 some learned citizens of Prato brought them to light, an astonishing number still remained: some 150,000 letters, over 500 account-books and ledgers, 300 deeds of partnership (some of the other small companies connected with his own), 400 insurance policies, and several thousand bills of lading, letters of advice, bills of exchange, and cheques. Thus has been preserved, in the very house of the man whose life-work it represented, an invaluable and indeed, in its fullness and homogeneity, a unique record of medieval trade.

The picture of commercial activity which these letters present is very remarkable. When Datini returned to Italy from Avignon in 1382, his branch in that city (entrusted to two Tuscan partners) continued to be as active as before; and he at once opened a central house in Prato, as well as branches in Florence, Pisa, and Genoa, in Barcelona and Valencia, and finally in Majorca and Ibiza, all managed by his own partners or *fattori* on the spot but controlled by his own untiring pen. Between these *fondachi* sailed the ships which carried his wares: lead and alum and pilgrims' robes from Roumania, slaves and spices from the Black Sea, English wool from London and Southampton and African or Spanish wool from Majorca and Spain, salt from Ibiza, silk from Venice, leather from Cordoba and Tunis, wheat from Sardinia and Sicily, oranges and dates and bark and wine from Catalonia. . . . Small wonder that Francesco's fellow citizens gaped as the great bales came pouring in, and whispered that he was "the greatest merchant who ever came out of Prato!" . . .

Francesco's own character is very sharply etched. It is impossible to imagine a more completely Tuscan figure. Intensely individualistic, he owed his success entirely to his own personal enterprise, to an audacity always tempered at just the right moment by shrewdness and mistrust of his neighbour. A hard businessman, he gathered his golden florins wherever he could find them: he traded in armour, wool, metals, and wheat; he made cloth and bought slaves; he opened (though this laid him open to the accusation of being a usurer) a bank. But he also never failed to conform to the conventions of pious practice: he neglected no fast-days, assigned a due proportion of his profits to alms and charity, built chapels and adorned churches. Self-indulgent during his prosperous years in Avignon—"keeping women and living on partridges," and begetting several little bastards—he was also capable, in the pursuit of his business, of a life as industrious and exacting as a monk's. . . .

Francesco's outstanding trait as a merchant is the variety of his activities. First an armourer and then a mercer in Avignon, he had become a cloth-maker in Prato and was now again a shopkeeper in Florence; next he founded a flourishing import-and-export business, and became the chief partner of a number of different trading-companies: he dealt in wool, cloth, veils, wheat, metals, and hides, in spices and pictures and jewels. In 1404 he joined yet another guild—that of the cloth-finishers, the *Arte di Calimala*. He even took over, for a short time, the city tolls for meat and wine in Prato; he did some under-writing; and finally (against the advice of all his friends) he set up a bank.

Such varied ventures were entirely characteristic of his time, when the fundamental distinction between the international merchant and the "little man" did not consist in whether his trade was wholesale or retail, or even in the quantity of his merchandise, but rather in the outlook of two different kinds of men. The local merchant was still, in his way of life, his lack of enterprise, and his parsimony, a man with the outlook of a craftsman—trading with a number of familiar clients, strictly subservient to the rules of his guild, taking small risks and expecting small profits. The international trader—whether he was the chief partner of a great company like the Alberti's, or a small one like Datini's—still retained something of the enterprise and audacity of his ancestor, the travelling peddler; he was prepared to take great risks, but diminished them by spreading them over the widest possible field; he acquainted himself with foreign languages and foreign ways, adapted himself to the needs of foreign markets, was both merchant and banker, dealt simultaneously in both wholesale and retail trade. As the Bardi had continued to run a draper's shop in Via di Calimala even while they were exporting enough wheat from Puglie to feed a whole city and financing the

English campaigns in France, so Datini, even at the time of his most successful foreign ventures, never closed his little mercer's shop in Por S. Maria.

But to his timid Florentine partners the variety of his enterprises was most alarming; they could not forget how many other great trading-houses, in recent years, had ended in bankruptcy. The following letter from Domenico di Cambio is typical of their warnings:

> Francesco, I have heard you would embark on a new enterprise. Before God, I beseech you, open your eyes wide and look well to what you do! You are rich and at ease, and not a boy any more, that you should need to undertake so much—and bethink you how we are mortal, and the man who does many things will assuredly meet with disaster. . . . Bethink you how Donato Dini must feel, who is now over seventy, and because he has tried to do too much is bankrupt, and gets only five *soldi* in the *lira!*

But Francesco did not heed. The opening of his new branches followed each other swiftly; first the Pisan *fondaco* in 1382, the Florentine in 1386, and the Genoese in 1388. Then came new branches in Spain and in the Balearic Islands in 1393 and 1394, while at the same time the company in Avignon prospered and trade with both the Black Sea and the Balkans increased. . . .

It is after the opening of the Spanish and Genoese branches, too, that we find reference to yet another line—the slave trade, of which the Balearic Islands were then the chief centre in the western Mediterranean. This trade was, of course, nothing new. In the eleventh and twelfth centuries Spain had been the great slave-market of western Europe, and as early as 1128 traders from Barcelona were selling Moslem slaves in the markets of Genoa. But it was the labour shortage after the Black Death of 1348 that suddenly caused a demand for domestic slaves to revive, and brought them to Italy not only from Spain and Africa, but from the Balkans, Constantinople, Cyprus and Crete, and, above all, from the shores of the Black Sea. In Florence a decree of the *Signoria,* issued in 1336, officially authorized their importation—provided only that they were infidels, not Christians, and they were also soon to be found in most prosperous Genoese and Venetian households. Many of them mere children of nine or ten, they belonged to a great variety of different races: yellow-skinned, slanting-eyed Tartars, handsome fair Circassians, Greeks, Russians, Georgians, Alans, and Lesghians. Sold by their parents for a crust of bread, or kidnapped by Tartar raiders and Italian sailors, they were brought from the slave-markets of Tana and Caffa, of Constantinople, Cyprus, and Crete to the Venetian and Genoese quays, where they were bought by dealers and forwarded to customers inland. By the end of the fourteenth century there was hardly a well-to-do household in Tuscany without at least one slave: brides brought them as part of their dowry, doctors accepted them from their patients in lieu of fees—and it was not unusual to find them even in the service of a priest. They were employed, too (as we shall see), in Francesco's own household, and he would sometimes oblige Tuscan friends by selecting one for them through his agents in Genoa or Venice; but the most active part in this trade was taken by his branches in Majorca and Ibiza, where both African slaves bound for Italy and eastern slaves bound for Spain were collected and sold.

Many letters in these files bear witness to these transactions, though they did not take place on any large scale; the most frequent entries refer rather to a few slaves included in a shipment of other assorted wares. The bill of lading, for instance, of a ship arriving in Genoa from Roumania on May 21, 1396, listed "17 bales of pilgrims' robes, 191 pieces of lead and 80 slaves." Another ship, sailing from Syracuse to Majorca, carried 1,547 leather hides and 10 slaves, and one sailing from Venice to Ibiza "128 sacks of woad, 55 bales of brass, 15 sacks of raw cotton, 5 sacks of cotton yarn, 4 bales of paper, 3 barrels of gallnuts, and 9 Turkish heads." The "9 heads" were then forwarded to Valencia to be sold, with a letter stating that one of them was a woman who could "sew and do everything," and who was therefore, in the writer's opinion, "too good for the people of Ibiza"—"for they are like dogs." "Your money," he added, "will be well placed in her." . . .

At the turn of the century Francesco—who had reached his sixty-fifth year—appears to us in a new aspect: wearing the garb of a penitent and a pilgrim. Clad in a long robe of coarse white cloth, with a cowl on his head, a friar's cord about his waist, and a lighted candle in his hand, he set forth barefoot, in a company of several thousand men, for a nine-day pilgrimage.

To none of Francesco's contemporaries did it seem strange to see him thus: the performance, in calamitous times, of such acts of devotion and self-abasement was part of an accepted pattern of life. The Datini papers, indeed, bring fresh confirmation of the extent to which a life of Christian conformity was led even by men (like Francesco himself) whose natural temperament was far from pious. Just as many of the laws they obeyed were still largely founded upon usage—*consuetudo*—so their devotional life rested upon a series of unquestioned, familiar acts, from the cradle to the grave. Hard-headed merchants not only gave lipservice to Christian doctrine, but paid tribute to it in their daily practice: they led their whole lives within an intricate framework of pious observance. During his whole youth and prime Francesco was not, and did not consider himself, a virtuous man; but he never questioned the necessity or the efficacy of these devout customs. His business contracts, like his private letters, began and ended with a pious formula; the Ten Commandments stood at the head of his ledgers; a fresco of St. Christopher guarded his front door. In Lent and on other fast-days both he and his wife fasted so strictly that Domenico di Cambio said his health would not permit to come and stay with them, and if he sometimes worked on a Sunday, he blamed himself most severely in the year in which he had attended only *six* Lenten sermons! Though he often scoffed at priests and monks, he went regularly to confession, and, in sickness, called five Franciscans to his bedside; though ungenerous by nature, he gave alms freely, paid his tithes regularly, built shrines and chapels. There was hardly a rich man of his time who did not do the same, and the few who failed to fulfill these duties were considered wicked men.

Many of these acts, of course, had a strong propitiatory character; it was through them that men hoped to receive protection from the terrors and mysteries of life in this world, as well as God's mercy in the next. Man is at all times a fear-ridden animal; and certainly many Tuscans of the *trecento* had good reason to dread a sudden death. The persistence of the tradition of vengeance by bloodshed—still considered not only a sacred duty but a pleasure—the permanent sense of insecurity produced by party strife and civil war, the frequent recurrence of famine, and, above all, the constant, haunting menace of the Black Death—this was the dark background of their lives. . . .

# Raymond de Roover: The Doctrine of Usury and Renaissance Business

The intensive examination of the organization and operations of the Medici Bank from which this reading is taken is the result of years of research in the Florentine archives by Professor de Roover, Belgian-born American economic historian. Here the author considers the impact of the Church's position on usury upon economic growth. Reprinted by permission of the publishers from Raymond de Roover, *The Rise and Decline of the Medici Bank, 1397–1494,* Cambridge, Mass.: Harvard University Press, Copyright 1963 by the President and Fellows of Harvard College, pp. 10–13.

Medieval banking cannot be understood without keeping in mind the usury doctrine of the Church. Since the bankers, in this regard, tried as much as possible to comply with religious precepts, they had to operate without incurring the censure of the theologians. As a result banking in the Middle Ages and even much later—on the Continent until far into the eighteenth century—was quite different from what it is today. It would be erroneous to believe that the usury doctrine was simply disregarded and had scarcely any effect on banking practices: on the contrary, as the available evidence proves, it exerted an enormous influence. First of all, the need for evading the usury prohibition, by legitimate means if possible, affected the entire structure of medieval banking. Second, it determined how the banks operated. And third, the usury doctrine, by recognizing certain transactions as licit and declaring others to be illicit, influenced business ethics and public opinion. . . .

The ban against usury did not halt the growth of banking, but recent research has shown that it certainly diverted the course of this development. Since the taking of interest was ruled out, the bankers had to find other ways of lending at a profit. The favorite method was by means of exchange by bills (*cambium per litteras*). It did not consist in discounting as practiced today, but in the negotiation of bills payable in another place and usually in another currency. Interest, of course, was included in the price of the bill which was fittingly called a "bill of exchange." Although the presence of concealed interest is undeniable, the merchants argued—and most of the theologians accepted these views—that an exchange transaction was not a loan (*cambium non est mutuum*) but either a commutation of moneys (*permutatio*) or a buying and selling of foreign currency (*emptio venditio*). In other words, the exchange transaction was used to justify the credit transaction, and speculative profits on exchange served as a cloak to cover interest charges. Nevertheless, it was argued that cambium was not usurious, since there could be no usury where there was no loan.

The practical consequence was to tie banking to exchange, be it manual exchange or exchange by bills. It is perhaps significant that the bankers' gild of Florence was called the Arte del Cambio, or the Moneychanger's Gild. In the account books of the Italian merchant-bankers, including those of the Medici, one rarely, if ever, finds traces of discount, but there are thousands and thousands of entries relating to exchange transactions. There is no account for interest income, but an account entitled *Pro e danno di cambio* (Profit and Loss on Exchange). . . .

It is untrue that the bankers openly disregarded the teachings of the Church. To be sure, they were not always consistent and often violated the precept against usury in private contracts. It does not follow, however, that there were many who pertinaciously questioned a doctrine erected into a dogma by the Church. On the contrary, many a banker had an uneasy conscience about his unholy deals. Overwhelming evidence is given in the numerous medieval testaments in which the testator ordered restitution of all usury and ill-gotten gains. True, such clauses became scarcer after 1350 because the merchant-bankers, while still continuing to make bequests to the Church for the salvation of their souls, were less and less eager to be branded as self-confessed usurers by referring specifically to restitution in their wills.

Moreover, they contended, with a semblance of truth, that they were engaged in legitimate business and not in usurious activities. In fact, they did shun illicit contracts as much as possible. Even the Pratese merchant-banker, Francesco di Marco Datini (1335–1410), although ruthless and grasping, boasted in letters to his wife that he had never made illicit profits. When his branch manager in Barcelona became involved in questionable exchange dealings, he was promptly rebuked by an irate master and told to desist. . . . In the partnership agreements of the Medici, illicit exchange was as a rule expressly forbidden, although this provision was not always carried out, as account books and other records prove. It is, therefore, understandable that Cosimo de' Medici himself was troubled by qualms about ill-acquired wealth and secured a papal bull which allowed him to atone for his covetousness by endowing the monastery of San Marco in Florence. . . .

If it had not been for the usury doctrine, why would the merchants have adopted a cumbersome procedure when simpler methods were available? It is far easier to discount instruments of debt than to work with bills of exchange payable abroad in foreign currencies. First of all, this procedure complicates bookkeeping. Next, it requires the bankers to operate with a network of correspondents in other places. Another drawback is that lenders, as well as borrowers, have to speculate and to run the risks of adverse exchange fluctuations. Moreover, the purchaser of a bill is exposed to loss not only through the insolvency of his debtor, but also through the failure of the correspondent to whom he sends a remittance. This is perhaps why the big bankers preferred to operate with their own branches. As for the borrower, if he had no funds standing to his credit in another place, he had to find some one willing to accept his drafts and to pay them when due. The drawee or payer would then have to recover his outlay at his own risk. The use of the bill of exchange thus increased both trouble and expense, so that the practical result of the usury prohibition, intended to protect the borrower, was to raise the cost of borrowing. To this extent the Church's legislation on usury may have retarded economic growth. . . .

# The Church as a Business Organization

Medieval Churchmen may have considered profit seductive and interest sinful, but efficient administration of the Church's income from her vast properties and the Christian congregation required efficient business organization. The papal camera (office of fiscal administration) seems to date from the Cluniac reform period of the mid-eleventh century. One of its major tasks was to oversee the collecting and transferring of Church income to Rome. Such income came from many sources: rents (census) for Church property, feudal dues (tribute), membership contributions (Peter's Pence), income taxes, a proportion of the annual income of bishops, abbots, etc. (common services), and others. The first reading describes the use made by the camera of available Italian merchants. The second consists of documents illustrating that relationship. From William E. Lunt, *Papal Revenues in the Middle Ages* (New York: Columbia University Press, 1934), I, pp. 51–53, 55–56, 301–302, 323–324, 338–340; II, 300–302.

## I

## Merchants as Agents of Church Finance

As early as the second half of the twelfth century the papacy was using agents outside the camera [Papal department of fiscal administration] for the deposit, transport and exchange of money, and for the contract of loans. At first the Templars performed these functions, and throughout the major portion of the thirteenth century the houses of the Templars continued to serve as places of deposit. . . . When the rising Italian capitalists began to establish agencies in the various commercial centers of Europe, they offered better facilities for the transaction of the growing fiscal business of the papacy. In the early years of the thirteenth century the papacy began to use Italian merchants concurrently with the Templars for the deposit and transportation of funds. By the time of Gregory IX (1227–1241), Italian merchants had become the principal bankers of the camera. For the remainder of the middle ages firms of bankers, which were for the most part Italian, took a large part in handling the finances of the papacy. . . .

The bankers supplied a variety of services. Their agents received deposits from the collectors, either for safe-keeping or for transportation to the camera. For these sums they gave receipts in which they promised to restore the amounts in full in any designated place on the demand of the collector or of an accredited agent of the pope. They took all risks such as those of fire, robbery and shipwreck, and pledged the possessions of the whole firm as a guarantee of repayment. The deposits might sometimes be kept for a long period, during which the merchants could use the money profitably in their own enterprises. In the fourteenth century, however, it became customary to require delivery of money assigned to them within a stated interval. Long before the close of the thirteenth century the bankers had become the principal agents for the conveyance of funds to the camera. . . . The cameral merchants might transport the actual specie, or make the transfer by order on the representative of the firm at the papal court or by bill of exchange. For this service they received a portion of the money transferred, and they might also charge for the exchange of the money from the currency of the country in which it was received into the money current at the papal court.

The papal bankers might be empowered to receive from the payers revenues that were owed to the papacy. Payments of census and services occasionally reached the camera in that manner throughout the period. The use of cameral merchants as collectors, however, was of comparatively rare occurrence.

The papal merchants were constantly called upon to lend money to the camera. Often the loans anticipated the receipt of taxes, which were pledged to the merchants for repayment. . . .

The patronage and protection of the papacy aided the cameral merchants greatly in the development of their banking operations. The numerous ecclesiastics, who, on coming to Rome, were obliged to borrow in order to meet papal charges, turned naturally to the bankers standing in relations with the curia [papal government]. Such loans were ordinarily made only with the permission of the pope, who gave the creditor special rights of recovering from the debtor. The latter was compelled to pledge as security not only his own property but also that of his church. If the debt was not paid within a month of the time specified, the creditor could obtain a special executory process for speedy recovery to be carried out by officials appointed at the papal court and enforced by ecclesiastical censures. If clergy outside the curia needed money to meet papal taxation or other expenses, they also were likely to place business with the accredited agents of the holy see. Some of these debts bore interest, of which the popes were sometimes aware, though they seem seldom to have taken official cognizance of the fact. The bankers were privileged to employ the ecclesiastical courts to enforce the payment of such debts, and might require the borrower to agree to submit to the jurisdiction of the auditor of the camera. The cameral merchants were accredited to sovereigns by the papacy, and, when occasion demanded, papal diplomacy was used in their behalf, not only with prelates and clergy but also with rulers and peoples. The prominent position held by the Italian bankers in European financial affairs must be attributed in no small degree to the business and the protection of the papacy. . . .

## II

### 1. Early Instance of the Association of Merchants with a Papal Collector (1229)

Moreover, the same Master Stephen [i.e., the papal collector] had with him certain most wicked usurers, who called themselves merchants, cloaking usury under the name of the business of banking, who offered money to those who were poor and vexed with exactions; and the said Stephen urging, many were forced under the severest penalty to accept a loan, who afterward fell into their snares, incurring irreparable damages.

### 2. Papal Order to a Collector To Deliver His Receipts to Specified Cameral Merchants (1262)

To the beloved son, brother John of Kent, of the order of Friars Minors, greeting, etc.

By the authority of the present we command that whatever you may receive or have received from the census of our dearest son in Christ, the illustrious king of the English, or from Peter's pence, which we have committed to you to be collected through our other letters, you assign with due caution to Deutaviva Guidi and Rayner Bonaccursi, merchants of Siena, as we have ordered you by those letters, but with the knowledge of the beloved son, Master Leonard, cantor of Messina, our chaplain, whom we are sending into England on certain business.

Given at Viterbo, II nones February, in the first year.

### 3. Papal Order for the Sequestration of the Goods of a Deceased Cameral Merchant Who Was Indebted to the Roman Church (1300)

Boniface, bishop, servant of the servants of God, to the venerable brother, the bishop of Lucca, greeting and apostolic benediction.

Recently it has come to our hearing that the late Labrus Vulpelli, of the society of Riczardi of Lucca, closed his last day. Therefore, since the said Labrus and the aforesaid society were and are debtors to us and the Roman church in large sums of money, we command your fraternity by apostolic writing, ordering you strictly in virtue of your obedience, that on the receipt of the present, without the obstacle of difficulty and delay, by you and others, you take care to take, receive, hold and keep by our authority, . . . all and each of the movable and immovable goods, with whomever they may be, which you are able to learn about and discover, invoking the aid of the secular arm for this, if need should be, . . . notwithstanding . . . if the aforesaid goods or any of them should be obligated in any way to another or others, by whom we do [not] wish [them] to be carried away against this our mandate, without our special knowledge.

Do you write back to us faithfully by your letters containing the sequence of these whatever you do and find about this.

Given at the Lateran, II kalends December, in the sixth year of our pontificate.

### 4. Action Taken by the Papacy To Secure the Release of Cameral Merchants from Prison (1251)

To . . . archbishop of Besançon and . . . the elect of Lyons.

Since on Holy Thursday at Lyons we caused Ponzardus de Duno to be cited by a formal proclamation that before the festival of the apostles Peter and Paul last past he should return to the command of the church prepared to give full satisfaction concerning the wrongs, excesses and enormous offenses, on account of which he was held bound by the chain of excommunication, or else we should proceed against him more severely, because he neither returns to the devotion of the church, nor comes to us, nor sends sufficient or suitable answer, but, raging into greater offense and adding enormities upon enormities, taking Hugolinus Belmontis, Orlando Bartholomei, Theobald Thebalducii and Rainer Tetii, merchants of Siena, whom we sent for the affairs of the church, he holds them in captivity to the offense of the apostolic see, we, not being able to tolerate further in patience his bold presumption and hardened iniquity, command that each of you, laying all of the land of [Ponzardus] under ecclesiastical interdict, do not permit baptisms, the eucharist, or any other ecclesiastical sacraments to be administered to any in that land. . . . Furthermore, do you place under ecclesiastical interdict any cities, towns, villas and places to which [Ponzardus] may happen to come, in which divine services may not afterward be celebrated in any wise without the special license of the apostolic see.

Given at Milan, VIII kalends September, in the ninth year.

### 5. Papal Intercession with the King of France in Behalf of Cameral Merchants (1291)

To the dearest son in Christ, Philip, illustrious king of France.

. . . Whereas you are said to have caused the Italian merchants staying in your said kingdom to be arrested, we ask and earnestly exhort your royal serenity that those merchants, and particularly those of the societies of the sons of Bonsignoris of Siena, of Thomas Spiliati and Lapus Hugonis, of the Spina, of the Pulici and Rimbertini and of the Lambertinii of the Friscobaldis of Florence, of the Riczardi of Lucca and of the Clarentini of Pistoia, who and the colleagues of whom are special merchants of our camera and have long served the Roman church advantageously, . . . you free from the restraint of this arrest and from any burden imposed on them anywhere, and restore to them their rightful liberty. When goods have been restored to them in full, do you, from the royal clemency, allow them to sojourn freely in the parts of the said kingdom, to be free to carry on legal commerce, and hold them committed favorably to your care in their opportunities. . . .

Given at Orvieto, V kalends June, in the fourth year of our pontificate.

## 6. A Pledge by the Camera of Church Income as Security for a Loan from the Fuggers (1501)

To the most admirable men, Ulrich Fucher [Fuggers] and Brothers, German merchants following the Roman court, greeting in the Lord.

You have lent to our most holy lord, for the necessities of him, the see and the apostolic camera, 6,000 gold ducats; and his holiness wished and ordered to be given to you as a gift 400 of the same: which sum, including in all 6,400 gold ducats, our same most holy lord wished, promised and ordered to be restored to you, namely, one-half at the end of two and one-half months and the other half at the end of five months to be calculated from the twentieth day of the present month of December, with authority and license, in the event that satisfaction should not be given to you . . . [the Fuggers served as transferers of Papal funds] of removing from the account and retaining for yourselves from the common services of the churches and monasteries, which may happen to be expedited by your hands from Germany and Hungary and Poland only, until you have been fully satisfied for the said 6,400 ducats. . . .

Given at Rome in the apostolic camera, on the last day of December entering January 1502, in the tenth year of the pontificate of our aforesaid most holy lord. . . .

### *Marginal Notes Made by Official of Papal Camera*

For the loan made to our most holy lord.

Assignment of 6,400 gold ducats of the camera for Ulric Fucher and Brothers, German merchants.

In deduction. Note that by mandate by receipt and issue, under the day 15 April 1502, they had 247½ ducats.

Item by another mandate, under the day 15 July 1502, they had 700 ducats 10 s. 8 d. of gold of the camera.

Item, in another mandate, under the day 6 August 1502, for the common service of the pope of the church of Schleswig 427½ ducats.

Item, in another mandate, under the day 27 December 1503 (*sic*), for common service of the church of Hildesheim 475 ducats.

Item, in another mandate, under the day 22 March 1503, for the common service of the church of Basel 475 ducats.

Item, in another mandate, under the day 24 June 1503, 902½ ducats for the common service of the churches of Verden and Transylvania.

From Lord John Conarii for the common service of the church of Cracow 1272 florins.

From Lord John Turzo for the common service of the church of Breslau 1,900 florins.

Constituting in all the sum of 6,400 ducats, in which he [Fugger] was creditor by the force of these patents, which is acknowledged by the lord's depositaries, and here accounted formally.

TOPIC 31

# THE NEW POLITICS

The appearance of a money economy strengthened the reassertions of central political authority that had begun in the late Middle Ages. Kings in France, England, and Spain pushed forward their efforts to uproot feudalism and establish national monarchies. In Italy, by contrast, where the commercial revolution had first developed, the city-state in the fourteenth and fifteenth centuries once again became the dominant political form. For two centuries Italy was free from foreign invasion while other sections of Europe were preoccupied with their own affairs. At the same time, the ties of traditional society and the medieval Church were steadily loosening. Without these restraints, the values of the new capitalist spirit—competition, enterprise, and success—openly governed Italian political life and fashioned an approach to government that served as a model for later state systems. The readings are thus concerned with the transfer of these values to political organization.

**Reading 163**

## The City-States of Italy

From *The Renaissance* by Wallace K. Ferguson. Copyright 1940 by Holt, Rinehart and Winston, Inc. Copyright © 1968 by Wallace K. Ferguson. Reprinted by permission of Holt, Rinehart and Winston, Inc.

### I

At the end of the thirteenth century the urban classes were still a minority in European society, and would long remain so. Even in Northern Italy and the Netherlands, the cities contained only a relatively small proportion of the total population. Yet the burghers had already exerted an influence out of all proportion to their numerical strength, and the future was theirs. . . .

The most obvious and the most immediately significant aspect of the transformation [that followed] was the change that took place in political organization. The expansion of money economy enabled the feudal monarchs of the West to assert their authority effectively and to transform amorphous feudal kingdoms into strongly centralized territorial states. And this new political organization, in turn, exercised an ever increasing influence on social and economic life. By the end of the fifteenth century the monarchs of England, France and the kingdoms of the Spanish peninsula had succeeded in destroying all but the last vestiges of political feudalism, while a similar result was accomplished in the Netherlands by the Dukes of Burgundy. The collapse of the Holy Roman Empire in the thirteenth century paralyzed central government in both Germany and Italy and prevented the rise of a national state in either country. . . . Yet even in Germany feudal chaos was mitigated by the consolidation of central government in the larger fiefs, which transformed them for all practical purposes into territorial principalities. . . .

The dynamic forces which transformed and finally destroyed medieval civilization began to operate first in Italy and developed there much more rapidly and intensively than in the northern countries. Before the end of the thirteenth century, feudalism had disappeared in central and northern Italy, giving place to a vigorous urban society in politically independent city-states. . . .

Italy owed her wealth and the early rise of her cities in the first place to her geographical position, which made her the natural entrepôt between the East and the West. From the beginning of the commercial revival in the eleventh century, it was the international trade of Italy that formed the basis for her extraordinary economic activity and kept for her the undisputed economic hegemony of Europe, until the explorations of the late fifteenth century and the growth of commerce and industry in the northern and western states combined to shift the centre of European commerce from the Mediterranean to the Atlantic coast. Moreover, it was the unique preponderance of foreign over domestic trade in Italy, the wide geographical scope of her commercial enterprises, and the unusual opportunities for profit arising from the luxury trade with the East that enabled

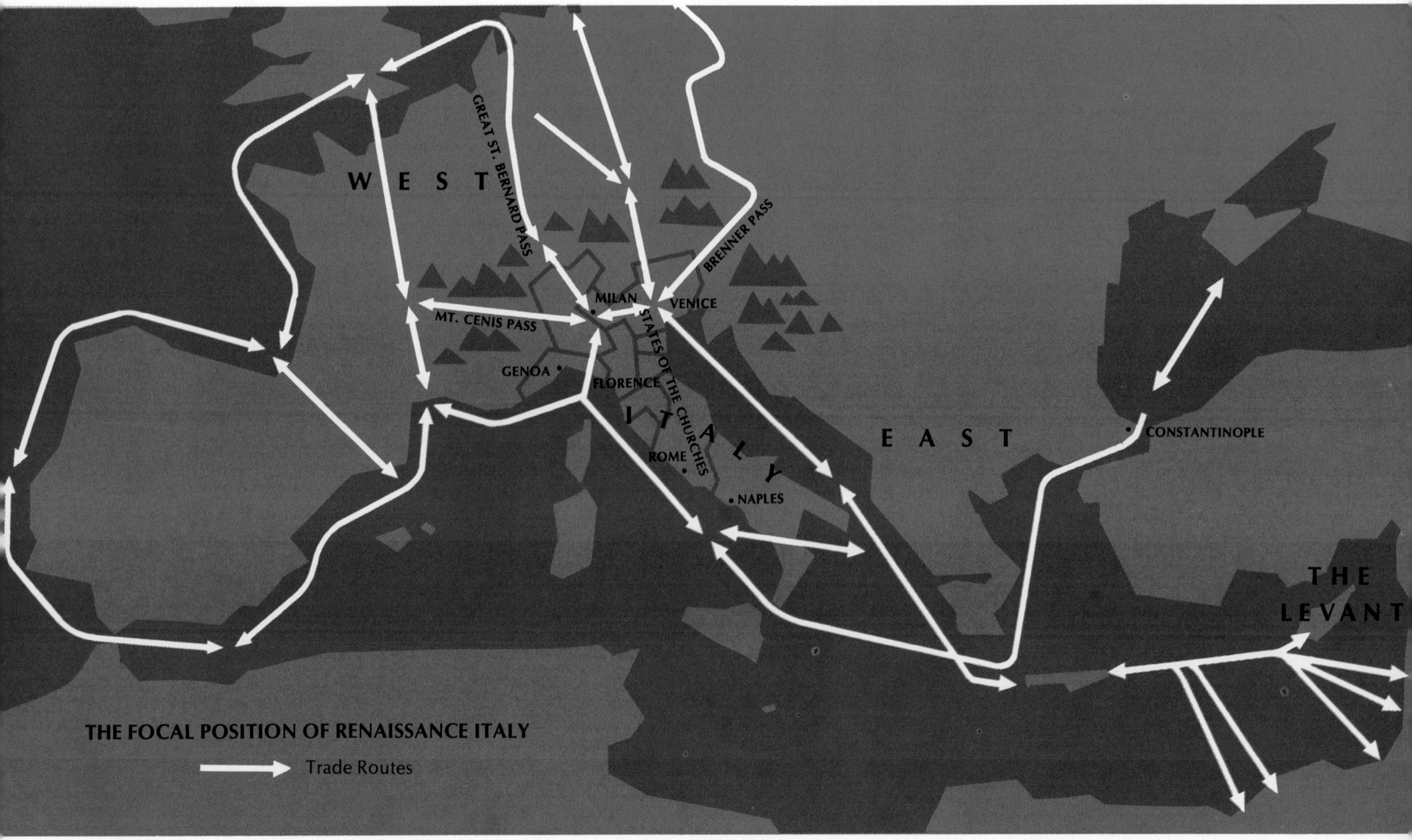


THE FOCAL POSITION OF RENAISSANCE ITALY

the Italian merchants to accumulate fortunes of unprecedented size, and to work out techniques for handling capital and credit far in advance of their northern neighbors. The concentration of wealth, which resulted from this early evolution of Italian capitalism, exercised a profound influence on the formation of Renaissance society and culture. . . .

### The Political Evolution of the Italian States

The political like the economic evolution of Italy was in many respects exceptional, though the same forces were at work there that transformed the feudal states beyond the Alps. But, whereas in the North the rise of money economy and city life led to the growth of central government and to the creation of great territorial or national states, in Italy the cities helped to destroy what central government there was. By the end of the High Middle Ages, each city, save in the southern Kingdom of Naples, had become the center of a separate little territorial state. . . .

Another factor in the exceptional character of Italy's political evolution was the early destruction of feudalism. Everywhere the rise of the cities and of money economy brought about the eventual decline of the nobility, but in Italy the influence of the cities was direct and overwhelming. By the twelfth century, the cities dominated the Italian scene and the feudal nobles were drawn into them by the irresistible attraction of their wealth and political power. The nobles combined with the rich merchants to form a patrician ruling class, contributing their military skill to the struggle for independence. Many of the nobles intermarried with the wealthy burgher families, engaged in trade, and gradually abandoned their feudal way of life. Those of the old nobility, indeed, who could not adjust themselves to urban economy did not survive. Their lands passed into the hands of the merchants and money-lenders, for land alone, when cultivated without capital and in the customary feudal fashion, could not produce enough money to meet the rising standard of living set by the rich urban classes. The ownership of land was thus concentrated in the cities, either by the migration of the old landholders or by purchase. A natural corollary of this was the extension not only of the city's economic control but also of its political authority over the surrounding country districts. No similar extension of the political power of the cities occurred in other parts of Europe, for elsewhere the feudal nobles kept to the land and retained their jurisdiction over it until the growth of central government vested all political power in the state. In Italy there was neither a bellicose landed nobility nor a strong central government to prevent the communes from acquiring full political rights over the surrounding countryside. The rural population, thus subjected to the rule of the cities, received no political rights and played no active part in the political life of the state.

Since every city was an independent city-state with its own tumultuous history of party strife and war with its neighbors, the political history of Italy during the early Renaissance is a bewildering story. Later, the confusion became somewhat less confounded as Venice, Milan and Florence expanded their subject territory and between them conquered nearly all of Lombardy and Tuscany. Toward the end of the Renaissance, too, the popes finally succeeded in restoring their authority over the Papal States and so destroyed the independence of the numerous little city-states which had sprung up in central Italy. Even then, the story is still too complex for brief summary. Nevertheless, some common characteristics may be observed and one may hazard certain generalizations regarding the course of political development in all the states. In the first place, the political evolution of each state was determined, more or less, by the nature of the city's economic life and by the conflicting interests of the various classes. And secondly, in nearly every state republican government broke down, to be replaced by the rule of a despot.

The Italian communes began their career as urban republics. In the early period of their existence they were in theory burgher democracies, but in almost every instance they were actually ruled by a patriciate of rich merchants and nobles. These old wealthy families, who were referred to indiscriminately as *grandi,* nobles or magnates, enjoyed the prestige of having led the cities triumphantly through the struggle for independence. With greater security, however, their government became increasingly selfish, and during the thirteenth century their domination was challenged by a rising class of new rich—merchants, industrial capitalists and bankers—who felt that their wealth entitled them to political influence and who were eager to direct state policy in accordance with their own economic interests. In Florence, these latter were aptly named the *popolo grasso,* the fat people. Below them were the middle class of small burghers—guild masters, shop-keepers and professional men. These were the *popolo.* Their interests centred about local trade and they were generally opposed to the economic imperialism of the great merchants, which so often involved the city-states in expensive wars. On the whole, however, they were in closer sympathy with the new rich who had arisen from their midst than with the aristocratic *grandi* on the one hand, or the propertyless industrial proletariat on the other. These last were the *popolo minuto,* the little people, strong in numbers but usually devoid of political rights. As the cities grew in population and wealth, the relative importance of the long-established patrician families declined, and each of the classes strove, singly or in combination with others, to seize control of the government.

The purely mercantile patriciate of Venice, where commerce was all important, formed the outstanding exception. There, the old merchant families succeeded in maintaining a rigid control of both the economic and political life of the city for centuries, so that Venice remained throughout the Renaissance a republic ruled by an aristocratic merchant oligarchy. The *grandi* of Florence were less fortunate. The industrial and commercial growth of the Tuscan city in the thirteenth century produced an exceptionally powerful class of new capitalists, who by 1293 were strong enough to exclude the *grandi* from office. This new oligarchy kept up the forms of democracy by admitting the *popolo* of the lesser guilds to a minor share in the government, but they excluded the growing class of proletarian workers who were the employees of the industrial capitalists. A successful rising of the weavers and other workers (the Ciompi) in 1378 gave them a brief political power, but in 1382 the *popolo grasso* regained control and kept it until 1434, when Cosimo de' Medici gathered the strings of the republican machine into his own capable hands. . . .

In most of the Italian cities, wealth was not so largely concentrated in the hands of one class as in Venice and Florence. As the political importance of the *grandi* began to decline, therefore, a fairly even balance of classes produced an unstable state of equilibrium in which no one class could dominate. Short-sighted selfishness and family pride prevented the old patrician families from sharing their traditional political privileges with the new rich, so that the wealthy classes remained divided and lost the opportunity to establish a secure plutocracy. . . . Security and internal peace are necessary to the welfare of a business community, and these the old republican administrations seemed unable to provide. Nor, while weakened by internal strife, could they give the strong leadership needed by cities perennially at war with one another in a struggle for more land, for control of trade routes or merely to ruin economic competitors.

Before the end of the thirteenth century there was a growing conviction that the only solution to this troubled situation was the rule of one man, who could suppress factional strife and give consistent direction to state policy. . . .

Despots rose to power in a variety of ways, and the legal foundation of their authority was often a rather feeble structure. Yet they all owed their power, in a sense, to the popular will, and they could continue to rule only with the tacit consent of the citizens. They could not, however, depend upon a long tradition of loyalty as could the northern monarchs. There was always danger of revolution or of assassination at the hands of some eager aspirant to the despot's office, often enough a member of his own family. Ruling an Italian state was a hazardous occupation, and the mortality rate among despots was high. On the other hand, the despotic princes were not hampered by feudal traditions and laws, nor had they to meet the problems involved in the transformation of a feudal régime into a centralized state. They took over states in which the government was already centralized. In these urban states money had long been the instrument of power and there was a long-established tradition of taxation. The Italian despots had merely to take over personal control of a going concern. They were the practically minded products of a business community and, if they were not all the self-made supermen of popular conception, most of them were intelligent enough to realize that their own prosperity depended on the prosperity of their subjects. The final justification of their government was that they fostered business, kept order and gave the states greater stability than had the old faction-torn republics. And they expended their wealth freely in the patronage of arts and letters. The concentration of wealth allied with political power in the princely courts was a very significant factor in the cultural and social development of the Renaissance.

## II

The government of the Italian states was in many respects more rational than that of the northern monarchies that were just emerging from feudalism. The despots grew up in a society that had lost the personal loyalties of the feudal régime and had abandoned many of the moral conceptions of the Middle Ages regarding the conduct of business and politics. They were inclined to regard any means as justifiable that led to the ultimate end of increasing the power of the state, which was embodied in themselves. The conception of the state as a law unto itself and of public morality as something entirely distinct from private morality appeared earlier and in more complete form in Italy than in the rest of Europe. Long before Machiavelli wrote *The Prince,* the despots were working on the conviction that an act of clemency or the keeping of a promise that might harm the state was little short of silly. In both government and diplomacy the calculated subordination of means to ends gave to the Italian states an air of practical efficiency that was in part an illusion, for there were disadvantages in this uninhibited virtuosity. Intricate diplomacy based on treachery often defeated its own ends, and the ruthless government of the despots failed to build up public spirit among the citizens of the state.

One of the most unfortunate results of this, as Machiavelli pointed out, was that the Italian states were forced to depend exclusively upon mercenary soldiers for defence or aggression. Neither the despots nor the oligarchies dared arm their subjects, nor would even the most loyal citizens be willing to fight for a government which they accepted, but for which they felt no active responsibility. The government had no choice but to bargain with one of the professional condottieri to supply it with an army. This was a straight business transaction. The condottieri were in reality military entrepreneurs, the capitalists of warfare. Many of them were skilled strategists, but they owed no real loyalty to the state they fought for and they usually preferred not to risk decisive battles, since in that event either a defeat or a victory meant the termination of a lucrative contract. The most successful condottieri were not the best generals but the best businessmen. However effective they might appear in action against one another, they proved quite incapable of defending the Italian states against the great national armies of France and Spain, when the foreign invasions began at the end of the fifteenth century.

Italy had escaped invasion, during the period when she was least united and therefore most helpless, largely because the great northern and western states were otherwise engaged. Until the latter part of the fifteenth century, France was involved in the Hundred Years' War and the struggle with Burgundy, and Spain was divided among five separate kingdoms. Meanwhile the expansion of the richest Italian states had restored a certain degree of unity to Italy. At the time of the first French invasion in 1494, five large states, Venice, Milan, Florence, the Papal States, and the Kingdom of Naples occupied most of the peninsula. . . . For half a century these states had kept a reasonable degree of peace through maintaining a balance of power. But they all regarded one another with suspicion and never dreamt of uniting, even when threatened by foreign conquest. The lack of Italian national patriotism and the selfish policy of states and princes sealed the doom of Italy in the following century.

# Alfred von Martin: The Dynamic Spirit of Capitalism

Alfred von Martin (1882–      ), German sociologist, is the author of numerous sociological interpretations of historical periods. In this reading he discusses the impact of a money economy on politics in the Renaissance. Of importance is his observation that here for the first time one meets the modern concept that time is money. From Alfred von Martin, *Sociology of the Renaissance* (Oxford University Press, 1944), pp. 1–3, 15–16.

The centre of gravity of medieval society was the land, was the soil. With the Renaissance the economic and thus the social emphasis moves into the town: from the conservative to the liberal, for the town is a changeable and changing element. . . . As the burghers became a power with the rise of a money economy, as the small artisan became the great merchant, we find a gradual emancipation from the traditional forms of society and the mediaeval outlook: there was a revolt against those sections of society which were most dependent upon this structure and upon these ways of thought, by virtue of which they exercised their authority. We find arising against the privileged clergy and the feudal nobility the bourgeoisie, which was throwing off their tutelage and emerging on the twin props of money and intellect as a bourgeoisie of "liberal" character. By revolting against the old domination they also freed themselves from the old community ties which had been interlinked with it. Blood, tradition and group feeling had been the basis of the community relationships as well as of the old domination. The democratic and urban spirit was destroying the old social forms and the "natural" and accepted divine order. It thus became necessary to order the world starting from the individual and to shape it, as it were, like a work of art. The guiding rules in this task accorded with those liberal aims set by the constructive will of the bourgeoisie.

Life in a primary community is apt to produce a conservative type of thought, a religious way of thought which orders the world in an authoritarian manner. Everything temporal is to it no more than a parable, a symbol of the metaphysical, and nature is but a reflection of the transcendental. But the bourgeois world as seen from the coolly calculating, realist point of view of the city-state is a world that has lost its magic. The liberal mode of thought of the emancipated individual attempts to control the outside world more and more consciously. Thus community becomes society, and thus arises the new domination by a new oligarchy, the capitalist domination by the moneyed great bourgeoisie, which exploits those "democratic" tendencies which had destroyed feudalism, as the best way to ensure its own domination. In the Middle Ages political power with religious sanction had prevailed: now comes the era of an intellectually supported economic power. Religion as well as politics becomes a means, just as previously commerce and secular culture had been no more than the means to an end.

The Middle Ages in their social structure as well as in their thought had a rigidly graduated system. There was a pyramid of Estates as well as a pyramid of values. Now these pyramids are about to be destroyed, and "free competition" is proclaimed as the law of nature. God and blood, the traditional powers, are deposed, and though they maintain some of their importance their dominance is shattered.

The spirit of capitalism which begins to rule the modern world with the Renaissance deprives the world of the divine element in order to make it more real. But the spirit of early capitalism did not as yet dehumanize it. Reason was not as yet rated above humanity; it was not yet the be-all and end-all of all action. Riches were, as yet, no more than a means to independence, respect and fame. . . .

### NEW MODES OF THOUGHT

Money capital and mobile property naturally linked up with the kindred power of time for, seen from that particular point of view, time is money. Time is a great "liberal" power as opposed to the "conservative" power of space, the immobile soil. In the Middle Ages power belonged to him who owned the soil, the feudal lord; but now Alberti could say that he who knew how to exploit money and time fully could make himself the master of all things: such are the new means to power of the bourgeois. . . . Money, because it circulates, as landed property cannot, shows how everything became more mobile. Money which can change one thing into another brought a tremendous amount of unrest into the world. The tempo of life was increased. Only now was formulated the new interpretation of time which saw it as a value, as something of utility. It was felt to be slipping away continuously—after the fourteenth century the clocks in the Italian cities struck all the twenty-four hours of the day. It was realized that time was always short and hence valuable, that one had to husband it and use it economically if one wanted to become the "master of all things." Such an attitude had been unknown to the Middle Ages; to them time was plentiful and there was no need to look upon it as something precious. It became so only when regarded from the point of view of the individual who could think in terms of the time measured out to him. . . .

# Cosimo de Medici Rules Florence

The best example of the relation between wealth and political power at this time is found in the Medici family of Florence. The Medici had accumulated a large fortune from trade and moneylending in the fourteenth century. Members of the family had long played an active political role in the city, but in 1434 their then head, Cosimo (1389–1464), gained permanent control of the city by astutely playing rival political factions against one another. Not holding office himself, Cosimo ran the city in the manner of a modern political boss, rewarding his supporters with political appointments and money gifts, while lavishly patronizing religion and art and turning a ready ear to popular demands. This account of the life of the great merchant prince is found in Niccolo Machiavelli's history of Florence, a work which marks the beginning of modern critical historical scholarship. The section on Cosimo is, nonetheless, a eulogy of one man who fit Machiavelli's standard for effective political leadership. From Niccolo Machiavelli, *History of Florence and of the Affairs of Italy* (New York, 1901), pp. 314–319.

Of all who have left memorials behind them, and who were not of the military profession, Cosimo was the most illustrious and the most renowned. He not only surpassed all his contemporaries in wealth and authority, but also in generosity and prudence; and among the qualities which contributed to make him prince in his own country, was his surpassing all others in magnificence and

Palazzo Riccardi, built in 1430, was one of several Medici townhouses in Florence. Note the fortress-like nature of the lower story to guard against popular riots.

This Medici country villa in Poggio a Caiano was built for Lorenzo the Magnificent, grandson of Cosimo.

generosity. His liberality became more obvious after his death, when to Piero, his son, wishing to know what he possessed, it appeared there was no citizen of any consequence to whom Cosimo had not lent a large sum of money. . . . His magnificence is evident from the number of public edifices he erected; for in Florence are the convents and churches of St. Marco and St. Lorenzo, and the monastery of Santa Verdiana; in the mountains of Fiesole, the church and abbey of St. Girolamo; and in the Mugello, he not only restored, but rebuilt from its foundation, a monastery of the Frati Minori, or Minims. . . . To these sacred edifices are to be added his private dwellings, one in Florence, of extent and elegance adapted to so great a citizen, and four others . . . each, for size and grandeur, equal to royal palaces. And, as if it were not sufficient to be distinguished for magnificence of buildings in Italy alone, he erected an hospital at Jerusalem, for the reception of poor and infirm pilgrims. Although his habitations, like all his other works and actions, were quite of a regal character, and he alone was prince in Florence, still everything was so tempered with his prudence, that he never transgressed the decent moderation of civil life; in his conversation, his servants, his traveling, his mode of living, and the relationships he formed, the modest demeanor of the citizen was always evident; for he was aware that a constant exhibition of pomp brings more envy upon its possessor than greater realities borne without ostentation. . . .

No one of his time possessed such an intimate knowledge of government and state affairs as himself; and hence amid such a variety of fortune, in a city so given to change, and among a people of such extreme inconstancy, he retained possession of the government thirty-one years; for being endowed with the utmost prudence, he foresaw evils at a distance, and therefore had an opportunity either of averting them, or preventing their injurious results. He thus not only vanquished domestic and civil ambition, but humbled the pride of many princes with so much fidelity and address, that whatever powers were in league with himself and his country, either overcame their adversaries, or remained uninjured by his alliance; and whoever were opposed to him, lost either their time, money, or territory. . . .

After the age of forty, he enjoyed the greatest felicity; and not only those who assisted him in public business, but his agents who conducted his commercial speculations throughout Europe, participated in his prosperity. Hence many enormous fortunes took their origin in different families of Florence, as in that of the Tornabuoni, the Benci, the Portinari, and the Sassetti. Besides these, all who depended upon his advice and patronage became rich; and, though he was constantly expending money in building churches, and in charitable purposes, he sometimes complained to his friends that he had never been able to lay out so much in the service of God as to find the balance in his own favor, intimating that all he had done or could do, was still unequal to what the Almighty had done for him. He was of middle stature, olive complexion, and venerable aspect; not learned but exceedingly eloquent, endowed with great natural capacity, generous to his friends, kind to the poor, comprehensive in discourse, cautious in advising, and in his speeches and replies, grave and witty. . . . Some [opponents] gave him to understand they were "not dreaming." He said, "he believed it, for he had robbed them of their sleep." When Pope Pius was endeavoring to induce the different governments to join in an expedition against the Turks he said, "he was an old man, and had undertaken the enterprise of a young one." . . . A few hours before his death, his wife asked him why he kept his eyes shut, and he said, "to get them in the way of it." Some citizens saying to him, after his return from exile, that he injured the city, and that it was offensive to God to drive so many religious persons out of it; he replied, that, "it was better to injure the city, than to ruin it; that two yards of rose-colored cloth would make a gentleman, and that it required something more to direct a government than to play with a string of beads." These words gave occasion to his enemies to slander him, as a man who loved himself more than his country, and was more attached to this world than to the next. . . . He died, however, at the zenith of his glory and in the enjoyment of the highest renown. The city, and all the Christian princes, condoled with his son Piero for his loss. His funeral was conducted with the utmost pomp and solemnity, the whole city following his corpse to the tomb in the church of St. Lorenzo, on which, by public decree, he was inscribed, "FATHER OF HIS COUNTRY." . . .

# Machiavelli Advises Princes How To Govern (1513)

Niccolo Machiavelli (1469–1527), Renaissance writer and statesman, is best known for his little book of advice for princes, in which Renaissance reliance on individualism is translated into practical examples of conduct for those in authority. The term "machiavellian" has come to describe one who is crafty or deceitful. From *The Prince* by Niccolo Machiavelli. Translated by W. K. Marriott. Everyman's Library Edition. Reprinted by permission of E. P. Dutton & Co., Inc. This is published in Canada by J. M. Dent & Sons Ltd.

## I. CONCERNING CRUELTY AND CLEMENCY, AND WHETHER IT IS BETTER TO BE LOVED THAN FEARED

I say that every prince ought to desire to be considered clement and not cruel. Nevertheless he ought to take care not to misuse this clemency. . . . A prince, so long as he keeps his subjects united and loyal, ought not to mind the reproach of cruelty; because with a few examples he will be more merciful than those who, through too much mercy, allow disorders to arise, from which follow murder or robbery; for these are wont to injure the whole people, whilst those executions which originate with a prince offend the individual only.

And of all princes, it is impossible for the new prince to avoid the imputation of cruelty, owing to new states being full of dangers. . . . Nevertheless he ought to be slow to believe and to act, nor should he himself show fear, but proceed in a temperate manner with prudence and humanity, so that too much confidence may not make him incautious and too much distrust render him intolerable.

Upon this a question arises: whether it be better to be loved than feared or feared than loved? It may be answered that one should wish to be both, but, because it is difficult to unite them in one person, it is much safer to be feared than loved, when, of the two, either must be dispensed with. Because this is to be asserted in general of men, that they are ungrateful, fickle, false, cowards, covetous, and as long as you succeed they are yours entirely; they will offer you their blood, property, life, and children, as is said above, when the need is far distant; but when it approaches they turn against you. And that prince who, relying entirely on their promises, has neglected other precautions, is ruined; because friendships that are obtained by payments, and not by greatness or nobility of mind, may indeed be earned, but they are not secured, and in time of need cannot be relied upon; and men have less scruple in offending one who is beloved than one who is feared, for love is preserved by the link of obligation which, owing to the baseness of men, is broken at every opportunity for their advantage; but fear preserves you by a dread of punishment which never fails.

Nevertheless a prince ought to inspire fear in such a way that, if he does not win love, he avoids hatred; because he can endure very well being feared whilst he is not hated, which will always be as long as he abstains from the property of his citizens and subjects and from their women. But when it is necessary for him to proceed against the life of some one, he must do it on proper justification and for manifest cause, but above all things he must keep his hands off the property of others, because men more quickly forget the death of their father than the loss of their patrimony. Besides, pretexts for taking away the property are never wanting; for he who has once begun to live by robbery will always find pretexts for seizing what belongs to others; but reasons for taking life, on the contrary, are more difficult to find and sooner lapse. But when a prince is with his army, and has under control a multitude of soldiers, then it is quite necessary for him to disregard the reputation of cruelty, for without it he would never hold his army united or disposed to its duties. . . .

Returning to the question of being feared or loved, I come to the conclusion that, men loving according to their own will and fearing according to that of the prince, a wise prince should establish himself on that which is in his own control and not in that of others; he must endeavour only to avoid hatred, as is noted.

## II. CONCERNING THE WAY IN WHICH PRINCES SHOULD KEEP FAITH

Every one admits how praiseworthy it is in a prince to keep faith, and to live with integrity and not with craft. Nevertheless our experience has been that those princes who have done great things have held good faith of little account, and have known how to circumvent the intellect of men by craft, and in the end have overcome those who have relied on their word. You must know there are two ways of contesting, the one by the law, the other by force; the first method is proper to men, the second to beasts; but because the first is frequently not sufficient, it is necessary to have recourse to the second. Therefore it is necessary for a prince to understand how to avail himself of the beast and the man. This has been figuratively taught to princes by ancient writers, who describe how Achilles and many other princes of old were given to the Centaur Chiron to nurse, who brought them up in his discipline; which means solely that, as they had for a teacher one who was half beast and half man, so it is necessary for a prince to know how to make use of both natures, and that one without the other is not durable. A prince, therefore, being compelled knowingly to adopt the beast, ought to choose the fox and the lion; because the lion cannot defend himself against snares and the fox cannot defend himself against wolves. Therefore, it is necessary to be a fox to discover the snares and a lion to terrify the wolves. Those who rely simply on the lion do not understand what they are about. Therefore a wise lord cannot, nor ought he to, keep faith when such observance may be turned against him, and when the reasons that caused him to pledge it exist no longer. If men are entirely good this precept would not hold, but because they are bad, and will not keep faith with you, you too are not bound to observe it with them. Nor will there ever be wanting to a prince legitimate reasons to excuse this non-observance. Of this endless modern examples could be given, showing how many treaties and engagements have been made void and of no effect through the faithlessness of princes; and he who has known best how to employ the fox has succeeded best.

But it is necessary to know well how to disguise this characteristic, and to be a great pretender and dissembler; and men are so simple, and so subject to present necessities, that he who seeks to deceive will always find some one who will allow himself to be deceived. One recent example I cannot pass over in silence. [Pope] Alexander the Sixth did nothing else but deceive men, nor ever thought of doing otherwise, and he always found victims; for there never was a man who had greater power in asserting, or who with greater oaths would affirm a thing, yet would observe it less; nevertheless his deceits always succeeded according to his wishes, because he well understood this side of mankind.

Therefore it is unnecessary for a prince to have all the good qualities I have enumerated, but is very necessary to appear to have them. And I shall dare to say this also, that to have them and always to observe them is injurious, and that to appear to have them is useful; to appear merciful, faithful, humane, religious, upright, and to be so, but with a mind so framed that should you require not to be so, you may be able and know how to change to the opposite.

And you have to understand this, that a prince, especially a new one, cannot observe all those things for which men are esteemed, being often forced, in order to maintain the state, to act contrary to fidelity, friendship, humanity, and religion. Therefore it is necessary for him to have a mind ready to turn itself accordingly as the winds and variations of fortune force it, yet, as I have said above, not to diverge from the good if he can avoid doing so, but, if compelled, then to know how to set about it.

# The Venetians Turn down a Crusade

In the fourteenth century a new menace from the East, the Ottoman Turks, began the gradual conquest of the Byzantine Empire that culminated in the fall of Constantinople in 1453. Pope Pius II (1458–1464), a brilliant writer and orator, called a congress in Mantua in 1459 at which he hoped to repeat the success of Pope Urban in organizing a crusade against the infidel. Essential to his efforts was the cooperation of the rich mercantile city-state of Venice that had extensive commercial interests in the eastern Mediterranean. Venetian hesitation to associate themselves in hostilities against the Turks unless they were assured of united action on the part of the Western nations doomed the papal efforts. In 1463 Pius dramatically took the Cross himself but died before he could set off on his crusade. This reading consists of comments on the congress dictated by the Pope himself. Reprinted by permission of G. P. Putnam's Sons from *Memoirs of a Renaissance Pope: The Commentaries of Pius II,* translated by Florence Gragg, edited by Leona C. Gabel. Copyright © 1959 by Florence A. Gragg.

We wish at this point to speak more fully of the Venetians, since they are today the most powerful state on both land and sea and seem not unfitted for the larger empire to which they aspire. . . .

Venetia originally occupied almost all the islands between Grado and Loredo which constituted one body politic composed of a number of towns. Today the buildings are continuous, forming one city divided by canals flooded with salt water which serve as streets. The large canals are broad enough to permit a galley to be rowed in them. There are paths paved with brick for pedestrians. Merchandise is shipped here from almost the entire world and there is no more famous trading center in all Europe. Merchants from all over the West bring their wares here and carry away the wares of the East. They have an armory and a magnificent dockyard called the Arsenal protected by all sorts of engines where they are ceaselessly building galleys and other craft. It is thought that at a moment's notice they could at pleasure equip 100 galleys and as a matter of fact they have sometimes done so.

The entire city is constructed of brick, but if their empire continues to flourish, it will soon be of marble, and indeed at the present time the palaces of the nobles are veneered with marble and glitter with gold. The celebrated church of St. Mark the Evangelist is constructed of eastern marble, its many gilded domes adorned with the work called mosaic. They say that in this church there is a treasury which surpasses the wealth of kings, containing rubies, diamonds, and all kinds of precious stones. . . .

So much for the Venetians. Though they long refused to send their ambassadors to the Congress of Mantua, finally on learning that the Duke of Clèves had arrived, that the French envoys were expected soon, that Francesco Sforza, Duke of Milan, himself was present, and that they alone of all Italy were missing, fearing public infamy they sent two envoys with a picked company of young nobles, accompanied as a mark of honor by some 500 knights. Francesco Sforza out of respect to the city of Venice met them outside the walls and entered the city riding between the two envoys. One of them, Lodovico, delivered a brilliant speech in a public consistory, for he was not only a jurist but an eloquent orator. The purport of the speech was as follows: The Venetians execrated the insolence of the Turks in invading the lands of others, but they accused the Christians of cowardice in not defending their own possessions or daring to take arms for their religion. They had only praise for the Pope, who in his anxiety for the common weal had come to

Several of the principal buildings of St. Mark's Square seen from the vantage point of the Grand Canal. The gilded palace of the Doge faces the canal to the right; behind it are the domes of St. Mark's Cathedral. To the left the *campanile* (bell tower) soars above the square. Painting by Giovanni Antonio Canaletto (1697–1768).

Mantua at the cost of toil and money. They urged a crusade against the Turks if it could be undertaken by the united forces of all Christians and they promised to do great things to bring that about.

In answer Pius, after some preliminary words about the origin of the Venetians and their glorious history, praised their offers in defense of religion even though they were made on a condition very difficult to fulfill. He rebuked the lateness of the ambassadors, who had been the last to arrive though they were nearest the place of the Congress. He recalled the great affection of Pope Alexander III for the Venetians and assured them that he himself would hold them in no less regard if they stoutly did their part, as they should, to defend the Faith. . . .

The following day all the ambassadors and princes from Italy who were present were summoned before the Pope. The Genoese were not as yet officially present but had secretly promised their aid. The cardinals sat to the right and left of the Pope; the princes and the ambassadors were seated by districts. When they were ready to listen, the Pope said, "My sons, on your advice we have determined to declare war against the Turks and we have no doubt that if Christians come to the defense of their own salvation there will be horses, men, ships, and money in abundance. Now we must consider whether we are to attack the enemy by land or sea or both together; how large a fleet and land army is needed; from what nations soldiers are to be levied: whether we desire to aid the Hungarians with money or with men. Take counsel for the good of all and state openly what help you can promise."

After this there was a long argument with the Venetian ambassadors, whose words were very different from their feelings. They favored the war against the Turks with their lips but condemned it in their hearts. They are not people who embrace splendid projects. They are mostly merchants whose nature, intent on gain, usually shrinks from noble aims which cannot be achieved without expense. The Venetians thought that if war were declared against the Turks, all their trade with the East, on which their livelihood depended, would cease and that after Greece was freed the western princes would not allow the Venetian republic to have sovereignty in Dalmatia and the East. They feared too that while they were occupied with a war with the Turks, the Duke of Milan would attack them; for men always suspect others of their own designs. They had therefore instructed their ambassadors to prolong the discussion and hold out fair hopes, but to promise nothing definite or binding. When however they were pressed more insistently they said that the Venetians would join in the war only on condition that they be allowed the sole conduct of naval matters; that they should have the spoils taken from the enemy; that a large fleet be raised; that an army of 50,000 cavalry and 20,000 infantry should march from Hungary against the Turks. They said a fleet of sixty galleys and twenty saette was needed and 8,000 soldiers besides rowers and other sailors to man them though before they had said that a much smaller number would suffice. They promised only that they would furnish the ships themselves and their equipment. For everything else they expected pay and for this purpose they demanded the tenths, twentieths, and thirtieths raised within their jurisdiction, which they thought would amount to 150,000 ducats. Not satisfied even with this they demanded from the general treasury 1,500,000 more. Such was the liberality of the Venetians.

The Pope answered them as follows: "Ambassadors of the Venetians, we see that it is not your purpose to defend religion, since you ask an almost impossible price. It is a matter for sorrow that your state has so degenerated that she who in the past has gladly armed great fleets for the defense of the Faith is now unwilling, if we take everything into account, to arm even a single ship. Against the Pisans and the Genoese, against kings and emperors you have often waged great wars at your own expense in behalf of your allies and subjects. You now demand a price to fight for Christ against the impious Turks, but even if it were given you you would not arm. Alas! Venetian race, how much of your ancient character have you lost! Too much intercourse with the Turks has made you the friends of the Mohammedans and you care no more for religion."

Much was said to this same effect and often more severely. The envoys being cautious made answers more specious than true. Nothing on their lips matched what was in their hearts.

They opened one line of argument after another, exaggerating the strength of the enemy and belittling ours and trying to take up time till the Congress should be dissolved. Nor did they come to the palace except by appointment. Their bearing was full of pomp and pride. They knelt reluctantly in the Pope's presence and though they saw the ambassadors of kings and of the Emperor himself and mighty princes lie prostrate long after kissing the Pope's feet, they themselves, either from their inveterate pride or the rudeness inherited from their fishermen ancestors, rose immediately. If they were kept waiting a sin-

Despite the hesitation of the Venetians, Pius determined to carry out his crusade. Here the pope (in a sedan chair) arrives at the seaport of Ancona where he died suddenly of fever in August 1464.

gle minute in the Pope's anteroom they at once complained as if insulted and wrote to their senate that they were no more honored by the Pope than if they had been ambassadors from Ancona [a small town]. . . . But as a matter of fact he was excessive and lavish in the honors shown the Venetians rather than remiss. They made these and countless other misrepresentations, in order to pile trouble on trouble. . . .

# Worldliness of the Renaissance Papacy

From pp. 30–33, 161–163 *The World of Humanism 1453–1517* by Myron P. Gilmore. 

The economic and political changes . . . produced serious strains in that most comprehensive of all governmental systems, the Christian church. The growing powers of secular states made compromises inevitable. Economic pressures and an expanding standard of wealth accelerated the scramble for the accumulation of benefices. The resulting decline in moral and institutional standards was felt in all parts of the great ecclesiastical organization, but was most dramatically apparent at the apex of the system in the papacy itself. To the long history of opposition to Roman financial exactions and papal control of appointments was now added an increasing lack of respect for the head of the church and his immediate court. Never had the gap appeared so wide between the pretensions of the incumbents of the see of Peter and their actual performance.

The two humanist popes of the mid-fifteenth century, Nicholas V and Pius II, had maintained a high sense of the responsibilities of their position, and if their patronage of the new learning had created precedents that in the long run might be dangerous, yet their pontificates had been free from serious scandals. Beginning, however, with the pontificate of Sixtus IV in 1471, the decline was rapid.

Sixtus IV, born Francesco della Rovere, was the son of a poor and large family. He had distinguished himself in the Franciscan order and in theological disputes on the currently debated doctrine of the Immaculate Conception. Strong, intelligent, ambitious, he embarked on a career of political activity motivated in part by the desire to provide in a suitably splendid way for his eleven nephews and two nieces. Melozzo da Forli's celebrated picture of the pope receiving Platina, the papal librarian, shows us, symbolically enough, Sixtus attended by his favorite nephews, whose faces reveal their greed, complacency, and ruthlessness. It was a family which had "arrived." During this pontificate significant steps were taken toward enlarging

TEMPLA DOMVM EXPOSITIS: VICOS FORA MOENIA PONTES:
VIRGINEAM TRIVII QVOD REPARARIS AQVAM.
PRISCA LICET NAVTIS STATVAS DARE COMMODA PORTVS:
ET VATICANVM CINGERE SIXTE IVGVM:
PLVS TAMEN VRBS DEBET: NAM QVAE SQVALORE LATEBAT:
CERNITVR IN CELEBRI BIBLIOTHECA LOCO.


Pope Sixtus IV (right) receives Platina (kneeling). The pope's nephews are in the background.

Michelangelo spent four and a half years (1508–1512) lying on his back on scaffolding, to complete the magnificent ceiling of the Sistine Chapel, commissioned by Pope Julius II. The painting retells the story of Genesis from the Creation to the Flood and contains hundreds of massive figures. On the end wall of the chapel is the dramatic "Last Judgment" painted by the artist between 1534 and 1541.

the papal control of the Romagna, where lordships were created for the various nephews . . . and when he died in 1484 he left the inheritance of a papacy increasingly dedicated to its position as a princely power in Italy. The tone of his court had become more and more magnificent and an extravagant luxury the common order of high ecclesiastical life in Rome.

His successor, Giovanni Cibo, who took the title of Innocent VIII, was elected at a conclave distinguished for the openly political struggle between the rival candidates. He was weak, compliant, undistinguished, and dominated by the influence of Giuliano della Rovere [nephew of Pope Sixtus IV], who was considered pope in all but name. Innocent's pontificate was notable because of the extent to which the pope's own children were avowed and openly provided for. His death in 1492 fell at a critical turning point in Italian political history, but it can hardly be supposed that if he had continued to live he would have had a very great influence on the evolution of the system of alliances.

Roderigo Borgia came to the throne in 1492 and took the name of Alexander VI. He reigned for eleven years. Although many of the famous scandals associated with his name and pontificate are highly colored versions of the truth, yet he has long since ceased to have any serious defenders. One of the most ambitious and aggressive of all the popes, he centered his hopes on the position of his family rather than on the institution which he presumably served. For over a decade his maneuvers, bargains and shifts of alliance occupied the center of the stage of European diplomacy, but in the end his favorite son, Caesar, failed to hold the position it had cost so much to win. This disastrous pontificate marked the lowest point of corruption and immorality in the Vatican itself.

After the short reign of Pius III, who died less than four weeks after his election, Giuliano della Rovere at last came to the papal throne as Julius II. The most famous of Renaissance popes, the "papa terribile" devoted himself to the enlargement of the states of the church on lines laid down by his predecessors. By a tremendous effort of energy and will be triumphed over a series of crises and lived to see the defeat of the French and the failure of the attempted council of Pisa. He had in a sense delivered the church, but at the price of opening the way to the Spanish domination of the Italian peninsula. One of the greatest patrons in the whole history of the arts, Julius commissioned the work of Michelangelo, Bramante and Raphael. Indeed, the sudden flowering of the style of the High Renaissance in Rome has been attributed to his personal inspiration. It has been suggested that this style was the appropriate expression of the pontiff's religious ideals, the product of a sincere conversion. Whatever the personal religious beliefs of Julius II and their relationship to the artistic achievements of his age, there were many contemporaries who considered the pope's career and ambitions far removed from Christian example. Perhaps no document better illustrates this aspect of contemporary opinion than the satire, *Julius Exclusus,* attributed to Erasmus. . . . Although the satire was not published until 1514 and was always denied by its author, it had a rapid circulation and must have made a profound impression on all who read it. It is cast in the form of a dialogue between Julius II and Saint Peter, in which the former, contrary to his expectation, finds himself excluded from Heaven. Every resource of the author's irony is directed to making manifest the incompatibility between the aims and achievements of this greatest of Renaissance popes and the ideals of the founder of Christianity. Julius finds that he is equipped only with the keys of his money box and of his political power, not with those of the Kingdom of Heaven. Saint Peter refuses to recognize in the warlike figure with his magnificent tiara and pallium the representative of the apostolic succession he had established. The success of this satire, and of others like it, is an indication of the degree to which the prestige of the papacy was declining among the intellectuals. . . .

TOPIC 32

# THE CLASSICAL REVIVAL

The literal meaning of Renaissance is "rebirth" and the most unifying feature of the period known as the Renaissance was the revival of interest in Greek and Roman literature and art. Italian writers of the fourteenth and fifteenth centuries viewed the medieval past as a thousand years of cultural obscurity and ignorance and were convinced that their own age was heir to the greatness of antiquity, that had been interrupted by barbarian invasion and the subsequent loss of ancient learning. The readings examine the relationship of this classical revival to the scholarly, artistic, and Christian life.

**Reading 169**

## The Rise of Humanism



Although there is division of opinion among historians on almost everything else concerned with the Renaissance, including the question of whether there was a Renaissance at all, there is consensus that it started in Italy. . . . There is also no doubt that the Renaissance was most exclusively an urban phenomenon. The medieval nobility had chivalry as its ideal; its pastimes were rudely physical, not to say rustic. Its primary interest was in fighting, not in books. The medieval noble, even in Italy, was rarely literate; even if he lived in a city he was likely to retain his feudal tastes. Most of the Renaissance leaders sprang from a bourgeois background, and had made enough money to be able to afford a life of some leisure and to indulge their taste for literature and the arts. . . .

Italy had never experienced the full pressure of the barbarian invasions at the end of the Roman Empire. Though Ostrogoths and Lombards ruled much of Italy, Italians—descended directly from the Romans—remained in the majority. So the Renaissance Italians believed themselves to be the direct inheritors of the Romans. Their language was the nearest of the European languages to Latin. It was not difficult for them to learn it, and many of the Latin classics were still easily available, even before the humanists began their search for manuscripts. Moreover, there were far more Roman remains in Italy than elsewhere. Thus it was that the Italians, seeking for new ideals suitable to the new situation, had no further to look for examples of secular living than their own Roman ancestors; and it is not surprising that the first stirrings of the Renaissance spirit found expression in the search for ancient manuscripts and the accumulation of libraries of works in the Latin language—not, of course, medieval Latin, which to a true humanist was a barbarous Germanized hodge-podge, but the stately periods of Cicero and the works of the Augustan age.

The consistent ideal of the Renaissance was humanism, which in its widest sense meant the cultivation of the human personality, the regarding of man as the earthly creature he apparently is, and not exclusively as a candidate for salvation. The Greeks in this sense were humanists, as were some of the better-educated Romans, such as Cicero, who had been permeated by Greek culture. It was, however, not unnatural for the men of the Renaissance to give humanism a more restricted meaning. They used it to mean especially the cultivation of the classics, or what are called the humanities. When one speaks therefore of the humanists as a class at this period, the reference is particularly to the scholars who cultivated the use of classical Latin and Greek, and sought for ancient manuscripts in these languages.

Probably the earliest example of this type of humanist was Francesco Petrarca (usually called Petrarch, 1304-1374), a man of varied talents and complex character, who, without being a great genius, was to set the fashion for generations of later humanists, some of whom surpassed him in talent. He wrote some of the best love lyrics in the Italian tongue, but valued far more highly his often pedantic and uninspired Latin epics, because Latin was the language of his beloved Cicero. He was worried in later life about the salvation of his soul because he had loved Laura and addressed to her his exquisite lyrics. He searched for manuscripts, found one of Homer and adored it, but could not bring himself to learn Greek in order to read it. He climbed a minor mountain for the purpose of enjoying nature in the raw and himself expatiating upon that pleasure. He allowed himself to be crowned with laurel as a poet, and accepted with due humility this uncontested title given to him by a self-appointed group of unauthorized donors. But when all this is admitted, the Italian lyrics and odes remain; the self-advertisement did advertise to all that the profession of letters could lead to fame and was thus worthy of pursuit by others; he did initiate the search for manuscripts, and they were safer in the hands of humanists than in fourteenth-century monasteries. Moreover, there can be little doubt that the humanists appreciated them more than did the monks, and they made them available to others who would likewise appreciate them. . . .

### THE IDEAL OF THE "UNIVERSAL MAN"

Ultimately more important than the much publicized recovery of antiquity was the idea of the *uomo universale,* or universal man—the man of versatility who was learned and skilled in all things to which he set his hand. Such a man was Leonardo da Vinci, painter, scientist, and inventor; or Lorenzo the Magnificent, the Medici prince of Florence, poet and literary artist, munificent patron of the arts, soldier, administrator, and businessman. In the great period of the Italian Renaissance few aspired to be specialists, with only one skill highly developed and the remainder left unused. The ideal expressed by a young noble, Pico della Mirandola who, if he had lived to maturity, might well have been among the great universal men of the Renaissance—was the ideal of all. In his *Oration on the Dignity of Man* he gave fine expression to the ideal of man's latent powers to create of himself what he would: "Restrained by no narrow bonds, according to thy own free will . . . thou, thy own free maker and molder, mayest fashion thyself in whatever manner thou likest best." . . .

Petrarch, crowned with a laurel wreath in emulation of the Roman poets of the Classical past. Detail in Palazzo Vecchio, Florence.

Unquestionably this was a reaction against the medieval and Christian ideal—the monk whose task was to work and pray, the scholastic philosopher who concentrated his thought on a limited field of knowledge and added little to it from his experience, the feudal noble with his martial ideals and activities, and his total ignorance of almost everything that lay beyond them. . . .

# Paul Kristeller: The Renaissance Study of the Humanities

Reprinted by permission of the publishers from Paul O. Kristeller, *The Classics and Renaissance Thought,* Cambridge, Mass.: Harvard University Press, Copyright 1955 by the Board of Trustees of Oberlin College. Pp. 9-13, 18-21, 25, 27-28, 30-34.

The term *humanista,* coined at the height of the Renaissance period, was in turn derived from an older term, that is, from the "humanities" or *studia humanitatis.* This term was apparently used in the general sense of a liberal or literary education by such ancient

Roman authors as Cicero and Gellius, and this use was resumed by the Italian scholars of the late fourteenth century. By the first half of the fifteenth century, the *studia humanitatis* came to stand for a clearly defined cycle of scholarly disciplines, namely grammar, rhetoric, history, poetry, and moral philosophy, and the study of each of these subjects was understood to include the reading and interpretation of its standard ancient writers in Latin and, to a lesser extent, in Greek. This meaning of the *studia humanitatis,* remained in general use through the sixteenth century and later, and we may still find an echo of it in our use of the term "humanities." Thus Renaissance humanism was not as such a philosophical tendency or system, but rather a cultural and educational program which emphasized and developed an important but limited area of studies. This area had for its center a group of subjects that was concerned essentially neither with the classics nor with philosophy, but might be roughly described as literature. . . .

The central importance of literary preoccupations in Renaissance humanism might be illustrated by the professional status of the humanists, most of whom were active either as teachers of the humanities in secondary schools or universities, or as secretaries to princes or cities, and by the bulk of their extant writings, which consist of orations, letters, poems, and historical works and which are in part still unpublished or even unsifted. It cannot be our task . . . to give an account of these professional activities of the humanists, or of their contributions to Neolatin literature and to the various vernacular literatures. I merely want to point out that Renaissance humanism must be understood as a characteristic phase in what may be called the rhetorical tradition in Western culture. This tradition is as old as the Greek Sophists, and it is very much alive in our own day, although the word "rhetoric" has become distasteful to many people. For the studies of speech and composition, of English and creative writing, of advertisement and business correspondence are nothing but modern varieties of the age old rhetorical enterprise that tries to teach oral and written expression by means of rules and models. . . . It was the novel contribution of the humanists to add the firm belief that in order to write and to speak well it was necessary to study and to imitate the ancients. Thus we can understand why classical studies in the Renaissance were rarely, if ever, separated from the literary and practical aim of the rhetorician to write and to speak well. This practical and professional connection provided a strong incentive towards classical studies and helped to supply for them the necessary manpower for their proper development. For I cannot help feeling that the achievements of a given nation or period in particular branches of culture depend not only on individual talents, but also on the available professional channels and tasks into which these talents can be drawn and for which they are trained. . . .

The humanist treatises are important in many ways and deserve a more thorough study than they have received. They please through the elegance and clarity of their style and their vivid personal and historical flavor as well as through their well-selected and mellowed classical wisdom. They also air or express interesting opinions on matters that occupied the heart and thought of the authors and their contemporaries. They derive added importance from the fact that some of the genuine and more concrete problems of moral philosophy were apparently neglected by the professional philosophers of the time, and thus the humanists prepared the ground for a more systematic treatment of the same problems by later philosophers. This seems to be the function of poets, writers, and amateur thinkers at any time when the professional philosophers are absorbed in technicalities and refuse to discuss certain basic problems.

If we remember the range and extent of humanist scholarship and literature, we shall not be surprised to learn that Isocrates, Plutarch, and Lucian were among their favorite authors, but that the ancient writer who earned their highest admiration was Cicero. Renaissance humanism was an age of Ciceronianism in which the study and imitation of Cicero was a widespread concern, although the exaggeration of this tendency also found its critics. Cicero's influence in the Renaissance has been the subject of more than one study, and we can merely try to state in a few words some of the main features of this influence. Above all, Cicero's rhetorical works provided the theory, and his orations, letters, and dialogues the concrete models for the main branches of prose literature, whereas the structure of his well-cadenced sentences was imitated in all kinds of literary compositions. Through his philosophical writings, he served as a source of information for several schools of Greek philosophy and also as a model of that eclectic type of thinking which was prepared to take its crumbs of knowledge wherever it could find them, and which also characterizes many of the humanist treatises. Finally, the synthesis of philosophy and rhetoric in his work provided the humanists with a favorite ideal, namely the combination of eloquence and wisdom, an ideal which pervades so much of Renaissance literature. . . .

After the middle of the fifteenth century, the influence of humanistic learning spread outside the limits of the *studia humanitatis* into all areas of Renaissance culture, including philosophy and the various sciences. This was due not only to the fashionable prestige of the humanities, but also the fact that practically every scholar received a humanistic training in secondary school before he acquired a professional training in any of the other disciplines at the university. On the other hand, some of the humanists also began to realize that a thorough study of philosophy should be added to the *studia humanitatis.* Consequently, we find a number of important thinkers in the fifteenth century, such as Cusanus, Ficino, and Pico, and many more in the sixteenth, who combined a more or less thorough-going humanist background with solid philosophical achievements which were derived from different origins. I believe that the discussion of Renaissance humanism in its original meaning has been confused by the attempts to claim these philosophers as an integral part of it, and thus to identify humanism with all or most of Renaissance philosophy. On the other hand, these thinkers should be taken into account if we wish to understand the indirect influence of humanism on Renaissance thought, an influence which in many ways was even more important than its direct contribution.

The pervasive influence of humanism on all aspects of Renaissance culture and especially on its philosophical thought is a vast subject of which we can mention only a few major points. Some influential aspects of Renaissance humanism are characteristic of the age, and not necessarily due to classical influences. There is the emphasis on man, on his dignity and privileged place in the universe, which was forcefully expressed by Petrarch, Manetti, and other humanists, and later elaborated or criticized by many philosophers. This idea was undoubtedly implied in, and connected with, the concept and program of the *studia humanitatis,* and it has provided the opening entry for many modern interpretations of humanism, whenever the specific content of the humanities was left out of account. Another characteristic feature is the tendency to express, and to consider worth expressing, the concrete uniqueness of one's feelings, opinions, experiences, and surroundings, a tendency which appears in the biographical and descriptive literature of the time as well as in its portrait painting, which is present in all the writings of the humanists, and which finds its fullest philosophical expression in Montaigne, who claims that his own self is the main subject matter of his philosophy. This tendency has been adequately described by Burckhardt, who called it "individualism," and those who have debated the individualism of the Renaissance have missed this point entirely when they understand by individualism merely the existence of great individuals. . . .

# The Spread of Learning

The enthusiasm of the humanists for classical learning is shown in a letter of Petrarch (1304–1374) to a friend who had lent him a copy of Cicero. In the days before the printing press, books had to be copied by hand. The second selection describes the founding of the Vatican Library by Pope Nicholas V (1447–1455). From J. H. Robinson, *Readings in European History* (Boston, 1904), I, pp. 527–530.

## I. PETRARCH ON CICERO (14TH CENTURY)

Your copy of Cicero has been in my possession four years and more. There is a good reason, though, for so long a delay; namely, the great scarcity of copyists who understand such work. It is a state of affairs that has resulted in an incredible loss to scholarship. . . . But I must return to your Cicero. I could not do without it, and the incompetence of the copyists would not let me possess it. What was left for me but to rely upon my own resources, and press these weary fingers and this worn and ragged pen into the service? The plan that I followed was this. I want you to know it, in case you should ever have to grapple with a similar task. Not a single word did I read except as I wrote. But how is that, I hear some one say; did you write without knowing what it was that you were writing? Ah! but from the very first it was enough for me to know that it was a work of Tullius [Cicero], and an extremely rare one too. And then as soon as I was fairly started, I found at every step so much sweetness and charm, and felt so strong a desire to advance, that the only difficulty which I experienced in reading and writing at the same time came from the fact that my pen could not cover the ground so rapidly as I wanted it to, whereas my expectation had been rather that it would outstrip my eyes, and that my ardor for writing would be chilled by the slowness of my reading.

So the pen held back the eye, and the eye drove on the pen, and I covered page after page, delighting in my task, and committing many and many a passage to memory as I wrote. For just in proportion as the writing is slower than the reading does the passage make a deep impression and cling to the mind.

### II. POPE NICHOLAS V FOUNDS THE VATICAN LIBRARY (15TH CENTURY)

Owing to the jubilee of 1450 a great quantity of money came in by this means to the apostolic see, and with this the pope commenced building in many places, and sent for Greek and Latin books, wherever he was able to find them, without regard to price. He gathered together a large band of writers, the best that he could find, and kept them in constant employment. He also summoned a number of learned men, both for the purpose of composing new works and of translating such existing works as were not already translated, giving them most abundant provision for their needs meanwhile; and when the works were translated and brought to him, he gave them large sums of money, in order that they should do more willingly that which they undertook to do.

He made great provision for the needs of learned men. He gathered together great numbers of books upon every subject, both Greek and Latin, to the number of five thousand volumes. So at his death it was found by inventory that never since the time of Ptolemy had half that number of books of every kind been brought together. All books he caused to be copied, without regard to what it cost him, and there were few places where his Holiness had not copiers at work. When he could not procure a book for himself in any way, he had it copied.

After he had assembled at Rome, as I said above, many learned men at large salaries, he wrote to Florence to Messer Giannozzo Manetti . . . urging him to attempt the translation of the books of the Bible and of Aristotle, and to complete the book already commenced by him, *Contra Judoeos et gentes;* a wonderful work, if it had been completed, but he carried it only to the tenth book. . . .

It was Pope Nicholas' intention to found a library in St. Peter's, for the general use of the whole Roman curia, which would have been an admirable thing indeed, if he had been able to carry it out, but death prevented his bringing it to completion. He illumined the Holy Scriptures through innumerable books, which he caused to be translated; and in the same way with the works of the pagans, including certain works upon grammar, of use in learning Latin,—the *Orthography* of Messer Giovanni Tortelle, who was of his Holiness' household and worked upon the library, a worthy book and useful to grammarians; the *Iliad* of Homer; Strabo's *De situ orbis* he caused to be translated by Guerrino, and gave him five hundred florins for each part,—that is to say, Asia, Africa, and Europe; that was in all fifteen hundred florins. Herodotus and Thucydides he had translated by Lorenzo Valla, and rewarded him liberally. . . .

# The Invention of Printing

From Sir George Clark, *Early Modern Europe from About 1450 to About 1720* (New York, 1960: Oxford University Press), pp. 52–60.

### I

In the year after the fall of Constantinople [1454] Pope Nicholas V proclaimed an indulgence, a remission of spiritual penalties for their sins, for all who would contribute money to the defence of Cyprus against the Turks. It happens that the announcement of this indulgence is the earliest piece of paper printed from movable type in Europe to which we can assign a definite date. We have no reason to suppose that anyone foresaw the full significance of this new technological contrivance. Certainly Mahomet II [the Turkish conqueror], if he ever heard of it, did not infer that the west had new reserves of strength and inventiveness which in time would reverse its relations with the east. . . .

We cannot be certain whether the Europeans learnt printing directly or indirectly from the Chinese or found it out for themselves. We do not even know exactly when or where it was first practised in Europe, but our ignorance of these matters reinforces the knowledge that the new art was not brought full-grown from outside to a western civilization wholly unprepared for it, as the telephone was brought to nineteenth-century Africa. There had been a series of preparatory stages on the technical side. As early as the thirteenth, or even the twelfth, century designs had been printed on textile fabrics from wood blocks cut in relief. Until the beginning of the fifteenth century writing had to be done on parchment and similar materials made from skins, of which the quantity was necessarily limited and the price comparatively high. From that time, however, there were ample supplies of rag-paper, and these made it possible for book-production and writing in general to expand indefinitely. Block-printing on paper came in: there were woodcut pictures of saints, and playing-cards.

The laborious and time-consuming task of writing a manuscript by hand was greatly simplified by the invention of the printing press. Left, a medieval German scholar; right, a scene from a printer's shop in Amsterdam about 1600.

Then only a few adaptations of presses and block-making were necessary to perfect the art, and the final steps were taken most likely in Mainz, a rich trading town and a cultivated ecclesiastical capital. . . .

Works of art became familiar which were not unique, or approximately like their originals, as hand-drawn copies may be, but so nearly identical that for ordinary purposes there was no difference. Many people could possess the same picture. That was a very great change, but there were others. By constantly seeing woodcuts and other engravings, people acquired a new habit or power of seeing not in colour but in black and white, which in some ways enriched and in other ways impoverished their mode of seeing. The world of sight and imagination altered. . . .

No sooner was printing discovered than a great demand for printed books and papers made itself effective throughout all the Latin area. Within a generation there were presses at work in France, Italy, Spain, the Netherlands, England, and Denmark. Before the end of the century Portugal and Sweden had them, and even Montenegro, the Balkan outpost. Books, of course, could be exported to countries where there was no printing; in the sixteenth century a well-organized international book-trade grew up, serving most of the western countries. . . .

Books could now be produced far more quickly, far more cheaply, and in far greater

Facsimile page from the Gutenberg Bible, 1454. Note that although the work was printed with movable type, the pages are illuminated in order to imitate a handcopied manuscript.

numbers. This was a revolution, a revolution continuing until, in our own time, the new inventions for reproducing sound have ended the age in which the printed word has been the main vehicle for spreading knowledge, information, ideas, and even emotions abroad. Beneath all the events of these centuries there has gone on the change from the first printers, who could put out a few hundred copies of a book in a few weeks, to the modern printers who can make a million copies of a newspaper in a few hours. The world has been filled with these uncountable printed sheets and volumes, large and small, cheap or costly, rare or universally familiar, durable or ephemeral, treasured or neglected, commonplace or exquisitely beautiful. Every one of them has left some result behind it, and the sum of these results is far beyond calculation.

It is easy to see that printing made the spread of literacy much easier; and the power to read and write is an instrument of authority if it belongs to a few, but a stepping-stone to equality if it belongs to many. As the number of readers increased, the influence of writers grew with it. In universities, in public affairs, and among general readers there were more books to be had, and so the more personal influence of the teacher or expositor gave way before the might of the book, of the unseen author. Literary reputations could be made and spread as quickly as ships and horses could carry packages of books. Erasmus had a European reputation, and every book he published was known from one end of the continent to the other as soon as it was ready. Every man who could read or be read to was accessible to persuasions, propaganda, from far and near, perhaps authorized, perhaps directed against established ideas and institutions. Governments and the Church, trying, in accordance with their traditions, to keep their control of men's minds, made rules of censorship and new institutions for enforcing them; but the simple machinery of government . . . was often unable to dam the rising streams. From clandestine presses, through secret channels of distribution, writers could still appeal to their readers against the established order. . . .

## II

Perhaps the greatest changes which printing brought with it were not these social changes, but the changes in language and literature themselves. Printed books set the standards of uniformity for languages, and so the multiplicity of dialects began to give way before a few great standard literary languages, centred on the political or academic or trading capitals. All Englishmen came to write the language of London; all Frenchmen that of Paris; most of the Spaniards that of Castile. This took time, and it happened more or less quickly according to circumstances. . . . Wherever it did emerge the metropolitan language had a binding and inspiring force of its own, and strengthened the national feeling that was already growing.

In literature the changes were subtle, but radical. It was much easier than before to bring together many books in one place, and so masses of information could be assembled quickly, and the apparatus of learning was transformed. Great books of reference, dictionaries, encyclopaedias, histories, and collections of texts, put at the disposal of every student knowledge which once could not have been gathered in a lifetime. Knowledge of the present was deepened, but also complicated and hindered, by an ever-present consciousness of the past. At the same time standards of correctness became more exacting. With so many identical copies of books before them, not varied by the little touches of individuality which scribes and copyists always introduced intentionally or by accident, readers learnt a new strictness in verbal accuracy and grammatical correctness. The individual work of an author was distinguished more sharply from the inherited or borrowed elements. Copyright became a legal fact, while authorship and plagiarism, as literary and ethical conceptions, were more clearly defined. The Renaissance was helped on not only as an intellectual movement but as a movement in the art of letters as well. The commonest way of enjoying poetry had been to hear it recited; the commonest way of using a book had been to read it aloud. Now there was so much reading that more and more people read silently to themselves, and books came to be written so that they could best be taken in by the eye and not the ear. Prose gained at the expense of verse; sense gained at the expense of sound. Memory lost some of its value. The story that can be followed without a teller has to be told in a special way: the words themselves, without a voice to clothe them in expression, without accent or intonation, must create their own illusion. So printing set new problems for literature, and as skilful writers devised means of solving them, the range of literature increased until it became, for millions of human beings, almost a substitute for thought and imagination. In the beginning of pre-history speech had given the power of communicating experience, of imagining oneself as a different being, in another time or place. Long afterwards writing had made imagination fixed and lasting and able to add one fancy to another beyond the range of memory, far away from the personal present. Printing set the works of imagination, along with those of thought and emotion, still more securely outside the chances of the present time and place.

# Petrarch Is Torn between the Spirit and the World

Francesco Petrarch (1304–1374), one of the greatest humanists, wrote extensively in both Latin and Italian and was one of the first to realize the potential of classical literature in providing men with a new cultural framework. Nonetheless, born in the High Middle Ages, he was torn by the conflict of spiritual and secular values which he reveals in this imaginary conversation between himself and St. Augustine. From Francesco Petrarch, *The Secret, or the Soul's Conflict with Passion,* trans. by William H. Draper. (London, 1911), pp. 175–192.

[St. Augustine] . . . But let us take for granted (what is quite impossible) that the duration of life will be long and assured: still, do you not find it is the height of madness to squander the best years and the best parts of your existence on pleasing only the eyes of others and tickling other men's ears, and to keep the last and worst—the years that are almost good for nothing—that bring nothing but distaste for life and then its end—to keep these, I say, for God and yourself, as though the welfare of your soul were the last thing you cared for?

Even supposing the time were certain, is it not reversing the true order to put off the best to the last?

[Petrarch] I do not think my way of looking at it is so unreasonable as you imagine. My principle is that, as concerning the glory which we may hope for here below, it is right for us to seek while we are here below. One may expect to enjoy that other more radiant glory in heaven, when we shall have there arrived, and when one will have no more care or wish for the glory of earth. Therefore, as I think, it is in the true order that mortal men should first care for mortal things; and that to things transitory things eternal should succeed; because to pass from those to these is to go forward in most certain accordance with what is ordained for us, although no way is open for us to pass back again from eternity to time.

[St. Augustine] O man, little in yourself, and of little wisdom! Do you, then, dream that you shall enjoy every pleasure in heaven and earth, and everything will turn out fortunate and prosperous for you always and everywhere? But that delusion has betrayed thousands of men thousands of times, and has sunk into hell a countless host of souls. Thinking to have one foot on earth and one in heaven, they could neither stand here below nor mount on high. Therefore they fell miserably, and the moving breeze swept them suddenly away, some in the flower of their age, and some when they were in midst of their years and all their business. . . .

[Petrarch] What must I do, then? Abandon my unfinished works? Or would it be better to hasten them on, and, if God gives me grace, put the finishing touches to them? If I were once rid of these cares I would go forward, with a mind more free, to greater things; for hardly could I bear the thought of leaving half completed a work so fine and rich in promise of success.

[St. Augustine] Which foot you mean to hobble on, I do not know. You seem inclined to leave yourself derelict, rather than your books.

As for me, I shall do my duty, with what success depends on you; but at least I shall have satisfied my conscience. Throw to the winds these great loads of histories; the deeds of the Romans have been celebrated quite enough by others, and are known by their own fame. Get out of Africa* and leave it to its possessors. You will add nothing to the glory of your Scipio [Roman leader] or to your own. He can be exalted to no higher pinnacle, but you may bring down his reputation, and with it your own. Therefore leave all this on one side, and now at length take possession of yourself; and to come back to our starting point, let me urge you to enter upon the meditation of your last end, which comes on step by step without your being aware. . . .

When your eyes behold some ancient building, let your first thought be, Where are those who wrought it with their hands? and when you see new ones, ask, Where, soon, the builders of them will be also? If you chance to see the trees of some orchard, remember how often it falls out that one plants it and another plucks the fruit; for many a time the saying of the *Georgics* comes to pass—

> "One plants the tree, but ah, the slow-grown shade
> His grandchild will enjoy."

*Petrarch was writing a history of the war between Rome and Carthage.

And when you look with pleased wonder at some swiftly flowing stream, then, that I bring no other poet's thought, keep ever in mind this one of your own—

> "No river hurries with more rapid flight
> Than Life's swift current." . . .

[Petrarch] Ah! would that you had told me all this before I had surrendered myself over to these studies! . . .

I will be true to myself, so far as in me lies. I will pull myself together and collect my scattered wits, and make a great endeavour to possess my soul in patience. But even while we speak, a crowd of important affairs, though only of the world, is waiting my attention.

[St. Augustine] For the common herd of men these may be what to them seem more important; but in reality there is nothing of more importance, and nothing ought to be esteemed of so much worth. For, of other trains of thought, you may reckon them to be not essential for the soul, but the end of life will prove that these we have been engaged in are of eternal necessity.

[Petrarch] I confess they are so. And I now return to attend to those other concerns only in order that, when they are discharged, I may come back to these.

I am not ignorant that, as you said a few minutes before, it would be much safer for me to attend only to the care of my soul, to relinquish altogether every bypath and follow the straight path of the way of salvation. But I have not strength to resist that old bent for study altogether. . . .

# Pico Della Mirandola Extols the Uniqueness of Man (1486)

Giovanni Pico Della Mirandola (1463–1494), a brilliant young Italian philosopher, wrote this praise of man at the age of twenty-four. The "Oration on the Dignity of Man" introduced 900 theses in which Pico tried to reconcile Greek and Christian thought, a daring attempt which led to trouble with the Church. From G. Pico Della Mirandola, *Oration on the Dignity of Man,* trans. A. R. Caponigri (Chicago: Gateway, 1956), pp. 1–5.

Most esteemed Fathers, I have read in the ancient writings of the Arabians that Abdala the Saracen on being asked what, on this stage, so to say, of the world, seemed to him most evocative of wonder, replied that there was nothing to be seen more marvelous than man. And that celebrated exclamation of Hermes Trismegistus, "What a great miracle is man, Asclepius," confirms this opinion.

And still, as I reflected upon the basis assigned for these estimations, I was not fully persuaded by the diverse reasons advanced by a variety of persons for the preeminence of human nature; for example: that man is the intermediary between creatures, that he is the familiar of the gods above him as he is lord of the beings beneath him; that, by the acuteness of his senses, the inquiry of his reason and the light of his intelligence, he is the interpreter of nature, set midway between the timeless unchanging and the flux of time; the living union (as the Persians say), the very marriage hymn of the world, and, by David's testimony but little lower than the angels. Their reasons are all, without question, of great weight; nevertheless, they do not touch the principal reasons, those, that is to say, which justify man's unique right to such unbounded admiration. Why, I asked, should we not admire the angels themselves and the beatific choirs more: At long last, however, I feel that I have come to some understanding of why man is the most fortunate of living things and, consequently, deserving of all admiration; of what may be the conditions in the hierarchy of beings assigned to him, which draws upon him the envy, not of the brutes alone, but of the astral beings and of the very intelligences which dwell beyond the confines of the world. A thing surpassing belief and smiting the soul with wonder. Still, how could it be otherwise? For it is on this ground that man is, with complete justice, considered and called a great miracle and a being worthy of all admiration.

Hear then, oh Fathers, precisely what this condition of man is; and in the name of your humanity, grant me your benign audition as I pursue this theme.

God the Father, the Mightiest Architect, had already raised, according to the precepts of His hidden wisdom, this world we see, the cosmic dwelling of divinity, a temple most august. He had already adorned the supercelestial region with Intelligences, infused the heavenly globes with the life of immortal souls and set the fermenting dung-heap of the inferior world teeming with every form of animal life. But when this work was done, the Divine Artificer still longed for some creature which might comprehend the meaning of so vast an achievement, which might be moved with love at its beauty and smitten with awe at its grandeur. When, consequently, all else had been completed (as both Moses and Timaeus testify), in the very last place, He bethought Himself of bringing forth man. Truth was, however, that there remained no archetype according to which He might fashion a new offspring, nor in His treasure-houses the wherewithal to endow a new son with a fitting inheritance, nor any place, among the seats of the universe, where this new creature might dispose himself to contemplate the world. All space was already filled; all things had been distributed in the highest, the middle and the lowest orders. Still, it was not in the nature of the power of the Father to fail . . . nor was it in the nature of that supreme Wisdom to hesitate through lack of counsel in so crucial a matter; nor, finally, in the nature of His beneficent love to compel the creature destined to praise the divine generosity in all other things to find it wanting in himself.

At last, the Supreme Maker decreed that this creature, to whom He could give nothing wholly his own, should have a share in the particular endowment of every other creature. Taking man, therefore, this creature of indeterminate image, He set him in the middle of the world and thus spoke to him:

"We have given you, Oh Adam, no visage proper to yourself, nor any endowment properly your own, in order that whatever place, whatever form, whatever gifts you may, with premeditation, select, these same you may have and possess through your own judgment and decision. The nature of all other creatures is defined and restricted within laws which We have laid down; you, by contrast, impeded by no such restrictions, may, by your own free will, to whose custody We have assigned you, trace for yourself the lineaments of your own nature. I have placed you at the very center of the world, so that from that vantage point you may with greater ease glance round about you on all that the world contains. We have made you a creature neither of heaven nor of earth, neither mortal nor immortal, in order that you may, as the free and proud shaper of your own being, fashion yourself in the form you may prefer. It will be in your power to descend to the lower, brutish forms of life; you will be able, through your own decision, to rise again to the superior orders whose life is divine.

Oh unsurpassed generosity of God the Father, Oh wondrous and unsurpassable felicity of man, to whom it is granted to have what he chooses, to be what he wills to be! The brutes, from the moment of their birth, bring with them, as Lucilius says, "from their mother's womb" all that they will ever possess. The highest spiritual beings were, from the very moment of creation, or soon thereafter, fixed in the mode of being which would be theirs through measureless eternities. But upon man, at the moment of his creation, God bestowed seeds pregnant with all possibilities, the germs of every form of life. Whichever of these a man shall cultivate, the same will mature and bear fruit in him. If vegetative, he will become a plant; if sensual, he will become brutish; if rational, he will reveal himself a heavenly being; if intellectual, he will be an angel and the son of God. And if, dissatisfied with the lot of all creatures, he should recollect himself into the center of his own unity, he will there, become one spirit with God, in the solitary darkness of the Father, Who is set above all things, himself transcends all creatures. . . .

# Jacob Burckhardt: Leon Battista Alberti

The classic interpretation of the Italian Renaissance was formulated by the Swiss cultural historian Jacob Burckhardt (1818–1897) in *The Civilization of the Renaissance in Italy* (1860). Burckhardt believed that each time period has its own pattern of culture, and he felt that the fourteenth and fifteenth centuries in Italy marked the beginning of the modern world. For him the new era was characterized most notably by man's rediscovery of the world about him and his reassessment of his own potential. In the reading Burckhardt describes the varied capabilities of one such Renaissance man. From Jacob Burckhardt, *The Civilization of the Renaissance in Italy,* trans. S. Middlemore (London: Phaidon Press Ltd., 1951), pp. 85–87.

The fifteenth century is, above all, that of the many-sided man. . . . But among these many-sided men, some, who may truly be called all-sided, tower above the rest. Before analysing the general phases of life and culture of this period, we may here, on the threshold of the fifteenth century, consider for a moment the figure of one of these giants—Leon Battista Alberti (b. 1404, d. 1472). His biography, which is only a fragment, speaks of him but little as an artist, and makes no mention at all of his great significance in the history of architecture. We shall now see what he was, apart from these special claims to distinction.

In all by which praise is won, Leon Battista was from his childhood the first. Of his various gymnastic feats and exercises we read with astonishment how, with his feet together, he could spring over a man's head; how, in the cathedral, he threw a coin in the air till it was heard to ring against the distant roof; how the wildest horses trembled under him. In three things he desired to appear faultless to others, in walking, in riding, and in speaking. He learned music without a master, and yet his compositions were admired by professional judges. Under the pressure of poverty, he studied both civil and canonical law for many years, till exhaustion brought on a severe illness. In his twenty-fourth year, finding his memory for words weakened, but his sense of facts unimpaired, he set to work at physics and mathematics. And all the while he acquired every sort of accomplishment and dexterity, cross-examining artists, scholars and artisans of all descriptions, down to the cobblers, about the secrets and peculiarities of their craft. Painting and modelling he practised by the way, and especially excelled in admirable likenesses from memory. Great admiration was excited by his mysterious 'camera obscura', in which he showed at one time the stars and the moon rising over rocky hills, at another wide landscapes with mountains and gulfs receding into dim perspective, and with fleets advancing on the waters in shade or sunshine. And that which others created he welcomed joyfully, and held every human achievement which followed the laws of beauty for something almost divine. To all this must be added his literary works, first of all those on art, which are landmarks and authorities of the first order for the Renaissance of Form, especially in architecture; then his Latin prose writings—novels and other works—of which some have been taken for productions of

1.

2.

3.

**4.**

**1.** "Bindo Altoviti" by Raphael, about 1515.

**2.** "David" by Donatello, about 1453. This is the first nude statue since Roman times.

**3.** "Adoration of the Magi" by Boticelli, completed in 1478. Piero, Cosimo and Giovanni di Medici appear in the painting as the Three Wise Men.

**4.** "Birth of Saint John the Baptist" by Ghirlandaio, completed about 1490. The ladies in the painting are members of the Tornabuoni family which commissioned the painting.

**5.** "The Descent From the Cross" by Pontormo, c.1526–28. Later Renaissance art called Mannerism.

**5.**

antiquity; his elegies, eclogues, and humorous dinner-speeches. He also wrote an Italian treatise on domestic life in four books; and even a funeral oration on his dog. His serious and witty sayings were thought worth collecting, and specimens of them, many columns long, are quoted in his biography. And all that he had and knew he imparted, as rich natures always do, without the least reserve, giving away his chief discoveries for nothing. But the deepest spring of his nature has yet to be spoken of—the sympathetic intensity with which he entered into the whole life around him. At the sight of noble trees and waving cornfields he shed tears; handsome and dignified old men he honoured as 'a delight of nature', and could never look at them enough. Perfectly formed animals won his goodwill as being specially favoured by nature; and more than once, when he was ill, the sight of a beautiful landscape cured him. No wonder that those who saw him in this close and mysterious communion with the world ascribed to him the gift of prophecy. He was said to have foretold a bloody catastrophe in the family of Este, the fate of Florence and that of the Popes many years beforehand, and to be able to read in the countenances and the hearts of men. It need not be added that an iron will pervaded and sustained his whole personality; like all the great men of the Renaissance, he said, 'Men can do all things if they will'. . . .

# Alberti Praises His Fellow Artists

Leon Battista Alberti (1404–1472) wrote the letter from which the following excerpts are taken to another renowned architect, Filippo Brunelleschi (1377–1446), designer of the famous dome of the Cathedral of Florence. From *Literary Source of Art History: An Anthology of Texts from Theophilus to Goethe,* ed. by Elizabeth Holt (Copyright 1947 by Princeton University Press), pp. 109–110. Reprinted by permission of Princeton University Press.

I used to be at once amazed and grieved that so many fine and godly arts and sciences, which we know, from their works and histories, flourished in those most virtuous ancients of old, are now lacking and almost entirely lost: painters, sculptors, architects, musicians, geometricians, rhetoricians, soothsayers, and similar most noble and wonderful minds are very rare and of little account. Hence I believed that it was as many people told me, that nature, the mistress of things, had now indeed grown old and weary, and, just as she no longer brought forth giants, so with talents, which in her younger and more glorious times, so to speak, she brought forth plentifully and wonderfully.

But after I was brought back here to this city of ours, adorned above all others, from the long exile in which we Alberti have grown old, I realized that in many, but especially in you, Filippo, and in our dear friend Donato the sculptor, and in those others, Nencio, Luca, and Masaccio, there was talent for every noble thing not to be ranked below any who was ancient and famous in these arts. Therefore I perceived that the power to gain praise consists in our industry and diligence no less than in the benefit of nature and the times. And I reveal to you, that if it was less difficult for the ancients, having as they had so very many to learn from and imitate, to rise to a knowledge of those supreme arts that are so toilsome for us today, then so much the more our fame should be greater if we, without teachers or any model, find arts and sciences unheard of and never seen. Who is so stubborn or so envious that he would not praise Pippo the architect, when he sees such a big building here, set aloft above the heavens, ample to cover all the peoples of Tuscany with its shade, made without any aid from scaffolding or quantity of timber?—a skillful construction which, if my opinion is right, as in our times it was unbelievable that it could be done, so among the ancients it was perhaps not known or known about.



# J. H. Randall: The Humanistic Spirit

In *The Making of the Modern Mind,* John Herman Randall (1899– ) tried to "make the thought of the present more intelligible by entering sympathetically into the spirit of the past." In this reading Randall comments on the gradual growth of the humanistic spirit that underlay the Renaissance. *The Making of the Modern Mind.* Copyright renewed, 1954, by John Herman Randall, Jr. Reprinted by permission of the publisher, Houghton Mifflin Company.

It is, of course, impossible to speak of *the* Renaissance, as though it were a single age or a single force, and had a definite date, like the French Revolution. Moreover, dramatic and painfully beautiful as were the life and the products of the Italy of the fifteenth and sixteenth centuries, the age of the humanists and of the noontide of Italian art does not mark one of the major intellectual events of the Western peoples. The earlier renaissance of the twelfth and thirteenth centuries was a much more unmistakable rebirth of the mind, while the forces at work in the Middle Ages, which in the sixteenth century were clearly revealed as disruptive of the old order, did not produce their fundamental revolution in men's ways of thinking until the seventeenth and eighteenth. Nevertheless, though the old forms and the old beliefs persisted relatively unchanged, that period which we loosely call the Renaissance was marked by the increasing prevalence of attitudes and interests that had hitherto played but a minor role in the life of Western Europe. These growing interests burst the bonds of the narrow if intricately carved medieval world and left men toying with the fragments. . . .

If, then, the central feature of the period of the Renaissance is an outgrowing, a freeing from ties that have proved to be bonds, it is evident that we have to do with new forces arising within an old order, with stresses and strains, with unstable attempts to effect some kind of adjustment between traditional allegiances and modern appeals. The age of the Renaissance and the Reformation was above all others an age of compromise. If in the joy of widened vistas many were intoxicated by the beauty and the lusts of life at its richest, many more were caught half-hesitant, reluctant, like Bruno, both to leave the Father's house, and not to venture into the glorious world. What was best in Renaissance and Reformation could not last; it was the noble enthusiasm of youth, and what was needed was the hard and painful work of maturity. Nor could what was worst endure; it was the incongruous compromise between elements neither of which was clearly understood, the Christian tradition and the natural, pagan, view of man's life and its scene. The Western peoples were leaving the old world; eagerly they snatched at the treasures of Greece and Rome as they moved onward to the new. But not till the turn of the seventeenth century did any man realize the nature of that new world, and not till the nineteenth did its features impress the average man. . . .

This rapid growth involved fundamental readjustments in every institution of society; it also demanded thoroughgoing intellectual reconstruction. The changes that came over the mind of Europe during this period, its new knowledge and new ideals, were conditioned by a multitude of other factors, but every new belief, every changed view of man and his destiny, was worked out by men living in such a society and powerfully influenced at every turn by the forces of this society. Only against this background is it possible to understand the new aspirations of the European nations, their achievements and their errors. But if the roots of the new world of the Renaissance are to be sought in economic conditions, its justification and its meaning are to be found in the new spirit and knowledge, that destroyed monasticism and Aristotelian science as capitalism was destroying feudalism and the guilds.

This new spirit consisted at bottom in an increasing interest in human life as it can be lived upon earth, within the bourne of time and space, and without necessary reference to any other destiny in the beyond or the hereafter. It meant the decay of that Oriental dualism in which the flesh for so many long years had lusted against the spirit, and the growth in its stead of the conviction that the life of flesh and spirit merged into one living man is not evil, but good. It meant that when society offered more than a rude mining-camp existence of blood and toil, the monastic temper declined, and gave way to a new and vital perception of the dignity of man, of the sweetness and glory of being a rational animal.

It happened that those who felt the call of human experience had a great literature to which they could turn, a literature written by peoples who had been stirred by the same passion for the free life of man in its natural setting. The frenzied zeal with which they did find in this literature a confirmation of their own inward stirrings in the face of a rich urban society, has left an indelible impress on the form taken by this interest in the natural man. But if the manuscripts of Greece and Rome had perished every one beneath the monk's missal, the outcome would not have been essentially different. Men would still have turned to man and nature, and if the modern world might not so soon have come into being, it is quite possible that men would not have wandered down so many blind alleys. Of a truth the Renaissance discovered the humanities, but it found them in Florence or Augsburg or Paris, not in ancient books. The books had always been there; they were discovered when men had grown fit to appreciate them. The polished and urbane Cicero, he who had taken the intellectual world of Greece and translated it from the idiom of free and heaven-questioning Athens into the Roman tongue of the market-place and the law-court, he who had dropped from the already fundamentally anthropomorphic wisdom of Hellas all that led the mind away from the passions and the will of the moral life of man, became naturally the idol of those whose days were passed in palace or piazza; and his conception of culture as essentially *Studia humanitatis ac litterarum,* the study of humanity and letters, was acclaimed by those dissatisfied with Acquinas' "truths of God."

TOPIC 33

# THE CURRENT OF CHRISTIAN REFORM

The striving of the late medieval Church for wealth and power produced a counter-current of reformist agitation. At issue was the very definition of the Christian Church and its relationship to the values of an increasingly commercial world. The Reformers drew inspiration from the ideals of the early Church, the popular desire for direct communication with God, and growing national feelings. The leaders of the reform movement wanted to change the Church from within, but the nature of their quest threatened, against their own will, to split the Church before they could change it. The readings describe the conditions that weakened the authority of the Church and introduce the programs of reform.

**Reading 178**

## Struggle for Reform in the Church



In the light of world history, as we see it today, one of the most momentous experiences that can befall any civilization is for it to break loose from its religious base. . . . It is not, in most cases, that peoples reject their ancestral religion. On the contrary, they often reaffirm it; but they try also to modernize it, to adapt it, to make room for new and non-religious interests, to bring it about that religion instead of being the womb or matrix from which all else comes, shall be one interest among many.

Latin Christendom was the first modern society to embark on the momentous, troublesome, and long drawn out process of "secularization." In 1300 Europe was still primarily a religious community. The clergy were the prestige-enjoying class. All else was somehow oriented to or pervaded by religious belief. Three centuries later religion was one interest among many. The church itself was divided. The Christian faith still stood; indeed it was purified and reaffirmed both by . . . Protestant and . . . Catholic. But other interests made equal claims upon men's attention. Government, law, philosophy, science, the arts, material and economic activities were pursued without regard to Christian values. Power, order, beauty, wealth, knowledge, control of nature were all accepted as desirable in themselves. . . .

### THE DECLINE OF THE CHURCH

At the close of the thirteenth century the church of the High Middle Ages, centralized in the papacy, stood at its zenith. But the church (as good Catholics always remind us) was staffed by mortal men who were no different from others. The church faced the danger that besets every successful institution—a form of government, an army or navy, a business corporation, a labor union, a university, to choose modern examples—the danger of believing that the institution exists for the benefit of those who conduct its affairs. The papacy, being at the top, was the most liable to this danger. The papacy became "corrupt," set in its ways, absorbed by the possession of wealth and authority, afflicted by a self-perpetuating bureaucracy, out of touch with public opinion, more concerned with maintaining papal grandeur than with spiritual religion, unable to reform itself, and unwilling to let anyone else reform it. At the same time, forces quite outside the papacy or the church, forces which had been growing up for generations before 1300, became too strong after 1300 to be held in the old containers, asserted themselves with ever more insistence, and clashed with the official clergy of the international church. Such forces, especially, were the new national monarchies and the commercial classes in the towns.

The decline of the papacy can be readily dated, from the time when Pope Boniface VIII ran into trouble with the kings of England and of France. These two kings, needing money for war, undertook to tax the clergy in their respective kingdoms, in both of which the clergy were substantial owners of land. Boniface prohibited the taxation of clergy by the civil ruler. In the ensuing altercation, in 1302, he issued the famous bull *Unam Sanctam,* the most extreme of all assertions of papal supremacy, declaring that outside the Roman church there was no salvation, and that "every human creature" was "subject to the Roman pontiff." The French king, Philip the Fair, retorted by sending soldiers to arrest Boniface, who soon died. French influence in the college of cardinals brought about the election of a pope who was subservient to Philip, and who took up his residence, with his court and officials, at Avignon on the lower Rhone river, on the then borders of France. Thus began the "Babylonian Captivity" of the church. The rest of Europe regarded the popes at Avignon throughout the century as tools of France. The prestige of the papacy as a universal institution was badly dimmed.

Attempts to correct the situation made matters worse. In 1378 the college of cardinals, torn by French and anti-French factions within it, elected two popes. Both were equally legitimate, being chosen by the cardinals, but one lived at Rome, one at Avignon, and neither would resign. The French and their supporters recognized the Avignon pope, England and most of Germany, the Roman. For forty years both lines were perpetuated. There were now two papacies, estranged by the Great Schism of the West, and it seemed as if the schism might become permanent, as the earlier schism between Rome and Constantinople had proved to be. All agreed that the situation was scandalous and must be ended, but no one in an influential position would make the sacrifice necessary to put it to an end.

Never had the papacy been so externally magnificent as in the days of the Captivity and the Schism. The papal court at Avignon surpassed the courts of kings in splendor. The papal officialdom grew in numbers, ignoring the deeper problems while busily transacting each day's business. Papal revenues mounted, and new papal taxes were devised, for example the "annates," by which every bishop or abbot in Christendom had to transmit to Rome most of the first year's income of his office. In the continuing movement of funds from all over Europe to the papal court, from the thirteenth century on, a new class of international bankers rose and prospered.

But the papacy, never so sumptuous, had never since the tenth century rested on such shaky foundations. People pay willingly for institutions in which they believe, and admire magnificence in leaders whom they respect. But before 1378, with the pope submissive to France, and after 1378, with two popes and two papacies to support, there was growing complaint at the extravagance and worldliness of papal rule. The most pious Christians were the most shocked. To them the behavior of the cardinals was disgraceful. Earnest souls were worried in conscience. To obtain God's grace was to them of all things the most vital, but with two churches under two popes, each claiming to hold the keys of Peter, how could anyone be certain that his church gave him true salvation? In a society that was still primarily a religious community, this sense of religious insecurity was a source of unutterable uneasiness and dread.

It was widely agreed, in this afflicted society, that the true church must be restored in its purity. Led by men like the Italian Marsiglio of Padua, or the Englishmen Ockham and Wycliff, reformers declared that the church consisted in the whole body of the faithful, not merely or even primarily in the clergy. If the clergy, they said, were not performing their spiritual duties to the laity, then either a secular ruler or a general council representing the whole church might enforce reform upon the clergy, and even upon the pope. John Wycliff went even further. He taught, about 1380, that no visible church was needful for salvation, that ordinary persons might obtain divine grace by reading the Bible, without the ministrations of any clergy whatsoever. This doctrine, which, if pursued far enough, would explode any church as an authoritative institution, was promptly branded as heresy. Wycliff nevertheless won many adherents. In England itself they were mostly "poor men," called Lollards, who sought escape from all forms of established authority. In Bohemia, John Huss took up Wycliff's ideas, and here the doctrine became a national movement. The Hussites were both a religious party and at the same time a Slavic or Czech party protesting against the supremacy of the Germans who lived in Bohemia. The Hussite wars ravaged central Europe for decades in the early part of the fifteenth century.

## THE CONCILIAR MOVEMENT AND ITS FAILURE

Settled, influential, educated, and established persons did not turn to heresy, nor yet to witchcraft or flagellation. Their answer to the needs of the day was the conciliar movement. Professors at the universities, advisers to kings, enlightened bishops, thoughtful burghers, about 1400, believed the pope (or rather, popes) to be incapable of reforming existing abuses. They demanded a great Europe-wide council of the entire church at

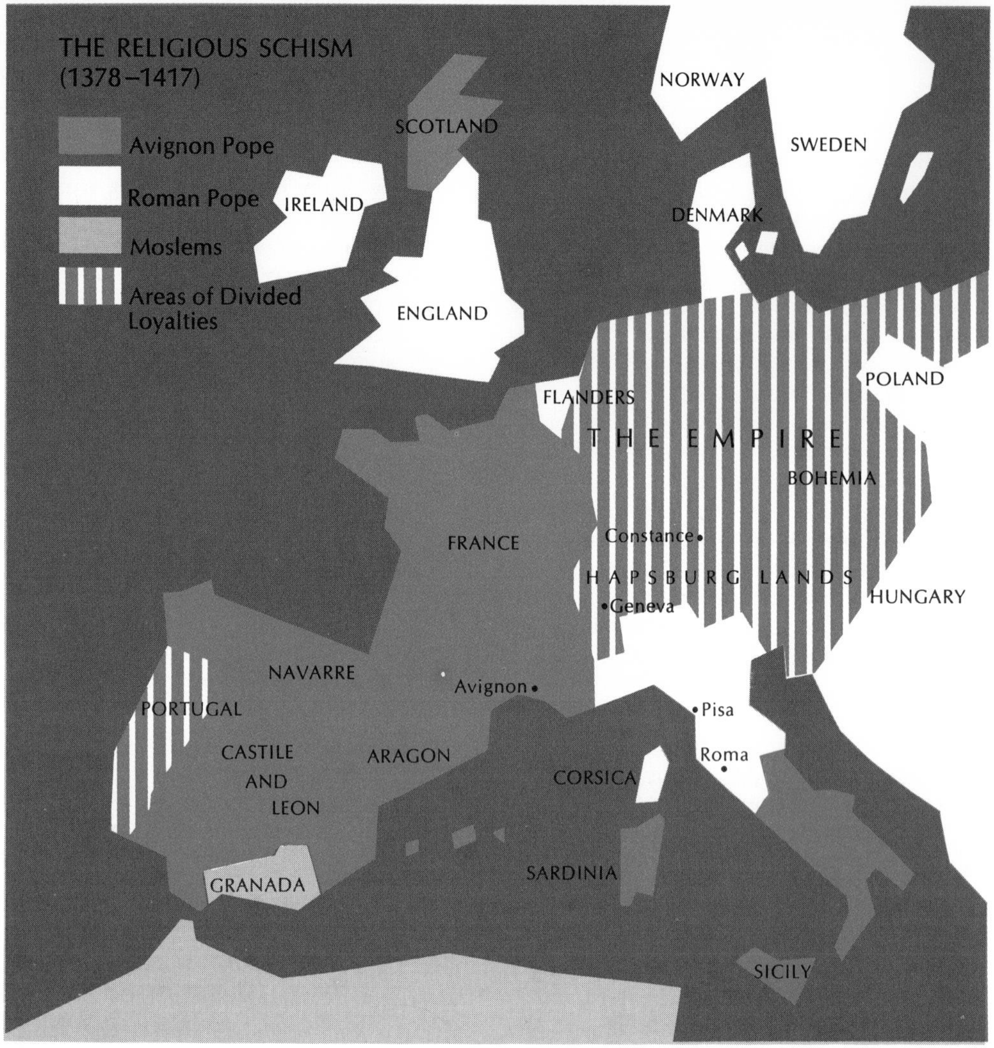


which all the gravest matters that were troubling Christendom might be discussed and decided. They would introduce into the church, that is to say, the type of parliamentary institutions which at this time were functioning in the civil affairs of almost all countries.

In 1409 such a church council met at Pisa. All parts of the Latin West were represented. The council declared both reigning popes deposed, and obtained the due election of another, but since the first two refused to resign there were now three. In 1414 an even greater and more fully attended council met at Constance. Its aims were three: to end the now threefold schism, to extirpate heresy, and to reform the church "in head and members," from top to bottom. Not much was accomplished in reform. To discourage heresy, John Huss was interrogated, condemned, and burned at the stake. The schism was ended. All three popes were at last persuaded or compelled to withdraw, and another, Martin V, was elected. The unity of the church, under the papacy, was at last restored.

The majority at the Council of Constance wished to make general councils part of the permanent apparatus of the church for all time in the future. They regarded the pope as, so to speak, a constitutional monarch, and the general body of the faithful as self-governing in religious matters. In its decree *Sacrosancta,* the Council solemnly declared that a council was superior to a pope, and, in the decree *Frequens,* that councils should be assembled every ten years in the future.

Martin V, however, no sooner elected pope, reaffirmed the prerogatives of the papal office. He dissolved the Council of Constance, and repudiated its decrees. The next thirty years saw a continuing tug of war between successive popes and successive councils. On the one hand, with the pope, stood the papal court and central bureaucracy, supported by the monastic orders, and by scattered individuals for various reasons. On the other, with the councils, stood most Catholic bishops from all countries (outside of Italy), together with representatives of the Emperor and the kings. Popes argued that theirs was the true apostolic authority derived from Peter, and that in any case to entrust power to the territorial bishops, exposed as they were to local pressure from kings and princes, would endanger the unity and independence of the church. Councils argued that the bishop of Rome was fundamentally only a bishop like any other; that the authority of Christ was vested in the whole church as a collective body, over which the pope was no more than a symbolic or merely administrative head.

In this acrimonious battle for jurisdiction few reforms could be adopted, and fewer still enforced. Increasingly the life of the church was corrupted by money. No one believed in bribery; but everyone knew that many high churchmen (like many high civil officials of the day) could be bribed. To buy or sell a church office was a crime in the canon law, known as "simony"; but it was a crime which in the fifteenth century could not be suppressed. For churchmen to live with mistresses was considered understandable, if unseemly; the standards of laymen in such matters were not high; but for a bishop or other ecclesiastic to give lucrative church positions to his own children (or other relatives) was the abuse known as nepotism, and it, too, could not be eradicated. To sell divine grace, for money, all agreed, was not only wrong but impossible. In 1300 Boniface VIII had given encouragement to the practice of "indulgences." A person, if properly confessed, absolved, and truly repentant, might, by obtaining an indulgence, be spared certain of the temporal punishments of purgatory. One obtained such an indulgence, almost always, in return for a donation of money. Indulgences were never "sold", but many unenlightened persons thought they were; and a protest arose all over Europe, among both laity and clergy, that the abuse of indulgences was discrediting the sacraments and undermining common morals. But to raise money in this way was fatally easy, and this practice, too, could not be stopped.

The councils insisted that such conditions be reformed, to which popes replied, while agreeing in principle, that the papal authority must be upheld first. Gradually the popes prevailed. The conciliar movement, for Christendom as a whole, was greatly weakened when the powerful French element secured its aims by a local national arrangement. In the Pragmatic Sanction of Bourges, in 1438, the Gallican (or French) church affirmed the supremacy of councils over popes, declared its administrative independence from the Holy See, suppressed the payment of annates to Rome, and forbade papal intervention in the appointment of French prelates. The papacy thus lost influence in France, but the conciliarists themselves were divided. In 1449, with the dissolution of the Council of Basel, the conciliar movement came to an end. In 1450 a great Jubilee was held to celebrate the papal triumph.

The papacy, its prestige and freedom of action thus secured, now passed into the hands of a series of cultivated gentlemen, men of the world, men of "modern" outlook in tune with their times—famous popes of the Renaissance. Some, like Nicholas V (1447–55) or Pius II (1458–64) were accomplished scholars and connoisseurs of books. Some were like Innocent VIII (1484–92), a pleasant man who was the first pope to dine in public with ladies. Alexander VI (1492–1503) exploited his office in the vain attempt to gratify his avaricious relatives who swarmed from Spain. He schemed also to make his son Caesar Borgia the ruler of all Italy. Julius II (1503–13) was a capable general, and Leo X (1513–21) a superb patron of the arts. . . .

# Wyclif Explains His Position to the Pope (1384)

John Wyclif (1320–1384) was educated and taught at Oxford during the period of the Avignonese Papacy. He criticized not only the wealth of the clergy, but also the character of the sacraments and the authority assumed by the priesthood. The simplicity of his preaching and its clear appeal to the poor gave his followers, known as Lollards, an important role in the peasant uprising of 1381. When Wyclif was summoned to Rome on charges of heresy in 1384, the last year of his life, he wrote the following letter to Pope Urban VI. From Guy Carleton Lee, *Source Book of English History* (New York, 1900).

I have joyfully to tell what I hold, to all true men that believe, and especially to the pope; for I suppose that if my faith be rightful and given of God, the pope will gladly confirm it; and if my faith be error, the pope will wisely amend it.

I suppose over this that the gospel of Christ be heart of the corps [body] of God's law; for I believe that Jesus Christ, that gave in His own person this gospel, is very God and very man, and by this heart passes all other laws.

I suppose over this that the pope be most obliged to the keeping of the gospel among all men that live here; for the pope is highest vicar that Christ has here in earth. For moreness of Christ's vicar is not measured by worldly moreness, but by this, that this vicar follows more Christ by virtuous living; for thus teacheth the gospel, that this is the sentence of Christ.

And of this gospel I take as believe, that Christ for time that He walked here, was most poor man of all, both in spirit and in having [possessions]; for Christ says that He was made needy for our love. And more poor might no man be, neither bodily nor in spirit. And thus Christ put from Him all manner of worldly lordship. For the gospel of John telleth that when they would have made Christ king, He fled and hid Him from them, for He would none such worldly highness.

And over this I take it as believe, that no man should follow the pope, nor no saint that now is in heaven, but in as much as he [the pope] follows Christ. For John and James erred when they coveted worldly highness; and Peter and Paul sinned also when they denied and blasphemed in Christ; but men should not follow them in this, for then they went from Jesus Christ. And this I take as wholesome counsel, that the pope leave his worldly lordship to worldly lords, as Christ gave them—and more speedily all his clerks [clergy] to do so. For thus did Christ, and taught thus His disciples, till the fiend [Satan] had blinded this world. And it seems to some men that clerks that dwell lastingly in this error against God's law, and flee to follow Christ in this, [are] open heretics, and their fautors [supporters] been partners. . . .

# John Huss Attacks the Papacy

Wyclif's doctrines had far-reaching consequences in their influence on John Huss (c.1369–1415), a scholar at the University of Prague in Bohemia. Huss made so fundamental a criticism of the worldliness of the Papacy that the authority of the existing Church was brought into question. The theological arguments in his treatise, *The Church,* furnished the grounds for which he was condemned and burned as a heretic at the Council of Constance. Some of his arguments became important to the Lutheran movement a century later. Reprinted with the permission of Charles Scribner's Sons from *The Church: A Treatise* by John Huss, pages 143–149, by David S. Schaff. Copyright 1915 Charles Scribner's Sons.

From these and other sayings it is evident that no pope is the manifest and true successor of Peter, the prince of the apostles, if in morals he lives at variance with the principles of Peter; and, if he is avaricious, then is he the vicar of Judas, who loved the reward of iniquity and sold Jesus Christ. And by the same kind of proof the cardinals are not the manifest and true successors of the college of Christ's other apostles unless the cardinals live after the manner of the apostles and keep the commands and counsels of our Lord Jesus Christ. For, if they climb up by another way than by the door of our Lord Jesus Christ, then are they thieves and robbers. . . .

Hence, if the cardinals heap up to themselves ecclesiastical livings and barter with them and take money for their sale either themselves or through others, and so devour and consume in luxurious living the goods of the poor, and if they do not do miracles or preach the Word of God to the people or pray sincerely or fill the place of deacons . . . in how far, I ask, are they the vicars of the apostles? [Not when] in the morning they come into the pope's presence clad in the most splendid apparel, and attended with the most sumptuous retinue of horsemen—thus attended, not on account of the distance of place or difficulty of the journey but to show their magnificence to the world and their contrariety to Christ and his apostles, who went about the towns, cities, and castles clad in humble garb, on foot, preaching the kingdom of God.

Nor in this are they the true and manifest vicars of Christ that they permit themselves to be adored of men on bended knee or that they surround the pope with visitors from abroad, that while he sits on high, splendidly apparelled even down to his feet, yea and far beyond his chair, they with bended knee humbly seek the kisses of his blessed feet, as if the sanctity of this father, the pope, would descend even to the place where his foot is planted. . . .

It is said goodness in a pope is like salt for all, and badness in him inures to the damnation of persons without number. If, therefore, the pope and the cardinals by pompous equipages, resplendence of dress, exquisite and wonderful furnishings, by excessive anxiety to heap up benefices or money, and by the manifest ambition for honour in greater measure than secular laymen—if they offend those who believe in Christ—how is it that they always and necessarily continue to be essential "for the government of the universal church as manifest and true successors in the office of Peter and Christ's other apostles?" Never was the office of the apostles other than one of following Christ in good living and in teaching the church, baptizing men, healing the sick, casting out devils, offering up the sacrifice of Christ's body and everywhere exercising the power connected with their office for the perfecting of the church. If therefore, the pope and his cardinals exercise that office, then the pope holds the Office of Peter.But, if he with the cardinals falls away from it, who doubts that he falls away from the true vicariate of Christ and his apostles?

# Should the Councils or the Pope Have Greater Authority?

When Nicholas of Cusa (1401–1464), a German churchman and humanist reformer, later Roman cardinal, wrote *De Concordantia Catholica,* from which the first selection is taken, the Council of Basel (1431–1438) was still in session. The goal of Church reform was not attained, however, at either the Council of Basel or its continuation at Florence (1438–1458), and Pope Pius II, who had been a supporter of the conciliar movement at Basel, dealt it a heavy blow in the Bull, "Execrablis," part of which is excerpted in the second selection. I. From *De Concordantia Catholica,* trans. F. W. Coker, in *Readings in Political Philosophy* (New York, 1938), pp. 261–263. Reprinted by permission of Macmillan Company. II. From Henry Bettenson, ed., *Documents of the Christian Church* (New York: Oxford University Press, 1947), pp. 193–194.

## I. NICHOLAS OF CUSA: ON THE SUPREMACY OF THE GENERAL COUNCILS (1433)

We know that Peter received from Christ no more authority than the other apostles; for nothing was said to Peter that was not also said to the others. Is it not true that just as it was said to Peter, "Whatsoever thou shalt bind upon the earth," it was also said to the others, "Whomsoever ye shall bind?" And although it was said to Peter, "Thou art Peter and upon this Rock" nevertheless by rock we understand Christ, whom Peter confessed. And if by *petra* ("rock"), Peter is to be understood as the foundation stone of the church, then, according to St. Jerome, all the other apostles were similarly foundation stones of the church (concerning which there is a discussion in next to the last chapter of the Apocalypse, wherein by the twelve foundation stones of the city of Jerusalem—that is the holy Church—no one doubts that the apostles are meant). If it was said to Peter, "Feed the sheep," it is nevertheless clear that this feeding is by word and example. So also, according to St. Augustine in his gloss upon the same passage, the same command was given for all. In the verse—"Go ye into all the world" (Matthew and Mark, at the end), it does not appear that anything was said to Peter that implied any supremacy. Therefore, we rightly say that all the apostles are equal in authority with Peter. It should also be remembered that at the beginning of the Church there was only one general episcopate, diffused throughout the whole world, without division into dioceses. . . .

Therefore, since the power of binding and loosing, on which all ecclesiastical jurisdiction is founded, is immediately from Christ, and since from this power comes the power of divine jurisdiction, it is evident that all bishops, and perhaps even presbyters, are of equal authority in respect to jurisdiction, although not in respect to the execution, which is confined within certain positive limits. . . .

Every constitution is founded on natural law (*jure naturali*), and if it contradicts this it cannot be valid. Wherefore, since natural law exists by nature in reason, every law (*lex*) is basically congenital with man. Accordingly, those who are wiser and more excellent than others are chosen as rulers, in order that, endowed with a naturally clear reason and with wisdom and prudence, they may choose just laws and by these govern others and hear cases, so as to preserve the peace; such are the judgments of the wise. . . .

Since by nature all men are free, all government—whether based on written law or on law embodied in a ruler through whose government the subjects are restrained from evil deeds and their liberty regulated, for a good end, by fear of punishment—arises solely from agreement and consent of the subjects. For if men are by nature powerful and equally free, a valid and ordained authority of any one person, whose power by nature is like that of the rest, cannot be created save by election and consent of the others, just as law is established by consent. . . .

Wherefore we see that in councils, canons issue from agreement, acceptance, consent, and approval; and that decretals or judicial decisions of the Roman pontiffs, or of contested incumbents in emergencies, have received the strength of stability and justness, not from a merely powerful will, but from the fact that in accordance with the canons it was right that those decisions should be made. . . .

## II. PIUS II: AN EXECRABLE ABUSE (1460)

There has sprung up in our time an execrable abuse, unheard of in earlier ages, namely that some men, imbued with the spirit of rebellion, presume to appeal to a future council from the Roman pontiff, the vicar of

Jesus Christ, to whom in the person of blessed Peter it was said, 'Feed my sheep' and 'Whatsoever thou shalt bind on earth shall be bound in heaven'; and that not from a desire for a sounder judgment but to escape the penalties of their misdeeds. Anyone who is not wholly ignorant of the laws can see how this contravenes the sacred canons and how detrimental it is to Christendom. And is it not plainly absurd to appeal to what does not now exist and the date of whose future existence is unknown? Wishing therefore to cast out from the Church of God this pestilent poison and to take measures for the safety of the sheep committed to our care, and to ward off from the sheepfold of our Saviour all that may offend. . . . We condemn appeals of this kind and denounce them as erroneous and detestable: . . .

# Thomas à Kempis Advises Christians To Imitate Christ (c. 1427)

*The Imitation of Christ,* written by a German monk, Thomas à Kempis (1379–1471), has probably been the second most widely read book in the Christian world (after the Bible). For fifteenth-century Christians it counselled a mystical devotion to Christ as the most important effective way of obtaining salvation. From *The Imitation of Christ,* in J. Scott, A. Hyma, A. Noyes, *Readings in Medieval History* (New York: Appleton-Century-Crofts Division of Meredith Publishing Company, 1933), pp. 548–549.

"The Kingdom of God is within you," says the Lord.

Turn yourself with your whole heart to the Lord, and forsake this wretched world; and your soul will find rest.

Learn to despise outward things and to give yourself to things within; and you will see the Kingdom of God coming within you.

For the Kingdom of God is peace and joy in the Holy Ghost, which is not given to the wicked.

Christ will come to you and will show you this consolation, if you prepare for him a worthy mansion within you.

All his glory and beauty is from within, and there is his delight.

He frequently visits the inner man; sweet discourse, pleasant solace, much peace, familiarity exceedingly wonderful.

Go to, faithful soul, make ready your heart for this Bridegroom, that he may vouchsafe to come to you and dwell in you.

For thus he says: "If any man love me, he will keep my Commandments; and my Father will love him, and we will come to him and make our abode with him."

Make therefore room for Christ, and deny entrance to all others.

When you have Christ, you are rich, and you have enough.

He will be your provider and faithful watchman in all things, so that it will not be necessary to trust in men.

For men soon change, and swiftly pass away, but Christ remains forever, and stands firmly by us till the end. . . .

Christ was also . . . despised of men, and when in greatest need, forsaken by friends and acquaintances, in the midst of slander.

Christ was willing to suffer and be despised; and dare you complain of any man?

Christ had adversaries and backbiters, and do you wish all men as your friends and benefactors?

Whence will your patience get its crown if no adversity befall you?

If you wish to suffer nothing, how will you be the friend of Christ?

Suffer with Christ and for Christ, if you desire to reign with Christ. . . .

A lover of Jesus, and inwardly true, and free from inordinate affections, can freely turn himself to God, and lift himself above himself in spirit, and rest fruitfully.

He who judges things as they are, not as they are said or esteemed to be, is truly wise, and taught more by God than by men.

He who knows how to walk, and to set little value upon outward things, neither requires places nor expects times for the performing of religious exercises. . . .

# Savonarola Suffers for Attacking Renaissance Worldliness

What could happen to the religious reformer is seen in the case of Girolamo Savonarola (1452–1498). Savonarola entered a Dominican monastery in 1475, explaining that "the reasons which drove me to become a religious are the miserable conditions of the world and the evils of which men are guilty such as rape, immorality, robbery, pride, idolatry, cursing, all in so grave measure that almost no one can be found who has any regard for what is good."

In Florence, after 1481, he found himself in a position to do something about the evils of mankind. With the French invasion of Italy in 1494 and the exile of the Medici family, Savonarola became the spiritual ruler of Florence. Horrified by the scandalous Roman court of Pope Alexander VI, the friar sided with the French invaders against the pope. A fiery, effective preacher, he pressed moral reform in Florence itself and organized gangs of children to spy out and report on the sins of their elders. For a while the city government was under his thumb. The readings describe Savonarola's approach to reform and the terrible final consequences. The first reading is taken from a biography of the friar which contains many quotations from his sermons to the excitable Florentine masses. The second reading consists of excerpts from the diary of a contemporary Florentine druggist. I. From *The Life of Girolamo Savonarola,* by Roberto Ridolfi, trans. by Cecil Grayson. © Copyright 1959 by Routledge & Kegan Paul. Reprinted by permission of Alfred A. Knopf. II. From *Luca Landucci. A Florentine Diary from 1450 to 1516,* ed. Iodoco del Badia, trans. Alice Jervis (London: J. M. Dent & Sons Ltd., 1927), pp. 122–123, 138, 139, 142–143.

## I. SAVONAROLA PUSHES REFORM IN FLORENCE (1497)

For the time being, the Friar triumphed, and his name stood above all things. Some part of the reform of women and children was approved after great difficulty, but it remained a dead letter. Gambling and sodomy were pursued with terrible laws. That these were not issued merely 'for show' . . . is shown by the effects which this chronicler himself has to record a few pages later. . . .

Then came the Christian festivities of the Savonarolan Carnival and the first 'burning of the vanities', celebrated in the Piazza de' Signori on the 7th of February, 1497. There had been erected a wooden construction in the shape of a pyramid with eight sides rising in steps, on which were displayed the 'anathema' that the Friar's lads had gone from house to house collecting: obscene books and pictures, lutes, women's false hair, cosmetics, perfumes, mirrors, dolls, playing-cards, dice, gaming-tables. A Venetian merchant tried to buy up all these beautiful things for 20,000 ducats, but all he achieved was that a fine picture of himself was put on the top of the edifice to share with the effigy of Carnival the rule of the vanities.

The procession of boys formed at San Marco (the Dominican convent) and came down to the square, each quarter of the city represented by a group with its own banner. They took up their positions on the steps and in the loggia of the Signori, singing *laudi* (hymns) in the vulgar tongue recently composed in praise of Jesus Christ and against Carnival. Finally they set fire to the wooden structure, which was full of brushwood, straw, and gunpowder, and with a joyful mingling of the music of the fifes and trumpets of the Signoria, the ringing of bells, the crackle of the flames, and the songs of the children, the burning was celebrated amid the great enthusiasm of the entire population. This has sometimes been exaggeratedly represented as the symbol of iconoclastic barbarism; it appears rather to us to symbolize the triumph of Savonarola and of his civil and religious reforms in the city of the Medici. . . .

During Lent Savonarola ['s] . . . criticisms of prelates and the Court of Rome became more frequent, his expression harsher. After the just but hard punishment he gave them in the sermons of the 13th, 14th, 21st, and 22nd of February and others, came the more violent scourges of the 4th of March: 'There is a proverb among friars: "He comes from Rome, don't trust him." . . . O wicked Church, listen to me! In the courts men are always dying [spiritually], they are all finished. Wretched people! I do not say this is true for everyone, but few remain good. When you see that they gladly stay on in Rome, you say they are cooked. He's cooked. You understand me.' I believe that when he passes from the plural to the singular, and particularly with his pointed 'you understand me', he was alluding to the Pope. If I am wrong, then I think that many of the Friar's audience that morning made the same mistake, even though the preacher added at once: 'I am not speaking of anyone in particular.'

He went on: 'You, harlot Church, you used to be ashamed of pride and lasciviousness. Now you are ashamed no longer. See how once the priests called their children "nephews"; now they are called sons, not nephews: sons everywhere.' This is the infamy that attaches to Borgia, the first of Roman Pontiffs to do such a thing. In that very year 1497, or at the end of 1496, the last son of Alexander VI was born, and it is likely that Savonarola, always well informed, knew something about it. . . .

Over and above the petty jealousies and mediocre monastic differences, Fra Girolamo appealed in [another] sermon to monks of all Orders to unite with him in the great work of reform. . . .

> Come, for Christ wishes to revive His Church. Come, I call on you, but I will cry in a loud voice and name no names.

> O priests, *Magister adest*—the Master is at hand, He is come, and He calls and desires you to reform His Church. He calls you to prayer, for the axe is laid to the root. O monks, black, white, or brown, all of whatever colour: the Orders have been abased. *Magister adest,* the Master is here, and calls for reform. O mendicant friars, the Lord wishes to renovate His Church: *Magister adest,* the Master is here. O nuns, *Magister adest.* You who cannot believe, pray, for the Master is here and will renew all things. Go to all the priests, monks, and nuns, and speak in their ear this good news: soon there will be reform, and they must pray. . . .

The body of the Church was rotten, but he had courage enough to revive it:

> You who are in France, in Germany, who have friends in those parts, send letters everywhere, write that they should go to their churchmen and say: 'That Friar says that he bids you on behalf of God to turn to the Lord and pray, for the Lord is coming.' Come, send off messengers, for this dead body cannot be revived otherwise! . . . Many of you say that there will be excommunications. . . ; do you not know who they are that seek them? Last year it did not succeed. Did I not tell you that, though it may come, those who do this, seek to do worse harm than merely excommunicate? I pray God it may come soon. 'Are you not afraid?' Not I, for they would excommunicate me because I do no evil. Bear it upon a lance, open the gates to it. And I will answer it; and if I do not astonish you, then say what you will. I will cause so many faces there and here to turn pale that you will be well pleased, and we shall utter a great cry, like that of Lazarus, and you will see the whole body tremble. . . . Lord, cause me to be persecuted: I ask Thee this favour—that I may not die in my bed, but that I may shed my blood for Thee, as Thou has done for me. . . .

## II. THE EXCOMMUNICATION AND EXECUTION OF FRA GIROLAMO (1497-1498)

*1497 18th June* An excommunication came from the Pope excommunicating Fra Girolamo, which was published this morning in Santo Spirito, in Santa Maria Novella, in Santa Croce, in the Badia, and at the Servi. I heard it read and proclaimed in Santo Spirito, in the chancel, between two lighted tapers, and amidst a number of friars. It was read and proclaimed by Fra Leonardo, their preacher, and the adversary of Fra Girolamo. It declared that the said *Frate* [monk] had not obeyed a certain Brief which had been sent as far back as the November of 1496, summoning him on his vow of obedience to go to the Pope; and if he did not choose to obey the excommunication, no one was to give him aid or support, and no one must go and hear him, nor go to any place where he was, on pain of excommunication. . . .

*1498 11th February* Fra Girolamo began to preach in *Santa Maria del Fiore,* and the stands (for the boys) were made as before. Many people went there, and it was much talked of, on account of his excommunication; and many did not go, for fear of being excommunicated. . . . I was one of those who did not go. . . .

*1498 10th April* At 9 in the evening (5 p.m.) the *Frate* was carried to the Bargello by two men on their crossed hands, because his feet and hands were in irons, and Fra Domenico also; and they seized them and put Fra Girolamo to the rack three times and Fra Domenico four times; and Fra Girolamo said: "Take me down, and I will write you my whole life." You may imagine that it was not without tears that right-minded men who had faith in him, heard that he had been tortured; he who had taught this prayer, *Fac bene bonis et rectis corde.* No, it was not without tears and grief, and urgent prayers to God. . . .

*19th April* The protocol of Fra Girolamo, written by his own hand, was read in Council, in the Great Hall; he whom we had held to be a prophet, confessed that he was no prophet, and had not received from God the things which he preached; and he confessed that many things which had occurred during the course of his preaching were contrary to what he had given us to understand. I was present when this protocol was read, and I marvelled, feeling utterly dumbfounded with surprise. My heart was grieved to see such an edifice fall to the ground on account of having been founded on a lie. Florence had been expecting a new Jerusalem, from which would issue just laws and splendour and an example of righteous life, and to see the renovation of the Church, the conversion of unbelievers, and the consolation of the righteous; and I felt that everything was exactly contrary, and had to resign myself with the thought: *In voluntate tua Domine omnia sunt posita.* . . .

*22nd May* (*Wednesday morning*) The sacrifice of the three *Frati* was made. They took them out of the Palagio and brought them on to the Square, where were assembled the

In this early painting Savanarola and his companions are shown hanging and being burned in the main square of Florence. Unknown Florentine, sixteenth century.

"Eight" and the *Collegi,* the pàpal envoy, the General of the Dominicans, and many canons, priests and monks of divers Orders, and the Bishop . . . who was deputed to degrade the three monks; and here on the Square the said ceremony was to be performed. They were robed in all their vestments, which were taken off one by one, with the appropriate words for the degradation, it being constantly affirmed that Fra Girolamo was a heretic and schismatic, and on this account condemned to be burnt; then their faces and hands were shaved, as is customary in this ceremony.

When this was completed, they left the *Frati* in the hands of the "Eight", who immediately made the decision that they should be hung and burnt; and they were led straight on to the platform at the foot of the cross. . . . This all happened without a word from one of them, which was considered extraordinary, especially by good and thoughtful people, who were much disappointed, as everyone had been expecting some signs, and desired the glory of God, the beginning of righteous life, the renovation of the Church, and the conversion of unbelievers; hence they were not without bitterness and not one of them made an excuse. Many, in fact, fell from their faith. When all three were hung, Fra Girolamo being in the middle, facing the *Palagio,* the scaffold was separated from the Square, and a fire was made on the circular platform round the cross, upon which gunpowder was put and set alight, so that the said fire burst out with a noise of rockets and cracking. In a few hours they were burnt, their legs and arms gradually dropping off; part of their bodies remaining hanging to the chains, a quantity of stones were thrown to make them fall, as there was a fear of the people getting hold of them; and then the hangman and those whose business it was, hacked down the post and burnt it on the ground, bringing a lot of brushwood, and stirring the fire up over the dead bodies, so that the very least piece was consumed. Then they fetched carts, and accompanied by the mace-bearers, carried the last bit of dust to the Arno, by the Ponte Vecchio, in order that no remains should be found. Nevertheless, a few good men had so much faith that they gathered some of the floating ashes together, in fear and secrecy, because it was as much as one's life was worth to say a word, so anxious were the authorities to destroy every relic. . . .

# Erasmus Satirizes the Practice of Religion in the Renaissance

One of the most slashing attacks on popular Christianity and the clergy of his day was made by the Dutch scholar Desiderius Erasmus (1466–1536). Known to his peers as the prince of humanists, Erasmus was not only a lover of the Greek and Roman classics but also a noted Biblical scholar and translator. His writing style, the biting wit of his pen, and the solid content of his essays made him the most famous publicist of his day and the favored guest of princes and other pillars of society. *The Praise of Folly,* from which this reading is drawn, was written in 1509. Its popularity was such that the first printed version appeared in the following year. Erasmus took the precaution of not signing his name to the work, although the authorship was widely known. No action against him was taken by the Church authorities, and he remained a loyal Catholic amidst the uproar of the religious revolt that broke out only a few years later. From *The Praise of Folly,* by Desiderius Erasmus, trans. by Hoyt Hopewell Hudson (Princeton University Press, 1941). Reprinted by permission of Princeton University Press.

[20] Next come the folk who have arrived at the foolish but gratifying belief that if they gaze on a picture of Polyphemus-Christopher they will not die that day, or that whoever salutes in certain prescribed words an image of Barbara will come through a battle unharmed, or that by making application to [St.] Erasmus on certain days, using a certain kind of candles and certain prayers, one will shortly become rich. . . . Then what shall I say of the people who so happily fool themselves with forged pardons for sins, measuring out time to be spent in purgatory as if with an hour-glass, and figuring its centuries, years, months, days, and hours as if from a mathematical table, beyond possibility of error? Or I might speak of those who will promise themselves any and every thing, relying upon certain charms or prayers devised by some pious impostor either for his soul's sake or for money, to bring them wealth, reputation, pleasure, plenty, good health, long life, and a green old age, and at last a seat next to Christ's in heaven—but they do not wish to get it too soon. That is to say, when the pleasures of this life have finally failed them, willy-nilly, though they struggled tooth and nail to hold on to them, then it is time for the bliss of heaven to arrive.

I fancy that I see some merchant or soldier or judge laying down one small coin from his extensive booty and expecting that the whole cesspool of his life will be at once purified. He conceives that just so many perjuries, so many lustful acts, so many debauches, so many fights, murders, frauds, lies, and so many breaches of faith, are bought off as by contract; and so bought off that with a clean slate he may start from scratch upon a new round of sins. . . . And is it not almost as bad when the several countries each lay claim to a particular saint of their own, and then assign particular powers respectively to the various saints and observe for each one his own peculiar rites of worship? One saint assists in time of toothache, another is propitious to women in travail, another recovers stolen goods, a fourth stands by with help in a shipwreck, and still another keeps the sheep in good repair; and so the rest, though it would take too long to specify all of them. Some of them are good for a number of purposes, particularly the Virgin Mother, to whom the common people tend to attribute more than to the Son. . . .

[33] Our popes, cardinals, and bishops for some time now have earnestly copied the state and practice of princes, and come near to beating them at their own game. Let a bishop but consider what his alb, the white emblem of sincerity, should teach him, namely, a life in every way blameless; and what is signified on his part by the two-horned miter, the two peaks bound by the same knot—I suppose it is a perfect knowledge of the Old and New Testaments; what is meant by covering his hands with gloves, a clean administration of the sacrament and one unsullied by any taint of human concerns; what the crozier symbolizes, most watchful care of the flock put under his charge; what is indicated by the cross that is carried before him, to wit, a victory over all carnal affections. If he would contemplate these and other lessons of the sort, I say, would he not lead a sad and troubled life? . . .

As to these Supreme Pontiffs who take the place of Christ, if they tried to emulate His life, I mean His poverty, labors, teaching, cross, and contempt for safety, if even they thought upon the title of Pope—that is, Father—or the addition "Most Holy," who on earth would be more afflicted? Who would purchase that seat at the price of every resource and effort? Or who defend it, when purchased, by the sword, by poison, or by anything else? Were wisdom to descend upon them, how it would inconvenience them! Wisdom did I say? Nay, even a grain of salt would do it—a grain of that salt which is spoken of by Christ. It would lose them all that wealth and honor, all those possessions, triumphal progresses, offices, dispensations, tributes, and indulgences; it would lose them so many horses, mules and retainers; so many pleasures. . . . In place of these it would bring vigils, fasts, tears, prayers, sermons, studies, sighs, and a thousand troublesome tasks of the sort. Nor should we pass over the circumstance that all those copyists and notaries would be in want, as would all those lawyers, promoters, secretaries, muleteers, grooms, bankers, and pimps—I was about to add something more tender, though rougher, I am afraid, on the ears. In short, that great host of men which burdens—I beg your pardon, I mean adorns—the Roman See would beg for their bread. . . .

As it is now, what labor turns up to be done they hand over to Peter and Paul, who have leisure for it. But the splendor and the pleasure they take care of personally. And so it comes about . . . that scarcely any kind of men live more softly or less oppressed with care; believing that they are amply acceptable to Christ if with a mystical and almost theatrical finery, with ceremonies, and with those titles of Beatitude and Reverence and Holiness, along with blessing and cursing, they perform the office of bishops. To work miracles is primitive and old-fashioned, hardly suited to our times; to instruct the people is irksome; to interpret the Holy Scriptures is pedantry; to pray is otiose; to shed tears is distressing and womanish; to live in poverty is sordid; to be beaten in war is dishonorable and less than worthy of one who will hardly admit kings, however great, to kiss his sacred foot; and finally, to die is unpleasant, to die on the cross a disgrace. . . .

## Norman Cantor: Why the Reformation Did Not Occur Earlier



There is nothing, or almost nothing, in the writings of Martin Luther or of any of the Protestant reformers of the sixteenth century that cannot be found in fourteenth-century literature. The question is not why the Protestant Revolt and schism came in the sixteenth century, but why it did not come a hundred or a hundred and fifty years before. This is perhaps the most important question which can be asked with regard to the later middle ages. Five reasons can be given for the failure of the heretical movement of the fourteenth century to produce a schism in Christendom. In the first place, the fourteenth century did not have the printing press, which did not come into use until just before 1500. It was very hard for the heretical theorists to disseminate their doctrines. In the early sixteenth century the same ideas spread like wildfire across Europe. Wyclif's doctrines were carried into Bohemia, presumably as the result of a dynastic marriage and consequent relations between England and that distant country, but he did not gain disciples in France and Germany. Second, the long depression of the later middle ages, while it produced discontent, sapped men's energy and distracted their interests, making them unlikely to get involved in a major struggle with ecclesiastical authority. Third, there is the paradoxical fact that the papacy was so weak in the fourteenth century that it did very little to combat the heretical movements. By not forcing the issue, the papacy allowed the new wave of heresy to run its course.

The last two reasons are undoubtedly the most important. The wealthier classes in Europe were frightened by the apparent social implications of heresy. It seemed to foment social revolt, and this led them around 1400 to turn against the heretical movements. The fourteenth century was the era of the first social revolts in medieval Europe. The industrial proletariat spawned by the textile industry in Flanders and Florence engaged in bitter, and ultimately unsuccessful, struggles against the oligarchies who dominated urban life. Even the peasant, whose economic position had been ameliorated in many parts of Europe because of a labor shortage, lifted up his head for the first time. Wherever the hitherto docile and mute peasant thought he was being ill-treated or the new freedom which seemed to be coming his way impeded by desperate landlords, he resorted to savage rebellion—the Jacquerie in France, the Peasants' Revolt in England. The English peasant uprising certainly was encouraged, and perhaps even led, by itinerant heretical preachers, and this caused the English government and nobility to turn against Wyclif's disciples. Similarly, the proto-Protestants of Bohemia made their doctrines into a national religion, raised armies, and terrified Germany. Even after the heretical leader John Huss had been burned by order of the Council of Constance, his disciples continued to harass southern Germany. What happened, then, was that the heretical movements unleashed feelings of social discontent and national hatred, as they were to do in the sixteenth century. But there was no Luther in the late middle ages to stem the tide of reaction and dissociate the religious radicalism from social and political extremism. Antisacerdotal doctrines did not entirely disappear in the fifteenth century, but they had been discredited by such terrifying events as the Peasants' Revolt and the Hussite wars, and they were driven underground for another century.

The final reason why the Reformation did not occur in the fourteenth or early fifteenth century is that the royal governments were so inept and distracted by other problems that they failed to take advantage of the religious situation as many sixteenth-century kings were to do. In the first decade of the fourteenth century the national monarchies of France and England appeared destined for continual and unlimited accretion of power, but the next one hundred and fifty years turned out to be disastrous for the royal governments in both countries. Europe had to wait until the late fifteenth century for the territorial sovereign state to secure its position of leadership in European society. In the interval the aristocracy was given a final chance to dominate the governments of the two most centralized states; but the great lords exhibited only greed and laziness in their role as the dominant force in the fourteenth- and fifteenth-century political life. The result was a degree of social disorder not experienced in Europe since the tenth century. . . .

TOPIC 34

# THE LUTHERAN PROTEST

The movement for reform, contained for more than two hundred years within the Roman Church, splintered Latin Christendom in the sixteenth century. No single figure assumes more responsibility for this than the stocky Augustinian monk from Wittenberg, Martin Luther. Echoing charges made by many reformers before him, Luther also gave expression to fresh and raw feelings of public anger at a foreign-dominated, wealthy, and corrupt Church. From the depth of his own religious conviction, Luther appealed for support to all elements of German society. Powerful forces of political and social unrest, shored up by strong religious feeling, produced a series of civil wars and compelled a realignment of the religious and political map of Central Europe. The readings trace the lines of Luther's attack and his response to those who found in a renewed religion the grounds for a general assault on the order of late medieval society.

Reading 186

## Luther's Revolt



Though all aspects of the past arouse our emotions to some extent at least, most of us can remain relatively detached until we come to the issues that engage us in this chapter. Here even the terms in common use betray involvement: the Protestant refers to the Protestant *"Reformation,"* the Catholic to the Protestant *"Revolt."* Even the secularist or skeptic can hardly claim to be impartial, for he inevitably feels that Protestantism, if only because it did shatter the unity and conformity of mediaeval Catholicism, prepared the way for such as him to exist. Old exaggerations, old slanders from the partisan struggle of the times are still bandied about: that Luther led a revolt against the Church so that he, a monk, could marry; that the Catholic clergy sold salvation; that Henry VIII broke with the Pope so that he might marry; and many more.

On October 31, 1517, Martin Luther (1483–1546) nailed his 95 Theses to the door of the court church at Wittenberg in Saxony. The action touched off what proved to be a major social, economic, and intellectual revolution. Neither Luther nor other later major leaders like Calvin intended such a revolution. They conceived of themselves not as starting *new* churches but as going back to the true old church, as reformers. Again and again, as we know, the Catholic church had faced reform movements like the Cluniac, the Cistercian, the Franciscan, and had absorbed them. In the fourteenth and fifteenth centuries Wyclif and Hus had almost created separate, or schismatic churches. The Conciliar movement, in the early fifteenth century, had challenged papal authority, though it had failed to subordinate the pope to the views of a general council.

This time, however, Luther's action led to the organization of a separate church outside the Catholic communion. Within a generation after 1517, dozens of sects or denominations in addition to the Lutheran came into existence: Anglican, Calvinist, Anabaptist, and many others. We take this multiplicity so much for granted today that it is worth emphasizing how great a departure this was in the sixteenth century, what a real revolution from mediaeval religious unity.

Son of a German peasant who became a miner and eventually a prosperous investor in mining enterprises, Luther studied law in his youth; then in 1505, at the age of 22, he had a shattering experience. Caught in a severe thunderstorm and greatly frightened, he prayed to St. Anne for help, and pledged himself to become a monk. Once in the monastery, however, he underwent a major personal crisis: He was sure he was a lost soul without hope of salvation. Though he submitted to the monastic discipline of his order and made a pilgrimage to Rome in 1510, none of the good works he did could free him from the fear that he could not attain God's grace and so was destined for hell. It was only when his confessor told him to study the Bible that Luther, from his readings in the Epistles of St. Paul and in St. Augustine, found an answer to his anxiety: He must have faith in God, faith in the possibility of his own salvation. The Roman Church had of course always taught this. What was new about Luther was his emphasis on *faith alone, to the exclusion of works*. The promise that faith alone might mean salvation had a particular attraction in an age of doubt and gloom rather like the era when men had first turned to Christianity.

Luther then began to question certain practices which in his view were abuses tending to corrupt or weaken faith. He cast his questions in the form of the 95 Theses, written in Latin and in the manner of the mediaeval scholastics as a challenge to debate. The specific abuse that he attacked he called the "sale" of "indulgences," particularly the activities of Tetzel, a Dominican, who, with papal authorization, was conducting a "drive" for contributions to rebuild St. Peter's in Rome.

The theory of indulgences concerned the remission of the punishment for sins: Since only God can forgive a sin, no indulgence can assure such forgiveness. A repentant sinner has to undergo punishment on earth in the form of penance and after death in purgatory, where he atones by temporary but painful punishment and is prepared for heaven. The Church claimed that Christ, the Virgin, and the Saints had performed so many good works that the surplus constituted a Treasury of Merit. A priest could secure for a layman a draft, as it were, on this heavenly treasury. This was an indulgence and could remit penance and part or all of the punishment in purgatory. According to Catholic theory, an indulgence was "granted" by the priest, and any monetary contribution thereupon made by the recipient was a free-will offering. Luther called Tetzel's activity the sale of indulgences.

The doctrine of indulgences was too complex for the ordinary layman to grasp completely. To the man in the street in sympathy with the reformers, it seemed as though a sinner could obtain *not only* remission of punishment *but also* forgiveness of sin, *if only* he secured enough indulgences, and that this depended on his money-gifts to Tetzel. In the 95 Theses Luther objected vehemently both to Tetzel's perversion of indulgences and to the whole doctrine behind them. He thus minimized the importance of good works at a moment when many ordinary believers were trying to increase their stock of such works by drawing on the Treasury of Merit. Christian theory usually insists on the need for *both* faith and good works. Luther's emphasis on faith drove his papal opponents into a corresponding extreme emphasis on works, and this in turn drove him, in moments of excitement, to deny the uses of works and to insist on faith alone. Since "works" include all earthly ecclesiastical organization and the priestly way of doing things, Luther before long was denying that priests are necessary. He had enunciated the doctrine of the priesthood of all believers, in popular terms, "every man his own priest."

In 1518, Luther defied a papal emissary, and refused to recant some of his propositions on indulgences. In 1519, at Leipzig, in debate with a learned theologian, John Eck, who accused him of disobeying the authority of the popes and church councils, Luther said that popes and councils were not necessarily authoritative. He said he accepted certain views of Hus, which the Council of Constance had declared heretical. In 1520, in his *Appeal to the Christian Nobility of the German Nation,* Luther called the term "spiritual estate," as used to describe the clergy, a "lie," and declared that "all Christians are truly of the spiritual estate, and there is no difference among them save the office." When Pope Leo X issued a bull condemning Luther's teaching, Luther burnt it. In 1521 he was excommunicated, and the Emperor Charles V and the imperial diet solemnly declared him an outlaw at Worms. Once again he was asked whether he would recant. His reply contained his most famous words:

> Your Imperial Majesty and Your Lordships demand a simple answer. Here it is, plain and unvarnished. Unless I am convicted of error by the testimony of Scripture or (since I put not trust in the unsupported authority of Pope or of councils, since it is plain that they have often erred and often contradicted themselves) by manifest reasoning I stand convicted by the Scriptures to which I have appealed, and my conscience is taken captive by God's word. I cannot and will not recant anything, for to act against our conscience is neither safe for us, nor open to us.
>
> *Hier stehe ich. Ich kann nicht anders. Gott helff mir. Amen.* (On this I take my stand. I can do no other. God help me. Amen.)

The empire and the papacy took their drastic actions in vain, for Luther was already gathering a substantial following and becoming a national hero. He had the protection of the ruler of his own German state, the Elector Frederick the Wise of Saxony, and was soon to secure the backing of other princes.

In the next few years he translated the Bible into vigorous and effective German, and remodeled the church in Saxony according to his own views. His revolt was a success.

## THE REASONS FOR LUTHER'S SUCCESS

More than theology was at issue in Luther's revolt. The Catholic Church that Luther attacked was, as many Catholic historians grant, at the time in one of its more worldly periods. Especially in its center at Rome, it had come under the influence of the new wealth of the Renaissance and the new fashions of good living. The papacy, triumphant over the councils, had been drawn into Italian politics, and the Rome Luther visited in his younger days was a shocking spectacle of intrigue, display, and corruption. Some part of Luther's success lay in the fact that he was attacking practices revolting to decent men, and reasserting the primacy of the spirit over materialism.

There was a second great reason for his success: In the name of good Germans he was attacking the practices of Italians and Italianate Germans. In the eyes of Luther and his followers Tetzel was not only extending an abuse theologically and morally outrageous; he was raising money to enrich Italy. . . . What Luther started, a good many German princes soon took out of his hands. They stood to gain, not only by cutting off the flow of German money to Italy, but by confiscating Catholic property, especially monastic property, which was not needed for the Lutheran church. Moreover, Luther gave them a new weapon in the eternal struggle against their feudal overlord, the emperor. The princes were also moved by Luther's German patriotism; some, like Frederick the Wise of Saxony, sympathized with many of his ideas.

Luther preaches from the Bible while his congregation receives both bread and wine. In the right foreground, other members of the clergy, including the Pope, are swallowed up in the mouth of hell. Woodcut by Cranach, sixteenth century.

Luther's personal energy, courage, and intelligence were also of major importance. He wrote the pamphlets that did for this revolution what Tom Paine and the Declaration of Independence did for the American. He put his *Appeal to the Christian Nobility of the German Nation* in the vernacular German, not the academic Latin, so that it became a "best-seller." Luther's translation of the Bible made that book a part of German life, and made Luther's language one of the bases of modern literary German. His marriage to a former nun and his raising of a large family dramatized the break with Rome. And behind all this was his passionate conviction that he was doing what he had to do. . . .

The forces that opposed Luther were relatively weak. Clerical opposition centered in the top levels of the Catholic bureaucracy: Pope Leo X was only its willing instrument. Moderate Catholics, anxious to compromise and avert a schism, existed. Had there been at the head of the Catholic Church a pope willing to reform and to make concessions not harmful to the Church's basic position as God's chosen instrument on earth, even Luther might perhaps have been reconciled. Yet, as in all the great modern revolutions, the moderates—gifted, numerous, and active though they were—could not hold up against the extremists. Once Leo X had excommunicated Luther in 1521, the way to compromise was probably blocked, for Luther's associates could have been won away from him only by concessions too great for a Catholic to make.

Politically, the opposition in these critical years centered in the young Emperor Charles V (reigned 1519–1556). . . . Together with the Habsburgs' lands in Austria and elsewhere and their claim to the title of Emperor he inherited the Low Countries, Spain and the Spanish lands overseas, and parts of Italy. This was the nearest approach to a European superstate since Charlemagne, and Charles V wanted to make it a reality. The activities of Luther's princely German supporters threatened his hold over Germany; moreover, Charles, though by no means a mere papal instrument, was Catholic. He decided to fight.

## WAR AND REBELLION IN THE 1520'S

Charles V entrusted the government of the Germans to his younger brother Ferdinand, who formed alliances with Bavaria and other Catholic German states to oppose the Lutheran states. Thus began a long series of combinations, the fruits of which were the religious wars of the next few generations, and the enduring territorial division of Germany into, roughly, a Protestant north and east and a Catholic south and west. But the imperial Habsburg power also had to fight against the French, and so could not steadily concentrate on defeating the Lutherans in Germany. In 1529 the Lutheran princes protested against the sudden new imperial severity against them. It is from this protest that the term "Protestant" arose.

In Germany, below the level of the princes, the knights espoused Luther's cause. Some of them held castles and small estates direct from the Emperor and were in theory just as "independent" as a greater prince. Others were vassals of some greater lord; some were younger sons, who were feeling the decline of their status caused by changing economic and social conditions. Under the leadership of Ulrich von Hutten and Franz von Sickingen they rose in 1522, in what is called the "Knights' War." Troops of the western German archbishoprics put them down, but their struggle added to the confusion of the period.

Worse still was the Peasants' Rebellion of 1524–1525, not unlike the French Jacquerie of 1358 or the English Peasants' Revolt of 1381: like them directed against the remaining burdens of the manorial system, like them without competent military commanders, and like them ruthlessly suppressed. It centered, not in the eastern German regions where serfdom had been completely enforced, but in the southwest, where the peasants had begun to emancipate themselves and wanted to finish the process. Much as Wyclif and the Lollards had influenced the English peasants, Luther's preaching stirred those in Germany. More than their English counterparts of the fourteenth century, the German peasants had educated leaders, who had a revolutionary program of their own, which they embodied in the "Twelve Articles." Couched in Biblical language, the articles seem moderate enough today: each parish should choose its own priest; tithes and taxes should be cut; the peasants should have the right to take game and firewood from the forests; and so on.

## LUTHERAN CONSERVATISM

Horrified at the peasants' interpretation of the Bible that he had translated into German for them, Luther denounced the rebels in unbridled terms. He intended his church to be respectful of established political authority. . . . This conservatism is quite consistent with Luther's fundamental spiritual position. If the visible external world is subordinate to the invisible spiritual world, the best one can hope for here on earth is that good order be maintained. Kings, princes, authority, custom, law: All existing institutions are preferable to discussion and dissension.

The princes of northern Germany and the Scandinavian kingdoms reciprocated. They superintended and hastened the process of converting the willing to Lutheranism and evicting the unwilling. By the mid-sixteenth century Lutheranism had become the state religion of these regions, and as such, it was often the docile instrument of political rulers.

In organizing his own church, Luther showed the same conservatism. After all, the logical extreme of the priesthood of all believers is no church at all, or as many churches as there are individual human beings; in Saxony reformers influenced by Luther tried out these anarchical concepts before Luther and the moderates intervened. The new

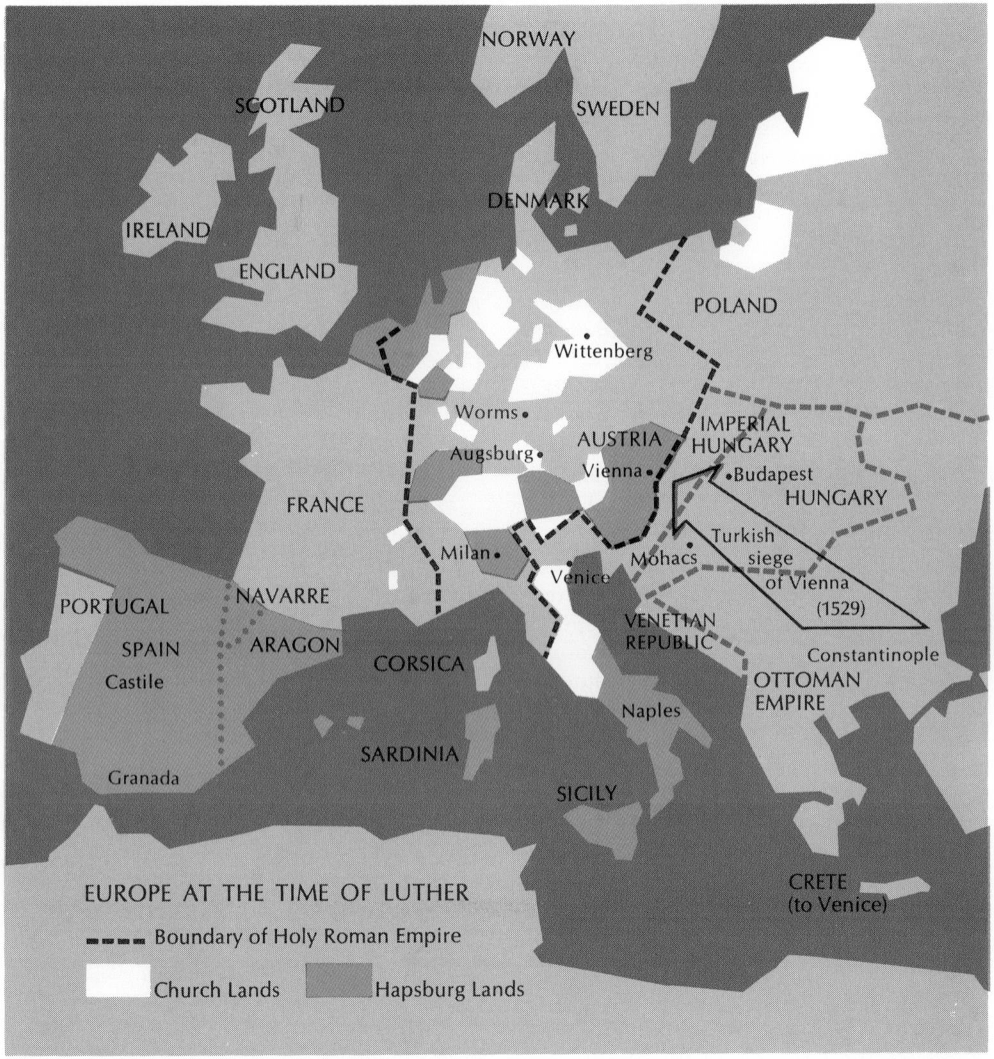

EUROPE AT THE TIME OF LUTHER

church Luther established, often by simply taking over the existing church buildings, did have priests; but they were free to marry, a sign that they had no more sacramental powers than other men. The Lutherans retained two of the sacraments: baptism and the Eucharist, both specifically mentioned in the Bible, but deprived them of their miraculous quality. Veneration of saints and relics, fasts, pilgrimages, monastic orders all vanished. Though the changes were great, the forms of worship retained much that had been traditional. To Luther this new church was not merely an alternative to the Church of Rome, it was the *one true church,* a return to early Christianity before Rome had corrupted it.

# Martin Luther Attacks the Papacy

Martin Luther was a master of the written word. The two works drawn on in part in this reading, set in print and read by tens of thousands of Germans and other dissatisfied Europeans, had a mjaor impact on the Protestant revolt. In the *Ninety-Five Theses* Luther attacked certain practices of the Church. In the *Address to the German Nobility,* he sought, as the title implies, the support of the secular powers in Germany for his definition of the Christian Church. I. From Henry Bettenson, ed., *Documents of the Christian Church* (New York: Oxford University Press, 1947), pp. 263, 267, 270–271. II. From J. H. Robinson, *Readings in European History* (Boston, 1906), II, pp. 75–80.

## I. THE NINETY-FIVE THESES (1517)

A disputation of Master Martin Luther, Theologian, for the elucidation of the virtue of Indulgences.

From a zealous desire to bring to light the truth, the following theses will be maintained at Wittenberg, under the presidency of the

Rvd. Fr. Martin Luther, Master of Arts, Master of Sacred Theology and official Reader therein. He therefore asks that all who are unable to be present and dispute with him verbally will do so in writing. In the name of our Lord Jesus Christ, Amen. . . .

43. Christians are to be taught that to give to the poor or to lend to the needy is a better work than the purchase of pardons.

44. And that because through a work of charity, charity is increased and a man advances in goodness; whereas through pardons there is no advance in goodness but merely an increased freedom from penalty.

45. Christians are to be taught that a man who sees a brother in need and passes him by to give his money for the purchase of pardon wins for himself not the indulgences of the pope but the indignation of God. . . .

48. Christians are to be taught that in dispensing pardons the pope has more desire (as he has more need) for devout prayer on his behalf than of ready money.

49. Christians are to be taught that the pope's pardons are useful if they do not put their trust in them, but most harmful if through them they lose the fear of God.

50. Christians must be taught that if the pope knew the exactions of the preachers of indulgences he would rather have S. Peter's basilica reduced to ashes than built with the skin, flesh and bones of his sheep.

51. Christians are to be taught that the pope (as is his duty) would desire to give of his own substance to those poor men from many of whom certain sellers of pardons are extracting money; that to this end he would even, if need be, sell the basilica of Saint Peter.

52. Confidence in salvation through letters of indulgence is vain; and that even if the commissary, nay, even if the pope himself, should pledge his soul as a guarantee. . . .

81. This wanton preaching of pardons makes it hard even for learned men to defend the honor of the pope against calumny, or at least against the shrewd questions of the laity.

82. They ask: Why does not the pope empty purgatory on account of most holy charity and the great need of souls, the most righteous of causes, seeing that he redeems an infinite number of souls on account of sordid money, given for the erection of a basilica, which is a most trivial cause? . . .

86. The pope's riches at this day far exceed the wealth of the richest millionaires, cannot he therefore build one single basilica of S. Peter out of his own money, rather than out of the money of the faithful poor?

87. What does the pope remit or dispense to those who through perfect contrition have the right to plenary remission and dispensation?

88. What greater good would be gained by the Church if the pope were to do a hundred times a day what he does once a day; i.e. distribute these remissions and dispensations to any of the faithful?

89. If the pope by means of his pardons now seeks the salvation of souls rather than payment, why does he suspend letters and pardons formerly granted, since they are equally efficacious?

90. To suppress these careful arguments of the laity merely by papal authority, instead of clearing them up by a reasoned reply, is to expose the Church and the pope to the ridicule of the enemy and to render Christians unhappy.

91. Now if pardons were preached according to the spirit and mind of the pope all these questions would easily be disposed of; nay, they would not arise.

92. And so let all those prophets depart who say to Christ's people 'Peace, peace' and there is no peace.

93. And farewell to all those prophets who say to Christ's people 'the cross, the cross' and there is no cross.

94. Christians are to be exhorted to endeavor to follow Christ, their head, through pains, deaths, and hells.

95. And so let them trust to enter heaven rather through many tribulations than through the false confidence of peace. . . .

## II. ADDRESS TO THE GERMAN NOBILITY (1520)

The Romanists have with great dexterity built themselves about with three walls, which hitherto have protected them against reform; and thereby is Christianity fearfully fallen.

In the first place, when the temporal power has pressed them hard, they have affirmed and maintained that the *temporal power has no jurisdiction over them,—that, on the contrary, the spiritual is above the temporal.*

Secondly, when it was proposed to admonish them from the Holy Scriptures they said, *"It beseems no one but the pope to interpret the Scriptures."*

And thirdly, when they were threatened with a council, they invented the idea that *no one but the pope can call a council.* . . .

And whenever they have been compelled to call a council, they have made it of no avail, by binding the princes beforehand with an oath to let them alone. Besides this they have given the pope full power over the ordering of the council, so that it is all one, whether we have many councils or no councils, for in any case they deceive us with pretenses and false tricks, so grievously do the Romanists tremble for their skins before a true, free council; and thus they have overawed kings and princes, so that these believe that they would be offending God if they refused to believe in all their knavish tricks.

Now may God help us, and give us one of those trumpets that overthrew the walls of Jericho, so that we may also blow down these walls of straw and paper, and that we may regain possession of our Christian rods for the chastisement of sin, and expose the craft and deceit of the devil; thus may we amend ourselves by punishment and again obtain God's favor.

Let us, in the first place, attack the first wall.

It has been discovered that the pope, bishops, priests, and monks should be called the "spiritual estate," while princes, lords, artisans, and peasants form the "temporal estate,"—a very fine hypocritical invention. But let no one be made afraid by it; and that for this reason: All Christians are truly of the spiritual estate, and there is no difference among us, save of office alone. As St. Paul says (1 Cor. xii), we are all one body, though each member has its own work to do, whereby it may serve the others. This is because we have one baptism, one gospel, one faith, and are all Christians alike; for baptism, gospel, and faith, these alone make spiritual and Christian folk. . . .

We see then that those we call churchmen, be they priests, bishops, or popes, are not set apart from or above other Christians, except in so far as they have to do with the word of God and the sacraments, for that is their calling and office. And moreover the temporal authorities wield the sword and the rod to chastise the wicked and protect the good. A cobbler, a smith, a peasant—every man has his own calling and office, just like the consecrated priests and bishops: and every one in his office or calling must help and serve the rest, so that all may work together for the common good, as the various members of the body all serve each other. . . .

The second wall is even more flimsy and tottering than the first,—namely, the claim that they alone are masters of the Scriptures. . . . But that we fight not with our own words, let us bring forth the Scriptures. St. Paul says: "If any thing be revealed to another that sitteth by, let the first hold his peace" (I Cor. xiv. 30). What would be the use of this commandment if we were to believe him alone who speaks first or sits in the highest seat? Christ himself says that all Christians shall be taught of God (John vi. 45). . . .

The third wall falls of itself as soon as the first two have fallen; for if the pope acts contrary to the Scriptures, we are bound to stand by the Scriptures and to punish and restrain him, in accordance with Christ's commandment (Matt. xviii. 15). . . . Moreover there is nothing in the Scriptures to show that the pope has the sole right to summon and confirm a council; the Romanists have nothing but their own laws, and these hold good only so long as they are not opposed to Christianity and the laws of God; but when the pope deserves punishment these laws cease to exist, since Christianity would suffer if he were not punished by means of a council. . . .

What is the use in Christendom of those who are called "cardinals"? I will tell you. In Italy and Germany there are many rich convents, endowments, holdings, and benefices; and as the best way of getting these into the hands of Rome they created cardinals, and gave to them the bishoprics, convents, and prelacies, and thus destroyed the service of God. . . .

Now that Italy is sucked dry, they come to Germany and begin very quietly but we shall soon see Germany brought into the same state as Italy. We have a few cardinals already. What the Romanists really mean to do, the "drunken Germans" are not to see until they have lost everything. . . .

# Social Consequences of the German Reformation: The Peasant Uprising (1524-1525)

Luther's successful break with the Church encouraged others to take similar steps. The peasantry in southern Germany, in the name of religion, demanded an end to serfdom and economic repression. The following selections contain: I. some of the Articles expressing the position of the peasants, II. Luther's reaction to the Articles, III. some excerpts from a contemporary diary describing the peasant uprising, and IV. Luther's final statement on civil uprising. In James H. Robinson, *Readings in European History* (Boston: Ginn & Co., 1906), Vol. II, pp. 94–108.

## I. THE ARTICLES OF THE PEASANTS (1524)

There are many evil writings put forth of late which take occasion, on account of the assembling of the peasants, to cast scorn upon the gospel, saying, "Is this the fruit of the new teaching, that no one should obey but that all should everywhere rise in revolt, and rush together to reform, or perhaps destroy altogether, the authorities, both ecclesiastic and lay?" The articles below shall answer these godless and criminal fault-finders, and serve, in the first place, to remove the reproach from the word of God and, in the second place, to give a Christian excuse for the disobedience or even the revolt of the entire peasantry.

In the first place, the gospel is not the cause of revolt and disorder, since it is the message of Christ, the promised Messiah; the word of life, teaching only love, peace, patience, and concord. Thus all who believe in Christ should learn to be loving, peaceful, long-suffering, and harmonious. This is the foundation of all the articles of the peasants (as will be seen), who accept the gospel and live according to it.

*The Third Article.* It has been the custom hitherto for men to hold us as their own property, which is pitiable enough, considering that Christ has delivered and redeemed us all, without exception, by the shedding of his precious blood, the lowly as well as the great. Accordingly it is consistent with Scripture that we should be free and should wish to be so. Not that we would wish to be absolutely free and under no authority. God does not teach us that we should lead a disorderly life in the lusts of the flesh, but that we should love the Lord our God and our neighbor. We would gladly observe all this as God has commanded us in the celebration of the communion. He has not commanded us not to obey the authorities, but rather that we should be humble, not only towards those in authority, but towards every one. We are thus ready to yield obedience according to God's law to our elected and regular authorities in all proper things becoming to a Christian. We therefore take it for granted that you will release us from serfdom as true Christians, unless it should be shown us from the gospel that we are serfs. . . .

*The Sixth Article.* Our sixth complaint is in regard to the excessive services which are demanded of us and which are increased from day to day. We ask that this matter be properly looked into, so that we shall not continue to be oppressed in this way, but that some gracious consideration be given us, since our forefathers were required only to serve according to the word of God.

*The Seventh Article.* Seventh, we will not hereafter allow ourselves to be farther oppressed by our lords, but will let them demand only what is just and proper according to the word of the agreement between the lord and the peasant. The lord should no longer try to force more services or other dues from the peasant without payment, but permit the peasant to enjoy his holding in peace and quiet. The peasant should, however, help the lord when it is necessary, and at proper times, when it will not be disadvantageous to the peasant, and for a suitable payment. . . .

## II. LUTHER'S COMMENTS ON THE PEASANT ARTICLES (1525)

There should be no serfs, because Christ has freed us all! What is that we hear? That is to make Christian freedom wholly bodily. Did not Abraham and the other patriarchs and prophets have serfs? Read what St. Paul says of servants, who in all times have been serfs. So this article is straight against the gospel, and moreover it is robbery, since each man would take his person from his lord to whom it belongs. A serf can be a good Christian and enjoy Christian liberty, just as a prisoner or a sick man may be a Christian although he is not free. This article would make all men equal and convert the spiritual kingdom of Christ into an external worldly one; but that is impossible, for a worldly realm cannot stand where there is no inequality; some must be free, others bond; some rulers, others subjects. . . .

My counsel would be that a few counts and lords should be chosen from the nobles, and from the towns a few councilors, who should settle the matter peacefully. You lords should unbend your stiff minds a bit,—for you will have to do that sooner or later whether you will or no,—and give up a little of your oppression and tyranny, so that the poor man can have a little space and air. On the other hand, the peasants will have to let a few of their articles go, which are screwed up too high. In this way the matter, even if it cannot be treated in a Christian spirit, can at least be adjusted according to human laws and agreements. . . .

## III. A DESCRIPTION OF THE PEASANT UPRISING IN ROTHENBURG (SPRING, 1525)

On March 21, a Tuesday, thirty or forty peasants got together in a mob in Rothenburg, bought a kettledrum, and marched about the town, a part going to Pretheim and a part toward Orenbach. They got together again on Thursday and on Friday, as many as four hundred.

The working classes in the town now begin to revolt. They cease to obey the authorities and form a committee of thirty-six to manage affairs. Cunz Eberhardt and George Bermeter are meanwhile dispatched to learn what the peasants are doing; but the peasants will give

The gulf in life-style between noble and peasant is evident in this portrait of Margrave Joachim of Brandenburg (1499–1535) by Lucas Cranach and in the scene of peasants harvesting grain by Pieter Bruegel.

no reply, for they say that they have not all got together yet. A letter is received from Margrave Casimir [of Brandenburg]. This is read to the community. He offers to aid the town authorities and if necessary come in person to reëstablish peace and harmony. The community and their committee of thirty-six treat this scornfully and do not accept the offer.

*March 24.* This evening . . . some one knocked off the head of Christ's image on a crucifix and struck off the arms.

*March 25.* The town councils are in great danger and anxiety, for they are oppressed by the community and its committee of thirty-six.

*March 27.* The councilors are forced to pledge their obedience to the community, for they are taken out one by one, guarded by members of the committee of thirty-six. Each thought he was going to be killed, but after taking the pledge he was secretly sent home without his companions' knowledge.

*March 26.* Chrischainz, the baker, knocked the missal out of the priest's hand in the chapel of our Lady and drove away the priest from mass. To-day the peasants let themselves be seen in the field outside the Galgenthor [city-gate]. . . .

On [March 31] all the artisans were to lay all their complaints and demands before a committee. The taxes, wages, and methods of weighing were discussed. The peasants encamped near Santhof. Friday, April 7, Kueplein, during the sermon, threw the lighted oil lamps about the church. Some of the peasants came into Rothenburg and the neighboring towns, everywhere plundering cupboards and cellars.

On Good Friday all services were suspended in the churches of Rothenburg, for there was neither chanting nor preaching except that Dr. John Teuschel preached against emperor, kings, princes, and lords, ecclesiastical and lay, with foul abuse and slander, on the ground that they were hindering God's word. . . .

*Friday.* All priests are forced to become citizens, otherwise whey would have lost all their goods. They are to take their share of guard duty and work on the fortifications.

On Wednesday [April 26] Lorenz Knobloch was hewn to pieces by the peasants at Ostheim; and then they pelted one another with the fragments. They said he was a traitor and that he wanted to mislead them. . . .

*April 30.* The monastery of Anhausen was plundered and burned in the night, also that near Dinkelsbühl. The peasants also attacked the monastery of Schwarzach, and the castle of Reichelsberg was burned.

Peasants prepare to murder a knight in this scene from the peasant war. On the raised banner is a peasant's ungainly shoe, symbol of the revolt.

*May 6.* Early in the morning the great bell rang three times, summoning the people to hear a message from Margrave Casimir, brought by three noblemen, and inviting all to take refuge in Rothenburg under his protection. The greater part refused, and some were noted by the Margrave's representative, and afterward lost their heads.

*Monday.* The peasants approach Neuhaus, and next day plunder and burn. . . .

On the next Monday Margrave Casimir proceeds with his forces to subdue and punish the peasants. Hans Krelein the older, priest at Wernitz, was beheaded, with four peasants, at Leutershausen. Seven have their fingers cut off. Likewise at Neuenstat eighteen burghers and peasants are beheaded. At Kitzingen fifty-eight have their eyes put out and are forbidden to enter the town again.

On Friday before Whitsuntide the forces of the Swabian League slay four thousand peasants at Königshofen. . . .

On June 6 messengers are sent from Rothenburg to Casimir to ask for pardon. Next day others are sent to the League, but they are told that they must surrender unconditionally.

On Thursday following, after the League had retaken the town of Würzburg, they beheaded sixty-two.

On Friday after Corpus Christi, mass was once more chanted in Rothenburg, as formerly. . . .

On the eve of Peter and Paul's day Margrave Casimir rides into Rothenburg with four hundred horsemen, a thousand footmen, and two hundred wagons full of arms and equipments. . . .

### IV. LUTHER URGES THE ANNIHILATION OF REBELS

In my preceding pamphlet [on the "Twelve Articles"] I had no occasion to condemn the peasants, because they promised to yield to law and better instruction, as Christ also demands.

But before I can turn around, they go out and appeal to force, in spite of their promises, and rob and pillage and act like mad dogs. From this it is quite apparent what they had in their false minds, and that what they put forth under the name of the gospel in the "Twelve Articles" was all vain pretense. . . .

Since, therefore, those peasants and miserable wretches allow themselves to be led astray and act differently from what they declared, I likewise must write differently concerning them; and first bring their sins before their eyes, as God commands, whether perchance some of them may come to their senses; and, further, I would instruct those in authority how to conduct themselves in this matter. . . .

. . . They cause uproar and sacrilegiously rob and pillage monasteries and castles that do not belong to them, for which, like public highwaymen and murderers, they deserve the twofold death of body and soul. It is right and lawful to slay at the first opportunity a rebellious person, who is known as such, for he is already under God's and the emperor's ban. Every man is at once judge and executioner of a public rebel; just as, when a fire starts, he who can extinguish it first is the best fellow. Rebellion is not simply vile murder, but is like a great fire that kindles and devastates a country; it fills the land with murder and bloodshed, makes widows and orphans, and destroys everything, like the greatest calamity.

. . . They cloak their frightful and revolting sins with the gospel, call themselves Christian brethren, swear allegiance, and compel people to join them in such abominations. Thereby they become the greatest blasphemers and violators of God's holy name, and serve and honor the devil under the semblance of the gospel, so that they have ten times deserved death of body and soul, for never have I heard of uglier sins. . . .

## Carl Gustavson: The Causes of the Reformation

In *A Preface to History* Carl Gustavson (1915–     ) of Ohio University sought to present college freshmen with "an outline of the nature of historical-mindedness." Each chapter dealt with an aspect of historical reasoning; his chapter on causation focused on the Reformation. Gustavson wanted his readers to recognize that no single cause "ever adequately explains a historical episode." From *A Preface to History* by Carl G. Gustavson. (Copyright 1955 McGraw-Hill.) Used with permission of McGraw-Hill Book Company. Pp. 56–62.

Quite obviously the immediate cause for the Reformation is to be found in the activity of Luther between 1517 and 1521, although the selection of a specific event may bring differences of opinion; the most likely choices would be the nailing of the ninety-five theses, the Diet of Worms, or the famous disputation with Eck, in which Luther first clearly crossed the line between Catholicism and heresy. Identifying the initial spark, however, by no means explains the enormous extent of the conflagration which followed.

Luther's ninety-five theses immediately became the best seller of that day. Great crowds gathered to applaud him as he went to the Diet of Worms. If we can decide why he suddenly experienced this popularity, we may also gain some idea of the reason for his success. . . . Luther had been denouncing the outrageous methods used in the sale of indulgences, an issue everyone could understand far better than discussions of abstruse theology. He was hitting out at unpopular figures, always a good way to attract a following. The friar of Wittenberg was a German, a son of the people, courageously talking up to pope and emperor, speaking for the common people and expressing what many of them felt. . . .

The career of John Hus of Prague is apt to come to mind. His life story bears several marked resemblances to that of Luther, and his proposals were very similar to those of his successors; there was a major difference however—he was burned for his temerity. A whole century before the Lutheran Reformation some of its principles were already widely approved, as witness the obstinate refusal of the Bohemians to give up the reforms of Hus. (Note, also, that Bohemia borders on Saxony, Luther's home district.)

Other reformers had also preceded Luther: Peter Waldo, Wyclif, Savonarola, to mention the most prominent. Nor should the criticism of the Church by such writers as Erasmus and Valla be forgotten. Evidences of Protestant ideas appear everywhere in Western Europe during the preceding century. . . .

One point to note is that the criticism of the Church usually did not carry with it a threat to leave the institution. It was criticized, its officials castigated, its practices and policies assailed in the same spirit in which Americans treat their governmental institutions. The object was reform, not separation, the attacks representing no more a desire to destroy the Church than we expect to abolish Congress. Some people might dislike papal authority in much the same way as some Americans suspect the power of a strong President. When Luther appeared at Worms, he had no expectation of founding a separate church, and in fact he may have gone to the diet with the lurking hope of converting Charles V to his own viewpoint. Had this happened, a sweeping reform within the Church could have resulted and the universal Church remained united at least for a longer time. Even after the break had occurred, the Lutheran and Anglican churches insisted that it was the Roman Catholics who had abandoned the original idea of the Church, while they themselves were simply purifying it of impure accretions.

Only a rugged, roughhewn, obstinate man could have shouldered his way to success in the circumstances—the looming figure of Luther makes the personal factor important in the causation of the Reformation. Unless the odds are too great, the victory is likely to go to the side inspired by genuine zeal for a cause. Historical movements, however much they are impelled by economic and social factors, after all are carried through by men. Their states of mind are important. Even Luther, however, could have accomplished little more than propagate his ideas if he had not found many others in the same mood. Had Luther alone, or a small circle of disciples only, held Protestant ideas, no social force of sufficient magnitude to create historical events would have existed. When tens of thousands, however, were possessed of the same general outlook, the scene was set for action, and it took only Luther's words and actions to precipitate the formation of a spiritual force of enormous extent and potency. . . .

The circumstances were ready for the man, and his religious zeal furnished a focal point for the hitherto diffused causes for the Reformation. One may legitimately question if any one single force, albeit as powerful as this one, could in itself have altered the course of history. From our perspective . . . a number of social forces seem to converge upon the . . . events and carry them forward.

We have seen gunpowder and the better ocean-going vessels make possible the expansion of the European into other parts of the world. The printing press, another technological advance, served as a tool of incalculable importance in the Reformation. Someone might argue very plausibly that no Reformation could have occurred had it not been for the invention of the printing press. Without this method of spreading ideas, the Lutheran doctrines could not have been disseminated so rapidly, and, if support had not quickly manifested itself, the emperor and Church might have succeeded in suppressing the movement. The press also aided the reformers by undermining the claim of the Church to pose as the custodian of final truth, since it was now becoming possible for more persons to acquire a copy of the Bible.

Social forces emerging from economic motives, powerful as they were, must have exercised an important influence on these events. The kind of merchant that we encountered in Florence or in sixteenth-century England, and who was also active in Germany, would deplore the constant flow of money to Rome. Most people, indeed, would feel indignation at this continual drain on the national wealth, and any rebel against papal authority would find useful ammunition here. The incessant sniping at the wealth of the bishops and the monasteries was partly due to the unfortunate contrast with the early ideal of the Church, but the criticisms were also likely to remind people that their contributions were not always usefully applied. Especially would the growing middle class deplore the drag on productivity caused by the clerical possession of land, the numerous church festivals, and the presumed idleness of the monks. With their ideals of thrift and industry, the middle class found many church habits irritating. Luther appealed to these feelings, with violent and exaggerated words, in his *Address to the Christian Nobility of the German Nation:* "What has brought us Germans to such a pass that we have to suffer this robbery and this destruction of our property by the pope?. . . Do we still wonder why princes, cities, foundations, convents, and people grow poor? We should rather wonder that we have anything left to eat."

We know that the nobles were always eager to expand their holdings. They had long eyed the lands of the Church, and the Reformation, with its expropriation of clerical wealth, offered the awaited opportunity. Many of

England's noble families had their origin in grants of this kind, and these were likely to remain Protestant, since any reversion to the old order would jeopardize their new acquisitions. The princes of Germany likewise benefited in this fashion, and the Crown in England and the Scandinavian countries added to its wealth at the expense of the Church. . . .

Why did Luther "get away with it" when others before him had failed? The truth is that Charles V was in a dilemma. New on the throne, he was uncertain of his support and would hesitate before alienating his German subjects. Luther's own prince, the Elector of Saxony, was friendly to the reformers and possessed the force and prestige to raise a rebellion. The loud acclaim of the friar must have alarmed Charles and dissuaded him from a highly unpopular move. He undoubtedly underestimated the potentialities of the movement, the more so since he had grave political problems to grapple with elsewhere. The Ottoman Turks were approaching the far-flung borders of his realm, and Charles needed German unity in order to meet this threat. All in all, "the king *was* weak," not so much because of his own personality as in his inheritance of an enfeebled government from his predecessors.

The Crown was one of the institutions which should have suppressed the rebellion. The other was the Church itself. After many centuries as the universal Church of Western Europe, it had undergone both a loss of positive vitality and a diminishing strength in comparison with new emerging forces. It had failed to suppress the Hussite heretics. The internecine struggle between two organs of the Church, the papacy and the council, in the conciliar movement might be seen as a portent of disruption. Perhaps most significant of all, the Renaissance was having a debilitating spiritual effect upon the papacy; popes who were using spiritual resources for temporal ends were blunting their own swords. Having centralized the Church, they failed to live up to their responsibilities. By making the papacy synonymous with the Church, they drew upon the Church itself a shower of invective. The fact that many believed the Church to be corrupt shook the all-important allegiance of the great masses of the people.

The Church no longer possessed as much power, proportionately, either. New forces were rising which had long challenged the Church and which now overwhelmed it. One of these was the national state. Even at the height of the Middle Ages potent secular authorities had challenged the papacy. A king might possess the men and swords, the brute force, which could humiliate a pope, as Philip IV's men did Boniface VIII. . . .

During the fourteenth and fifteenth centuries, national kings continued to add to their power, and in France, England, and Spain these rulers arrogated to themselves increasing control over the national churches. Seen in the light of later events, the rivalry of nations during the Avignon period, the schism, and the conciliar movement betoken a growing national feeling which would burst asunder the ancient bonds. The Catholic Church was faced with its perennial problem, how to keep its international character although threatened by national feelings and provincial attachments. The Church, after all, was essentially an institution of the southland. From thence it had come, there it had matured and built up its customs and symbols. At one time, the cultural inferiority of the north caused these peoples to accept southern leadership as natural; as the northern peoples developed, however, the subservience to the south began to rankle.

In the northern countries, a sense of nationalism was a strong factor in the break with Rome. In Germany, where other national aspirations went unsatisfied, this was particularly true. The Reformation passed into effect in Sweden coincident with the overthrow of Danish rule. The English struggle against Spain would tend to associate the state church with national existence in that country. The native language was substituted for Latin in the churches of these regions. In nearly all instances, the advent of the Reformation brought added power and wealth to the kings or territorial princes. The institutional factor is a powerful one in the causation of the Reformation; one institution, the Church, was losing ground to another institution, the national monarchy, and the spiritual crisis precipitated by Luther offered the territorial princes of Germany and the kings of northern Europe a splendid opportunity to establish state control over the Church. . . .

TOPIC 35

# CALVIN'S CITY OF GOD

In the wake of the Lutheran protest, Protestant reform movements mushroomed. Of the ideas at work in these movements, the doctrines of the brilliant but stern Frenchman, John Calvin, had the greatest impact on the future development of Western civilization. Calvin went far beyond Luther, who was some thirty years his senior, in establishing the rule of religion in everyday life. In Geneva, the Swiss community he dominated, laymen played an important role in enforcing a strict code of personal behavior. Tolerance found no new defenders in the closed climate of Geneva, but where Calvinists were in a minority their own self-interest made them defenders of religious, and hence often political freedom. In the world of commerce, Calvinist thinking seemed at home with the new affluence and social mobility bred by economic opportunity. The readings examine the relevance of Calvinism to the great religious, economic, social, and political questions of the day.

**Reading 190**

## Calvinism in Theory and Practice

From *Civilization Past and Present* by T. Walter Wallbank, Alastair M. Taylor, Nels M. Bailkey,  Pp. 298–299, 300.

The most famous sixteenth-century Protestant leader after Luther was John Calvin (1509–1564). A Frenchman of the middle class, Calvin studied theology and law at Paris, where he became interested in Luther's teachings. About 1533 he had what he called a "conversion," whereby he abandoned Catholicism. When Francis I began to persecute heretics, Calvin fled to Switzerland and settled first at Basel, a Protestant city. There he published in 1536 the first edition of his great work the *Institutes of the Christian Religion,* unquestionably one of the most significant books of systematic theology ever written. His capacity for creative thinking was overshadowed by his ability as an organizer and synthesist. Influenced by his legal training as well as by humanistic scholarship and the doctrines of Luther, Calvin set forth a system that was a masterpiece of logical reasoning.

Whereas Luther's central doctrine was justification by faith, Calvin's was the sovereignty of God. "The great text for Luther was 'Thy sins are forgiven,' but for Calvin it was 'If God is for us who can be against us?' Both Calvin and Luther had an overwhelming sense of the majesty of God, but whereas for Luther this served to point up the miracle of forgiveness, for Calvin it gave rather the assurance of the impregnability of God's purpose." God was omnipotent and for His own purposes had created the world and also man in His image. Since Adam and Eve had fallen from a state of sinlessness, man was utterly depraved and lost.

Carrying these doctrines to their logical conclusions, Calvin defined man's relations to God in his famous doctrine of predestination. Since God is omniscient, He knows the past, present, and future. Consequently, He must always know which men are to be saved by Him and which men are to be damned eternally. Man's purpose in life, then, is not to try to work out his salvation—for this has already been determined—but to honor God. While Calvin did not profess to know absolutely who among men were to be God's chosen—the elect—he believed that the following three tests constituted a good yardstick by which to judge who might be saved: participation in the two sacraments—Baptism and the Lord's Supper; an upright moral life; and a public profession of the faith.

It was the duty of the living members of the church to glorify God by establishing a theocracy that would be governed according to scriptural precept. The Bible was the supreme authority, and the community should discipline or remove any found guilty of blasphemy or unseemly behavior. . . .

Pains were taken to provide instruction in the fundamentals of faith, to prepare the young for useful Christian citizenship, to safeguard the purity of the faith, to extirpate any remnant of Catholicism. Although the regime was high-minded, it carried its zeal to ridiculous lengths. Penalties were inflicted for being absent from sermons or laughing during the church service, for wearing bright colors, for swearing or dancing, for inability to recite prayers, for playing cards, or for having one's fortune told by gypsies. Such regulations had also existed in medieval times, but in Calvin's Geneva they were energetically enforced.

In regard to more serious offenses, especially in the religious sphere, Calvin and his associates acted with the utmost severity. Torture was used to obtain some confessions, and citizens of Geneva were banished for heresy, blasphemy, witchcraft, and adultery. When Servetus, a scholarly anti-Trinitarian, appeared in Geneva, Calvin prosecuted him for heresy, saying that his defense was:

> . . . no better than the braying of an ass, and that the prisoner was like a villainous cur wiping his muzzle.

### THE SPREAD OF CALVINISM

From Geneva, Calvinism spread far and wide, imbued with its founder's austerity of spirit, power of mind, and high purpose. Much of this influence stemmed from the Academy (today the University of Geneva), which trained students from other countries in Calvin's theology. In France, Calvinism made influential converts among both the bourgeoisie and the nobility. . . .

Carried down the Rhine River to the northern Netherlands, Calvin's teachings formed the basis for the Dutch Reformed religion. In the latter half of the sixteenth century and the first half of the seventeenth, the Dutch struggle for independence against a Catholic king of Spain strengthened Protestantism in their country. And in Scotland the authority of the Roman Church was challenged by John Knox. . . .

### PRESBYTERIANISM IN SCOTLAND

The religious revolt in Scotland was largely the work of the zealous reformer John Knox (1505?–1572), who had become acquainted with Calvin in Geneva and frequently consulted him concerning church doctrine and civil authority. After returning to his native Scotland in about 1559, Knox became leader of the Lords of the Congregation, a group of Protestant nobles who wished to overthrow the jurisdiction of the Roman Catholic Church in their land. In 1560 Knox drew up the Articles of the Presbyterian Church, which abolished the authority of the pope and condemned the creeds and practices of the old Church. With the help of English troops, he effected a religious revolution.

One year later, the beautiful but ill-fated Mary Stuart returned from France to find her bleak kingdom alienated from her own Catholic views. From his pulpit and in his debates with Mary about questions of theology and the loyalty owed by a subject to his monarch, Knox defied the queen's authority and thundered against her religious principles. Although Mary showed amazing skill and logic in her arguments with him, the fiery reformer gained the support of the Scottish people in his denunciation of the queen. By the time Mary had been executed by Elizabeth [of England] in 1587, Scotland had been won over to Calvinistic Presbyterianism.

## Calvin Explains God's Will

The key to Calvin's beliefs is found in the *Institutes of the Christian Religion,* published in 1536 when he was twenty-seven. Extracts in this reading present Calvin's views on predestination and on what he called man's calling. (I) From the *Institutes of the Christian Religion* in *Documents of the Christian Church,* Henry Bettenson, ed. (New York, 1947), p. 302. Reprinted by permission of the Oxford University Press. (II) From *Institutes of the Christian Religion,* John Calvin, Vol. I, translated by John Allen, edited by Benjamin B. Warfield. Published 1936 by the Presbyterian Board of Christian Education, Philadelphia, U.S.A. Pp. 789–791.

### I. PREDESTINATION

No one who wishes to be thought religious dares outright to deny predestination, by which God chooses some for the hope of life, and condemns others to eternal death. But men entangle it with captious quibbles; and especially those who make foreknowledge the ground of it. We indeed attribute to God both predestination and foreknowledge; but we call it absurd to subordinate one to the other. When we attribute foreknowledge to God we mean that all things have ever been, and eternally remain, before his eyes; so that to his knowledge nothing is future or past, but all things are present; and present not in the sense that they are reproduced in imagination (as we are aware of past events which are retained in our memory), but present in the sense that he really sees and observes them placed, as it were, before his eyes. And this foreknowledge extends over the whole universe and over every creature. By predestination we mean the eternal decree of God, by which he has decided . . . what he wishes to happen in the case of each individual. For all men are not created on an equal footing, but for some eternal life is pre-ordained, for others eternal damnation. . . .

### II. MAN'S PLACE IN LIFE

The Scripture has . . . a third rule, by which it regulates the use of earthly things; of which something was said, when we treated of the precepts of charity. For it states, that while all these things are given to us by the Divine goodness, and appointed for our benefit, they are, as it were, deposits intrusted to our care, of which we must one day give an account. We ought, therefore, to manage them in such a manner that this alarm may be incessantly sounding in our ears, "Give an account of thy stewardship." Let it also be remembered by whom this account is demanded; that it is by him who has so highly recommended abstinence, sobriety, frugality, and modesty; who abhors profusion, pride, ostentation, and vanity; who approves of no other management of his blessings, than such as is connected with charity; who has with his own mouth already condemned all those pleasures which seduce the heart from chastity and purity, or tend to impair the understanding.

Lastly, it is to be remarked, that the Lord commands every one of us, in all the actions of life, to regard his vocation. For He knows with what great inquietude the human mind is inflamed, with what desultory levity it is hurried hither and thither, and how insatiable is its ambition to grasp different things at once. Therefore, to prevent universal confusion being produced by our folly and temerity, He has appointed to all their particular duties in different spheres of life. And that no one might rashly transgress the limits prescribed, He has styled such spheres of life *vocations,* or *callings.* Every individual's line of life, therefore, is as it were, a post assigned him by the Lord, that he may not wander about in uncertainty all his days. And so necessary is this distinction, that in His sight all our actions are estimated according to it, and often very differently from the sentence of human reason and philosophy.

There is no exploit esteemed more honorable, even among philosophers, than to deliver our country from tyranny; but the voice of the celestial Judge openly condemns the private man who lays violent hands on a tyrant. It is not my design, however, to stay to enumerate examples. It is sufficient if we know that the principle and foundation of right conduct in every case is the vocation of the Lord, and that he who disregards it will never keep the right way in the duties of his station. He may sometimes, perhaps, achieve something apparently laudable; but however it may appear in the eyes of men, it will be rejected at the throne of God; besides which, there will be no consistency between the various parts of his life.

Our life, therefore, will then be best regulated, when it is directed to this mark; since no one will be impelled by his own temerity to attempt more than is compatible with his calling, because he will know that it is unlawful to transgress the bounds assigned to him. He that is in obscurity will lead a private life without discontent, so as not to desert the station in which God has placed him.

It will also be no small alleviation of his cares, labors, troubles, and other burdens, when a man knows that in all these things he has God for his guide. The magistrate will execute his office with greater pleasure, the father of a family will confine himself to his duty with more satisfaction, and all, in their respective spheres of life, will bear and surmount the inconveniences, cares, disappointments, and anxieties which befall them, when they shall be persuaded that every individual has his burden laid upon him by God. Hence also will arise peculiar consolation since there will be no employment so mean and sordid (provided we follow our vocation) as not to appear truly respectable, and be deemed highly important in the sight of God.

# The Lives of the Genevans Are Regulated (1547)

Some idea of what life in Calvin's heavenly city was like can be gained by reading the city ordinances to which all inhabitants of Geneva had to conform. In *Translations and Reprints from the Original Source of European History,* Merrick Whitcomb, ed. (Philadelphia, n.d.), III, No. 3, pp. 10–11.

### CONCERNING THE TIME OF ASSEMBLING AT CHURCH

That the temples be closed for the rest of the time, in order that no one shall enter therein out of hours, impelled thereto by superstition; and if any one be found engaged in any special act of devotion therein or near by he shall be admonished for it: if it be found to be of a superstitious nature for which simple correction is inadequate, then he shall be chastised.

### BLASPHEMY

Whoever shall have blasphemed, swearing by the body or by the blood of our Lord, or in similar manner, he shall be made to kiss the earth for the first offence; for the second to pay 5 sous, and for the third 5 sous, and for the last offence be put in the pillory for one hour.

## DRUNKENNESS

1. That no one shall invite another to drink under penalty of 3 sous.

2. That taverns shall be closed during the sermon, under penalty that the tavern-keeper shall pay 3 sous, and whoever may be found therein shall pay the same amount.

3. If any one be found intoxicated he shall pay for the first offence 3 sous and shall be remanded to the consistory, for the second offence he shall be held to pay the sum of 6 sous, and for the third 10 sous and be put in prison. . . .

## SONGS AND DANCES

If any one sing immoral, dissolute or outrageous songs, or dance the *virollet* or other dance, he shall be put in prison for three days and then sent to the consistory.

## USURY

That no one shall take upon interest or profit more than five per cent, upon penalty of confiscation of the principal and of being condemned to make restitution as the case may demand.

## GAMES

That no one shall play at any dissolute game or at any game whatsoever it may be, neither for gold nor silver nor for any excessive stake, upon penalty of 5 sous and forfeiture of stake played for.

A Calvinist church in Lyons, France, in the sixteenth century. The building and the clothing of the congregation reflect the simplicity and severity of this Protestant creed.

# Protestants Persecute a Heretic: Michael Servetus' Sentence (1553)

Miguel Serveto (1511–1553), or as he latinized his name, Michael Servetus, a frequent practice among Renaissance scholars, was a Spanish physician who, while living in France, wrote a book attacking the Trinity and the belief that Jesus had existed from eternity. Arrested, Servetus escaped to Geneva but there Calvin found his theological views as abhorrent as the Catholics had. Servetus was tried as a heretic. The sentence of the Calvinist judges contains a statement of the case against him, a statement that in most particulars could have been written five centuries earlier. From R. H. Bainton, trans., *Hunted Heretic: The Life and Death of Michael Servetus* (Boston: Beacon Press, 1953), pp. 207–209.

This is the sentence pronounced against Michel Servet de Villeneufve of the Kingdom of Aragon in Spain who some twenty-three or twenty-four years ago printed a book at Hagenau in Germany against the Holy Trinity containing many great blasphemies to the scandal of the said churches of Germany, the which book he freely confesses to have printed in the teeth of the remonstrances made to him by the learned and evangelical doctors of Germany. In consequence he became a fugitive from Germany. Nevertheless, he continued in his errors and, in order the more to spread the venom of his heresy, he printed secretly a book in Vienne of Dauphiny [France] full of the said heresies and horrible, execrable blasphemies against the Holy Trinity, against the Son of God, against the baptism of infants and the foundations of the Christian religion. He confesses that in this book he called believers in the Trinity Trinitarians and atheists. He calls this Trinity a diabolical monster with three heads. He blasphemes detestably against the Son of God, saying that Jesus Christ is not the Son of God from eternity. He calls infant baptism an invention of the devil and sorcery. His execrable blasphemies are scandalous against the majesty of God, the Son of God and the Holy Spirit. This entails the murder and ruin of many souls. Moreover he wrote a letter to one of our ministers in which, along with other numerous blasphemies, he declared our holy evangelical religion to be without faith and without God and that in place of God we have a three-headed Cerberus. He confesses that because of this abominable book he was made a prisoner at Vienne and perfidiously escaped. He has been burned there in effigy together with five bales of his books. Nevertheless, having been in prison in our city, he persists maliciously in his detestable errors and calumniates true Christians and faithful followers of the immaculate Christian tradition.

Wherefore we Syndics, judges of criminal cases in this city, having witnessed the trial conducted before us . . . and having seen your voluntary and repeated confessions and your books, judge that you, Servetus, have for a long time promulgated false and thoroughly heretical doctrine, despising all remonstrances and corrections and that you have with malicious and perverse obstinacy sown and divulged even in printed books opinions against God the Father, the Son and the Holy Spirit, in a word against the fundamentals of the Christian religion, and that you have tried to make a schism and trouble the Church of God by which many souls may have been ruined and lost, a thing horrible, shocking, scandalous and infectious. And you have had neither shame nor horror of setting yourself against the divine Majesty and the Holy Trinity, and so you have obstinately tried to infect the world with your stinking heretical poison. . . . For these and other reasons, desiring to purge the Church of God of such infection and cut off the rotten member, having taken counsel with our citizens and having invoked the name of God to give just judgment . . . having God and the Holy Scriptures before our eyes, speaking in the name of the Father, Son and Holy Spirit, we now in writing give final sentence and condemn you, Michael Servetus, to be bound and taken to Champel and there attached to a stake and burned with your book to ashes. And so you shall finish your days and give an example to others who would commit the like.



# A Witch Is Tracked down in Germany (1628)

Religious division among Christians reinforced men's resolves to be on their guard against the machinations of the Devil. A side effect of these fears was the increase in persecution of persons suspected of witchcraft. The reading presents one such case, that of the Burgomaster (Mayor) of Bamberg in southeastern Germany, Johannes Junius. The minutes of the trial are followed by a letter of Junius to his daughter. The bracketed commentary to this letter was written by the editor of the English translation. From *Translations and Reprints from the Original Sources of European History,* George Burr, ed. (Philadelphia: University of Pennsylvania, n.d.) Vol. III, No. 4, pp. 23–24, 25–28.

## I. MINUTES OF THE WITCH TRIAL OF JOHANNES JUNIUS

. . . On Wednesday, June 28, 1628, was examined without torture Johannes Junius, Burgomaster at Bamberg, on the charge of witchcraft: how and in what fashion he had fallen into that vice. Is fifty-five years old, and was born at Niederwaysich in the Wetterau. Says he is wholly innocent, knows nothing of the crime, has never in his life renounced God; says that he is wronged before God and the world, would like to hear of a single human being who has seen him at such gatherings [as the witch-sabbaths].

Confrontation of Dr. Georg Adam Haan. Tells him to his face he will stake his life on it, that he saw him, Junius, a year and a half ago at a witch-gathering in the electoral council-room, where they ate and drank. Accused denies the same wholly.

Confronted with Hopffens Elsse. Tells him likewise that he was on Hauptsmoor at a witch-dance; but first the holy wafer was desecrated. Junius denies. Hereupon he was told that his accomplices had confessed against him and was given time for thought.

On Friday, June 30, 1628, the aforesaid Junius was again without torture exhorted to confess, but again confessed nothing, whereupon, . . . since he would confess nothing, he was put to the torture, and first the

*Thumb-screws* were applied. Says he has never denied God his Saviour nor suffered himself to be otherwise baptized; will again stake his life on it; feels no pain in the thumb-screws.

*Leg-screws.* Will confess absolutely nothing; knows nothing about it. He has never renounced God; will never do such a thing; has never been guilty of this vice; feels likewise no pain.

Is stripped and examined; on his right side is found a bluish mark, like a clover leaf, is thrice pricked therein, but feels no pain and no blood flows out.

*Strappado.* He has never renounced God; God will not forsake him; if he were such a wretch he would not let himself be so tortured; God must show some token of his innocence. He knows nothing about witchcraft. . . .

On July 5, the above named Junius is without torture, but with urgent persuasions, exhorted to confess, and at last begins and confesses:

When in the year 1624 his law-suit at Rothweil cost him some six hundred florins, he had gone out, in the month of August, into his orchard at Friedrichsbronn; and, as he sat there in thought, there had come to him a woman like a grass-maid, who had asked him why he sat there so sorrowful; he had answered that he was not despondent, but she had led him by seductive speeches to yield him to her will. . . . And thereafter this wench had changed into the form of a goat, which bleated and said, "Now you see with whom you have had to do. You must be mine or I will forthwith break your neck." Thereupon he had been frightened, and trembled all over for fear. Then the transformed spirit had seized him by the throat and demanded that he should renounce God Almighty, whereupon Junius said, "God forbid," and thereupon the spirit vanished through the power of these words. Yet it came straightway back, brought more people with it, and persistently demanded of him that he renounce God in Heaven and all the heavenly host, by which terrible threatening he was obliged to speak this formula: "I renounce God in Heaven and all the heavenly host, and will henceforward recognize the Devil as my God." . . .

*Of crimes.* His paramour [female witch] had immediately after his seduction demanded that he should make away with his younger son Hans Georg, and had given him for this purpose a gray powder; this, however, being too hard for him, he had made away with his horse, a brown, instead.

His paramour had also often spurred him on to kill his daughter, . . . and because he would not do this he had been maltreated with blows by the evil spirit.

Once at the suggestion of his paramour he had taken the holy wafer out of his mouth and given it to her. . . .

A week before his arrest as he was going to St. Martin's church the Devil met him on the way, in the form of a goat, and told him that he would soon be imprisoned, but that he should not trouble himself—he would soon set him free. Besides this, by his soul's salvation, he knew nothing further; but what he had spoken was the pure truth; on that he would stake his life. On August 6, 1628, there was read to the aforesaid Junius this his confession, which he then wholly ratified and confirmed, and was willing to stake his life upon it. And afterward he voluntarily confirmed the same before the court.

A late seventeenth-century torture chamber of the Inquisition. The hanging figure at the left is in strappado.

## II. JUNIUS WRITES THE TRUE FACTS TO HIS DAUGHTER

[So ended the trial of Junius, and he was accordingly burned at the stake. But it so happens that there is also preserved in Bamberg a letter, in quivering hand, secretly written by him to his daughter while in the midst of his trial (July 24, 1628):]

Many hundred thousand good-nights, dearly beloved daughter Veronica. Innocent have I come into prison, innocent have I been tortured, innocent must I die. For whoever comes into the witch prison must become a witch or be tortured until he invents something out of his head and—God pity him—bethinks him of something. I will tell you how it has gone with me. When I was the first time put to the torture, Dr. Braun, Dr. Kötzendörffer, and two strange doctors were there. Then Dr. Braun asks me, "Kinsman, how come you here?" I answer, "Through falsehood, through misfortune." "Hear, you," he says, "you are a witch; will you confess it voluntarily? If not, we'll bring in witnesses and the executioner for you." I said "I am no witch, I have a pure conscience in the matter; if there are a thousand witnesses, I am not anxious, but I'll gladly hear the witnesses." Now the chancellor's son was set before me . . . and afterward Hoppfens Elsse. She had seen me dance on Haupts-moor. . . . I answered: "I have never renounced God, and will never do it—God graciously keep me from it. I'll rather bear whatever I must." And then came also—God in the highest Heaven have mercy—the executioner, and put the thumbscrews on me, both hands bound together, so that the blood ran out at the nails and everywhere, so that for four weeks I could not use my hands, as you can see from the writing. . . . Thereafter they first stripped me, bound my hands behind me, and drew me up in the torture.* Then I thought heaven and earth were at an end; eight times did they draw me up and let me fall again, so that I suffered terrible agony. . . .

And this happened on Friday, June 30, and with God's help I had to bear the torture. . . . When at last the executioner led me back into the prison, he said to me: "Sir, I beg you, for God's sake confess something, whether it be true or not. Invent something, for you cannot endure the torture which you will be put to; and, even if you bear it all, yet you will not

*This torture of the strappado, which was that in most common use by the courts, consisted of a rope, attached to the hands of the prisoner (bound behind his back) and carried over a pulley at the ceiling. By this he was drawn up and left hanging. To increase the pain, weights were attached to his feet or he was suddenly jerked up and let drop.

escape, not even if you were an earl, but one torture will follow after another until you say you are a witch. Not before that," he said, "Will they let you go, as you may see by all their trials, for one is just like another." . . .

And so I begged, since I was in wretched plight, to be given one day for thought and a priest. The priest was refused me, but the time for thought was given. Now, my dear child, see in what hazard I stood and still stand. I must say that I am a witch, though I am not,—must now renounce God, though I have never done it before. Day and night I was deeply troubled, but at last there came to me a new idea. I would not be anxious, but, since I had been given no priest with whom I could take counsel, I would myself think of something and say it. It were surely better that I just say it with mouth and words, even though I had not really done it; and afterwards I would confess it to the priest, and let those answer for it who compel me to do it. . . . And so I made my confession as follows; but it was all a lie.

Now follows, dear child, what I confessed in order to escape the great anguish and bitter torture, which it was impossible for me longer to bear.

[Here follows his confession, substantially as it is given in the minutes of his trial. But he adds:]

Then I had to tell what people I had seen [at the witch-sabbath]. I said that I had not recognized them. "You old rascal, I must set the executioner at you. Say—was not the Chancellor there?" So I said yes. "Who besides?" I had not recognized anybody. So he said: "Take one street after another; begin at the market, go out on one street and back on the next." I had to name several persons there. Then came the long street. I knew nobody. Had to name eight persons there. Then the Zinkenwere—one person more. Then over the upper bridge to the Georgthor, on both sides. Knew nobody again. Did I know nobody in the castle—whoever it might be, I should speak without fear. And thus continuously they asked me on all the streets, though I could not and would not say more. So they gave me to the executioner, told him to strip me, shave me all over, and put me to the torture. "The rascal knows one on the market-place, is with him daily, and yet won't name him." By that they meant Dietmeyer: so I had to name him too.

Then I had to tell what crimes I had committed. I said nothing. . . . "Draw the rascal up!" So I said that I was to kill my children, but I had killed a horse instead. It did not help. I had also taken a sacred wafer, and had desecrated it. When I had said this, they left me in peace.

Now, dear child, here you have all my confession, for which I must die. And they are sheer lies and made-up things, so help me God. For all this I was forced to say through fear of the torture which was threatened beyond what I had already endured. For they never leave off with the torture till one confesses something; be he never so good, he must be a witch. Nobody escapes, though he were an earl. . . .

Dear child, keep this letter secret so that people do not find it, else I shall be tortured most piteously and the jailers will be beheaded. So strictly is it forbidden. . . . Dear child, pay this man a dollar. . . . I have taken several days to write this: my hands are both lame. I am in a sad plight. . . .

Good night, for your father Johannes Junius will never see you more. July 24, 1628.

[And on the margin of the letter he adds:]

Dear child, six have confessed against me at once; the Chancellor, his son, Neudecker, Zaner, Hoffmaisters Ursel, and Hoppfens Elsse—all false, through compulsion, as they have all told me, and begged my forgiveness in God's name before they were executed. . . . They know nothing but good of me. They were forced to say it. . . .

# John Knox Debates Religion with Queen Mary of Scots

**(c. 1562)**

The teachings of Calvin, spread by his disciple John Knox (1505–1572), were soon adopted by the majority of the hard-working inhabitants of the poor northern kingdom of Scotland. The return of the Scottish queen, Mary (1542–1587), in 1561 after the death of her husband, the king of France, initiated a hard-hitting debate between the twenty-one-year-old Catholic queen and the dour Calvinist minister. At issue was the question of ultimate authority. Although this account of the debate was written by Knox himself, the exchange of opinion accurately reflects the difference between the lay and spiritual positions. From John Knox, *The History of the Reformation in Scotland,* ed. W. M'Gavin (Glasgow, 1832), pp. 250, 252–253.

Whether it was by counsel of others, or the queen's own desire, we know not; but the queen spake with John Knox, and had long reasoning with him, none being present, except the lord James—two gentlemen stood in the other end of the house. The sum of their reasoning was this. . . .

"But yet," said she, "ye have taught the people to receive another religion, than their princes can allow: and how can that doctrine be of God, seeing, that God commands subjects to obey their princes?"

"Madam," said he, "as that right religion takes neither origin or authority from worldly princes, but from the eternal God alone, so are not subjects bound to frame their religion according to the appetite of their princes; for oft it is, that princes are the most ignorant of all others in God's true religion, as we may read as well in the histories before the death of Christ Jesus, as after. If all the seed of Abraham should have been of the religion of Pharaoh, to whom they were long subjects, I pray you, madam, what religion should there have been in the world? For, if all men, in the days of the apostles, should have been of the religion of the Roman emperors, what religion should have been upon the face of the earth? Daniel and his fellows were subjects to Nebuchadnezzar, and unto Darius, and yet, madam, they would not be of their religion, neither of the one nor of the other: for the three children said, 'We make it known unto thee, O king, that we will not worship thy gods.' And Daniel did pray publicly unto his God, against the express commandment of the king. And so, madam, ye may perceive, that subjects are not bound to the religion of their princes, albeit they are commanded to give them obedience."

"Yea," said she, "none of those men raised the sword against their princes." "Yet, madam," said he, "ye cannot deny but that they resisted: for these that obey not the commandments that are given, in some sort they resist." "But yet," said she, "they resisted not by the sword." "God," said he, "madam, had not given unto them the power and the means." "Think ye," said she, "that subjects having power may resist their princes?" "If their princes exceed their bounds," said he, "madam, and do against that wherefore they should be obeyed, it is no doubt but they may be resisted, even by power." . . .

At these words, the queen stood as it were amazed, more than a quarter of an hour; her countenance altered, so that lord James began to entreat her, and to demand, "What has offended you, madam?" At length, she said, "Well, then, I perceive, that my subjects shall obey you, and not me; and shall do what they list, and not what I command: and so must I be subject to them, and not they to me." "God forbid," answered he, "that ever I take upon me to command any to obey me, or yet to set subjects at liberty to do what pleases them. But my travail is, that both princes and subjects obey God. And think not," said he, "madam, that wrong is done unto you, when you are willed to be subject unto God: for, it is He that subjects the people under princes, and causes obedience to be given unto them; yea, God craves of kings, 'That they be, as it were, foster-fathers to His kirk, and commands queens to be nurses unto His people.' And this subjection, madam, unto God, and unto His troubled kirk, is the greatest dignity that flesh can get upon the face of the earth, for it shall carry them to everlasting glory."

"Yea," said she, "but ye are not the kirk that I will nurse. I will defend the kirk of Rome, for it is, I think, the true kirk of God."

"Your will," said he, "madam, is no reason; neither doth your thought make that Roman harlot to be the true and immaculate spouse of Jesus Christ. And wonder not, madam, that I call Rome a harlot; for that kirk is altogether polluted with all kind of spiritual fornication, as well in doctrine as in manners. Yea, madam, I offer myself farther to prove, that the kirk of the Jews, that crucified Christ Jesus, when that they manifestly denied the Son of God, was not so far degenerated from the ordinances and statutes which God gave by Moses and Aaron unto His people, as that the kirk of Rome is declined, and more than five hundred years hath declined from the purity of that religion, which the apostles taught and planted."

"My conscience," said she, "is not so." "Conscience, madam," said he, "requires knowledge; and I fear that right knowledge you have none." "But," said she, "I have both heard and read." "So, madam," said he, "did the Jews who crucified Christ Jesus, read both the law and the prophets, and heard the same interpreted after their manner. Have ye heard," said he, "any teach, but such as the pope and the cardinals have allowed? And ye may be assured, that such will speak nothing to offend their own estate." "Ye interpret the scriptures," said she, "in one manner, and they in another; whom shall I believe, and who shall be judge?" "You shall believe God," said he, "that plainly speaketh in His word: and farther than the word teacheth you, you neither shall believe the one nor the other. The word of God is plain in the self; and if there appear any obscurity in any place, the Holy Ghost, who is never contrarious to Himself, explains the same more clearly in other places: so that there can remain no doubt, but unto such as will remain obstinately ignorant."

# Erich Fromm: The Theology of Anxiety

Erich Fromm (1900– ), a social philosopher and psychoanalyst, left his native Germany in protest against the Nazi take-over. His best-selling *Escape From Freedom* (1941) applied the techniques of psychoanalysis to the social process. In this reading Fromm seeks the psychological motivations for religious change. He explores these motivations in their social and economic context and, in his book, sees parallels between the sixteenth and twentieth centuries. From *Escape from Freedom* by Erich Fromm. Copyright 1941, © 1949 by Erich Fromm. Reprinted by permission of Holt, Rinehart & Winston, Inc., pp. 39, 79–81, 90–93.

## I. THE LUTHERAN CONCEPT OF FREEDOM

Ideological similarity is not the only one that makes the study of the fifteenth and sixteenth centuries a particularly fruitful starting point for the understanding of the present scene. There is also a fundamental likeness in the social situation. I shall try to show how this likeness is responsible for the ideological and psychological similarity. Then as now a vast sector of the population was threatened in its traditional way of life by revolutionary changes in the economic and social organization; especially was the middle class, as today, threatened by the power of monopolies and the superior strength of capital, and this threat had an important effect on the spirit and the ideology of the threatened sector of society by enhancing the individual's feeling of aloneness and insignificance. . . .

What is the connection of Luther's doctrines with the psychological situation of all but the rich and powerful toward the end of the Middle Ages? As we have seen, the old order was breaking down. The individual had lost the security of certainty and was threatened by new economic forces, by capitalists and monopolies; the corporative principle was being replaced by competition; the lower classes felt the pressure of growing exploitation. The appeal of Lutheranism to the lower classes differed from its appeal to the middle class. The poor in the cities, and even more the peasants, were in a desperate situation. They were ruthlessly exploited and deprived of traditional rights and privileges. They were in a revolutionary mood which found expression in peasant uprisings and in revolutionary movements in the cities. The Gospel articulated their hopes and expectations as it had done for the slaves and laborers of early Christianity, and led the poor to seek for freedom and justice. In so far as Luther attacked authority and made the word of the Gospel the center of his teachings, he appealed to these restive masses as other religious movements of an evangelical character had done before him.

Although Luther accepted their allegiance to him and supported them, he could do so only up to a certain point; he had to break the alliance when the peasants went further than attacking the authority of the Church and merely making minor demands for the betterment of their lot. They proceeded to become a revolutionary class which threatened to overthrow all authority and to destroy the foundations of a social order in whose maintenance the middle class was vitally interested. For, . . . the middle class, even its lower stratum, had privileges to defend against the demands of the poor; and therefore it was intensely hostile to revolutionary movements which aimed to destroy not only the privileges of the aristocracy, the Church, and the monopolies, but their own privileges as well.

The position of the middle class between the very rich and the very poor made its reaction complex and in many ways contradictory. They wanted to uphold law and order, and yet they were themselves vitally threatened by rising capitalism. Even the more successful members of the middle class were not wealthy and powerful as the small group of big capitalists was. They had to fight hard to survive and make progress. The luxury of the moneyed class increased their feeling of smallness and filled them with envy and indignation. As a whole, the middle class was more endangered by the collapse of the feudal order and by rising capitalism than they were helped.

Luther's picture of man mirrored just this dilemma. Man is free from all ties binding him to spiritual authorities, but this very freedom leaves him alone and anxious, overwhelms him with a feeling of his own individual insignificance and powerlessness. This free, isolated individual is crushed by the experience of his individual insignificance. Luther's theology gives expression to this feeling of helplessness and doubt. The picture of man which he draws in religious terms describes the situation of the individual as it was brought about by the current social and economic evolution. The member of the middle class was as helpless in face of the new economic forces as Luther described man to be in his relationship to God.

But Luther did more than bring out the feeling of insignificance which already pervaded the social classes to whom he preached—he offered them a solution. By not only accepting his own insignificance but by humiliating himself to the utmost, by giving up every vestige of individual will, by renouncing and denouncing his individual strength, the individual could hope to be acceptable to God. Luther's relationship to God was one of complete submission. In psychological terms his concept of faith means: if you completely submit, if you accept your individual insignificance, then the all-powerful God may be willing to love you and save you. If you get rid of your individual self with all its shortcomings and doubts by utmost self-effacement, you free yourself from the feeling of your own nothingness and can participate in God's glory. Thus, while Luther freed people from the authority of the Church, he made them submit to a much more tyrannical authority, that of a God who insisted on complete submission of man and annihilation of the individual self as the essential condition to his salvation. . . .

## II. CALVIN AND THE COMPULSION TO WORK

. . . The particular emphasis on a virtuous life which was characteristic for Calvinism had also a particular psychological significance. Calvinism emphasized the necessity of unceasing human effort. Man must constantly try to live according to God's word and never lapse in his effort to do so. This doctrine appears to be a contradiction of the doctrine that human effort is of no avail with regard to man's salvation. The fatalistic attitude of not making any effort might seem like a much more appropriate response. Some psychological considerations, however, show that this is not so. The state of anxiety, the feeling of powerlessness and insignificance, and especially the doubt concerning one's future after death, represent a state of mind which is practically unbearable for anybody. Almost no one stricken with this fear would be able to relax, enjoy life, and be indifferent as to what happened afterwards. One possible way to escape this unbearable state of uncertainty and the paralyzing feeling of one's own insignificance is the very trait which became so prominent in Calvinism: the development of a frantic activity and a striving to do something. Activity in this sense assumes a compulsory quality: the individual has to be active in order to overcome his feeling of doubt and powerlessness. This kind of effort and activity is not the result of inner strength and self-confidence; it is a desperate escape from anxiety.

This mechanism can be easily observed in attacks of anxiety panic in individuals. A man who expects to receive within a few hours the doctor's diagnosis of his illness—which may be fatal—quite naturally is in a state of anxiety. Usually he will not sit down quietly and wait. Most frequently his anxiety, if it does not paralyze him, will drive him to some sort of more or less frantic activity. He may pace up and down the floor, start asking questions and talk to everybody he can get hold of, clean up his desk, write letters. He may continue his usual kind of work but with added activity and more feverishly. Whatever form his effort assumes it is prompted by anxiety and tends to overcome the feeling of powerlessness by frantic activity.

Effort in the Calvinist doctrine had still another psychological meaning. The fact that one did not tire in that unceasing effort and that one succeeded in one's moral as well as one's secular work was a more or less distinct sign of being one of the chosen ones. The irrationality of such compulsive effort is that the activity is not meant to create a desired end but serves to indicate whether or not something will occur which has been determined beforehand, independent of one's own activity or control. This mechanism is a well-known feature of compulsive neurotics. Such persons when afraid of the outcome of an important undertaking may, while awaiting an answer, count the windows of houses or trees on the street. If the number is even, a person feels that things will be all right; if it is uneven, it is a sign that he will fail. Frequently this doubt does not refer to a specific instance but to a person's whole life, and the compulsion to look for "signs" will pervade it accordingly. Often the connection between counting stones, playing solitaire, gambling, and so on, and anxiety and doubt, is not conscious. A person may play solitaire out of a vague feeling of restlessness and only an analysis might uncover the hidden function of his activity: to reveal the future.

In Calvinism this meaning of effort was part of the religious doctrine. Originally it referred essentially to moral effort, but later on the emphasis was more and more on effort in one's occupation and on the results of this effort, that is, success or failure in business. Success became the sign of God's grace; failure, the sign of damnation.

These considerations show that the compulsion to unceasing effort and work was far from being in contradiction to a basic conviction of man's powerlessness; rather was it the psychological result. Effort and work in this sense assumed an entirely irrational character. They were not to change fate since this

1 Tidore, valued for its cloves, was the site of the first Spanish garrison in the Spice Islands. Control of this important island was assumed by the Portuguese in 1529, and the Dutch tried to wrest it from them at the turn of the century. This etching by the Flemish artist De Bry offers a contemporary view of a Dutch attack on the garrison.

## The Expansion of the West

It is a vanity of Europeans in their Age of Exploration that they took to themselves responsibility for the "discovery" of already inhabited lands. This was no innocent conceit, however, for their pride in discovery reflected a sense of legitimate possession and a determination to assert title to territory. Two centuries of piracy and colonial warfare did not terminate the struggle among Western powers for the lands revealed to Europeans in the first voyages to Asia, Africa, and the New World. The voyages were explosive and productive, bringing to the parochial consciousness of Western Europeans a knowledge of tastes and life styles largely denied them since the end of the West's earlier outpouring in the Crusades. At the same time they established a world-wide colonial economy in service to the needs of a European market. Its effects would take centuries to measure. The collision of cultures has been recorded in the pictorial archives of the mother country as well as in the art of the native, silent witness to an alien encounter. From this mirror of exploration come a few shocks of recognition and a sense of participation in the creation of a more universal history.

1 A sober but satisfied Dutch trader points with a malacca cane to the ships of the Dutch East India Company in the harbor of Batavia (now Djakarta). By the middle of the seventeenth century, when this picture was painted, one hundred vessels in regular commerce linked Holland with the spice depots in the East Indies. A native servant shields the couple from the sun with a parasol.

2 The fine porcelains of China, like the fine silks, were highly valued in Europe. Porcelain of the Ming period, contemporary with the age of European exploration, are still collectors' items. This still life of a pewter flagon and two Ming bowls is the work of the Dutch artist Jan Treck, 1649.

3 The Meissen works, established near Dresden in 1710, imitated Chinese processes in the production of porcelains known as "china." Dresden is still famous in this connection. This Meissen grouping dates from the period 1725–1735. The decor is of Chinese inspiration, but note the European galleons at the lip of the plate (top).

1 Macao in the late sixteenth century was the main port for the European trade with China until the opening of Hong Kong in the mid-nineteenth century. The six square mile enclave is still under Portuguese control, though under Chinese suffrance with a predominantly Asian population. In De Bry's somewhat fanciful etching, European merchants adapt to their new circumstances. Note the parasols and sedan chairs, and also the church bells and the cross.

2 Chinese mandarin carried in a sedan chair from De Bry's collection. The chair is still used for transportation in portions of mainland China.

3 This early eighteenth-century etching opposite places an Indian next to a tobacco plant. Tobacco, an exotic crop of the New World, was used by the aborigines of America long before the arrival of Europeans. Natives smoking rolled leaves of the plant were seen by the crew of Christopher Columbus in a stopover in Cuba in 1492. Tobacco smoking spread to Europe in the sixteenth and seventeenth centuries and from there to Africa and Asia. The plant was used for a variety of purposes in early European medicine, largely because of its characteristics as a narcotic. By the beginning of the eighteenth century, however, it was being taken largely for pleasure. Some opposition to the use of the plant on moral and medical grounds followed closely upon its introduction to Europe. By 1828 nicotine had been isolated as a poisonous alkaloid.

Tobacco, in Europe, occasionally produced its own cult and rituals. Frederick William I of Prussia created his own somewhat notorious "tobacco parliment," shown in this painting by a contemporary artist. Foreign ambassadors were compelled to state their business before this gathering, and one of the king's chief delights was to sicken his guests with tobacco smoke. Frederick William sits at the table facing two of the younger princes who have entered the room to say good night. The fourteen-year-old Crown Prince, later known as Frederick the Great, sits at his right. (**4**) Coffee as a drink, made from roasted and ground beans, originated in Arabia in the fifteenth century and spread around the world. Recognized as a stimulant, and opposed initially by both Mohammedans and Catholics, it gained widespread acceptance in Europe by the mid-seventeenth century. The brew was first drunk outside the home in the coffeehouse, pictured below right, seed-bed of literary imagination, radicalism, and community in the seventeenth and eighteenth centuries. This etching of an eighteenth-century coffeehouse crowd, made from an old drawing, conveys a sense of the strong tempers, seditious literature, and leisurely routines that mixed at the tables. (**5**)

4

3

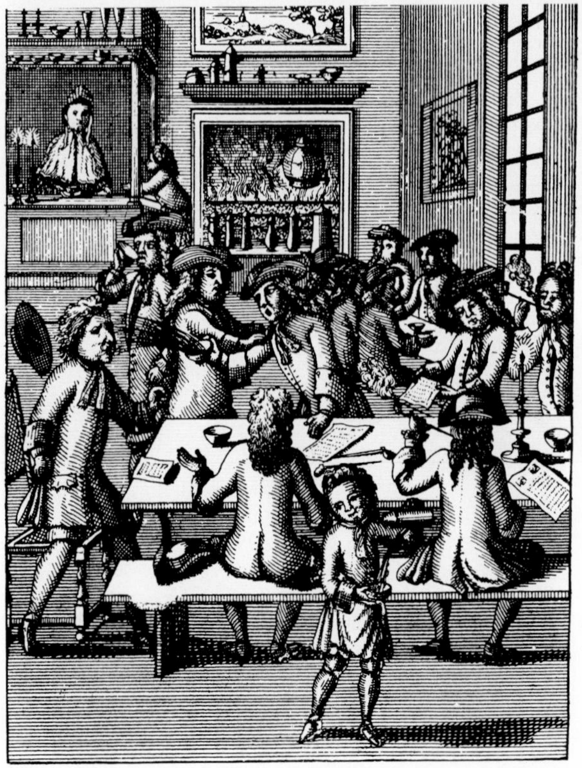

5

1 The passage of the martial European is clearly marked in native art. This sixteenth-century bronze plaque from Benin, Western Africa, shows a Portuguese soldier with a cross-bow across one shoulder and a bunch of arrows in his hand. Note the careful detail given the weaponry. Even in the sixteenth century, cross-bows were in wide-spread use. They could be loaded with a bolt and released as rapidly as a musket could be loaded and fired.

2 Here a European witnesses the traffic in slaves. A dug-out canoe brings a new shipment to the coast, in a nineteenth-century rendering.

3 Europeans in the developed civilizations of China and Japan in the seventeenth and eighteenth centuries were tolerated at the pleasure of the native rulers. As a class of missionaries, Jesuit priests from Portugal had reason to recognize the tenuousness of their position. Identified in the eyes of the rulers with the Portuguese traders, they were harassed, mistreated, and finally expelled from Japan in 1641. This Japanese screen revives the memory of the Portuguese in curiosity rather than rancor. For the Japanese, they belonged to the world of the exotic, just as the Oriental did for the European. In the lower part of the screen, Jesuit priests (left foreground) are visited by a group of Portuguese merchants. The latter enter with horses, dogs, and a retinue of African servants. The native artist portrays the Portuguese as he perceived them, with big noses and billowy pantaloons. A scene of the Jesuit mission is shown above the golden clouds.

4 In India, by contrast, the British reached a dominant position during the eighteenth century. The entire administration of Bengal lay in the hands of the British East India Company. The miniature shown here, by the Indian artist Dip Chand, is believed to be a portrait of the Scottish surgeon with the East India Company, Dr. William Fullerton. Here he reclines on stuffed cushions, draws on his hookah, and almost fades into the Oriental scene. The portrait was executed in Bengal in 1760.

was predetermined by God, regardless of any effort on the part of the individual. They served only as a means of forecasting the predetermined fate; while at the same time the frantic effort was a reassurance against an otherwise unbearable feeling of powerlessness.

This new attitude towards effort and work as an aim in itself may be assumed to be the most important psychological change which has happened to man since the end of the Middle Ages. In every society man has to work if he wants to live. Many societies solved the problem by having the work done by slaves, thus allowing the free man to devote himself to "nobler" occupations. In such societies, work was not worthy of a free man. In medieval society, too, the burden of work was unequally distributed among the different classes in the social hierarchy, and there was a good deal of crude exploitation. But the attitude toward work was different from that which developed subsequently in the modern era. Work did not have the abstract character of producing some commodity which might be profitably sold on the market. One worked in response to a concrete demand and with a concrete aim: to earn one's livelihood. There was, as Max Weber particularly has shown, no urge to work more than was necessary to maintain the traditional standard of living. It seems that for some groups of medieval society work was enjoyed as a realization of productive ability; that many others worked because they had to and felt this necessity was conditioned by pressure from the outside. What was new in modern society was that men came to be driven to work not so much by external pressure but by an internal compulsion, which made them work as only a very strict master could have made people do in other societies. . . .

TOPIC 36

# THE CATHOLIC REFORMATION

The search for religious renewal tore at the sinews of the Roman Church, dividing families and nations as it pulled at the European conscience. The reflex of the papacy, weakened by the seditious example of northern reformers and the amputation of large territories from its religious control, was to place its own house in order, while closing its doors to dissent and reaffirming its legitimacy and authority. New agencies were created to meet the menace of Protestantism and these helped the Church to slow the advance of its Christian rival, contain it, and even recover lost territories. But its answer to the challenge marked the Church with the stamp of conservatism. The Church remained responsive to the religious needs of the members, but not until the middle of the twentieth century would the institution be open to currents of radical change. The readings examine the movement for Catholic reform.

Reading 197

## The Persistence of Reform

From *Civilization Past and Present* by T. Walter Wallbank, Alastair M. Taylor, Nels M. Bailkey. Copyright © 1965 by Scott, Foresman and Company. Pp. 302-306.

The Catholic Reformation should not be viewed as only a retaliatory movement or a series of measures taken to stem the rising tide of Protestantism. The Roman Church had always retained latent forces of recuperation and strength which were drawn upon in challenging times. Before Luther had nailed his ninety-five theses to the church door at Wittenberg, renewed vitality and internal reform were apparent in the Roman Church.

One of the prime examples of this resurgence occurred in Spain, where humanistic energies were expended in the fields of religion and government. In this passionately orthodox country, royalty enlisted the services of the humanist Cardinal Ximenes de Cisneros (1436?-1517). At once a hairshirted Franciscan friar, a reformer of lax clergymen, the grand inquisitor, and the chancellor of the realm, Cardinal Ximenes was also a Renaissance scholar who founded the University of Alcala, where humanistic studies were pursued. The melding of his humanistic and religious interests is revealed in the careful scholarship involved in new translations of the Bible. Under the supervision and financial support of Ximenes, the famous Polyglot Bible was prepared. In what was the most scientific study of the Scriptures in the sixteenth century, the Polyglot Bible reproduced in its six large volumes all the original texts together with the Vulgate.

In a unique category of his own was Savonarola (1452-1498), a Dominican preacher and reformer in the city of Florence. A persuasive speaker, he induced the wealthy and pleasure-loving Florentines to make bonfires of their luxuries. When the discredited Medici fled before the invasion of Charles VIII of France, Savonarola organized Florence as a republic and managed to keep the French from sacking the city. He also attacked the iniquities of the Borgia pope, Alexander VI. But despite the fact that he was later hailed by Luther and the Protestants as a forerunner of their movement, Savonarola was actually attempting to return the papacy to its tradition of simple living and dedicated service. By this means he hoped to avert a real revolt against the Church. Unfortunately Savonarola did not possess the power to enforce his dictates. Publicly humiliated by having his Dominican garb torn from him in the great square of Florence, Savonarola was hanged and burned, a victim of political intrigue.

In Italy other forces were also at work to revitalize and purify the Church. In the same year that Luther issued his ninety-five theses, a group of clerics and laymen in Rome founded the Oratory of Divine Love. Its purpose was to use prayer, sermons, and good works to create a strong personal religious consciousness but at the same time to retain the traditional Catholic framework and the leadership of the papacy. Other oratories were founded in Italy, but their work was relatively short-lived.

By the middle of the sixteenth century, the inroads of Protestantism were apparent, and in retaliation the Church rallied its forces and prepared a powerful offensive. This renewal of strength is known as the Catholic Reformation. As we shall see, the reforming spirit penetrated almost all areas of the Church. New monastic orders infused with crusading zeal were organized, and a resurgence of mysticism occurred. The pope himself adopted a program of vigorous reform. Climaxing the whole movement was the Council of Trent, where the Church boldly reaffirmed its traditional doctrines and flatly refused to compromise in any way with the Protestants.

## REFORMING ORDERS

Reverting to methods which it had almost perfected during medieval eras of reform, the Church instituted new monastic orders. Springing up in the sixteenth century, several new orders performed useful work in a variety of fields—charitable works, education, and conversion.

In 1524, the order of the Theatines was founded in Italy by a member of the Oratory of Divine Love. By preaching and exemplary conduct, the Theatines undertook to check the spread of heresy. They also performed such good works as supporting hospitals and orphanages. The number of Theatines was small but their work proved highly influential.

Among other orders established at this time were the Capuchins, an offshoot of the Franciscan order. Seeking to return to the original Rule and spirit of St. Francis, they became notable for their preaching and for their care of the poor and sick. Still another successful movement was that of the Ursulines, founded in 1535 to educate girls.

A Spanish ex-soldier, Ignatius Loyola (1491–1556), founded in 1534 the Society of Jesus, better known as the Jesuit order, which played a vital role in the Catholic Reformation. In addition to the three vows of chastity, obedience, and poverty, the Jesuits took a special vow of allegiance to the pope. By means of preaching and education, this order intended to win back converts to the Roman Church. They succeeded remarkably well, recovering most of Poland and maintaining Catholicism in Bavaria, the southern Netherlands (now Belgium), Austria, and Ireland. Owing to their efforts and to the weight always lent by tradition, Italy, Spain, and Portugal remained loyally Catholic, while France saw Protestantism checked. In addition, the Jesuits performed excellent missionary work in North and South America, China, and India. . . .

## PAPAL REFORM: PAUL III

A new era was at hand for the Church when Paul III, who reigned from 1534 to 1549, ascended the papal throne. He chose outstanding men as cardinals and appointed a commission to look into the need for reform. Their report listed the evils requiring correction, including the appointment of worldly bishops and priests; the traffic in benefices, in indulgences, and other financial abuses; the venality of some cardinals; and the absence of others from the papal court. There was considerable opposition from various quarters to Paul's decision to begin acting upon this report. He persisted, however, and among other reforms improved the papal administrative machinery. Again ignoring the opposition of high churchmen who feared for their positions and incomes, Paul made plans to reform the entire Church organization of a general council.

## THE COUNCIL OF TRENT: CLIMAX OF THE CATHOLIC REFORMATION

Reviving the device of a Church council, so useful at the time of the Great Schism, the Catholic Reformation came to a climax in the Council of Trent (1545–1563). There, a clear enunciation of Catholic doctrines was set forth. In no point of dogma did the Catholic Church compromise with the Protestants. The successors of St. Thomas Aquinas, who had done so much to shape the dogmas of the medieval Church, reaffirmed the doctrines of the Church as the basis of Christianity and the role of the Church as the only interpreter of these vital elements. As proof of the fact that the Catholic Church in no wise departed from its age-old body of beliefs, the following statement reiterates the validity of the sacramental system:

> If any one saith that the sacraments of the new lay were not all instituted by Jesus Christ, our Lord; or that they are more or less than seven . . . or even that any one of these seven is not truly and properly a sacrament; let him be anathema.

At the same time, drastic reforms were made in Church discipline and administration. Such evils as simony, absenteeism, and secular pursuits on the part of the clergy were strictly forbidden. The Council forbade prelates and other holders of ecclesiastical offices to aid their kinsmen at the expense of the Church:

It [the Council] strictly forbids them . . . to strive to enrich their own kindred or domestics out of the revenues of the Church; seeing that even the canons of the apostles forbid them to give to their kindred the property of the Church, which belongs to God . . . yea, this holy Council, with the utmost earnestness, admonishes them completely to lay aside all this human and carnal affection towards brothers, nephews, and kindred, which is the seed plot of many evils in the Church.

## EFFECTS OF THE RELIGIOUS UPHEAVAL

Prior to 1517 there had been two religious divisions of Christendom—Greek Orthodox and Roman Catholic. By 1550 Christendom was composed of three divisions—Orthodox, Catholic, and Protestant. Protestantism had become uppermost in northern Europe, while Catholicism held sway in the south. This great religious division had struck a mortal blow at the medieval unity of Europe. The Catholics placed their faith in the infallibility of the pope and the need for a mediatory priesthood. The Protestants placed their faith in the infallibility of the Bible and individual interpretation of it; furthermore, every Christian could win salvation without priestly mediation. The Protestants differed among themselves in their interpretation of the Bible and the methods of church organization; in time hundreds of Protestant sects arose, many claiming to possess the one and only true interpretation and logical administration.

Although the religious upheaval irreparably split the unity of Christendom and in so doing fostered the religious diversity of modern times, it also represented in some aspects a return to medievalism. It was a great religious revival, a renewal of faith. After the Renaissance era of free and secular thought, of individualism and humanism, men's thoughts were turned again to salvation and the life hereafter. Free thought gave way again to authority—for Protestants it was the Bible; for Catholics, the Church. The Renaissance movement, having fostered doubt and criticism of medieval values, was now engulfed in a return to some of those values. Free thinkers were persecuted by both sides, and talented writers and thinkers who in Renaissance times might have followed the prevailing pattern of individualism and secularism now devoted their abilities to arguing one side or another of the burning conflict of the day. Thus, temporarily at least, the Renaissance spirit was stifled. But it was to prove stronger than this intense religious revival and in the end was to profit from the passing of the single religious authority of the universal Church.

In addition to renewing the surge of faith, the religious upheaval brought about a great deal of genuine religious reform. Protestant service of worship was simplified in an effort to return to the purity of early Christian times. Strict attention was given to conduct and morals. Within the Catholic Church a reform movement also took place in answer to the Protestant challenge, beginning, as we have seen, with the accession of Pope Paul III and culminating in the decrees of the Council of Trent. This movement changed neither doctrine nor organization but aimed at clarifying and reaffirming doctrine and purifying and strengthening discipline among the clergy and laity alike. . . .

While religious developments fostered a return to medieval attitudes in many ways, in the economic sphere the opposite was true. The Renaissance encouraged a new individualism in economic matters, which contributed to a breakdown of the guild system and to the rise of the individual entrepreneur. Protestantism did away with the old concept of the "just price" and the ban against receiving interest on money loaned (usury). Investment of capital and loaning of money became respectable. Calvinism especially encouraged enterprise; some Calvinists regarded prosperity as a sign of election to grace and poverty as evidence of damnation. The confiscation of monastic lands in Protestant countries also stimulated economic development. England in particular benefited from the use of former monastic lands. We have noted earlier that the business classes were among those that encouraged the revolt from Rome. We can now see that they were also among those that most benefited by it.

In many cases the religious division of Europe followed political lines. Just as the English king bound the national church and the national state together under his own leadership, so in Germany the Peace of Augsburg gave the ruler of each state the right to decide the faith of his subjects, thus controlling the church in his realm. Similarly, rulers of other countries, both Catholic and Protestant, developed national churches, so that Europe was divided religiously into an Anglican Church, a Dutch Church, a Swedish Church, and so on.

In many countries one effect of such division was to strengthen the hand of the king in building a unified state. The authority and prestige of the Protestant monarch was increased as he became the spiritual as well as the political ruler of his subjects. Even in Catholic countries, though the pope remained the spiritual ruler, the Church became

SCOTLAND
MIXED WITH CATHOLIC
Edinburgh
IRELAND
ENGLAND
London
NETHERLANDS
NORWAY
SWEDEN
DENMARK
FINLAND
ESTONIA
COURLAND
PRUSSIA
RUSSIA
HOLY ROMAN EMPIRE
Wittenberg
Wartberg
POLAND
Paris
Worms
BOHEMIA
FRANCE
PALATINATE
Augsburg
Vienna
SWISS CONFEDERATION
ARCHDUCHY OF AUSTRIA
Geneva
HUNGARY
PORTUGAL
SPAIN
ITALY
OTTOMAN EMPIRE
MIXED WITH ISLAMIC
RELIGIOUS DIVISIONS OF EUROPE IN 1600
Roman Catholic
Greek Orthodox
Islam
Lutheran
Anglican
Calvinist and Zwinglian

national in sentiment, and it was the king rather than the pope who enforced religious conformity among his subjects. Conversely, in countries where the split between Protestants and Catholics was deep, as in the Holy Roman Empire, the power of the central ruler was limited and national unity impeded.

Freedom of religion was still far from a reality. Protestants were persecuted in Catholic countries and Catholics in Protestant states, partly because of the intolerance engendered by the clash between faiths but even more because religious uniformity was the ideal of the rulers of the rising national states. Just as he sought to create a uniform system of law and justice throughout his realm, so the strong monarch endeavored to establish a single faith to which his subjects owed complete obedience. An incidental result of this policy was the emigration of religious minorities to areas where they could worship freely, as in the New World. . . .

# The Society of Jesus Seeks Converts to Catholicism (16th Century)

These documents illustrate two aspects of the Jesuit order: first, the complete obedience of its members to the wishes of the Pope, and second, its educational role in recovering Christians for the Catholic Church. The second selection is taken from the *Ratio Studiorum* which set forth methods of instruction for Jesuit professors. I. From Henry Bettenson, ed., *Documents of the Christian Church* (New York: Oxford University Press, 1947), p. 366. II. *St. Ignatius and the Ratio Studiorum,* ed. Edward Fitzgerald (New York: McGraw-Hill, Inc., 1933), pp. 280–282.

## I. JESUIT RULE OF OBEDIENCE (1539)

Let us with the utmost pains strain every nerve of our strength to exhibit this virtue of obedience, firstly to the Highest Pontiff [Pope], then to the Superiors of the Society; so that in all things, to which obedience can be extended with charity, we may be most ready to obey his voice, just as if it issued from Christ our Lord. . . , leaving any work, even a letter, that we have begun and have not yet finished; by directing to this goal all our strength and intention in the Lord, that holy obedience may be made perfect in us in every respect, in performance, in will, in intellect; by submitting to whatever may be enjoined on us with great readiness, with spiritual joy and perseverance; by persuading ourselves that all things [commanded] are just; by rejecting with a kind of blind obedience all opposing opinion or judgment of our own; and that in all things which are ordained by the Superior where it cannot be clearly held that any kind of sin intervenes. And let each one persuade himself that they that live under obedience ought to allow themselves to be borne and ruled by divine providence working through their Superiors exactly as if they were a corpse which suffers itself to be borne and handled in any way whatsoever; or just as an old man's stick which serves him who holds it in his hand wherever and for whatever purpose he wishes to use it. . . .

## II. REGULATIONS FOR JESUIT INSTRUCTION (1599)

### Rules of the Professor of Scholastic Theology

1. *Duty.* He shall realize that it is his duty to join a well-founded subtlety in disputation with an orthodox faith and devotion in such a way that the former shall especially serve the latter.
2. *Following St. Thomas.* All members of our Order shall follow the teaching of St. Thomas in scholastic theology, and consider him as their special teacher; they shall center all their efforts in him so that their pupils may esteem him as highly as possible. However, they should realize that they are not confined to him so closely that they are never permitted to depart from him in any matter, since even those who especially profess to be Thomists occasionally depart from him, and it would not befit the members of our Order to be bound to St. Thomas more tightly than the Thomists themselves.
3. *With Some Exceptions.* Therefore, in regard to the conception of Blessed Mary, and in regard to the solemnity of vows, let them follow the opinion which is more common at this time, and more generally received among theologians, and in questions merely philosophical and also in those which belong to Scripture and Canon Law, he will be allowed to follow other authorities also who have treated those subjects *ex professo.*
4. *Choice of Opinions on Doubtful Questions.* On those questions in which the

opinion of St. Thomas is not clear, or which he does not treat, if Catholic scholars do not agree, he may hold either side of the question, as provided in the Common Rules, Rule 5.

5. *Regard for Faith and Devotion.* In teaching, he shall first have regard for strengthening faith and fostering devotion. Wherefore, in those questions which St. Thomas does not explicitly treat, no one shall teach anything which does not accord with the interpretation of the Church and with her traditions, or which tends to weaken the foundation of true devotion. Whence it comes that they are not to reject the accepted arguments, even though they are only probable, by which matters of faith are accustomed to be proved; nor shall any form new opinions hastily, unless from firmly established principles.
6. *Not to Assert Views Which Offend Catholics.* If any opinions, regardless of authority, are known to be seriously offensive to the Catholics of any province or school, he shall not teach them or defend them there. When no doctrine of faith or uprightness of morals is involved, charitable prudence requires that the members of the Order accommodate their actions to those with whom they are dealing.

### Rules for the Professor of Philosophy

1. *Purpose.* Since the arts and the natural sciences prepare the mind for theology and help to a perfect knowledge and use of it and of themselves aid in reaching this end, the instructor, seeking in all things sincerely the honor and glory of God, shall so treat them as to prepare his hearers and especially ours for theology and stir them up greatly to the knowledge of their Creator.
2. *How Far Aristotle Is to Be Followed.* In matters of any importance let him not depart from Aristotle unless something occurs which is foreign to the doctrine which academies everywhere approve of; much more if it is opposed to the orthodox faith, and if there are any arguments of this or any other philosopher against the faith, he will endeavor earnestly to refute them according to the Lateran Council.
3. *Authors Hostile to Christianity.* He shall not read without careful selection or bring into class interpreters of Aristotle who are out of harmony with the Christian religion and he will take care that his students do not become influenced by them. . . .

## A Jesuit Explains His Motives (1580)

Robert Persons became disillusioned with English Protestantism while a student at Oxford. Crossing to the continent, he entered the Catholic Church and later joined the Society of Jesus. In 1580 Persons returned secretly to England to help English Catholics in their efforts to hold out against the Protestant current. The reading contains an excerpt from the confession of faith prepared by the Jesuit in anticipation of possible detection while on his dangerous mission. From *Letters and Memorials of Father Robert Persons, S.J.*, ed. L. Hicks, S.J. (London: Catholic Record Society, 1942), pp. 36–38.

With regard to my faith and considered religious principles, although the description of "Catholic" has adequately indicated them, yet I desire to explain them more clearly, if possible. Let Your Worships then know that *as a young man I had for long been led hither and thither by the misleading utterances of false preachers,* and this was accentuated after I had come to the University. There for many years I desired to accept the attitude newly adopted by my country [Protestantism] and by degrees to reconcile my conscience which was very opposed to it; for I perceived that all promotion in the service of the kingdom had been made to depend on this. I have to thank God, however, that He never allowed my wavering soul, though I was daily listening to and reading the new teachers, to adhere to them so obstinately as to be infected with this plague which it was God's will to keep from me. Yet the more I kept reading, ever the more uncertain and restless I seemed to become. But after I had begun to peruse the sacred writings of the Fathers, I perceived that everything they contained was so repugnant to this new doctrine that I was ashamed any longer to tempt God and do violence to my own convictions. . . .

And so be it known to you that I firmly believe all that which the Catholic Church of Christ in any way proposes for belief. And I mean by this that church which has always been acknowledged as the visible church of Christ on earth. Of this I hold the Roman church is to be the most honoured part, and

I hold the holy Bishop of that See to have been constituted by God, next after Himself, as the universal Pastor and supreme Governor of the whole of it; and all heretics, both ancient and modern, who have left the Church or shall leave it in the time to come, inventing some new form of belief, I hate to the death, and especially the heresiarchs of our day, *Luther, Zwingli, Calvin, Béza,* and men of the same kidney . . . for I am firmly convinced that there can no more be a new faith or religion than there can be some new God, or a Christ other than Him in whom we conscientiously believe.

*And now I will set down openly and truthfully what has been the motive of my coming* to these parts at this time. It is not unknown to you, I imagine, that there is a certain Society called, from its imitating in a special way the life of our Saviour, the Society of Jesus; and you have heard perhaps that by its profession it incurs the liability of being sent to any part of the whole world to preach the gospel of Christ, without taking any account of danger. It is with this end in view that so many men in these last few years have flocked to it through the various Colleges in which they arm themselves with the weapons necessary for so great a conflict. Here they spend their time partly in giving earnest attention to letters, partly also in taking stock of the strength for so great a labour as this; thereby fulfilling the counsel of Christ, who exhorts him who will build a tower to reckon the expense necessary for it, and so, too, him who is entering on a battle, especially when it is a most bloody one, to hold an inspection of his forces. And when this has been done and they perceive that they have laid aside all sensual love and have won a complete victory over themselves, so as to be resolved to despise for Christ's sake even the greatest advancement in this world, and to give up their own liberty and yield themselves wholly to the disposition of their superiors, holding no danger to be an excuse from carrying out their commands, then at length, when they have put off all earthly affections, whatever mission may be assigned to them, they welcome it invariably for the honour of God (always after the customary outpouring of prayer) without any dread at all, nay more, subjugating to the service of Christ their intellects and all their inclinations, and promising themselves the favour and help of Him for whose sake they are undertaking this enterprise. And that God has not failed them up to now, the many glorious deeds they have done in nearly all parts of the world bear witness. . . .

# Catholics Persecute Heretics: Sacred Procession in Paris (1535)

Protestantism spread rapidly in the decades after Luther's revolt. As in Germany, men dissatisfied with social, economic, and political, as well as religious, conditions were converted. Such religious rebels posed a threat to the stability of the state, especially in a country like France which had freed itself from papal administrative and financial control as early as 1438 (Pragmatic Sanction of Bourges). The reading describes how Francis I (reigned 1515–1547) dealt with this threat. From Roland H. Bainton, *The Age of the Reformation* (Princeton, N.J.: G. Van Nostrand Reinhold Company, 1956), pp. 180–181.

The most Christian king, our sovereign lord [Francis I], knowing that certain damnable heresies and blasphemies swarmed in his kingdom and desiring with the aid of God to extirpate the same decreed that a sacred procession should be held in this city of Paris on the twenty-first day of January 1535. The streets were adorned with gorgeous tapestries and the crowds held in order by archers in uniform. First came the crosses and banners of the Diocese of Paris followed by citizens and merchants carrying torches, then the four monastic orders with relics, next priests and canons of the parochial churches with relics, and the monks of Saint Martin with the head of that saint. Another carried the head of Saint Philip, one of the most precious relics in Paris. The body of Madame Saincte Genevieve was borne by six citizens in their shirts. Then followed the Canons of Notre Dame, the Rector of the University, and the Swiss Guard with their band of violins, trumpets, and cornets. Among the relics were the true cross of Christ and the crown of thorns and the lance that pierced his side. Then came a great number of the archbishops and bishops with the blood of our Saviour, the rod of Moses, and the head of John the Baptist. Next the cardinals. The precious body of our Lord was carried by archdeacons on a velvet cushion of violet adorned with *fleurs de lys.* Following the Holy Sacrament came the King alone with bare head carrying a lighted taper. After him marched Monseigneur the Cardinal of Lorraine, then all the princes and knights and members of the *Parlement,* etc. The Holy Sacrament was taken to the church of Notre Dame and there deposited with great reverence by the Bishop of Paris. Then the King and his children, the Queen and her attendants and many notables had dinner with the Bishop of Paris. After dinner the King made a speech against the execrable and damnable opinions dispersed throughout his kingdom. While the King, the Queen, and their court were with the Bishop of Paris, into their presence we brought six of the said heretics, and in front of the church of Notre Dame they were burned alive. A number of other heretics went to the stake during the days following so that all over Paris one saw gibbets by which the people were filled with terror.

# Catholics Combat Heresy with the Inquisition

The reforming Pope Paul III (1534–1549) sought to reverse the spread of Protestantism by correcting abuses within the Church and by combatting heresy. One instrument in the latter effort was the new Jesuit Order. Another was the creation of the Inquisition. The first reading, taken from the Pope's decree establishing the Inquisition, describes its functions. The second reading provides an example of the campaign against heresy in Spain, where the Inquisition was under the control of the king and was used to exterminate opposition to both papal and royal authority. I. From Roland H. Bainton, *The Age of the Reformation* (Princeton, N.J.: G. Van Nostrand Reinhold Company, 1956), p. 155. II. From Charles Lea, *A History of the Inquisition of Spain* (New York, 1906), III, pp. 437–442.

## I. THE ESTABLISHMENT OF THE ROMAN INQUISITION (1542)

Although from the beginning of our Pontificate we have been concerned for the flourishing of the Catholic faith and the expurgation of heresy that those seduced by diabolical wiles might return to the fold and unity of the Church and that those who persist in their damnable course should be removed and their punishment might serve as an example to others, nevertheless hoping that the mercy of God, the prayers of the faithful and the preaching of the learned would cause them to recognize their errors and come back to the Holy Catholic Church, and if any delayed they would be induced by the authority of the sacred, ecumenical and general council, which we hope speedily to convene, therefore we deferred the establishment of the Inquisition of heretical Pravity, but now, since for a variety of reasons, the council has not met and the enemy of the human race has disseminated even more heresy among the faithful and the robe of Christ is further rent, consequently, lest pending a council things grow worse, we have appointed our beloved sons, Giovanni Caraffa [*and five others*], Inquisitors General with jurisdiction throughout Christendom including Italy and the Roman Curia. They are to investigate by way of inquisition all and single who wander from the way of the Lord and the Catholic faith, as well as those suspected of heresy, together with their followers and abettors, public or private, direct or indirect. The guilty and the suspects are to be imprisoned and proceeded against up to the final sentence. Those adjudged guilty are to be punished in accord with canonical penalties. After the infliction of death goods may be put up for sale. The aid of the civil arm may be invoked to implement whatever measures the above named deem needful. Any who impede will incur the indignation of Almighty God and of the blessed Apostles, Peter and Paul.

## II. INQUISITION IN SPAIN: AUTO-DA-FÉ OF 1559

Nothing was spared to enhance the effect of the auto-da-fé of Trinity Sunday, May 21, 1559, in which the first portion of the Valladolid [northern Spanish city] prisoners were to suffer. It was solemnly proclaimed fifteen days in advance, during which the buildings of the Inquisition were incessantly patrolled, day and night, by a hundred armed men, and guards were stationed at the stagings in the Plaza Mayor, for there were rumors that the prison was to be blown up and that the stagings were to be fired. Along the line of the procession palings were set in the middle of the street, forming an unobstructed path for three to march abreast. . . . Every house-front along the line and around the plaza had its stagings; people flocked in from thirty and forty leagues around and encamped in the fields. . . .

The procession was headed by the effigy of Leonor de Vivero, who had died during trial, clad in widow's weeds and bearing a mitre with flames and appropriate inscriptions, and followed by a coffin containing her remains to be duly burnt. Those who were to be relaxed in person numbered fourteen, of whom one, Gonzalo Baez, was a Portuguese convicted of Judaism. Those admitted to reconciliation, with penance more or less severe, were sixteen in number, including an Englishman variously styled Anthony Graso or Bagor—probably Baker—punished for Protestantism, like all the rest, excepting Baez.

A seventeenth-century auto-da-fé in Spain. In the foreground convicted heretics are herded from the tribunal, where their cases have been judged, to their fiery death (left).

When the procession reached the plaza, Austin Cozalla was placed in the highest seat, as the conspicuous chief of the heresy, and next to him his brother, Francisco de Vivero. Melchor Cano at once commenced the sermon, which occupied an hour, and then Valdés and the bishops approached the Princess Juana and Prince Carlos, who were present, and administered to them the oath to protect and aid the Inquisition, to which the multitude responded in a mighty roar, "To the death!" Cozalla, his brother and Alonso Pérez, who were in orders, were duly degraded from the priesthood, the sentences were read, those admitted to reconciliation made the necessary adjurations and those condemned to relaxation were handed over to the secular arm. Mounted on asses, they were carried to the Plaza de la Puerta de Campo, where the requisite stakes had been erected, and there they met their end. . . .

Of these there were only two or three who merit special consideration. Cozalla, on his trial, had at first equivocated and denied that he had dogmatized, asserting that he had only spoken of these matters to those already converted. As a rule, all the prisoners eagerly denounced their associates; he may have been more reticent at first, for he was sentenced to torture . . . but when stripped he promised to inform against them fully, which he did, including Carranza among those who had misled him as to purgatory. He recanted, professed conversion and eagerly sought reconciliation. . . . He declared that, when opportunity offered in the auto, he would curse and detest Lutheranism and persuade everyone to do the same, with which purpose he took his place in the procession.

So great was his emotional exaltation that he fulfilled this promise with such exuberance during the auto that he had to be checked. . . . On the way to the brasero he continued to exhort the people and directed his efforts especially to the heroic Herrezuelo, who had steadfastly refused to abandon his faith and was to be burnt alive. . . .

It was otherwise with Herrezuelo, the only martyr in the group. He avowed his faith and resolutely adhered to it, in spite of all effort to convert him and of the dreadful fate in store for him. On their way to the brasero, Cozalla wasted on him all his eloquence. He was gagged and could not reply, but his stoical endurance showed his unyielding pertinacity. When chained to the stake, a stone thrown at him struck him in the forehead, covering his face with blood but, as we are told, it did him no good. Then he was thrust through the belly by a pious halberdier, but this moved him not and, when the fire was set, he bore his agony without flinching and, to the general surprise, he thus ended diabolically. Illescas, who stood so near that he could watch every expression, reports that he seemed as impassive as flint but, though he uttered no complaint and manifested no regret, yet he died with the strangest sadness in his face, so that it was dreadful to look upon him as on one who in a brief moment would be in hell with his comrade and master, Luther. . . .

The remainder of the Valladolid reformers were reserved for another celebration, October 8th, honored with the presence of [King] Philip II, who obediently took the customary oath, with bared head and ungloved hand. It was, if possible, an occasion of greater solemnity than the previous one. A Flemish official, who was present, estimates the number of spectators at two hundred thousand and, though he must have been hardened to such scenes at home, he could not repress an expression of sympathy with the sufferers. Besides a Morisco who was relaxed, a Judaizer reconciled and two penitents for other offences, there were twenty-six Protestants. The lesson was the same as in the previous auto, that few had the ardor of martyrdom. Thirteen had made their peace in time to secure reconciliation or penance. Even Juana Sánchez, who had managed to bring with her a pair of scissors and had cut her throat, recanted before death, but her confession was considered imperfect and she was burnt in effigy. . . . Only in two cases did this withstand the test of fire. Carlos de Seso was unyielding to the end and, when we are told that he had to be supported by two familiars to enable him to stand when hearing his sentence, we can guess the severity of the torture endured by him. Juan Sánchez was likewise pertinacious; when the fire was set it burnt the cord fastening him to the stake; he leaped down and ran in flames; it was thought that he wanted to confess but, when a confessor was brought, he refused to listen to him; one account says that the guards thrust him back into the flames, another, that he looked up and saw Carlos de Seso calmly burning and himself leaped back into the blazing pile. . . . Thus was exterminated the nascent Protestantism of Valladolid. . . .

# Religion and Life in the 16th Century: Letters of the Fugger Banking House

The Fuggers were the most important European banking house in the sixteenth century. Loyal Catholic subjects of the Hapsburgs, this family made use of its house as the principal financier of Hapsburg ventures. Its enterprises extended, however, throughout the known world and its agents were encouraged to solicit and report back to the main office the news and rumor of the day. Some dispatches of the 1580s and 1590s are printed below. Reprinted by permission of G. P. Putnam's Sons from *News and Rumor in Renaissance Europe: The Fugger Newsletters,* edited by George T. Mathews. Copyright © 1959, by G. P. Putnam's Sons, pp. 84, 157–159, 190–191, 202–203.

## I. PERSECUTION OF JESUITS IN ENGLAND

From Antwerp, the 16th
day of September, 1581

Several English Jesuits, who had come from Rouen to London, and, at the behest of the Pope, were trying to convert the people to their Faith, were taken prisoner in London. Three were hanged and two were quartered. They are said to have committed all manner of treachery and to have denounced the Queen shamefully.

## II. DISTURBANCES IN PRAGUE

From Prague, the 24th
day of December, 1590

During the past day a clamour was raised here that the Jesuits and the priests of the Pope are minded to take by force several churches of the Hussites on Christmas Eve, and retain them for the purpose of holding their services therein. It was also rumoured that the Jesuits have received outfits for war for some hundred men and have hidden them in their College. This alarm was raised by a monk, who said that he was awarded by the late Pope the privilege of obtaining possession of the monastery and church of St. Emaus, together with its revenue and appurtenances. This outcry came to the ears of His Imperial Majesty, who ordered inquiries to be made with reference to the matter. It has transpired that several artisans had spoken thus during a carousal. At the order of His Majesty they were examined by the councillors of the city of Prague. They were sent to court and questioned from whom they held such information. It resulted in a tanner being charged with spreading the rumour. He was put in prison in the Altstadt where he was questioned in kindly manner, but later put to the rack, as to where he had first heard these tales. But he pleaded ignorance. His journeymen were called and testified that he voiced such opinions before even they had partaken any wine. The aldermen condemned him to be executed with the sword. They submitted the sentence to the Emperor and asked him whether they should carry it out.

His Majesty issued a proclamation in the Bohemian language which was exhibited in all public places and, to some extent, has pacified the people, who were in an ugly temper. At first they had armed for resistance, although they had no grounds for so doing. In all parts of Prague there broke out disturbances. It has been ordered that a number of burgesses hold night-watch in all the suburbs of Prague. Likewise, a house-to-house visitation was carried out in order to ascertain how many strange guests there be with each citizen, how named, from whence, and of what nature their business. This had to be reported to His Majesty. Moreover, it was ordained that whosoever should know or hear of any danger should give tidings thereof to His Majesty or the Council. This scheme may lead to great bloodshed, theft and pillaging, if by chance a daring murderer or robber make use of this rumour to start an outcry and raise disorder in the town of Prague.

## III. BIRTH OF ANTICHRIST

From Venice, the 14th
day of April, 1592

This week a News-letter has been circulated here which is said to have been written by the Grand Master of Malta and divers other Christian princes. This News-letter reports that in a certain province of Babylon there has been born to a woman of evil repute a child whose father is unknown. The child is reported to be covered with cat's hair and to be a dreadful sight. It began to talk eight days after its birth and to walk after a month. It is said to have intimated that it is the Son of God. At its birth the sun grew dark at midday and on the previous night a mighty flame of fire appeared above its house. Many mountains opened, and in one of these there was seen a column covered with Hebrew script reading: "This is the hour of my birth!" On the next day there fell from Heaven a goodly quantity of manna and precious stones; at other places, howsoever, snakes and other horrible creatures. When the child was questioned as to the meaning of this, it made answer: that the precious stones stand for the supreme delight of those who will keep his commandments, the snakes for the martyrdom and castigation of the disobedient. Adoration of this infant has already begun because it has performed great miracles, awakening the dead and making the blind to see and the lame to walk. The populace is being encouraged by a bare-footed friar, who alleges that this is the true Son of God. For the sake of brevity I must omit further reports which do not sound very credible. It is said that the Rabbis have come to the conclusion that this is the Child of Perdition, the Antichrist.

## IV. PERSECUTION OF PROTESTANTS IN SALZBURG

Copy of the Princely
Mandate of Salzburg
concerning the exercise of the Religion,
on the 3rd day of
September 1588

We, Wolf Dietrich, Archbishop of Salzburg by the Grace of God, Legate of the Holy

Roman See, hereby declare and make known: In our Capital of Salzburg, we have found several of our citizens and inhabitants opposed to our old and true Catholic Faith, who after loyal and fatherly exhortation, information and instruction, in spite of the several weeks' respite granted, have stubbornly persisted in their pre-conceived and antagonistic opinions. On this account we bid them to leave the town and the Archbishopric, for the sake of preventing further trouble and embarrassment. So that they may know how it stands with their real and movable property and their merchandise, we have publicly announced the following articles:

Firstly: It is our earnest will that those who leave our town of Salzburg make a statement of all their real estate and property before their departure and omit nothing nor leave it unregistered. This also applies to those who have already left. This statement is to be handed to us in writing. Should any one show disobedience herein or hide anything, his property is to become forfeit to us as fiscal property and subject to our domain. So that those who are no longer here should not remain in ignorance, they are to be advised of this by our Civic Authorities, through their tenants, or their own messengers, otherwise we shall proceed against the recalcitrant with heavy fines.

Secondly: They are to sell their houses and property, in and around our town, within one month, to such persons as shall find favour in our eyes, or, after this time has lapsed, make them over to them for a reasonable sum until the latter can dispose of them. Since we shall not permit that the houses be closed or that we see bad servants and citizens within them, we shall let such houses and gardens through our Civic Authorities to others for a low rent. For as Prince and Ruler of these lands we are not willing to have our capital stand partly empty, but wish that it should be fully inhabited.

Thirdly: Those who leave this town for the sake of their faith are not to hold any civic rights or honours in our Archbishopric. They are to be treated here as foreigners and strangers, but if any one of them should again return to the Catholic Faith, and tender the customary allegiance, we will reinstate him fully in all things. In the meantime, however, they are to be allowed to take their goods and chattels through our Archbishopric, unhampered, as do other strangers and foreigners.

Fourthly: They are not to venture to trade in the outer town of Salzburg or any other town in our Archbishopric. But should they resort to smuggling or carry on their calling with their own servants or other citizens and inhabitants of this town in any other name, their wares are to be considered our fiscal property.

Fifthly: They are to be permitted, as need arises, to travel through our Archbishopric. But they must not cause any offence and must frequent only the open inns. Neither are they allowed to sojourn longer than three days without our Councillor's knowledge, especially within our town of Salzburg.

Sixthly: Whatever they have need to transact in our Archbishopric, this may they do, but only through Catholic proxies, and not through sectarian servants.

Seventhly: Those who hold guardianships and have foster-children are to make over their trust-moneys and render proper account of them. In their place are to be appointed Catholic guardians who will bring up the wards in the Catholic Faith.

Eighthly: Wards, who are not here, but live in sectarian places are to be cited and brought hither by our Town Council. They are to be sent to strange places only with our foreknowledge.

Ninthly: All those who have already put their property in order or do not hold any and are ready to depart, are to leave our town of Salzburg and our Archbishopric within fourteen days of this date and see to it that they are not encountered here any more.

All this is our Will, Wish and Command.

In true Testimony of this our Mandate we have signed and written it by our own hand.

Issued in our town of Salzburg on the 3rd day of September in the year 1588 after Christ our Lord and Redeemer's birth.

Wolf Dietrich m.p.

# The Tridentine Profession of Faith (1564)

A most important result of the Catholic reform movement was this clear statement on matters of faith. With slight modification it has remained the basic statement of Catholic doctrine to the present. From Henry Bettenson, ed., *Documents of the Christian Church* (New York, Oxford University Press, 1947), pp. 374–375.

I [Name] with steadfast faith believe and profess each and all the things contained in the symbol of faith which the Holy Roman Church uses, namely 'I believe in One God, etc. [The Nicene Creed.]

I most firmly acknowledge and embrace the Apostolical and ecclesiastical traditions and other observances and constitutions of the same Church. I acknowledge the sacred Scripture according to that sense which Holy Mother Church has held and holds, to whom it belongs to decide upon the true sense and interpretation of the holy Scriptures, nor will I ever receive and interpret the Scripture except according to the unanimous consent of the Fathers.

I profess also that there are seven sacraments. . . . I embrace and receive each and all of the definitions and declarations of the sacred Council of Trent on Original Sin and Justification.

I profess likewise that true God is offered in the Mass, a proper and propitiatory sacrifice for the living and the dead, and that in the most Holy Eucharist there are truly, really and substantially the body and blood, together with the soul and divinity of Our Lord Jesus Christ, and that a conversion is made of the whole substance of bread into his body and of the whole substance of wine into his blood, which conversion the Catholic Church calls transubstantiation. I also confess that the whole and entire Christ and the true sacrament is taken under the one species alone.

I hold unswervingly that there is a purgatory and that the souls there detained are helped by the intercessions of the faithful; likewise also that the Saints who reign with Christ are to be venerated and invoked; that they offer prayers to God for us and that their relics are to be venerated. I firmly assert that the images of Christ and of the ever-Virgin Mother of God, as also those of other Saints, are to be kept and retained, and that due honor and veneration is to be accorded them; and I affirm that the power of indulgences has been left by Christ in the Church, and that their use is very salutary for Christian people.

I recognize the Holy Catholic and Apostolic Roman Church as the mother and mistress of all churches; and I vow and swear true obedience to the Roman Pontiff, the successor of blessed Peter, the chief of the Apostles and the representative [*vicarius*] of Jesus Christ.

I accept and profess, without doubting, the traditions, definitions and declarations of the sacred Canons and Oecumenical Councils and especially those of the holy Council of Trent, and at the same time I condemn, reject and anathematize all things contrary thereto, and all heresies condemned rejected and anathematized by the Church. This true Catholic Faith (without which no one can be in a state of salvation), which at this time I of my own will profess and truly hold, I, *N*, vow and swear, God helping me, most constantly to keep and confess entire and undefiled to my life's last breath, and that I will endeavor, as far as in me shall lie, that it be held, taught and preached by my subordinates or by those who shall be placed under my care: so help me God and these Holy Gospels of God.

TOPIC 37

# AGE OF DISCOVERY

The fifteenth century witnessed both the contraction and the expansion of the European world. In 1453 Constantinople fell to the Ottoman Turks and a thousand years of Byzantine history came to an end. At almost the same time a sea captain in the service of the Portuguese reached the most western point of the African continent. By the end of the century Vasco da Gama had found the sea way to India and Columbus had landed in the Western Hemisphere. Europeans could never thereafter remain isolated from the world, for the voyages of discovery set Europe on a course that led to empire and the global dispersion of Western culture. The readings examine why and how this expansion began and what some of its consequences were.



## European Expansion in the Perspective of World History

From pp. 30–33, 161–163 *The World of Humanism 1453–1517* by Myron P. Gilmore. Copyright 1952 by Harper & Row, Publishers, Incorporated. By permission of Harper & Row, Publishers.

Seen in the perspective of world history, Latin Christendom occupied in the fifteenth century a territory relatively small and insignificant in comparison with the habitable areas of the earth's surface. It amounted in fact to no more than a western peninsula jutting out from the great Asiatic land mass. From time to time, and especially in the thirteenth and early fourteenth centuries, vistas had been opened toward the east. These vistas provided glimpses of societies whose territorial extent, population, material wealth, and political stability were superior to anything in recent European experience, and whose achievements in arts and letters bore at the very least a favorable comparison with the Latin west. This knowledge had never been shared by many and was now in the fifteenth century blurred and overlaid with a mass of legend. The most optimistic calculation taken in the middle of that century might have concluded that a society that had occupied western Europe for so long a time, with occasional if ephemeral bursts of outward expansion, might continue to survive and hold its own.

No one, however, in this general situation could have foreseen that before the fifteenth century was finished western Europeans would have discovered the vast lands of the western hemisphere that now lay open to exploitation, or would have established the new sea routes to the civilizations of the east, which this time were to be regular and permanent. By 1500 the greatest steps in this unique and dramatic expansion had been taken, and within two more decades—by the time the religious revolution was beginning in Germany—the Portuguese Empire had been established in India and southeast Asia; European Christians traded in Malacca and Canton, and in the New World the Aztec Empire was about to fall to a small band of Spanish adventurers. A man who remembered the fall of Constantinople as a boy could easily have lived to hear the news of the circumnavigation of the globe. Within the space of hardly more than a generation the horizon of Latin Christendom had lifted; Europe was in a position to take a view of the world, and this perspective was not again to be closed.

It is natural that history would have endowed the men and events associated with this achievement with a transcendent significance. Adam Smith in the eighteenth century declared that the discovery of America and of a passage to the East Indies by the Cape of Good Hope were the two greatest and most important events recorded in the history of mankind, and at least half of this judgment is enshrined in the memory of every American schoolboy. Succeeding generations, recalling these names and dates, have celebrated not only the triumphs of individual genius and persistence; they have also and more importantly registered a conviction that here began a new epoch in the history of Europe and the world. We are dealing here with the kind of events that become symbolic of dramatic and revolutionary change. What is often minimized or forgotten is the extent to which the voyages of Columbus and Da Gama rested upon the labors of countless predecessors in the European past, but what is never forgotten is the fact that they were succeeded by increasing numbers of followers who finally carried the civilization of Europe to the remotest parts of the earth. In this sense their historical significance depends upon the belief that they mark the beginning of a continuous process. It may seem unnecessarily obvious to suggest that if Columbus had returned from his first voyage and reported his results to a society absolutely indifferent whether the east was reached or not—if in other words there had been no encouragement, no response, no imitation—then the date 1492 would hardly occupy its present sacred place in the historical calendar. When we celebrate this date the emotional focus is on Columbus with all the drama justified by history and enriched by legend. We forget the extent to which we presuppose or imply the existence in fifteenth-century Europe of a society ready and eager to follow the paths which had been opened. So strongly do we feel that it was natural, indeed inevitable, to seize all the advantages that followed from the great voyages of the fifteenth century that we cannot imagine a condition of affairs in which the achievements of a Columbus or a Da Gama would have remained without consequences. Yet there have been other societies and other times in the history of Europe itself in which comparable achievements appear as isolated phenomena, irrelevant happenings, promising beginnings that led to nothing. The voyages of the Norsemen to North America left no perceptible mark except in literature either on the lands which they reached or on the society from which they came. The successes of the Polos inaugurated no permanent routes between Europe and the east.

If examples from the history of Europe are not convincing on this point, consider the case of China. The same fifteenth century in which the eastern Europeans began their successful expansion by sea to the east was the century in which the tribute fleets of the Chinese emperors accomplished their most remarkable voyages in the south and west. In the years between 1405 and 1433 seven great expeditions ordered by the Ming emperors sailed to the western seas under the command of the eunuch, Cheng Ho. Their purpose seems to have been the establishment of diplomatic relations and the collection of tribute from the barbarian kingdoms. They were official undertakings of formidable size. Typically each expedition consisted of over 27,000 men embarked in fifty or more huge ocean-going junks. These great fleets visited the East Indies, Malacca, Siam, Ceylon, India, Ormuz in the Persian Gulf, the Red Sea and the eastern coast of Africa. Aden and other Red Sea ports were reached several times and a delegation from at least one of the expeditions was sent to Mecca. The fleets touched at various places on the African coast at least as far south as Melinda and perhaps beyond.

During the years when the China Sea, the Indian Ocean, the Red Sea and the Persian Gulf were thus being swept by Chinese fleets, the Portuguese were inching along the western coast of Africa and, in 1434, the year after the last great recorded expedition of the Ming, Gil Eannes in the service of Prince Henry rounded Cape Bojeador, only a little more than eight hundred miles from Lisbon. In the long history of the relations between east and west there are few contrasts more dramatic than that presented by these two voyages, the Portuguese with its *barca* of twenty-five tons carrying a handful of men, and the Chinese fleet manned by thousands. Yet the Chinese voyages had no revolutionary consequences in the society from which they came, and in the end it was the west that conquered. Cheng Ho's ships visited over twenty countries and brought back many rare and costly things, but these results failed to stimulate in China the same aggressive impulse to expansion that was produced in the west by a handful of gold dust and a few slaves brought back from the Guinea coast.

The contrast between the achievements and attitudes of the Chinese and those of the Europeans in the fifteenth century is one of the striking coincidences of history, but the Chinese were of course not alone in failing to exploit possibilities of cultural and commercial expansion in the way that became characteristic of Europeans after the fifteenth century. Throughout the medieval and early modern period the civilization of Islam was in some ways in a uniquely favored position to undertake a program of further military, political or cultural conquests until its influence should circle the globe. The far-flung commerce of the Arabs stretched from China to western Europe. Their geographers knew more about the world than those of any other society. Their merchants were in direct contact with the greatest number and variety of religious and political systems. Yet with all this the Arab civilization failed to produce the same kind of thinking and action that developed in Europe. So it has been with others. The expansion of Latin Christendom, with all its fateful consequences, has been a unique phenomenon in the history of the world. . . .

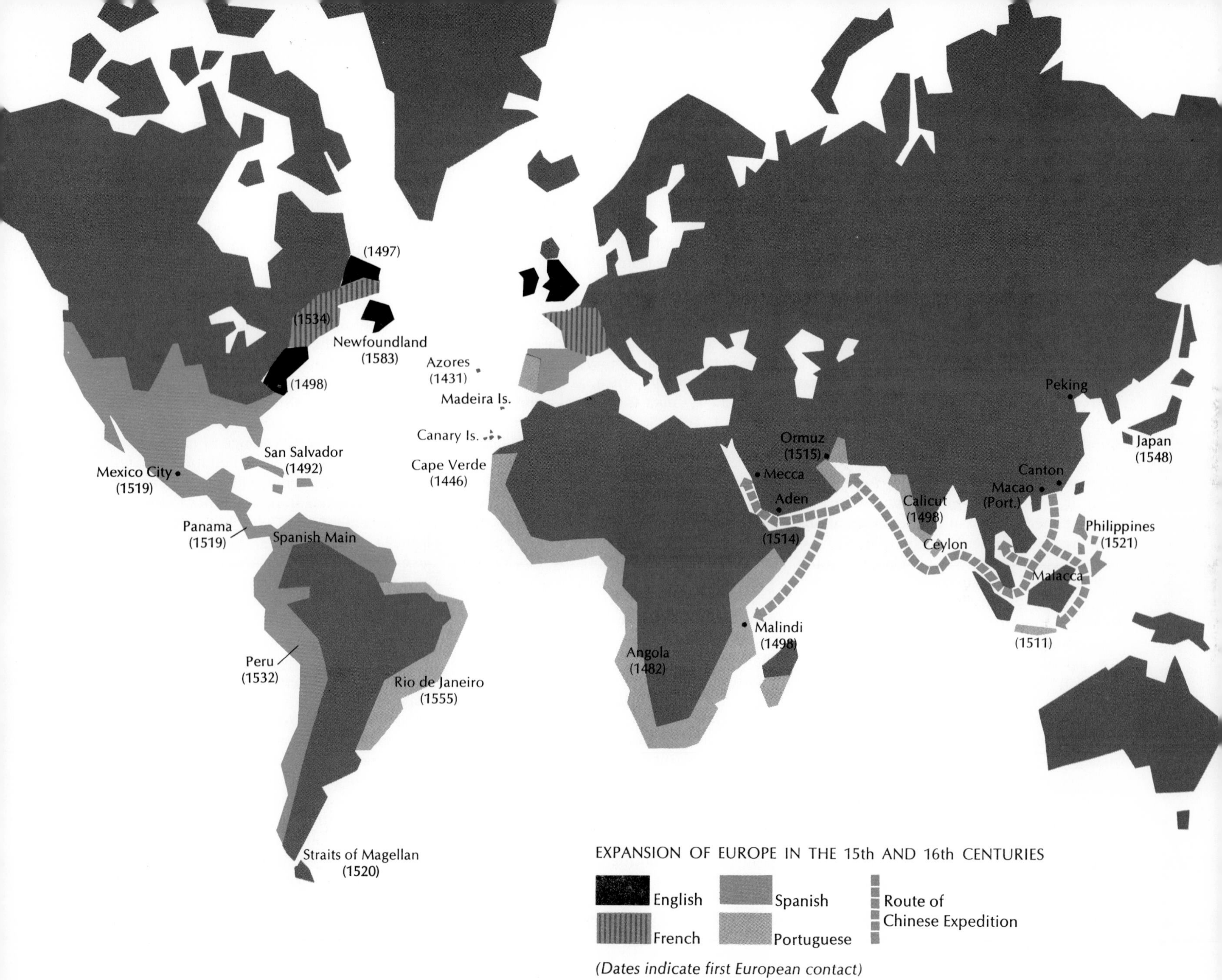


The map shows the areas broadly claimed by Portugal, Spain, England, and France in 1600 with the date of first contact. The routes of the seven great Chinese expeditions between 1405 and 1433 are also indicated.

# The Course of Expansion

L. S. Stavrianos, *The World Since 1500: A Global History,* © 1966. Reprinted by permission of Prentice-Hall, Inc., Englewood Cliffs, New Jersey.

## I. ROOTS OF SPANISH AND PORTUGUESE EXPANSIONISM

Religion was an important factor in European overseas expansion, but nowhere was it so important as in the Iberian Peninsula. Both the Spaniards and the Portuguese were impelled by memories of their long anti-Moslem crusade. To other peoples of Europe, Islam was a distant menace, but for the Iberians it represented a traditional and ever present enemy. Most of the peninsula at one time had been under Moslem rule, and now, in the fifteenth century, Granada in the south still remained a Moslem stronghold. Furthermore, the Moslems were in control of the nearby North African coast, while the growing Turkish seapower was making itself felt throughout the Mediterranean. Other Europeans were crusaders by fits and starts, but for the devout and patriotic Iberian, the struggle against Islam was a stern imperative—a combination of religious duty and patriotic necessity.

Prince Henry (1394-1460), called the Navigator, was a prime force in expanding the geographic bounds of the European world. Younger son of the King of Portugal, he was inspired by the stories of captured Arabs about the riches of the land south of the Sahara Desert to devote his life to exploring the sea routes around the west coast of Africa. From the observatory he established at the southern tip of Portugal, the Prince, surrounded by a new breed of map-makers and ship-designers, sent expedition after expedition into the Atlantic and laid the foundation for the onward movement of discovery.

Prince Henry the Navigator first won fame in 1415 for his gallant role in the capture of the town and fortress of Ceuta across the Straits of Gibraltar. Likewise Queen Isabella [of Spain], moved by intense religious conviction, was determined to wipe out Moslem Granada and to carry the war into the enemy's territory in North Africa, as the Portuguese had done at Ceuta. Isabella began her crusade against Granada in 1482, and pressed on, village by village, until final victory in 1492. Immediately thereafter, the Spaniards crossed the Straits and captured the city of Melilla. In this same year, 1492, a royal decree required all Jews in Spain to accept the Catholic faith or leave the realm. Ten years later a similar decree was issued against the Moslems remaining in Castile. . . .

The Iberians were lured overseas also by four groups of islands—the Canaries, the Madeira, the Azores, and the Cape Verde—stretching westward across the Atlantic and southward down the coast of Africa. These were highly attractive, partly because they were fertile and productive, but also because they provided strategic bases and ports of call. When the Portuguese began settling Madeira in 1420, they first obtained high quality timber; next they produced sugar very profitably, and, when this was undercut by Brazilian sugar, they introduced from Crete the Malvoisie grape, from which the characteristic dessert wines of Madeira are made to the present day.

In contrast to Madeira, which was indisputably Portuguese, the Canaries were claimed by both Spain and Portugal. After appeals to the Pope and savage local fighting, the Portuguese dropped their claim to the Canaries, and the Spaniards conceded the other three island groups to the Portuguese. This settlement forced the Portuguese to sail far out into the Atlantic on their way south, to avoid Spanish privateers based on the Canaries. Their first port of call, therefore, was the Azores, which they explored systematically, until by the mid-fifteenth century they had reached the westernmost islands, about a quarter of the way across the Atlantic.

Throughout the fifteenth century, then, sailors had been discovering islands located far out into the ocean. It was natural that they should assume the existence of more islands awaiting discovery and exploitation. Atlantic charts were peppered with such imaginary islands, providing stepping stones to the East. The agreement that Columbus reached with Isabella in 1492 provided that he should head an expedition "to discover and acquire islands and mainland in the Ocean Sea."

It was Portugal, however, rather than Spain, that took the lead in overseas enterprise during the fifteenth century. Spain moved belatedly, and usually in reaction to Portuguese initiative. There were two reasons for Portugal's head start. One was its small size and its location on the Atlantic coast, surrounded on three sides by Spanish territory. This effectively safeguarded the Portuguese from temptation to squander their resources in European wars. Thanks to the leadership of Prince Henry, they turned instead to oceanic projects. The other was Portugal's superior knowledge of navigation, gained primarily from the Italians. Lisbon was on the route of Genoese and Venetian sea traffic with Flanders through the Straits of Gibraltar; and the

## THE WORLD ACCORDING TO BEHAIM IN 1492

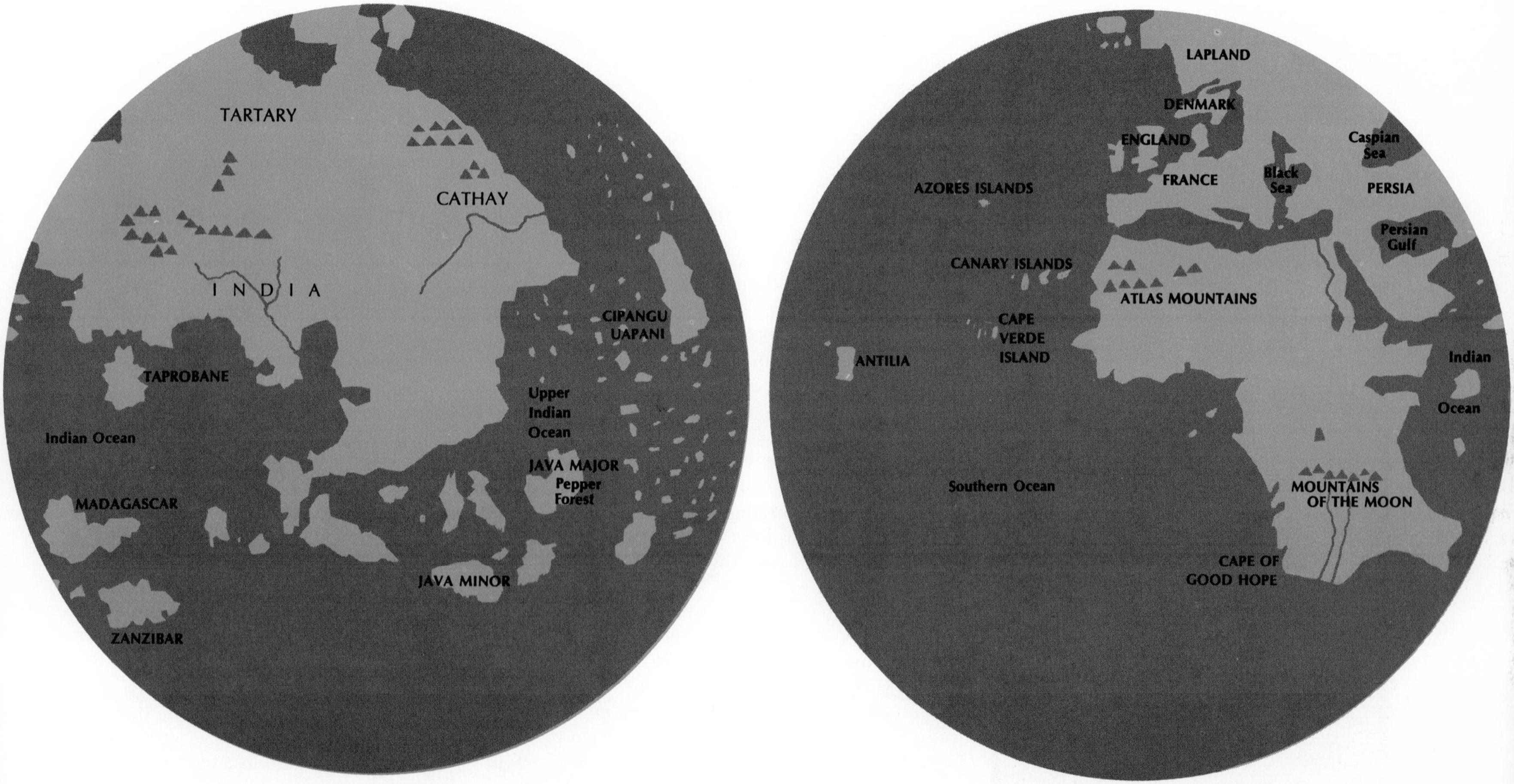


Martin Behaim (1459?–1506?), German traveler and cosmographer, fashioned this globe in 1492 and gave it to his native city of Nuremberg. It was such a view of the world that motivated Columbus to consider the Atlantic the shortest route to Asia.

Portuguese took advantage of this, by employing Italian captains and pilots in the royal navy. Prince Henry followed up by assembling a galaxy of talented seamen, including Italians, Catalans, and even a Dane. Furthermore, Henry's work was continued by the crown following his death, so that the Portuguese became the most knowledgeable of all Europeans in seamanship and geography. It was this steady and consistent government direction and support that gave the Portuguese a decisive advantage over their Spanish neighbors and rivals.

Portugal's interest in exploration quickened following the capture of Ceuta in 1415. Moslem prisoners divulged information concerning the ancient and profitable trade across the Sahara with the Negro kingdoms of the Sudan. For centuries the latter had provided ivory, slaves, and gold in return for various manufactured goods and salt. Since Western Europe in general and Portugal in particular were then suffering from a serious shortage of bullion, Prince Henry was intrigued by the possibility of tapping this gold trade. . . .

One of Columbus' ships on his voyage of discovery. Woodcut published in Basel in 1496.

A major step forward in early Portuguese exploration was taken when Prince Henry's captains passed the desert coast in 1445 and found below it a verdant new land "covered with palms and other green and beautiful trees, and it was even so with the plains thereof." By the time of Henry's death, the coast had been explored down to Sierra Leone, and a number of coastal stations had been established which enabled the Portuguese to attract at least a part of the caravan trade that they were after. Later on, in 1487, they established a factory at Wadan, an inland entrepôt, which enabled them to obtain a larger share of the north-south caravan traffic.

Meanwhile, even before Henry's death, Portuguese aspirations had come to encompass India as well as Africa. Because Europe at this time was blocked from access to the East by the Moslem power that controlled all of North Africa and the Middle East, the Mediterranean was for the Europeans a prison rather than a highway. Therefore, with the exception of the Venetians, who profited as middlemen, they eagerly sought a new route "to the Indies where the spices grow." Prince Henry had not thought of India when he first began his operations, but as his ships crept further and further down the African coast, it was natural that his horizon should expand from the African caravan trade to the Indies spice trade. From then on, the discovery and the domination of the spice route was the prime objective of Portuguese policy. It is significant that when Albuquerque urged his followers before Malacca to "quench the fire of the sect of Mahamede," he also emphasized the prospects for material gain. "I hold it certain that if we take this trade of Malacca away from them (the Moors) Cairo and Mecca will be entirely ruined and Venice receive no spiceries unless her merchants go and buy them in Portugal."

## II. COLUMBUS DISCOVERS AMERICA

In view of Portugal's pioneering work in the theory and practice of oceanic navigation, it is paradoxical that the first great discovery—that of the New World—was effected under Spanish auspices. It is even more paradoxical that the reason for this outcome is that the Portuguese were more advanced in their geographical knowledge than the Spaniards and figured correctly that Columbus was wrong in his calculations. It was common knowledge among informed people by the fifteenth century that the world was round. The question was not the shape of the world but its size, and the relationship of the continents to the oceans. By combining Marco Polo's estimate of the east-west extent of Asia, which was an overestimate, the same traveler's report of the distance of Japan from the Asian mainland—1,500 miles—an extreme overestimate, and Ptolemy's estimate of the circumference of the globe, which was an underestimate, Columbus concluded that less than 3,000 miles of ocean separated Europe from Japan. Accordingly, he believed that the shortest and easiest route to Asia was by a short voyage across the Atlantic, and this was the project that he proposed before various courts. The Portuguese, thanks to Prince Henry, had more practical experience and were better informed of the most advanced knowledge of the day. They were convinced that the globe was larger than Columbus held, that the oceans were wider, and that the shortest route to the Orient was around Africa rather than across the Atlantic. For this reason the Portuguese king turned Columbus down

Poma de Ayala (1535–1616), who traveled with the Spanish forces, sketched scenes of the Spanish conquest of the Incas. At left, Atahualpa and his retinue receive the Spaniards; at right, Atahualpa is held prisoner and in chains by one of Pizarro's band.

when he applied for financial assistance in 1484. Two years later Columbus was at the Spanish court where, after a preliminary rejection, he finally won the support of Queen Isabella.

On August 2, 1492, Columbus set sail from Palos with three small ships manned by reliable crews with capable and seasoned officers. By September 6 the expedition had left the Canary Islands behind and sailed into the open ocean. Luckily there was a fair wind all the way out, but as the days and weeks went by, the men became restless. To calm their apprehension, Columbus gave out false information about the distances covered. Birds were sighted on October 7, but still no land appeared on the horizon. Even Columbus became worried, for he had now sailed so far west that, according to his calculations, he should have sighted Japan. On October 9 he promised to turn back in three days if land were not found. Just before time ran out, the lookout sighted one of the Bahaman Islands, which Columbus named San Salvador. It was an hour fraught with destiny for all of mankind.

One of the supreme ironies of world history is that Columbus was convinced until the end of his life that he had reached Asia. He was certain that San Salvador was very near to where Japan ought to be, and the next step was to find Japan itself. When he sailed southwest to the mainland of the New World, he believed that he was somewhere near the Malacca Straits. The fact that Columbus persisted in his delusion had momentous consequences: it spurred on further exploration of the Americas until the great prizes in Mexico and Peru were discovered. But if the Spaniards had realized from the outset that they had merely chanced upon a New World far away from the Continent of Asia, they might very well have turned away from what appeared at first to be an unattractive and unprofitable wilderness. In that case, the New World might have been ignored for many decades, particularly because Portugal's Vasco da Gama had in the meantime opened the extremely profitable Cape route to India.

The Spanish monarchs loyally supported Columbus and invested large sums in outfitting him for three additional expeditions. But not till 1518 did the Spaniards stumble upon the rich Aztec Empire in Mexico. During the quarter century between this windfall and Columbus' first expedition, disappointment followed disappointment as the Spaniards explored the innumerable and unpromising islands of the West Indies. . . .

### III. PORTUGAL IN ASIA

The Portuguese in the meantime had been making considerable profit from their trade along the African Guinea Coast. Coarse pepper, gold, ivory, cotton, sugar, and slaves now entered European commerce through Portugal. The slave trade alone supported fifty to sixty merchants in Lisbon. It is significant that when the conquistador Bernal Díaz observed the sale of slaves in the Aztec capital, he was moved to remark, "This slave market was upon as great a scale as the Portuguese market for negro slaves at Guinea."

Prince Henry's successors continued his work of opening up the West African coast. A breakthrough occurred in 1487 when Bartholomeu Dias, while probing along the coast, was caught by a gale that blew his ships south for thirteen days out of sight of land. When the wind moderated, Dias steered for the West African coast but discovered that he had already passed the Cape without knowing it. He landed at Mossel Bay on the Indian Ocean, and wished to explore further, but his weary and frightened men forced him to return. On the homeward passage he first sighted the great cape, and named it the Cape of Storms. It was the Portuguese king who, upon Dias' return, renamed it the Cape of Good Hope. . . .

These expeditions, and several others by both land and sea, made the Portuguese the best informed in Europe on global geography and trade routes. But they failed to follow up on Dias' rounding of the Cape because of political and financial complications. The result, as noted, was that Columbus was the first to reach the New World, which he persisted in claiming to be the Orient. The more knowledgeable Portuguese were dubious from the beginning, but they now hastened to open and secure the Cape route to India. On July 8, 1497, Vasco da Gama sailed from Portugal with four ships, and at the end of May, 1498, he entered Calicut harbor. This was not so great a feat of navigation as that of Columbus. Da Gama had been able to stop at various Portuguese stations on the way south, and he knew from various sources of the Arab cities on the East African coast. . . .

Da Gama did not receive a warm welcome in Calicut. The resident Arab merchants were naturally alarmed by this threat to their traditional monopoly and did their best to throw obstacles in the way of European intruders. Furthermore, the Portuguese trade goods—mostly trinkets and woolen cloth—were unsuitable for the Indian market. The fact is that the Portuguese had completely underestimated the level and sophistication of Indian civilization. This is evident in the nature of the presents that da Gama offered to the ruler of Calicut—woolen cloth, hats, strings of coral beads, washbasins, and jars of oil and honey—which definitely did not make a favorable impression. . . .

With much effort da Gama collected a cargo of pepper and cinnamon and cleared for home, arriving in September, 1499. The cargo proved to be worth sixty times the cost of the entire expedition. Dazzling horizons opened up before the delighted Portuguese, and King Manuel assumed the titles "Lord of the Conquest, Navigation, and Commerce of Ethiopia, Arabia, Persia, and India." These titles were taken quite seriously. The Portuguese were determined to monopolize the trade along the new route and to exclude, not only other Europeans, but also the Arabs and other Eastern peoples who had traded in the Indian Ocean for centuries. To enforce their claims, the Portuguese resorted to ruthless terrorism, particularly when they encountered the hated Moslems. Da Gama, on a later voyage, found some unarmed vessels returning from Mecca. He captured the vessels and, in the words of a fellow Portuguese, "after making the ships empty of goods, prohibited anyone from taking out of it any Moor and then ordered them to set fire to it." Another contemporary Portuguese declared,

> It is true that there does exist a common right to all to navigate the seas and in Europe we recognize the rights which others hold against us; but the right does not extend beyond Europe and therefore the Portuguese as Lords of the Sea are justified in confiscating the goods of all those who navigate the seas without their permission.

Such was the nature of the epochal meeting of two Eurasian cultures brought face to face for the first time after millennia of regional isolation. The Europeans were the aggressive intruders. They were the ones who seized the initiative and retained it until gradually, but inexorably, they emerged the masters in every quarter of the globe. . . .

# An Arab Traveler Reports on Africa

The Portuguese learned about the land in Africa south of Sahara from the stories of Arab merchants and travelers and the tales told by mariners. In addition to wealth, legend had it that beyond the recesses of the Saharan desert lay Prester John's Christian kingdom. These expectations spurred the exploration of Africa's western coast and permitted the discovery of a sea route to India. Ibn Battúta (1304–c.1368) from whose *Travels in Asia and Africa* this reading is taken was a widely traveled North African Moslem. His first-hand report of life in West Africa added substance to the dreams of gold, and remains an important source for our knowledge of the West African empires before the European organization of the slave trade. Ibn Battúta, *Travels in Asia and Africa, 1325–1354,* trans. H. A. R. Gibb (London: Routledge & Keagan Paul Ltd., 1929), pp. 317–318, 324, 326–330.

From Marrákush I travelled with the suite of our master [the Sultan] to Fez, where I took leave of our master and set out for the Negrolands. . . . At Sijilmása I bought camels and a four months' supply of forage for them. Thereupon I set out on the Ist Muharram of the year [seven hundred and] fifty-three [18th February 1352] with a caravan including, amongst others, a number of the merchants of Sijilmása. After twenty-five days we reached Tagházá. . . . No one lives at Tagházá except the slaves of the Massúfa tribe, who dig for the salt; they subsist on dates imported from Dar'a and Sijilmása, camels' flesh, and millet imported from the Negrolands. The negroes come up from their country and take away the salt from there. At Iwálátan a load of salt brings eight to ten *mithqáls;* in the town of Mállí it sells for twenty to thirty, and sometimes as much as forty. The negroes use salt as a medium of exchange, just as gold and silver is used [elsewhere]; they cut it up into pieces and buy and sell with it. The business done at Tagházá, for all its meanness, amounts to an enormous figure in terms of hundredweights of golddust. . . .

## II

The sultan of Mállí is Mansá Sulaymán, *mansá* meaning [in Mande] sultan, and Sulaymán being his proper name. . . . On certain days the sultan holds audiences in the palace yard, where there is a platform under a tree, with three steps; this they call the *pempi.* It is carpeted with silk and has cushions placed on it. [Over it] is raised the umbrella, which is a sort of pavilion made of silk, surmounted by a bird in gold, about the size of a falcon. The sultan comes out of a door in a corner of the palace, carrying a bow in his hand and a quiver on his back. On his head he has a golden skull-cap, bound with a gold band which has narrow ends shaped like knives, more than a span in length. His usual dress is a velvety red tunic, made of the European fabrics called *mutanfas.* The sultan is preceded by his musicians, who carry gold and silver guimbris [two-stringed guitars], and behind him come three hundred armed slaves. He walks in a leisurely fashion, affecting a very slow movement, and even stops from time to time. On reaching the *pempi* [a richly carpeted platform] he stops and looks round the assembly, then ascends it in the sedate manner of a preacher ascending a mosque-pulpit. As he takes his seat the drums, trumpets, and bugles are sounded. Three slaves go out at a run to summon the sovereign's deputy and the military commanders, who enter and sit down. Two saddled and bridled horses are brought, along with two goats, which they hold to serve as a protection against the evil eye. . . .

## III

I was at Mállí during the two festivals of the sacrifice and the fast-breaking. On these days the sultan takes his seat on the *pempi* after the midafternoon prayer. The armour-bearers bring in magnificent arms—quivers of gold and silver, swords ornamented with gold and with golden scabbards, gold and silver lances, and crystal maces. At his head stand four amirs driving off the flies, having in their hands silver ornaments resembling saddle-stirrups. The commanders, qádí, and preacher sit in their usual places. The interpreter Dúghá comes with his four wives and his slave-girls, who are about a hundred in number. They are wearing beautiful robes, and on their heads they have gold and silver fillets, with gold and silver balls attached. A chair is placed for Dúghá to sit on. He plays on an instrument made of reeds, with some small calabashes at its lower end, and chants a poem in praise of the sultan, recalling his battles and deeds of valour. The women and girls sing along with him and play with bows. Accompanying them are about thirty youths, wearing red woollen tunics and white skull-caps; each of them has his drum slung from his shoulder and beats it. Afterwards come his boy pupils who play and turn wheels in the air, like the natives of Sind. They show a marvellous nimbleness and agility in these exercises and play most cleverly with swords. Dúghá also makes a fine play with the sword. Thereupon the sultan orders a gift to be presented to Dúghá and he is given a purse containing two hundred *mithqáls* of gold dust, and is informed of the contents of the purse before all the people. . . .

The negroes dislike Mansá Sulaymán because of his avarice. His predecessor was Mansá Maghá, and before him reigned Mansá Músá, a generous and virtuous prince, who loved the whites and made gifts to them. It was he who gave Abú Isháq as-Sáhilí four thousand *mithqáls* in the course of a single day. I heard from a trustworthy source that he gave three thousand *mithqáls* on one day to Mudrik ibn Faqqús, by whose grandfather his own grandfather, Sáraq Játa, had been converted to Islám.

The negroes possess some admirable qualities. They are seldom unjust, and have a greater abhorrence of injustice than any other people. Their sultan shows no mercy to anyone who is guilty of the least act of it. There is complete security in their country. Neither traveller nor inhabitant in it has anything to fear from robbers or men of violence. They do not confiscate the property of any white man who dies in their country, even if it be uncounted wealth. On the contrary, they give it into the charge of some trustworthy person among the whites, until the rightful heir takes possession of it. They are careful to observe the hours of prayer, and assiduous in attending them in congregations, and in bringing up their children to them. On Fridays, if a man does not go early to the mosque, he cannot find a corner to pray in, on account of the crowd. . . .

Vasco da Gama as Viceroy of India. From a Portuguese manuscript c.1524.

Another of their good qualities is their habit of wearing clean white garments on Fridays. Even if a man has nothing but an old worn shirt, he washes it and cleans it, and wears it to the Friday service. Yet another is their zeal for learning the Koran by heart. They put their children in chains if they show any backwardness in memorizing it, and they are not set free until they have it by heart. I visited the qádí in his house on the day of the festival. His children were chained up, so I said to him "Will you not let them loose?" He replied "I shall not do so until they learn the Koran by heart." . . .

# Vasco da Gama Sails around Africa to India

**(1498)**

This account of da Gama's visit to Calicut on his epic voyage around Africa is by an unknown member of the expedition. From *A Journal of the First Voyage of Vasco da Gama, 1497–1499,* ed. and trans. E. G. Ravenstein (London, 1898).

When we arrived at Calicut [May 1498] the king was fifteen leagues away. The captain-major sent two men to him with a message, informing him that an ambassador had arrived from the King of Portugal with letters, and that if he desired it he would take them to where the king then was. . . .

The king was in a small court, reclining upon a couch covered with a cloth of green velvet, above which was a good mattress, and upon this again a sheet of cotton stuff, very white and fine, more so than any linen. The cushions were after the same fashion. In his left hand the king held a very large golden cup [spittoon], having a capacity of half an almude [8 pints]. At its mouth this cup was two palmas [16 inches] wide, and apparently it was massive. Into this cup the king threw the husks of a certain herb which is chewed by the people of this country because of its soothing effects, and which they call *atambor* [betel nut]. On the right side of the king stood a basin of gold, so large that a man might just encircle it with his arms; this contained the herbs. There were likewise many silver jugs. The canopy above the couch was all gilt. . . .

And the captain told him he was the ambassador of a King of Portugal, who was Lord of many countries and the possessor of great wealth of every description, exceeding that of any king of these parts; that for a period of sixty years his ancestors had annually sent out vessels to make discoveries in the direction of India, as they knew that there were Christian kings there like themselves. This, he said, was the reason which induced them to order this country to be discovered, not because they sought for gold or silver, for of this they had such abundance that they needed not what was to be found in this country. He further stated that the captains sent out travelled for a year or two, until their provisions were exhausted, and then returned to Portugal, without having succeeded in making the desired discovery. There reigned a king now whose name was Dom Manuel, who had ordered him to build three vessels,

Babar the Tiger, Mongul emperor of India (1483–1530), receives visitors.

of which he had been appointed captain-major, and who had ordered him not to return to Portugal until he should have discovered this King of the Christians, on pain of having his head cut off. . . .

On Tuesday [May 29] the captain got ready the following things to be sent to the king, viz., twelve pieces of *lambel* [striped cloth], four scarlet hoods, six hats, four strings of coral, a case containing six wash-hand basins, a case of sugar, two casks of oil, and two of honey. And as it is the custom not to send anything to the king without the knowledge of the Moor, his factor, and of the *bale* [Governor] the captain informed them of his intention. They came, and when they saw the present they laughed at it, saying that it was not a thing to offer to a king, that the poorest merchant from Mecca, or any other part of India, gave more, and that if he wanted to make a present it should be in gold, as the king would not accept such things. When the captain heard this he grew sad, and said that he had brought no gold, that, moreover, he was no merchant, but an ambassador; that he gave of that which he had, which was his own [private gift] and not the king's; that if the King of Portugal ordered him to return he would intrust him with far richer presents. . . .

On Wednesday morning the Moors returned, and took the captain to the palace, and us others with him. The palace was crowded with armed men. Our captain was kept waiting with his conductors for fully four long hours, outside a door, which was only opened when the king sent word to admit him. . . . The king then said that he had told him that he came from a very rich kingdom, and yet had brought him nothing. . . .

The king then asked what kind of merchandise was to be found in his country. The captain said there was much corn, cloth, iron, bronze, and many other things. The king asked whether he had any merchandise with him. The captain replied that he had a little of each sort, as samples, and that if permitted to return to the ships he would order it to be landed, and that meantime four or five men would remain at the lodgings assigned them. The king said no! He might take all his people with him, securely moor his ships, land his merchandise, and sell it to the best advantage. Having taken leave of the king the captain returned to his lodgings, and we with him. . . .

# Columbus Discovers India in the Atlantic (1492)

Columbus wrote the following letter to a Spanish official in 1493 upon his return from the Western hemisphere. From *Select Letters of Christopher Columbus,* ed. R. H. Major (London, 1870), pp. 1–18.

As I know that it will afford you pleasure that I have brought my undertaking to a successful result, I have determined to write you this letter to inform you of everything that has been done and discovered in this voyage of mine.

This woodcut appeared in the first published edition (1496) of Columbus' letter to Sanchez, a Spanish official. The scene is Columbus' landing on the island (now known as Santo Domingo).

On the thirty-third day after leaving Cadiz I came into the Indian Sea, where I discovered many islands inhabited by numerous people. I took possession of all of them for our most fortunate King by making public proclamation and unfurling his standard, no one making any resistance. To the first of them I have given the name of our blessed Saviour, trusting in whose aid I had reached this and all the rest; but the Indians call it Guanahani. To each of the others also I gave a new name, ordering one to be called Sancta Maria de Concepcion, another Fernandina, another Hysabella, another Johana; and so with all the rest. . . . From there I saw another island to the eastwards, distant 54 miles from this Johana, which I named Hispana, and proceeded to it. . . .

In the island, which I have said before was called Hispana, there are very lofty and beautiful mountains, great farms, groves and fields, most fertile for cultivation and for pasturage, and well adapted for constructing buildings. The convenience of the harbors in this island, and the excellence of the rivers, in volume and salubrity, surpass human belief, unless one should see them. In it the trees, pasture-lands, and fruits differ much from those of Johana. Besides, this Hispana abounds in various kinds of spices, gold, and metals. The inhabitants of both sexes of this and of all the other islands I have seen, or of which I have any knowledge, always go as naked as they came into the world, except that some of the women cover parts of their bodies with leaves or branches, or a veil of cotton, which they prepare themselves for this purpose. They are all, as I said before, unprovided with any sort of iron, and they are destitute of arms, which are entirely unknown to them, and for which they are not adapted; not on account of any bodily deformity, for they are well made, but because they are timid and full of terror. They carry, however, canes dried in the sun in place of weapons, upon whose roots they fix a wooden shaft, dried and sharpened to a point. But they never dare to make use of these, for it has often happened, when I have sent two or three of my men to some of their villages to speak with the inhabitants, that a crowd of Indians has sallied forth; but, when they saw our men approaching, they speedily took to flight, parents abandoning their children, and children their parents. This happened not because any loss or injury had been inflicted upon any of them. On the contrary, I gave whatever I had, cloth and many other things, to whomsoever I approached, or with whom I could get speech, without any return being made to me; but they are by nature fearful and timid. . . .

I was informed that there is another island larger than the aforesaid Hispana, whose inhabitants have no hair; and that there is a greater abundance of gold in it than in any of the others. Some of the inhabitants of these islands and of the others I have seen I am bringing over with me to bear testimony to what I have reported. Finally, to sum up in a few words the chief results and advantages of our departure and speedy return, I make this promise to our most invincible Sovereigns, that, if I am supported by some little assistance from them, I will give them as much gold as they have need of, and in addition spices, cotton, and mastic, which is found only in Chios, and as much aloes-wood, and as many heathen slaves as their Majesties may choose to demand. . . .

Therefore let King and Queen and Princes, and their most fortunate realms, and all other Christian provinces, let us all return thanks to our Lord and Saviour Jesus Christ, who has bestowed so great a victory and reward upon us; let there be processions and solemn sacrifices prepared; let the churches be decked with festal boughs; let Christ rejoice upon earth as he rejoices in Heaven, as he foresees that so many souls of so many people heretofore lost are to be saved; and let us be glad not only for the exaltation of our faith, but also for the increase of temporal prosperity, in which not only Spain, but all Christendom is about to share. . . .

# The Spaniards Exploit the West Indians

Columbus' discovery of the Indies was followed by a rush to the New World of adventurers and others eager to gain quick profit. Finding the natives unwilling to work for them, the first settlers persuaded Queen Isabella to issue a decree commanding forced labor from the Indians. Isabella's decree is the first selection; the second contains excerpts from a sermon by Bishop Bartholomew de Las Casas (1474–1566), who was known as the "Apostle of the Indians," and who devoted his life, in vain, to winning more humane treatment for them. I. From Lesley Simpson, *The Encomienda in New Spain: Forced Native Labor in the Spanish Colonies, 1492–1550* (Berkeley: University of California Press, 1929). Reprinted by permission of The Regents of the University of California, pp. 30–31. II. From Francis A. MacNutt, *Bartholomew de Las Casas: His Life, His Apostolate, and His Writings* (New York, 1909), pp. 314–318.

## I. A ROYAL DECREE (1503)

Medina del Campo, Dec. 20, 1503. Isabella, by the Grace of God, Queen of Castile, etc. In as much as the King, my Lord, and I, in the instruction we commanded given to Don Fray Nicolás de Ovando, [Governor of Espanola] at the time when he went to the islands and mainland of the Ocean Sea, decreed that the Indian inhabitants and residents of the island of Espanola, are free and not subject . . . and as now we are informed that because of the excessive liberty enjoyed by the said Indians they avoid contact and community with the Spaniards to such an extent that they will not even work for wages, but wander about idle, and cannot be had by the Christians to convert to the Holy Catholic Faith; and in order that the Christians of the said island . . . may not lack people to work their holdings for their maintenance, and may be able to take out what gold there is on the island . . . and because we desire that the said Indians be converted to our Holy Catholic Faith and taught in its doctrines; and because this can better be done by having the Indians living in community with the Christians of the island, and by having them go among them and associate with them, by which means they will help each other to cultivate and settle and increase the fruits of the island and take the gold which may be there and bring profit to my kingdom and subjects:

I have commanded this my letter to be issued on the matter, in which I command you, our said Governor, that beginning from the day you receive my letter you will compel and force the said Indians to associate with the Christians of the island and to work on their buildings, and to gather and mine the gold and other metals, and to till the fields and produce food for the Christian inhabitants and dwellers of the said island; and you are to have each one paid on the day he works the wage and maintenance which you think he should have . . . and you are to order each cacique to take charge of a certain number of the said Indians so that you may make them work wherever necessary, and so that on feast days and such days as you think proper they may be gathered together to hear and be taught in matters of the Faith. . . .

After the decimation of the Indian population, slaves from Africa were brought in for the gold mines of Santo Domingo. Here Spaniards supervise the mining operations. Etching, seventeenth century.

## II. A BISHOP CHARGES GENOCIDE (1552)

The Indies were discovered in the year fourteen hundred and ninety-two. The year following, Spanish Christians went to inhabit them, so that it is since forty-nine years that numbers of Spaniards have gone there: and the first land, that they invaded to inhabit, was the large and most delightful Isle of Hispaniola, which has a circumference of six hundred leagues. . . .

Among these gentle sheep, gifted by their Maker with the above qualities, the Spaniards entered, as soon as they knew them, like wolves, tigers, and lions which had been starving for many days, and since forty years they have done nothing else; nor do they otherwise at the present day, than outrage, slay, afflict, torment, and destroy them with strange and new, and divers kinds of cruelty, never before seen, nor heard of, nor read of, of which some few will be told below: to such extremes has this gone that, whereas there were more than three million souls, whom we saw in Hispaniola, there are today, not two hundred of the native population left.

The island of Cuba is almost as long as the distance from Valladolid to Rome; it is now almost entirely deserted. The islands of San Juan [Puerto Rico], and Jamaica, very large and happy and pleasing islands, are both desolate. The Lucaya Isles lie near Hispaniola and Cuba to the north and number more than sixty, including those that are called the Giants, and other large and small Islands; the poorest of these, which is more fertile, and pleasing than the King's garden in Seville, is the healthiest country in the world, and contained more than five hundred thousand souls, but to-day there remains not even a single creature. All were killed in transporting them, to Hispaniola, because it was seen that the native population there was disappearing. . . .

The reason why the Christians have killed and destroyed such infinite numbers of souls, is solely because they have made gold their ultimate aim, seeking to load themselves with riches in the shortest time and to mount by high steps, disproportioned to their condition: namely by their insatiable avarice and ambition, the greatest, that could be on the earth. These lands, being so happy and so rich, and the people so humble, so patient, and so easily subjugated, they have had no more respect, nor consideration nor have they taken more account of them (I speak with truth of what I have seen during all the aforementioned time) than—I will not say of animals, for would to God they had considered and treated them as animals—but as even less than the dung in the streets.

In this way have they cared for their lives—and for their souls: and therefore, all the millions above mentioned have died without faith, and without sacraments. And it is a publicly known truth, admitted, and confessed by all, even by the tyrants and homicides themselves, that the Indians throughout the Indies never did any harm to the Christians: they even esteemed them as coming from heaven, until they and their neighbours had suffered the same many evils, thefts, deaths, violence and visitations at their hands.

# Hawkins Brings Slaves to the New World (1568)

John Hawkins (1532–1595) made a reputation as one of the dogged English sailors who defeated the mighty Spanish Armada in 1587. Earlier, he made a fortune as one of the many slave traders who purchased (or seized) Africans and sold them to the Spaniards in the Caribbean to take the place of the native peoples. This reading is taken from Hawkins' own account of a trip made in 1567–1568. From *Voyages of the Elizabethan Seamen,* ed. E. J. Payne (London, 1880), pp. 52–53.

The Third troublesome Voyage made with the *Jesus of Lubeck,* the *Minion,* and four other ships, to the parts of Guinea and the West Indies, in the years 1567 and 1568, by Master John Hawkins.

The ships departed from Plymouth, the 2nd day of October, Anno 1567, . . . and arrived at Cape Verde on the 18th day of November: where we landed 150 men, hoping to obtain some negroes, where we got but few, and those with great hurt and damage to our men, which chiefly proceeded of their envenomed arrows. And although in the beginning they seemed to be but small hurts, yet there hardly escaped any that had blood drawn of them, but died in strange sort, with their mouths shut some ten days before they died, and after their wounds were whole; where I myself had one of the greatest wounds, yet, thanks be to God, escaped. From thence we passed the time upon the coast of Guinea, searching with all diligence the rivers from Rio Grande unto Sierra Leone, till the 12th of January, in which time we had not gotten together a hundred and fifty negroes. . . . But even in that present instant, there came to us a negro, sent from a king, oppressed by other kings his neighbours, desiring our aid, with promise that as many negroes as by these wars might be obtained, as well of his part as of ours, should be at our pleasure. Whereupon we concluded to give aid, and sent 120 of our men, which on the 15th of January assaulted a town of the negroes of our ally's adversaries, which had in it 8,000 inhabitants, being very

Europeans constructed strongholds along the West African coast to serve as trading posts and slave warehouses. This sketch by a Dutch officer of El Mina Castle and its attached settlement has a very European appearance.

This sketch of a cross-section of a slave ship was made during a parliamentary investigation of the slave trade in England in 1788. English law permitted a ship of 320 tons to carry 454 persons. Inspection of an actual 320-ton ship, the BROOKES (sketch), demonstrated that in fact only 451 persons could be crammed aboard. The viewer should draw his own conclusions about the conditions of transport.

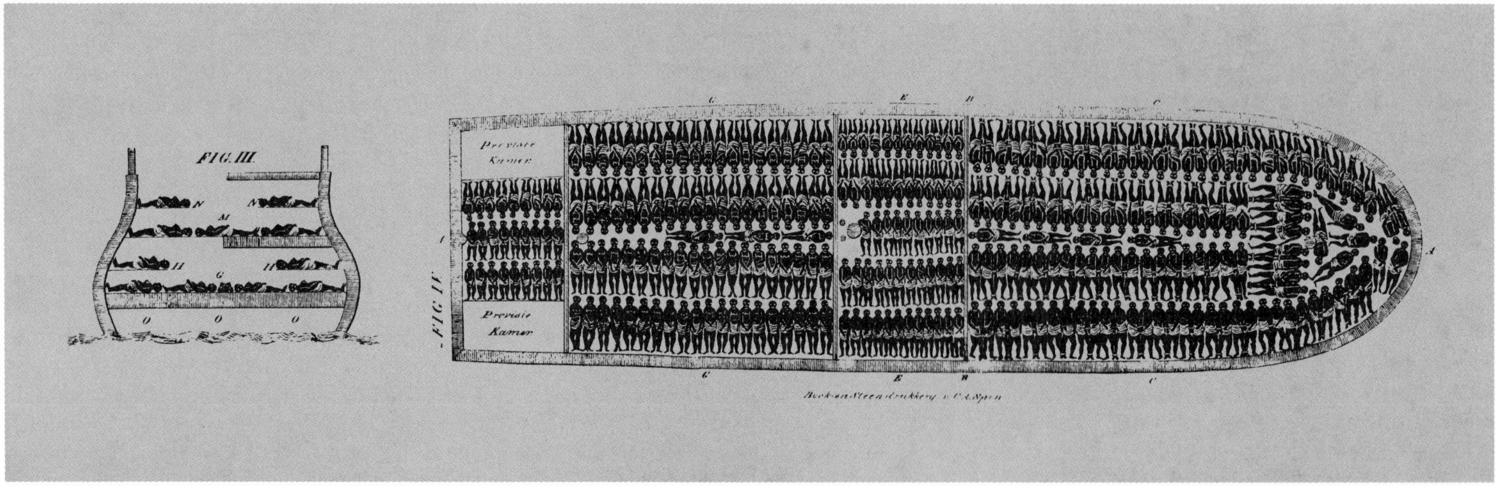

strongly impaled and fenced after their manner. But it was so well defended, that our men prevailed not, but lost six men and forty hurt: so that our men sent forthwith to me for more help. Whereupon, considering that the good success of this enterprise might highly further the commodity of our voyage, I went myself, and with the help of the king of our side, assaulted the town, both by land and by sea and very hardly with fire (their houses being covered with dry palm leaves) obtained the town and put the inhabitants to flight, where we took 250 persons, men, women, and children, and by our friend the king of our side, there were taken 600 prisoners, whereof we hoped to have our choice. But the negro (in which nation is seldom or never found truth) meant nothing less: for that night he removed his camp and prisoners, so that we were fain to content us with those few which we had gotten ourselves.

Now had we obtained between four and five hundred negroes, wherewith we thought it somewhat reasonable to seek the coast of the West Indies; and there, for our negroes, and our other merchandise, we hoped to obtain whereof to countervail our charges with some gains. Whereunto we proceeded with all diligence, furnished our watering, took fuel, and departed the coast of Guinea on the 3d of February, continuing at the sea with a passage more hard than before hath been accustomed till the 27th day of March, which day we had sight of an island, called Dominica, upon the coast of the West Indies, in fourteen degrees. From thence we coasted from place to place, making our traffic with the Spaniards as we might, somewhat hardly, because the king had straitly commanded all his governors in those parts by no means to suffer any trade to be made with us. Notwithstanding, we had reasonable trade, and courteous entertainment, from the Isle of Margarita unto Cartagena, without anything greatly worth the noting, saving at Capo de la Vela, in a town called Rio de la Hacha, from whence come all the pearls. The treasurer, who had the charge there, would by no means agree to any trade, or suffer us to take water. He had fortified his town with divers bulwarks in all places where it might be entered, and furnished himself with an hundred arquebusiers, so that he thought by famine to have enforced us to have put on land our negroes. Of which purpose he had not greatly failed, unless we had by force entered the town; which (after we could by no means obtain his favour) we were enforced to do, and so with two hundred men brake in upon their bulwarks, and entered the town with the loss only of two men of our part, and no hurt done to the Spaniards, because after their volley of shot discharged, they all fled. Thus having the town with some circumstance, as partly by the Spaniards' desire of negroes, and partly by friendship of the treasurer, we obtained a secret trade: whereupon the Spaniards resorted to us by night, and bought of us to the number of 200 negroes. In all other places where we traded the Spanish inhabitants were glad of us and traded willingly.